T0189239

Communications in Computer and Information Science 1274

Commenced Publication in 2007
Founding and Former Series Editors:
Simone Diniz Junqueira Barbosa, Phoebe Chen, Alfredo Cuzzocrea,
Xiaoyong Du, Orhun Kara, Ting Liu, Krishna M. Sivalingam,
Dominik Ślęzak, Takashi Washio, Xiaokang Yang, and Junsong Yuan

Editorial Board Members

More information about this series at http://www.springer.com/series/7899

Juan Carlos Figueroa-García ·
Fabián Steven Garay-Rairán ·
Germán Jairo Hernández-Pérez ·
Yesid Díaz-Gutierrez (Eds.)

Applied Computer Sciences in Engineering

7th Workshop on Engineering Applications, WEA 2020
Bogota, Colombia, October 7–9, 2020
Proceedings

 Springer

Editors
Juan Carlos Figueroa-García 🆔
Universidad Distrital Francisco José
de Caldas
Bogotá, Colombia

Germán Jairo Hernández-Pérez
National University of Colombia
Bogotá, Colombia

Fabián Steven Garay-Rairán 🆔
Infantry School of the National
Colombian Army
Bogotá, Colombia

Yesid Díaz-Gutierrez
Corporación Unificada Nacional CUN
Bogotá, Colombia

ISSN 1865-0929 ISSN 1865-0937 (electronic)
Communications in Computer and Information Science
ISBN 978-3-030-61833-9 ISBN 978-3-030-61834-6 (eBook)
https://doi.org/10.1007/978-3-030-61834-6

This Springer imprint is published by the registered company Springer Nature Switzerland AG
The registered company address is: Gewerbestrasse 11, 6330 Cham, Switzerland

Preface

The 7th edition of the Workshop on Engineering Applications (WEA 2020) was jointly organized with the International Congress on Technology and Innovation for the Infantry (CITINF 2020), both events focused on applications in computer science, computational intelligence, military applications, optimization, simulation, IoT, and bioengineering. WEA/CITINF 2020 was one of the flagship events of the Faculty of Engineering of the Universidad Distrital Francisco José de Caldas and the Infantry School of the National Colombian Army.

WEA/CITINF 2020 was held online due to the COVID-19 pandemic which affected global life. We received 136 submissions from 14 countries on topics such as computer science, military applications, computational intelligence, bioengineering, operations research/optimization, simulation systems, IoT/networks, power and electrical applications, among others. The Program Committee organized all papers into different sections in order to improve the readability of this volume published by Springer in the *Communications in Computer and Information Sciences* (CCIS) series. Therefore, the main topic of the conference was "Applied Computer Sciences in Engineering."

All submissions were rigorously peer-reviewed by the reviewers who provided constructive comments, and as a result of their work, 44 papers were accepted for presentation at WEA/CITINF 2020. The Faculty of Engineering of the Universidad Distrital Francisco José de Caldas, the Infantry School of the National Colombian Army, the Corporación Unificada Nacional (CUN), the Faculty of Engineering of the National University of Colombia, and the Secretary of Science, Technology and Innovation of the Cundinamarca Regional Governorate made significant efforts to guarantee the success of the conference considering the global impact of COVID-19.

We would like to thank all members of the Program Committee and the referees for their commitment to help in the review process, and for spreading our call for papers which was an especially hard job due to the pandemic. We would like to thank Alfred Hofmann and Jorge Nakahara from Springer for their helpful advice, guidance, and their continuous support in publicizing the proceedings. Moreover, we would like to thank all the authors for supporting WEA/CITINF 2020, without all their high-quality submissions the conference would not have been possible. Finally, we are especially grateful to the IEEE Universidad Distrital Francisco José de Caldas student branch, the Laboratory for Automation and Computational Intelligence (LAMIC), GITUD research groups of the Universidad Distrital Francisco José de Caldas, Center for Simulation and Research for the Infantry (CISI) of the National Colombian Army, BIOINGENIERÍA, GIBIO, and GEPRO research groups of the Antonio Nariño University, the Algorithms and Combinatory (ALGOS) research group of the National University of Colombia, the

Secretary of Science, Technology and Innovation of the Cundinamarca Regional Governorate, and the AXON group of the Corporación Unificada Nacional (CUN).

October 2020

Juan Carlos Figueroa-García
Fabián Steven Garay-Rairán
Yesid Díaz-Gutierrez
Germán Jairo Hernández-Pérez

Organization

General Chair

Juan Carlos Figueroa-García   Universidad Distrital Francisco José de Caldas, Colombia

Finance Chair/Treasurer

Fabián Steven Garay-Rairán   Infantry School of the National Colombian Army, Colombia

Technical Chairs

Yesid Díaz-Gutierrez   Corporación Unificada Nacional de Educación Superior (CUN), Colombia

Julio Barón   Universidad Distrital Francisco José de Caldas, Colombia

Publication Chair

Germán Jairo Hernández-Pérez   Universidad Nacional de Colombia, Colombia

Track Chairs

Yesid Díaz-Gutierrez   Corporación Unificada Nacional de Educación Superior (CUN), Colombia

Lindsay Alvarez   Universidad Distrital Francisco José de Caldas, Colombia

Elvis Eduardo Gaona   Universidad Distrital Francisco José de Caldas, Colombia

Sebastián Jaramillo Isaza   Universidad Antonio Nariño, Colombia

Logistic Chairs

José Luis Jiménez-Useche   Infantry School of the National Colombian Army, Colombia

Yesid Díaz-Gutierrez   Corporación Unificada Nacional de Educación Superior (CUN), Colombia

Plenary Speakers

José Luis Verdegay	Universidad de Granada, Spain
Martine Ceberio	The University of Texas at El Paso, USA
Philippe Dufort	Saint Paul University, Canada
Robert Lummack	Royal Military College Saint-Jean, Canada
Nelly Yolanda Russi	Cundinamarca Governorate, Colombia

Program Committee

Adil Usman	Indian Institute of Technology, Mandi, India
Adolfo Jaramillo-Matta	Universidad Distrital Francisco José de Caldas, Colombia
Alvaro David Orjuela-Cañon	Universidad del Rosario, Colombia
Andrés Ernesto Salguero	Universidad Antonio Nariño, Colombia
Andrés Felipe Ruiíz	Universidad Antonio Nariño, Colombia
Andres Gaona	Universidad Distrital Francisco José de Caldas, Colombia
Andrés Guillermo Molano	Universidad Antonio Nariño, Colombia
Andres M. Alvarez Mesa	Universidad Nacional de Colombia, Colombia
Carlos Franco-Franco	Universidad del Rosario, Colombia
Carlos Osorio-Ramírez	Universidad Nacional de Colombia, Colombia
DeShuang Huang	Tongji University, China
Diana Ovalle	Universidad Distrital Francisco José de Caldas, Colombia
Eduyn López-Santana	Universidad Distrital Francisco Jose de Caldas, Colombia
Elvis Eduardo Gaona	Universidad Distrital Francisco José de Caldas, Colombia
Feizar Javier Rueda-Velazco	Universidad Distrital Francisco José de Caldas, Colombia
Francisco Ramis	Universidad del Bío-Bío, Chile
Germán Jairo Hernández-Pérez	Universidad Nacional de Colombia, Colombia
Gloria Jeanette Rincón	Universidad Cooperativa de Colombia, Colombia
Guadalupe González	Universidad Tecnológica de Panamá, Panama
Gustavo Puerto-Leguizamón	Universidad Distrital Francisco José de Caldas, Colombia
Gustavo Suárez	Universidad Pontificia Bolivariana, Colombia
Henry Diosa	Universidad Distrital Francisco José de Caldas, Colombia
Heriberto Román-Flores	Universidad de Tarapacá, Chile
I-Hsien Ting	National University of Kaohsiung, Taiwan
Jair Cervantes-Canales	Universidad Autónoma de México, Mexico
Jairo Soriano-Mendez	Universidad Distrital Francisco José de Caldas, Colombia

Contents

Computational Intelligence

Computer Science

Bioengineering

Computational Intelligence

Testing the Intermediate Disturbance Hypothesis in Concurrent Evolutionary Algorithms

J. J. Merelo[1][(✉)], Mario García Valdez[2], and Sergio Rojas-Galeano[3]

[1] Universidad de Granada, Granada, Spain
jmerelo@ugr.es
[2] Instituto Tecnológico de Tijuana, Tijuana, Baja California, Mexico
mario@tectijuana.edu.mx
[3] Universidad Distrital Francisco José de Caldas, Bogotá, Colombia
srojas@udistrital.edu.co

Abstract. Concurrency is a powerful abstraction that can be used to model and implement multi-deme evolutionary algorithms, opening up additional design questions such as what the different populations in various threads can do and how they interact with each other (via a combination of populations). One approach is synchrony: although threads can run asynchronously, they often perform the same amount of work, which brings a (rough) synchrony to appear within them. Our intention in this paper is to test if the intermediate disturbance hypothesis holds: this kind of synchrony is a small disturbance, which likewise big disturbances will not boost diversity; however, moderate disturbances will. We tested several ways of creating this intermediate disturbance by changing how different threads operate or modifying its working in alternative ways.

Keywords: Intermediate disturbance hypothesis · Evolutionary algorithms · Concurrency · Distributed algorithms

1 Introduction

The intermediate disturbance hypothesis was introduced by several researchers in the seventies [2] to explain the diversity found in different ecosystems; it states [18] that

> ... Moderate levels of disturbance foster greater species diversity than do low or high levels of disturbance

These levels refer to amplitude as well as frequency; a disturbance happening too often will wipe out all diversity, if it happens rarely the system reaches equilibrium bringing species that have some competitive advantage to dominate the ecosystem; in the same way, a high level of disturbance like sudden changes in temperature will not allow species to thrive except those that can stand them.

© Springer Nature Switzerland AG 2020
J. C. Figueroa-García et al. (Eds.): WEA 2020, CCIS 1274, pp. 3–15, 2020.
https://doi.org/10.1007/978-3-030-61834-6_1

In contrast, a moderate temperature range across day and night will allow a whole lot of adapted species to survive together, in the same way as it happens in the rainforest. This disturbance may also refer to changes in the genetic pool brought in by the introduction of new populations.

Wider diversity is something that is much sought after in evolutionary algorithms, since diversity helps to avoid falling in local optima. This is also truth in multi-deme distributed or concurrent evolutionary algorithms, where *disturbances* will usually take the form of changes in the population, commonly selection or insertion policies. As a matter of fact, we investigated this kind of hypothesis in [14], finding that by evolving populations asynchronously (and thus, being in a different state of evolution), can result in an *intermediate* disturbance by interchanging members of the population; the latter in turn helps to boost the performance of the algorithm, obtaining better results than synchronously evolving populations or other scenarios with a lesser degree of disturbances.

Concurrent evolutionary algorithms are placed at a different level of abstraction than distributed algorithms; they can be run in parallel or not, distributed over many computers or simply many processors; nonetheless, they use high-level language constructs such as channels and messages that ensure that there are no deadlocks and every task runs smoothly until it's finished. Languages such as Raku (formerly known as Perl 6) [10], include channels as a built-in data structure, so by using them, it is feasible to implement concurrent evolutionary algorithms following Hoare's Communicating Sequential Processes model [8].

In this kind of evolutionary algorithms [11–13,16] there is no *migration per se*, and although populations are not moved from one *island* to another, but *merged*, the intermediate disturbance principle may hold; therefore we should *let nature be our guide* [5] and apply it to validate if certain level of performance, scaling or both can be achieved.

However, there seems no way to introduce those intermediate disturbances from first principles, in such a way that it does not really change the nature of the algorithm in fundamental ways. For starters, in several occasions this intermediate disturbances happens inherently in asynchronous evolutionary algorithms [15], so adding further intermediate disturbance devices may probably amount to induce too much disturbance indeed, or maybe not. Thus, if we want to find out what actually works we should observe its effects and discard other possible causes; in a word, we will be trying to heuristically measure the effects of different types of disturbances on the population, which can only be made by changing the degree of evolution a population undergoes in every task. We will do that via alterations in the number of generations or in the population. In this way, we will pick the one that has the more positive outcome in algorithmic, performance terms, or both.

What we expect by altering the evolution degree of different populations is to create a disturbance, possibly of moderate size, when these populations mix. We will measure the effect and size of this disturbance indirectly by comparing the changes in the performance of the algorithm: higher diversity will mean better performance. Besides, we will check how this performance boost behaves when we scale from two to eight or ten simultaneous tasks.

The rest of the paper is organized as follows. Next, we will present the state of the art in the use or observation of the intermediate disturbance hypothesis in bioinspired algorithms; next we will describe the experimental setup for this paper. Section 4 will present the results, followed by a section with discussions and future lines of work that will close the paper.

2   State of the Art

The intermediate disturbance hypothesis [2,6] has not really had a long run in the area of bioinspired algorithms; instead, using *big* disturbances such as hyper-mutation, has been a preferred approach. This technique was popularized by another bioinspired methodology, immune systems, [9], which has been adopted under many different names such as the *plague* method that was proposed for genetic programming [3]. Even as their names suggest a degree of perturbation of the system that is beyond moderation, it is very likely that their real effect is that of a mild disturbance. The *plague*, for instance, just removes some individuals in the population; hypermutation does generate new (faulty) copies of some specific individuals, generating a moderate disturbance yielding the generation of diversity.

The same happens in the area of distributed evolutionary algorithms; these moderate disturbances are introduced, although not really by name. Pelta et al. [17] propose a "cooperative multi-thread strategy", where every thread runs a different optimization algorithm. The results of every thread will be a *moderate* disturbance to the solutions of the other threads, and this is achieved explicitly by using fuzzy rules to update thread method parameters as well as the starting point of the algorithm; however, while this strategy avoids low disturbance, it does not guarantee that catastrophic high disturbance happens, causing that a new solution much better than the existing ones, will *invade* the whole system.

This is why a more explicit approach to the observation or implementation of the intermediate disturbance hypothesis might help to better apply it to distributed evolutionary algorithms. As such, it has been used with a certain frequency by evolutionary algorithms, although mainly in the area of particle swarm optimization. Gao et al. [4] mention a *moderate disturbance strategy*, which adds exploration to the PSO algorithm; this *moderate* disturbance has the effect of increasing exploration and thus diversity, at least in a local scale; that is also the intention of the *intermediate disturbance* PSO proposed by He et al. [7], which perturbs the position of particles using the value initially proposed by Gao et al.

However, in the context of distributed evolutionary algorithms, it was introduced explicitly by us in the above-mentioned paper, [14], although we focused more on the algorithmic effects than in the real time-wise performance, since the implementation was not actually parallel. In that case, we compared populations operating synchronously with others that operated asynchronously by starting at different points in time; this simple procedure had the effect of a decrease in the number of evaluations needed.

A different implementation of the same concept was made in what we called a *multikulti* algorithm [1], which used an explicitly parallel population. This created the intermediate disturbance by using genotypic differences to select migrants from one island (in an island-based GA) to another; in that study, the moderate perturbation created by this inflow of population was explicitly proved to increase diversity, and consequently, performance.

In this paper we aim at adding to the state of the art by first, testing the intermediate hypothesis in a concurrent setting, trying to create different conditions that produce a moderate disturbance, and measuring its algorithmic as well as performance effects. We'll describe the setup next.

3   Experimental Setup

The overall architecture of the algorithm used in this paper was presented in [16]. Essentially, it's a concurrent evolutionary algorithm written in Raku that uses channels for interchange of information among different tasks.

There are two kinds of tasks:

- The evolutionary task run a classical evolutionary algorithm for a number of generations with a fixed population. This is the task that we will scale.
- The mixer task will be used to interchange information among the evolutionary tasks; it picks up pairs of vectors representing probability distributions of populations, from the "mixer" channel, and then cross them over to create a new probability vector. The resulting vector along with a randomly chosen member of the original pair, will be sent back to the "evolutionary" channel.

The data flow is as follows.

- A set of probability vectors are initially generated. These will be the gene-wise Bernoulli probability distributions used to generate an initial binary population. We will generate 1 or 2 sets of probabilities more than the number of (evolutionary) threads; for instance, 12 vectors for 10 evolutionary threads.
- These sets are sent to the mixer thread, that mixes and sends them to the evolutionary channel.
- The evolutionary tasks pick up one probability vector, rebuild the population using it, and run an evolutionary algorithm for a fixed number of generations or until solution is found. If that's not the case, the top 25% fittest individuals of the population are used to estimate a new distribution probability vector, that is sent back to the mixer channel.
- Each task is event driven, so that they "react" when there's a vector available in the channel; it's implemented as a promise that will be fulfilled when the solution is found in that specific thread.

The timeline of this concurrent algorithm is shown in Fig. 1; this monitor shows tasks as bars and specific events as triangles. The mixer task bar can be seen intermittent since every time it reacts it takes a very short time, but nonetheless it keeps running in a single thread, and it starts before the others.

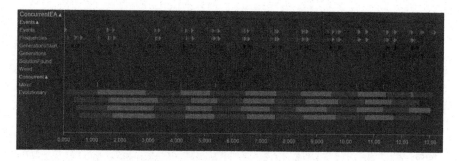

Fig. 1. Monitor showing the execution of the baseline concurrent evolutionary algorithm with 4 threads, as shown by the Comma IDE concurrency tool

Since generation (and mixer) start concurrently with evolution, new threads *wake up* as new information is available in the channel; they end at different points in the timeline, but their state of evolution should be approximately the same, since they have been arranged with the same number of evaluations and the population is the same. The monitor also shows that there are few gaps (except at the beginning) and that concurrency is use quite efficiently throughout all the run.

We will run every program 15 times with the same parameters, and will evaluate from 2 to 10 threads. For parametrizations where performance plateaus at 8, we will stop there. All experiments have been performed on a 8 CPU, 16 core system running Ubuntu 18.04 and Raku 2020.02.1. Experiment logs and resulting data are available in GitHub under a free license, as well as the scripts used to perform it. The version of Algorithm::Evolutionary::Simple used is 0.0.7. The benchmark problem used is Leading Ones with 60 bits; this problem is difficult enough to require a good-sized population to be solved. Results are probably extensible to other binary benchmark problems such as Royal Road or OneMax. In any case, since we are more interested in evaluating aspects of concurrent operation rather than the solving effectiveness of the algorithm, the specific problem is probably not as important. Population will be 1024, split among threads in the baseline configuration; for instance, there will be 512 individuals per thread for the 2-threads configuration.

In the next section, we will subject this baseline operation to different kinds of perturbations, looking for that Goldilocks zone where perturbations are moderate and wider diversity emerges.

4   Results

The number of generations was established in the initial papers as one with the best communications/computation tradeoff. However, here we decided to establish a baseline of non-perturbed values for comparison. A boxplot of the number of evaluations vs. threads is shown in Fig. 2. First, we can check that the number of evaluations scales down with the number of threads, although it plateaus

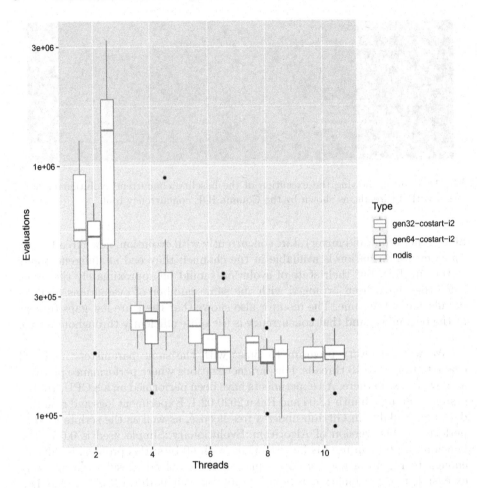

Fig. 2. Boxplot of the number of evaluations for 16 (labeled "nodis"), 32 and 64 generations.

at 16 generations. Parallelism also evens out the differences between different parameters: while stopping for transmission at 16 generations is notably worse at 2 and 4 threads, the difference is not remarkable beyond that. Differences for 32 and 64 generations are never noticeable. We don't show figures for wall clock time taken, but it is notably worse; this is simply explained by the fact that longer stretches of running mean less communication between tasks.

From this baseline, subsequently we introduced a small perturbation: a single thread will use 9 or 25 generations; the rest of the threads will use 16. We will show results in Fig. 3. Essentially, this change does not seem to affect the average number of evaluations, and when it does, it is for the worse. The "late" thread, labeled dis, actually needs more evaluations to find the solution, but only for 4 threads. The rest of the results are basically the same. Thus we reason this

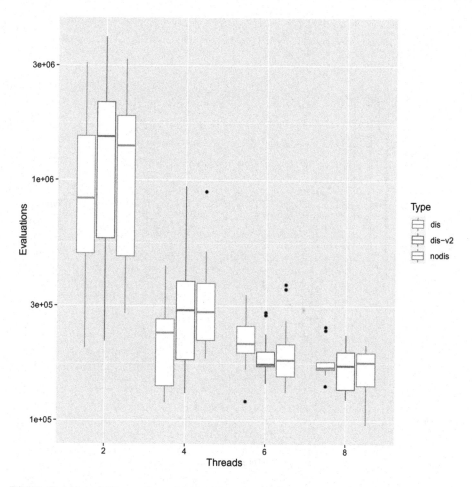

Fig. 3. Boxplot of the number of evaluations for 16 (labeled "nodis") and a "disturber" task that ends after 9 (`dis-v2`) or 25 (`dis`) generations.

qualifies as a small disturbance: it does not cause a noticeable change; this implies that the introduction of populations with differentiated phases in the evolution, as was done in [14], does not have any impact in this setting. It could be due to the fact that we are scaling up to 8 threads, but as a matter of fact, it does not make any difference for 2 threads either. Notice that, as previously, there's no improvement from 6 to 8 threads, which is why we have not scaled up to 10 threads this time.

Let us try now another approach to creating disturbances. We will randomly vary the number of generations ranging randomly from 8 to 24, or the population, which will be sampled from the probability distribution vector to a number between half the baseline value (1024/number of threads) to twice that value.

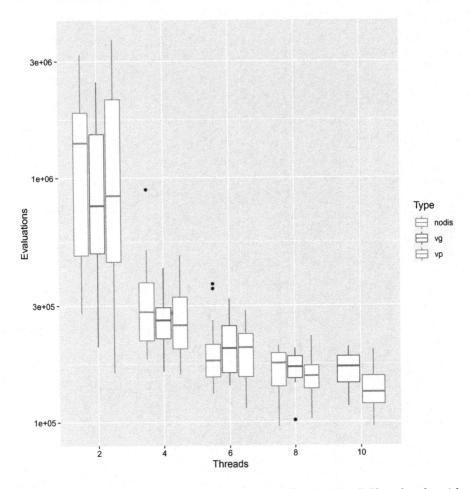

Fig. 4. Boxplot of the number of evaluations for 16 (labeled "nodis") and tasks with a variable population **vp** and variable number of generations **vg**

A boxplot of the number of evaluations is shown in Fig. 4 and the wall clock time is shown in Fig. 5.

Despite the median being slightly better when we use a variable population, the statistical variability of the results show no significant difference in the number of evaluations obtained for up to 8 threads between the baseline and the variable population version (there might be some improvement for 10 threads, but we didn't measure that); however, there is a significant difference in time (at the 10% level) for 4 and 8 threads; this can also be appreciated in the chart.

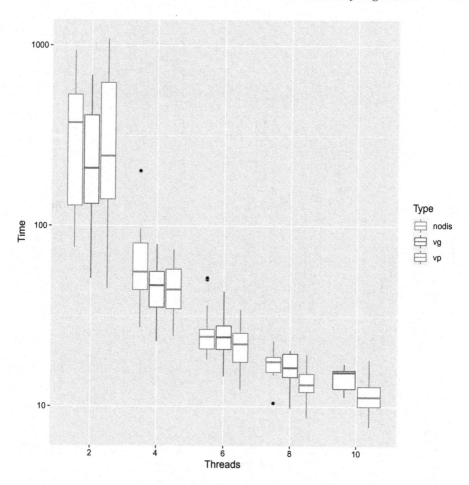

Fig. 5. Boxplot of the clocked time for experiments for 16 (labeled "nodis") and tasks with a variable population **vp** and variable number of generations **vg**. Please notice that the y axis is logarithmic.

On the other hand, the difference in the number of evaluations is significant between variable population and variable number of generations for 10 threads, with the time needed showing a significant difference for 8 and 10 threads. Both effects are compounded in the number of evaluations per second, which is shown in Fig. 6. In this case, the difference is significant for 2 to 8 threads; the median number of evaluations per second for variable population tops up at 12254.234, while it's 9408.067 for the baseline without any kind of disturbance.

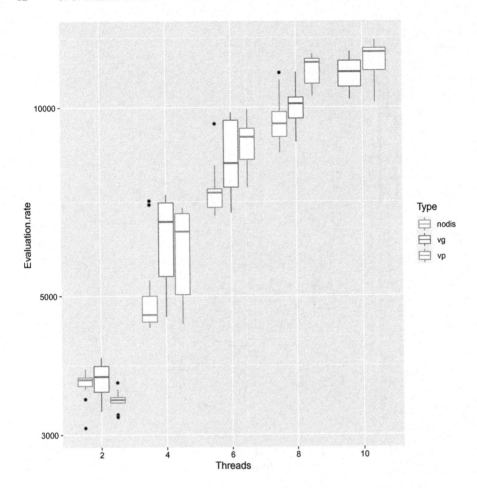

Fig. 6. Boxplot of the evaluation rate (evaluations per second) for experiments for 16 (labeled "nodis") and tasks with a variable population **vp** and variable number of generations **vg**, with a logarithmic y axis.

5   Discussion and Conclusions

In this paper, we evaluated how creating a moderate amount of disturbance in a concurrent and multi-threaded evolutionary algorithm contributed to the diversity, and indirectly to the results of the algorithm across a wide scale; we have made several experiments changing the degree of evolution that every individual population undergoes, with the intention of introducing disturbances by mixing populations that had been in different stages. In some cases, minimal differences were achieved with respect to the baseline system, and only for some parts of the scale-up to 10 threads.

However, using a strategy that generated a population of random size in a range that decreased with the number of threads proved to be computationally more efficient (finding the problem solution in fewer evaluations across a whole range of scales) but also faster (by boosting the number of evaluations per second), achieving a result that is overall much faster by an order of magnitude; while the median time for the baseline system and 2 threads was 372.4505 s, the variable population with 10 threads managed to find the solution in a median time of 11.27906, 33 times faster (instead of just 5 times faster, which would be expected by the scale-up of the number of threads). This leads us to note that, at least this strategy, is efficient enough to be on a par with the state of the art.

Nonetheless, the interesting question is if it is a moderate disturbance or some other factor that achieved the result. Since we are using a random value in a range that goes from half the baseline population to twice the baseline population, on average, the population will have a bigger size; the ratio of evaluations to communications is then lower, and that might explain the small edge when the number of evaluations is not significantly better. However, there are cases when the number of evaluations is actually better, mainly at higher concurrency values. Arguably, this could constitute a moderate disturbance. As the population gets smaller, the range of variation with respect the total population also gets smaller; while for two threads, for instance, we could have one thread with 300 and the other with 900, and the difference between them is going to be 60% of the total population, for 8 threads the differences of a population between tasks is going to be a moderate size with respect to the total population. This would explain the good results happening at the bigger scales, and also the fact that there is an improvement for that strategy across all scales, from 2 to 10.

We conclude that intermediate disturbance in concurrent evolutionary algorithms introduces many different degrees of freedom in the system, and exploring them looking for good performance and scaling is still a challenge once we've established a good baseline performance measure. However, once we know the degree of disturbance that works the best, we could extend measurements to other benchmark functions, and also try to max out the number of threads available in a single machine. This is left as future work.

Acknowledgements. We are grateful to Jonathan Worthington and the rest of the Edument team for their disposition to help with implementation problems and provide suggestions to make this work correctly. This is extended to the rest of the Raku development team, which is an excellent and technically knowledgeable community committed to creating a great language. This paper has been supported in part by projects DeepBio (TIN2017-85727-C4-2-P).

References

1. Araujo, L., Guervós, J.J.M.: Diversity through multiculturality: assessing migrant choice policies in an Island model. IEEE Trans. Evol. Comput. **15**(4), 456–469 (2011)

2. Connell, J.H.: Diversity in tropical rain forests and coral reefs. Science **199**(4335), 1302–1310 (1978)
3. Fernandez, F., Vanneschi, L., Tomassini, M.: The effect of plagues in genetic programming: a study of variable-size populations. In: Ryan, C., Soule, T., Keijzer, M., Tsang, E., Poli, R., Costa, E. (eds.) EuroGP 2003. LNCS, vol. 2610, pp. 317–326. Springer, Heidelberg (2003). https://doi.org/10.1007/3-540-36599-0_29
4. Gao, H., Zang, W., Cao, J.: A particle swarm optimization with moderate disturbance strategy. In: Proceedings of the 32nd Chinese Control Conference, pp. 7994–7999. IEEE (2013)
5. Goldberg, D.E.: Zen and the art of genetic algorithms. In: Schaffer, J.D. (ed.) ICGA, pp. 80–85. Morgan Kaufmann (1989)
6. Grime, J.P.: Competitive exclusion in herbaceous vegetation. Nature **242**(5396), 344–347 (1973)
7. He, Y., Wang, A., Su, H., Wang, M.: Particle swarm optimization using neighborhood-based mutation operator and intermediate disturbance strategy for outbound container storage location assignment problem. Math. Probl. Eng. **2019** (2019)
8. Hoare, C.A.R.: Communicating sequential processes. Commun. ACM **21**(8), 666–677 (1978). https://doi.org/10.1145/359576.359585
9. Jansen, T., Zarges, C.: Analyzing different variants of immune inspired somatic contiguous hypermutations. Theoret. Comput. Sci. **412**(6), 517–533 (2011)
10. Lenz, M.: Perl 6 Fundamentals. Apress, Berkeley (2017). https://doi.org/10.1007/978-1-4842-2899-9
11. Merelo, J.J., García-Valdez, J.-M.: Going stateless in concurrent evolutionary algorithms. In: Figueroa-García, J.C., López-Santana, E.R., Rodriguez-Molano, J.I. (eds.) WEA 2018. CCIS, vol. 915, pp. 17–29. Springer, Cham (2018). https://doi.org/10.1007/978-3-030-00350-0_2
12. Merelo, J.J., García-Valdez, J.M.: Mapping evolutionary algorithms to a reactive, stateless architecture: using a modern concurrent language. In: Proceedings of the Genetic and Evolutionary Computation Conference Companion, GECCO 2018, pp. 1870–1877. ACM, New York (2018). https://doi.org/10.1145/3205651.3208317. http://doi.acm.org/10.1145/3205651.3208317
13. Merelo, J.J., Laredo, J.L.J., Castillo, P.A., García-Valdez, J.-M., Rojas-Galeano, S.: Scaling in concurrent evolutionary algorithms. In: Figueroa-García, J.C., Duarte-González, M., Jaramillo-Isaza, S., Orjuela-Cañón, A.D., Díaz-Gutierrez, Y. (eds.) WEA 2019. CCIS, vol. 1052, pp. 16–27. Springer, Cham (2019). https://doi.org/10.1007/978-3-030-31019-6_2
14. Merelo, J.J., et al.: Testing the intermediate disturbance hypothesis: effect of asynchronous population incorporation on multi-deme evolutionary algorithms. In: Rudolph, G., Jansen, T., Beume, N., Lucas, S., Poloni, C. (eds.) PPSN 2008. LNCS, vol. 5199, pp. 266–275. Springer, Heidelberg (2008). https://doi.org/10.1007/978-3-540-87700-4_27
15. Merelo-Guervós, J.J., García-Sánchez, P.: Modeling browser-based distributed evolutionary computation systems. CoRR abs/1503.06424 (2015). http://arxiv.org/abs/1503.06424
16. Merelo, J.J., Laredo, J.L.J., Castillo, P.A., García-Valdez, J.-M., Rojas-Galeano, S.: Exploring concurrent and stateless evolutionary algorithms. In: Kaufmann, P., Castillo, P.A. (eds.) EvoApplications 2019. LNCS, vol. 11454, pp. 405–412. Springer, Cham (2019). https://doi.org/10.1007/978-3-030-16692-2_27

17. Pelta, D., Sancho-Royo, A., Cruz, C., Verdegay, J.L.: Using memory and fuzzy rules in a co-operative multi-thread strategy for optimization. Inf. Sci. **176**(13), 1849–1868 (2006)
18. Reece, J.B., Urry, L.A., Cain, M.L., Wasserman, S.A., Minorsky, P.V., Jackson, R.B., et al.: Campbell Biology, no. 1309. Pearson, Boston (2014)

An Interpretable Automated Machine Learning Credit Risk Model

Gabriel Patron[1], Diego Leon[2(✉)], Edwin Lopez[1], and German Hernandez[1]

[1] Universidad Nacional de Colombia, Bogotá, Colombia
{gapatron,edlopez,gjhernandezp}@unal.edu.co
[2] Universidad Externado de Colombia, Bogotá, Colombia
diego.leon@uexternado.edu.co

Abstract. Credit risk prediction is one of the most recurrent problems in the financial industry. While machine learning techniques such as Neural Networks can have a stunning power of prediction accuracy when done right, the results of such models are not easily interpretable and hence, are difficult to explain and to integrate into financial regulation. Building strong and robust models requires a high degree of expertise, time and testing, and as the list of the available model grows, their complexity also increases. This is why meta-heuristic search and optimization techniques are being built to tackle this task. However, this often means that such models may not be easily interpretable. This work proposes a fast, reproducible pipeline that targets these two salient needs: solid, comparable model-building and reliable interpretability. An automated machine learning process is implemented via Genetic Algorithms to obtain a locally optimal model for our data that is comparable to top Kagglers' performance for the same classification problem and then, an interpretation engine is added on top to perform sanity checks on our results and identify the most important causals of prediction. This process greatly reduces time, cost and barrier of entry for model-building while providing the reasons for prediction, which can be easily contrasted with expert knowledge to check for correctness and extracting key insights.

Keywords: Automated Machine Learning · Interpretable machine learning · Credit risk

1 Introduction

In recent years we have witnessed the widespread application of a growing variety of Machine Learning algorithms and their combinations, that learn (extract knowledge and insights) from data. Machine Learning algorithms today form an eclectic and powerful collection originating from a wide variety of disciplines such as statistics, computer science, signal processing, computer vision, and control, among others. This usually means that the qualified practitioner has spent lots of time and resources learning about these various algorithms and models:

© Springer Nature Switzerland AG 2020
J. C. Figueroa-García et al. (Eds.): WEA 2020, CCIS 1274, pp. 16–23, 2020.
https://doi.org/10.1007/978-3-030-61834-6_2

their respective advantages or strengths, and also their weaknesses. Also, their implementation usually involves hyper-parameter tuning, data preprocessing and many very high-level tasks. But this high barrier of entry usually means that domain experts are left out of this cycle of experimentation and most importantly, left out of the validation process: how then can we know if the predictions of our models are made for the right reasons? How can we incorporate new knowledge into our domain if the only measure of success is prediction accuracy regardless of explainability?.

We, therefore, find ourselves amid a crucial dilemma: should we leave out domain experts and miss on their knowledge, but train highly accurate models, or include them and sacrifice speed, and maybe some precision, for the interpretability (and conceptual validation) they provide. Can we have the best of both worlds?. Certainly, with some caveats.

In the present work, we propose an easy-to-use pipeline designed for fast, reproducible and most importantly, Automated Machine Learning (AutoML) with interpretable explanations. This reduces the barrier of entry for rigorous implementation: it opens the door for domain experts to perform autonomous experimentation and efficiently contrast the results with their knowledge [5].

Regarding credit risk, credit assignment should be interpretable and consistent. This, to make suggestions and simulate conditions for loans to aid decision-makers' risk assessment. Decision Trees are easy to understand [3], and provide a simple tree graph about model decisions. This paper aims to predict if a customer falls into a category of default, evaluate decision tree model performance and interpret those predictions with an interpretation engine [15]. Future research.

1.1   Automated Machine Learning

In a typical machine learning application the practitioner's first step starts either with an unclassified data set (unsupervised learning task), an input-output classified dataset (supervised learning task) or an environment where the algorithms can interact to collect the data (reinforcement learning task); the second is to prepare the data that includes formatting (binary, numeric, ranking categorical, etc.) and encoding the information in appropriate data structures; the third step is model and hyperparameter selection. Finally, results are evaluated, interpretations are extracted (if possible), this feedback is sent back into the model and the process is iterated to satisfaction.

In summary, the usual Machine Learning process can be (naively) stated as:

1. Data preparation
2. Feature engineering
3. Model and hyperparameter selection
4. Model training
5. Model testing

Given the complexity of the tasks of finding a competitive ML model, there have been multiple efforts to automate the stages of the ML process and more recently to the complete ML process with end-to-end automation. The challenges involve the data, model selection, hyperparameters, among others.

The raw data itself may not be in a format that all algorithms may apply to it out of the box. An expert may have to apply the appropriate data preprocessing, feature engineering, feature extraction, and feature selection methods that make the dataset amenable for machine learning. Following those preprocessing steps, practitioners must then perform algorithm selection and hyperparameter optimization to maximize the predictive performance of their final machine learning model. As many of these steps are often beyond the abilities of non-experts, AutoML was proposed as an artificial intelligence-based solution to the ever-growing challenge of applying machine learning [11]. Automating the process of applying machine learning end-to-end offers the advantages of producing simpler solutions, faster creation of those solutions, and models that often outperform models that were designed by hand.

However, AutoML is not a silver bullet and can introduce additional parameters of its own, called hyperparameters, which may need some expertise to be set themselves [1]. But it does make application of Machine Learning easier for non-experts. Genetic algorithms are optimization algorithms inspired by natural selection. Successive generations evolve towards a locally optimal solution based on a cost function. The algorithm replicates evolution by establishing selection, mutation and crossover rules to an initially random population [14]. This process converges to, after several generations, more well-adapted individuals. This means individuals whose solutions are more optimal relative to their cost functions than their ancestors [9].

This idea was put into place by the creators of the TPOT Python library, the population is initialized with a random set of models with random sets of hyperparameters [12]. Applying a genetic algorithm to this population will result in a model, or combination of models, with fine-tuned hyperparameters that optimize cross-validated accuracy [13]. This we use to automatically find satisfactory models without much manual intervention.

1.2   Model Interpretability

Machine learning methods, especially those from the Deep Learning subfield, are widely recognized as black-box predictors. It is almost impossible to trace their decision processes and for this reason, they can't be blindly introduced into the already complex models of highly regulated fields, such as banking and finance. LIME (Linear Interpretable Model-Agnostic Explanations) has surged as a partial remedy to this situation [15]. It works by generating linear models around specific instances via random perturbations of the input. This way they can approximate which features were the biggest influencers of the final prediction for that instance.

The creators of the method also made it into an easy-to-use Python library with the technique's name. This way we have provided much desired interpretable explanations for the predictions in a way that shows relative contributions in a human-friendly way, making it easy for anyone to contrast with either common sense or field expertise from the model and extract valuable insights.

2   Results

2.1   Model Results

We performed our tests with the "Give me some credit" open dataset. We chose it based on the diversity of techniques historically used for processing and also comparability [10]; performance of a wide variety of models can be found at Kaggle, organized from best to worst based on the ROC score criterion [4, 7]. Missing values were filled with the mean or the mode, depending on the type of variable. Several sampling techniques were used to balance the training data, which is highly skewed as can be seen in Fig. 5, and reduce the bias. Undersampling provided us with the best results. The evolutionary search for a model was performed three times, each taking less than two hours to complete. The models obtained were (hyperparameters in the Appendix):

– Random Forest Classifier with Gradient Boosting model
– Random Forest Classifier
– XGB Classifier

We chose the best predictor of defaults, that is, the model that proved most accurate for Default prediction in the test set. This turned out to be the **Random Forest model** [2], with an accuracy of 78%. This and all other relevant prediction values can be appreciated in Fig. 1.

Next, we calculate the Area Under Receiver Operating Curve, also known as AUC ROC. The top prediction scores can be found in the leaderboard on Kaggle's "Give Me Some Credit" competition's page. Top score and our score are compared in Table 1. The corresponding ROC curve can be found in Fig. 2.

Table 1. AUC ROC scores

Top Kaggle	Ours
0.869	0.861

Clearly there is not much difference between our score and the top Kaggle score. It all becomes more relevant when considering that convergence to this satisfactory model took less than two hours and didn't actively involve manual tunning nor any kind of specialized knowledge.

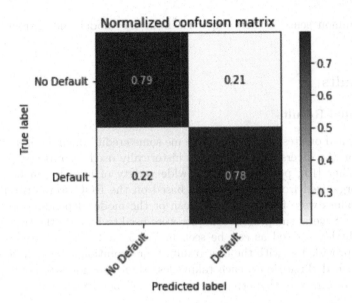

Fig. 1. Confusion matrix

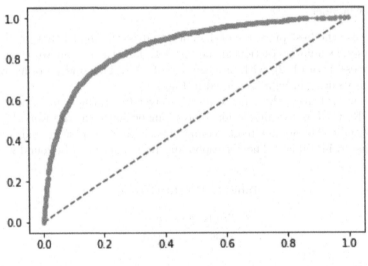

Fig. 2. ROC curve

2.2 Interpretability Results

We are interested in the Interpretable Explanations of Defaults, first to perform a sanity check on the reasons for prediction and second, to extract valuable knowledge from them. In Fig. 3 we find the explanation for a Default prediction *close to the decision threshold*. The figure shows that the variable representing the number of times that the borrower has been 90 days or more past due, and the variable corresponding to the total balance on credit cards and personal lines of credit except for real estate and no installment debt like car loans divided by the sum of credit limits, these two variables define about 50% of probability to fall in default for a borrower.

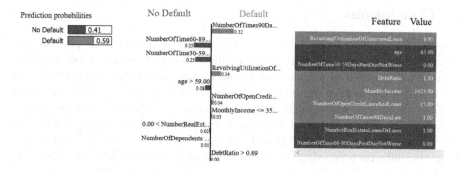

Fig. 3. Intepretable explanations for default

Finally, in Fig. 4 we can appreciate an overwhelming Default prediction, if we need to predict a borrower with *98% probability to fall in default*, our model finds that the number of times that the borrower has been 90 days or more past due, the number of times borrower has been 30–59 days past due but no worse in the last 2 years, the number of times borrower has been 60–89 days past due but no worse in the last 2 years, and again, the revolving utilization of unsecured lines are a good predictor giving the 95% of predictability. These two exemplary cases here shown can provide clear and actionable knowledge.

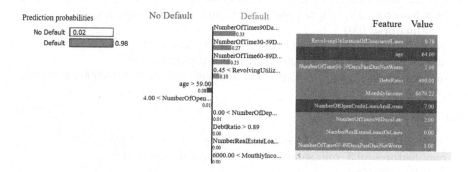

Fig. 4. Interpretable explanations for default

From both previous Figures, we can extract the following key insights:

– The biggest predictor of Default is having been past due for some period.

– Age work in your favor: the older you are the more likely you are to pay on time.
– Revolving Utilization of Unsecured Lines is also a key predictor for default. Higher values are correlated with higher probabilities of Defaulting on a loan.

3   Conclusions

The present work it was shown that the proposed pipeline can provide satisfactory results without much human input and with interpretable explanations. This is essential as financial regulations require better explanations on the detailed mechanism of credit scoring tools for transparency with the client [6,8]. This proves valuable for any domain expert who may not be closely acquainted with the powerful Machine Learning techniques available but still needs to extract the knowledge and insights that can be derived from them. However, data preprocessing is still one of the major hurdles for easy, automatic implementation. As an example, we had to experiment with several resampling algorithms to rebalance the notably unbalanced data that was used. It remains to be explored in future work the possibilities for automatic data preprocessing; both its potential and limitations.

4   Apendix: Hyperparameter Values

All these modeling hyperparameters come in the form of Python code for immediate reproducibility.

4.1   Random Forest with Boosting

– mod_rf=RandomForestClassifier(bootstrap=True, criterion='entropy', max_features=0.1, min_samples_leaf=8, min_samples_split=15, n_estimators=100)
– mod_gb=GradientBoostingClassifier(learning_rate=0.01, max_depth=8, max_features=0.7500000000000001, min_samples_leaf=11, min_samples_split=15, n_estimators=100, subsample=0.9000000000000001)

4.2   Random Forest

– model_rf=RandomForestClassifier(bootstrap=False, criterion='gini', max_features=0.3, min_samples_leaf=3, min_samples_split=15, n_estimators=100)

4.3   XGB Classifier

– model_xgb=xgb.XGBClassifier(learning_rate=0.001, max_depth=7, min_child_weight=19, n_estimators=100, nthread=1, subsample=0.6500000000000001)

References

1. Bergstra, J.S., Bardenet, R., Bengio, Y., Kégl, B.: Algorithms for hyper-parameter optimization. In: Advances in Neural Information Processing Systems, pp. 2546–2554 (2011)
2. Breiman, L.: Random forests. Mach. Learn. **45**(1), 5–32 (2001)
3. Dumitrescu, E., Hue, S., Hurlin, C., Tokpavi, S.: Machine learning for credit scoring: improving logistic regression with non linear decision tree effects. Ph.D. thesis, Paris Nanterre University, University of Orleans (2018)
4. ElMasry, M.H.A.M.T.: Machine learning approach for credit score analysis: a case study of predicting mortgage loan defaults. Ph.D. thesis (2019)
5. Feurer, M., Klein, A., Eggensperger, K., Springenberg, J., Blum, M., Hutter, F.: Efficient and robust automated machine learning. In: Advances in Neural Information Processing Systems, pp. 2962–2970 (2015)
6. Goodman, B., Flaxman, S.: European union regulations on algorithmic decision-making and a "right to explanation". AI Mag. **38**(3), 50–57 (2017)
7. Gulsoy, N., Kulluk, S.: A data mining application in credit scoring processes of small and medium enterprises commercial corporate customers. Wiley Interdiscip. Rev. Data Min. Knowl. Discov. **9**(3), e1299 (2019)
8. Guszcza, J., Rahwan, I., Bible, W., Cebrian, M., Katyal, V.: Why we need to audit algorithms. Harv. Bus. Rev. (2018). https://hbr.org/2018/11/why-we-need-to-audit-algorithms
9. Hernandez, G.J.: Asymptotic behavior of evolutionary algorithms. The University of Memphis (2000)
10. Khandani, A.E., Kim, A.J., Lo, A.W.: Consumer credit-risk models via machine-learning algorithms. J. Bank. Finance **34**(11), 2767–2787 (2010)
11. Komer, B., Bergstra, J., Eliasmith, C.: Hyperopt-Sklearn: automatic hyperparameter configuration for scikit-learn. In: ICML Workshop on AutoML, vol. 9. Citeseer (2014)
12. Olson, R.S., Bartley, N., Urbanowicz, R.J., Moore, J.H.: Evaluation of a tree-based pipeline optimization tool for automating data science. In: Proceedings of the Genetic and Evolutionary Computation Conference 2016, GECCO 2016, pp. 485–492. ACM, New York (2016). https://doi.org/10.1145/2908812.2908918
13. Olson, R.S., Urbanowicz, R.J., Andrews, P.C., Lavender, N.A., Kidd, L.C., Moore, J.H.: Automating biomedical data science through tree-based pipeline optimization. In: Squillero, G., Burelli, P. (eds.) EvoApplications 2016. LNCS, vol. 9597, pp. 123–137. Springer, Cham (2016). https://doi.org/10.1007/978-3-319-31204-0_9
14. Reif, M., Shafait, F., Dengel, A.: Meta-learning for evolutionary parameter optimization of classifiers. Mach. Learn. **87**(3), 357–380 (2012)
15. Ribeiro, M.T., Singh, S., Guestrin, C.: Why should I trust you?: explaining the predictions of any classifier. In: Proceedings of the 22nd ACM SIGKDD International Conference on Knowledge Discovery and Data Mining, pp. 1135–1144. ACM (2016)

IRBASIR-B: Rule Induction from Similarity Relations, a Bayesian Approach

Lenniet Coello[1], Yaima Filiberto[2(✉)], Rafael Bello[3], Mabel Frias[4],
and Rafael Falcon[5]

[1] Ryder, Miami, USA
Lenniet_m_coello@ryder.com
[2] AMV Soluciones, Avenida de Madrid 40, Oficina 14, Vigo, Spain
yaima.filiberto@amvsoluciones.com
[3] Central University of Las Villas Carretera Camajuaní km 5.5, Santa Clara, Cuba
rbellop@uclv.edu.cu
[4] University of Camaguey Carretera de Circunvalación Norte entre Camino Viejo de
Nuevitas y Ave Ignacio Agramonte, Camagüey, Cuba
mabel.frias@reduc.edu.cu
[5] University of Ottawa, Ottawa, Canada
rfalcon@uottawa.ca

Abstract. IRBASIR is a recently proposed algorithm that, inspired on
one of the extensions of classical Rough Set Theory, employs similarity
relations to learn classification rules. By using similarity relations as
its underlying building blocks, IRBASIR is able to process datasets with
both nominal and numerical features. In this paper we propose IRBASIR-
Bayes, a modification to the IRBASIR method that relies on Bayesian
Networks to construct the reference vector used to generate the rules.
This scheme has demonstrated satisfactory performance compared to
other rule induction algorithms.

Keywords: IRBASIR · Bayesian approach · Similarity relations

1 Introduction

Technological innovation continues to grow at a fast pace, thus giving rise to
modern computational tools that make capturing, storing and processing a myr-
iad of data a much straightforward endeavor than in previous generations; this
fact, together with the overwhelming volume of data being generated in the last
two decades, has sparked a renewed interest in different scientific branches like
Machine Learning [12].

Machine Learning is a very active research field within Artificial Intelligence that seeks to develop automated techniques capable of learning from the
vast oceans of data available nowadays; in other words, the goal is the automatic extraction of meaningful and representative knowledge from the raw data
streams in a particular domain of consideration [15].

© Springer Nature Switzerland AG 2020
J. C. Figueroa-García et al. (Eds.): WEA 2020, CCIS 1274, pp. 24–34, 2020.
https://doi.org/10.1007/978-3-030-61834-6_3

Inducing classification rules from data is a classical Machine Learning problem. Most approaches follow a sequential covering strategy in order to come up with and then refine the rule base. They do this by working on a training set consisting of objects that are characterized through a list of conditional attributes (that represent the antecedents of the ensuing rules). These methods use the conditional attributes to arrive at a conclusion regarding the decision (class/label) attribute, often expressed at the consequent of rules. On the other hand, uncertainty management as well as knowledge representation, remain pivotal issues for Artificial Intelligence. Uncertainty is very pervasive and inherent to the real world and may emerge in multiple fashions caused by: (i) inaccurate information due to wrong measurements or transmission errors; (ii) incomplete information owing to forbidden or expensive access to data sources and (iii) ambiguous concept descriptions.

Bayesian reasoning emerged in the 1980s as a probabilistic model for reasoning with uncertainty in Artificial Intelligence and in just a few years, became popular. Different successful applications of Bayesian reasoning have been reported in fields as medicine, information retrieval, computer vision, information fusion, agriculture and so on.

In this study we employ Bayesian reasoning to improve the performance of the a recently proposed rule induction algorithm, named IRBASIR, by rewriting the aggregation function from a Bayesian angle. The new method, IRBASIR-Bayes, shows superior classification accuracy in comparison to other well-known rule induction methods. The rest of the paper is structured as follows. Section 2 elaborates on the technical background while Sect. 3 focuses on the application of Bayesian concepts to the IRBASIR algorithm. The empirical analysis is reported in Sect. 4. Conclusions and further remarks are stated in Sect. 5.

2   Technical Background

In this section we briefly review some foundational concepts in this study such as Bayesian networks as well as the Naïve-Bayes and IRBASIR algorithms.

2.1   Bayesian Networks

An increasing number of studies have to cope with a large number of variables that exhibit complex relationships among them. Bayesian Networks, (BNs) are a class of probabilistic networks that model precisely these interactions. Probabilistic networks are graphical representations of a problems variables and their relationships [14]. Simply put, BNs have a topological/structural component and a parametric/numerical component. The former is realized via a Directed Acyclic Graph (DAG) that encodes the qualitative knowledge of the model through probabilistic relationships of conditional dependence and independence. This knowledge is articulated in defining these dependence/independence relationships among the model variables. These relationships range from complete independence to a functional dependence. The fact that the model is specified in a graph-based fashion makes BNs really attractive among other peer knowledge representation formalisms. BNs not only qualitatively model the domain knowledge but also quantitatively express the "strength" of the relationships among the variables by means of probability distributions as the extent of the belief we hold on the underlying relations among the model variables.

A Directed Acyclic Graph is composed of nodes denoting the problem variables, which could be descriptive features or attributes. Each pair of nodes is connected by directed edges. These edges represent probabilistic dependencies between the variables. In terms of probabilities, linking X to Y means there is a conditional dependence of Y with respect to X, i.e., $Y's$ probability distribution is different from that of Y given X. These variables will be linked to the decision class that would act as the root variable. The parametric component of a BN take the form of Conditional Probability Tables (CPTs) established from the information encoded in the DAG. The Bayes theorem is given by Eq. 1,

$$P(h|O) = \frac{P(O|h)P(h)}{P(O)} \tag{1}$$

where h is a hypothesis, O is an observation (or set of observations) and $P(hO)$, $P(Oh)$ are conditional probabilities. The latter is the *likelihood* that hypothesis h may have produced the set of observations $O.P(h)$ is called the *prior* probability and represents the initial degree of belief in h. For a classification problem with the class variable C and set of input attributes $A = \{A_1, A_2, \cdots, A_n\}$ the Bayes theorem adopts the form in Eq. 2,

$$P(c|A) = \frac{P(A|c)P(c)}{P(A)} \tag{2}$$

What we want is to identify the most plausible decision class c_* in the set $C = \{c_1, c_2, \cdots, c_k\}$ for an observation O that needs to be classified. In the Bayesian framework, the most plausible hypothesis is the one with the maximum a posteriori (MAP) probability. In other words, the decision class c_* to be assigned to O is computed by means of Eq. 3,

$$c_* = \arg\max_{c \in C}\{P(A|c)P(c)\} \tag{3}$$

Notice that the denominator in Eq. 2 has not been included in Eq. 3 for simplification purposes. Bayes' theorem hence provides a neat and interpretable way to solve a classification problem.

2.2 Naïve-Bayes

A Bayesian classifier that is usually quite accurate despite its simplicity is known as Naïve-Bayes (NB) [11]. NB is actually one of the most widely used methods among the BN family of classification techniques.

The core of the NB classifier is the underlying assumption that all attributes are independent given the value of the class variable. NB's name stems from the assumption that predictive variables are conditionally independent given the decision variable; this assumption gives rise to a simplified form of Eq. 2, hence we will only need to learn the conditional probabilities of the attributes given the class values [15]. The simplified expression used by NB for classification purposes is given in Eq. 4,

$$c_* = \arg\max_{c \in C} \prod_{i=1}^{n} P(A|c) \tag{4}$$

This procedure is known as *maximum likelihood estimation*. Unfortunately, it requires a large sample size and tends to overfit the data. More complex estimators like Laplace succession are applied to counter this limitation.

NB deals with the numerical data assuming all attributes are generated from different normal or Gaussian probability distributions. The mean and standard deviation for each decision class and numeric attribute is then calculated [15]. The probability density function for a normal distribution with mean μ and standard deviation σ is given by Eq. 5,

$$f(x, \mu, \sigma) = \frac{1}{\sigma\sqrt{2\pi}} e^{-\frac{(x-\mu)^2}{2\sigma^2}} \tag{5}$$

NB is one of the strongest and most popular classifiers. Several studies confirm that its classification results are competitive with regards to, or even surpass, those produced by other models such as decision trees, neural networks, etc.

2.3 IRBASIR

IRBASIR (Induction of Rules BAsed on SImilarity Relations) is an algorithm [4, 5,7] for the automatic generation of classification rules in decision systems that may contain both nominal and numerical attributes. The algorithm leans upon the learning of similarity relations [3] for building similarity classes of objects, which is accomplished by extending the canonical Rough Set Theory (RST). The overall similarity relation learned from data encompasses attribute-wise similarity functions for both nominal and numerical descriptors. Algorithm 1 depicts the operational workflow of the IRBASIR algorithm introduced in [7].

Algorithm 1. The IRBASIR Algorithm

Input : a decision system $D = (U; A \cup \{d\})$ with $|U| = m \neq 0$ objects and $|A| = n \neq 0$ attributes
Output : a set of classification rules
1: Define the set of attribute-wise similarity functions
2: Build the similarity relation R
3: Generate classification rules and their associated confidence values by using *GenRulesRST*()

In step 1, we need to specify the set of functions $\delta_i(x, y)$ that determine the similarity between two objects x and y based on their values for the attribute A_i.

Equations 6 show the expressions used in [7] to deal with numerical and nominal attributes, respectively,

$$\partial_i(x,y) = \begin{cases} 1 & \text{if } x \text{ and } y \text{ are real and } |x_i - y_i| \leq \varepsilon \\ & \text{or } x \text{ and } y \text{ are discrete and } x = y \\ 0 & \text{otherside} \end{cases} \tag{6}$$

To build the similarity relation R Eq. 7 are employed,

$$xRy \text{ if and only if } F_1(x,y) \geq \varepsilon \text{ and } F_2(x,y) = 1 \tag{7}$$

where ε denotes a threshold. For the experiment the value of $\varepsilon = 0.85$ was used for all datasets suggested by [8]. The functions F_1 and F_2 are defined by Eqs. 8 and 9:

$$F_1(x,y) = \sum_{i=1}^{n} w_i * \partial_i(x,y) \tag{8}$$

$$F_2(x,y) = \begin{cases} 1 & \text{if } class(x) = class(y) \\ 0 & \text{otherside} \end{cases} \tag{9}$$

where n is the number of features, w_i is the weight of feature i calculated according to the method proposed in [5,6] and ∂_i is a features comparison function which calculates the similarity between the values of objects x and y with respect to the feature instances i, is defined by expression 10,

$$\partial_i(x_i, y_i) = \begin{cases} 1 - \dfrac{|x_i - y_i|}{\max(D_i) - \min(D_i)} & \text{if } i \text{ is continuous} \\ 1 & \text{if } i \text{ is discrete and } x_i = y_i \\ 0 & \text{if } i \text{ is discrete and } x_i \neq y_i \end{cases} \tag{10}$$

where D_i is the domain of feature i.

The third step is the automatic learning of classification rules based on Algorithm 2. This procedure is to generate classification rules and it's *certidumbre value*.

In the pseudo code of Algorithm 2, $[x_i]_R$ returns the set of decision classes of all objects in a set passed as input argument. Upon calculation of the similarity class $[x_i]_R$ for an object x_i, if the objects in the similarity class all share the same value of the decision class, a rule for that decision class is created; otherwise, the most frequent class in that object set is taken and a rule is created for it.

Then the objects in $[x_i]_R$ are all flagged as used and the rule generation process carries on. The *GenRulSim()* procedure is given in Algorithm 3.

Algorithm 2. The GenRulesRST Algorithm

Input : a decision system $D = (U; A \cup \{d\})$ with $|U| = m \neq 0$ objects and $|A| = n \neq 0$ attributes

Output : a set of classification rules (ruleBase)

1: objectUsed[j] ← false $\forall j \in \{1, \ldots, m\}$;
2: $ruleBase \leftarrow \emptyset$;
3: i ← index of the first unused object;
4: **if** i==0 **then**
5:     stop; return ruleBase
6: **else**
7:     objectUsed[i] ← true;
8: compute similarity class $[x_i]_R$;
9: rule ← $GenRulSim(k, [x_i]_R, C)$;
10: ruleBase ← ruleBase $\cup$ rule;
11: objectUsed[j] ← true $\forall j : x_j \in C \bigwedge d(x_j) == k$
12: Go to line 3;

Algorithm 3. The GenRulesSim Algorithm

Input : decision class k, similarity class object set O_s, objects in O_s with class O_s^k

Output : a classification rule as well as its accuracy and coverage

1: create a vector p for the objects in O_s^k, $p(i) = f(V_i[O_s^k]); \forall i \in \{1, \ldots, n\}$
2: generate the rule from the vector p, rule ← IF $w_1 \partial_1(x_1, p_1) + \cdots + w_n \delta_n(x_n, p_n) \geq \varepsilon$
   THEN $d \leftarrow k$;
3: compute the rule accuracy $acc(rule) \leftarrow \dfrac{|A(rule) \cap O_s|}{|A(rule)|}$;
4: compute the rule coverage $cov(rule) \leftarrow \dfrac{|A(rule) \cap O_s|}{|O_s|}$;
5: return $\langle rule, acc(rule), cov(rule) \rangle$;

The term $V_i[O_s^k]$ in Step 1 denotes the set of values of the attribute V_i for those objects belonging to the set O_s^k. The function $f(V_i[O_s^k])$ aggregates the set of values in $V_i[O_s^k]$ depending on the type of the attribute V_i, e.g., the mode in case of V_i being a nominal attribute or the mean/median if it is a numerical attribute.

Hence, the vector p could be thought of as a prototype (or centroid) for all objects in O_s^k. Additionally, the weight vector $(w_1, \ldots, w_n)$, the similarity threshold ε and the attribute-wise similarity functions δ_i and come from Eqs. 7 and 8.

3   The IRBASIR-Bayes Algorithm

In order to improve the performance of the IRBASIR algorithm, a modification in Step 1 of the *GenRulSim()* method is introduced. The idea is to vary the aggregation function $f(\cdot)$ to find the vector p with n components for the set of reference objects in O_s^k, from which the rules are generated.

The main idea of the proposed IRBASIR-Bayes approach is to rewrite the function $f(\cdot)$ by switching from a purely statistical aggregation method, such as the mean or the mode of a set, to a probabilistic scheme like the one used in the NaïveBayes classifier.

Each component $p(i), i = 1, \cdots, n$, of the reference (central tendency) vector p is now calculated as shown in Eq. 11 if V_i is a nominal attribute and by means of Eq. 11 if V_i is a numerical attribute,

$$p_{(i)} = \arg \max_{v \in V_i[O_s^k]} \left\{ \frac{|x \in O_s^k : x_i == v|}{O_s^k} \right\} \tag{11}$$

$$p_{(i)} = \arg \max_{v \in V_i[O_s^k]} \left\{ \frac{1}{\sigma\sqrt{2\pi}} e^{-\frac{(x-\mu)^2}{2\sigma^2}} \right\} \tag{12}$$

In the nominal/discrete case portrayed in Eq. 11, the estimation of the conditional probability is based on the frequencies with which the different values for the attribute V_i appear in the objects of the set O_s^k. The reader may notice that this approach is equivalent to the calculation of the mode of V_i over O_s^k. Semantically, this means that the vector component $p(i)$ will take the most frequently occurring value in that attribute for the objects under consideration. Therefore, the reference vector p is made up by the most frequent values of all nominal attributes in the decision system.

When it comes to numerical attributes, however, the NB method assumes they follow an underlying Gaussian probability distribution; hence, the first step is the calculation of the sample mean μ_i and the sample standard deviation σ_i for the objects in the similarity class O_s^k. Then, Eq. 12 applies to each numeric value x of the attribute V_i over the objects in O_s^k. From a semantic standpoint, this means that the representative value for that attribute captured by the vector component $p(i)$ will be the one with the highest probability distribution value among all other values of V_i for the objects under consideration.

4   Experimental Results

For the empirical analysis, we relied on 13 UCI Machine Learning Repository data sets[1] in .ARFF format. They were used to gauge the efficacy and efficiency of the algorithms under consideration. Table 1 lists the data sets.

We will empirically compare the classification accuracy of the following classifiers: C4.5 [13], EXPLORER [10], MODLEM [10], LEM2 [9], IRBASIR [4] and IRBASIRBayes for each of the datasets using 10-fold cross validation. Table 2 reports these results. To calculate the measurement accuracy there was used the measure that is typically used in these cases, as shown in expression 13:

$$Accuracy = \frac{TP + TN}{TP + TN + FP + FN} \tag{13}$$

where: TP (True Positives), TN (True Negatives), FP (False Positives) and FN (False Negatives).

---

[1] http://www.ics.uci.edu/~mlearn/MLRepository.html.

Table 1. Description of the datasets used in the experiments.

Datasets	#Instances	#Attributes
ecoli	336	7
iris	150	4
pima	768	8
heart-statlog	270	13
balance-scale	625	4
haberman	306	3
biomed	194	8
breast-w	699	9
wisconsin	699	9
optdigits	5620	64
waveform	5000	21
diabetes	768	8
vehicle	845	18

Table 2. Classification accuracy results for all rule induction algorithms

Datasets	IRBASIR-Bayes	IRBASIR	C4.5	LEM2	EXPLORE	MODLEM
ecoli	**80.14**	80.09	79.47	52.97	0.6	75.7
iris	**96.06**	96	94.67	94	88	94
pima	**75.29**	75.26	75.26	65.89	60.29	74.23
heart-statlog	**82.04**	79.63	77.78	75.19	81.85	75.19
balance-scale	**85.95**	84.95	77.9	83.67	84.78	80.47
haberman	**73.25**	72.87	70.97	71.48	67.91	70.27
biomed	**88.14**	87.16	86.53	66.5	66.63	85
breast-w	**84.7**	80.46	75.1	59.82	0	70.26
wisconsin	**96.25**	95.15	94.57	95.16	89.13	93.99
optdigits	**96.51**	96.3	95.56	95.75	89.41	94.28
waveform	93.88	**93.98**	90	79.59	0	78.72
diabetes	75.19	**75.66**	74.62	64.83	59.9	75.27
vehicle	**72.01**	71.78	71.81	49.76	58.27	53.66

To statistically validate the results, we employed non-parametric multiple-comparison tests in order to identify the best algorithm. The Friedman test is the non-parametric standard test for comparison among several classifiers. This test works by assigning ranks in ascending order, i.e., the first rank for the best obtained results, the second rank for the second best result and so on [2].

The null hypothesis states that all algorithms behave similarly, so the ranks should be similar. In the experimental study conducted in this investigation, the p-value found using the Friedman statistic was zero, while the critical point for a Chi-square distribution with five degrees of freedom was 44.241758. As the value obtained by the Friedman statistic is much lower than this latter value, there is enough evidence to reject the null hypothesis and conclude that there are indeed statistically significant differences among the groups. Table 3 displays the ranks produced by the Friedman test upon the set of algorithms under comparison, with IRBASIS-Bayes topping the list.

Table 3. Friedman ranks for each algorithm

Algorithms	Ranks
IRBASIR-Bayes	1.2308
IRBASIR	2.1154
C4.5	3.5
LEM2	4.4615
MODLEM	4.4615
EXPLORER	5.2308

Table 4. Holm post-hoc procedure results with IRBASIR-Bayes as the control method

Algorithm	$z = (R_0 - R_i)/SE$	p	Holm	Hypothesis
EXPLORER	5,451,081	0	0.01	Rejected
LEM2	4,402,796	0.000011	0.0125	Rejected
MODLEM	4,402,796	0.000011	0.016667	Rejected
C45	309,244	0.001985	0.025	Rejected
IRBASIR	1,205,528	0.228	0.05	Rejected

Table 4 displays the results of the Holm post-hoc procedure used to compare the control algorithm (IRBASIR-BAYES) with the rest at a 5% significance level. The test statistic for comparing the ith algorithm and jth algorithm, z, depends on the main nonparametric procedure used; where R_0 and R_i are the average rankings by the Friedman test of the algorithms compared [1]. Holm test rejects those hypotheses having a p-value ≤ 0.05. The test rejects all cases in favor of the best-ranked algorithm; hence we can claim that the proposed algorithm is statistically superior to the other ones in terms of classification accuracy.

5 Conclusions

The IRBASIR algorithm allows inducing classification rules for mixed data (i.e., numerical and nominal attributes). It is characterized by not requiring the discretization of the numerical attributes, neither as a preprocessing step nor during the learning process. IRBASIR generates the rules from a reference or prototype vector that allows constructing similarity classes for the objects in the training set. This vector is simply calculated as the mean/median for each numerical attribute.

IRBASIR-Bayes is a spin-off from IRBASIR that alters the way in which prototype vectors are constructed, namely by switching from the mean/median statistical approach to a probabilistic approach through the classification functions used by Naïve-Bayes. IRABASIR-Bayes has the disadvantage of assuming normality and independence among data. Nevertheless, the results obtained with 13 publicly available Machine Learning repositories evidence a statistically verified superiority in terms of classification accuracy to other well-known rule induction algorithms (C4.5, MODLEM, EXPLORER, LEM2, and IRBASIR itself); another benefit is that the method allows processing attributes with missing values. Future work will concentrate on the parametric tuning of IRBASIR and IRBASIR-Bayes so as to obtain even higher accuracy marks.

References

1. Daniel, W.: Applied Nonparametric Statistics, 2nd edn. Duxbury Thomson Learning, Pacific Grove (2000)
2. Derrac, J., García, S., Molina, D., Herrera, F.: A practical tutorial on the use of nonparametric statistical tests as a methodology for comparing evolutionary and swarm intelligence algorithms. Swarm Evol. Comput. **1**(1), 3–18 (2011)
3. Fernandez, Y., Coello, L., Filiberto, Y., Bello, R., Falcon, R.: Learning similarity measures from data with fuzzy sets and particle swarms. In: 2014 11th International Conference on Electrical Engineering, Computing Science and Automatic Control (CCE), pp. 1–6 (2014)
4. Filiberto, Y., Bello, R., Caballero, Y., Frias, M.: Algoritmo para el aprendizaje de reglas de clasificacion basado en la teoria de los conjuntos aproximados extendida. Dyna **78**(169), 62–70 (2011)
5. Filiberto, Y., Bello, R., Caballero, Y., Frias, M.: An analysis about the measure quality of similarity and its applications in machine learning. In: Fourth International Workshop on Knowledge Discovery, Knowledge Management and Decision Support (2013)
6. Filiberto, Y., Bello, R., Caballero, Y., Larrua, R.: Using PSO and RST to predict the resistant capacity of connections in composite structures. In: González, J.R., Pelta, D.A., Cruz, C., Terrazas, G., Krasnogor, N. (eds.) Nature Inspired Cooperative Strategies for Optimization (NICSO 2010). Studies in Computational Intelligence, vol. 284, pp. 359–370. Springer, Heidelberg (2010). https://doi.org/10.1007/978-3-642-12538-6_30
7. Filiberto, Y., Caballero, Y., Larrua, R., Bello, R.: A method to build similarity relations into extended rough set theory. In: 2010 10th International Conference on Intelligent Systems Design and Applications (ISDA), pp. 1314–1319 (2010)
8. Fras, M., Filiberto, Y., Fernndez, Y., Caballero, Y., Bello, R.: Prototypes selection based on similarity relations for classification problems, October 2015
9. Grzymala-Busse, J.W.: A new version of the rule induction system LERS. Fundamenta Informaticae **31**(1), 27–39 (1997)

10. Grzymala-Busse, J.W.: Mining numerical data – a rough set approach. In: Peters, J.F., Skowron, A. (eds.) Transactions on Rough Sets XI. LNCS, vol. 5946, pp. 1–13. Springer, Heidelberg (2010). https://doi.org/10.1007/978-3-642-11479-3_1

11. Keerthika, G., Priya, D.S.: Feature subset evaluation and classification using Naive-Bayes classifier. J. Netw. Commun. Emerg. Technol. (JNCET), **1**(1) (2015). www.jncet.org

12. Kodratoff, Y., Michalski, R.S.: Machine Learning: An Artificial Intelligence Approach. Springer, Heidelberg (2014). https://doi.org/10.1007/978-3-662-12405-5

13. Quinlan, J.R.: C4.5: Programs for Machine Learning. Morgan Kaufmann Publishers Inc., San Mateo (1993)

14. Whittaker, J.: Graphical Models in Applied Multivariate Statistics. Wiley, Chichester (2009)

15. Witten, I.H., Frank, E.: Data Mining: Practical Machine Learning Tools and Techniques. Elsevier, San Francisco (2005)

Using Numerical Modelling and Artificial Intelligence for Predicting the Degradation of the Resistance to Vertical Shear in Steel – Concrete Composite Beams Under Fire

Rafael Larrua Quevedo[1], Yisel Larrua Pardo[1], Valdir Pignatta Silva[2], Yaima Filiberto Cabrera[3(✉)], and Yaile Caballero Mota[4]

[1] Department of Civil Engineering, University of Camaguey,
Carretera Circunvalación Norte km 5 1/2., 74650 Camaguey, Cuba
{rafael.larrua,yisel.larrua}@reduc.edu.cu
[2] Department of Structural and Geotechnical Engineering,
Polytechnic School of the University of Sao Paulo (EPUSP),
Av. Prof. Almeida Prado TRAV. 2, 83, 05508-900 São Paulo, SP, Brazil
valpigss@usp.br
[3] Research and Development Department, AMV Soluciones,
Avenida de Madrid 40, Oficina 14, 36204 Vigo, Spain
yaima.filiberto@amvsoluciones.com
[4] Department of Computer Sciences, University of Camaguey, Camaguey,
Cuba. Carretera Circunvalación Norte km 5 1/2., 74650 Camaguey, Cuba
yaile.caballero@reduc.edu.cu

Abstract. In this paper the combination of numerical modelling and artificial intelligence for predicting the degradation of the resistance to vertical shear in composite beams under fire is exposed. This work presents a technique that integrates the backpropagation learning method with a method to calculate the initial weights in order to train the Multilayer Perceptron Model (MLP). The method used to calculate the initial weights of the MLP is based on the quality of similarity measure proposed on the framework of the extended Rough Set Theory (RST). The artificial neural network models were trained and tested using numerical results from the thermal-structural analysis carried out by the two-dimensional fire-dedicated FE software Super Tempcalc and the computational tool SCBEAM which was developed by the authors for the resistances determinations. The results revealed that the proposed approach accurately permits the prediction of the degradation of the resistance to vertical shear in steel – concrete composite beams under fire.

Keywords: Fire design · Composite beams · Vertical shear resistance · Artificial intelligence · MLP · Measure quality of similarity

© Springer Nature Switzerland AG 2020
J. C. Figueroa-García et al. (Eds.): WEA 2020, CCIS 1274, pp. 35–47, 2020.
https://doi.org/10.1007/978-3-030-61834-6_4

1   Introduction

A composite construction is essentially characterized by the presentation in its structure of elements having resistant sections in which the structural steel and concrete work jointly. Exposure of these structural materials at high temperatures results in the degeneration of the physical and chemical characteristics, generating reduction in strength and stiffness, which causes the degradation of the resistance of cross sections of structural elements. For the verification of resistance to vertical shear in steel-concrete composite beams, the main international standards tends to consider only the contribution of the steel web at room temperature or in fire [1–3]; for the second situation, it is essential to have the temperature distribution in the steel web at each considered fire exposition time. For the thermal analysis, different standards, such as EN 1994-1-2 (2005) [3] or ABNT NBR 14323: 2013 [4], present analytical simplified formulations for determining the evolution of the temperatures, which can lead to uneconomical results. Therefore, in the present paper the finite-element approach (FE) is adopted for such purpose. On the other hand, Artificial Neural Networks (ANNs) construct a functional relationship between input and output patterns through the learning process; relationship in the form of weights are memorised, and recalled in applications [5]. The crucial part in ANN-based modelling is ANN training. Many learning algorithms are used for the neural networks to learn the relationship between input and output patterns; among them, the backpropagation (BP) algorithm is most widely used to train the Multilayer Perceptron (MLP), which is one of the most popular models in artificial neural networks, where neurons are grouped in layers and only forward connections exists. In supervised problems, the learning algorithms are based on the output error; this error is the difference between the neural network output and the desired output, and it is a function of the weights; the algorithms minimize the output error by adjusting neural networks' weights [5]. There are permanent efforts to integrate ANN with the Fuzzy Set Theory, Genetic algorithms, Rough Set Theory (RST) and other methodologies in the Soft Computing paradigm. This is the case of [6], in which the basic idea of the proposed method is to set the initial weights from the input layer to the hidden layer using the weights of conditional features which are calculated to build the similarity relation that maximize the measure quality of similarity proposed in the framework of the RST. ANN method has recently been used to solve a diversity of structural engineering problems. Some of the problems deals with the prediction of the magnitude and distribution of different kinds of loads [10], diverse properties of structural materials [11,14], the resistance of structural sections [15,16] and the structural damage [19,21]. Though many researchers have applied ANNs for the prediction of the structural responses at room temperature, there is a limited number of works reported on ANNs applications in the field of the predictions in fire situation [23]. Besides, there is no research reported in literature on predicting resistances in steel – concrete composite beams in fire. This study is concerned with not only the prediction of the response of composite beams in fire, specifically the degradation of the resistance to vertical shear, but also the performance of a combined approach, using FE and artificial intelligence (AI), for solving fire engineering problems.

2 Applied Artificial Intelligence (A.I) Approach to Predict the Degradation of the Resistance

In this paper a method in which the equivalence classic relation RST [26] is replaced by a weaker binary relation [29] was used in [6–9]. The similarity between two objects (x, y) from the description of the problems (according to n condition features) and the similarity regarding the solution of the problems (feature of decision) is set according to the relations R_1 and R_2 respectively, as defined by the expressions 1 and 2:

$$x R_1 y \; if \; and \; only \; if \; F_1(x, y) \geq \varepsilon_1 \tag{1}$$

$$x R_2 y \; if \; and \; only \; if \; F_2(x, y) \geq \varepsilon_2 \tag{2}$$

The function F_1 is a function for comparing the values of the feature decision. Note that two objects in classification problems are similar objects according to F_2 if they belong to the same class; e_1 and e_2 are thresholds, and the function F_1 is defined by the expression 3:

$$F_1(x, y) = \sum_{i=1}^{N} w_i * \partial_i(x_i, y_i) \tag{3}$$

where w_i is the weight of feature i and $\partial_i()$ is the comparison function for the feature i. The purpose is to find relations R_1 and R_2 such that similar objects to any object x of the universe according to R_1 and R_1 are practically the same, i.e. the set N_1 and N_2, defined by the expressions 4 and 5, should be similar (optimal case is $N_1(x) = N_2(x)$, for any object x).

$$N_1(x) = \{y \in U : x R_1 y\} \tag{4}$$

$$N_2(x) = \{y \in U : x R_2 y\} \tag{5}$$

The degree of similarity between both sets for an object x is expressed by the following measure 6:

$$\varphi(x) = \frac{|N_1(x) \cap N_2(x)|}{0.5 * |N_1(x)| + 0.5 * |N_2(x)|} \qquad 0 \leq \varphi(x) \leq 1 \tag{6}$$

From which is defined, by the 7, the quality of the similarity measure of a decision system (DS) with a universe of M objects:

$$\theta(DS) = \left\{ \frac{\sum\limits_{\forall X \in U} \varphi(x)}{|U|} \right\} \tag{7}$$

The objective is to maximize the value of $\theta(DS)$. The value of this measure depends on the function F_1. Using the weighted sum defined by (3), and given the comparison functions for each feature, the problem is reduced to finding the set of weights $W = \{w_1, w_2, ..., w_n\}$, to construct F_1. In order to find the set of weights W associated with the condition features, a method is proposed in [30]. This method uses the metaheuristic Particle Swarm Optimization (PSO) [31], in which the particles are real vectors with dimension n and the evaluation function of the particles is defined by 7. At the end of the search process, the particle with maximum value of the measured quality of similarity is used as weights for the condition features. In this research, a method to calculate the initial weights in the MLP network consists of using the set of weights W as the initial weights between the input layer and the hidden layer in the MLP network.In general, MLPs can have several hidden layers. However, a three-layer neural network with n inputs (features), q outputs (categories), and one hidden layer with a variable number of nodes $(n + q)/2$ is adopted. (see Fig. 1)

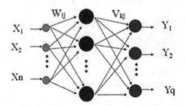

Fig. 1. The topology of the MLP in this research.

The initial values for the MLP are the following: W_{ji} (weight of the connection between the jth hidden node and the ith input node) are assigned in the following way: $W_{ji} = W_i$ for all j, where W_i is the calculated weight for the feature i. Note, all links from the ith input node have the same value (the weight calculated for the ith feature using the method described before). V_{kj} (weight of the connection between the jth hidden node and the kth output node) are random values in the interval [0, 1].

In [6], an experimental study for problems of function approximation in which 12 databases were used from the UCI repository [32] was exposed. The results show a superior performance of the MLP when the initial weights from the input layer to the hidden layer were established using the weights of conditional features which are calculated to build the similarity relation that maximize the measure quality of similarity proposed in the framework of the RST (MLP + RST + PSO approach), compared to other previously reported methods to calculate the weight of features.

3 Resistance to Vertical Shear in Steel Concrete – Composite Beams. Thermo – Structural Analysis

For the purposes of thermal analysis, different standards, such as EN 1994-1-2: 2005 [3] or ABNT NBR 14323: 2013 [4], recommend the thermal properties of the materials and present analytical formulations for determining the temperatures in the component parts of the steel section, for unprotected and protected steel beams. This analytical approach does not consider heat transfer between the different parts of the steel profile or from the profile to the concrete slab. These models can lead to uneconomical results, since they consider uniform temperature in each element. On the other hand, a number of previous studies have demonstrated the applicability of Super Tempcalc – Temperature Calculation and Design v.5 (TCD) [36] to the modelling of heat transfer problems in structural fire engineering. This software is a two-dimensional fire-dedicated FE software, in which the heat flow is derived from the conservation of energy, describing the fact that the total inflow equals the total outflow per unit time. The constitutive relation invoked is Fourier's constitutive law of heat conduction which describes the heat flow within the material. However, SuperTempcalc does not contain a calculation module for determining structural analyses of composite cross sections in fire situation. So, it was necessary to implement a computational tool (SCBEAM), with the ability to determine the resistance to vertical shear at room temperature and in fire situation from the results issued by the thermal analysis module of TCD. The thermal analysis was carried out using TCD based on the following criteria:

- In the geometric modelling, domain coincided with the cross section of the composite section. Models formed by a steel rolled W section and a solid concrete slab were analysed. In addition when fire protection is included protection material thicknesses of 0.01, 0.025 0.040 m were considered.
- Thermal properties of materials recommended in EN 1994-1-2 [3] were considered. Also, values of conductivities and capacitances representing a wide range of protection materials usually used in international practice were considered, that is, thermal conductivities between 0.1 and 0,3 W/(K.m) and an average capacitance of 625 000 J/mK.
- All cross sections were subjected to standard fire exposure and the initial temperature was adopted equal to 20 °C. A time step equal to 0.002 hours. In this study the fire exposure was limited to 40 and 120 min for unprotected and protected sections, respectively.
- For the boundary conditions it is assumed that three sides, under slab, are exposed to standard fire ISO 834 [37], while lateral and upper sides of the slab are at room temperature (20 °C).
- To select the type of finite element and defining the mesh density it was taken into account that the cross sections are composed by rectangular geometries; for this reason, an automatically generated mesh, comprising of rectangular elements with the longest side $L \leq 0.01$ m was adopted.

However, according to the essential purposes of the present work, outputs in Microsoft Excel format containing the evolution of the temperatures on all the nodes of the section is especially relevant and are the basic inputs for the computational tool SCBEAM implemented in the present research in order to determine the resistances, at room temperatures and under fire, of the considered sections. SCBEAM permits the study of the degradation of different types of resistances in composite steel – concrete beams under fire. The software gives detailed information about temperatures in different parts of the cross section and their averages, the forces involved in the resistance responses, the moments and shear resistances at ambient temperature and in fire and the relative values between the responses in these two situations.

4   Degradation of Resistance to Vertical Shear

4.1   Generalities

To characterise the degradation of the resistance the relative parameter ν is defined 8:

$$\nu = \frac{V_{Rd,fi}}{V_{Rd}} \tag{8}$$

where:

$V_{Rd,fi}$: design resistance to vertical shear of the cross section in a fire situation.

V_{Rd}: design resistance to vertical shear of the cross section at room temperature.

For the study, a selection of 32 profiles from American Wide Flange Beams (W profiles) were used, taking into account their ample international use, specifically the types: W310, W360, W410, W460, W530 and W610, with appropriate characteristics to the field of application of composite beams in buildings construction.

4.2   Unprotected Beams

In order to facilitate the study of the degradation of resistance to vertical shear, the design resistance at room temperature (VRd) and in fire situation ($V_{Rd,fi}$) were determined. Also, relative parameter $\nu(V_{Rd,fi}/V_{Rd})$ was calculated and ν vs time of exposure to standard fire ISO-834 [36] curves were constructed in the range of 0 to 40 min. It was demonstrated that the degradation of the resistance to vertical shear is not significantly influenced by the steel strength. This resistance is also independent of other factors such as the effective width and the thickness of the concrete slab, the characteristic concrete compressive strength and the degree of interaction.

4.3   Protected Beams

In protected beams, the analysis of the resistance degradation takes into account both the protection material thickness (10, 25 and 40 mm) and the protection material conductivity (0.1, 0.2 and 0.3 (W/K•m). As expected, both the protection material thickness and the thermal conductivity have a marked influence on the degradation of the resistance to vertical shear.

5   Prediction of the Degradation of the Resistance to Vertical Shear by MLP + RST + PSO Approach

5.1   Generalities

The main objective of this section is to demonstrate the effectiveness of the approach MLP + RST + PSO in predicting degradation of resistance to vertical shear of composite sections in fire. Firstly, the solutions for all instances in unprotected beams were determined by TCD + SCBEAM approach. Then, a database was defined in order to establish the minimum number of numerical data required for effective predictions. Subsequently, such results were considered in the more complex case of protected beams with the final intention of the combined use of the predictions made by MLP + RST + PSO with the numerical results from TCD + SCBEAM in assessing the degradation of the resistance.

5.2   Unprotected Beams

A database with 288 instances, involving 9 input variables related to the geometry of the 32 included profiles, an input variable related with the time of fire resistance (from 0 to 40 min) and an output variable (ν) was created (see Table 1). The study was conducted in two phases. Initially the k – Fold Cross – Validation method was used, subdividing each dataset into 10 subsets. Subsequently, the effectiveness was achieved with different ratios of instances considered training or testing, in order to establish criteria for the minimum number of numerical data required for effective predictions to be applied in protected beams. The analysis taken into account four statistical measures: PMD (according to Eq. 9), PC (according, to Eq. 10), correlation coefficient (c.c) and the coefficient of multiple determination (R^2).

$$PMD = \frac{\sum\limits_{i=1}^{N} |ak - bk|}{N} \qquad (9)$$

$$PC = \frac{\sum\limits_{i=1}^{N} ak/bk}{N} \qquad (10)$$

where: ak is desired output (calculated by TCD + SCBEAM), bk the predicted output (calculated by MLP + RST + PSO) and N is a number of determinations.

Table 1. Input variables.

Description	Range of values
Total depth	(303−612) mm
Web total depth	(276.6−573) mm
Web partial depth	(245−547) mm
Web thickness	(5.1−13) mm
Flange width	(101−324) mm
Flange thickness	(5.7−21.7) mm
Web area	(1487.16−7277.1) mm^2
Flanges area	(1151.4−12312.0) mm^2
Total area	(2638.56−19589.1) mm^2
Time of fire resistance	$(0, 5, 10, 15, 20, 25, 30, 35, 40)$ min

Also, the definition of the instances considered as training or testing was done randomly and the three alternatives considered were: a) Training set: 75% (24 profiles and 216 instances); Test set: 25% (8 profiles and 72 instances), b) Training set: 59,4% (19 profiles and 171 instances); Test set: 40,6% (13 profiles and 117 instances) and c) Training set: 50,0% (16 profiles and 144 instances); Test set: 50,0% (16 profiles and 144 instances).

In the study, PROCON 4.0 software developed at the University of Camaguey, in which the above-mentioned techniques are implemented, was used. The results achieved in the first phase are shown in Table 2.

Table 2. Summary of the results of the first phase.

Statistical measures	Values
PMD	0.010
PC	0.990
c.c	0.999
R^2	0.998

Table 3 summarizes the results achieved in the second phase when MLP + RST + PSO was used to predict the output values of instances that are part of different test set, according to the proportions described above.

It can be clearly seen that the approach MLP + RST + PSO offers great precision, with a low values of PMD and values close to 1 of PC, c.c and R^2. Also, it can be perceived that there were no significant changes in the results, when the number of instances that are part of the training set are reduced, that is, excellent accuracy can be achieved considering as training set 50% of the total data,

Table 3. Unprotected beams. Prediction of the degradation of resistance to vertical shear with different training/test ratios.

Statistical measures	Training (instances)/Test (instances)		
	216/117	171/117	144/144
PMD	0,011	0,011	0.013
PC	1.028	0.981	0.969
c.c	0.999	0.999	0.999
R^2	0.998	0.998	0.998

leading to the feasibility of reducing the number of cases performed by thermal – structural modelling (TCD + SCBEAM), which contributes significantly to the optimization of the research process. Figures 2 a) and b) show the correspondence between the results by TCD + SCBEAM and A.I (MLP + RST + PSO) for two profiles included in the test set when the training/test ratio is 144 /144.

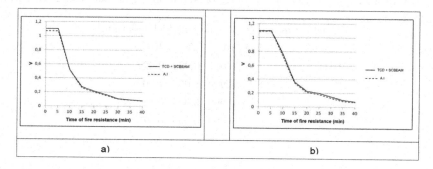

a)   b)

Fig. 2. Unprotected beams. Comparison of the degradation of resistance to vertical shear. TCD + SCBEAM vs A.I (MLP + RST + PSO). a) W310 × 165 × 38.7; b) W530 × 210 × 92.

6   Protected Beams

Given the strong dependence of the degradation on the thickness and conductivity of the protection material, separated graphics for each of the nine combinations of these variables were developed. The information required to generate the graphics, takes into account the 32 profiles and 9 exposure times (0, 15, 30, 60, 75, 90, 105 and 120 min), which involves making 288 thermal models and the generation of 2592 instances. So, it is reasonable to take into account the excellent results shown in 5.2 and using a strategy to reduce the number of laborious TCD + SCBEAM determinations.

This was conceived as follows: a) Considering training sets with 50% of the data, and therefore test sets composed with the remaining 50%. Besides, it was necessary to define validation instances, into the test sets and determine their responses by TCD + SCBEAM procedures. The definition of the instances that make up the training or test sets takes into account the same random selection considered before for the case 50%/50%. Therefore, the training (or test) sets includes 16 profiles (1296 instances), b) To evaluate the results, the same statistical measures described in 5.2 were used, and also the comparison between graphics elaborated by TCD + SCBEAM results and by MLP + RST + PSO approach was carried out, for validation profiles (W310 × 100 × 28.3; W460 × 150 × 60; W610 × 325 × 155). A total of 27 graphical verifications were performed and c) The final result consists in 9 sets of graphics (ν vs time of fire resistance), in which the results from numerical modelling and from artificial intelligence predictions were jointly used for elaboration.

Table 4 presents a summary of the results achieved in predicting resistance degradation in validation profiles.

Table 4. Protected beams. Prediction of the degradation of resistance to vertical shear.

Statistical measures	Protection thickness (mm)		
	10	25	40
PMD	0,017	0,039	0.027
PC	0.988	1.056	1.007
c.c	0.999	0.995	0.987
R^2	0.999	0.999	0.973

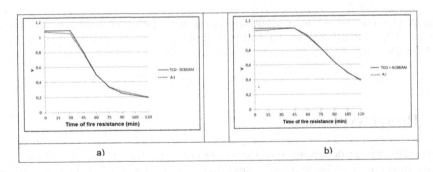

a)   b)

Fig. 3. Protected beams. Comparison of the degradation of resistance to vertical shear. TCD + SCBEAM vs MLP + RST + PSO. Protection thickness: 10 mm / protection material conductivity: 0,1 W/(Km). a) W460 × 150 × 60; b) W310 × 310 × 117.

It can be noticeably seen that low values of PMD and values close to 1 for PC, c.c and R^2 were achieved. It validates the effectiveness of the results and justifies the combined use of the predictions made by MLP + RST + PSO with the results of TCD + SCBEAM in assessing the degradation of the resistance. Figures 3a) and b) corroborate the above statements, for two validation cases.

7   Conclusions

Artificial neural networks (ANNs) are a potent tool for solving diverse structural engineering problems. In this study, they were used, in combination with the FE numerical modelling, for predicting the degradation of the resistance to vertical shear in composite beams in fire. Besides, the backpropagation learning method was integrated with a method to calculate the initial weights, in order to train the MLP, taking into account the weights of conditional features which are calculated to build the similarity relation that maximize the measure quality of similarity proposed in the framework of the RST. It was shown that the artificial neural network prediction model obtained is an effective tool for predicting resistance degradation under fire. Also, the combined use of data from numerical origin and from artificial intelligence predictions allowed the optimization of the research process, by the substitution of several laborious numerical models, which effectively contribute to the generation of new data in order to improve the design methods or the generation of graphic aids. Subsequently, the results of the present research can be successfully applied in solving different problems related with the behaviour and design of the structural members in fire.

Acknowledgements. The authors gratefully acknowledge the support provided by CAPES (Coordination for the Improvement of Higher Level Personnel, Brazil) and FAPESP (São Paulo Research Foundation, Brazil). The authors would also like to thank Eng. Natoya Corneilla Thomas for her appreciated assistance.

References

1. American institute of steel construction. specification for structural steel buildings, ANSI/AISC (2010)
2. European Committee for Standardization. EN 1994-1-1: 2004. Eurocode 4. Design of Composite Steel and Concrete Structures, Part 1–1: General Rules and Rules for Buildings (2004)
3. European Committee for Standardization. EN 1994-1-2: 2005. Eurocode 4. Design of Composite Steel and Concrete Structures, Part 1. 2: General Rules - Structural Fire Design (2005)
4. Comitê Brasileiro da Construção Civil ABNT/CB-2. ABNT NBR 14323. Associação Brasileira de Normas Técnicas. Rio de Janeiro, Brasil. Projeto de estruturas de aço e de estruturas mistas de aço e concreto de edifícios em situação de incêndio (2012)
5. Hocenski, Z., Antunovic, M., Filko, D.: Accelerated gradient learning algorithm for neural network weights update. In: Lovrek, I., Howlett, R.J., Jain, L.C. (eds.) KES 2008. LNCS (LNAI), vol. 5177, pp. 49–56. Springer, Heidelberg (2008). https://doi.org/10.1007/978-3-540-85563-7_12

6. Filiberto Cabrera, Y., Bello Pérez, R., Mota, Y.C., Jimenez, G.R.: Improving the MLP learning by using a method to calculate the initial weights of the network based on the quality of similarity measure. In: Batyrshin, I., Sidorov, G. (eds.) MICAI 2011. LNCS (LNAI), vol. 7095, pp. 351–362. Springer, Heidelberg (2011). https://doi.org/10.1007/978-3-642-25330-0_31

7. Filiberto, Y., Frias, M., Larrua, R., Bello, R.: Induction of rules based on similarity relations for imbalance datasets. A case of study. In: Figueroa-García, J.C., López-Santana, E.R., Ferro-Escobar, R. (eds.) WEA 2016. CCIS, vol. 657, pp. 65–73. Springer, Cham (2016). https://doi.org/10.1007/978-3-319-50880-1_6

8. Arias, D., Filiberto, Y., Bello, R.: Methods for generating contexts based on similarity relations to multigranulation. In: Figueroa-García, J.C., López-Santana, E.R., Rodriguez-Molano, J.I. (eds.) WEA 2018. CCIS, vol. 915, pp. 114–123. Springer, Cham (2018). https://doi.org/10.1007/978-3-030-00350-0_10

9. Alvarez, Y.R., Mota, Y.C., Cabrera, Y.F., Hilarión, I.G., Hernández, Y.F., Dominguez, M.F.: Similar prototype methods for class imbalanced data classification. In: Bello, R., Falcon, R., Verdegay, J.L. (eds.) Uncertainty Management with Fuzzy and Rough Sets. SFSC, vol. 377, pp. 193–209. Springer, Cham (2019). https://doi.org/10.1007/978-3-030-10463-4_11

10. Chen, Y., Kopp, G.A., Surry, D.: Prediction of pressure coefficients on roofs of low buildings using artificial neural networks. J. Wind. Eng. Ind. Aerodyn. **91**, 423–441 (2003)

11. Raghu Prasad, B.K., Eskandari, H., Venkatarama Reddy, B.V.: Prediction of compressive strength of SCC and HPC with high volume fly ash using ANN. Constr. Build. Mater. **23**(1), 117–128 (2009)

12. SarIdemir, M.: Prediction of compressive strength of concretes containing metakaolin and silica fume by artificial neural networks. Adv. Eng. Softw. **40**(5), 350–355 (2009)

13. Ashu, J., Sanjeev Kumar, J., Sudhir, M.: Modeling and analysis of concrete slump using artificial neural networks. J. Mater. Civil Eng. **20**(9), 628–633 (2008)

14. Topçu, I.B., Karakurt, C., Sandemir, M.: Predicting the strength development of cements produced with different pozzolans by neural network and fuzzy logic. Mater. Des. **29**, 1986–1991 (2008)

15. Caglar, N.: Neural network based approach for determining the shear strength of circular reinforced concrete columns. Constr. Build. Mater. **23**(10), 686–691 (2009)

16. Garzón-Roca, J., Adam, J.M., Sandoval, C., Roca, P.: Estimation of the axial behaviour of masonry walls based on artificial neural networks. Comput. Struct. **125**, 145–152 (2013)

17. Ahn, N., Jang, H., Park, D.K.: Presumption of shear strength of steel fiber reinforced concrete beam using artificial neural network model. J. Appl. Polym. Sci. **103**, 2351–2358 (2007)

18. Inel, M.: Modeling ultimate deformation capacity of RC columns using artificial neural networks. Eng. Struct. **29**, 329–335 (2007)

19. Hasançebi, O., Dumlupınar, T.: Linear and nonlinear model updating of reinforced concrete t-beam bridges using artificial neural networks. Comput. Struct. **119**, 1–11 (2013)

20. Miller, B.: Application of neural networks for structure updating. Comput. Assist. Mech. Eng. Sci. **18**, 191–203 (2011)

21. Zhang, S., Chen, S., Wang, H., Wang, W.: Model updating of a steel truss based on artificial neural networks. Appl. Mech. Mater. **121–126**, 363–366 (2012)

22. Ukrainczyk, N., Pecur, I.B., Bolf, N.: Evaluating rebar corrosion damage in RC structures exposed to marine environment using neural network. Civ. Eng. Environ. Syst. **24**(1), 15–32 (2007)
23. Luongo, A., Contento, A.: Nonlinear elastic analysis of steel planar frames under fire loads. Comput. Struct. **150**, 23–33 (2015)
24. Cachim, P.B.: Using artificial neural networks for calculation of temperatures in timber under fire loading. Constr. Build. Mater. **25**, 4175–4180 (2011)
25. Erdem, H.: Prediction of the moment capacity of reinforced concrete slabs in fire using artificial neural networks. Adv. Eng. Softw. **41**, 270–276 (2010)
26. Pawlak, Z.: Rough sets. Int. J. Inf. Comput. Sci. **11**, 145–172 (1982)
27. Skowron, A.: Logic, algebra and computer science. In: Rasiowa, H., Rauszer, C. (eds.) Memoriam, pp. 1–215 (1996). Bulletin of the Section of Logic
28. Slowinski, R., Vanderpooten, D.: A generalized definition of rough approximations based on similarity. IEEE Trans. Data Knowl. Eng., 331–336 (2000)
29. Pawlak, Z., Skowron, A.: Rough sets: some extensions. Inf. Sci. **177**, 28–40 (2007)
30. Filiberto, Y., Bello, R., Caballero, Y., Larrua, R.: Using PSO and RST to predict the resistant capacity of connections in composite structures. In: González, J.R., Pelta, D.A., Cruz, C., Terrazas, G., Krasnogor, N. (eds.) NICSO, vol. 284, pp. 359–370. Springer, Heidelberg (2010). https://doi.org/10.1007/978-3-642-12538-6_30
31. Kennedy, J., Eberhart, R.C.: Particle swarm optimization. In: Proceedings of the 1995 IEEE International Conference on Neural Networks, Piscataway, New Jersey, IEEE Service Center, pp. 1942–1948 (1995)
32. Asuncion, A., Newman, D.: UCI machine learning repository. A study of the behaviour of several methods for balancing machine learning training data. SIGKDD Explor. **6**(1), 20–29 (2007)
33. Anderberg, Y.: SUPER-TEMPCALC. a commercial and user friendly computer program with automatic fem-generation for temperature analysis of structures exposed to heat. In: Fire Safety Design (1991)
34. Silva, V.P.: Determination of the steel fire protection material thickness by an analytical process-a simple derivation. Eng. Struct. **27**, 2036–2043 (2005)
35. Correia, A., Rodrigues, J.P., Silva, V.: A simplified calculation method for temperature evaluation of steel columns embedded in walls. Fire Mater. J. **35**, 431–441 (2011)
36. Larrua, R., Silva, V.: Thermal analysis of push-out tests at elevated temperatures. Fire Saf. J. **55**, 1–14 (2013)
37. International organization for standardization. Fire-resistance tests. Elements of building construction, Part 1.1: General requirements for fire resistance testing. ISO 834. Revision of first edition ISO (1990)

Machine Learning for Cup Coffee Quality Prediction from Green and Roasted Coffee Beans Features

Javier Andrés Suarez-Peña[1] , Hugo Fabián Lobaton-García[2] ,
Jose Ignacio Rodríguez-Molano[1] , and William Camilo Rodriguez-Vazquez[2(✉)]

[1] Research Group GICOECOL, Universidad Distrital Francisco José de Caldas,
Carrera 7 No. 40B–53, Bogotá D.C., Colombia
[2] Research Group GEICOS, Universitaria Agustiniana, Ak. 86 #11b-95, Bogotá D.C., Colombia
William.rodriguez.v@gmail.com

Abstract. Coffee is one of the main exported products of Colombia. It is grown in different regions throughout the territory and is recognized worldwide for its flavor and freshness. Its quality is evaluated by professional tasters, who taste the coffee drink obtained from roasted coffee beans. They qualify it according with the platform or method requested by customers. This study proposes the use of different Machine Learning (ML) algorithms for the prediction of cup coffee quality, based on a set of measurements made to almond and roasted coffee beans. The data was obtained with the support of Almacafé, a company belonging to the National Federation of Coffee Growers (FNC) of Colombia. The classification results with the validation set, showed a higher accuracy with the Neural Network algorithm, with an average score of 81% for a 10-fold stratified cross validation. This work demonstrates the possibility of qualifying cup coffee quality with ML algorithms.

Keywords: Cup coffee quality · Machine Learning · Neural network · Classification · SVM

1 Introduction

Colombia is the third-largest producer of coffee in the world and the main producer of Arabian coffee [1], recognized by its coffee quality, which goes through rigorous selection processes and a final qualification that allows its definition for exportation [2]. Coffee exports in Colombia for 2017 were 710,440 Metric tons and 710,836 for 2018, representing 7% and 5% of total exports for their respective years [3]. Colombian coffee is produced by more than 560,000 small coffee producers, who are grouped in the National Federation of Coffee Growers (FNC) and follow standards to guarantee coffee quality [2]. To assess the quality of coffee, professional tasters are required, specialized in recognizing the different cup coffee features, who transfer their sensory experience to a score. His knowledge is based on empirical models of interpretation of coffee quality [1], however, human errors can occur in some of the measurements made,

© Springer Nature Switzerland AG 2020
J. C. Figueroa-García et al. (Eds.): WEA 2020, CCIS 1274, pp. 48–59, 2020.
https://doi.org/10.1007/978-3-030-61834-6_5

which requires standardized statistical methods, forms, and analyzes, in addition to the experience of the tasters in interpreting the results [2]. It is necessary to find statistical methods based on numerical measurements of physicochemical properties that can be performed by a wider range of professionals, with reproducible results and with less variation. Alternatively, ML techniques emerge as a novel alternative given their ability to emulate human activities and operations.

Among the examples of ML applications related to coffee, we found works such as the one proposed by [3], who proposed a model capable of classifying green coffee beans by differences in their color, using neural networks first to convert RGB space colors to CIELab. Later they use a Bayesian classifier, to classify the images of coffee in four colors white, green, blue green and cane green. This study was justified in the importance of color for coffee quality definition, associated with a greater market value. [4] made a classifier using a neural network algorithm for green coffee samples containing several grains, corresponding to Indonesian standards. [5], performs a segmentation of coffee fruits to classify them according to their maturation state. To do this, the author uses a connectivity algorithm, which uses homogeneity criteria to group pixels.

Another example is an electronic selection system for specialty coffee ("excelso") based on color through image processing from [6], where they trained a neural network to recognize a coffee with defects (bad) of one without defects. [7] presented a method to classify coffee based on its color. A similar approach is addressed by [8], who, using a sphere spectrophotometer, quantitatively determined the color of the fruit during its different stages of development, which, although they do not use ML algorithms, their results can be used for the application of classifiers.

According to the articles reviewed, it can be inferred that most authors have aimed their studies towards the classification of coffee after harvest, working with fruits or grains due to their importance in quality definition, either by building mobile identification systems, models or algorithms, for segmentation or segregation of defects, such as immature or overripe fruits. In addition, no articles were found that use ML to predict cup coffee quality by analyzing the characteristics of fruits, almonds, green beans or roasted coffee beans. Therefore, the objective of this article is to propose a ML model that allows to predict cup coffee quality as high or low, based on variables measured in green coffee beans in Colombia.

2 Materials and Methods

2.1 Coffee Samples and Collected Data

The experimental data were provided by Almacafé. The data correspond to measurements made on samples from different parts of Colombia of almond coffee beans. It obtained by wet process and analyzed as they arrived at the facilities of the Almacafé laboratory, located in the city of Bogotá during the period from May to August 2019. Each sample is received in packages of 500 gr of parchment coffee beans according to FNC definitions. From this sample 250 gr has taken, to the wrap or parchment of the grain. This it is removed by a process called threshing. The process leaves the green almond coffee an average weight of 210 gr per sample. Table 1 lists the measurements made. In total 56 samples were analyzed.

Regarding the humidity measurement, it has done in equipment calibrated according to ISO 6673 method. The particle size distribution gives an idea of superior quality if its size is above the 15/64-inch mesh. According to the experience of Almacafé, a small grain would likely to be a not fully developed grain, causing its attributes being not optimal. The color is measured with a spectrophotometer on the CIELAB and CIEXYZ scale defined by the Commission Internationale de lÉclairage (CIE), as to [9]. The spectrophotometers collect the entire spectrum of each wavelength and by means of an algorithm they transform it into values that resemble human perception. For this work the color of green coffee beans and roasted beans was measured. For each of these two grains, the color space coordinates L *, a *, b *, X, Y and Z are recorded in the database. As for sensory evaluation, 10 coffee quality descriptors are measured on an ordinal scale from 1 to 10. These are aroma, taste, residual taste, acidity, body, balance, uniformity, cup cleaning, sweetness and overall cup score (overall). To make this measurement, the roasting of the green coffee beans of each sample is carried out, under a standardized method and with controlled conditions of Almacafé. Then, the roasted coffee is ground and 5 cups of coffee are prepared, which are evaluated by professional tasters. An important precision regarding the tasters is that they perform the evaluation, without any prior knowledge of the physical analyzes results carried out on the coffee beans, or on the traceability of the crop, allowing them to have no bias at the time of making the qualifications to the respective cups of coffee.

Considering the empirical evidence and the experience of Almacafé, a high correlation between the measured variables and the results of the cupping would be expected. According to Siswoputrano (1993) cited by [4], the main aspects for determining the quality of coffee are size, shape, color, defects and other materials.

Table 1. Summary of measurements made to coffee samples

Variable	Unit of measurement	Measurement equipment	Measurement method	Sample size
Altitude	meters	Google Earth	Approximate location according to the sample place location	500 g taken from several sacks
Moisture	percentage	MOISTURE KAPPA AK-60-B	AL-CC-EC-P-0003 Parchment coffee - Excelso coffee: Moisture determination (kappa)	400 g
Initial parchment weight	grams	Digital Scales	Direct weight on digital scale	250 g

(*continued*)

Table 1. (*continued*)

Variable	Unit of measurement	Measurement equipment	Measurement method	Sample size
Green almond weight	grams	Digital Scales	Direct weight on digital scale	210 g approx.
Waste (peel)	percentage	Manual	It is the percentage resulting from dividing the difference between the weight of the parchment and the almond, divided by the weight of the parchment	210 g approx.
Defective grains group 1	Units and grams	Manual	The beans are spread on a table, where is proceeded to identify, separate, count and weigh the beans with color defects	210 g approx.
Defective grains group 2	Units and grams	Manual	The beans are spread on a table, where is proceeded to identify, separate, count and weigh the beans with physical defects other than color	210 g approx.
Granulometric distribution	Mesh retention percentage	ZARANDA MECANICA	AL-CC-EC-P-0008 Green Coffee: Granulometric Distribution. Mesh sizes	210 g approx.
Color	Cielab	spectrophotometer LABSCAN EX	Direct scale measurement CIELAB y CIEXYZ	210 g approx.
Sensory assessment	Ordinal scale	Professional taster	AL-CC-EC-I-0002 SENSORY ANALYSIS PREPARATION OF THE TEST	5 coffee cups

2.2 Support Vector Machine

SMV are supervised learning algorithms (MathWorks, s.f.), proposed by [10], used for binary classification or regression, in pattern recognition problems. This classification is based on the basis of optimal separation between classes, so that if the classes are subject to separation, the result is chosen to segregate the classes as much as possible. [11]. The SVM builds a hyperplane in a space of very high dimensionality (which can become infinite) that separates the classes that are held in a data set. A good dissociation between classes will generate a correct categorization of the new sample, in other words, it is required to find the maximum separation to the points closest to the generated hyperplane [12]. Because SVMs are a known method of ML implemented in various fields of knowledge, libraries and tools have emerged to facilitate their use, one of them is LIBSVM (SVM library), used within the Python-based Scikit-Learn library. The LIBSVM allows several SVM formulations for classification, regression and distribution estimation [13]. One of these formulations is the Classification of support vectors C, in which, there are two training vectors Xi that belongs to the set Rn, where i = 1, ..., l, in two classes, and an indicator vector and that belongs to the set Rl such that yi belongs to {1,−1}, C-SVM solve the primary optimization problem, according with Boser et al.,1992; Cortes & Vapnik, 1995; cited by [13], as follows,

$$\min_{w,b,\xi} \frac{1}{2} w^T w + C \sum_{i=1}^{l} \xi_i \tag{1}$$

Subject to,

$$y_i \left(w^T \emptyset(x_i) + b \right) \geq 1 - \xi_i, \xi_i \geq 0, i = 1, \ldots, l \tag{2}$$

where $\emptyset(x_i)$ Assign xi to a space of larger dimensions and C > 0 is the regularization parameter. In view of the possible high dimensionality of the variable W, the dual problem is solved with the following equation [13],

$$\min_{\alpha} \frac{1}{2} \alpha^T Q \alpha - e^T \alpha \tag{3}$$

Subject to,

$$0 \leq \alpha_i \leq C \quad i = 1, \ldots, l \tag{4}$$

Where e = [1, ...,1] T is the vector of each one of these, Q is a positive semi-defined matrix l by l and α is Lagrange multiplier that acts as an inverse of the C term, which solves the problem of dual optimization. After the application of the previous equation, the optimal satisfaction equation (w) is applied [13],

$$w = \sum_{i=1}^{l} y_i \alpha_i \emptyset(x_i) \tag{5}$$

And finally the decision function [13],

$$sgn\left(w^T \emptyset(x) + b \right) = sgn\left(\sum_{i=1}^{l} y_i \alpha_i K(x_i, x) + b \right) \tag{6}$$

2.3 Neural Networks

In ML one of the most used models is neural networks (NN). An artificial neural network, is a computational model consisting of a number of basic computational units called neurons, that are connected to each other forming a network of communication, allowing complex computations [14]. Where each node is a neuron and the arcs represent the connections between them. Neurons are grouped in layers. An input layer that receives the input data of the model, which passes through the next group, called hidden layers. In this group, we can find as many layers as the complexity of the problem or the data requires. Finally, an output layer, where the values to the functions resulting from the network processing will be obtained. The way in which networks acquire their knowledge is contained in the connection weights that each neuron (node) possesses within the network. They compute their values (connection weights) during the training phase [15].

The way in which neurons interconnect allows two types of architecture to be distinguished [15]: The feedback architecture, in which there are connections between neurons of the same or the previous layer; The feedforward architecture [16], without feedback connections, that is, the signals go only to the neurons of the next layer. Neural networks can be configured in multiple ways (the possibilities become infinite), so the choice of the optimal configuration for the data or problem handled, must be primarily an objective function of the application. The most common neural networks are Perceptron and Multilayer Perceptron.

Perceptron: t is the simplest network, which is made up of a single neuron, with n inputs and a single output Rosenblatt (1958) Minsky and Papert (1969) cited by [15].

Multilayer Perceptron (MLP): networks with an input layer, intermediate layers (which may range from one to those required) and an output layer are called multilayer perceptron [16].

2.4 Programming Tools

The development of this work is achieved using the free execution environment of Google Colaboratory web books. It allows users to write and execute the Python programming language, access to hosted execution environments, providing free use of up to 25 GB of RAM, and large capacity GPU processors, which reduce the execution time of the algorithms. The link to the Colab book is shared in Appendix A. The Keras API is used for the implementation of the neural network [17], and the Scikit-Learn module of SVM for the SVC algorithm [18].

2.5 Coffee Quality Classification

The authors [1], mention that there are different methods to evaluate coffee quality, most of them are based on a score scale of 0 to 100, similar to the wine ratings. Score augmentations are obtained from the ratings assigned to non-standardized descriptors qualified on a smaller scale, which together give a result relative to 100 according to their quality score. Among the methods mentioned by these authors, there is a use of similar descriptors to those used by Almacafé for this work. The first step to define the classification categories is to add the scores selected in the different descriptors, grouping them into a variable called "Sum". Then a separation of the data is performed looking for a balance between the data. Although there are scores of great interests than others, like scores greater than 80 points for the qualification of a coffee as excellent, in this work scores were obtained between the range of 32.5 to 63.5, because the sample selection was random. Therefore, it is decided to divide the results into two groups, samples with low quality scores and samples with high quality scores, with the differentiating value being a score of 51.5. In this way, 28 data were obtained in each group. Subsequently, the variables "X" and "y" are created to store in "X" the input data and in "y" the respective labels for each sample. With the "train_test_split" function of Scikit-Learn, the data is separated in training and validation, using a validation set size of 20% of the total samples and a seed of 4 to obtain a balanced amount of the categories in the validation data.

2.6 Model Validation

Following [19, 20], a stratified cross validation is applied with 10 folds for model validation. This method divides the whole dataset in 10 groups, where it uses 9 for training and one for test, interchanging the test set with each one of the 10 groups, until it evaluates all of them. This method has the advantage that considers the elements of each subset of categories defined and is designed to have the same number of examples from each class, on both training and test sets.

3 Results and Discussion

For data processing through defined ML algorithms, a statistical analysis of the data was carried out in first place, the categorical variables were transformed into numerical. With the purpose of validating if the normalized data would improve the prediction, a normalization of the data was performed as suggested by [21]. A correlation analysis between the variables was also conducted.

In this work, the color coordinates on green coffee beans and roasted coffee beans were measured. Additionally, this information was used to predict the quality of the coffee drink in the defined groups. Similarly [3], measured the coordinates of the CIELAB space in green coffee beans to classify them with the help of a neural network and a Bayesian classifier. [22] used an electronic tongue (ET) for coffee quality prediction, trained a neural network with the measurements obtained with the ET and the quality scores assigned by professional tasters, to classify in the defined groups. In this work the quality scores assigned by professional tasters were also used, with the difference that the variables or input measurements, were not made on the coffee drink, but on the beans, resembling the filter and quality evaluation performed by Almacafé and secondly because it could generate savings by reducing the need for beverage preparation. [6] they developed a machine capable of selecting defective coffee beans from good ones, from the implementation of the multilevel thresholding segmentation method, applied to images of good and defective beans, which allowed to determine the ranges of each color of the RGB space for the categories defined. In contrast, in this work the CIELAB space was used, where the values of each component of the color space, together with the other variables, contribute a weight to each cupping result obtained.

3.1 Programming Tools

The neural network was made using the Keras API [17]. An input layer of 36 nodes was defined, corresponding to each of the measurements made per sample. Then the size was reduced by half to match the defined classes. Table 2 lists the parameters used in the neural network. The dataset used was the normalized version.

Table 2. Neural network parameters

PARAMETERS	VALUE
Input size	36
Number of layers	4
NN architecture	Input layer 36 nodes – dense layer 18 nodes – Dropout layer 50% - dense output layer with 2 nodes and activation function "Softmax" [23]
Activation function (Dense layer)	ReLu [24]
Kernel initializer	he-normal [25]
Optimizer	Adam [26]
Learning rate	$1e-2$
Learning rate reduction	50% after 4 epochs without improvement in validation accuracy (val_acc)
Loss function	"categorical_crossentropy"
Early stopping (callback)	Patience de 20 epochs monitoring validation accuracy with a maximum number of 100 epochs
Reduce (callback)	Factor = 0,5, patience = 3, min = $1e-8$
Batch size	1
Epochs	26

The initial results of this network are shown in Fig. 1. The accuracy obtained was 83%. It is observed that this network was better classifying the low score samples, correcting in 100% of the cases, without modifying, that improvement in category 0 implied only 67% of successes in class 1, as shown in the Confusion matrix of Fig. 1. The classification metrics, confusion matrix and classification report were used. This lats one, groups the following metrics: accuracy, precision, recall and F1 score.

After evaluating the initial results and tuning the hyper parameters of the neural network, the next step was to run the stratified cross validation. A for loop was defined to visualize the elements of each fold and to let the use of the callbacks early and reduce, as well as some auxiliary functions to plot each epoch and the confusion matrix. On Table 3 are resumed the results of each fold in terms of accuracy and F1 scores.

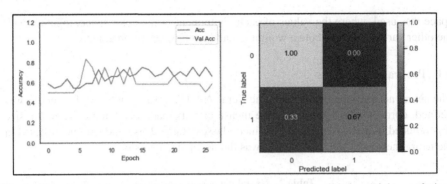

Fig. 1. Neural network results. Left, training precision curve and validation. Right, confusion matrix. Source: self-made.

Table 3. Results of the stratified cross validation

Iteration	Accuracy	F1-0	F1-1	Test samples selected	Class of test samples
1	1	1	1	[0 1 2 3 4 8]	[1. 1. 0. 1. 0. 0.]
2	0,67	0,75	0,5	[5 6 7 11 12 13]	[1. 1. 1. 0. 0. 0.]
3	0,83	0,8	0,86	[9 10 14 15 16 17]	[1. 1. 0. 0. 0. 1.]
4	0,67	0,75	0,5	[18 19 20 21 22 24]	[0. 1. 1. 0. 1. 0.]
5	0,67	0,75	0,5	[23 25 26 27 31 32]	[1. 0. 0. 0. 1. 1.]
6	0,83	0,8	0,86	[28 29 30 33 39 42]	[0. 0. 0. 1. 1. 1.]
7	0,83	0,86	0,8	[34 35 36 43 45 47]	[0. 0. 0. 1. 1. 1.]
8	0,83	0,86	0,8	[37 38 40 48 49 50]	[0. 0. 0. 1. 1. 1.]
9	0,75	0,8	0,67	[41 44 51 52]	[0. 0. 1. 1.]
10	1	1	1	[46 53 54 55]	[0. 1. 1. 0.]

The average accuracy was 81%, showing a better F1 score for low quality samples in comparison with high quality coffee. From the results was of interest to analyze the reasons of the folds (or iterations) where the high-quality samples were misclassified, founding that those samples were close of the partition point defined which may confuse the neural network. This also shows that more classes could be defined with the corresponding incremental number of samples per class. In contrast the folds with 100% accuracy come from sets where the difference on the score of the test samples were at least 3 points or more away from the partition point of class definition.

3.2 SVM (SVC) Results

The SVC algorithm was implemented using the Scikit-Learn Libsvm library, additional "GridSearchCV" function was used to define the penalty parameter C and gamma, using a Kernel = "rbf" (radial basis function), obtaining a value of C = 1000, a gamma = 0.01. The other parameters of this algorithm were left as they come by default in the "SVC" function.

From Fig. 2 the resulting accuracy, was the same achieved with the neural network, however the F1 scores show more balance on the performance of the model for both classes. Alike the previous algorithm a stratified cross validation is conducted to check the performance of the model with different training and test sets. In Table 4, are shown the results of the cross validation using the SVC.

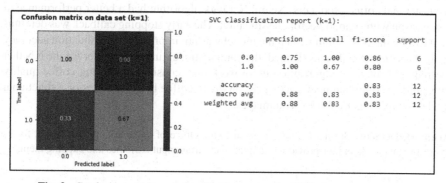

Fig. 2. Confusion matrix and classification report for SVC. Source: self-made.

Table 4. Cross validation results using SVC

Iteration	Accuracy	F1-0	F1-1	Test samples selected	Class of test samples
1	0,5	0,57	0,4	[0 1 2 3 4 8]	[1. 1. 0. 1. 0. 0.]
2	0,67	0,75	0,5	[5 6 7 11 12 13]	[1. 1. 1. 0. 0. 0.]
3	0,5	0,57	0,4	[9 10 14 15 16 17]	[1. 1. 0. 0. 0. 1.]
4	0,67	0,75	0,5	[18 19 20 21 22 24]	[0. 1. 1. 0. 1. 0.]
5	0,83	0,86	0,8	[23 25 26 27 31 32]	[1. 0. 0. 0. 1. 1.]
6	0,83	0,86	0,8	[28 29 30 33 39 42]	[0. 0. 0. 1. 1. 1.]
7	1	1	1	[34 35 36 43 45 47]	[0. 0. 0. 1. 1. 1.]
8	0,17	0	0,29	[37 38 40 48 49 50]	[0. 0. 0. 1. 1. 1.]
9	0,5	0,67	0	[41 44 51 52]	[0. 0. 1. 1.]
10	0,75	0,67	0,8	[46 53 54 55]	[0. 1. 1. 0.]

A 64% average accuracy resulted from the cross validation run. With this algorithm there was minimal difference between using the original dataset or the normalized version. It was also applied a Principal Component Analysis (PCA) to reduce dimensionality, however there was not any improvement on the results. One of most significant results was the computational time with 1 s (or less) for SVC and 20 to 60 s for NN algorithm.

4 Conclusions

This research shows that cup coffee quality can be predicted as high or low from the analysis of green coffee beans features. The neural network model defined can be an alternative to expert cup coffee qualification, reducing the cost of the evaluation, saving time in analysis and cup coffee preparation and providing an additional tool for coffee taster and coffee producers. Neural Network algorithm had a better performance in comparison with support vector classification. The early stopping callback was determinant to stop the NN training when the model was not improving the validation accuracy score. Despite the callbacks defined, the computational time was higher for the NN that the required for SVC algorithm. Future work may consider predicting coffee quality by using convolutional neural networks on green coffee beans pictures or a functional model to mix numerical data with images.

Acknowledgement. Special thanks are given to the Office of coffee quality Almacafé, for its interest in this work and for providing samples, measuring input attributes and cupping them.

Appendix A

Link to the notebook used in Colab and the corresponding database:
https://github.com/Javiersuing/GitHub/blob/master/AlmacafeDataBase_CrossV_v4.ipynb.

References

1. Thomas, E., Puget, S., Valentin, D., Songer, P.: Sensory Evaluation-Profiling and Preferences. Elsevier Inc., London (2017)
2. Salamanca, C.: Métodos Estadísticos Para Evaluar La Calidad Del Café. Universitat de Girona (2015)
3. de Oliveira, E.M., Leme, D.S., Barbosa, B.H.G., Rodarte, M.P.: A computer vision system for coffee beans classification based on computational intelligence techniques. J. Food Eng. **171**, 22–27 (2015). https://doi.org/10.1016/j.jfoodeng.2015.10.009
4. Faridah, F., Parikesit, G.O.F., Ferdiansjah, F.: Coffee bean grade determination based on image parameter. TELKOMNIKA (Telecommun. Comput. Electron. Control) **9**, 547–554 (2011). https://doi.org/10.12928/telkomnika.v9i3.747
5. Montes, N.: Segmentación De Imágenes De Frutos De Café En El Proceso De Beneficio. Universidad Nacional de Colombia, sede Manizales (2003)
6. Ruge, I.A., Pinzon, A.S., Moreno, D.E.: Sistema de selección electrónico de café excelso basado en el color mediante procesamiento de imágenes. Rev Tecnura **16**, 84–93 (2012). http://dx.doi.org/10.14483/udistrital.jour.tecnura.2012.4.a06
7. Ramos Giraldo, P.J., Sanz Uribe, J.R., Oliveros Tascón, C.E.: Identificación y clasificación de frutos de café en tiempo real, a través de la medición de color. Cenicafé **61**, 315–326 (2010)
8. Carvajal, J.J., Aristizábal, I.D., Oliveros, C.E., Mejía, J.W.: Colorimetría del Fruto de Café (Coffea arabica L.) Durante su Desarrollo y Maduración. Rev Fac Nac Agron Medellín **1**, 37–48 (2006)

9. Tobijaszewska, B., Mills, R., Jons, J.: El uso de la espectrometría para la medición simultánea del color y la composición en muestras de alimentos. In: FOSS (2018). https://www.fossanalytics.com/-/media/files/documents/papers/meat-segment/using-spectrometry-for-simultaneous-measurement_es.pdf
10. Cortes, C., Vapnik, V.: Support-vector networks. In: Saitta, L. (ed.) Machine Learning, pp. 273–297. KlugerAcademic Publishers, Boston (1995)
11. Nascimento, R.F.F., Alcântara, E.H., Kampel, M., et al.: O algoritmo SVM: avaliação da separação ótima de classes em imagens CCD-CBERS-2. XIV Simpósio Bras Sensoriamento Remoto 2079–2086 (2009)
12. Gala, Y.: Algoritmos SVM para problemas sobre big data. Universidad Autonoma de Madrid (2013)
13. Chang, C.C., Lin, C.J.: LIBSVM: a library for support vector machines. ACM Trans. Intell. Syst. Technol. 2 (2011). https://doi.org/10.1145/1961189.1961199
14. Shalev-Shwartz, S., Ben-David, S.: Understanding Machine Learning: From Theory to Algorithms. Cambridge University Press, New York (2014)
15. Gallo, C.: Artificial Neural Networks: tutorial (2015)
16. Hornik, K., Stinchcombe, M., White, H.: Multilayer feedforward networks are universal approximators. Neural Netw. (1989). https://doi.org/10.1016/0893-6080(89)90020-8
17. Chollet, F.: Keras (2015) (2017). http://keras.io/
18. Pedregosa, F., Varoquaux, G., Gramfort, A., et al.: Scikit-learn: machine learning in Python. J. Mach. Learn. Res. 12, 2825–2830 (2011)
19. Forman, G., Forman, G., Scholz, M., Scholz, M.: Apples-to-apples in cross-validation studies: pitfalls in classifier performance measurement. HP Labs 12, 49–57 (2009). https://doi.org/10.1145/1882471.1882479
20. Zhang, Y.D., Yang, Z.J., Lu, H.M., et al.: Facial emotion recognition based on biorthogonal wavelet entropy, fuzzy support vector machine, and stratified cross validation. IEEE Access 4, 8375–8385 (2016). https://doi.org/10.1109/ACCESS.2016.2628407
21. Kotsiantis, S.B., Kanellopoulos, D.: Data preprocessing for supervised leaning. Int. J. Comput. Sci. 1, 1–7 (2006). https://doi.org/10.1080/02331931003692557
22. Ferreira, E.J., Pereira, R.C.T., Delbem, A.C.B., et al.: Random subspace method for analysing coffee with electronic tongue. Electron. Lett. (2017) https://doi.org/10.1049/el:20071182
23. Dunne, R., Campbell, N.: On the pairing of the Softmax activation and cross-entropy penalty functions and the derivation of the Softmax activation function. In: Proceedings of 8th Australian Conference Neural Networks (1997). https://doi.org/10.1.1.49.6403
24. Agarap, A.F.: Deep learning using rectified linear units (ReLU), pp. 2–8 (2018)
25. He, K., Zhang, X., Ren, S., Sun, J.: Delving deep into rectifiers: surpassing human-level performance on imagenet classification. In: Proceedings of IEEE International Conference Computer Vision 2015, pp. 1026–1034 (2015). https://doi.org/10.1109/ICCV.2015.123
26. Kingma, D.P., Ba, J.: Adam: a method for stochastic optimization, pp. 1–15 (2014)

Predictive Analysis and Data Visualization Approach for Decision Processes in Marketing Strategies: A Case of Study

Andrés García-Pérez⬡, María Alejandra Millán Hernández(✉)⬡,
and Daniela E. Castellón Marriaga⬡

Programa de Ingeniería Industrial, Universidad Tecnológica de Bolívar,
Cartagena de Indias, Colombia
agarcia@utb.edu.co, marialeja-9805@hotmail.com,
castellonmarriga@gmail.com

Abstract. In this paper, we perform a new strategy for recommender systems in online entertainment platforms. As a case of study, we analyzed the reading preferences based on users of Goodreads, a social network for readers, to classify the books depending on their associated with variables as average rating, rating count, and text review count. Multivariate techniques cluster analysis and benchmarking for comparison of predictive models were used. Graphs and data are presented, allowing optimal evaluation of the number of clusters and the precision of models. Finally, we show the existence of groups of elements that can be forgotten by traditional recommendation systems, due to their low visualization on the platform. It is proposed to use promotional strategies to highlight these high-quality articles but with little visibility. All in all, consider the classification of books that predictive models can offer, it can favor the authors, readers, and investors of Goodreads, by the retention and attraction of users.

Keywords: Machine Learning · Predictive analytics · Data visualization · Recommender systems · Marketing strategies

1 Introduction

The creation of the concept of digital reading with the entry of electronic books brings transformations to the relationship between author and reader. [1] manifests the challenges facing the publishing industry today, claiming that this industry requires a high capital investment, referring to the costs of publishing and promoting books in physical format, while the low prices of electronic publishing remove barriers to entry. These economic costs make e-books affordable and show a competitive advantage against the publishing industry. On the other hand, there is another scenario that also encompasses digital publication: self-publishing, where authors without an editor intervention publicize his books through the internet making it easily accessible to readers.

Social networks have promoted the author-reader relationship, promoting feedback between them, and expanding the possibilities of an idea exchange. Likewise, readers

© Springer Nature Switzerland AG 2020
J. C. Figueroa-García et al. (Eds.): WEA 2020, CCIS 1274, pp. 60–70, 2020.
https://doi.org/10.1007/978-3-030-61834-6_6

from any part of the world can meet on digital platforms in spaces such as virtual reading clubs, where topics of the books are commented and criticized, and especially books recommendations are made. Goodreads is a readers social network, which was born as a proposal for readers who wanted to have a virtual library with the books they had read, the ones who were reading, and those who wanted to read. It offers, among its basic functions adding ratings and reviews to books read, also making friends with other readers with similar literary preferences.

The platform has around 90 million users. It was sold to Amazon six years after its launching and helps authors to make themselves known doing giveaways of books that have just released. Due to all its functionalities, Goodreads draws attention not only from readers but also from authors, who establish links with readers, get feedback on their books, know their popularity in the community and can assess their positioning as writers. To keep the reader up to date on the latest books, it´s needed to select and filter the books of greatest interest. In response, recommendation systems are integrated since they study current people predilections to predict future ones, saving them the time invested, and generating higher conversion rates.

Various ways of creating generic recommendation systems have been proposed [2]. Collaborative filtering, for example, assumes if a user has rated two books, then to another user who has read one of these books, can be recommended the other one. In [3] describes how Amazon and Netflix use algorithms to offer quality recommendations to their users, using the collaborative filtering recommendation system. In this way, through this method, it is intended to generate a list of similar items. However, the user experience translates that recommendations are made based only on the previous interests that the reader may have had, regardless of the incredible variety of other options that this type of platform can offer. This opens up the possibility of creating user interest lists that allow low-view authors to be promoted to keep readers more interested in the recommendations.

The present work tries to expose a new approach recommendations system in virtual entertainment platforms. Our proposal uses data visualization and machine learning techniques for the creation of experimental lists of items that along together with the inclusion of other features, can generate a higher conversion rate and maintain user traffic on the platform. This methodology is applied to the Goodreads case study to identify lists of books to be prioritized when trying to generate innovative recommendations that favor Goodreads authors, readers, and investors.

2   Related Works

The recommendation systems are based on the relationship between products or users. With this, there are two main techniques used for that task, collaborative filtering and content-based recommendation. [4–6] evaluated their studies based on the collaborative filtering system, where they focused on the description of the products to make the recommendations. These authors based their work on the use of algorithms like KNN to find the similarities between the items. On the other hand, [7–9] used a content-based recommendation system, using the feedback collected from users on products and using clustering or clustering algorithms in their research. While [10–12] suggest the combination of these two systems, exposing a hybrid approach that combines techniques from the previous recommenders to try to cover their deficiencies.

[13] propose adding a third level of user interests to the typical characteristics of users and products. In this way, over-specialization is aided, thus personalizing the recommendations. Recently, works have used the power of Artificial Neural Networks for learning about users or product features. This technique has also been used to retrieve missing values as ratings and develop hybrid recommender systems [14, 15]. [16] suggests using three similarity measures to avoid co-rated items: users, rating choice weight, and the ratio of co-rated items, obtaining good results to minimize the deviation of similarity calculation.

From the works analyzed, it is possible to observe the interest in generating emotion in the users about the recommendations made, which can generate higher conversion rates. On entertainment platforms, boredom can arise among users due to the always similar recommendations. In this way, it is intended to start a discussion on the inclusion in the list recommendation systems that allow exploring the wide range of options that an entertainment platform can offer, without losing the quality of these.

3   Methodology

The study used the K-Means grouping technique and benchmarking for comparison of supervised Machine Learning techniques. The analyzed data was taken from the Goodreads database stored in [17], which has 11 127 book records that have been read by platform users until 2019. To classify the books, we consider the preference of the readers. Three characteristics were chosen, which represent the most significant variability among the books to carry out the segmentation. Features such as identifier code and ISBN were left out. The variables considered were:

- Average rating (average_rating): The average rating that the book has received in total (users can rate according to their perception from 1 to 5, with 1 being "very bad" and 5 "very good").
- Ratings_count: Total number of ratings received by the book.
- Comment count (text_reviews_count): Total number of comments the book got.

The perception of users on this platform is that the recommendations made are often based on similar authors, so growing authors with excellent ratings are ignored. The type of recommendation proposed is aimed at the marketing team, to promote the promotion of little-known writers, but with great potential in topics of interest to the user. In this way, it is proposed that these types of recommendations that benefit authors and readers by offering them a greater diversity of books be incorporated into marketing strategies.

As it was told, growing authors are overshadowed by famous authors. Figure 1 shows the Top Ten famous authors in Goodreads. This violin chart illustrates the relationship between authors and their book scores. It is observed that the scores given to the author Rumiko Takahashi are highly concentrated around the median, that means majority of people who read his books agree they are good. Also is noticed the scores given to Stephen King are more spread out, so the rating presented a high standard deviation. In other terms there is people who liked his books and rate it low, and they are people who loved and rate it high. All previous support the fact that if there is a group of well-rated authors, they deserve the opportunity to be known.

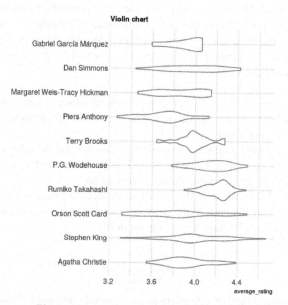

Fig. 1. Top ten famous authors in Goodreads

Figure 2 shows the proposed method. The mass of data should be grouped by its characteristics, such as score and count of ratings and comments. The score received quality of work, while the score count and comment count, the author's rating. The cluster is then assigned to the records in the original database. The cluster to attack is identified, and the promotional strategies are generated. Finally, classification techniques are used to evaluate new data received and thus maintain the system.

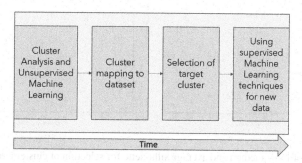

Fig. 2. The workflow of the proposed method.

4 Results and Discussion

For this study, the R language was used. A pre-processing of the data was performed, choosing the characteristics shown in Sect. 3, the missing values were removed, and the data were normalized. The percentage of variance explained according to the number of clusters is analyzed [18]. The variation in the number of clusters is evaluated with the sum of squares of the residuals, as shown in Fig. 3. We determine the optimal number, using the Silhouette Coefficient presented by [19]. For each observation i, the silhouette coefficient (s_i) is obtained as follows:

1. Calculate the average of the distances (a_i) between observation i and the rest of the observations that belong to the same cluster. The smaller ai, the better the assignment of i to its cluster has been.
2. Calculate the average distance between observation i and the other clusters. Understanding by the average distance between i and a given cluster (K) as the mean of the distances between i and the cluster observations
3. Identify as b_i the smallest of the average distances between i and the rest of the clusters, that is, the distance to the nearest cluster (neighborhood cluster).
4. Calculate the value of silhouette, as shown in Eq. 1.

$$s_i = \frac{b_i - a_i}{\max(a_i, b_i)} \tag{1}$$

The average silhouette method considers as the optimal number of clusters, the one that maximizes the mean of the silhouette coefficient of all the observations. In this way, the maximum Average Silhouette Width (see Fig. 3). It is presented for $K = 7$ clusters.

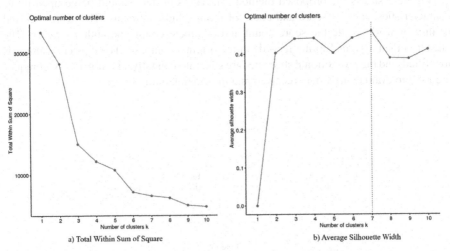

a) Total Within Sum of Square   b) Average Silhouette Width

Fig. 3. Elbow method and average silhouette for selection of cluster number.

After choosing the optimal number of clusters, it is possible to carry out an adequate classification of the books, which will be divided into seven categories.

Figure 4, shows the resulting clusters for the Goodreads database. There is a large concentration of books for high average rating. Besides, a positive correlation is presented for variations in the rating count and text review count, which represent the number of people who evaluated the books.

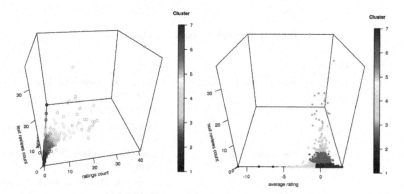

Fig. 4. Goodreads book clusters

Clusters are shown in Fig. 5, for average rating and ratings count. With this, the aim is to identify the cluster with well-ratings books, but little known/evaluated on the platform. There are very popular books with high average ratings, such as those belonging to cluster 3. At the same time, there are very little-known books with low ratings, as in the case of cluster 1. The cluster of interest is presented as being 6, which presents a range of evaluations similar to that of very popular books, but which are little commented or evaluated.

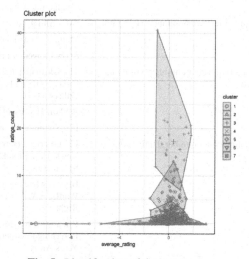

Fig. 5. Identification of the target group.

In this way, the target cluster that should be prioritized has been visually identified. For the present study, the two characteristics used for identification represented the popularity and quality of work. Other possible approaches may include visualizing data in multiple dimensions and factor rating system. Table 1 shows some examples of books belonging to each cluster along with the characteristics present in each one of these.

Table 1. Example of books by clusters.

Book category	Description	Title
Cluster 1	Low rating count number, Low rating average	Out to Eat London 2002 (Lonely Planet Out to Eat)
		Juiced Official Strategy Guide
		Open City 6: The Only Woman He Ever Left
Cluster 2	Low rating count number, High rating average	Harry Potter and the Chamber of Secrets (Harry Potter #2)
		Harry Potter Boxed Set Books 1-5 (Harry Potter #1-5)
		Harry Potter Collection (Harry Potter #1-6)
Cluster 3	High rating count number, High rating average	Harry Potter and the Half-Blood Prince (Harry Potter #6)
		Harry Potter and the Order of the Phoenix (Harry Potter #5)
		Harry Potter and the Prisoner of Azkaban (Harry Potter #3)
Cluster 4	Low rating count number, Medium rating average	Bill Bryson's African Diary
		Hatchet Jobs: Writings on Contemporary Fiction
		Changeling (Changeling #1)
Cluster 5	Medium rating count number, High rating average	Atlas Shrugged
		Memoirs of a Geisha
		Snow Flower and the Secret Fan
Cluster 6	Medium rating count number, High rating average	The Ultimate Hitchhiker's Guide to the Galaxy (Hitchhiker's Guide to the Galaxy #1-5)
		A Short History of Nearly Everything
		In a Sunburned Country
Cluster 7	Low rating count number, High rating average	Unauthorized Harry Potter Book Seven News: Half-Blood Prince Analysis and Speculation
		Bryson's Dictionary of Troublesome Words: A Writer's Guide to Getting It Right
		I'm a Stranger Here Myself: Notes on Returning to America After Twenty Years Away

With clusters assigned by book, it is possible to process new data. In this way, it is intended to determine when a book is moved from one cluster to another. We are especially interested when a book enters to cluster 6, to be considered in the promotion strategy. For this purpose, k-fold cross-validation was performed with k = 10, with the examples called dataset for four models: Random Forests, Support Vector Machines (svm), KNN and Extreme Gradient Boosting (xgboost). The performance measures to choose the best model are Classification Accuracy (acc), Balanced Accuracy (bacc), and Classification Error (ce). The results are presented in Fig. 6.

The Support Vector Machines model, on average, shows maximums with better performance, as well as their average and, in general, offers a good relationship between the minimum and maximum values for the different performance measures.

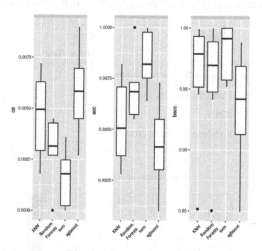

Fig. 6. Model performance.

To find out which model performed better in all tasks simultaneously, performance statistics were calculated for each one. The positions occupied by each model, according to the Table 2 are shown in Table 3. In this work, the Support Vector Machines model presents the best evaluation in the test set, getting a rank of 1; and the second position for the train set, getting a rank of 2. Contrarily, the Extreme Gradient Boosting model presents the worst evaluation in the train and test set, getting a rank of 4 in both.

Figure 7 shows the classification of books using the Support Vector Machines model, from the perspective of average rating and ratings count. In this way, the items (books) on the platform that can be prioritized for promotional activities could be identified through the proposed methodology. These activities can be manifested with more visualization on the platform or a more significant number of recommendations to users, depending on their interest.

This approach will increase the diversity of options offered, which can promote further exploration of the platform. As it could be verified, the predictive model presents a high hit rate. So, for system maintenance, this classification model can be used to identify candidates for these promotions. This information can be used by a recommendation system, which takes into account content diversification and other variables such as common characteristics of users, products, and the user's interests.

Table 2. Measures of each model for the test and training data set.

Model	Train			Test		
	acc	bacc	ce	acc	bacc	ce
Random Forest	1.000	1.000	–	0.997	0.960	0.003
Support Vector Machines	0.999	0.993	0.001	0.998	0.981	0.002
KNN	0.999	0.988	0.001	0.995	0.965	0.005
Extreme Gradient Boosting	0.998	0.982	0.002	0.994	0.937	0.006

Table 3. Positions occupied by each model according to their average performance.

Model	Rank	
	Train	Test
Support Vector Machines	2	1
Random Forests	1	2
KNN	3	3
Extreme Gradient Boosting	4	4

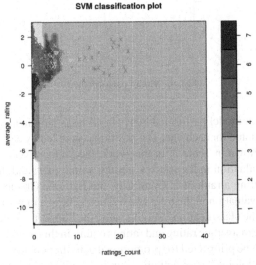

Fig. 7. Support Vector Machines in Goodreads book ranking.

5   Conclusions and Future Work

The results obtained in the study serve as a decision-making tool that can favor the Goodreads community. Developers are proposed to place greater emphasis on the group of books that are not very popular but are highly rated, using marketing strategies to make them more known, giving these writers a position.

The presence of user authors on the platform could increase if they achieve their objective: to reach the critical mass of readers. Goodreads developers can support authors who produce good content but are not yet highly recognized. With this, the reading users and investors will also obtain benefits. The former will have new books in their reading suggestions that are recommended for their excellent evaluation, and that can offer them a different experience, the latter on their part will have greater profits as they have more traffic on their platform generated by users who are motivated to stay on Goodreads or by new users who come to the platform.

Future Work

Consider readers' dissatisfaction with specific recommendations. When the scanning option is enabled on the platform, the possibility of implementing a hybrid model combining the collaborative and content-based filtering recommendation system with the proposed prioritization system can be evaluated.

References

1. Shatzkin, M., Riger, R.: The Book Business, 1st edn. Oxford University Press, New York (2019)
2. Rana, A., Deeba, K.: Online book recommendation system using collaborative filtering (with Jaccard similarity). Nano Sci. J. Phys. Conf. Ser. **1362**, 12130 (2019). https://doi.org/10.1088/1742-6596/1362/1/012130
3. Adomavicius, G., Tuzhilin, A.: Toward the next generation of recommender systems: a survey of the state-of-the-art and possible extensions. IEEE Trans. Knowl. Data Eng. **17**(6), 734–749 (2005). https://doi.org/10.1109/TKDE.2005.99
4. Resnick, P., Iakovou, N.: GroupLens: an open architecture for collaborative filtering of netnews. In: Computer Supported Cooperative Work Conference (1994)
5. Hill, W., Stead, L., Rosenstein, M., Furnas, G.: Recommending and evaluating choices in a virtual community of use. In: Proceedings of Conference on Human Factors in Computing Systems (1995)
6. Sarwar, B., Karypis, G., Konstan, J.: Item-based collaborative filtering recommendation algorithms. In: Proceedings of 10th International WWW Conference (2001)
7. Lang, K.: Newsweeder: learning to filter netnews. In: Proceedings of 12th International Conference Machine Learning (1995)
8. Balabanovic, M., Shoham, Y.: Fab: content-based collaborative recommendation. Comm. ACM **40**(3), 66–72 (1997)
9. Pazzani, M., Billsus, D.: Learning and revising user profiles: the identification of interesting web sites. Mach. Learn. **27**, 313–331 (1997)
10. Claypool, M., Gokhale, A., Miranda, T.: Combining content-based and collaborative filters in an online newspaper. In: Proceedings of ACM SIGIR 1999 Workshop Recommender
11. Tran, T, Cohen., R.: Hybrid recommender systems for electronic commerce. In: Proceedings of Knowledge-Based Electronic Markets. Papers from the AAAI Workshop, Technical report WS-00-04, AAAI Press (2000)
12. Melville, P., Mooney, R.: content-boosted collaborative filtering for improved recommendations. In: Proceedings of 18th National Conference Artificial Intelligence (2002)

13. Liu, Q., Chen, E., Xiong, H., Ding, C.H.Q., Chen, J.: Enhancing collaborative filtering by user interest expansion via personalised ranking. IEEE Trans. Syst. Man Cybern. Part B Cybern. **42**(1), 2012 (2012)
14. Strub, F., Gaudel, R., Mary, J.: Hybrid recommender system based on autoencoders. In: Proceedings of the 1st Workshop on Deep Learning for Recommender Systems, ACM, pp. 11–16 (2016)
15. Zhang, S., Yao, L., Sun, A.: Deep learning based recommender system: a survey and new perspectives. arXiv preprint arXiv:1707.07435 (2017)
16. Feng, J., Fengs, X., Zhang, N., Peng, J.: An improved collaborative filtering method based on similarity. PLoS ONE **13**(9), e0204003 (2018)
17. Kaggle (2020). https://www.kaggle.com/jealousleopard/goodreadsbooks
18. Bholowalia, P., Kumar, A.: EBK-means: a clustering technique based on elbow method and k-means in WSN. Int. J. Comput. Appl. **105**(9), 17–24 (2014)
19. Rousseeuw, P.: Silhouettes: a graphical aid to the interpretation and validation of cluster analysis. J. Comput. Appl. Math. **20**, 53–65 (1987). https://doi.org/10.1016/0377-0427(87)90125-7. ISSN 0377-0427

Computer Science

State Observer for a Chemical Process Using Modern Discretization Algorithms

Juan Sebastián Molina-Gómez$^{(\boxtimes)}$ and Héctor Antonio Botero-Castro

Facultad de Minas, Grupo de Investigación en Procesos Dinámicos - Kalman,
Universidad Nacional de Colombia, Bogota, Colombia
{jsmolinag,habotero}@unal.edu.co

Abstract. State estimation using sliding modes allows taking advantage of finite time convergence and robustness for the design of virtual sensors. The goal of this paper is to design observers for a chemical process by using robust differentiators, based on high-order sliding mode, but using modern discretization algorithms, in such a way that low sampling rates and high estimation precision can be obtained. In addition, it seeks to preserve the convergence properties in finite time and avoid the chattering effects due to the discretization time. The results obtained are verified by means of simulation, by comparing the performance of different discretization algorithms.

Keywords: Virtual sensor · State estimation · Sliding modes · Robust differentiator

1 Introduction

State estimation is a technique, which allows reconstructing the state of a dynamic system from the knowledge of input and output. State observers are designed by using a model of a system and control techniques in order to achieve a desired behavior in the error of estimation. In the case of sliding mode observers, it is possible to obtain finite-time, fixed-time, or predefined-time convergence, and robustness in the dynamic of error [8]. However, many algorithms require high-order derivatives of the output, which make the observer very sensitive to measurement noise. Therefore, it is necessary to use robust filtering and differentiation techniques in order to achieve noise rejection [1]. Numerical differentiation is a special class of application, which proposes a classic problem with sliding mode control (SMC) [5,14]. The idea is to extract the base signal and the derivatives from the original signal $f(t)$ contaminated with noise [9].

Particularly, for the design of observers for nonlinear systems, transformations of the models to an observable triangular shape are used, by making that the estimated variables correspond to those derived from the measured output [4,13]. Therefore, it is necessary to find those derivatives online, and thus, be able to implement estimation algorithms. Then, this type of solution poses two

© Springer Nature Switzerland AG 2020
J. C. Figueroa-García et al. (Eds.): WEA 2020, CCIS 1274, pp. 73–84, 2020.
https://doi.org/10.1007/978-3-030-61834-6_7

challenges: a) obtaining the derivatives of the output, and b) finding an invertible transformation in real time in order to obtain the estimates of the original state variables [4].

Therefore, in this paper the design of a nonlinear observer is applied in a model of chemical process [10], which uses a method for the solution of a variant algebraic equation in time and does not need non-linear transformations. The observer's performance is enhanced, by using a discrete sliding-mode-based differentiator in order to find state variables. To achieve this, three types of high-order discretization algorithms proposed in the literature are implemented: a) the explicit algorithm, b) the implicit algorithm, and c) the Robust Exact Differentiator (RED) by its acronym in English [2]. The latter is the discretization of the robust differentiator, which uses the Zero Order Hold (ZOH) technique developed in [12]. The idea of these algorithms is to avoid the chattering generated by the use of the traditional Euler's method when implementing very low sampling frequencies, by maintaining the properties of finite-time convergence, accuracy, and robustness regarding disturbances and modeling uncertainties when applied in state estimation for nonlinear models [3,8].

This paper is organized as follows: In Sect. 2, a nonlinear state observer, reported in [10], is briefly explained, which requires the knowledge of the derivatives of the measured variables to be implemented. Section 3 takes up the robust differentiator in continuous time and its model in state space, as well as explicit and implicit differentiators in discrete time and the Robust Exact Differentiator (RED). Section 4 explains a case of study in which the differentiators were applied to the nonlinear observer, on a Continuous Stirred Tank Reactor (CSTR) model. Finally, Sect. 5 shows the conclusions.

2   Structure of the Nonlinear Observer

In this paper, a finite-time sliding mode observer for nonlinear system is used [10]. The observer is based on a method for the solution of time-varying algebraic equations to estimate the states variables so that the theoretical output derivatives are equal to the actual derivatives provided by sliding mode differentiator. In this sense, by considering the following time-varying system

$$\mathbf{H}(\mathbf{z}(t)) - \mathbf{G}(t) = \mathbf{0} \qquad (1)$$

Where $\mathbf{z} \in \mathbf{Z} \subseteq \mathbf{R}^\eta$ is the vector of variables to be determined, $\mathbf{H} : \mathbf{R}^\eta \to \mathbf{R}^q$ and $\mathbf{G} : [0, \infty) \to \mathbf{R}^q$ are known. Let system (1) satisfy the assumptions in [10]. A method to solve (1) could involve a sliding mode technique, which drives $\mathbf{z}$ to a manifold, where the sliding variable $\boldsymbol{\sigma} = \boldsymbol{\sigma}(\mathbf{z}, t) = \mathbf{H}(\mathbf{z}) - \mathbf{G}(t)$ is zero. By the lemma proposed in [10], the dynamical system for variable $\mathbf{z}$ is given by

$$\dot{\mathbf{z}} = \frac{\boldsymbol{\sigma}^T \dot{\mathbf{G}} - r||\boldsymbol{\sigma}||^{3/2}}{||(\frac{\partial \mathbf{H}}{\partial \mathbf{z}})^T \boldsymbol{\sigma}||^2} (\frac{\partial \mathbf{H}}{\partial \mathbf{z}})^T \boldsymbol{\sigma} \qquad (2)$$

Where $|| \cdot ||$ is the Euclidean norm and $r > 0$ is a tuning parameter. The Lyapunov function $V(\boldsymbol{\sigma}) = \frac{1}{2}||\boldsymbol{\sigma}||^2$ and its derivative satisfy some conditions for finite-time stability. Therefore, the sliding manifold $\boldsymbol{\sigma} = \mathbf{0}$ is finite-time attractive for system (2) (see proof in [10]). If the output derivatives of the system are known, the observation problem can be reduced to a time-varying system of algebraic equation as the one proposed in (1). For the design of an observer, consider the following dynamical system

$$\dot{\mathbf{x}} = \mathbf{f}(\mathbf{x}, \mathbf{u})$$
$$\mathbf{y} = \mathbf{h}(\mathbf{x}) = [h_1(\mathbf{x}), h_2(\mathbf{x}), \cdots, h_m(\mathbf{x})] \tag{3}$$

Where $\mathbf{x} \in \mathbf{R}^n$ is the state vector, $\mathbf{u} \in \mathbf{R}^p$ is the input vector and $\mathbf{y} \in \mathbf{R}^m$ is output vector. Let the functions $\mathbf{H}$ and $\mathbf{G}$ be defined as:

$$\mathbf{H}(\hat{\mathbf{z}}) = \begin{bmatrix} L_f^0 h_1(\hat{\mathbf{z}}) \\ \vdots \\ L_f^{v_1-1} h_1(\hat{\mathbf{z}}) \\ \vdots \\ L_f^0 h_m(\hat{\mathbf{z}}) \\ \vdots \\ L_f^{v_m-1} h_m(\hat{\mathbf{z}}) \end{bmatrix}, \mathbf{G}(t) = \begin{bmatrix} y_1 \\ \vdots \\ y_1^{(v_1-1)} \\ \vdots \\ y_m \\ \vdots \\ y_m^{(v_m-1)} \end{bmatrix}$$

Where $\hat{\mathbf{z}}$ is the estimated vector state, $\mathbf{H}(\hat{\mathbf{z}})$ is computed, by using the Lie derivative, the integers $v_1, v_2, ..., v_m$ must be such that the conditions in [10] are satisfied. To obtain $\mathbf{G}(t)$, a sliding mode differentiator is computed in real time using the modern discretization algorithms for their implementation as explained below.

3   Discretization Algorithms

In this section, modern algorithms to discretize higher-order differentiators proposed in literature, which use state space representation, are presented.

3.1   Continuous-Time Higher-Order Differentiators

The objective of higher-order sliding mode differentiators is to calculate the nth derivatives for the measurement signal $f(t)$ which, could have noise with $f(t)$ defined on $[0, \infty)$ and the nth derivatives have a known Lipschitz constant $L > 0$ [8]. The nth derivatives $f^{(1)}(t), f^{(2)}(t), \cdots, f^{(n)}(t)$ are obtain as a state space model, by defining variables $x_i = f^{(i)}(t)$ and $\mathbf{x} = \begin{bmatrix} x_0\ x_1\ x_2 \cdots x_n \end{bmatrix}^T \in \mathbf{R}^{n+1}$. State space model is defined as follows [2]

$$\dot{\mathbf{x}} = \mathbf{A}\mathbf{x} + \mathbf{e}_{n+1} f^{n+1}(t)$$
$$\mathbf{y} = \mathbf{e}_1 \mathbf{x} \tag{4}$$

With vectors $\mathbf{e}_1 = \begin{bmatrix} 1 & 0 & \cdots & 0 & 0 \end{bmatrix}^T$, $\mathbf{e}_{n+1} = \begin{bmatrix} 0 & 0 & \cdots & 0 & 1 \end{bmatrix}^T$ and matrix $\mathbf{A}$:

$$\mathbf{A} = \begin{bmatrix} 0 & 1 & 0 & \cdots & 0 \\ 0 & 0 & 1 & \cdots & 0 \\ \vdots & \vdots & \vdots & \ddots & \vdots \\ 0 & 0 & 0 & \cdots & 1 \\ 0 & 0 & 0 & \cdots & 0 \end{bmatrix}$$

The representation (4) allows finding the derivatives of $f(t)$ through the design of a state observer. From [8] and [9] the proposed observer to estimate the nth derivatives of $f(t)$ is

$$\dot{z}_0 = -\lambda_n L^{\frac{1}{n+1}} |z_0 - f(t)|^{\frac{n}{n+1}} sign(z_0 - f(t)) + z_1$$
$$\dot{z}_1 = -\lambda_{n-1} L^{\frac{2}{n+1}} |z_0 - f(t)|^{\frac{n-1}{n+1}} sign(z_0 - f(t)) + z_2 \tag{5}$$
$$\vdots$$
$$\dot{z}_n = -\lambda_0 L sign(z_0 - f(t))$$

Where $\mathbf{z} = \begin{bmatrix} z_0 & z_1 & z_2 & \cdots & z_n \end{bmatrix}^T$ are the estimated states of the state vector $\mathbf{x}$ and the parameters λ_i y L are defined on [8]. Defining the estimation errors as $\sigma_i = z_i - x_i$ with $i = 0, 1, 2, ..., n$, the differentiator (5) can be rewritten as:

$$\dot{\mathbf{z}} = \mathbf{A}\mathbf{z} + \mathbf{B}u(\sigma_0) \tag{6}$$

where $\mathbf{B}$ is the identity matrix $(n+1) \times (n+1)$ and $u(\sigma_0)$ is defined as follows:

$$\mathbf{u}(\sigma_0) = \begin{bmatrix} \Psi_0(\sigma_0) & \Psi_1(\sigma_0) & \cdots & \Psi_n(\sigma_0) \end{bmatrix}^T$$
$$\Psi_i(\sigma_0) = -\lambda_{n-i} L^{\frac{i+1}{n+1}} |\sigma_0|^{\frac{n-i}{n+1}} sign(\sigma_0) \tag{7}$$

The error vector is $\boldsymbol{\sigma} = \mathbf{z} - \mathbf{x}$ and its dynamics is given by:

$$\dot{\boldsymbol{\sigma}} = \mathbf{A}\boldsymbol{\sigma} + \mathbf{B}u(\sigma_0) - \mathbf{e}_{n+1} f^{n+1}(t) \tag{8}$$

3.2   Explicit Discretization Algorithm

In this discretization algorithm, Taylor's series are used because they apply a higher-order method compared to the one used by Euler's method, the numerical error, and the chattering effects are much less for low sampling frequencies [2,6].

To compute this algorithm, signal $f(t)$ is measured at the time instants $t_k = k\tau$ for $k = 0, 1, 2, 3, \cdots$, where τ is the sampling time. Let us denote $x_i(t_k) = x_{i,k}$ and $z_i(t_k) = z_{i,k}$ discrete-time system states of (4) and (6) respectively and $\sigma_i(t_k) = \sigma_{i,k}$ error at the time instants. With this definitions and using (7) to

$u_k = u(\sigma_{0,k})$, Taylor's series are used to discretize (6) (see [6]) obtaining the following discrete-time observer:

$$\mathbf{z}_{k+1} = \boldsymbol{\Phi}(\tau)\mathbf{z}_k + \mathbf{B}^*(\tau)\mathbf{u}_k$$

$$\mathbf{u}_k = \left[\Psi_0(\sigma_{0,k})\ \Psi_1(\sigma_{0,k})\ \cdots\ \Psi_n(\sigma_{0,k})\right]^T \qquad (9)$$

$$\Psi_i(\sigma_{0,k}) = -\lambda_{n-i}L^{\frac{i+1}{n+1}}|\sigma_{0,k}|^{\frac{n-i}{n+1}}sign(\sigma_{0,k})$$

Where $\boldsymbol{\Phi}(\tau)$ and $\mathbf{B}^*(\tau)$ are matrices with the following representation:

$$\boldsymbol{\Phi}(\tau) = \begin{bmatrix} 1 & \tau & \frac{\tau^2}{2!} & \cdots & \frac{\tau^{n-1}}{(n-1)!} & \frac{\tau^n}{n!} \\ 0 & 1 & \tau & \cdots & \frac{\tau^{n-2}}{(n-2)!} & \frac{\tau^{n-1}}{(n-1)!} \\ \vdots & \vdots & \vdots & \ddots & \vdots & \vdots \\ 0 & 0 & 0 & \cdots & 1 & \tau \\ 0 & 0 & 0 & \cdots & 0 & 1 \end{bmatrix}, \mathbf{B}^*(\tau) = \begin{bmatrix} \tau & \frac{\tau^2}{2!} & \frac{\tau^3}{3!} & \cdots & \frac{\tau^n}{n!} & \frac{\tau^{n+1}}{(n+1)!} \\ 0 & \tau & \frac{\tau^2}{2!} & \cdots & \frac{\tau^{n-1}}{(n-1)!} & \frac{\tau^n}{n!} \\ \vdots & \vdots & \vdots & \ddots & \vdots & \vdots \\ 0 & 0 & 0 & \cdots & \tau & \frac{\tau^2}{2!} \\ 0 & 0 & 0 & \cdots & 0 & \tau \end{bmatrix}$$

Equation (9) and the above matrices represent the explicit discretization algorithm with the same structure as the one in [2]. It is called an explicit method because the variable $\mathbf{z}_{k+1}$ depends only on the previous values.

Since function $f^{(n+1)}$ can be variable over the time interval $[t_k, t_{k+1})$, then a discrete system of (4) is obtained, by using Taylor's series expansion with Lagrange's remainders [7]

$$\mathbf{x}_{k+1} = \boldsymbol{\Phi}(\tau)\mathbf{x}_k + \mathbf{h}_e \qquad (10)$$

with

$$\mathbf{h}_e = \left[\frac{\tau^{n+1}}{(n+1)!}f_0^{(n+1)}(\zeta_n),\ \frac{\tau^n}{(n)!}f_0^{(n+1)}(\zeta_{n-1}),\ \cdots\ \tau f_0^{(n+1)}(\zeta_0)\right]^T$$

Where $\zeta_i \in (t_k, t_{k+1})$ y $|f_0^{(n+1)}(\zeta_0)| \leq L$. By using (9) and (10), the discrete form of the error system is given as [2]:

$$\boldsymbol{\sigma}_{k+1} = \boldsymbol{\Phi}(\tau)\boldsymbol{\sigma}_k + \mathbf{B}^*(\tau)\mathbf{u}_k - \mathbf{h}_e \qquad (11)$$

3.3 Implicit Discretization Algorithm

This algorithm is based on the implicit discretization method which is able to avoid the chattering effects due to low sampling frequencies [2]. The implicit discretization algorithm for the differentiator (6) has the same form of the differentiator from the previous subsection. The difference between both is that in the implicit algorithm, the error $\sigma_{0,k+1}$ is used, instead $\sigma_{0,k}$. Therefore, the vector $\mathbf{u}$ for the error $\sigma_{0,k+1}$ is defined as follows

$$\mathbf{u}_{k+1} = \left[\Psi_{0,k+1}\Psi_{1,k+1}\cdots\Psi_{n,k+1}^T\right]$$

$$\Psi_{i,k+1} = -\lambda_{n-i}L^{\frac{i+1}{n+1}}|\sigma_{0,k+1}|^{\frac{n-i}{n+1}}sign(\sigma_{0,k+1})$$

The discretization obtained for the differentiator is as follows:

$$\mathbf{z}_{k+1} = \boldsymbol{\Phi}(\tau)\mathbf{z}_k + \mathbf{B}^*\mathbf{u}_{k+1}$$
$$\boldsymbol{\sigma}_{k+1} = \boldsymbol{\Phi}(\tau)\boldsymbol{\sigma}_k + \mathbf{B}^*\mathbf{u}_{k+1} - \mathbf{h}_e \tag{12}$$

Notice that σ_{k+1} cannot be calculated, by using (12) due to the impossibility of measuring the states $x_{1,k}, x_{2,k}, \cdots, x_{n,k}$, vector $\mathbf{h}_e$, and $f^{(n+1)}(\zeta_i)$. Therefore, these terms are taken into account as disturbances for the estimation of $\sigma_{0,k+1}$. Now, in order to implement (12) the variables $\tilde{\sigma}_{0,k+1}$ and $\xi_{k+1} = sign(\tilde{\sigma}_{0,k+1})$ are defined to solve the equations proposed in [2] and by using the variables

$$b_k = -\sigma_{0,k} - \sum_{m=1}^{n} \frac{\tau^m}{m!} z_{m,k}$$
$$a_l = \frac{\tau^{n-l+1}}{(n-l+1)!} \lambda_l L^{\frac{n-l+1}{n+1}} \tag{13}$$

Once the above variables have been found, the following lemma is used in order to compute the discrete differentiator [2].

Lemma 1: For parameters $a_i \in \mathbb{R}^-$ and $b_k \in \mathbb{R}$, there is an unique pair $\tilde{\sigma}_{0.k+1} \in \mathbb{R}$ and $\xi_{k+1} \in [-1, 1]$ which have the following solution:

– **Case 1**: $b_k > a_0$
  $\xi_{k+1} = -1$, $\tilde{\sigma}_{0,k+1} \in \mathbb{R}^-$ and is determined by $\tilde{\sigma}_{0,k+1} = -(r_0)^{n+1}$, where r_0 is the unique positive root of the polynomial equation (14).
– **Case 2**: $b_k \in [-a_0, a_0]$
  $\tilde{\sigma}_{0,k+1} = 0$ y $\xi_{k+1} = -\frac{b_k}{a_0}$.
– **Case 3**: $b_k < -a_0$
  $\xi_{k+1} = 1$, $\tilde{\sigma}_{0,k+1} \in \mathbb{R}^+$ and is determined by $\tilde{\sigma}_{0,k+1} = r_0^{n+1}$, where r_0 is the positive root of the polynomial equation (15).
  The polynomial equations are the following:

$$p(r) = r^{n+1} + a_n r^n + \cdots + a_1 r + (-b_k + a_0) \tag{14}$$

$$p(r) = r^{n+1} + a_n r^n + \cdots + a_1 r + (b_k + a_0) \tag{15}$$

Therefore, the discrete-time observer is expressed as follows:

$$\mathbf{z}_{k+1} = \boldsymbol{\Phi}(\tau)\mathbf{z}_k + \mathbf{B}^*(\tau)\mathbf{v}_{k+1}$$
$$\mathbf{v}_{k+1} = \begin{bmatrix} \tilde{\Psi}_{0,k+1} & \tilde{\Psi}_{1,k+1} & \cdots & \tilde{\Psi}_{n,k+1} \end{bmatrix}^T \tag{16}$$
$$\tilde{\Psi}_{i,k+1} = -\lambda_{n-i} L^{\frac{i+1}{n+1}} |\tilde{\sigma}_{0,k+1}|^{\frac{n-i}{n+1}} \xi_{k+1}$$

As ξ_{k+1} and $\tilde{\sigma}_{0,k+1}$ are calculated using only a_i, $\sigma_{0,k}$ y $z_{i,k}$, then the differentiator (16) is non-anticipative. Finally, the estimation error of observer (16) is expressed as follows:

$$\boldsymbol{\sigma}_{k+1} = \boldsymbol{\Phi}(\tau)\boldsymbol{\sigma}_k + \mathbf{B}^*(\tau)\mathbf{v}_{k+1} - \mathbf{h}_e \tag{17}$$

4   Case of Study

In this paper, a nonlinear model of Continuous Stirred Tank Reactor (CSTR) is used. This plant performs an exothermal chemical reaction from reactant A to product B ($A \rightarrow B$). The CSTR model was taken from [11], and it consists of two state equations: temperature and concentration. This model considers that the dynamics of the jacket temperature is faster than the dynamics of temperature inside the reactor and the concentration. Therefore, this temperature is kept constant, by using a control loop. Other modeling assumptions are perfect mixing in reactor and jacket, constant volume reactor and jacket (the level is perfectly controlled), constant parameter values, and negligible heat retained by the walls. The state equations of CSTR are

$$\frac{dT}{dt} = \frac{F}{V}(T_{in} - T) + \frac{-\Delta H}{\rho C_p}k_0 C_A exp(\frac{-E}{RT}) - \frac{UA}{\rho C_p V}(T - Tj)$$
$$\frac{dC_A}{dt} = \frac{F}{V}(C_{in} - C_A) - k_0 C_A exp(\frac{-E}{RT})$$

$$(18)$$

where F is the flow into the reactor, V is the volume of the reaction mass, C_{in} is the reactive input concentration, C_A is the concentration of reactive, k_0 is the Arrhenius's kinetic constant, E is the activation energy, R is the universal gas constant, T is the temperature inside the reactor and the measurement variable, T_{in} is the inlet temperature of the reactant, ΔH is the reaction heat, ρ is the density of the mixture in the reactor, C_p is the heat capacity of food, U is the overall coefficient of heat transfer, A is the heat transfer area, and T_j is the temperature inside the jacket. The Table 1 shows the values of the parameters.

Table 1. Parameters of CSTR [11]

Parameters	Values	Units
F	0.1605	$m^3 \cdot min^{-1}$
V	2.4069	m^3
C_{in}	2114.5	$gmol \cdot m^{-3}$
k_0	2.8267×10^{11}	min^{-1}
E	75361.14	$Jgmol^{-1}$
R	8.3174	$Jgmol^{-1}K^{-1}$
T_{in}	295.22	K
ΔH	-9.0712×10^4	$Jgmol^{-1}$
ρ	1000	$kg \cdot m^{-3}$
C_p	3571.3	Jkg^{-1}
U	2.5552×10^4	$J \cdot (s \cdot m^2 \cdot K)^{-1}$
A	8.1755	m^2
T_j	430, 0	K

For observer design, consider the CSTR nonlinear system model in the form:

$$\dot{x}(t) = f(x(t), u(t))$$
$$y(t) = h(x(t))$$

(19)

Where $x(t) = \begin{bmatrix} T(t) \ C_A(t) \end{bmatrix}^T$, $u(t) = F(t)$ and $y(t) = T(t)$. The aim of this observer is to estimate $C_A(t)$ using the observer model (2), where $\mathbf{z} = \hat{x}$, $\mathbf{H}(\hat{z})$ is shown in (20) and is obtained using Lie derivatives for nonlinear system outputs (19) and $\dot{\mathbf{G}}$ is estimated using higher order differentiator [10].

$$\mathbf{H}(\hat{z}) = \begin{bmatrix} \hat{T} \\ \frac{F}{V}(T_{in} - \hat{T}) + \frac{-\Delta H}{c_p \rho} k_0 \hat{C}_A exp(\frac{-E}{RT}) - \frac{UA}{\rho C_p V}(\hat{T} - T_j) \end{bmatrix}$$

(20)

For the simulations without measurement noise, a fourth-order differentiator ($n = 4$) and $L = 1$ was used. Parameters tuning λ_i are taken from [8] and for the dynamic observer (2) $r = 1$ is chosen. The initial conditions are taken so that the dynamics of the differentiator is already in a stable state. That is, the differentiator has already subsequently calculated the value of the output and its derivatives. The initial condition of the plant $x(0) = \begin{bmatrix} 375.649 \ 14.493 \end{bmatrix}^T$ is the equilibrium point and the observer's initial condition is 5% above of $x(0)$ with a sampling time and simulation time $\tau = 0.1$ min. In Figures 1 and 2, the temperature and concentration estimation are shown, by using the Robust Exact Differentiator Toolbox (RED) for Matlab®/Simulink ® [12], the explicit differentiator, and the implicit differentiator applied to the state observer of Sect. 2. In Fig. 3 the error dynamics for both variables is shown. In $t = 30$ min a 10% change is made at the plant input (F) above steady state value to show observer's behavior.

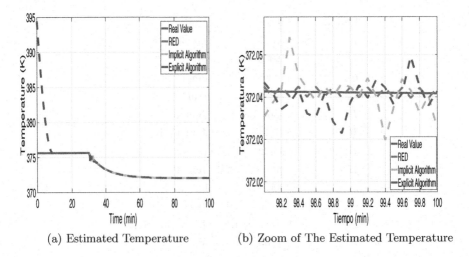

(a) Estimated Temperature   (b) Zoom of The Estimated Temperature

Fig. 1. Estimated temperature

Figure 1a shows the estimated temperature by using the different discretization algorithms for the high-order differentiators applied to the observer (2). In all three cases, the temperature starts with a value different from that measured temperature, and in approximately 10 min, it converges to the real value. After 30 min, the input changes, and the observer responds satisfactorily, by following approximately the same measured temperature value. Temperatures between 98 and 100 min are shown in Fig. 1b, by zooming in. When the observer uses the differentiator with the RED algorithm, it shows better performance compared to the others, although for all three cases, the error does not exceed $0.0115K$ for that time interval. In Fig. 2, the estimated concentration is shown. This variable is more important than temperature since it is the variable to estimate. Temperature was used as a measured variable. In Fig. 2a, it can be seen how concentration converges to the reference or real value for all three cases. When the input changes in 30 min, the observer responds faster with the RED algorithm. The performance of concentrations between 96 and 100 min is shown in Figure 2b by zooming in. The observer with the best performance is the observer with the RED algorithm, although for the three algorithms, the error does not exceed $0.05\ gmol^{-3}$. Figure 3 shows the error dynamics for temperature and concentration. When the change in the input variable occurs, the observer responds accordingly to all cases, and the error is close to zero again.

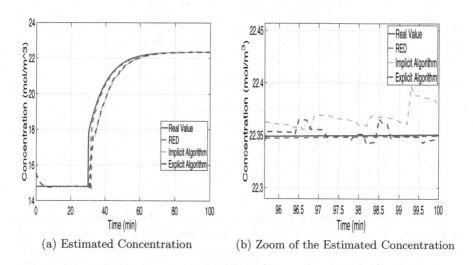

(a) Estimated Concentration   (b) Zoom of the Estimated Concentration

Fig. 2. Estimated concentration

In order to check how the observer works for the case in which the measured signal has noise, the behavior of each variable is shown in Fig. 4. For this case, a new tuning for the value L is made ($L = 1 \times 10^{-4}$) since the value is smaller, it was verified by simulation that it takes longer to the observer to approach the actual value. The change on plant input F is 10% below steady state value. However, the signal is better filtered than with a larger value.

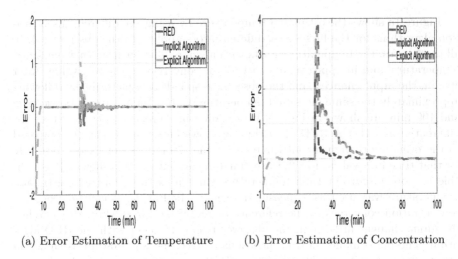

(a) Error Estimation of Temperature   (b) Error Estimation of Concentration

Fig. 3. Error estimation

Table 2. Sum of Squares Error

Discretization Algorithms	SSE
Explicit Algorithm	66, 354
Implicit Algorithm	67, 248
RED	39, 102

Table 3. Sum of Squares Error in Steady State

Discretization Algorithms	SSE
Explicit Algorithm	0.0031
Implicit Algorithm	0.0056
RED	0.0007

Table 2 shows the result of calculating the sum of the squared errors (SSE) for the concentration variable, without noise measurement, at the set simulation time, in order to obtain a quantitative comparison between observers. This analysis yields better results for the RED algorithm since the value of SSE is the lowest. Finally, Table 3 shows the same SSE calculated, but on the interval time [96–100] min, with the aim to obtain this value in the steady sate. The result shows again the lowest value of SSE for the RED algorithm, which implies the reduction of chattering.

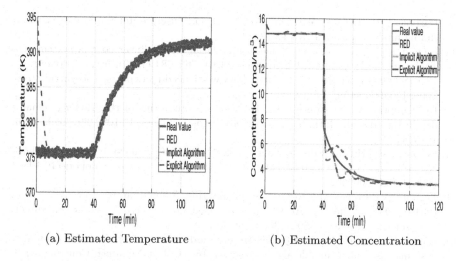

(a) Estimated Temperature   (b) Estimated Concentration

Fig. 4. Behavior of the estimated variables with noise measurement

5   Conclusions

In this paper, three different discretization algorithms were used in a nonlinear observer in order to eliminate the chattering, which is produced, by using very low sample rates and discretization. In this case, a discretization time 0.1 min was used. For the three study cases, the results obtained were satisfactory regarding to the convergence of the error. The RED differentiator was the best result for having a better response and less error in steady state. However, in order to implement RED algorithm in a digital device, it has a higher degree of difficulty than the other discrete differentiators, because for its implementation is necessary to compute an algorithm to find the roots of a polynomial at each instant of time.

References

1. Atassi, A., Khalil, H.: Separation results for the stabilization of nonlinear systems using different high-gain observer designs. Syst. Control Lett. **39**, 183–191 (2000). https://doi.org/10.1016/S0167-6911(99)00085-7
2. Carvajal-Rubio, J.E., Loukianov, A.G., Sánchez-Torres, J.D., Defoort, M.: On the discretization of a class of homogeneous differentiators. In: 2019 16th International Conference on Electrical Engineering, Computing Science and Automatic Control (CCE), pp. 1–6 (2019)
3. Drakunov, S., Utkin, V.: On discrete-time sliding modes. IFAC Proc. Volu. **22**(3), 273–278 (1989). https://doi.org/10.1016/S1474-6670(17)53647-2. http://www.sciencedirect.com/science/article/pii/S1474667017536472. Nonlinear Control Systems Design, Capri, Italy, 14–16 June 1989
4. Fridman, L., Shtessel, Y., Edwards, C., Yan, X.: State estimation and input reconstruction in nonlinear systems via higher order sliding mode observer. In: 2007 American Control Conference, pp. 3807–3812 (2007)

5. Barbot, J.-P., Levant, A., Livne, M., Lunz, D.: Discrete differentiators based on sliding modes. Automatica **112** (2020)
6. Kazantzis, N., Kravaris, C.: Time-discretization of nonlinear control systems via Taylor methods. Comput. Chem. Eng. **23**(6), 763–784 (1999). https://doi.org/10.1016/S0098-1354(99)00007-1. http://www.sciencedirect.com/science/article/pii/S0098135499000071
7. Kechriniotis, A., Anastasiou, K., Kotsos, B.: New forms of the Taylor's remainder. J. Interdiscip. Math. **9**, 37–48 (2006). https://doi.org/10.1080/09720502.2006.10700426
8. Levant, A.: Higher-order sliding modes, differentiation and output-feedback control. Int. J. Control **76**, 924–941 (2003). https://doi.org/10.1080/0020717031000099029
9. Levant, A., Livne, M.: Robust exact filtering differentiators. Eur. J. Control (2019). https://doi.org/10.1016/j.ejcon.2019.08.006. http://www.sciencedirect.com/science/article/pii/S0947358019301517
10. López, E., Botero, H.: Finite-time sliding mode observer for uncertain nonlinear systems based on a tunable algebraic solver. Int. J. Rob. Nonlinear Control (2017). https://doi.org/10.1002/rnc.3806
11. Osorio, B.G., Castro, H.B., Torres, J.D.S.: State and unknown input estimation in a CSTR using higher-order sliding mode observer. In: IX Latin American Robotics Symposium and IEEE Colombian Conference on Automatic Control, 2011 IEEE, pp. 1–5 (2011)
12. Reichhartinger, M., Koch, S.K., Niederwieser, H., Spurgeon, S.K.: The robust exact differentiator toolbox: improved discrete-time realization. In: 2018 15th International Workshop on Variable Structure Systems (VSS), pp. 1–6 (2018)
13. Shen, Y., Shen, W., Jiang, M., Huang, Y.: Semi-global finite-time observers for multi-output nonlinear systems. Int. J. Rob. Nonlinear Control **20**, 789–801 (2010). https://doi.org/10.1002/rnc.1471
14. Yu, X., Xu, J.: Nonlinear derivative estimator. Electron. Lett. **32**(16), 1445–1447 (1996)

A Comparison of Wavelet, LPC and Cepstrum Techniques for Formant Estimation in Spanish and English Speakers

Simón Orellana and Juan P. Ugarte$^{(\boxtimes)}$ (iD)

Universidad de San Buenaventura, Medellín, Colombia
`juan.ugarte@usbmed.edu.co`

Abstract. Vowel formant estimation is the most common procedure to extract information from human speech. The formants prove to be an useful feature to characterize the vocal tract acoustics with direct practical applications, such as the study of vowel perception, speakers identification and synthetic voice production. Moreover, the first two formants yield vowels characterization and articulatory and acoustic features specifically related to a given language. There are several techniques to implement this process. An important issue that is normally overlooked, is that these techniques performance depend on a single o several parameters. A proper vowel characterization depends on the correct choice of these parameters. In this work, the parameter effect on formants extraction is studied. For this purpose, the Discrete Wavelet Transform, LPC, and Cepstrum techniques are assessed. Two datasets of Spanish and English recordings are used for the comparative analysis. The results indicate a nonlinear relation between the parameters of each method and the capability of correctly identifying the frequency formants. Moreover, the formants space for the Spanish dataset evinces a better discrimination among vowels. These results suggest that the implementation of a formant extraction technique requires an initial stage of configuration of the parameters playing a role in the spectrum estimation. Furthermore, from the assessed techniques the wavelet analysis parameters can afford a specific configuration for estimating the formants for a given language.

Keywords: Vowels · Formant · Frequency spectrum envelope · Vowel triangle

1 Introduction

The human voice can be regarded as the container of specific information related to its respective speaker. The acoustic features yielded by a speech signal enables establishing a personalized signature that has been widely exploited in technological solutions, such as cellphones, entertainment systems, security systems, and so on. Among the main speech features, the vowel formants are of primary

© Springer Nature Switzerland AG 2020
J. C. Figueroa-García et al. (Eds.): WEA 2020, CCIS 1274, pp. 85–96, 2020.
https://doi.org/10.1007/978-3-030-61834-6_8

interest. Vowel formants characterization are relevant in the study of perception of vowels [9,20], speaker identification [6,13] and they provide a direct practical application to synthetic speech production [14,19]. Moreover, the relation between the multidimensional space where formants coordinates are confronted (i.e the formant space plot) and the locus formed by those values (i.e vowel triangle) enables the vowel formants as inputs for descriptive linguistic purposes [11,12,16].

The vowel formants are attributed to the resonant frequencies of the vocal tract [10]. In terms of systems and signals theory, the vowel sound generation can be interpreted as the output signal of a system established by the vocal tract and whose input or excitation comes from the vocal chords. Thus, the frequency formants can be identified as the resonant peaks of the frequency response of the filter system that represents the vocal tract. Following the source-filter theory, distinct methods have been proposed for estimating the vowels formants.

The non-invasive quantitative methods for estimating vowel formants process the speech signal in order to approximate the spectrum of the source (i.e. the vocal chords) and the frequency response of the filter (i.e. the vocal tract). Since the formants are identified by the prominent peaks, the filter frequency response is enough to extract the relevant information. The vowel triangle can be constructed by using the first (F1) and second (F2) formants as coordinates within a cartesian plot. Such representation suggest that the first two formants provide enough information for vowel characterization. Furthermore, it has been established that language specific features, such as articulation and acoustics, can be studied through the vowel formants. Bearing this ideas in mind, this works aims to provide a comparative study of three methods for estimating vowel formants F1 and F2. Spanish and English vowels recordings are characterized in order to evaluate the possibility of vowel discrimination within the formants space. For this purpose, the implemented methods are specifically parameterized for the signals under study so that the frequency spectrum envelope allows a clear peaks formants identification and the global behavior of the formants outcomes is assessed.

2   Materials and Methods

In this section, the procedure of the analysis and comparison between Spanish and English vowel formants is presented. In short, two datasets of recordings from Spanish and English speakers uttering isolated vowels are considered. Three techniques for formants estimation are implemented: linear predictive coding (LPC), Cepstrum analysis and wavelet analysis. The LPC and Cepstrum approaches are commonly used for formants estimation, while the wavelet analysis requieres further assessment in solving this problem. Each approach parameters are adjusted for Spanish vowels characterization. Format frequencies are calculated for each dataset and a comparative analysis is performed. A detailed description of this procedure is presented below.

2.1   Spanish and English Datasets

The Spanish dataset includes 30 speakers, 16 females and 14 males from Antio-quia, Colombia. Such population have unique features in the utterance, as explained in [15]. Participants were asked to utter each Spanish vowel by sustaining pitch and volume during 6 s. This database was recorded in an ordinary room using an M-audio back-electret condenser microphone. It was recorded using the Digital Audio Workstation Fl Studio 20 which uses standardize music industry sample rates, such as 44,1 kHz, 48kHz, 96kHz. Therefore, signals are resampled to obtain a final sampling frequency of 10 kHz. The hVd Database: Spoken vowels in context from the CMU Artificial Intelligence Repository was used as the English dataset. This database is freely available at [1]. In this work, only the recordings that resemble the Spanish vowels sound were considered. It includes 29 speakers, 13 females and 16 males. Each recording has a duration of approximately 0.5 s with a sampling frequency of 10kHz. In both databases, each signal is segmented into seven intervals. The representative formant for each signal is obtained from the average of the seven calculated formants. Since Spanish signals are longer than English signals, the intervals are set to 512 and 450 samples in length for each dataset, respectively. Such interval lengths represent approximately 50 ms of duration and they allow quasi-periodicty of the signals and the same quantity of processed intervals per signal.

2.2   Discrete Wavelet Transform Analysis

Discrete wavelet transform (DWT) relies on short oscillatory waves called wavelets. A signal can be represented by a linear combination of scaled and translated versions of such wavelets [3,5,24]. In DWT a pair of waveforms allow signal analysis: the mother wavelet and father wavelet. The former represents quick changes in the signal (i.e high frequency content) and the latter represents slow signal changes (i.e low frequency content). Under such scheme, signals can be decomposed into detail and approximation coefficients.

Formant estimation through DWT is accomplished by reconstructing the speech signal using the approximation and detail coefficients from a given decomposition level N. According to previous works [4,21,22], a speech signal is preprocessed by applying a Hamming window and calculating the logarithm of the magnitude of the discrete Fourier transform (DFT). The DWT is then applied until decomposition level N. For reconstructing the signal, the detail coefficients from the first $N - 1$ levels are set to zero, leaving the approximation and detail coefficients from level N without modifications. The resulting signal corresponds to the frequency spectrum envelope, where formants can be identified. The parameters to be adjusted in the DWT analysis are level of decomposition N and the wavelet family.

2.3   Linear Predictive Coding Analysis

The LPC relies on an all-pole model, also known as an auto-regressive model. This model states that a function output depends linearly on its own p previous values [23], as shown in the following expression:

$$s(n) = \sum_{k=1}^{p} a_k s(n - k),\tag{1}$$

where $s(n)$ is the current signal prediction and a_k are the LPC coefficients. The a_k values are calculated by minimizing the total squared error.

The implementation of the LPC analysis for formants estimations is as follows: the signal is pre-emphasizes through a high-pass finite impulse response filter. A Hamming window is applied and the LPC coefficients are calculated by a least squares procedure. The following transfer function is built:

$$H(z) = \frac{1}{1 - \sum_{k=1}^{p} a_k z^{-k}}\tag{2}$$

The frequency response of system $H(z)$ corresponds to the frequency spectrum envelope. The LPC order p is the parameter to be adjusted for the formants characterization.

2.4   Cepstrum Analysis

Cepstrum analysis assumes the speech signal as the result of the convolution between an excitation signal and a linear and time-invariant system [8]. The vocal tract can be considered as a system that filters the excitation signal in order to produce speech [17], and can be modeled by the following equation:

$$y(t) = x(t) * h(t),\tag{3}$$

where $y(t)$ is the voice signal, $x(t)$ is the excitation signal and $h(t)$ is the vocal tract impulse response. The Cepstrum approach transforms the Eq. (3) aiming to separate the vocal tract contribution from the excitation signal originated at the vocal chords. Through the Fourier transform, the Eq. (3) turns into a multiplication and by applying the natural logarithm, the factors can be splitted into a logarithm addition. Accordingly, the complex Cepstrum signal Y_C can be calculated as follows:

$$Y_C = \mathcal{F}^{-1}\left\{\log|\mathcal{F}\{x(t) * h(t)\}|\right\} = \mathcal{F}^{-1}\{\log|X|\} + \mathcal{F}^{-1}\{\log|H|\},\tag{4}$$

where X and H are the Fourier transform of $x(t)$ and $h(t)$, respectively, and $\mathcal{F}\{\cdot\}$ is the Fourier transform operator. A temporal filter must be applied to Y_C in order to eliminate the pitch component. The spectrum envelope is reconstructed by calculating the exponential of the Fourier transform of the temporal-filtered version of Y_C.

Spanish and English datasets are processed using a Hamming window and the same pre-emphasis filter used in the LPC analysis. Complex cepstrum is obtained by applying Eq. (4). The temporal filter cut-off value T_c is defined as a percentage of the pitch period T_p [2]. The pitch period is estimated by means of the autocorrelation function. The spectrum envelope is obtained by calculating the exponential of the DFT of the resulting signal. In this method, the cut-off value T_c is the parameter to be adjust in order to estimate the vowel formants.

3   Results

In this section, the parameterization of the methods and the corresponding implementation are presented. Each analysis is adjusted using the Spanish database. The English database is used to assess the behavior of the three formants estimation procedures with the Spanish-based parameterization.

3.1   Wavelet Analysis

In order to determine the optimal wavelet family configuration, several DWT parameters arrangements were tested. The software Praat is used as reference procedure for adjusting the DWT parameters. This software is a widely used tool in phonetics and acoustics research [7,18,25] The adjusment criterion is the similarity between the formants yielded by each wavelet configuration and the estimations obtained using the Praat software. In this manner, different wavelets families are selected for vowel characterization process: Bior3.5 for /a/, Db15 for /e/, Dmey for /i/ and /u/, and Sym7 for /o/. The DWT decomposition level was adjusted so that the spectral envelope clearly represent the first and second formants peaks. Figure 1 depicts the influence of the decomposition level on the frequency spectrum envelope.

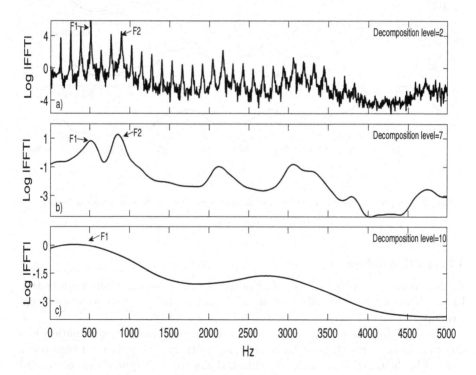

Fig. 1. Frequency spectrum envelope comparison using different Wavelet decomposition level.

Figures 1(a) and 2(c) evince a detailed and smoothed envelope, respectively, if an incorrect decomposition level is used, causing formant identification problems. In Fig. 1(b), the formants peaks can be clearly identified. Thus, after several tests using the five vowels, for a 50 ms signal interval, the decomposition level is set to 4.

The effect of the window length is also tested. Several power-of-two lengths were tested. Figure 2 shows five averaged envelopes using distinct window lengths for vowel /o/. It can be seen that the formants locations remain approximately invariant.

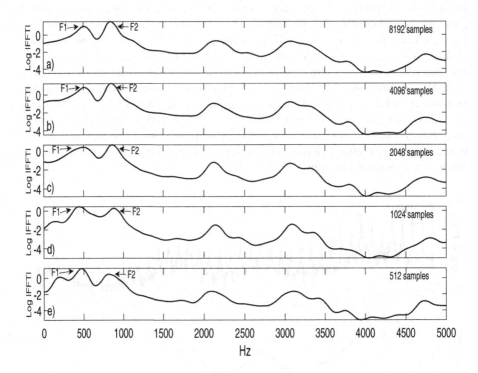

Fig. 2. Frequency spectrum envelope comparison using different window length.

3.2   LPC Analysis

To determine the optimal LPC filter order, several configurations were tested. Figure 3 illustrates the effect of ht LPC order on the frequency spectrum envelope.

The Fig. 3(a) shows that a low filter order causes formant information loss due to a highly smoothed envelope. On the contrary, by applying a high order filter (Fig. 3(b)), the formants are masked due to the appearance of several peaks. In Fig. 3(c) formants can be clearly identified. Therefore, a 32 LPC filter order is selected to perform the analysis.

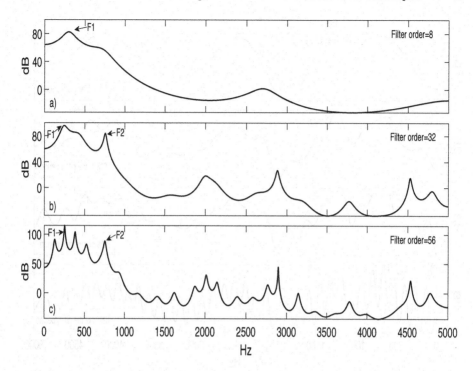

Fig. 3. Frequency spectrum envelope comparison using different LPC filter order.

3.3 Cepstrum Analysis

Figure 4 shows the effect of the cut-off quefrency of the temporal filter applied in the Cepstrum analysis. The cut-off value is set as a percentage of the pitch of the signal. The pitch is estimated through the autocorrelation function, as reported in [2].

The cut-off value of 50% of the pitch period for the temporal filter was established after testing distinct configurations using the datasets. Figure 4 (b) shows the optimal smoothed envelope where formant peaks can be easily identified. If the cutoff value approaches the pitch period, the formants are masked by the spectral details (Figs. 4(c)–(d)), else if the cut-off value is to low (Fig. 4(a)), the formants are lost in a smoothed version of the envelope. Therefore, the cut-off value of 50% of the pitch period is used for the analysis.

3.4 Wavelet vs LPC vs Cepstrum

Formants estimation was performed using the parameterized DWT, LPC and Cepstrum methods for both datasets. Figure 5 illustrate the formant space distribution obtained by each formants analysis method. The Spanish and English datasets results are depicted in the left and right column, respectively. The five vowels are presented with different colors.

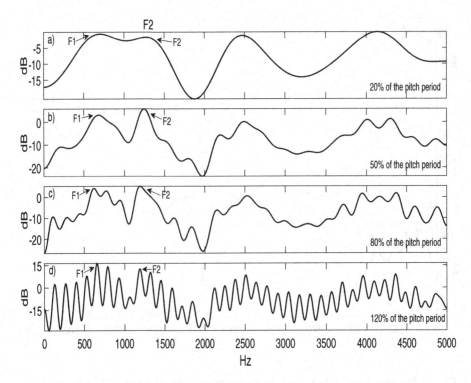

Fig. 4. Frequency spectrum envelope comparison using different cut-off values for the temporal filter in the Cepstrum analysis.

Figures 5(a), 5(c) and 5(e) show the formants space of Spanish database characterized by the three studied procedures. For DWT and Cepstrum analysis it is possible to identified well defined clusters for each vowel. The LPC analysis is able to concentrate clusters for vowels /a/, /e/ and /i/, but discrimination between /o/ and /u/ is not possible. For the case of English dataset in Figs. 5(b), 5(d) and 5(f), none of the methods generate a clustered formants space. The vowels points are broadly scattered, so that vowel identification is not possible. It is noteworthy that, the LPC analysis generates identifiable regions for the group of vowels /a/, /o/ and /u/ and the group /e/ and /i/, through lower and higher values for F2.

In addition, the following can be concluded:

- If only vowels /e/ and /i/ are considered, LPC analysis is the one that provides better results in both languages.
- If only vowels /o/ and /u/ are considered, Cepstrum and wavelet analysis are the ones that provides better results in Spanish language, due to a smaller cluster mix. While the LPC analysis has the best performance for English language.

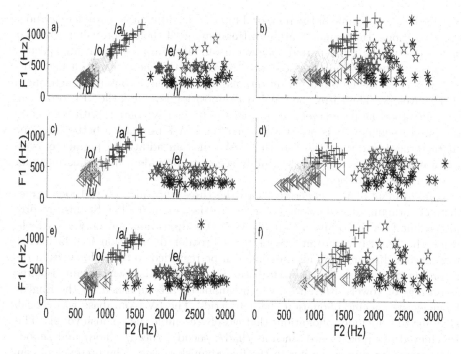

Fig. 5. Formants space generated using the DWT ((a) and (b)), LPC ((c) and (d)) and Cepstrum ((e) and (f)) methods for Spanish (left column) and English (right column) datasets. The colors indicate distinct vowels.

- For vowel /a/, all methods provide favorable results in Spanish language. While Wavelet analysis has the best performance in the English dataset.

4   Discussion

In this work, three formant estimation approaches are assessed using Spanish and English vowels recordings. The three procedures rely on reconstruction of the spectrum envelope in which formants can be identified. The results evinced that each approach has a parameter that non-linearly modulates the smoothness and sharpness o the resulting envelope. Additionally, the characterization of Spanish speakers provides a better distribution of each vowel formants pair within the formants space. Specifically the DWT analysis generates clusters allowing vowels discrimination.

The parameterization process of the three implemented methods evince that the decomposition level (DWT), the filter order (LPC) and the cut-off temporal filter value (Cepstrum) have a similar effect on the spectral envelope: lower or higher values of these parameters degenerates the morphology of the envelope and formants can be easily identified only by applying intermediate values. Such nonlinear behavior can be explained through the Cepstrum fundamentals, in which, the cut-off value of the temporal filter is the adjustable parameter. Under this conditions, the formants are indistinguishable if the cut-off value is too far or to close to the pitch period. A low cut-off value implies discarding spectral details and thus obtaining a smoothed envelope. On the contrary, a high cut-off value close to the pitch period retains high frequency content, generating a sharp envelope. Therefore, the DWT decomposition level and the LPC order can be understood as parameters regulating the frequency content with respect to the pitch frequency. It is noteworthy that the DWT provides a better envelope characterization due to the fact that DWT has an additional parameter with the wavelet family. The wavelet family seems to provide a fine adjustment for the formants estimation.

The formants space generated with the three implemented methods evince distinct formants distributions according to the language. The Spanish recordings result in a distribution that allows better discrimination between vowels, while the English recordings generates a broader distribution in which clusters are not discernible. This outcome can be regarded to the differences in the recording procedures for each database. The Spanish dataset contains isolated recordings of vowels utterances, which cannot be accomplished for the English language its specific phonation characteristics. The hVd Database was considered due to it includes phonations that closely resemble the Spanish vowels. This is achieved by spoken words such as /had/, /head/, /heed/, /hod/ and /hood/ which generate sounds similar to the five Spanish vowels. The presence of consonants during the phonation has an important effect in the frequency content. Therefore, the vowels characterization resulted in a mixed space. In spite of this, the LPC analysis allows certain clustering degree which can be exploited to further improve the English vowels quantification. Moreover, the versatility of DWT analysis in regard to its parameters, can be exploited in order generate a specific-English parameterization for formants extraction.

5 Conclusions

In this work, a comparison between three formants extraction techniques is performed. The DWT analysis proves to be the most reliable method for characterizing Spanish vowels due to its clustering capability within the formants space. Such feature can be exploited for training a machine learning using a larger database for speakers identification applications. Moreover, the results suggest that it would be possible to set a specific parameterization of the formants extraction technique for a given language. Since this study was performed with Colombian Spanish speaker, future studies should evaluate the proposed adjustment procedure with Spanish speakers from distinct regions and countries and non-Spanish speakers. Although there are more advanced tools for formants estimation, compared with the software Praat, this work results evinced that a proper parameterization can be achieved using the latter. Future works should assess if the use of other tools may yield a significant improvement in the performance of formants extraction.

References

1. Andy Hewett, D.D.: HVD database (1987). http://www.cs.cmu.edu/Groups/AI/util/areas/speech/database/hvd/
2. Benesty, J., Sondhi, M., Huang, Y.: Springer Handbook of Speech Processing. Springer Handbook of Speech Processing. Springer, Heidelberg (2017). https://doi.org/10.1007/978-3-540-49127-9
3. Benhmad, F.: A wavelet analysis of oil price volatility dynamic. Econ. Bull. **31**(1), 792–806 (2011)
4. Bensaid, M., Schoentgen, J., Ciocea, S.: Estimation of formant frequencies by means of a wavelet transform of the speech spectrum. In: Proceedings of the ProRISC Workshop on Circuits, Systems and Signal Processing, pp. 43–46 (1997)
5. Crowley, P.M.: A guide to wavelets for economists. J. Econ. Surv. **21**(2), 207–267 (2007)
6. Daqrouq, K., Tutunji, T.A.: Speaker identification using vowels features through a combined method of formants, wavelets, and neural network classifiers. Appl. Soft Comput. J. **27**, 231–239 (2015). https://doi.org/10.1016/j.asoc.2014.11.016
7. Deliyski, D.D., Evans, M.K., Shaw, H.S.: Influence of data acquisition environment on accuracy of acoustic voice quality measurements. J. Voice **19**(2), 176–186 (2005). https://doi.org/10.1016/j.jvoice.2004.07.012
8. Drugman, T., Bozkurt, B., Dutoit, T.: Causal-anticausal decomposition of speech using complex cepstrum for glottal source estimation. Speech Commun. **53**(6), 855–866 (2011)
9. Fernàndez Planas, A.: Estudio del campo de dispersión de las vocales castellanas. Estudios de fonética experimental **5**(5), 129–162 (1993)
10. Gargouri, D., Hamida, A.B.E.N.: A comparative study of formant frequencies estimation techniques. In: Proceedings of the 5th WSEAS International Conference on Signal Processing, vol. 2006, pp. 15–19 (2006)
11. Gordon, M., Barthmaier, P., Sands, K., Sands, K.: A cross-linguistic a cross-linguistic acoustic study of voiceless fricatives. J. Int. Phonetic Assoc. **32**(02), 141–174 (2003). https://doi.org/10.1017/S0025100302001020
12. Hillenbrand, J., Getty, L.A., Clark, M.J., Wheeler, K., Acoust, P.B.J.: Acoustic characteristics of American English vowels. J. Acoust. Soc. Am. **97**(5), 3099–3111 (1995)
13. Juan, E.S., Jamett, M., Kaschel, H., Sánchez, L.: Sistema de reconocimiento de voz mediante wavelets, predicción lineal y redes backpropagation. Ingeniare **24**(1), 8–17 (2016)
14. Klatt, H.: Software for a cascade/parallel formant synthesizer. J. Acoust. Soc. Am. **67**(3), 971–995 (1979)
15. López, S.M.: El habla de la comunidad paisa de Medellín en Montreal. Master's thesis, Université de Montréal (2013)
16. Maddieson, I., Emmorey, K.: Relationship between semivowels and vowels: cross-linguistic investigations of acoustic difference and coarticulation. Phonetica **42**(4), 163–174 (1985)
17. Kammoun, M.A., Gargouri, D., Frikha, F., Hamida, A.B.: Cepstral method evaluation in speech formant frequencies estimation. Technology, 1612–1616 (2004)
18. Moura, C.P., et al.: Voice parameters in children with down syndrome. J. Voice **22**(1), 34–42 (2008). https://doi.org/10.1016/j.jvoice.2006.08.011
19. Narendranath, M., Murthy, H.A., Rajendran, S., Yegnanarayana, B.: Transformation of formants for voice conversion using artificial neural networks. Speech Commun. **16**(2), 207–216 (1995). https://doi.org/10.1016/0167-6393(94)00058-I

20. Peterson, G.E., Barney, H.L.: Control methods used in a study of the vowels. J. Acoust. Soc. Am. **24**, 175–184 (1952)
21. Hamzenejadi, S., Goki, S.A.Y.H., Ghazvini, M.: Extraction of speech pitch and formant frequencies using discrete wavelet transform. In: 2019 7th Iranian Joint Congress on Fuzzy and Intelligent Systems (CFIS), pp. 1–5 (2019). https://doi.org/10.1109/CFIS.2019.8692150
22. Schoentgen, J., Bensaid, M., Bucella, F.: Multivariate statistical analysis of flat vowel spectra with a view to characterizing dysphonic voices. J. Speech Lang. Hear. Res. **43**(6), 1493–1508 (2000). https://doi.org/10.1044/jslhr.4306.1493
23. Spratling, M.W.: A review of predictive coding algorithms. Brain Cogn. **112**, 92–97 (2017). https://doi.org/10.1016/j.bandc.2015.11.003
24. Sundararajan, D.: Discrete Wavelet Transform: A Signal Processing Approach. Wiley, Course Smart Series (2016)
25. Ubul, K., Hamdulla, A., Aysa, A.: A digital signal processing teaching methodology using Praat. In: Proceedings of 2009 4th International Conference on Computer Science and Education, ICCSE 2009, pp. 1804–1809 (2009). https://doi.org/10.1109/ICCSE.2009.5228251

Smoothing of Robotic Navigation Trajectories, Based on a Tessellation Generated Weighted Skeleton, Based on Wavefront Dilation and Collisions

I. Ladino[1]([⊠]), O. Penagos[2]([⊠]), B. Sáenz-Cabezas[1]([⊠]), and Y. Pastrana[3]([⊠])

[1] Fundación Universitaria Los Libertadores, Bogotá, Colombia
{idladinov,bjsaenzc}@libertadores.edu.co
[2] Universidad Nacional de Colombia, Bogotá, Colombia
openagose@unal.edu.co
[3] Universidad Tecnológica de Bolívar, Bolívar, Colombia
ypastrana@utb.edu.co
http://www.ulibertadores.edu.co
http://www.unal.edu.co
http://www.utb.edu.co

Abstract. Discretization processes adapted to robotic configuration spaces designed to limit the possible positions and movements of a robot in a continuous environment, have been based mainly on four methods for robotic motion planning: potential fields based, cell decomposition, roadmaps and sampling. However, these methods are not suitable for finding smooth routes through obstacles, and at he same time, avoiding collisions and taking into account the dimensions of the robot. This work proposes a new tessellation method using Bézier curves, which facilitates drawing of smooth curves while respecting restrictions imposed by the environment. The method takes into account the dimensions of the robot and, through a vector description of the configuration space, it constructs a skeleton of the configuration space between obstacles, where each point of the skeleton, in addition to having information on its coordinate, includes information about the transverse distance between objects at each point of the skeleton.

Keywords: Voronoi diagrams · Tessellation · Bezier curves · Navigation

1 Introduction

The accelerated progress of artificial intelligence [3], sensors [1] and the increase in the performance of computer systems [13], have promoted the development of

---

Fundación Universitaria Los Libertadores, Universidad Nacional de Colombia, Universidad Tecnológica de Bolívar.

J. C. Figueroa-García et al. (Eds.): WEA 2020, CCIS 1274, pp. 97–108, 2020.
https://doi.org/10.1007/978-3-030-61834-6_9

mobile robotics technology and autonomous vehicles in applications of different kinds [11], from those related to people's daily lives to those typical of industrial processes. One of the basic tasks of these vehicles or robots, is to move autonomously in an environment where there are fixed as well mobile obstacles.

A robot or mobile vehicle, to fulfill a certain task, must navigate on a map of the environment, for this it is required to draw a path or a set of paths that make up the total navigation route. The layout of each path basically consists of finding a route from an origin point to a destination point, this, taking into account the obstacles, but also, considering the dynamic limitations of the robot [8, 9].

Various types of algorithms have been proposed for tracing routes on discrete representations of space, one of these representations consists of the use of cells or Voronoi diagrams, these algorithms have been sufficiently analyzed, establishing their advantages and disadvantages in different types of applications [2, 4]. However, the dynamic limitations of the robot or in the case of autonomous vehicles with passengers, the comfort of people, determine a set of characteristics or restrictions in the geometry of the routes followed by the robot or the vehicle, that is, routes made up of straight paths and vertices cannot be tolerated, since they can lead to different inconveniences, for example that the robot must stop completely and make rotations about its axis or that its route cannot be predicted by another vehicle to be able to plan its own route [11].

Due to the aforementioned limitations, it is essential to look for the construction of smooth routes, which comply with the limitations imposed by the dynamics of the robot or the mobile vehicle. In [10] it is presented a review of the state of the art, regarding planning smooth routes, where smoothing based on polynomial interpolations are contemplated, Bézier curves, Nurbs curves, Dublin curves, B-splines curves, Hypocycloids and Clotoids, among others.

The process of obtaining a smooth route depends on several factors, first, the limitations or restrictions imposed by the environment, that is, the configuration space with its obstacles, second, the geometric characteristics of the robot and finally, the restrictions related to vehicle dynamics. Regarding this last factor, in [13] several algorithms related to obtaining smooth curves are presented, under a set of restrictions that include not only the extreme points of the paths, but also slopes or curvatures of trajectories in a set of control points, the latter, allows to take into account, in a certain way, the restrictions imposed by the dynamic characteristics of the robot.

In article [5] a method for obtaining smooth Bezier curves is proposed, the method starts with a set of constraints, among which are a set of points called via points, through which the smoothed curve must transit. Bezier curves are used to smooth the curve under the conditions imposed by the constraints and via points. This work determines a substantial improvement to that delivered in previous works, since in addition to obtaining the smooth curve, the curve is also forced to travel through the via points, regarding a set of restrictions to shape the curve, this allows taking into account the conditions of the robot's dynamics, however, the procedure to take into account, the limitations established by the edges of the obstacles and the dimensions of the robot, is not clearly developed.

In the work presented in this article, in first instance, a new strategy is conceived to obtain a representation of the configuration space, this, from a tessellation of the space by means of two processes, the first, a basic expansion to absorb the size of the robot in such a way that thereafter, the robot can be considered as a point in the configuration space and, the second, a process of expansion of objects from rectangular wave fronts, each one of them originated, at the points of the edges of the objects, this process is developed until obtaining a skeleton of the configuration space between obstacles in such a way that each point that is part of the skeleton, in addition to its coordinates, includes information about the distance transversal between adjacent objects, that is, the border between obstacles, consists of a discreet and compact way of representing the configuration space. In second instance, a smooth route between the origin and destination is calculated, this process, part of the skeleton obtained and its distance weights between objects, initially a set of routes are drawn on the nodes of the skeleton, the shortest is selected from these, subsequently, the obtained route is adjusted by taking nodes over the configuration space until obtaining an even shorter route. Finally, a smoothing process was developed, based on the application of Bézier functions and taking account, a set of restrictions that includes the skeleton, its distance information as between objects, and the via points.

2 Stages of the Algorithm

The proposed algorithm is made up of three components, the first for the configuration space tiles construction process, the second is aimed at generating the route based on the configuration space skeleton, and the third is aimed at the reduction and smoothing of the final route using Bezier curves.

2.1 Tessellation Algorithm Description

With this first algorithm a discrete representation of the space is constructed, it is made up of two parts, one, the skeleton of the space between the obstacles, that is, the border between the objects, the second part, consists of the set of transversal distances to each point of the skeleton. Based on this compact representation of space, the routing algorithms for the routes and the smoothing algorithm for the final route are developed.

For the generation of the Voronoi diagrams, that is, the construction of the space mosaic, a configuration space tessellation model was conceived and implemented through two processes: the first, a simultaneous expansion of the obstacles from the edges of these, taking into account, the radius of the circumference that circumscribes the robot; with this, it is guaranteed that the configuration space obtained will always have sufficient dimensions to contain the robot, therefore from that point onwards, the robot can be considered as a point in the space.

The second process consists of the dilation of the objects resulting from the first process, by means of the simultaneous generation of wave fronts at each of the points of the border, these wave fronts propagate out of the obstacles, this process develops from such that, when a point on one wavefront has been reached, by wavefronts from other non-adjacent points; the point will be marked as part of the skeleton, it does not continue expanding and all the wave fronts that reach it are counted, this allows obtaining the border and additionally the width of the configuration space for each point of the skeleton.

The environment tiling process is carried out as follows (see Fig. 2):

1. The variables are initialized, based on the following data: robot diameter D, the rectangular dimensions of the environment, the panoramic image of the environment with the obstacles in white and the background in black, the starting point (S) and the point of arrival (T) (see Figure 2a).
2. *Segment* the environment image, to obtain a binary matrix M_b, where the objects are represented by the value 1 and the background by the value 0.
3. Perform the initial expansion of the obstacles by an amount $D/2$ and update the matrix M_b. At this point, the already segmented obstacles have absorbed the size of the robot, so from now on the robot is considered as a point. This step ensures that there are no collisions between the robot and the obstacles, when determining the routes (ver ejemplo en la Figure 2b).
4. Tiling the environment by iteratively expanding through wave fronts, over the points that make up each of the edges of the obstacles, in each iteration it is validated if each point of the wave fronts has been reached by another wavefront, if This happens, these points will not generate more wavefronts and will be marked as part of the skeleton (border), in detail:
   - Expand the edges from each of its points by means of square wave fronts (see Fig. 2c)
   - It is evaluated whether each new point on the edges of the obstacles has been reached by wavefronts from other points, on the edges of the objects, in this case, a counter is increased for each point on the edge, so, in the process associates to each point (of the edges) the number of dilations p required to reach it. In the next step, the coordinate of each point and its value p are stored in the array M_b. Hereinafter p will be called *weight*.

The last stage of the algorithm is to find the nodes of the configuration space, these nodes represent the intersection points of three or more tiles, for this, at each point in the configuration space, it is determined how many wave fronts are in each point, that number of wave fronts corresponds to the number of tiles found at that point. The importance of these nodes in the algorithm lies in the fact that the initial routes (not reduced or smoothed) of navigation are traced on them. The location of the nodes is represented as follows: $\eta_i(f_i, c_i)$, where $\eta_i = \eta_S$ equals the starting point of the route and $\eta_i = \eta_T$ represents the end point, f_i and c_i corresponds to the row and column respectively of node η_i in the matrix M_b. The nodes and the borders of the tiles can be seen in the Fig. 2e. In the Fig. 2f, the weights of each one of the points of the skeleton can be seen graphically, these are stored in the matrix M_b.

The flow chart of the algorithm implemented in Matlab, can be seen in the Fig. 1, As explained in the previous paragraphs, the first step consists of data entry (data entry label), then the segmentation stage is proceeded to separate the obstacles from the bottom, the result of this step consists of the binary matrix M_b (see Segmentation box Fig. 1). Then proceed with the initial dilation (*Initial dilatation*), through which the objects expand an amount equivalent to the size of the robot, to avoid collisions of the robot with the obstacles. From this step, an iterative tessellation loop is generated, which in each iteration, on the matrix M_b (binary matrix of the configuration space), the edges of the obstacles are dilated, avoiding overlaps between wave fronts, and subsequently updated the value of the weights for each point on the edges. In the case that the entire configuration space was covered, then the tessellation process has ended (*Complete tessellation?*). Once the tessellated space is obtained, two results are available, one, the matrix M_b, where the skeleton and the nodes are available, without binarization, on the other the matrix M_p with the weights of each of the points of the configuration space.

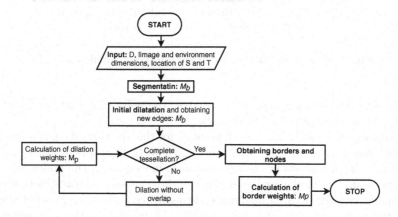

Fig. 1. Tessellation flow diagram

The block *Obtaining borders and nodes* from the matrices M_b and M_p calculates the skeleton and the nodes of the configuration space. Then through the block *Calculation of borders weights* the weights of each of the points that make up the skeleton are calculated. In this step there is a skeleton of the configuration space (between obstacles), where each point is represented by a coordinate, it also contains a weight that indicates the transverse distance between the obstacles adjacent to each point.

2.2 Generation of the Path on the Configuration Space Skeleton

The initial route generation, that is, without smoothing, is built from the following information, the skeleton and the intersection nodes of three or more

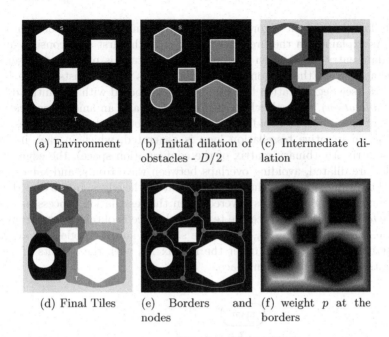

(a) Environment   (b) Initial dilation of (c) Intermediate di-
                    obstacles - $D/2$ lation

(d) Final Tiles   (e)   Borders   and (f) weight p at the
                    nodes   borders

Fig. 2. Tessellation process to obtain the skeleton and weights p

tiles (Matrix M_b) and the end points, that is, the point of departure S and the destination point T (see example Fig. 2).

The process starts at the starting point S, for this the variable η_i is initialized with the coordinates of that point ($\eta_i = S$), from this, an iterative cycle is performed, which consists in the first instance, in evaluating the nodes adjacent to the point η_i, by calculating the distance of these nodes to the destination node T, the node with the smallest distance is then selected and it is concatenated with the initial node S, in this step, the variable η_i is updated with the coordinates of the selected node. This process is carried out iteratively until the destination node is reached, that is, when $\eta_i = T$. At this point in the process, an initial route is available (see Fig. 3.a), made up of a series of n nodes and a total of $n-1$ connections between those nodes.

In the next phase of the algorithm, other $n-1$ routes are calculated, using the following process: a connection is provisionally removed from the initial route and the same procedure previously described is executed until the new route is obtained, this process repeats with each of the connections of the initial route, until obtaining a set of $n-1$ additional routes to the initial route, that is, a total of n routes. Of these n routes, the shortest is selected for the next stage of the algorithm.

Next, the flow diagram (Fig. 3) of the algorithm for generating the shortest route for the discretized space is described.

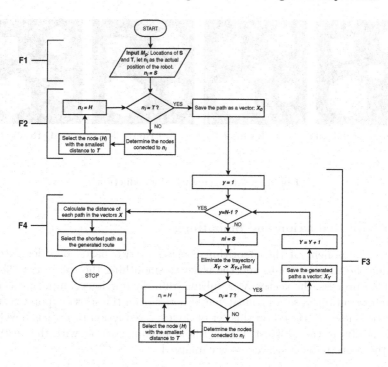

Fig. 3. Flow diagram for route generation

1. In the first phase (F1) of this algorithm, the locations S, T and the array M_b are stored, the variable η_i is initialized with the coordinates of the point S.

2. The second phase (F2) of this diagram consists, in a loop where, initially, the nodes adjacent to η_i are located, then the distances of all those nodes to the destination node T are calculated, and select the node with the shortest distance. This step will be repeated until $\eta_i = T$, thus obtaining an initial route composed of n nodes and $n - 1$ connections. The coordinates of the nodes of the initial path found are stored in the vector X_0.

3. In the third phase (F3), based on the vector X_0 of the initial route previously generated, we proceed to eliminate one by one the $y = n - 1$ connections between the n nodes, for each connection eliminated, a new route is generated following the same procedure of the second phase of the algorithm, these new routes are stored in vectors X_y ($y = 1, \cdots, n-1$), reaching a total of $y = n-1$ new routes.

4. In the fourth and last phase of this algorithm (F4), the n routes X_0, X_1, X_{n-1} are taken and the length of each one is calculated, finally the selected route is that with the shortest length and is stored in the vector X_c (Fig. 4).

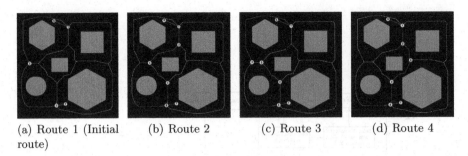

(a) Route 1 (Initial   (b) Route 2   (c) Route 3   (d) Route 4
route)

Fig. 4. Routes generated for reduction

2.3   Route Reduction and Smoothing

The last component of the algorithm consists of two parts, one dedicated to obtaining the shortest route and the other to smoothing the route. For the first part of the process, the vector X_c resulting from the previous component is used, this vector contains a set of concatenated nodes from the starting point S to the destination node T. Based on this set of nodes, a reduction process is developed seeking to obtain the shortest route without making contact with the obstacles. Next, the route reduction process is explained.

1. From the route obtained from the two previous algorithms, the reduction process is performed (see Fig. 5a). For this, a η_i and η_j are selected as the initial comparison nodes, where $\eta_i = S$ and $\eta_j = \eta_{i+2}$, that is, the following node to the neighbor of η_i.
2. The first step of the reduction is to draw a straight line between η_i and η_j and, from the matrix M_p, it is determined if that line, crosses an obstacle at some point, if not that is, the node η_{i+1} will be removed from the path and, the nodes η_i and η_j will connect directly, in otherwise η_j will be updated as the midpoint between η_j and η_{i+1} and the process will be repeated; this process will stop if the distance between η_j and η_{i+1} is less than the diameter of the robot D. If it is not possible to remove nodes, the node η_{i+1} will be marked as irreducible node.
3. The previous step is performed simultaneously from the other end of the route, in which $\eta_i = T$ and $\eta_j = \eta_{i-2}$ taking into account the same established criteria and procedures.
4. This process will stop once $\eta_i = \eta_{n/2}$ ($\eta_i = \eta_{n+1/2}$, in the case that the number of nodes that compose the path is odd), this means that the reduction at both ends of the path converges to node $n/2$. At the end of this step, one route reduction cycle will have been performed (see Fig. 5b).
5. Subsequently, the entire route reduction cycle will be repeated again (Phases 1–4) and will be carried out iteratively until all the nodes present in the route reach the irreducible character (see Fig. 5c y Fig. 5d).
6. Finally, the reduced path is stored in M_b.

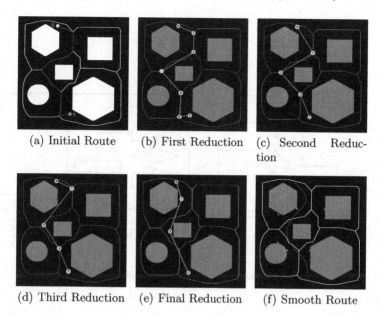

(a) Initial Route   (b) First Reduction   (c) Second Reduction

(d) Third Reduction   (e) Final Reduction   (f) Smooth Route

Fig. 5. Determination of the final route through the reduction process

Route Smoothing: Bezier curves, are commonly used, in robotics navigation algorithms for the smoothing of the trajectories [5], are based on a representation of the route using polynomial approximations of degree n and a set of $n+1$ checkpoints [10]. A N dimensional Bezier curve can be represented by the Eq. [1].

$$^nB(u) = \sum_{i=0}^{n} J_{n,i}(u)^n P_i \qquad (0 \leq u \leq 1, P_i \in \mathbf{R}^N) \qquad (1)$$

Where the control points are represented by $(P_0, P_1, ..., P_n)$, $J_{n,i}(u)$ corresponds to the intrinsic parameter (2) and the points $^nP_0$ and ^nP_n represent the end points of the route.

$$J_{n,i}(u) = \binom{n}{i} u^i (1-u)^{n-i} I_N \qquad (u \in [0,1]) \qquad (2)$$

The generation of the Bezier curves consists simply in the implementation of the function (1), where the control points $(P_0, P_1, \cdots, P_n)$ correspond to the end points located in transverse lines to the nodes of the reduced curve, the distance of those points to each node of the curve corresponds to the respective weight stored in the matrix M_p, in the Fig. 5f, it is appreciated, the smoothed final curve of the entire process for a given configuration space (Fig. 6).

3   Results and Discussion

When comparing the proposed algorithm, with respect to other Voronoi diagram-based navigation algorithms, such as [7] and [6], it is determined that, the

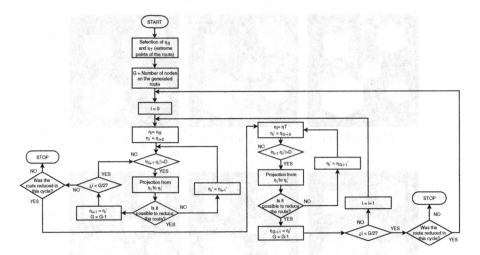

Fig. 6. Flow diagram for route reduction.

reduction of the route in the proposed method reduces the path length, the number of nodes and the angular movements, thereby ensuring that the calculated initial path for the smoothing process is the shortest in space decomposition, in addition, the proposed algorithm solves the problem of the generation of smooth routes with control points on Voronoi diagrams.

With respect to strategies such as the one proposed in [12], the expansion of the tessellations is carried out in environments with multi-agents, and the origin of each expansion corresponds to the centroid of each of the robots, subsequently the algorithm of Lloyd is used, to establish the movement area of each robot; On the other hand, the generation of the routes is carried out from the groups of homotopic and homological trajectories, the former are used to know the path and the direction the robot is traveling, the latter are used to establish the exact trajectory for the minimization of the distance traveled. In our proposal, we expanded the tessellations from the obstacles and the edges, to obtain a single path for each possible path between the obstacles, the result is similar to the group of homotopic paths, however, the implemented method originates one path for each group of homotopic trajectories. To minimize the distance of the total route, groups of homological is not used in this work for calculate trajectories or functions with similar objectives, for this we use the weight diagram (Fig. 2f), which allows us to calculate the shortest route, between two points without the need to generate a large number of additional paths or perform point-to-point movements (PTP). It should be noted that in order to consider the movement of the other robots in space, it is enough to consider each of the other robots as an additional obstacle and then recalculate the route each time a change in the environment is detected.

Thus, the proposed method guarantees finding a smooth route between two points in a robotic environment, the process is based on the tessellation of the environment based on variants of the Voronoi diagrams from processes of dilation of obstacles, then a short route is calculated, to later perform the reduction of nodes of the generated route. Despite the fact that the algorithm does not focus on detecting the shortest curve, the reduction of the route allows minimizing the distance and the number of nodes necessary to calculate the smooth curve. Furthermore, this proposed method is capable of being used for most Sampling methods in the planning of robotic routes that are made from movements by nodes. The dilation of the edges in the tessellation process ensures that the algorithm is capable of generating routes between edges and obstacles, contrary to decomposition algorithms based on Voronoi diagrams, without modifications in their geometric structure, which generate nodes and edges only among the obstacles [6]. The path weights provide the necessary information to know the degree of flexibility of the route at any point, thus, the process of reducing the route can be carried out (avoiding collisions) without the need to use PTP movements from the nodes of the route.

4   Conclusions

For the discretization of environments in robotic navigation algorithms, the expansion of tessellations with the proposed method offer advantages over others traditionally used such as: triangulation, overlapping of square meshes, decomposition of the environment into geometric patterns, among others.

The advantages of the proposed algorithm arises mainly in three aspects:

- A new method of space tessellation based on two dilation processes, one to absorb the size of the robot and thus, be able to consider it from now on as a point; The other dilation process consists of expanding the objects from rectangular wave fronts, which ultimately allow us to obtain a skeleton of the configuration space, where each of the points that make it up have weights that determine the width of the configuration space at each point.
- An iterative method of reducing routes by drawing straight lines between the skeleton nodes.
- And, a smoothing method, based on Bézier curves and the control points, generated by the skeleton weights of space.

The advantages of the proposed method consist of:

- Fewer paths and nodes are generated for the skeleton or tessellation border.
- The execution time required by some of its internal processes is lower since the centroid calculation is not required.
- It does not require special conditions or additional variables to perform the tiling of the environment, other methods of expansion from points on the configuration space require knowing the way of expansion, calculating the appropriate number of points and the location in the environment.
- Additionally, by having the weights of the skeleton nodes, the ends determined by them can be used as the control points for the generation of the Bézier curve.

References

1. Ubiquitous sensor networks (USN) (2018). https://www.itu.int/dms$_$pub/itu-t/oth/23/01/T23010000040001PDFE.pdf. Accessed 22 June 2020
2. Barraquand, J., Latombe, J.C.: Robot motion planning: a distributed representation approach. Int. J. Robot. Res. IJRR **10**, 628–649 (1991). https://doi.org/10.1177/027836499101000604
3. Brunette, E.S., Flemmer, R.C., Flemmer, C.L.: A review of artificial intelligence. In: 2009 4th International Conference on Autonomous Robots and Agents, pp. 385–392 (2009)
4. Delling, D., Sanders, P., Schultes, D., Wagner, D.: Engineering route planning algorithms. In: Lerner, J., Wagner, D., Zweig, K.A. (eds.) Algorithmics of Large and Complex Networks. LNCS, vol. 5515, pp. 117–139. Springer, Heidelberg (2009). https://doi.org/10.1007/978-3-642-02094-0_7
5. Kawabata, K., Ma, L., Xue, J., Chengwei, Z., Zheng, N.: A path generation for automated vehicle based on Bezier curve and via-points. Robot. Auton. Syst. **74** (2015). https://doi.org/10.1016/j.robot.2015.08.001
6. Milos, S., Pich, V.: Robot motion planning using generalised voronoi diagrams, pp. 215–220, August 2008
7. Mo, H., Xu, L.: Research of biogeography particle swarm optimization for robot path planning. Neurocomputing **148**(C), 91–99 (2015)
8. Ravankar, A., Ravankar, A., Kobayashi, Y., Emaru, T.: Avoiding blind leading the blind: uncertainty integration in virtual pheromone deposition by robots. Int. J. Adv. Robot. Syst. **13** (2016). https://doi.org/10.1177/1729881416666088
9. Ravankar, A., Ravankar, A., Kobayashi, Y., Emaru, T.: Symbiotic navigation in multi-robot systems with remote obstacle knowledge sharing. Sensors **17**, 1581 (2017). https://doi.org/10.3390/s17071581
10. Ravankar, A., Ravankar, A.A., Kobayashi, Y., Hoshino, Y., Peng, C.C.: Path smoothing techniques in robot navigation: state-of-the-art, current and future challenges. Sensors (Basel, Switzerland) **18**, 3170 (2018)
11. Silva Ortigoza, R., et al.: Wheeled mobile robots: a review. IEEE Lat. Am. Trans. **10**(6), 2209–2217 (2012)
12. Suhbrajit, B.: Topological and geometric techniques in graph search-based robot planning (2012)
13. Vu, A., Ramanandan, A., Chen, A., Farrell, J.A., Barth, M.: Real-time computer vision/DGPS-aided inertial navigation system for lane-level vehicle navigation. IEEE Trans. Intell. Transp. Syst. **13**(2), 899–913 (2012)

Computational Plane Strain Tests of Epoxy Resin Reinforced with Glass Fibers

Valeria Ferrer[1] , Manuela Palacio[1] , John Del Rio[1] , Juan Mejia[1] ,
Gustavo Suarez[1(✉)] , and Juliana Niño[2]

[1] Grupo de Investigación sobre Nuevos Materiales, Universidad Pontificia Bolivariana,
Cir.1 70-01, 050031 Medellín, Colombia
{valeria.ferrer,manuela.palacio,john.del,juanc.mejiam,
gustavo.suarez}@upb.edu.co
[2] Grupo de Investigación en Ingeniería Aeroespacial, Universidad Pontificia Bolivariana,
Cir.1 70-01, 050031 Medellín, Colombia
juliana.nino@upb.edu.co

Abstract. The global industry has found great advantages in composite materials in comparison with monolithic conventional materials. Glass fiber reinforced polymer (GFRP) is widely used in the construction, aeronautics and automotive industries due to its high strength and low density. In this article, computational simulations were performed in order to analyze the behavior of four GFRP specimens or plaques with different fiber orientations and lengths. The specimens were subjected to mechanical tensile loads. A constitutive model for materials with a linear-elastic behavior was established for both fibers and resin. The mechanical properties, such as Young's modulus and Poisson's ratio, were determined for each component material, and tensile load conditions were established in order to carry out the simulations. A numerical grid of 2601 nodes was designed and the constitutive law of materials equations were solved using the Finite Difference Method (FDM). The computational implementations were executed for the 4 specimens on MATLAB. The results indicate an excellent mechanical contribution on the composite when tensile loads were applied in the same direction as the fiber orientation, while separation or delamination of the material may occur if the load is applied in a different direction. The fibers positioned in a random matter presented a more isotropic behavior. These simulations may contribute to the analysis of the behavior of different types of composite materials and facilitate testing for diverse mechanical tests, and additionally, it could help in reducing the high costs generated by experimental testing.

Keywords: Computational simulation · Plane strain · Epoxy resin · Glass fiber · MATLAB

1 Introduction

Composite materials are made of strong fibers of specific materials (such as glass, aramid, or carbon) that are usually placed in a polymeric or epoxy resin matrix. The fibers, also

© Springer Nature Switzerland AG 2020
J. C. Figueroa-García et al. (Eds.): WEA 2020, CCIS 1274, pp. 109–117, 2020.
https://doi.org/10.1007/978-3-030-61834-6_10

called reinforcement, provide high resistance, while the matrix transfers the applied loads to the fibers and protects them from the environment [1, 2]. The maximum load that the matrix is capable of withstanding is much smaller than what the reinforcement can resist, but this difference is what will allow the matrix to transfer the loads to the fibers in order for them to support the great amounts of tensile and compressive stresses [3, 4].

These materials present an anisotropic nature, meaning that its properties will vary according to the direction in which the load is applied in relation to the orientation of its fibers. For this reason, it is common to pile multiple laminae in order to ensure mechanical properties will be maintained in all directions of load application. Composite material is made by combining a minimum of two or more materials, often with different properties. Composite materials usually present unique properties in which the strength-to-weight ratio is high. Another advantage of composite material is that it provides flexibility in design because the composites can be molded into complex shapes [5, 6].

It is known that composites fail in a brittle manner, which is characterized by very little or absence of plastic deformation and the rapid propagation of a crack. A physical indication of this type of failure is the lack of change in size, or reduction of area, of the cross-sectional area of a specimen. For this reason, these materials fail when their elastic limit is exceeded, resulting in a stress-strain curve that presents no plastic behavior. It is important to note that in a stress-strain curve for a composite material, its ultimate tensile strength typically coincides with its fracture strength.

Evidently, for the fibers to provide the desired properties, they must be harder, more rigid and have a higher strength than the matrix. The reinforcement may be present in the form of fibers or particles, however, composites that have particle reinforcement will be less resistant than those with fiber reinforcement, as the particles will be present in lower volume, nonetheless, they will be an asset when cost is an important consideration. Fibers have a length (l) value much higher than its diameter (d), and this l/d ratio is known as aspect ratio. Due to their small diameter, fibers present a low number of defects while still providing high strength and flexibility, but as the diameter decreases in size, the manufacture cost will inevitably increase. Fibers can also be classified as continuous or discontinuous: if fibers are continuous, they will be oriented in a principal direction, but if they are discontinuous, it is common that they be randomly oriented.

Composites have a very wide range of applications in engineering. The aerospace industry was one of the first to be interested in the development of composite materials for their use in space and aeronautical models. This is because these materials present desirable characteristics that are hard to obtain from other typical structural materials, for example, composites have a very high strength-to-density ratio, known as specific strength, compared to other structural materials such as aluminum and titanium, which allows for the design of lighter components that maintain a high strength. The notable demand for composites in the aerospace industry is attributed to aeronautics. Currently, composites are highly relevant because of the necessity to implement materials with outstanding mechanical properties without sacrificing other desirable ones such as low weight, reduced cost, high formability, etc. The implementation of composites as structural materials translates as a high cost reduction, not only because of the significant weight savings, which therefore lead to the reduction of fuel required for operation, but also because of the lower amount of maintenance required for these components due to they are immune to corrosion. Although composites provide a great amount of benefits, they can sometimes result in high expenses if a component is exposed to impact, as they cannot be repaired and therefore the part must be replaced. Other important applications for composites have been developed for use in many industries such as Automotive, Naval, Sports, and Construction.

This article seeks to analyze the behavior of four GFRP plaques with different fiber orientations when subjected to tensile loads under a plane strain condition, this based on the results from computational testing with the aid of MATLAB. The constitutive law of this material was solved using the finite difference method (FDM). This is a classical method with applications in elasticity, which Timoshenko and Goodier detailed in 1970 [7]. The FDM is simple due to its lack of integration techniques, resulting in less software processing time in comparison with other finite methods available for the solution of partial linear differential equations. Another advantage of the FDM is its extremely accurate results for spatial discretization thanks to its high-order approximations, relying on the expansion of Taylor series for the discretization of the derivatives of the flow variables [8]. This method is especially applicable to simple geometries like the plaques analyzed in this article.

2   Materials and Methods

2.1   Material Constitutive Laws

In order to simulate the behavior of the beforementioned composite material, a model based on Hooke's law was implemented, keeping in mind simple hypotheses of anisotropic elasticity and the constitutive stiffness tensor that depends on the type of material and the directions of application of the load. The formulation of the constitutive law is defined as [9, 10]:

$$\sigma_{ij} = C_{ij} \, \epsilon_j \tag{1}$$

The stress for each component material is given by:

$$\sigma_f = E_f \, \epsilon \tag{2}$$

$$\sigma_m = E_m \, \epsilon \tag{3}$$

Where σ_f is the stress in the direction of the fibers, σ_m is the stress on the matrix, E_f is the fibers' modulus of elasticity, E_m is the matrix's modulus of elasticity, and ϵ is the strain in the direction of the fibers or matrix.

The relationship between the constitutive laws of each material is obtained through the following equations:

Longitudinal modulus:

$$E_{22} = \frac{E_f E_m}{E_m V_f + E_f V_m} \tag{4}$$

Transverse modulus:

$$E_{11} = E_f V_f + E_m V_m \qquad (5)$$

Where V_f is the fiber volume percentage and V_m is the matrix volume percentage.

2.2 Load Considerations and Mechanical Properties

Four 2D computational test plaque geometries were made to represent the 1x1m plaques. Subsequently, the patterns for the reinforcement distributions were determined: unidirectional fibers, fibers oriented at 45° (and −45°), orthotropic fibers 0° (and 90°) and randomly positioned fibers. The configurations are illustrated in Fig. 1.

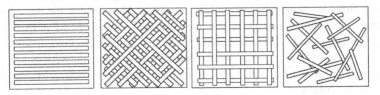

Fig. 1. Plaques with the different fiber orientations established for computational testing.

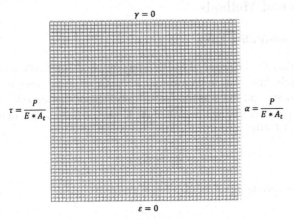

$$\gamma = 0$$

$$\tau = \frac{P}{E * A_t} \qquad\qquad \alpha = \frac{P}{E * A_t}$$

$$\varepsilon = 0$$

Fig. 2. Representative mesh of the computational test plaque and its boundary conditions.

The specimens are composed of an epoxy resin matrix and a glass fiber reinforcement. The following table lists the modulus of elasticity of each component material of the Glass Fiber Reinforced Plastic (GFRP) [11–15] (Table 1).

The load conditions that were used in the computational implementation for the flat tension test on the plaques were (Fig. 2):

Where P is the pressure applied on the plaque [Pa], E is the resin's elasticity modulus [Pa], and A_t is the transverse area of the plaque [m]. The top and bottom boundaries are fixed.

Each plaque is subjected to plane tensile load conditions to evaluate the behavior of the composite under these stresses by developing a square mesh of 2601 nodes.

Table 1. Elasticity Modulus of GFRP.

Material	Elasticity Modulus [GPa]
Glass fiber type E	75
Epoxy resin	2.8–3.4

2.3 Numerical Design of the Plaques

To make a discretization of the material's domain, numerical meshing of 2601 nodes was constructed for the four plaques, in which a representative design of the different fiber orientation models was implemented for the computational analysis of tensile testing under a plane strain condition. The representative models are illustrated in Fig. 3.

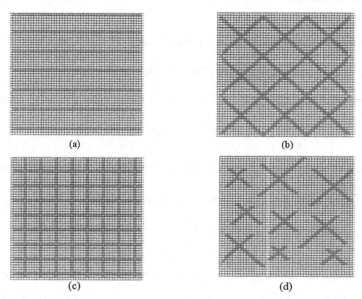

Fig. 3. Discretization of the plaque domain and fiber orientation models in the epoxy resin matrix.

Hooke's law can be mathematically represented as a partial differential equation to be solved using the finite difference method and is implemented by using algorithms developed in MATLAB. To carry out the simulation of the tensile test of the plaques through this model, and under the beforementioned conditions, the constants of the finite difference equation are replaced by the constants that represent Hooke's law of elasticity, which is described as:

$$EA_t \left(\frac{\partial^2 u}{\partial x^2} + \frac{\partial^2 u}{\partial y^2} \right) = P \tag{6}$$

Where E is the material's elasticity modulus, P the pressure applied on the plaque, and A_t is the cross sectional area of the plaque.

In order to find the values of the internal nodes, a mesh as seen in Fig. 4 must be solved.

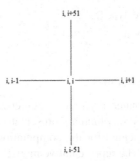

Fig. 4. Representation of the mesh to be solved through the finite difference method.

The system of matrix equations is represented as:

$$[A_{i,i}][u_{i,i}] = [B_i] \tag{7}$$

The central differences can be broken down, resulting in the following equation:

$$EA_t \left(\frac{A_{i,i+1}u_{i,i+1} - 2A_{i,i}u_{i,i} + A_{i,i-1}u_{i,i-1}}{hx^2} + \frac{A_{i,i+51}u_{i,i+51} - 2A_{i,i}u_{i,i} + A_{i,i-51}u_{i,i-51}}{hy^2} \right) = P \tag{8}$$

Where A represents the material's properties, u represents displacement, and h is the step.

And by reorganizing (8), the following equation is obtained:

$$\frac{u_{i,i+1}}{hx^2} - \frac{2u_{i,i}}{hx^2} + \frac{u_{i,i-1}}{hx^2} + \frac{u_{i,i+51}}{hy^2} - \frac{2u_{i,i}}{hy^2} + \frac{u_{i,i-51}}{hy^2} = \frac{P}{EA_t} \tag{9}$$

By grouping, the values $\frac{1}{hx^2} = r$ y $\frac{1}{hy^2} = s$ can be replaced. The equation results in:

$$ru_{(i,i+1)} - 2(r+s)u_{(i,i)} + ru_{(i,i-1)} + su_{(i,i+51)} + su_{(i,i-51)} = \frac{P}{EA_t} \tag{10}$$

This final equation is implemented on MATLAB to carry out the simulations of the mechanical tests.

3 Results

Figure 5 shows the behavior of the different composite plaques when subjected to a tensile stress. Based on the results obtained with the implementation of the algorithm solved using the finite difference method (FDM) on the computational program MATLAB, it is possible to distinguish the strain in millimeters that each of the test specimens studied would undergo in a tensile test.

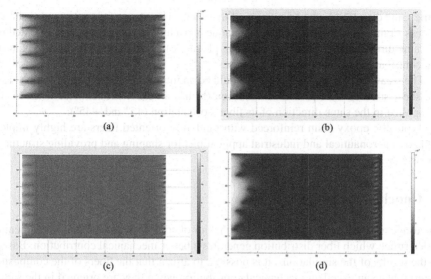

Fig. 5. Plane strain simulation results on glass fiber reinforced epoxy resin test specimens.

The results of the simulations showed the following strain values in terms of the displacement: (a) u = 0.2 mm (b) u = 0.25 mm (c) u = 0.15 mm, and (d) u = 0.4 mm.

As shown in the simulations, the deformation energy is lower in the plaques that have a greater volume percentage of glass fiber reinforcement. This is because this reinforcement helps in reducing displacement and provides a better distribution of stress in the composite.

The closeness of the fibers in plaque (c) makes the plaque's strain ratio very low in comparison to the other fiber configurations. On the other hand, the distribution of the fibers in plaque (d) allowed greater displacement, product of the application of the load, and therefore resulted in a greater deformation energy.

These results explain how the orientation of the fibers within a resin matrix is fundamental when analyzing the deformations in a plaque and how for each configuration, regardless of whether it is made of the same material, the matrix/reinforcement ratio has a notorious impact on the results.

4   Analysis

Plaque (c) underwent the least amount of strain, it is then evident that (c), with fibers at 0° and 90°, is the plaque that presents the best behavior under an applied tensile load. Consecutively, specimen (a), with horizontally oriented fibers, showed a good mechanical behavior. Specimen (b) had an intermediate mechanical behavior due to its weaving at 45° and −45°. The specimen with randomly oriented fibers (d) had the lowest mechanical behavior.

Because composites usually have an anisotropic behavior, it would have been expected for (a) to have the best behavior under this test, since the load was applied in the same direction as the orientation of the fibers. The reason for specimen (c) showing less strain is due to the fact that this plaque had a higher amount of fibers oriented in the same direction of load application than plaque (a), in addition to the weave pattern that contributed in supporting shear stresses.

The weaving pattern present in (b) would be an important contributor given the case that shear stresses were present. In addition (b) has an excellent behavior when loads are applied in the same direction of its fiber's orientation (45° and −45°).

Typically, epoxy resin reinforced with randomly oriented fibers are highly implemented in aeronautical and industrial applications for shaping and providing structural consistency.

5 Conclusions

The usage of simulations to analyze the behavior of composite materials is fundamental to determine which fiber distribution generates a better mechanical contribution. Based on the results of the simulations, it is possible to affirm that the fibers of the composite material have an excellent mechanical contribution when they are oriented in the same direction of application of the load, and that a higher volume percentage of fibers will also aid in this mechanical contribution.

These computational simulations, related to the analysis of the behavior of different types of composite materials, are useful to determine which fiber distribution and matrix/reinforcement ratio is the most adequate to resist the stresses that a certain structure can withstand, in addition, it allows to identify, in a general matter, the optimal configuration in which the reinforcement can better distribute the stresses and dissipate the applied loads without suffering considerable permanent deformation or strain. The improvement of their mechanical behavior under certain loads and according to the variation and the positioning of the fibers within the matrix is an important advantage that composite materials have, providing the possibility to pile multiple laminae with different orientations in order to build a structure from composites.

Similarly, by the analysis of results obtained from algorithms within computational simulation programs, it is possible to reduce the cost of experimental mechanical tests, while obtaining concise and effective predictions for the behavior that parts or structures built with composite materials will show in practice.

References

1. ASM Handbook.: Composites. Vol 21. ASM International, Materials Park, OH (1995)
2. Matthews, F., Rawlings, R.: Composite Materials: Engineering and Science. CRC Press, London (1999)
3. Clyne, T., Hull, D.: An Introduction to Composite Materials, 2nd edn. Cambridge University Press, New York (2019)
4. Chawla, K.: Composite Materials: Science and Engineering. Springer Science & Business Media, New York (2012)
5. Amir, S., et al.: Nondestructive testing method for kevlar and natural fiber and their hybrid composites. Durability and Life Prediction in Biocomposites, Fibre - Reinforced Composites and Hybrid Composites, pp. 367–388. Elsevier, Amsterdam (2018)

6. Raju, A., Shanmugaraja, M.: Recent researches in fiber reinforced composite materials: a review. Materials Today: Proceedings (2020)
7. Sadd, M.: Formulation and solution strategies. Elasticity, pp. 531–535 (2014)
8. Blazek, J.: Principles of Solution of the Governing Equations. Computational Fluid Dynamics: Principles and Applications, pp. 29–72. Butterworth-Heinemann, Oxford (2015)
9. Yarrapragada, R., Mohan, R., Kiran, B.: Composite pressure vessels. Int. J. Res. Eng. Technol. **1**(4), 597–618 (2002)
10. Patiño-Pérez, D., Corz-Rodríguez, A.: Optimum design of a toroidal pressure vessel of composite material for gas (CNG) powered vehicles, pp. 546–553 (2019)
11. Savage, G.: Formula 1 composites engineering. Eng. Fail. Anal. **17**(1), 92–115 (2010)
12. Mikitaev, A.K., Yanovskii, Y.G., Kozlov, G.V.: Description of mechanical properties of particulate-filled nanostructured polymer composites using fractal analysis. Phys. Mesomech. **18**(2), 149–157 (2015). https://doi.org/10.1134/S1029959915020071
13. Lozano, C.: Deformación y fractura de una resina epóxica reforzada con fibras de algodón, Tesis Doctoral. Universidad Nacional de Colombia, Bogotá (2016)
14. Estrada, M., Xometl, O., Aguilar, G., Rosas, R., Caselis, V.: Preparación y caracterización de recubrimientos resina epóxica/montmorillonita curados por UV sobre acero al carbón. Superficies y Vacío **29**(3), 74–77 (2016)
15. Pertuz, A., Monroy, D., Monsalve, S., León, J., González-Estrada, A.: Study of fatigue in sheets of composite pipe of epoxy matrix with glass fiber for tensile loads. Scientia et Technica, pp. 479–488 (2018)

Design and Structural Analysis of a Machine for Characterizing Strain Gauge on Paper Substrate

Luiz Antonio Rasia[1]($\boxtimes$) (iD), Edmilton Oliveira Stein[1] (iD), Humber Furlan[2] (iD), and Carlos Eduardo Andrades[1] (iD)

[1] Regional University of the Northwest of the State of Rio Grande do Sul, Ijuí, Brazil
rasia@unijui.edu.br, e_stein@outlook.com,
carloseduardoandrades@gmail.com
[2] Faculty of Technology of São Paulo - CEETEPS, São Paulo, Brazil
humber@fatecsp.br

Abstract. This work shows the design and structural analysis of a tensile testing machine for paper used as a substrate for the manufacture of piezoresistive sensors similar to strain gauges. This article also discusses the manufacturing process and the performance analysis of a low cost machine to characterize electromechanical structures made of graphite on polymeric substrate. Graphite in thin paper films have been investigated for a wide range of applications due to their excellent electrical and mechanical properties. Graphite sensors on flexible polymer substrates can be applied to portable wearable devices, as well as sensors for the Internet of things, bioengineering and applications in various areas of science and technology.

Keywords: Traction machine · Graphite on paper (GoP) · Strain gauge · Paper electronics

1 Introduction

Extensometers, also known as strain gauges, are devices capable of converting mechanical deformations into electrical signals, having applications in the most diverse areas such as aeronautics, medicine, civil construction, robotics and other fields [1].

Strain sensors have a wide range of applications directly measure strain in structural health monitoring of critical infrastructure to prevent catastrophic failure and identify any initiation of damage in real-time.

The strain gauge is the fundamental component of sensors for mass, pressure, acceleration, inertia, among others, since its function is to convert mechanical loads into an electrical signal, that is, it is from this device that the variables in the environment start to be measured and can be controlled. In addition to the strain gauge in an electronic device, as described, there are diaphragms, electronic signal conditioning components and encapsulations that together form a MEMS - microelectromechanical system.

© Springer Nature Switzerland AG 2020
J. C. Figueroa-García et al. (Eds.): WEA 2020, CCIS 1274, pp. 118–125, 2020.
https://doi.org/10.1007/978-3-030-61834-6_11

In general, strain gauges are manufactured using the deposition of metallic or semi-conductor films on the silicon substrate. However, new technologies are being used to manufacture these sensors [2].

Electronics using paper as a substrate is an emerging field of interest in the development of new electronics due to its low cost, lightweight, flexibility and biocompatible and recyclable nature. It is possible to deposit different materials on paper and, in particular, pencil graphite by mechanical exfoliation without using chemical solvents. This technique is known as GoP - Grafite on Paper [2–4].

The diversity of applications ends up arousing interest in researching different materials, manufacturing techniques and conceptions of several transducers and sensors for this purpose [2].

In this work, a machine is proposed for the characterization of piezoresistive sensor elements, in particular extensometers deposited on the paper substrate according to the technical characterization standards [4].

1.1 Strain Gauges Model and Processing Steps

The resistance, R, of a strain gauge is determined by Eq. (1) according to the literature [10]:

$$R = \frac{\rho L}{A} = \frac{\rho L}{wt} \tag{1}$$

where, $\rho = \rho_0$, is the resistivity of the graphite, L, length, w, the width and, t, thickness of the sensor element.

The resistance, R, of a strain gauge, shown in Fig. 1, can be calculated according to [7] by Eq. (2):

$$R = R_{ref} + \rho_0 \pi_l \int_{xd}^{xu} T_l(x)dx + \rho_0 \pi_t \int_{xd}^{xu} T_t(x)dx \tag{2}$$

where, R_{ref}, represents the value of the piezoresistor value without applying mechanical stresses, π_l, π_t, are the longitudinal and transverse piezoresistive coefficients, respectively. The mechanical stress applied to the crimped beam is given by, T_l (x), and, T_t (x), longitudinally and transversely.

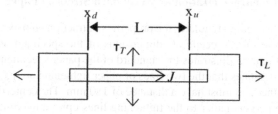

Fig. 1. Strain gauge model

The piezoresistive effect can be described expressing the change of electrical resistance, $\Delta R/R$, of macroscopic form as a function of mechanical stress, mechanical deformation, ε, and the sensitivity factor or gauge factor, GF, [6] given by Eq. (3):

$$GF = \frac{\Delta R/R}{\varepsilon} \tag{3}$$

Hooke's law relates the longitudinal strain to mechanical stress by Eq. (4):

$$T = E\varepsilon_L \tag{4}$$

where, E, is the Young's modulus or the modulus of elasticity of the material [8]. The Young's modulus of elasticity of the graphite crystal varies up to two orders of magnitude with the directions $1060 - 36.5$ GPa.

For the fabrication of the sensor elements a few steps were followed presented by [4, 10]: polymer substrate sizing, GoP deposition, copper contact fixation and encapsulation, shown in Fig. 2.

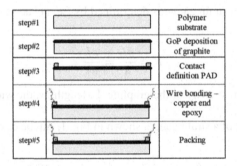

Fig. 2. Description of the processing steps of graphite sensor elements

Using the manufacturing steps described in Fig. 2, in a clean environment, air temperature of 26 °C and humidity of 59%, the sensor elements were made in accordance with the model shown in Fig. 1.

1.2 Standard for Characterization of Mechanical Stress on Paper

The ISO 1924-2 [9] standard regulates the properties of traction on paper and cardboard, including data acquisition procedures, dimensions of the specimen and the constant stretching speed. Figure 3 illustrates the standard of the paper specimen.

This standard regulates that the two lines of paper tightening are parallel with up to 1° angle to each other and must have a distance of 180 mm. The centerline of the paper specimen must be perpendicular to the tightening lines up to a maximum angle of 1°. The traction force must be parallel to the centerline of the specimen with a maximum angle of 1°. The width must be 15 mm and may be 1.1 mm more or less as an acceptable limit. The tensile test consists of applying a uniaxial load until the paper breaks.

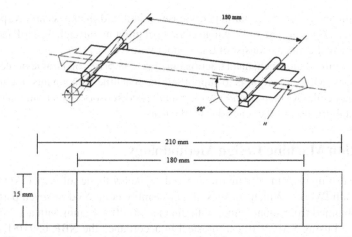

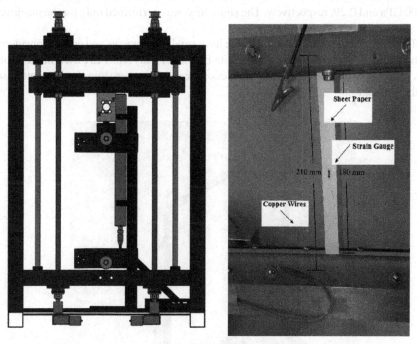

Fig. 3. Illustration adapted from the standard for tensile tests on paper [9]

Fig. 4. CAD design of the machine and photograph of the application of the standard for uniaxial tensile testing materials testing.

Figure 4 illustrates this test process according to specific standards for each type of material and shows the CAD design of the complete machine.

The samples use commercial paper, whose weight and thickness are, respectively, 75 g/m^2 and 0.088 mm. The strain gauge is made of graphite through the GoP technique, and the electrical contacts consist of thin copper wires.

The structure of the mechanical traction machine comprises of a frame of rectangular metallic tubes, whose function is to support all the machine components, including the standard load cell, DC motors and position and speed sensors. This frame needs to be robust enough to support the loads during the tests.

2   Traction Machine Design Methodology

The tensile testing machine's main frame was designed with the software CAD Dassault Systèmes SolidWorks. Which consists of an assembly composed of seven parts, six of them are obtained from square tubes with dimensions 40 x 40 mm with a 1.2 mm wall, manufactured using SAE 1010 carbon steel in accordance the NBR 6591/81. And the remaining part is obtained from a 50.8 mm x 3.175 mm thick flat bar of the same material. SAE 1010 carbon steel is known to have an elastic modulus and average Poisson's ratio of 200 GPa and 0.29, respectively. The simulation was performed only for the machine's chassis as shown in Fig. 4.

The components of the metallic frame have small thicknesses and can be considered, mathematically, as a shell during the Finite Element Analysis - FEA used in this work. This procedure saves time and requires less processing power from the computer used for the simulation.

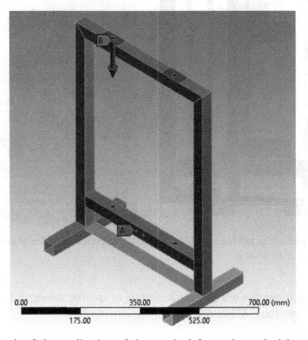

Fig. 5. Photograph of the application of the standard for testing uniaxial tensile testing of materials.

The numerical analysis is done using the features of the CAE software (Computer Aided Engineering) ANSYS Mechanical. This process can be summarized in three stages, mesh generation, application of loads and restrictions and analysis of the results.

Figure 5 illustrates the traction machine's metallic frame showing the location of the supports (A), as well as the applied force (B), where the specimens' evaluation happens.

The simulation uses a force range between 10 N and 100 N located in the area highlighted in red pictured in Fig. 5 exactly at point (B). That is the position of the reactions generated by the traction of the threaded rods coupled to the electric motors.

3   Results and Discussions

In this work, the displacement of point A of Fig. 6 was verified, where the paper test samples are fixed in relation to the base where the displacement sensor is fixed. This sensor measures the mechanical deformation of the samples up to the breaking point of the graphite sensor device.

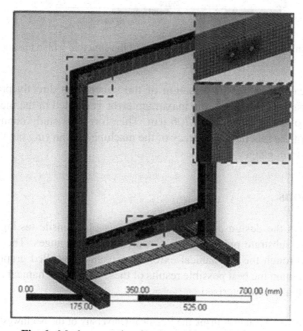

Fig. 6. Mesh generation for the traction machine frame

The mesh is generated using two-dimensional parabolic elements and as an evaluation metric, its skewness is used, whose value should not be greater than 0.75 and, preferably, less than 0.5 in areas with a high stress gradient. The resulting mesh is pictured in Fig. 6.

Figure 7 illustrates the result of the vertical displacement analysis, using the maximum load of 100 N with the mesh already refined where it is verified that the displacement between points (A) and where the sensor is located (B) is 13.706 μm.

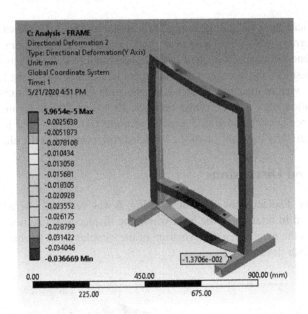

C: Analysis - FRAME
Directional Deformation 2
Type: Directional Deformation(Y Axis)
Unit: mm
Global Coordinate System
Time: 1
5/21/2020 4:51 PM

5.9654e-5 Max
-0.0025638
-0.0051873
-0.0078108
-0.010434
-0.013058
-0.015681
-0.018305
-0.020928
-0.023552
-0.026175
-0.028799
-0.031422
-0.034046
-0.036669 Min

-1.3706e-002

0.00   450.00   900.00 (mm)
        225.00   675.00

Fig. 7. Analysis of the vertical deformation of the structure with a load of 100 N.

The error caused by the deformation of the structure is directly proportional to the test force used. In this work, the maximum error generated in the measurement of the elongation of the samples is 13.706 µm. Therefore, this study contributed to the understanding of the functional accuracy of the machine for carrying out the tests of the manufactured strain gauges sensors.

4 Conclusions

This work shows the design and structural analysis of a tensile testing machine for paper used as a substrate piezoresistive sensor like strain gauges. These devices are manufactured through the mechanical exfoliation technique called graphite on paper, and in order to obtain the best possible results of these electromechanical elements, they must be individually characterized.

Acknowledgments. The authors thank the Regional University of the Northwest of the State of Rio Grande do Sul and the Foundation for Research Support – FAPERGS and CNPq for financial support.

References

1. Liu, H., et al: A promising material for human-friendly functional wearable electronics (2017). https://doi.org/10.1016/j.mser.2017.01.001

2. Mahadeva, S.K., Walus, K., Stoeber, B.: Paper as a platform for sensing applications and other devices: a review. ACS Appl. Mater. Interfaces. **7**(16), 8345–8362 (2015). https://doi.org/10.1021/acsami.5b0037

3. Lin, C.W., Zhao, Z., Kim, J., Huang, J.: Pencil drawn strain gauges and chemiresistors on paper. Sci. Rep. **4**(3812), 2–6 (2014). https://doi.org/10.1038/srep03812

4. Gabbi, R., Rasia, L.A., Valdiero, A.C., Gabbi, M.T.T.: An aproach for computational simulation of the elements piezoresistives of graphite. Int. J. Dev. Res. **8**(02), 19150–19155 (2018)

5. Dinh, T., et al.: Graphite on paper as material for sensitive thermoresistive sensors. J. Mater. Chem. C **3**(34), 8776–8779 (2015)

6. Kanaparthi, S., Badhulika, S.: Low cost, flexible and biodegradable touch sensor fabricated by solvent-free processing of graphite on cellulose paper. Sens. Actuators B Chem. **242**, 857–864 (2017)

7. Gniazdowski, Z., Kowalski, P.: Practical approach to extraction of piezoresistance coefficient. Sens. Actuators, A **68**, 329–332 (1998)

8. Rasia, L.A., Leal, G., Koberstein, L.L., Furlan, H., Massi, M., Fraga, M.A.: Design and analytical studies of a DLC thin-film piezoresistive pressure microsensor. In: Figueroa-García, J.C., López-Santana, E.R., Villa-Ramírez, J.L., Ferro-Escobar, R. (eds.) WEA 2017. CCIS, vol. 742, pp. 433–443. Springer, Cham (2017). https://doi.org/10.1007/978-3-319-66963-2_39

9. ISO. 1924–2: Paper and board – Determination of tensile properties – Part 2: Constant rate of elongation method (20 mm/min). 3 ed. 20 pp. Switzerland: ISO Copyright Office (2008)

10. Rasia, L.A., Pedrali, P.C., Furlan, H., Fraga, M.A.: Design and characterization of graphite piezoresistors in paper for applications in sensor devices. In: Figueroa-García, J.C., Duarte-González, M., Jaramillo-Isaza, S., Orjuela-Cañon, A.D., Díaz-Gutierrez, Y. (eds.) WEA 2019. CCIS, vol. 1052, pp. 577–583. Springer, Cham (2019). https://doi.org/10.1007/978-3-030-31019-6_48

Computational Analysis of an Electrodynamic Speaker and Implementation in 3D Printing

Julian Guillermo Rodriguez Mora[1], Mauricio Andrés Polochè Arango[2(✉)],
Manuel F. Torres Cifuentes[1], Oscar E. Acosta Agudelo[1],
and Héctor Fabián Guarnizo Méndez[3]

[1] Sound Engineering, Universidad de San Buenaventura, Bogotá, Colombia
jgrodriguezmora@academia.usbbog.edu.co,
{mtorres,oacosta}@usbbog.edu.co
[2] Electronic Engineering, Universidad de San Buenaventura, Bogotá, Colombia
mpoloche@usbbog.edu.co
[3] Electronic Engineering, Universidad El Bodque, Bogotá, Colombia
hguarnizo@unbosque.edu.co

Abstract. This article presents the use of two technologies as a methodology to design, study, and fabrication of electrodynamic speakers. The experiment setup consisted first in modeling and simulated the classical physical structure circular of a loudspeaker using ANSYS® and solved by the finite element method (FEM), the second part was manufacturing the loudspeaker using 3D printing technics and standard materials in this industry. The simulations, the physical structure implementation and the measurements of frequency response.

Keywords: FEM · Frequency response · 3D printing

1 Introduction

This paper presents a methodology for the design, construction, and testing of loudspeakers, making use of the finite element method (FEM) [1–3] and 3D printing [4, 5]. The motive is offer a reliable and fast procedure for the study of these systems to obtain results quickly and accurately, so can be study variations in the design like the geometry [6, 7]. This type implementation could be use in medical, industrial and entertainment applications allow evaluating big size devices till miniaturized devices, using 3D printing like a fast and economic technique.

In this research, first a loudspeaker is modeled with 3D printing materials for computational analysis of the modal and vibratory behavior in ANSYS®. With these results, some Thiele-Small parameters [8] necessary for the design of an acoustic box that avoids an acoustic short circuit [9] are computed. Modeling the box system, the mechanical simulation is performed taking into account the damping factor and its corresponding acoustic simulation, obtaining the frequency response. Second, once the computational analysis is completed, the prototype is manufactured and implemented, with which the physical measurements will be carried out for final validation of the results.

© Springer Nature Switzerland AG 2020
J. C. Figueroa-García et al. (Eds.): WEA 2020, CCIS 1274, pp. 126–138, 2020.
https://doi.org/10.1007/978-3-030-61834-6_12

2   Computational Simulation

2.1   Description of the Loudspeaker Model Structure

A 6.5″ diameter loudspeaker is modeled, for good low frequency performance [10] and not exceed the printing limits, based on a commercial cone 2.7 cm deep and 5.5 cm radius, obtaining, in addition, the other components that are required for the construction like the core, the magnet, voice coil, dust cover and spider, which are easy and cheap to get. Figure 1 shows the modeled prototype in CAD software.

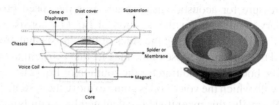

Fig. 1. CAD model of prototype loudspeaker

Tension tests on ABS (acrylonitrile butadiene styrene) and PLA (polylactic acid) [4], showed that the latter has better mechanical characteristics, which makes this material suitable for implementation. The suspension must be flexible so that the system can move and return to its resting point. The TPU (Thermoplastic Polyurethane) is one of the few materials in 3D printing that meets this requirement and is easily accessible. The materials and physical characteristics used in the simulation are show in Table 1.

Table 1. ANSYS® material library definitions.

Component	Material	Density (kg/mm^3)	Young's modulus (MPa)	Poisson's coefficient
Chassis	PLA	1.25E−06	3450	0.39
Core	Iron	7.13E−06	1.71E+05	0.275
Magnet	Ferrite	7.72E−06	2.00E+05	0.28
Voice coil	Copper	8.94E−06	1.24E+05	0.345
Spider	Rigid cloth	1.10E−06	20	0.4433
Diaphragm	PLA	1.25E−06	3450	0.39
Suspension	TPU	1.19E−06	55	0.3
Dust cover	Paperboard	1.79E−06	2828	0.3674

2.2   Boundary Conditions to Vibration Analysis

The vibratory analysis is performance by a modal module, where the natural frequencies of vibration of the system are obtained by solving the homogeneous wave equation expressed in (1); and a harmonic module that estimates speed with respect to frequency, solving the nonhomogeneous wave equation in (2) [11].

$$\nabla^2 \Phi - \frac{1}{v^2} \frac{\partial^2}{\partial t^2} \Phi = 0 \qquad (1)$$

$$\nabla^2 \Phi - \frac{1}{v^2} \frac{\partial^2}{\partial t^2} \Phi = f(x, y, z, t) \qquad (2)$$

In Eqs. (1) and (2), Φ represents a magnitude, like a displacement to mechanical analysis or the pressure for acoustic analysis, and v is the speed propagation of the wave. The boundary conditions for the solution of Eq. (1), consist in indicating the surfaces where the speed is zero, being the sides of the chassis that are in contact with the suspension and the spider and those of the magnet that is in contact with the nucleus and the chassis. The boundary condition for the solution of Eq. (2), is the magnitude of the variable force with which the voice coil is going to move the system, whose estimated value is 0.88 N. Normally, this magnitude is calculated by multiplying the current that it passes through the loudspeaker and the force factor Bl, according to Lenz Faraday's law, where B is the density of the flux of the magnetic field cross the voice coil and l the length of the winding [10]. Likewise, a force of 0.88 N corresponds to a Bl of 2.5 Tm and a current of 0.35 A, equivalent to 1 W RMS for a loudspeaker of 8 Ω of electrical resistance.

2.3 Meshing for Vibratory Analysis

For a computational analysis using the finite element method, it is always necessary evaluate the mesh results and mesh quality. Due to limits in software license, in this case only the mesh quality was considerate, where the elements size decreases to recreate the model. The Fig. 2 shows the selected mesh that has 2 mm element size for a range of analysis to 1 kHz. The bar on the left side denotes the quality of the mesh by relating the chosen element size to the final size created.

Fig. 2. Meshing for vibratory analysis.

2.4 Design and Modeling of the Acoustic Box

A first analysis is realized to obtain the curves speed of the diaphragm with respect to the frequency, without damping factor. Figure 3 shows these values obtained by ANSYS®. With this first approach, it is possible to estimate some of the Thiele-Small parameters (typical electromechanical parameters of a loudspeaker) that are necessary for the design of the loudspeaker box. The resonance frequency is where the system reaches its maximum speed, and according to Fig. 3, it is 157.66 Hz. With the speed of the resonance frequency, it is possible to compute the speed at the lower and upper cutoff frequencies (f_1, f_2) with (3); likewise, the values of the cutoff frequencies are compute using (4) [10].

$$V_{f_1, f_2} = \frac{1}{\sqrt{2}} V_{f_s} \qquad (3)$$

$$f_s = \sqrt{f_1 f_2} \qquad (4)$$

Without considering a damping factor, speed results in Fig. 3 are very high, making it impossible to obtain the cutoff frequency speeds. Therefore, the suggested procedure is to gradually decrease the speed at the resonant frequency, compute the speeds with Eq. (3), find those results on the simulation and verify the frequencies with Eq. (4). Thus, the speed curve is projected as shows in Fig. 3.

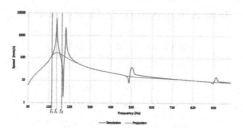

Fig. 3. Projection of the speed curve

According to Fig. 3 the final lower cutoff frequency is 133.14 Hz and the upper cutoff is 186.69 Hz. With these frequency values, the total loss factor of the loudspeaker (Q_{TS}) is computed with (5).

$$Q_{TS} = \frac{f_s}{f_2 - f_1} \qquad (5)$$

Afterwards the volume of air equivalent to compliance (V_{AS}) was computed to proceed with the design of the box, and for this, it is necessary to know the mechanical compliance of the system (C_{MS}), which is obtained from the resonance frequency and the total mechanical mass (M_{MS}) as seen in (6).

$$f_s = \frac{1}{2\pi \sqrt{C_{MS} M_{MS}}} \qquad (6)$$

Total mechanical mass is the sum of the mass of the diaphragm, voice coil, dust cover (M_{MD}), and the mechanical radiation mass (M_{MR}). ANSYS® was used to compute the mass of these components and the M_{MR} was computed with (7).

$$M_{MR} = \rho_0 S_D 0.85 a \qquad (7)$$

Where ρ_0 is the density of the propagation medium, approximately 1.2 kg/m^3, S_D the effective area of the diaphragm and a diaphragm radius. Table 2 shows the mass values. Solving for mechanical compliance with (6) and the V_{AS} with (8).

$$V_{AS} = \rho_0 C^2 S_D^2 C_{MS} \tag{8}$$

Table 2. Total mechanical mass

M_{MD} (kg)			M_{MR} (kg)	M_{MS} (kg)
Diaphragm	Voice coil	Dust cover	0,00053	0,0148
0.0108	0,00203	0,0014		

With this analysis, the obtained Thiele-Small parameters are presented in Table 3.

Table 3. Estimated Thiele-Small parameters

Parameter	Unit	Value
f_s	Hz	157.66
f_1	Hz	133.14
f_2	Hz	186.69
Q_{TS}		2.944
M_{MS}	g	14.8
C_{MS}	mm/N	0.069
S_D	cm^2	95.03
V_{AS}	l	0.878

Now it is proceeding to the design of the acoustic box [9]. This component in the model will avoid the acoustic short circuit that is produced by the interference of the front and rear waves of the loudspeaker [10]. However, the filter must not affect the behavior of the loudspeaker. The procedure consists of choosing an alignment (Q_{TC}) and computing the compliance ratio (α) with (9), afterwards, the new resonance frequency (f_c) is computed with (10) and if it is approximate to f_s, it is computed the volume of the box (V_{AB}) with (11). The results obtained are presented in Table 4.

$$\alpha = \left(\frac{Q_{TC}}{Q_{TS}}\right)^2 - 1 \tag{9}$$

$$f_c = f_s\sqrt{1+\alpha} \tag{10}$$

$$V_{AB} = \frac{V_{AS}}{\alpha} \tag{11}$$

Table 4. Acoustic box parameters.

Parameters	Unit	Value
Q_{TC}		2.967
α		0.016
f_C	Hz	158.89
V_{AB}	l	55

With the alignment factor, the total damping factor (ζ) that will restrict the movement of the system is compute with (12).

$$\zeta = \frac{1}{2Q_{TC}} \tag{12}$$

The dimensions of the box were using Bolt's criterion (Fig. 4, left), to obtain a homogeneous distribution of the frequencies that generate acoustic modes within the space [12].

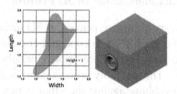

Fig. 4. Bolt's criterion (left) [12] and loudspeaker in acoustic box (right).

A length ratio of 1.5 and 1.2 of the width was considerate, taking into account the thickness of the wood of 1.5 cm, the external dimensions of the box are 50 cm long, 41 cm wide and 34 cm high (see Fig. 4).

2.5 Boundary Conditions for Acoustic Analysis

To solve the acoustic section, the propagation medium fluid must be created, so a spherical enclosure is created to emulate both the interior and exterior air of the model. The acoustic section is solved with (2) using as a source the speed results of the harmonic section at the modal frequencies of the system, and using Robin's condition expressed in (13).

$$\nabla P + jkP = 0 \tag{13}$$

Solving the differential equation with this condition, the surface where this condition is applied will be the point where the wave front will be flat.

2.6 Meshing for Acoustic Analysis

This mesh is 10 times greater than that used in the mechanical analysis study due to the large size of the box and the propagation medium fluid. However, the meshing of the loudspeaker area will be the same of the mechanical analysis. Figure 5 shows the selected mesh that has 38 mm element size.

Fig. 5. Meshing for acoustic analysis.

3   Manufacturing of the Loudspeaker Prototype

3.1   Implementation of the Loudspeaker in 3D Printing

The components of the loudspeaker were printed in 3D technique with materials used in the computational model design; PLA to cone and chassis, and TPU for suspension, the cost was 14 dollars, the printed time was approximately six hours and the printed machine used the Prusa I3™. The assembly process consisted of centering all the pieces avoiding that the voice coil rubbing against the other components to extend its useful life. In Fig. 6 is shows the manufactured loudspeaker prototype.

Fig. 6. Prototype of the electrodynamic speaker in 3D printing.

3.2   Thiele-Small Parameters

There are different techniques and software for measuring Thiele-Small parameters. In this works, a manual method was used, as suggested by Remberto-Gómez [8] (Fig. 7).

Fig. 7. Circuit for measuring the electrical input impedance of the speaker.

In this series circuit, the impedance in the loudspeaker (R_s) can be expressed as shows in (14).

$$R_S = \frac{V_S}{V_R} R \tag{14}$$

Where V_s is the voltage in the loudspeaker, V_R is the voltage in the power resistor, and R is the resistance. Using RMS multimeter, the voltages are measured and the impedance was computed with the frequency changes in the signal generator. The obtained curve is known as the input electrical impedance (Z_{ee}) and with it the other Thiele-Small parameters can be obtained. Figure 8 shows the impedance curve measure.

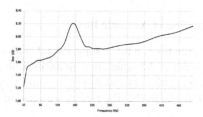

Fig. 8. Measure of impedance vs frequency response.

Table 5. Thiele-Small Parameters

Parameter	Computation	Unit	Value	Parameter	Computation	Unit	Value
R_E	Multimeter measurement	Ω	7.6	S_D	From CAD model	cm^2	95.03
R_m	Curve Z_{ee}	Ω	8.26	M_{MS}	Mass of the components	g	15.3
r_0	$\frac{R_m}{R_E}$		1.087	C_{MS}	Equation (6)	mm/N	0.0699
Z_i	$\sqrt{R_m R_E}$	Ω	7.924	V_{AS}	Equation (8)	l	0.892
f_s	Curve Z_{ee}	Hz	154.00	X_{MAX}	Manual measurement	mm	3
f_1	Curve Z_{ee}	Hz	130.00	V_D	$S_D X_{MAX}$	l	0.0285
f_2	Curve Z_{ee}	Hz	183.00	L_E	$\frac{\sqrt{R_S^2 - R_E^2}}{2\pi f}$	mH	0.939
Q_{MS}	$\frac{\sqrt{r_0} f_s}{f_2 - f_1}$		3.03	Bl	$\sqrt{\frac{2\pi f_s R_E M_{MS}}{Q_{ES}}}$	Tm	1.798
Q_{ES}	$\frac{Q_{MS}}{r_0 - 1}$		34.78	$\eta 0$	$\frac{4\pi^2 f_s^2 V_{AS}}{C^3 Q_{ES}}$	%	0.091
Q_{TS}	$\frac{Q_{ES} Q_{MS}}{Q_{ES} + Q_{MS}}$		2.787	S_D	From CAD model	cm^2	95.03

Each of the measured parameters are R_E (Voice coil electrical resistance or DC resistance), R_m (Impedance at resonance frequency of the loudspeaker), r_0 (Relationship between maximum impedance and electrical resistance), Z_i (Impedance that crosses the upper and lower cutoff frequencies), f_s (Resonance frequency), f_1 (Lower cutoff frequency), f_2 (Upper cutoff frequency), Q_{MS} (Mechanical loss factor), Q_{ES} (Electric loss factor), Q_{TS} (Total loss factor), S_D (Effective surface of the diaphragm), M_{MS} (Total mechanical mass), C_{MS} (Mechanical compliance), V_{AS} (Volume of air equivalent to compliance), X_{MAX} (Maximum displacement of the diaphragm), V_D (Volume of air that moves the loudspeaker), L_E (Electrical inductance of the voice coil), Bl (Force factor), η_0 (Loudspeaker efficiency like ratio of electrical input power and acoustic output power). The measurement results are presented in Table 5.

3.3 Design and Construction of Acoustic Box

Without modifying the design used in the computational analysis, it is verified that the volume of the 55 L box generates the same effect in the measured parameters. Knowing the V_{AS} y V_{AB}, α is compute with (11) and from this value, f_c y el Q_{TC} of the box are compute with (10) and (9) respectively. The results are show in Table 6.

Table 6. Final parameters of the acoustic box.

Parameter	Unit	Value
Q_{TC}		2.809
α		0.016
f_C	Hz	155.00
V_{AB}	1	55

Comparing the results of Table 4 and Table 6, the difference between the estimated and final values is 5.3%. The computational box simulated will have the same effect for the assembled prototype. Figure 9 shows the entire system built it.

Fig. 9. Final manufacture system.

3.4 Frequency Response Measurement

For the measurement of frequency response, the method suggested by Keele [13] was used, where the microphone is placed in the near field, pointing to the center of the acoustic radiation system and avoiding the effect of room reflections. Acoustic analysis software EASERA© was used, this software sends a sine sweep to the digital sound card Roland™ Studio Capture UA-1610 to adjust voltage levels easily and connected to power amplifier class D, 100 W power and THD of 10% TDA 7498. The signal amplified attacks the loudspeaker, that transforms the electrical signal into acoustic energy, that is captured by condenser microphone, omnidirectional and flat response from 3 Hz to 23 kHz Earthworks m23, ideal for acoustic measurements. The signal captured by the microphone sends the data to the analysis software. The software internally computes the transfer function of the system, obtaining the frequency response of the loudspeaker. Figure 10 shows a setup diagram of the measurement system implemented.

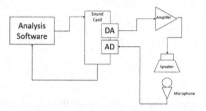

Fig. 10. Measurement setup.

4   Result Analysis

The measurement results and simulation results obtained were analyzed, finding the differences in magnitude and the percentage error to validate the reliability of the design method. The average error was 2.49% with a standard deviation of 1.28% for the results show in Table 7, acceptable range to validate the design method.

Table 7. Thiele-Small parameter comparison.

Parameter	Unit	Estimation	Measure	Magnitude difference	% error
f_s	Hz	157.66	154.00	3.66	2.32%
f_1	Hz	133.14	130.00	3.14	2.36%
f_2	Hz	186.69	183.00	3.69	1.98%
Q_{TS}		2.944	2.787	0.157	5.30%
M_{MS}	g	14.8	15.3	0.5	3.27%
C_{MS}	mm/N	0.0688	0.0699	0.011	1.57%
V_{AS}	l	0.878	0.892	0.014	1.57%

For the design of the acoustic box, the average error of estimated parameters is 1.95% with a standard deviation of 2.19%. Due to the rigidity of the suspension in TPU, the cone does not generate a good excursion and this in turn produces instability in the results, since the Q_{ES} is usually between 0.2 and 1.3. Likewise, the maximum impedance is not very far from the electrical resistance of the voice coil and, therefore, the impedance ratio is very close to one, which when computing like shows Table 5, the denominator less than one and the magnitude of the Q_{ES} is excessive. This makes TPU unfeasible as a suspension material. Table 8 shows the same analysis for the design parameters of the loudspeaker box.

Table 8. Comparison of parameters of the acoustic box.

Parameter	Unit	Estimated design	Obtains design	Magnitude difference	% error
Q_{TC}		2.967	2.809	0.158	5.30%
α		0.016	0.016	0	0%
f_C	Hz	158.89	155.00	3.89	2.45%
V_{AB}	1	55	55	0	0%

The graph of Fig. 11 shows the correlation of the simulated results with respect to the measured results together to commercial model Scanspeak classic p17wj00-08, that is similar size and mechanical mass, for a final comparation. Whit results of simulation and measurement, the resonance curves coincide in amplitude and is very approximate in the bandwidth, this corresponds to the high proximity in the resonance frequencies and damping factors, obtaining differences of maximum 1.5 dB between 120 Hz and 500 Hz. In Fig. 12 the correlation (R^2) between measurement and simulation is 0.97, indicating the results are very near, and the residue change between 2.6 dB and −3 dB.

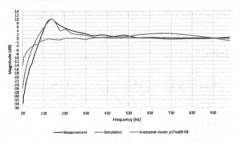

Fig. 11. Final frequency response analysis.

The differences are due to varied factors, like the reflections in the room that generate acoustic distortion, while the simulation is in an ideal condition, without noise or uncertainty, the frequency response of the power amplifier is not completely flat and the high harmonic distortion characteristics may be present when the speaker requires high power, the temperature that affects the speed and the wavelength; in this case, the simulation is contemplated at a temperature of 23 °C, and the differences between the CAD model and the physical loudspeaker, since in the CAD model the components are 100% centered, whereas the manual implementation may have millimeter errors in one or

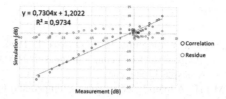

Fig. 12. Analysis correlation and residue to measurement and simulation.

more elements. Comparing the prototype with the Scanspeak's commercial model, starting for the technical characteristics, commercial model has a flatter frequency response and more efficiency in bass frequencies. This due to the great differences in the Q_{TS}, commercial model's 0.35 and prototype's 2.79, and resonance frequency, commercial model's 37 Hz and prototype's 154 Hz, whose origin is the deficiency of the TPU material. Economically, prototype is cheaper than Scanspeak's model, taking into account materials, printing and components, the prototype cost is 25 dollars while Scanspeak's model cost is 77 dollars. This means, the next step is the prototype optimization to be technically efficient and cheap.

5 Conclusions

This work presented the computational modeling and analysis of an electrodynamic speaker implemented with 3D printing materials. Thiele-Small parameters were estimated from the analysis and a box design was carried out that avoids the acoustic short circuit, without affecting the natural behavior of the loudspeaker and being able to estimate its frequency response. After the simulation, the construction of the prototype for physical measurements was developed. The results of the measurement of the Thiele-Small parameters showed a high correlation with the estimated parameters, both in the loudspeaker and in the design of the acoustic box and the frequency response, demonstrating the method efficiency. On the other hand, the use of TPU as a suspension material makes this prototype very rigid, hindering the excursion and giving atypical results. The differences in the frequency response functions are due to the power amplifier that affects the damping of the system and presents greater harmonic distortion at high power levels. In conclusion, designing and estimating the results of an electrodynamic speaker prototype from the computational analysis can be a reliable method, with which it can have different analyzes and carry out tests modifying the components materials or geometry in the model. The use of 3D printing for the manufacture and assembly of a prototype, allows quickly physical tests of a particular model to verify the simulation results, and although the TPU is not a material with which to obtain a good response, the possibility of adjusting a simulation based on physical results gives greater probabilities to future tests with different materials and so, obtain approximately the characteristics like commercial model Scanspeak classic p17wj00-08.

References

1. Hu, Y., Zhao, X., Yamaguchi, T., Sasajima, M., Sasanuma, T., Hara, A.: Effects of the cone and edge on the acoustic characteristics of a cone loudspeaker, 21 May 2017. https://doi.org/10.1155/2017/2792376. Accessed 17 Sep 2019
2. Marttila, P., Jensen, M.J.H.: A hybrid electroacoustic lumped and finite element model for modeling loudspeakers drivers. In: AES International Conference, Helsinki, Finland, vol. 51 (2013)
3. Ramis, J., Carbajo, E., Segovia, E., Espí, A., Martínez, J.: Analysis of the dynamic behavior of a double suspension in a electrodynamic speaker. In: Tecni Acústica - Spanish Acoustics Congress, version. 42 (2011). (Spanish version)
4. Agudelo, D., Díaz, D., Ibarra, A., Cruel, C., Montoya, M., Hernández, C.: Mechanical characterization to tensile of deposition modeled PLA and ABS 3D prints. In: Development and Innovation in Engineering, vol. 4, pp. 497–507 (2019). (Spanish version)
5. Ted, K.: The Ear to Hell: a 3D Printed Re-Imagining of the Classic Audio Speaker, 15 June 2015. https://3dprint.com/72675/ear-to-hell-3d-printed-speaker/. Accessed 07 Nov 2019
6. Diedrich, B.M., Kautz, C.A., Roemer, D.F.: Square speaker. United States Patent US 7275620 B1, 02 Oct 2007
7. Irby, S.M., Doerring, W.O.: Ultra low frequency transducer and loud speaker comprising same. Unites States Patent US 8023688 B2, 11 Sep 2011
8. Meda, R.G.: Measurement of thiele small parameters for a given loudspeaker, without using box. In: AES Convention New York, vol. 91 (1991)
9. Ortega, B.P., Romero, M.R.: Acoustics boxes. In: Electroacoustics: Loudspeakers and Microphones, Madrid, PEARSON, pp. 239–256 (2003). (Spanish version)
10. Beranek, L.L.: Direct-radiator loudspeakers. In: Acoustics. HASA, New York, pp. 194–254 (1993)
11. Guerrero, A.: Continuous limit. Traveling and evanescent waves. In: Oscillations and Waves, Bogotá, National University of Colombia, pp. 133–138 (2005). (Spanish version)
12. Carrion, A.: Sound propagation in a closed room. In: Acoustic Design of Architectural Spaces, Madrid, UPC, pp. 49–70 (1998). (Spanish version)
13. Keele, D.B.: Low-frequency loudspeaker assessment by nearfield sound-pressure measurement. J. Audio Eng. Soc. 1, 154–162 (1980)

Computational Analysis to Design Loudspeakers with Nonconventional Forms

Esteban Polania Gutierrez[1], Mauricio Andrés Polochè Arango[2]([⊠]),
and Héctor Fabián Guarnizo Mendez[3]

[1] Sound Engineering, Universidad de San Buenaventura, Bogotá, Colombia
epolania@academia.usbbog.edu.co
[2] Electronic Engineering, Universidad de San Buenaventura, Bogotá, Colombia
mpoloche@usbbog.edu.co
[3] Electronic Engineering, Universidad El Bosque, Bogotá, Colombia
hguarnizo@unbosque.edu.co

Abstract. This word presents the study of the frequency response between two loudspeaker configurations, where the first is a conventional circular form and the second a nonconventional form with modification over its geometry. This analysis was done using the FEM computational ANSYS® software. This goal surged from the necessity to research how to improve the esthetic and electro-acoustical properties of a loudspeaker while the geometry of its diaphragm is modified and to get a new nonconventional loudspeaker models for the industry. A hendecagon loudspeaker model was simulated and compared to a conventional circular loudspeaker. The results presented were the modal analysis, harmonic response and frequency response.

Keywords: Loudspeaker · Simulation · Acoustic analysis · FEM

1 Introduction

The first electrodynamic transducer was patented by Ernst Siemens on December the 14 TH in 1877, but only Alexander Bell used this device to play audio when he patented the first telephone in 1876. In 1925 Rice and Kellogg Researchers from General Electric, established the basic principles for the voice coil loudspeaker as a direct radiator with a mass-controlled diaphragm and a uniform medium band radiation ability. In the design, they also included a power amplifier to work with the loudspeaker [1]. Since then, the original speaker design has been almost identical. Brands like Sony and Kicker have been risking with new loudspeaker diaphragms and surround designs like the Kicker Solo-baric L7 [2]. The difference in these speakers is that the diaphragm and surround geometry is square shaped. Hence the objective of this simulation is to analyze the changes in frequency response when diaphragm's geometry is modified, to seek for new models and to work as a guide to simulate loudspeakers using the FEM method. For the present paper a preliminary simulation stage is done to define the simulation parameters based on some criteria. Second, the simulation of the reference model with the data analysis. As third, a hendecagon loudspeaker simulation is realized, and results are presented for both models.

© Springer Nature Switzerland AG 2020
J. C. Figueroa-García et al. (Eds.): WEA 2020, CCIS 1274, pp. 139–150, 2020.
https://doi.org/10.1007/978-3-030-61834-6_13

2 Electroacoustic Concepts for Loudspeakers

2.1 Components of and Equivalent Circuit of a Loudspeaker

Today, exist a lot of different materials, voice coils, magnets, chassis and sizes of loud-speakers, as there are multiple different applications such as live, car audio, recording studios, home audio, industrial audio and biomedical devices. Each loudspeaker design has also a specific audio frequency range and a defined power level to supply these applications. *Frequency response* is the range capability that the loudspeaker possesses, depending on its size, materials, etc. [12]. The *directivity* radiation describes the sound pressure behavior in a 360° far field for 1 m distance from the source. *Sensitivity* describes the acoustical output power of the speaker at a given wattage input [1, 11]. The *Q factor* is a parameter that describe how underdamped, is an oscillator as the loudspeaker. Damping ratio is another parameter that describes the oscillation decaying in a system after a disturbance. It can be related as inversely proportional to the Q factor as described (1) [3].

$$\zeta = \frac{1}{2 * Q} \tag{1}$$

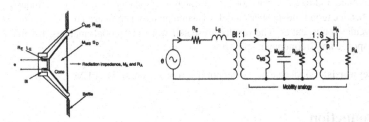

Fig. 1. The loudspeaker driver electro-mechano-acoustical transducer (Left). Equivalent electrical circuit with mobility analogy in mechanical and acoustical portions (Right) [4].

In Fig. 1, is presented the loudspeaker parts and the electro-mechano-acoustical equivalent circuit, were R_e is the electrical resistance of the voice coil, L_e is the voice coil inductance, Bl is the force factor, C_{ms} is the suspension mechanical compliance, Mms is the mechanical mass of the cone, R_{ms} is the mechanical damping, S is the cone area, M_a is the acoustic mass and R_a is the acoustic resistance.

2.2 FEM Simulation

The finite element method (FEM) or finite element analysis (FEA) is based on the idea of building complicated objects from smaller pieces making more manageable a mathematical analysis. This can be applied in solving mathematical models of many engineering problems, from structural analysis, to fluid dynamics, thermal analysis, etc. [5]. ANSYS® is one of these platforms designed for this purpose and is used in this work to analyze in a loudspeaker the modal, the harmonic response and the acoustic performance. This work takes like a reference a circular cone midrange loudspeaker model of 6.5″ from the commercial brand Challenger® that was disassembled to get the dimensions of each part of it. Next, the parts were designed and modeled in 3D CAD software and imported to ANSYS®. From this procedure, the dimensions of the diaphragm were the external diameter of the cone 130 mm, its height 25 mm, the voice coil diameter as 35 mm, the internal diameter of the diaphragm was 36 mm and to the external diameter an internal edge of 5 mm was added to allow the use of any regular loudspeaker surround. Using the same surround on both models implemented in simulation.

The computational simulation process is divided into two phases: first a mechanical part with two steps, analysis of *vibration modes* and *harmonic response*, and the second, *acoustic response* as shown in Fig. 2 [6].

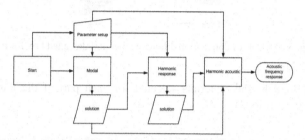

Fig. 2. Simulation workflow in ANSYS® Workbench.

Modal analysis is used to determine the vibration characteristics as natural frequencies and mode shapes of a structure; for this simulation, the basic equation solved in a typical undamped modal analysis is the eigenvalue problem, show in (2) [7]:

$$[K]\{\Phi_i\} = \omega_i^2[M]\{\Phi_i\} \tag{2}$$

Where K is the stiffness matrix, Φ_i is the mode shape vector (eigenvector of mode i), Ω_i is the natural circular frequency of mode i, ω_i^2 is the eigenvalue and M is the mass matrix. The harmonic response is a technique used to obtain the steady-state response of a linear structure to loads that vary sinusoidal with time, it allows to get a displacement versus frequency graph of the entire structure and the "peak" responses are stress reviewed. In this simulation the superposition method is used as it requires an initial modal analysis, it consist of the sum of eigenvectors from the previous modal analysis and in this case is faster than a full harmonic response, this is because the natural modes are already known during this analysis [8].

Lastly, the harmonic acoustics analysis is used to determine the steady-state response of a structure and the surrounding fluid medium to loads and excitations that vary sinusoidally with time. This module imports the velocity loads from the harmonic response using the modal analysis modes to interpolate them. The ruling equation are the acoustic and structural matrices coupled for fluid structure interaction problems as shows in (3).

$$\left(-\omega^2 \begin{bmatrix} Ms & 0 \\ P_0R^T & Mf \end{bmatrix} + j\omega \begin{bmatrix} C_s & 0 \\ 0 & C_f \end{bmatrix} + \begin{bmatrix} Ks & -R \\ 0 & Kf \end{bmatrix}\right)\begin{Bmatrix} u \\ p \end{Bmatrix} = \begin{Bmatrix} fs \\ Ff \end{Bmatrix} \tag{3}$$

Where P is the nodal pressure vector, u is the nodal displacement vector, Mf is the assembled fluid equivalent mass matrix, Kf is the assembled fluid equivalent stiffness matrix, Ms is the assembled structural mass matrix, Ks is the assembled structural stiffness matrix, Po is the density, R is the coupling matrix in the interface surface, Fs and Ff are the structural and fluid load vectors [9]. For the modal mechanical and the harmonic response five solids were defined: the box, the surround, the diaphragm, the spider and the dust-cap (Fig. 3).

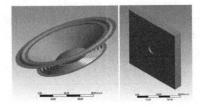

Fig. 3. Model for conventional loudspeaker and designed box for it.

Having the models, the materials selected for each part of the loudspeaker are presented in Table 1 (Fig. 4).

Fig. 4. Contacts loudspeaker parts.

The next step is the meshing of all solids; thus, it is necessary defining the frequency range for all the parts of the simulation. This will allow to find the sizing of the space between nodes for each mesh of the loudspeaker. Researching information about the disassembled loudspeaker allowed to determinate that its structure corresponds to a midrange loudspeaker, so, the frequency estimation is in the range of 60 Hz to 5 kHz, and such the computational analysis must be similar. Unfortunately, the software license of ANSYS® is limited, for this reason the computational simulation was implemented in the range of 20 Hz to 1 kHz. Achieving this, the procedure of determining the mesh size for the loudspeaker parts was with a maximum quantity of 10 elements per wavelength for the maximum frequency of the sine sweep according to (4) and (5).

Table 1. Loudspeaker materials.

	Diaphragm	Surround	Spider	Dust cap	Box
Material	PLA	Polyethylene foam	Polyester flexible	Paper	Plywood
Density (g/cm^3)	1.2550	0.032900	1.1010	0.89720	0.74800
Young modulus (MPa)	3447	0.84900	300	2828	6320
Mass (g)	13.407	0.15877	9.3196	1.5681	7612.5

$$\lambda = \frac{343.2\,\text{m/s}}{1600\,\text{Hz}} = 0.2145\,\text{m} \tag{4}$$

$$EPW = \frac{0.2145\,\text{m}}{10} = 0.02145\,\text{m} \tag{5}$$

Where EPW is the number of *Elements per Wavelength*. Thus, the distance between each node element must be 21.45 mm for the cone, the surround and the dust-cap that shares similar dimensions but in the simulation this is not possible because the real size of the speaker is too tiny to get an acceptable mesh, then, 100 elements are going to be used and corresponds to 2.145 mm. This was selected due to the quality of the mesh obtained while meshing these parts (Fig. 5).

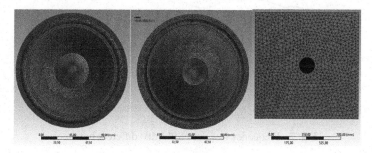

Fig. 5. Diaphragm, dust-cap and surround mesh and loudspeaker box mesh.

To avoid the acoustics short circuit (that is when the frontal and rear sound waves emitted from the diaphragm motion, encounter out of phase cancelling the low frequency response of a loudspeaker) [10] in free space by the loudspeaker radiation, a box was implemented too, being a huge part, the sizing was of 35.75 mm that corresponds to 6 elements per wavelength and this is enough to have appreciable results for the simulation. To the loudspeaker, a force was applied taking into consideration the force of a real 8 Ω voice coil. The force factor *BL* of this commercial loudspeaker is 7.949 N/A with a 120 mm diameter magnet, doing a relation with another magnet of 100 mm considering the current for a power of 1 W, the new force of 2.34 N was estimated, Fig. 6 shows the force applied.

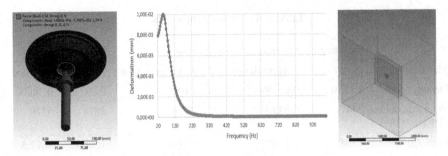

Fig. 6. Harmonic response force exerted on the spider (Left), Harmonic response, speaker deformation (Center), air enclosure (Right).

Implemented the simulation, the obtained result for the loudspeaker in terms of deformation is shown in Fig. 6. To be able to make an acoustic analysis, an air enclosure was made. The given dimensions should be at least be 2 times the wavelength of the maximum frequency used for the analysis. As the wavelength for 1 kHz at 20 °C is 343.3 mm, the size of the enclosure is 686.4 mm from the box surfaces, see Fig. 6. Finally, this procedure were applied to three plywood boxes to choose the best performance, an infinite baffle, a closed box of 50 L, and a closed box of 100 L, as show in Fig. 7.

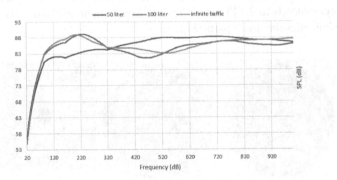

Fig. 7. Frequency response SPL (dB) different boxes.

As show the Fig. 7, the low frequency response for the 100 L box and the infinite baffle was acceptable, this can be due to the air volume that is big enough to avoid a rising on the acoustic compliance; instead, the 50 L box raised the resonant frequency making the low response deficient. The infinite baffle had the best result of the three, the frequency response was the most homogeneous presenting the less peak and valley variations. Thus, the 100 L box had a big valley around the 420 Hz and 520 Hz range. As the infinite baffle is known for not altering significantly loudspeaker frequency response it will be the one used for all the simulations. (The infinite baffle design was taken from the IEC 268-5 and the AES2-1984 for the sizing relations). Table 2 show the final parameter implemented in the computational analysis.

Table 2. Simulation parameters.

Heading level	Font size and style
Mechanical mass without voice coil	13.407 ± 1 g
Diaphragm, surround, dust cap mesh	2.145 mm
E. distance box mesh	35.75 mm
E. distance spider mesh	1.5 mm
Box type	Infinite baffle
Box fixed supports	8 faces
Fixed supports for surround and spider	2 faces
Frequency range modal	20 Hz–1600 Hz
Number of modes	600
Frequency range harmonic response	20 Hz–1000 Hz
Number of steps	1000
Force exerted on the spider	2.34 N
Damping ratio	0.454
Equivalent Q for damping ratio	1,1
E. distance enclosure	85.8 mm
Frequency range Harmonic acoustic	20 Hz–1000 Hz
Number of steps	400
Temperature	20 °C
Step type	Logarithmic
Enclosure axis size	686.4 mm

3   Model 1. Circular Reference Loudspeaker

In this section, the reference model is simulated based on the last section parameters; this design was made in base of a real 6.5″ loudspeaker model. The only difference is the diaphragm material, this will affect the mass of the system, Fig. 8 shows the 3D model of the loudspeaker reference. Using PLA for the cone, a mechanical mass of 13.407 g was achieved, this means that the resonant frequency will lower a bit, considering a normal paper diaphragm weight around 9 g and 11 g.

3.1   Vibration Modes Model 1. Reference Diaphragm

The most important vibration modes found on this section as show in Fig. 8. The first mode correspond to the resonant frequency and is the natural deformation movement of the loudspeaker, and the second mode, confirm a non-natural deformation.

Hence, the frequency 84.672 Hz could be the resonant frequency for this system without considering harmonic and acoustic parameters.

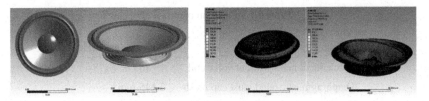

Fig. 8. Reference circular loudspeaker model (Left), first and second modes (Right).

3.2 Harmonic Response Model 1. Reference Diaphragm

An already defined force of 2.34 N is used over the spider. The deformation results are consequence of this force. The Fig. 9 shows the spider colliding with the diaphragm at the 458.08 Hz meaning that the spider center is out of phase meanwhile the resonant frequency is clearly in phase.

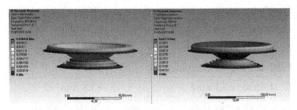

Fig. 9. Total deformation frequency of 458.06 Hz (Left), resonant frequency of 78.8 Hz (Right).

3.3 Acoustic Response Model 1. Reference Diaphragm

With the data from the harmonic response, the amplitude decay around the problematic frequency is expected. Then, the results for the frequency response are show in Fig. 10.

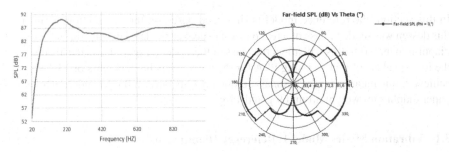

Fig. 10. Frequency response, reference model SPL (dB) (Left), directivity at resonant frequency SPL (dB) (Right).

The resonant frequency moved to 190.72 Hz; the spider design could be the reason for this erratic behavior; the problematic frequency found on the harmonic response created a problem around the 530 Hz frequency as seen in the valley from the Fig. 10. In Fig. 10, there are wave cancelations because the infinite baffle does not have a box to contain the back waves generated by the loudspeaker. These are evident in the 90° and 270° angles. As the speaker is not centered in the plywood wall, there is a cancelation in the 30° angle. Also, a dipole behavior can be seen in the overall directivity of the speaker.

These results are considered satisfactory as a real speaker with a $Q = 1.1$ corresponds to a strong oscillation pattern with a heavy amplification around the resonant frequency.

4   Model 2. Hendecagon Loudspeaker

The hendecagon is a polygon with 11 faces, the reason to choose this geometric figure is that there are not any parallel faces, the goal of this decision is to avoid any vibration mode that could be the result of a parallel face. Also, a hendecagon polygon was added to the center of the diaphragm and was rotated to make the vertices take form of helixes while extruding the solid in the 3D design software. As shown in Fig. 11.

The Fig. 11 shows that the diaphragm has a little edge where the surround is bonded, to maintain the same effective surface as the reference model and to easily connect the surround. This allowed to keep the mechanical mass almost equal to the reference model. The mechanical mass was 13.229 g with a 0.177 g difference, almost nothing, but could rise the resonant frequency.

4.1   Vibration Modes Model 2. Hendecagon Loudspeaker

The Fig. 11 shows the first mode corresponding to the resonant frequency and is the natural deformation movement of the hendecagon loudspeaker, and the second mode, confirm a non-natural deformation.

 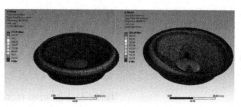

Fig. 11. Hendecagon model (Left), hendecagon first and second mode (Right).

4.2   Harmonic Response Model 2. Hendecagon Loudspeaker

The Fig. 12 shows that at the problematic frequency the spider is not entirely colliding, but it still is out of phase, meaning that the performance may be better than the reference loudspeaker.

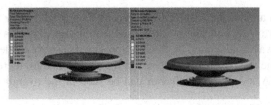

Fig. 12. Total deformation frequency of 458.06 Hz (Left), resonant frequency of 80.76 Hz (Right).

4.3 Acoustic Response Hendecagon Loudspeaker

For this case, the resonant frequency was of 194.49 Hz, it raised as expected. In the Fig. 13, the frequency response observed is similar in behavior to the reference model, there is a problematic valley in the 550 Hz mark caused by the spider design and material.

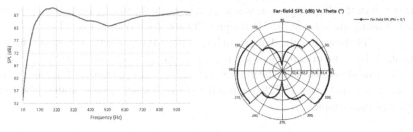

Fig. 13. Frequency response SPL (dB) Hendecagon loudspeaker (Left), directivity Resonant frequency SPL (dB) (Right).

A dipole behavior is shown, nothing different from the reference speaker with its same infinite baffle problems as the cancelations in the same angles.

5   Results

In the results comparison, the following modal differences are presented in Table 3.

Table 3. Vibration modes comparison.

Model	Speaker system modes	Diaphragm modes	Spider modes	Total
Reference	9	7	8	24
Hendecagon	7	6	9	22

In the Table 3, the speaker system modes refer to those modes found present in the overall speaker deformation, meanwhile the other modes from the other columns are from the ones that only where present in the parts without affecting the whole speaker deformation. These results show that the hendecagon presented less vibration modes than the reference model, this could be because the 11 vertices inclusion allowed to increase the diaphragm rigidity. The Fig. 14 show an important difference between the hendecagon and the reference loudspeaker:

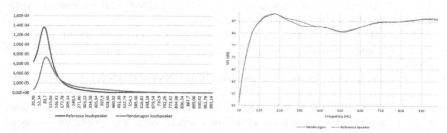

Fig. 14. Frequency response deformation comparison in mm (Left), acoustic frequency response comparison (Right).

Where the reference loudspeaker deformed more on its resonant frequency with a more visible decay after the peak, the hendecagon rigidity made it deform lesser, making the resonant frequency rise. Finally, for the acoustic comparison the Fig. 14 compares the overall performance of both speakers. Where the valley around the 550 Hz is present in the two models, but the hendecagon proved to have a better response toward the 320 Hz and the 1 kHz range. This is because the spider erratic behavior affected more the reference model than the hendecagon, a reason for this, could be that the lower mass made the spider deform less; although, the reference speaker deformed more, the hendecagon had a better sensitivity at the resonant frequency.

6 Conclusions

The speakers behave in a proper way to reality, as the $Q = 1.1$ corresponds to a Chebyshev filter response; the acoustic analysis results, show a tendency to strongly amplify the resonant frequency with marked peaks and valleys that denotes oscillations characteristic of an underdamped system. Both speakers performance were significatively worsened due to the spider design that altered their 550 Hz response; even more, in the reference model than in the hendecagon loudspeaker. This difference could be because the second model is lighter and more rigid. It can be estimated that is important to reduce the vibration modes quantity from the diaphragm, this can be achieved during the speaker design by choosing a more rigid material or adding a great quantity of vertices to the model. To get a better frequency response, is essential to combine these two characteristics and to try to maintain a low mass for the diaphragm. The use of the infinite baffle was effective to measure the frequency response but will not get satisfactory results in the directivity field, as there are wave cancelations at both sides. If a better computational engine is available, it's better to put the infinite baffle in the wall structure to avoid these cancelations and to get more realistic results.

References

1. Romero, M.R., Ortega, B.P.: Electroacústica: Altavoces y microfonos. Pearson Education S.A., Madrid (2003)
2. Irby, S.M., Doering, O.: Ultra low frequency transducer and loudspeaker comprising same. United States Patent US 7,916,890 B2, 29 March 2011
3. Siebert, W.M.: Circuits, Signals, and Systems. MIT Press, United States (1985)
4. Eargle, J.: Loudspeaker Handbook, p. 11. Springer Science & Business Media, New York (2013)
5. Liu, Y., Chen, X.: Finite Element and Simulation with ANSYS Workbench. CRC Press, Boca Raton (2014)
6. ANSYS, Inc.: «ANSYS HELP,» ANSYS, Inc. https://ansyshelp.ansys.com/account/secured?returnurl=/Views/Secured/corp/v201/en/wb_sim/ds_simulation_types.html. Accessed 26 May 2020
7. ANSYS Inc.: ANSYS Mechanical APDL Structural Analysis Guide 15, Southpointe (2013)
8. Harmonic Response Analysis of a Crankshaft. Int. J. Emerg. Technol. Adv. Eng. 5(6), 323–327 (2015)
9. ANSYS Inc.: Mechanical APDL acoustic analysis guide Release 15.0. ANSYS, Southpointe (2013)
10. Kuttruff, H.: «Acoustics an Introduction,» de Acoustics an Introduction, p. 411. CRC Press, Boca Raton (2007)
11. Hill, G.: «Loudspeaker Modelling and Design: A Practical Introduction,» de Loudspeaker Modelling and Design: A Practical Introduction, p. 82. Routledge, Milton Park (2018)
12. Dickanson, V.: Loudspeaker Design Cookbook. Audio Amateur Press, Peterborough (2006)

Optimization

Solving an Urban Goods Distribution Problem as the 2E-CVRP Model Using a MILP-based Decomposition Approach

Angie Ramirez-Villamil[1] , Jairo R. Montoya-Torres[2]([✉]) ,
and Anicia Jaegler[3]

[1] Maestría en Diseño y Gestión de Procesos, Universidad de La Sabana,
km 7 autopista norte de Bogota, D.C., Chia, Colombia
angieravi@unisabana.edu.co
[2] School of Engineering, Universidad de La Sabana,
km 7 autopista norte de Bogota, D.C., Chia, Colombia
jairo.montoya@unisabana.edu.co
[3] Kedge Business School, 40 Avenue des Terroirs de France, 75012 Paris, France
anicia.jaegler@kedgebs.com

Abstract. Distribution of goods in urban areas are complex logistics problems. To avoid the negative impacts of trucks within cities, Urban Distribution Centers (UDC) located at the periphery allows goods delivery by smaller vehicles. The problem can be modeled as a two-echelon vehicle routing problem. Since the problem is known to be NP-hard, metaheuristics have mainly been proposed in the literature. In this paper instead a solution approach based on mathematical programming is proposed. Experiments are carried out using real data from the distribution network of a convenience store company in Bogota, Colombia. Results show the impact of analyzing different network structures.

Keywords: Urban logistics · Two-echelon distribution network · Decomposition approach

1 Introduction

The urban distribution of goods is essential for the economic development of cities. However, it is one of the main generators of traffic congestion and interferes with the rest of the urban activities in terms of the use of public space [2]. As urban areas have increased in their population, the number of vehicles circulating in the cities has grown. Every day, hundreds of trucks must arrive into the cities to deliver the products to fulfill the demand. The amount of CO_2 that these trucks emit to the environment is very high and affects the quality of the air. Likewise, traffic jams also increases. This generates higher fuel consumption and

Work supported by Universidad de La Sabana under a master by research scholarship awarded to the first author, and by grant INGPHD-10-2019.

CO_2 emissions [5, 24, 30]. In addition, distribution-related costs make up about 10.5% of the U.S. economy and about 20% of the cost of manufacturing [7]. Hence, considerable efforts of the scientific community have aimed at designing efficient optimization models and algorithms capable of providing support to logistics decision-makers.

To face these issues and seeking for more efficiency of the logistics system and to reduce negative externalities of transport activities, the concept of logistics centers appeared offering services such as storage and consolidation-deconsolidation of goods, but adding value [2, 22]. One kind of these urban logistics spaces is the Urban Distribution Center (UDC), which is a facility that is located in the proximity of an urban area, allowing the consolidation and distribution of goods before delivering within the city. When the shipments are consolidated, a UDC can perform the last-mile delivery more efficiently than individual carriers [6].

When designing the last-mile distribution network, the most employed model is the two-echelon distribution system. The problem consists on delivering goods from one depot to a set of satellites and from there to a set of geographically dispersed customers. In the case of the capacitated version (2E-CVRP, two-echelon capacitated vehicle routing problem), each echelon is served by its own identical (heterogeneous) fleet of vehicles, those of the second echelon being smaller, but all with limited loading capacity. Satellites are capacitated also and can be visited by one or more 1st-level vehicles while the customers must be visited by only one 2nd-level vehicles [16].

The scientific literature has defined the two-echelon distribution problem as "a class of problems that study how to optimally route freight in two-echelon distribution systems, possibly considering also location decisions" ([12], page 185). Different applications have been reported in the academic literature, such as city logistics, multi-modal transportation, postal and parcel delivery, milk collection, press and grocery distribution; being city logistics probably the most frequently cited application [9, 12]. Several reviews of literature have been published. Two-echelon freight transportation optimization problems are analyzed in [15] with the aim at identifying the main concepts and issues, while other review papers deal with the presence of intermediate facilities in distribution networks [18], multi-echelon issues not explicitly related to goods routing [27], and two-echelon location and routing problems [12]. A review of multi-echelon distribution systems for city logistics problems is presented in [21].

Several variants of the 2E-VRP have been studied, including time windows (2E-VRPTW) [13], with satellite synchronization (2E-VRP-SS) [17], with multiple depots where the satellites are served by more than one depot, or with pickup and deliveries (2E-VRPPD) [4]. Integer-linear programming (ILP) formulations (without providing solution procedures) for the 2E-VRP with multiple depots, multiple products, heterogeneous fleet and time windows are presented in [9]. Problem-specific and branch-and-bound algorithms are proposed in [3, 20, 25, 26]. Meta-heuristics, such as GRASP (greedy randomized adaptive search procedure), ALNS () and multi-start heuristics are presented in [8, 10, 11, 19].

According to the current state of the research, approaches to solve the 2E-VRP are based on exact algorithms and meta-heuristics, also dealing mainly with experimental settings using benchmark instances using random-generated data. So, as pointed out in [31], one of the most relevant opportunities for research regarding the 2E-VRP is concerned with more real-life issues. In addition, mathematical-based solution procedures are scarce. Hence, the objective of this paper is to solve an application of the 2E-VRP in urban distribution of goods arising in the mega-city of Bogota, Colombia. The case study research approach is followed [32], in which the distribution problem of a company of convenience stores is analyzed, as described later in Sect. 2. The problem is modeled as a 2E-CVRP, which is known to be NP-hard. Because of this, an approximation algorithm is proposed, based on the decomposition of the problem in tractable subproblems, where each of them solved using mathematical programming. As objective functions, we consider both the minimization of travel time. Numerical experiments are run using real data for the delivery of goods to convenience stores in the city of Bogota, Colombia.

This paper is organized as follows. Section 2 describes the problem under study. Section 3 presents the proposed solution approach. Section 4 analyzes the results of numerical experiments based on a real-life application for a well-known brand of convenience stores (mini-markets) in the city of Bogota, Colombia. The paper ends in Sect. 5 by presenting some concluding remarks and outlining opportunities for further research.

2   Problem Description

Researchers and practitioners have proposed different strategies to deal with urban distribution of goods. Some of them include direct delivery of goods to customers or the use of delivery facilities such as depots, urban distribution centers or warehouses. This last consists on temporary storage of finished goods before being delivered to the final customer using its own fleet of vehicles or a third-party logistics provider or a mix of both.

For the purpose of this work, the case of a well-known brand of convenience stores (that is, like a mini-market) is studied. The delivery network is composed of a set of central depots located at the borders of the city, named urban distribution center (UDC), a set of smaller satellites depots located within the city and a set of sales points where customers buy the products. Goods are first delivered from the UDC to the satellites, and from there to the sales points. An example of the distribution network is shown in Fig. 1. This scenario can be implemented in some companies to reduce the travel distance between the depot and the clients, so that operational cost can be reduced too. This also contributes to the reduction of the number of big trucks in cities, which at the same time would minimize the invasion of the public space during freight unloading and consequently, it could decrease traffic congestion in cities.

This approach in urban freight delivery can be modeled as a 2E-CVRP, as proposed in [16]. This paper deals with the deterministic version of the problem, which is known to be NP-hard [26], since it reduces to a vehicle routing problem, meaning that obtaining optimal solution for large-sized datasets is likely hard when using exact algorithms. So, approximation solution procedures, based on heuristics or meta-heuristics are preferred.

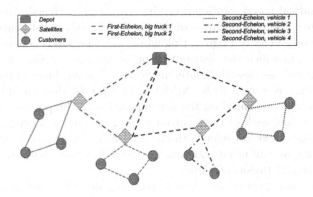

Fig. 1. An example of a two-echelon network system.

3   Solution Approach

As pointed out before, due to the NP-hardness of the 2E-CVRP, approximate algorithms are good solution approaches to find good solutions. Exact methods based in mathematical programming allow to optimally solve small-sized instances, as well as some parts of the problem. Real-life problems are very complex, but heuristic solution approaches allow the generation of high-quality solutions in relatively short computational times.

A flow diagram of the proposed solution approach consists is shown in Fig. 2. The 2E-CVRP is solved using an MILP-based decomposition algorithm. The decomposition algorithm splits the problem into four sub-problems to reduce its complexity, but aggregates them and their corresponding results to guarantee the quality and feasibility of the solutions. The first sub-problem is to find a set of routes starting from the depot to serve the satellites (first-echelon); the second one is the vehicle allocation to satellites; the third sub-problem is to cluster the clients to the satellites, and the last sub-problem solves the VRP from the satellites to serve the corresponding clients (second-echelon VRP).

3.1   Routing from Depots to Satellites and Vehicle Allocation to Satellites

This sub-section explains in more detail the mathematical models employed to solve the first two sub-problems. This subsection first presents the mathematical formulation for the VRP of the first level. The VRP is solved using the

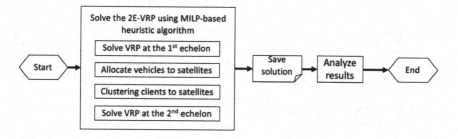

Fig. 2. Flow chart of the solution algorithm.

mixed-integer linear programming (MILP) model. Let i be the set of depots, $i = \{1, \ldots, n\}$; j be the set of satellites, $j = \{1, \ldots, m\}$; and k be the set of vehicles, $k = \{1, \ldots, l\}$. Sets h and f are also needed as alias of set j.

We define binary decision variables as follows: $A_i = 1$ if the depot i is opened, and 0 otherwise; $X_{ijk} = 1$ if the depot i serves the satellite j with vehicle k, and 0 otherwise; $Y_{jik} = 1$ if vehicle k goes from satellite j to depot i, and 0 otherwise; and $B_{jhk} = 1$ if vehicle k goes from satellite j to satellite h, and 0 otherwise. Auxiliary variables U_j are also defined to allow defining subtour elimination constraints.

The parameters of the model are: v is the speed of vehicles, De_j is the demand of satellite j, $CapT$ is the total loading capacity of a vehicle, N is the fleet size, M is the total number of satellites in the network, D_{ij} and DC_{jh} are the distances respectively between depot i and satellite j and between satellites j and h. The mathematical model is presented next. The objective function computes the minimization of the travel times:

$$
\min \sum_i \sum_j \sum_k \left(\frac{1}{v} D_{ij} X_{ijk} \right) + \sum_j \sum_i \sum_k \left(\frac{1}{v} D_{ji} Y_{jik} \right)
$$
$$
+ \sum_j \sum_h \sum_k \left(\frac{1}{v} DC_{jh} B_{jhk} \right) \tag{1}
$$

Constraints are described next. Constraints (2) ensure that only one depot is opened. Constraints (3) ensure that if the depot is opened it is possible to send freight from it. Constraints (4) ensure that one vehicle must leave the depot to do the routing. Constraints (5) ensure that if satellite j is served from depot i this route must be continued to another customer h with the same vehicle k. Constraints (6) define the route sequence per vehicle. Constraints (7) force that all satellites to be visited exactly once. Constraints (8) define that after a satellite is visited, the vehicle goes to another satellite or returns to the depot. Constraints (9) ensure that each route must start and end at the depot. Constraints (10) ensure that the maximum capacity of vehicles is not violated. Constraints (11) correspond to sub-tour elimination. Constraints (12) ensure that each vehicle has only one route. Constraints (13) ensure binary values of decision variables.

$$\sum_i A_i = 1 \tag{2}$$

$$N \times A_i \geq \sum_j \sum_k X_{ijk} \qquad\qquad \forall i \tag{3}$$

$$\sum_i \sum_j \sum_k X_{ijk} = 1 \tag{4}$$

$$\sum_i X_{ijk} = \sum_h B_{jhk} \qquad\qquad \forall j, k \tag{5}$$

$$\sum_i X_{ijk} + \sum_h B_{hjk} = \sum_i Y_{ijk} + \sum_f B_{jfk} \qquad\qquad \forall j, k \tag{6}$$

$$\sum_j \sum_k B_{jhk} = 1 - \sum_i \sum_k X_{ihk} \qquad\qquad \forall h \tag{7}$$

$$\sum_h \sum_k B_{jhk} = 1 - \sum_i \sum_k Y_{jik} \qquad\qquad \forall j \tag{8}$$

$$\sum_j X_{ijk} = \sum_j Y_{jik} \qquad\qquad \forall i, k \tag{9}$$

$$\sum_i \sum_j X_{ijk} De_j + \sum_h \sum_j B_{hjk} De_j \leq CapT \qquad\qquad \forall k \tag{10}$$

$$U_j - U_h + M \times B_{jhk} \leq M - 1 \qquad\qquad \forall j, h, k \tag{11}$$

$$\sum_i \sum_j X_{ijk} \leq 1 \qquad\qquad \forall k \tag{12}$$

$$A_i, X_{ijk}, Y_{jik}, B_{jhk}, \in \{0, 1\} \qquad\qquad \forall i, j, h, k \tag{13}$$

The allocation model of vehicles to satellites (second sub-problem) is solved using the allocation model proposed in [23].

3.2   Routing from Satellites to Clients

This section explains the last two sub-problems. In the third sub-problem, a clustering of the clients is made to allocate that clients to a specific satellite with a given coverage range. The model used for this clustering is the same as the used in the first sub-problem and it was based on the allocation model in [23]. Furthermore, to solve the VRP in the second echelon (last sub-problem) the previous mathematical formulation is employed, but some changes in both sets and binary variables are required. Thus, the VRP model of the second-level has the following sets: i corresponds to satellites and j corresponds to clients, while k remains to be the set of vehicles. Binary variables are defined as: $A_i = 1$ if the satellite is opened, and 0 otherwise; $X_{ijk} = 1$ if satellite i serves client j with vehicle k, and 0 otherwise; $Y_{jik} = 1$ if vehicle k goes from client j to satellite i, and 0 otherwise; and $B_{jhk} = 1$ if vehicle k goes from client j to client h, and 0 otherwise.

4   Numerical Experiments

Since the problem under study was inspired by a real-life situation of urban distribution of goods in Bogota, Colombia, numerical experiments were run using real locations from a recognized brand of retail stores, whose name is kept confidential. This company owns 94 stores in Bogota, D.C and 2 distribution centers (depots) outside the city. Figure 3 shows the geographical distribution of the nodes (UDC, satellites and stores). Bogota is the largest city in Colombia and also its capital. The population of Bogota is approximately 7.1 million inhabitants according to the last census [14]. We selected Bogota as the city under study because its configuration and size allow to have a complex scenario that can be an example of the behavior of cities with similar characteristics. The locations of the selected convenience stores were collected using Google Maps^{TM}. The origin-destination matrix with actual driving distances was obtained through Google Maps^{TM} Distance Matrix API, the shortest path was selected for calculations, following the approach proposed in [23,28]. We chose two types of vehicles: for the first-level, the JMC Carrying Plus, with 3.5 tons of payload, while for the second-level, the selected vehicle was the Renault Kangoo Van, with 750 kg of payload [29]. It is also assumed that availability of the necessary vehicles fleet achieves a 100% of service level.

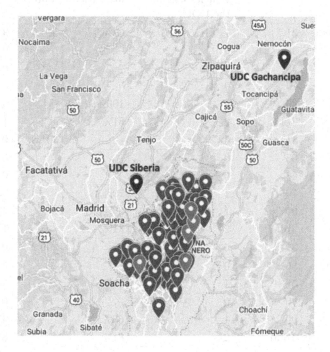

Fig. 3. Geographical distribution of nodes for the case study.

In order to compute the actual travel times, we used the value of the mean travel speed in the city that is 20 km/h, according the data reported by the Secretariat of Mobility [1]. Deterministic customers demand was generated from a normal distribution with $\mu = 60$ and $\sigma^2 = 6.6/De_i$. Satellites act as both satellite and store at the same time. Finally, different scenarios that results of the combination of both deposits and the use of each one separately (Gachancipa alone, Siberia alone, and Gachancipa-Siberia), with 5 satellites and the 94 stores were generated. In order to replicate the experiments, full origin-destination matrix and travel times sets are available upon request to the corresponding author of this paper.

The proposed procedure MILP models were coded in GAMS (General Algebraic Modeling System). Experiments were run on a personal computer with processor Intel® Core™ i3 CPU at 2.3 GHz and 8 GB RAM. Results of the experiments are presented in Tables 1 and 2. The former is devoted to the show the performance of the first echelon, while the latter shows the results for the second echelon.

Table 1. Results for the first echelon: routing from UDC to satellites

UDC location	Satellite ID	Number of vehicles leaving the UDC	% vehicle utilization	Time of route	Distance
Gachancipa	31	1	63%	274.5	33.5
	35	0	–		0
	58	0	–		0
	70	0	–		0
	90	1	100%		96.4
	Total	2	81%		129.9
Siberia	31	0	-	361.8	0
	35	0	–		0
	58	0	–		0
	70	1	79%		73.9
	90	1	83%		46.7
	Total	2	81%		120.6
Gachancipa & Siberia	31	0	0	250.2	0
	35	0	–		0
	58	1	100%		36
	70	0	–		0
	90	1	63%		47.2
	Total	2	81%		83.4

Table 2. Results for the second echelon: routing from satellites to clients

UDC location	Satellite ID	Number of vehicles leaving the satellite	% utilization vehicle 1	% utilization vehicle 2	Average utilization	Time of route (2nd echelon)	Distance (2nd echelon)	Number of served nodes	Served demand	Total distance
Gachancipa	31	1	88%	-	88%	228	76	12	722	109.5
	35	2	98%	90%	94%	288.9	96.3	24	1469	96.3
	58	2	71%	94%	83%	267.3	89.1	22	1298	89.1
	70	2	97%	91%	94%	250.8	83.6	24	1472	83.6
	90	1	89%	-	89%	203.7	67.9	12	724	164.3
	Total	8	89%	92%	90%	1238.7	412.9	94	5685	542.8
Siberia	31	1	88%	-	88%	228	76	12	722	76
	35	2	98%	90%	94%	288.9	96.3	24	1469	96.3
	58	2	71%	94%	83%	267.3	89.1	22	1298	89.1
	70	2	97%	91%	94%	250.8	83.6	24	1472	157.5
	90	1	89%	-	89%	203.7	67.9	12	724	114.6
	Total	8	89%	92%	90%	1238.7	412.9	94	5685	533.5
Gachancipa & Siberia	31	1	88%	-	88%	228	76	12	722	76
	35	2	98%	90%	94%	288.9	96.3	24	1469	96.3
	58	2	71%	94%	83%	267.3	89.1	22	1298	125.3
	70	2	97%	91%	94%	250.8	83.6	24	1472	83.6
	90	1	89%	-	89%	203.7	67.9	12	724	115.1
	Total	8	89%	92%	90%	1238.7	412.9	94	5685	496.3

In the first echelon, for all escenarios, two vehicles depart from the depot to the satellites. When using both UDC, Gachancipa and Siberia, there is a vehicle that goes from Gachancipa to satellite 58 and another one from Siberia to satellite 90 where the corresponding route begins. The average loading vehicle utilization rate is 81%, allowing some space if clients' demand increases. Results also show that the scenario that considers the use of both UDCs is the one that provides the shortest travel time which is 250.2 min and a traveled distance of 83.4 km. This may occur because these UDCs are located in different areas of the city (as shown previously in Fig. 3), and at the moment of distribution to the satellites, each one will make the delivery of freight to the nearby satellites. When only one UDC is used, either the located in Siberia or the one in Gachancipa, the vehicles must cross the city to supply the satellites located far away, thus increasing the distance traveled and the travel time.

As for the second echelon (distribution from satellites to clients or stores), results shown that distribution is not affected by the UDC from which the goods are supplied. The fleet size is 8 vehicles, which are able to satisfy the whole demand, with an average vehicle utilization rate of 90%. So, if customer demand increases, the distribution networks is still able to satisfy that demand without the need to incur in additional costs to include a new vehicle, human resources or travel costs for higher fuel consumption. Finally, the scenario that allows the total distribution of the goods to all the clients in a minimum total travel time of 1488.9 min and a minimum total traveled distance of 496.3 km is the one that includes the use of both UDCs (Gachancipa and Siberia), while the other two configurations obtain travel times of 1513.2 min and 1600.5 min when departing respectively from Gachancipa or Siberia.

5   Conclusions and Further Work

This paper studied a goods distribution problem in an urban setting inspired from a real case of convenience stores in the city of Bogota, Colombia, where Urban Distribution Centers (UDC) located at the periphery of the city are used to delivery goods to satellite facilities, and then to final sales points where customers can buy the products. The problem was modeled as a two-echelon vehicle routing problem with limited capacity of both vehicles and satellites (2E-CVRP). A heuristic procedure based on decomposing the problem in four sub-problems is applied. Each sub-problem was solved using mathematical programming to obtain their optimal solutions. The global approach finally searched to guarantee feasibility of the integrated solution. Numerical experiments were carried out using real data. Results were analyzed in terms of the impact of using either one or both of the urban distribution centers already available for delivery to the satellites.

Further research will study the problem in several lines. Since the proposed solution approach is used to generate a solution to the problem, the first line for further research will address the design of improvement heuristics. In a second line, other characteristics can be included, such as delivery time windows and heterogeneous fleet of vehicles. The inclusion of time windows will approach the model to more realistic situations in which the supply of goods is constrained by certain delivery schedules, while the heterogenous fleet can include the use of both electric and gasoline-based vehicles or vehicles with different loading capacities at any of the echelons. Another interesting line for further research is the inclusion of uncertainty, such as stochastic demand or variable travel speed.

References

1. Alcaldía Mayor de Bogotá. Programa de gestión de la velocidad para Bogotá - Documento base (2019). Alcaldí de Bogotá, Colombia
2. Antun, J.P.: Distribución Urbana de Mercancías: Estrategias con Centros Logísticos. Nota técnica IDB-TN-167, Banco Interamericano de Desarrollo (2013)
3. Baldacci, R., Mingozzi, A., Roberti, R., Wolfler Calvo, R.: An exact algorithm for the two-echelon capacitated vehicle routing problem. Oper. Res. **2**, 298–314 (2013)
4. Belgin, O., Karaoglan, I., Altiparmak, F.: Two-echelon vehicle routing problem with simultaneous pickup and delivery: mathematical model and heuristic approach. Comput. Ind. Eng. **115**, 1–16 (2017)
5. Benjelloun, A., Crainic, T.G., Bigras, Y.: Towards a taxonomy of City Logistics projects. Procedia Soc. Behav. Sci. **2**(3), 6217–6228 (2010)
6. Browne, M., Sweet, M., Woodburn, A., Allen, J.: Urban Freight Consolidation Centres: Final Report. Transport Studies Group, University of Westminster (2005)
7. Chopra, S., Meindl, P.: Supply Chain Management: Strategy, Planning, and Operation. Prentice Hall, Upper Saddle River (2009)
8. Crainic, T.G., Mancini, S., Perboli, G., Tadei, R.: Clustering-based heuristics for the two-echelon vehicle routing problem. Technical report CIRRELT-2008-46 (2008)
9. Crainic, T.G., Ricciardi, N., Storchi, G.: Models for evaluating and planning city logistics systems. Transp. Sci. **43**, 432–54 (2009)
10. Crainic, T.G., Mancini, S., Perboli, G., Tadei, R.: Multi-start heuristics for the two-echelon vehicle routing problem. In: Merz, P., Hao, J.-K. (eds.) EvoCOP 2011. LNCS, vol. 6622, pp. 179–190. Springer, Heidelberg (2011). https://doi.org/10.1007/978-3-642-20364-0_16
11. Crainic, T.G., Mancini, S., Perboli, G., Tadei, R.: GRASP with path relinking for the two-echelon vehicle routing problem. In: Di Gaspero, L., Schaerf, A., Stutzle, T. (eds.) Advances in Metaheuristics. Operations Research/Computer Science Interfaces Series, vol. 53, pp. 113–25. Springer, Heidelberg (2013). https://doi.org/10.1007/978-1-4614-6322-1_7
12. Cuda, R., Guastaroba, G., Speranza, M.G.: A survey on two-echelon routing problems. Comput. Oper. Res. **55**, 185–199 (2015)
13. Dellaert, N., Dashty, F., Van Woensel, T., Crainic, T.G.: Branch & price based algorithms for the two-echelon vehicle routing problem with time windows. Transp. Sci. **53**(2), 463–479 (2016)
14. Departamento Administrativo Nacional de Estadistica. 'Cuantos somos' Censo Nacional de Colombia (2018). https://www.dane.gov.co/index.php/estadisticas-por-tema/demografia-y-poblacion/censo-nacional-de-poblacion-y-vivenda-2018/cuantos-somos. Accessed 1 April 2020
15. Gonzalez-Feliu, J.: Two-echelon freight transport optimization: unifying concepts via a systematic review. Working Papers on Operations Management, vol. 2, pp. 18–30 (2011)

16. Gonzalez-Feliu, J., Perboli, G., Tadei, R., Vigo, D.: The two-echelon capacitated vehicle routing problem. Technical report OR/02/08, Politecnico di Torino (2008)

17. Grangier, P., Gendreau, M., Lehuédé, F., Rousseau, L.M.: An adaptive large neighborhood search for the two-echelon multiple-trip vehicle routing problem with satellite synchronization. Eur. J. Oper. Res. **254**(1), 80–91 (2016)

18. Guastaroba, G., Speranza, M.G., Vigo, D.: Designing service networks with intermediate facilities: an overview. Technical report, Department of Quantitative Methods, University of Brescia, Italy (2014)

19. Hemmelmayr, V.C., Cordeau, J.F., Crainic, T.G.: An adaptive large neighborhood search heuristic for two-echelon vehicle routing problems arising in city logistics. Comput. Oper. Res. **39**, 3215–3228 (2012)

20. Jepsen, M., Ropke, S., Spoorendonk, S.: A branch-and-cut algorithm for the symmetric two-echelon capacitated vehicle routing problem. Transp. Sci. **47**, 23–37 (2013)

21. Mancini, S.: Multi-echelon distribution systems in city logistics. Eur. Transp. - Trasporti Europei **54**, 1–24 (2013). Paper 2

22. Meza-Peralta, K., Gonzalez-Feliu, J., Montoya-Torres, J.R., Khodadad-Saryazdi, A.: A unified typology of Urban Logistics Spaces as interfaces for freight transport - a systematic literature review. Supply Chain Forum Int. J. (to appear)

23. Muñoz-Villamizar, A., Montoya-Torres, J.R., Vega-Mejía, C.A.: Non-collaborative versus collaborative last-mile delivery in urban systems with stochastic demands. Procedia CIRP **30**, 263–268 (2015)

24. Muñuzuri, J., Larrañeta, J., Onieva, L., Cortés, P.: Solutions applicable by local administrations for urban logistics improvement. Cities **22**(1), 15–28 (2005)

25. Perboli, G., Masoero, F., Tadei, R.: New families of valid inequalities for the two-echelon vehicle routing problem. Electron. Notes Discrete Math. **36**, 639–646 (2010)

26. Perboli, G., Tadei, R., Vigo, D.: The two-echelon capacitated vehicle routing problem: models and math-based heuristics. Transp. Sci. **45**(3), 364–380 (2011)

27. Pirkul, H., Jayaraman, V.: Production, transportation, and distribution planning in a multi-commodity tri-echelon system. Transp. Sci. **30**, 291–302 (1996)

28. Quintero-Araujo, C.L., Juan, A.A., Montoya-Torres, J.R., Muñoz-Villamizar, A.: A simheuristic algorithm for horizontal cooperation in urban distribution: application to a case study in Colombia. In: Proceedings of the 2016 Winter Simulation Conference, pp. 2193–2204 (2016)

29. Renault Kangoo van vehicle specifications. https://www.renault.com.co/gama/vehiculos-utilitarios/kangoo.html. Accessed 1 April 2020

30. Russo, F., Comi, A.: A classification of city logistics measures and connected impacts. Procedia Soc. Behav. Sci. **2**(3), 6355–6365 (2010)

31. Savelsbergh, M., Van Woensel, T.: City logistics: challenges and opportunities. Transp. Sci. **50**(2), 579–590 (2016)

32. Yin, R.K.: Case Study Research and Applications: Design and Methods. SAGE Publications Inc., Thousand Oaks (2013)

An Efficient Algorithm for Minimizing Regular Criteria in the Job-Shop Scheduling Multi-resource Resource Flexibility with Linear Routes

Andrés Alberto García-León$^{(\boxtimes)}$ (ID) and William Fernando Torres Tapia (ID)

Facultad de Ingeniería, Programa de Ingeniería Industrial,
Universidad de Ibagué, Ibagué, Colombia
{andres.garcia,william.torres}@unibague.edu.co

Abstract. The level of publications of extensions derived from the Job-shop scheduling problem is really low. The Flexible Job-shop scheduling problem is the most studied and the minimization of the makespan is the dominant approach in the literature. The level of the customer service cannot be measured efficiently minimizing makespan, since it does not consider relevant aspects like the due date of jobs and the importance between customers. In this paper, we propose an efficient and fast local search general algorithm to minimize regular criteria in the Job-shop Scheduling Multi-resource Resource Flexibility with Linear Routes Problem "JSMRFLR". JSMRFLR models situations in which an operation to be processed needs simultaneously several resources or machines, where each resource is selected from a given set of candidate resources. Our approach makes use of the disjunctive graph model to represent schedules or solutions and guide the search for an optimal solution by a fast estimation function. The transformation in the conjunctive graph is evaluated at swapping a critical arc (x, y) that affects the criterion and the reassignment of x and y separately. The efficiency of our approach is evidenced in instances of literature for the case of makespan criterion and a reference of results is proposed by the case of the total flow time, the maximum and total tardiness.

Keywords: Scheduling theory · Extension of the Job-Shop scheduling problem · Makespan · Total flow time · Maximum tardiness · Total tardiness and local search and linear routes

1 Introduction

In modern industrial environments, the decisions of scheduling must lead to improve the productivity and the competitiveness. The minimization of regular criteria considering the due date of jobs allows the optimization of the customer satisfaction. In scheduling theory, the Job-shop Scheduling Problem (JSP) and its extensions have attracted the attention for solving problems in more real configurations. This paper considers one extension of the JSP with two types of flexibility: Multi-resource and resource flexibility.

© Springer Nature Switzerland AG 2020
J. C. Figueroa-García et al. (Eds.): WEA 2020, CCIS 1274, pp. 165–180, 2020.
https://doi.org/10.1007/978-3-030-61834-6_15

Multi-resource considers that an operation needs several resources simultaneously to be performed and resource flexibility indicates that a resource may be selected in a given set. The problem that is studied in this paper is called Job-shop Scheduling Problem Multi-resource Resource Flexibility with linear routes "JSMRFLR". Linear route considers that an operation belongs only to a job. This situation is typical of metalworking activities, where the process of an operation needs several machines simultaneously and the processed or assembled parts are used for a job.

This paper addresses the minimization of any regular criterion by an efficient fast local search algorithm which uses the properties of the disjunctive graph model and an estimation function at reversing a critical arc (x, y), which connect critical resources from operation x to operation y that belong to the critical paths of jobs which affect a criterion, and the reassignment of the critical resources of x and y separately. To validate the quality of the results, we have calculated the makespan and our proposed approach gets better results respect to the best known values in some instances referenced in the literature. Additionally a benchmark of results for criteria derived from the analysis of the due date of jobs such as the maximum and total tardiness is presented. The paper is explained as follows. Section 2 presents a literature review; Sect. 3 describes and models the problem. In Sect. 4 the feasibility conditions and move evaluation are adapted to the problem at estimating the criterion without transforming the conjunctive graph. In Sect. 5, the algorithm is explained using an example to illustrate the efficiency of our approach. Finally the Sect. 6 shows computational experiments.

2 Literature Review

JSP has been widely studied in the literature. It considers a set of n jobs. Each job has a sequence of operations and each operation is processed exclusively by a unique machine [1]. The objective of the JSP is to determine a sequence of operations on each machine to optimize an objective function. JSP cannot model some real situations of the industry for example, the flexible Job-shop Scheduling problem "FJSP" considers that an operation can be processed by more than one machine, that leads to increase its complexity at solving two sub problems: sequence and assignment, which determines the machine where an operation is performed (see for example [1, 2]).

The FJSP has been analyzed considering constraints, assumptions and issues. For example, sequence-dependent setup and transportation times [3], batching machines, reentrant flows, and sequence-dependent setup times [4]. The blocking constraint, which requires holding machines used for an operation until machines needed for the next operation of the same job [5, 6], overlapping in operations [7], fuzzy processing times [8] and preventive maintenance [9].

The extension of the JSP considered in this paper is Multi-resource operation, which integrates many assumptions that can be found in real environment. It considers that every operation may need several resources to be performed. Therefore, a resource is chosen from a given set of candidates resources. It was proposed by [10] and additionally considered the alternative of non-linear routes, which implies that an operation could have more than one predecessor and/or more than one successor on the routing. In [11] two considerations are added. In the first, an operation that needs several resources might not need all the resources during its entire processing time. It allows a resource to be released before finishing the operation. The second extension considers the fact that, for a given operation, one might have to prevent a set of incompatible resources to be chosen.

The state of the art developed by [12] concluded that makespan is the most studied criterion, and in other regular criteria is really limited, which was verified by [13]. Minimizing other regular criteria than the makespan leads to measure the customer service and furthermore if the due date of jobs is considered [14]. It is important to highlight that our paper generates two contributions. The first is gotten at increasing the level of knowledge for a problem that has been little studied and it is typical of flexible manufacturing environments such as make to order philosophy. And the second is the development of an approach that can be used for optimizing any regular criterion in the JSMRFLR that is formulated considering a new disjunctive graph model adapted to regular criteria and a fast estimation function for the completion time of jobs. In the experiments, the quality of the estimation function is determined and a benchmark of results for four regular criteria is proposed for future research. An extension of our approach was presented by the case of Pareto Optimization in [15].

3   Problem Description and Modeling

The JSP is modeled as follows. A set of n jobs $J = \{J_1, \ldots . J_n\}$ are processed on a set $M = \{M_1, \ldots . M_m\}$ of m machines that are available. Each machine can only process one job at a time. A job J_i is obtained at performing sequentially n_i operations in a fix route. Preempting operations is not allowed. It means that an operation cannot be interrupted once started. J_i has a due-date d_i. JSMRFLR considers that an operation needs several resources simultaneously to be performed and resource flexibility indicates that a resource may be selected in a given set.

A representation of the disjunctive graph for the Multi-resource shop scheduling with resource flexibility considering linear and non-linear routes is detailed in [10]. The properties of linear routes are considered to represent the JSMRFLR adapted to minimize regular criteria proposed and validated in [13, 14]. This graph is noted $G = (V, A, E)$, where V is the set of nodes, A is the set of conjunctive arcs and E is the set of disjunctive arcs. The nodes in E represent operations of jobs (set O), plus a dummy node 0 that corresponds to the start of each job, and n dummy nodes ϕ_i, where ϕ_i models the completion time of J_i. The set A contains conjunctive arcs that connect two consecutive operations on the routing of jobs, the node 0 to every first operation of each job, and the last operation of J_i to ϕ_i. E contains disjunctive arcs between every pair of operations assigned to the same resource. Let E_k be the set of disjunctive arcs between pairs of operations that must be processed on k, $E = \cup E_k$.

The set of operations O has to be processed on a set of machines (resources) M. To be processed an operation $x \in O$, it requires $R(x)$ resources simultaneously and M_x^k is the resource subset in which the kth resource $(1 \leq k \leq R(x))$ must be selected. The M_x^k subsets are not necessarily disjoint, i.e., a resource may belong to several subsets. To obtain a feasible schedule for the JSMRFLR, two main decisions must be made on operations namely assignment and sequencing to solve the conflict in E. The assignment decision means determining a mapping $a : O \times N \to M$, where $a(x, k)$ is the kth resource assigned to x, $a(x, k) \in M_x^k$. Moreover $M_x^a = \{m \in M \,|\, \forall k \leq R(x), a(x, k) = m\}$ is the subset of resources of operation x is assigned.

As the M_x^k subsets are not necessarily disjoint, it is mandatory to ensure of not assigning a resource twice or more to the same operation. The processing time of an operation x (p_x) is determined by the maximum time of the resource where it was assigned. To explain it, in Fig. 1(a), the Operation x needs three resources simultaneously to be performed. The first resource has to be selected in the subset $M_x^1 = \{M_1, M_2, M_3\}$, besides, in parenthesis the processing time of each resource. The second resource in the sub set $M_x^2 = \{M_1, M_2, M_4\}$, and the third resource in the subset $M_x^3 = \{M_2, M_4\}$. In this case, the three subsets are not disjoint, x is assigned to the resources M_1, M_2 and M_4 (see Fig. 1(b)), and its processing time is 4 $(p_x = 4)$. The sequencing decision deals with determining a sequence of operations on each selected resource k to minimize any regular criterion that in our case we have validated makespan, total flow time, and maximum and total tardiness separately.

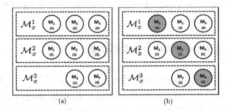

Fig. 1. Scheduling with resource allocation

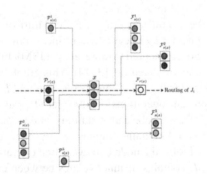

Fig. 2. Example of immediate predecessors and successors of an operation x

We denote P_x (resp. F_x) the set of immediate predecessors (resp. successors) of x. Besides, let $P_{r(x)} \in P_x$ (resp. $F_{r(x)} \in F_x$) be the immediate predecessor (resp. successor) on the routing of x. Let $P_{s(x)} \in P_x$ (resp. $F_{s(x)} \in F_x$) be the set of predecessors (resp. successors) on the sequence and $P_{s(x)}^k$ (resp. $F_{s(x)}^k$) be the immediate predecessor (resp. successor) on resource k^{th}. It means that $P_{s(x)} = \cup P_{s(x)}^k$ (resp. $F_{s(x)} = \cup F_{s(x)}^k$), $\forall k$ such that $1 \leq k \leq R(x)$). The Fig. 2 illustrates the immediate predecessors and successors of an operation x that belongs to J_i and needs three resources identified by colors.

When a solution is obtained and considering the properties from [15], an arc has a length equal to the processing time of the operation from which it starts. The starting time of x, $h_x = L(0, x)$, called head, that corresponds to the length of the longest path from 0 to x. The tail from a node x to ϕ_i (q_x^i) is equal to $[(x, \phi_i) - p_x]$, if a path exists from x to ϕ_i and $-\infty$ otherwise. A path from 0 to ϕ_i is called critical if its length is equal to C_i, and every node x belonging to this critical path is critical according to J_i. A critical node x for J_i satisfies $h_x + p_x + q_x^i = C_i$. An arc belonging to the critical path of J_i is called critical if it connects two operations x and. $(y \neq F_{r(x)})$ that are assigned to the same machine. Note that an arc may be critical for several jobs. The level l_x of a node x in G denotes the maximum number of arcs in a path from 0 to x. After obtaining the heads of the nodes of the graph, the criterion of a feasible schedule represented by the selection can be determined in $O(n)$ from the starting times of the dummy nodes. For instance, the makespan is obtained using the formula $C_{max} = \max C_i$, total flow time is $\sum C_i$, the tardiness (T_i), $T_i = \max(0, C_i - d_i)$. Then the maximum tardiness is $T_{max} = \max T_i$ and total tardiness (T) is the sum of the tardiness of jobs.

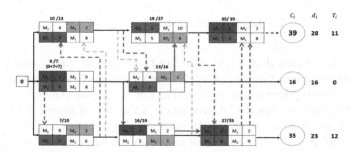

Fig. 3. Example of a solution for the proposed instance

The Fig. 3 illustrates the conjunctive graph for a solution of an instance with three jobs, three machines $(M_1, M_2$ and $M_3)$ and eight operations. The second job (see the second horizontal route in Fig. 3) has three operations and its due-date is 16 (see d_i column). The first operation of the second job needs two resources. Its first resource must be selected between M_1 and M_2 and its second resource between M_2 and M_3. In this case, M_1 and M_2 are selected respectively and 7 represents the processing time. This operation starts the processing activities for both resources $(M_1$ and $M_2)$ simultaneously, if it starts at time 0, its completion time is 7 (see 0/7, $0 + 7 = 7$ in Fig. 3). At solving the graph, the completion time of jobs (see C_iC_i column) are 39, 16 and 35 respectively and their tardiness (see T_iT_i column) are 19, 8 and 20. The critical path for all jobs is remarked with dashed arcs. The criteria calculated are $C_{max} = 39$. $T_{max} = 12$, total tardiness of 23 $(T = 23)$ and $\sum C_i = 90$.

4 Feasibility of Moves and Evaluation

Our approach uses two conditions for moving operations of a critical arc (x, y) in the JSMRFLR. The first condition consists on reversing the arc (x, y) which satisfies the properties of the JSP in [16]. Besides, at considering several resources, in [10] (see Lemma 2), all arcs that are connected from x to y are also critical and they must be reversed. The Fig. 4 illustrates the transformation in the conjunctive graph at reversing critical arcs from x to y. In this case, x and y have two disjoint resources (identified by colors). According to Lemma 2, the arcs from u and $v \in P_x$ after reversing critical arcs will be connected to y. From y the critical arcs will be connected to x. Then, x will be connected to z and r (see Fig. 4(b)).

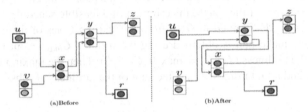

(a)Before   (b)After

Fig. 4. Reversing critical arcs (x, y)

At reversing a critical arc (x, y), we want to evaluate the new completion times of jobs after performing the move ($\hat{c}$). These new completion times will be estimated without transforming the graph, since it spends a significant computational effort. Before adapting the estimation function, the concept of set of critical resources K for the arc (x, y) is introduced, which represents the set of disjoint resources of x and y. Besides, let $P_{kx} \in P_x$ (resp. $F_{kx} \in F_x$) be the set of immediate predecessor (resp. successor) of x on resource k. The expression described in the Fig. 5 is used to estimate the completion time of jobs at reversing critical arc (x, y). It extends the results obtained in [14] for the swap move in the classical JSP by considering the operations that belong to the same level of l_x, i.e. operations ω for which $l_\omega = l_x$.

$$\hat{C}_i = \begin{cases} C_i & \text{if } q_x^i = -\infty \\ \max\{L_1, L_2, L_3\} & \text{otherwise} \end{cases}$$

With

$$L_1 = \hat{h}_y + p_y + \max_{v \in V}\{p_v + q_v^i\}$$
$$L_2 = \hat{h}_x + p_x + \max_{w \in W}\{p_w + q_w^i\}$$
$$L_3 = \max_{\omega \in S_x}\{h_\omega + p_\omega + q_\omega^i\}$$

Where

$$\hat{h}_y = \max_{u \in U}\{h_u + p_u\}$$
$$\hat{h}_x = \max\{\hat{h}_y + p_y, \max_{r \in R}\{h_r + p_r\}\}$$
$$U = \{\{\mathcal{P}_y - x\} \cup \mathcal{P}_{Kx}\}$$
$$V = \{\mathcal{F}_y - \mathcal{F}_{Ky}\}$$
$$W = \{\{\mathcal{F}_x - y\} \cup \mathcal{F}_{Ky}\}$$
$$R = \{\mathcal{P}_x - \mathcal{P}_{Kx}\}$$
$$S_x = \{\omega \neq x / l_\omega = l_x\}$$

Fig. 5. Estimation function for C_i at reversing a critical arc (x, y)

The second condition is based on the reassignment of the resource L to L' between operations j and k for a critical operation $\in$, $\in = x \vee \in = y$. For doing it, the feasibility of moving $\in$ is considered the concept of order of operation or maximum number of arcs from node 0 to $\in$ ($l_\in$) introduced by [16] and demonstrated at considering two sets $B = \left\{ F_\in - F^L_{s(\in)} \right\}$ and $C = \left\{ P_\in - P^L_{s(\in)} \right\}$. As consequence the reassignment of the resource L to L' between operations j and k for $\in$ (critical) is feasible, if there are no paths from $b(\forall b \in B)$ to j and simultaneously from k to $c(\forall c \in C)$. To ensure it, two expressions considering the number of arcs must be satisfied: $l_j \leq \min_{b \in B}\{l_b\}$ and $l_k \geq \max_{c \in C}\{l_c\}$. The Fig. 6 illustrates the estimation function at reassigning $\in$ between j and k. It is important to mention that L_3 is the same estimation at reversing the critical arc considering to $\in$

$$\hat{C}_i = \begin{cases} C_i & \text{if } q^i_\in = q^i_k = -\infty \\ \max\{L_1, L_2, L_3\} & \text{otherwise} \end{cases}$$

with

$$L_1 = h_{P^L_{s(\in)}} + p_{P^L_{s(\in)}} + p_{\mathcal{F}^L_{s(\in)}} + q^i_{\mathcal{F}^L_{s(\in)}}$$
$$L_2 = \hat{h}_\in + p'_\in + \max\{p_k + q^i_k, \max_{b \in B}\{p_b + q^i_b\}\}$$

where $p'_\in$ is the processing time of $\in$ after the move and

$$\hat{h}_\in = \max\{\hat{h}_j + p_j, \max_{c \in C}\{h_c + p_c\}\}$$
$$\hat{h}_j = \begin{cases} \max_{p \in \{P_j - \in\}}\{h_p + p_p\} & \text{if } j = \mathcal{F}^L_{s(\in)} \\ h_j & \text{otherwise} \end{cases}$$
$$B = \{F_\in - \mathcal{F}^L_{s(\in)}\}$$
$$C = \{P_\in - P^L_{s(\in)}\}$$

Fig. 6. Estimation function for C_i at reassigning $\in$ between j and k on resource L'

5 Description of the Algorithm

Our algorithm requires of an initial solution, which is performed as follows: the jobs are sorted in increasing order according to the due-date. At analyzing the example of the Fig. 3, the order of jobs is: $J_2 - J_3 - J_1$, since the due-dates (d_i column) are 16, 23 and 28 respectively. After that, for the assignment and sequence of operations on resources (machines) is solved at considering the operation in the path according to the sorted jobs. In this case, the first operation of J_2, the first of J_3 and the first of J_1. Then, the second operation of J_2, and so on. The assignment and sequence decisions on resources aim to get the lowest completion time. As example, the second operation of J_2 is the first operation to solve, here M_1 and M_2 are selected. Then, in the first operation of J_3, M_3 and M_2 are assigned. The results of the initial solutions are the same that are illustrated in Fig. 3. Note that the initial solution is a general approach and does not have distinction between criteria.

To optimize the criterion, two phases have been designed: Improvement and diversification. In the Improvement phase, the critical paths of the jobs which affect the criterion are considered to determine all critical arcs (x, y) into the paths. For each arc (x, y) the estimation functions illustrated in Fig. 5 and 6 are applied and the best moves generated from the estimation functions are saved. It means moves which estimation is less than the current criterion. When the best move is detected and a new solution is created. This move could be reversing a critical arc (x, y) or reassigning x or y between j and k on resource L'. The diversification phase starts when it is not possible to improve the criterion. Several strategies were tested. The best strategy consists on performing b random moves ($4 \leq b \leq 10$), which conducts to the search escapes from a local optimal.

6 Computational Experiments

To validate and evaluate the efficiency of our approach for the four criteria, the instances with linear routing studied in [10] have been considered. Our algorithm was developed in Java language. A PC with 3.40 GHz and 8 GB RAM was used for executing the experiments. The algorithm was executed for 300 s per criterion and ten times per instance.

6.1 Quality of the Estimation Function

The quality of our proposed estimation function is based on the moves at performing the algorithm during the improvement phase using the four criteria and evaluating four percentage performance measures and are illustrated for some instances in Table 1: *MRE, Non-imp, Exact and Same*. *MRE* represents the Mean Relative Error of the value obtained by the estimation function over the exact value when the estimation function does not give the exact value of the criterion. *Non-imp* gives the number of times the estimation function selects a non-improving move but the neighborhood contains at least an improving one. *Exact* is the number of times the estimation function gives the exact value of the criterion. *Same* determines the number of times the estimation function selects the same move in the neighborhood as the exact method. The results of the Table 1 evidence the good performance of the estimation function, since the percentage of non-improving moves is really low for the four criteria in the analyzed instances. For example, the instance *mjs01*, Non-imp is less than 1.0% for the four criteria. However, in some instances this percentage could be considered significant, but never greater than 12%. Concerning to *MRE* is possible to infer that the difference between real value of the criterion and the estimation is not representative, even though in the criteria T_{max} and T is on average 10% at considering the increasing of the tardiness. The last analysis conducts to affirm that, despite the complexity of the problem (configuration and criteria) never *Same* and *Exact* are zero.

6.2 Minimizing Regular Criteria

The Fig. 7 illustrates an evidence of the efficiency of our algorithm at minimizing total tardiness for the instance analyzed in Fig. 3 which solution is 14. It is obtained at adding the tardiness of each job illustrated in column Ti ($10 + 0 + 4 = 14$). The results of the four criteria are presented in two steps. In the first, the performance of makespan is compared to the best known values. Then, a benchmark of results for the other criteria is proposed.

The results for the criteria C_{max} and $\sum C_i$ are illustrated on Table 2. Concerning to C_{max}, column *BKV* represents the best known value of the criterion, *BS* means the

Table 1. Quality of the estimation function

Inst	C_{max}				$\sum C_i$				T_{max}				T			
	MRE	Same	Exact	Non-imp	MRE	Same	Exact	Non-imp	MRE	Same	Exact	Non-imp	MRE	Same	Exact	Non-imp
mjs01	2.4	24.1	72.1	0.9	4.6	6.7	9.1	0.8	14.3	25.0	85.4	0.9	15.3	8.8	3.5	0.8
mjs06	3.2	9.4	36.3	1.3	2.1	5.3	8.4	8.9	3.8	80.0	66.9	8.8	9.8	3.6	4.8	3.2
mjs12	1.8	7.2	10.6	1.3	3.1	8.0	8.6	6.4	12.8	17.1	47.3	7.4	4.4	2.3	6.9	7.6
mjs18	1.8	4.7	18.8	1.0	1.2	6.2	8.8	8.9	3.8	5.1	19.8	10.3	2.1	1.4	6.0	6.6
mjs21	2.3	4.5	18.4	1.6	3.3	9.5	6.8	9.2	13.9	7.7	27.9	8.5	5.1	2.5	7.5	7.2
mjs29	1.7	3.3	14.6	0.9	1.6	5.7	2.9	9.9	4.2	3.8	17.0	10.1	12.9	5.1	5.9	5.8
mjs33	4.7	4.2	17.1	1.4	0.2	1.1	2.3	3.8	11.3	2.0	18.6	8.6	2.9	1.6	1.6	3.5
mjs37	4.8	4.3	16.2	1.5	0.4	0.8	1.8	4.5	18.5	2.1	11.8	9.3	9.4	1.9	0.8	3.9
mjs41	4.2	3.5	13.2	1.2	0.5	1.0	2.9	6.7	15.8	4.8	17.0	8.5	4.5	2.2	1.9	4.8
mjs45	3.2	3.6	14.8	0.5	0.3	0.6	0.9	8.7	3.4	1.9	11.8	7.7	5.5	0.8	1.6	5.2
mjs50	2.9	1.0	5.7	0.7	0.6	0.9	0.8	5.6	7.4	1.7	7.9	4.6	2.9	0.9	0.7	1.3
mjs58	1.8	0.6	4.8	1.1	0.4	0.8	1.7	4.8	4.2	0.4	4.9	6.4	11.1	0.7	0.9	1.8
mjs60	3.9	3.0	13.3	0.8	0.3	0.7	1.6	9.6	14.1	1.4	8.9	5.3	17.0	0.9	3.2	2.7
mjs63	2.1	3.2	10.7	0.9	0.7	0.9	1.5	8.9	6.5	1.6	13.5	11.5	1.8	1.3	0.5	1.9

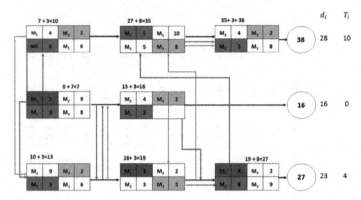

Fig. 7. The best known solution for all criteria considering the proposed instance in the Fig. 3

best solution of our algorithm. An asterisk (*) indicates that our algorithm got the *BKV* and the criterion. A number in **bold** indicates that a better solution was gotten. *DP(%)* represents the percent difference between the best solution of the search and the *BKV* when it is not gotten. Finally, the column *AV* represents the average of the criterion.

The results respect to C_{max} criterion is explained as follows. Our algorithm evidences a high performance in 17 of the 68 instances, for example in the instance *mjs02* where the best known value is improved, which represents the 25% of the experiments. The best known value is gotten in 7 of 68 (10.3%) instances (for example in the instance *mjs01*). In the other instances, in spite the best known value was not reached, the percent difference could not be considered as significant in 16 instances, which value is less than 2.1%, see the instances *mjs13, 22, 30, 31, 33, 34, 36, 43, 45, 63* and *64*. Besides in *mjs03, 16, 26* and *61*, this value is less or equal than 1.0%. Even though, our algorithm is general and it is not designed exclusively for makespan criterion, some instances motivate the formulation of new diversification strategies like optimizing a secondary criterion. It is evidenced in the instances *mjs50, 52, 55, 56, 57, 58* and *59*. Respect to criterion $\sum C_i$, the column *IS* represents the initial solution and $\Delta(\%)$ indicates the percentage change determined by the *IS* and *BS*. It is important to highlight that is quite high at reducing the criterion significantly during the search.

To calculate the maximum tardiness and the total tardiness, the due-date d_i is calculated at introducing a parameter f equals to 1.1, which is inspired from [16]. d_i is determined by multiplying the sum of the average processing times of operations belong to J_i by f. To determine the average processing time of an operation, it is calculated at considering the highest processing time per subset of resources. For example at considering the operation x in the Fig. 1, in each subset of resources the maximum processing time is referenced (5, 5 and 3 respectively). d_i was rounded to the next integer number. From the Table 3, it is possible to infer that in most instances optimal solution is gotten since the value is zero (0) for both criteria and in some instances the difference between obtained solution and the gotten one is significant. For example in the instance *mjs21*, the initial solution is 13814 and our algorithm got 4954 for T.

Table 2. Results for the criteria C_{max} and $\sum C_i$

Inst	C_{max}				$\sum C_i$			
	BKV	BS	DP(%)	Av	IS	BS	Av	Δ(%)
mjs01	361	*		379.2	5272	3174	3291.2	39.8
mjs02	384	**382**		388.8	5839	3321	3382.3	43.1
mjs03	378	379	0.3	389.0	5688	3344	3383.8	41.2
mjs04	394	**391**		438.8	6049	3321	3430.9	45.1
mjs05	643	**637**		700.7	9753	5900	6144.7	39.5
mjs06	585	**561**		583.7	8046	5375	5503.2	33.2
mjs07	644	**627**		685.8	11617	5991	6297.8	48.4
mjs08	575	**568**		602.3	10125	5185	5318.3	48.8
mjs09	568	**564**		587.2	8799	5103	5178.5	42.0
mjs10	928	**925**		1026.0	17825	8645	8912.5	51.5
mjs11	1057	**1004**		1143.0	18464	9559	9964.0	48.2
mjs12	859	**806**		970.7	16153	7525	7902.1	53.4
mjs13	827	875	5.8	912.7	14516	8048	8278.4	44.6
mjs14	946	966	2.1	1056.0	16307	9085	9481.2	44.3
mjs15	1469	**1418**		1515.5	25331	13179	13542.8	48.0
mjs16	1312	1314	0.2	1395.5	24686	12927	13070.9	47.6
mjs17	1572	**1562**		1649.0	27435	15007	15347.8	45.3
mjs35	265	*		265.0	4839	2182	2227.1	54.9
mjs36	225	228	1.3	243.0	5200	2085	2122.5	59.9
mjs37	207	214	3.4	221.2	5009	1943	2000.5	61.2
mjs38	241	*		308.0	4809	2155	2207.7	55.2
mjs39	210	216	2.9	221.2	4917	1982	2023.9	59.7
mjs40	241	*		241,4	4507	1884	1920.5	58.2
mjs41	218	223	2.3	233.8	5498	2054	2087.0	62.6
mjs42	250	*		250.0	4487	1901	1953.7	57.6
mjs43	219	223	1.8	227.8	4624	1816	1854.6	60.7
mjs44	258	256		260.2	6013	2110	2151.7	64.9
mjs45	296	301	1.7	323.4	6812	4295	4322.2	36.9
mjs46	300	320	6.7	337.8	7287	3449	3579.9	52.7
mjs47	333	348	4.5	366.0	7890	3550	3643.3	55.0
mjs48	327	335	2.4	348.8	6561	3578	3632.9	45.5
mjs49	356	*		366.8	6957	3563	3712.6	48.8
mjs50	327	362	10.7	421.6	10069	3997	4140.5	60.3
mjs51	373	407	9.1	437.4	11595	4604	4826.8	60.3

(continued)

Table 2. (continued)

Inst	C_{max}				$\sum C_i$				Irst	C_{max}				$\sum C_i$			
	BKV	BS	DP(%)	Av	IS	BS	Av	Δ(%)		BKV	BS	DP(%)	Av	IS	BS	Av	Δ(%)
mjs18	1544	**1532**		1634.8	27817	15005	15393.5	46.1	mjs52	317	364	14.8	381.2	10040	3410	3585.4	66.0
mjs19	1572	**1503**		1622.5	25849	14953	15226.7	42.2	mjs53	353	378	7.1	430.8	10535	4001	4191.5	62.0
mjs20	1033	**1003**		1113.5	19070	9448	9686.7	50.5	mjs54	311	337	8.4	373.8	10149	3827	3957.8	62.3
mjs21	916	**870**		935.7	17147	8062	8228.5	53.0	mjs55	493	590	19.7	759.0	15889	10058	10058.0	36.7
mjs22	924	943	2.1	998.2	19904	8331	8530.6	58.1	mjs56	508	572	12.6	725.4	17907	8710	8962.5	51.4
mjs23	957	**948**		1027.0	17842	8740	9006.2	51.0	mjs57	500	567	13.4	768.8	14691	9112	9336.9	38.0
mjs24	918	**848**		922.3	15270	7635	7968.0	50.0	mjs58	530	587	10.8	740.6	15818	9427	9452.9	40.4
mjs25	1513	**1505**		1582.5	28077	14592	14923.5	48.0	mjs59	490	547	11.6	754.6	16246	10854	10885.8	33.2
mjs26	1481	1486	0.3	1523.5	25342	13046	13268.3	48.5	mjs60	268	**262**		281.6	9206	3613	3668.4	60.8
mjs27	1566	**1322**		1629.0	27599	14389	14671.8	47.9	mjs61	303	306	1.0	332.6	9287	3344	3377.9	64.0
mjs28	1395	1513	8.5	1577.8	27635	13929	14091.6	49.6	mjs62	284	*		290.8	8319	3055	3065.3	63.3
mjs29	1336	1424	6.6	1467.4	27510	13220	13592.3	51.9	mjs63	289	294	1.7	308.0	7470	2987	3066.6	60.0
mjs30	218	221	1.4	227.0	4453	1973	2004.3	55.7	mjs64	240	245	2.1	256.8	7334	2516	2597.4	65.7
mjs31	218	221	1.4	231.8	5494	2049	2130.6	62.7	mjs65	381	406	6.6	460.0	10535	6492	6507.9	38.4
mjs32	219	224	2.3	242.0	5626	2081	2195.0	63.0	mjs66	423	444	5.0	524.8	12737	8036	8055.6	36.9
mjs33	224	227	1.3	235.2	5293	2121	2143.3	59.9	mjs67	408	448	9.8	505.4	11365	7833	7834.1	31.1
mjs34	213	217	1.9	225.0	4644	1938	1967.6	58.3	mjs68	400	429	7.3	503.4	12146	7094	7099.4	41.6

Table 3. Results for the criteria T_{max} and T

Inst	T_{max}			T		
	IS	BS	Av	IS	BS	Av
mjs01	249	18	31.6	1905	78	158.1
mjs02	321	58	62.1	2491	180	193.3
mjs03	269	17	19.1	2197	74	99.9
mjs04	322	67	77.5	2839	296	413.7
mjs05	475	118	143.0	4513	863	978.7
mjs06	363	56	78.0	2990	482	565.1
mjs07	700	128	153.8	6477	1034	1405.1
mjs08	569	92	115.5	5237	491	612.6
mjs09	433	72	88.6	3743	425	548.0
mjs10	1536	667	693.8	14423	5501	5747.9
mjs11	1623	711	767.6	15162	6669	7079.0
mjs12	1343	540	561.6	12607	4722	5316.6
mjs13	1185	543	575.6	11042	4681	4875.7
mjs14	1375	672	693.9	12819	6010	6196.9
mjs15	2089	947	974.8	20254	8712	9008.9
mjs16	2005	921	960.5	19624	7971	8450.1
mjs17	2305	1102	1169.6	22580	11050	11483.9
mjs18	2335	1088	1149.3	22698	10387	10668.0

Inst	T_{max}			T		
	IS	BS	Av	IS	BS	Av
mjs35	86	0	0.0	437	0	0.0
mjs36	121	0	0.0	782	0	0.0
mjs37	132	0	0.0	534	0	0.0
mjs38	65	0	0.0	381	0	0.0
mjs39	102	0	0.0	520	0	0.0
mjs40	52	0	0.0	207	0	0.0
mjs41	153	0	0.0	1118	0	0.0
mjs42	55	0	0.0	128	0	0.0
mjs43	65	0	0.0	258	0	0.0
mjs44	185	0	0.0	1438	0	0.0
mjs45	75	0	0.0	234	0	0.0
mjs46	114	0	0.0	741	0	0.0
mjs47	274	0	0.0	1540	0	0.0
mjs48	98	0	0.0	175	0	0.0
mjs49	45	0	0.0	241	0	0.0
mjs50	655	0	0.0	5491	0	0.0
mjs51	814	0	0.0	7168	0	0.0
mjs52	628	0	0.0	5602	0	0.0

(continued)

Table 3. (continued)

Inst	T_{max}			T			Inst	T_{max}			T		
	IS	BS	Av	IS	BS	Av		IS	BS	Av	IS	BS	Av
mjs19	2129	1051	1084.3	20858	9826	10544.0	mjs53	695	0	0.0	6061	0	0.0
mjs20	1634	741	770.5	15490	5856	6438.7	mjs54	636	0	0.0	5749	0	0.0
mjs21	1468	566	593.3	13814	4954	5083.1	mjs55	953	110	133.9	9183	4062	4122.8
mjs22	1743	653	676.5	16586	5481	5713.3	mjs56	1201	107	131.5	11215	3170	3511.3
mjs23	1533	615	666.1	14423	5556	5875.1	mjs57	868	96	158.4	7978	3818	3979.7
mjs24	1282	572	586.1	11941	4786	4970.7	mjs58	963	98	120.8	9032	3770	3792.3
mjs25	2349	988	1024.5	22946	9746	9868.0	mjs59	1068	173	209.5	9571	4706	4727.7
mjs26	2154	952	1001.1	20452	8686	9005.8	mjs60	572	0	0.0	4795	0	3.2
mjs27	2334	1280	1280.8	22604	9942	10490.5	mjs61	548	0	0.0	4916	0	0.0
mjs28	2404	988	1036.6	22733	9821	10098.0	mjs62	456	0	0.0	3791	0	0.0
mjs29	2315	943	1003.9	22500	9066	9253.7	mjs63	373	0	0.0	3038	0	0.0
mjs30	45	0	0.0	113	0	0.0	mjs64	344	0	0.0	2885	0	0.0
mjs31	148	0	0.0	1070	0	0.0	mjs65	481	0	0.0	3796	0	0.0
mjs32	221	0	0.0	1274	0	0.0	mjs66	705	0	0.0	6193	0	0.0
mjs33	148	0	0.0	915	0	0.0	mjs67	531	0	0.0	4785	0	0.0
mjs34	68	0	0.0	240	0	0.0	mjs68	579	0	0.0	5358	0	0.0

7 Conclusion

This paper presented a local search algorithm to solve the job shop scheduling Multi-resource resource flexibility with linear routes at minimizing regular criteria. We have presented results for four criteria: makespan, maximum tardiness, total flow time and total tardiness. To best of our knowledge, there is not any reference about of this extension of the job-shop scheduling problem to calculate regular criteria different than the makespan. The algorithm is supported in the adaptation of estimation functions as extensions of the classic Job-shop scheduling problem and the proposition of the conjunctive graph. In its formulation, the properties of heads, tails and levels of operations have been considered. Computational results show the efficiency of our algorithm at getting some best known values and better values in known instances for the makespan criterion. Additionally optimal solutions are gotten by the case of the maximum tardiness and the total tardiness. Finally, we are also extending our approach to the simultaneous optimization of multiple criteria and as perspectives the extension of our approach in other environments such as the multi-resource with no-linear routing. This research is supported by the project identified with the code 18-531-INT financed by the Universidad de Ibagué (Colombia).

References

1. Zeng, C., Tang, J., Yan, C.: Job-shop cell-scheduling problem with inter-cell moves and automated guided vehicles. J. Intell. Manuf. **26**(5), 845–859 (2014). https://doi.org/10.1007/s10845-014-0875-x
2. Brucker, P., Schlie, R.: Job-shop scheduling with multi-purpose machines. Computing **45**(4), 369–375 (1990)
3. Rossi, A.: Flexible job shop scheduling with sequence-dependent setup and transportation times by ant colony with reinforced pheromone relationships. Int. J. Prod. Econ. **153**, 253–267 (2014)
4. Knopp, S., Dauzère-Pérès, S., Yugma, C.: A batch-oblivious approach for complex job-shop scheduling problems. Eur. J. Oper. Res. **263**(1), 50–61 (2017)
5. Mati, Y., Rezg, N., Xie, X.: An integrated greedy heuristic for a flexible job shop scheduling problem. In: 2001 IEEE International Conference on Systems, Man, and Cybernetics, vol. 4, pp. 2534–2539. IEEE (2001)
6. Mati, Y., Lahlou, C., Dauzère-Pérès, S.: Modelling and solving a practical flexible job-shop scheduling problem with blocking constraints. Int. J. Prod. Res. **49**(8), 2169–2182 (2011)
7. Meng, T., Pan, Q.-K., Sang, H.-Y.: A hybrid artificial bee colony algorithm for a flexible job shop scheduling problem with overlapping in operations. Int. J. Prod. Res. **56**(16), 5278–5292 (2018)
8. Palacios, J.J., González, M.A., Vela, C.R., González-Rodríguez, I., Puente, J.: Genetic tabu search for the fuzzy flexible job-shop problem. Comput. Oper. Res. **54**, 74–89 (2015)
9. Khoukhi, F.E., Boukachour, J., Alaoui, A.E.H.: The dual-ants colony: a novel hybrid approach for the flexible job-shop scheduling problem with preventive maintenance. Comput. Ind. Eng. **106**, 236–255 (2017)
10. Dauzère-Pérès, S., Roux, W., Lasserre, J.: Multi-resource shop scheduling with resource flexibility. Eur. J. Oper. Res. **107**(2), 289–305 (1998)
11. Dauzère-Pérès, S., Pavageau, C.: Extensions of an integrated approach for multi-resource shop scheduling. IEEE Trans. Syst. Man Cybern. Part C Appl. Rev. **33**(2), 207–213 (2003)

12. Chaudhry, I.A., Khan, A.A.: A research survey: review of flexible job shop scheduling techniques. Int. Trans. Oper. Res. **23**, 551–591 (2016)
13. García-León, A.A., Dauzère-Pérès, S., Mati, Y.: An efficient Pareto approach for solving the multi-objective flexible job-shop scheduling problem with regular criteria. Comput. Oper. Res. **108**, 187–200 (2019)
14. Mati, Y., Dauzère-Pérès, S., Lahlou, C.: A general approach for optimizing regular criteria in the job-shop scheduling problem. Eur. J. Oper. Res. **212**(1), 33–42 (2011)
15. García-León, A.A., Torres Tapia, W.F.: A General Local Search Pareto Approach with Regular Criteria for Solving the Job-Shop Scheduling Problem Multi-resource Resource Flexibility with Linear Routes. In: Figueroa-García, J.C., Duarte-González, M., Jaramillo-Isaza, S., Orjuela-Cañon, A.D., Díaz-Gutierrez, Y. (eds.) WEA 2019. CCIS, vol. 1052, pp. 764–775. Springer, Cham (2019). https://doi.org/10.1007/978-3-030-31019-6_64
16. Singer, M., Pinedo, M.: A computational study of branch and bound techniques for minimizing the total weighted tardiness in job shops. IIE Trans. **30**(2), 109–118 (1998)

A Fast Pareto Approach to Minimize Regular Criteria in the Job-shop Scheduling Problem with Maintenance Activities, Sequence Dependent and Set-up Times

Andrés A. García-León[(⊠)] [iD] and William F. Torres Tapia[iD]

Facultad de Ingeniería, Programa de Ingeniería Industrial,
Universidad de Ibagué, Ibagué, Colombia
{andres.garcia,william.torres}@unibague.edu.co

Abstract. In the Job-shop scheduling problem minimizing the makespan has been the dominant approach in the literature. The level of the customer service cannot be measured efficiently for this criterion, since it does not consider relevant aspects like the due date of jobs to determine the tardiness. In this paper, we propose an innovate general approach for minimizing regular criteria in the Job-shop Scheduling which adds the conditions of maintenance activities and sequence dependent set-up times considering the Pareto optimization. Our approach makes use of the disjunctive graph model to represent schedules and support the search for an optimal solution using a classical estimation function at reversing a critical arc. The search is performed by two phases: improvement and diversification. In the improvement phase, initially, a random criterion is selected to create improving moves iteratively. When it is not possible to create a move using the selected criterion, it is penalized and a new criterion is selected. The diversification phase considers feasibility conditions to escape from a local optimal. In each move the set of solutions of the front is updated. The efficiency of our approach is illustrated on instances of literature at performing three sets of criteria. The first set considers makespan and maximum tardiness. In the second $\sum C_i$ is considered and in the third the total tardiness. As a contribution of our approach, a benchmark of results is proposed by future research.

Keywords: Scheduling theory · Extension of the Job-Shop scheduling problem · Regular criteria · Maintenance activity · Sequence dependent · Set-up times · Local search and pareto optimization

1 Introduction

The minimization of regular criteria considering the due date of jobs allows the optimization of the customer satisfaction. In scheduling theory, the Job-shop Scheduling Problem (JSP) can model real configurations presented in a workshop. This paper considers the JSP with maintenance activities, sequence dependent set-up times. This situation is typical of manufacturing activities, since, to maintain an efficient performance of machines

© Springer Nature Switzerland AG 2020
J. C. Figueroa-García et al. (Eds.): WEA 2020, CCIS 1274, pp. 181–193, 2020.
https://doi.org/10.1007/978-3-030-61834-6_16

needs periodically maintenance activities and normally the set-up times are affected by the complexity of the tasks between jobs (sequence dependent).

This paper proposes a Pareto approach to minimize regular criteria by a fast local search algorithm which uses the properties of the disjunctive graph model and an estimation function at reversing a critical arc (x, y) belong to the jobs which affect a criterion at considering the conditions of the problem. To validate the quality of the results, we have evaluated three sets of regular criteria to create a benchmark of results considering three instances.

The paper is explained as follows. Section 2 presents a literature review. Section 3 describes and models the problem. Section 4, the feasibility conditions and move evaluation are adapted to the problem to estimate the value of the criterion without transforming the graph. In Sect. 5 the guidelines of the Pareto optimization are detailed, in Sect. 6 the algorithm is described and an example is referenced to illustrate the set of non-dominated solutions. Finally, Sect. 7 shows computational experiments.

2 Literature Review

The objective of the maintenance activities is not only to increase the productivity, but also some performance indicators like machine efficiency [1]. Rarely, productivity and efficiency have been considered simultaneously in scheduling decisions [2]. However, recently some works have been published, which integrate both decisions in sceneries of a single machine [3–5], parallel machines [6, 7], flow-shop [8–10] and flow-shop with sequence-dependent and setup times [11–13]. Concerning to Job-shop, some maintenance activities have been added. However, there is not any benchmark that integrates with set-up times.

The reference of publications that considers maintenance activities to Job-shop configuration aims to minimize makespan [14] and the idle time [15]. Other works consider Pareto optimization with genetic algorithms [16] and artificial bee colony [17]. In local search algorithms reversing critical arcs have been the most used (see [18, 19]) by the case of regular criteria and disjunctive graph model. The main contribution of our paper is the extension of the classical estimation function at reversing critical arcs for regular criteria adapted to the Job-shop Scheduling problem with maintenance activities and sequence-dependent set-up times under a Pareto approach evaluated by quality metrics proposed in the literature (see for example [20, 21]). The best of our knowledge, this problem has not been studied.

3 Problem Description and Modeling

JSP is modeled as follows. A set of n jobs $J = \{J_1, \ldots J_n\}$ are processed on a set $M = \{M_1, \ldots M_m\}$ of m machines that are available. Each machine can only process one job at a time. A job J_i is obtained at performing sequentially n_i operations in a fix route. Each operation is processed on a unique machine. Preempting operations is not allowed. It means that an operation cannot be interrupted once started. Solving the JSP implies to determine the sequence of operations on machines to optimize an objective function.

The disjunctive graph proposed in [19] is used to represent the problem at considering criteria based on tardiness, which is necessary to determine the completion time of J_i (C_i), therefore the due date d_i of J_i is known. When the sequence on each machine is determined, it means solves the conflict on a disjunctive graph to create a conjunctive one, where the arcs are directed without creating a cycle and a sets of criteria are calculated. The Fig. 1 illustrates an example of an instance of the JSP with a disjunctive and a conjunctive graph. It represents an instance of three jobs. The node 0 is the beginning of operations and jobs. The nodes ϕ_1, ϕ_2 and ϕ_3 represent the finalization of the jobs. To explain briefly the structure of the graph, the nodes 1 and 2 represent the route of operations for the first job. The red arcs with double arrow in Fig. 1(a) represent the conflict on a specific machine at determining its sequence, which is solved on conjunctive graph (see Fig. 1(b)), where a cycle cannot be generated.

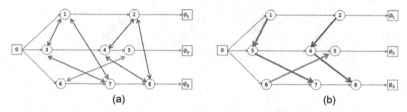

(a)   (b)

Fig. 1. Disjunctive and conjunctive graphs for an instance of the JSP

When a solution is obtained and considering the properties from [21], the length of an arc is equal to the processing time of the operation from which it starts. For an operation x, the processing time is p_x. The starting time of x, $h_x = L(0, x)$, called head, that corresponds to the length of the longest path from 0 to x. The tail from a node x to the dummy node $\phi_i(q_x^i)$ is equal to [L $(x, \phi_i) - p_x$] if a path exists from x to ϕ_i and $-\infty$ otherwise. A path from 0 to ϕ_i is called critical if its length is equal to C_i, and every node x belonging to this critical path is critical according to job J_i. A critical node x for job J_i satisfies $h_x + p_x + q_x^i = C_i$. An arc belonging to the critical path of J_i is critical if it connects two operations x and y that are assigned to the same machine and belong to different job. The level l_x of a node x denotes the maximum number of arcs in a path from 0 to x. After obtaining the heads of the nodes of the graph, the criterion of a feasible schedule represented by the selection can be determined in $O(n)$ from the starting times of the dummy nodes. For instance, the makespan is obtained using the formula $C_{max} = \max C_i$. The tardiness (T_i), $T_i = \max(0, C_i - d_i)$. Then the maximum tardiness is $T_{max} = \max T_i$ and total tardiness (T) is the sum of the tardiness of jobs. It is important to highlight that P_{rx}(resp. P_{sx}) is the predecessor in the route (resp. in the sequence) of x, and F_{rx}(resp. F_{sx}) is the sucessor in the route (resp. in the sequence) of x.

Concerning to the maintenance activities for machines, MA_m represents the maximum frequency of maintenance operation on machine m, $A_{(x)}$ is the current frequency of maintenance operation on machine where x is performed ($MA_m \geq A_x$). PM_m is the duration of the maintenance operation on m, S_{lkm} is the set-up time for preparing the machine m at changing from job l to job k. Let ST_{lm} be the preparing time for the machine m for the job l, if l is the first assigned job to m or, if l is the assigned job after a maintenance operation on m. Finally, let TM_{lm} be the time for preparing the machine m for the maintenance operation as soon as m has finished an operation that belongs to job l.

The Fig. 2(a) illustrate an instance for a problem with four machines (M1, M2, M3 and M4) and four jobs (J1, J2, J3 and J4) by a set of tables which information represents the times of maintenance activities. For example, considering the machine M1, the maximum frequency of maintenance operation is $MA_1 = 40$ (see frequency) and its duration $PM_1 = 6$ (see Maintenance time), the preparing times ST_{l1} where $l = 1, 2\ and\ 3$ are respectively 5, 1 and 3 (see start). Besides the TM_{l1} are 3, 2 and 1 (see column Maint). The other values on the same table are the set up times, for example the set time for changing the machine from J_1 to J_2 is 3 (see the cell with the underlined 3).

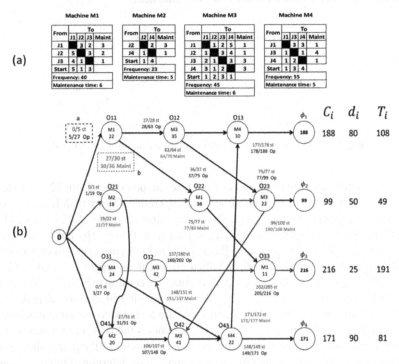

Fig. 2. Information of machines and solution for the proposed instance. (Color figure online)

Figure 2(b) shows a conjunctive graph that represents a solution for the proposed instance with the completion time of jobs (column C_i), the due date of jobs (column d_i) and their tardiness (column T_i). It is explained by an example as follows. The route of the first job is formed by three operations (O_{11}, O_{12} and O_{13}). The processing time for O_{11} is 22 and it is performed on machine M1. The sequence of operations on M1 is O_{11}, O_{22} and O_{33}. For explaining the structure of times, the operation O_{11} is analyzed and the information is located in the dashed rectangles (a and b). O_{11} is the first operation in the sequence of M1, the $ST_{11} = 5$, see start row in the table for machine M1 on Fig. 2(a). Therefore, if M1 starts at time 0, it finishes its preparing at time 5 (see letters in red color on rectangle a). After that, O_{11} is processed between the time 5 and 27 since the processing time is 22 (see letters in black color). The operation is finished and the machine goes to a maintenance operation, since $MA_1 = 40$ and the processing time for O_{22} is 38, it implies that the sum of their processing time $(22 + 38 = 60)$ must be lower than 40. M1 is prepared for a maintenance operation between the times 27 and 30 (see red letters on rectangle b) and finally from 30 to 36 on M1 the maintenance operation is performed. At solving the graph, the completion time of jobs are $C_1 = 188$, $C_2 = 99$, $C_3 = 216$ and $C_4 = 171$. In this instance, the makespan is 216 $(C_{max} = 216)$ and the critical path that affects the criterion is highlighted in purple color. The value for the maximum tardiness is 191 $(T_{max} = 191)$ and the Total flow time is 674 $(\sum C_i = 674)$.

4 Move Evaluation and Estimation Function

To transform the graph, our approach estimates the value of the criterion at reversing a critical arc (x, y) which affects it. The estimation function is inspired in [19], which estimates the completion time of J_i. Our contribution consists on adapting the expressions at considering the effect of maintenance activities and set-up times. The estimated completion time of J_i or for node ϕ_i $\tilde{C}_i$ is analyzed by three expressions: $L_{(1,i)}$, $L_{(2,i)}$ and $L_{(3,i)}$. $L_{(1,i)}$ considers all paths from the node F_{ry}. $L_{(2,i)}$ Estimates simultaneously the nodes F_{rx} and F_{sy} since after reversing critical arc (x, y), an arc from x to F_{sy} is created. $L_{(3,i)}$ is the estimation considering nodes $\omega/l_\omega = l_x$ and $\omega \neq x$, which is constant and expressed as $L_{(3,i)} = \max_{\omega \neq x}(h_\omega + P_\omega + q_{(w,i)})$.

For proposing the estimation, we denote the job J_r for P_{sx}, J_s for x, J_t for y and J_U for F_{sy}. To explain the situation before and after reversing the arc, Fig. 3 illustrates the transformation in the graph and the expression to estimate $\tilde{C}_i$. Besides, four cases that affect the completion of J_i and their expressions are detailed in Fig. 4. The first case considers that the maintenance activity does not affect the inversion of the arc (x, y). In the second case the maintenance activity is performed just before x. In the third case, the maintenance activity is located between x and y and finally just after y. Note that the start time for y and x (h_y and h_x) are estimated.

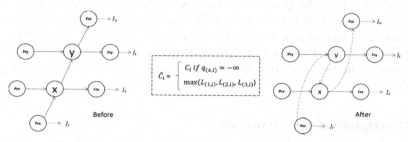

Fig. 3. Transformation in the graph at reversing critical arc (x, y)

An important aspect to analyze at reversing critical arc (x, y) is the condition of the maintenance activity. For example, in Case 1, Case 2 and Case 4 there is not any problem, since at reversing the arc (x, y) the maximum frequency (MA_m) is not affected. In case

$$\bar{h}_y = max(h_{psx} + P_{sx}, h_{pry} + P_{pry}) + S_{rt}$$
$$\bar{h}_x = max(\bar{h}_y + P_y, h_{prx} + P_{prx}) + S_{ts}$$
$$L_{(1,t)} = \bar{h}_y + P_y + P_{Fry} + q_{(Fry,t)}$$
$$L_{(2,t)} = \bar{h}_x + P_x + max(P_{Frx} + q_{(Frx,t)}, \; S_{su} + P_{Fsy} + q_{(Fsy,t)})$$

① ②

$$\bar{h}_y = max(h_{psx} + P_{psx} + TM_{rm} + PM_m + ST_{tm}, h_{pry} + P_{pry})$$
$$\bar{h}_x = max(\bar{h}_y + P_y, h_{prx} + P_{prx}) + S_{ts}$$
$$L_{(1,t)} = \bar{h}_y + P_y + P_{Fry} + q_{(Fry,t)}$$
$$L_{(2,t)} = \bar{h}_x + P_x + max(P_{Frx} + q_{(Frx,t)}, \; S_{su} + P_{Fsy} + q_{(Fsy,t)})$$

③

$$\bar{h}_y = max(h_{psx} + P_{psx}, h_{pry} + P_{pry}) + S_{rt}$$
$$\bar{h}_x = max(\bar{h}_y + P_y + TM_{tm} + PM_m + ST_{sm}, h_{prx} + P_{prx})$$
$$L_{(1,t)} = \bar{h}_y + P_y + P_{Fry} + q_{(Fry,t)}$$
$$L_{(2,t)} = \bar{h}_x + P_x + max(P_{Frx} + q_{(Frx,t)}, \; S_{su} + P_{Fsy} + q_{(Fsy,t)})$$

④

$$\bar{h}_y = max(h_{psx} + P_{psx}, h_{pry} + P_{pry}) + S_{rt}$$
$$\bar{h}_x = max(\bar{h}_y + P_y, h_{prx} + P_{prx}) + S_{ts}$$
$$L_{(1,t)} = \bar{h}_y + P_y + P_{Fry} + q_{(Fry,t)}$$
$$L_{(2,t)} = \bar{h}_x + P_x + max\begin{pmatrix} P_{Frx} + q_{(Frx,t)}, TM_{sm} + PM_m + \\ ST_{um} + P_{Fsy} + q_{(Fsy,t)} \end{pmatrix}$$

Fig. 4. Expressions for estimating $\tilde{C}_i$ considering the four cases

3, the processing times of x and y can affect the frequency of maintenance on machine m. Consequently, it must be satisfied that $A_y - P_y + P_x \leq MA_m$ and simultaneously $A_x - P_x + P_y \leq MA_m$.

5 Pareto Optimization and Quality of the Front

In a multi objective approach, regular criteria must be minimized. The objective of the Pareto optimization is to find a set of non-dominated solutions Q, which satisfies the dominance conditions described in [20, 21]. The Fig. 5 helps to illustrate three non-dominated solutions of the instance illustrated in Fig. 2 at minimizing makespan, maximum tardiness and total flow time simultaneously, where Fig. 5(a) aims to minimize makespan, 5(b) the maximum tardiness and 5(c) the total flow time. Note that neither of the solutions is dominant when comparing the three criteria.

To determine the quality of the Pareto Front, we adopted the set of metrics described in [20] at evaluating the convergence and diversity. Convergence leads to Q must be located nearest to the origin of coordinates and diversity conducts to find variety of solutions in sparsely space to make efficient decisions. For the convergence the hyper volume (HV), elite solutions and the Mean Ideal Distance (MID) are measured. HV is the volume covered by Q respect to the worst solution. Elite solutions are the best values of the criteria. MID is the average Euclidean distance obtained between each non-dominated solution and the origin. The maximum spread (D) and spacing (SP) are evaluated for the diversity. D is the longest diagonal of the hyper box formed by the extreme values of the criteria, and SP is the average distance between consecutive solutions.

6 Description of the Algorithm

Our algorithm is a local search process that uses the properties of the conjunctive graph explained in Sect. 3, using the estimation function described in Sect. 4 and an efficient procedure to update Q proposed in [20]. The search starts with an initial solution, which is the first solution added to Q. Then, iteratively two phases (improvement and diversification) are performed. In the initial solution, the jobs are collected according

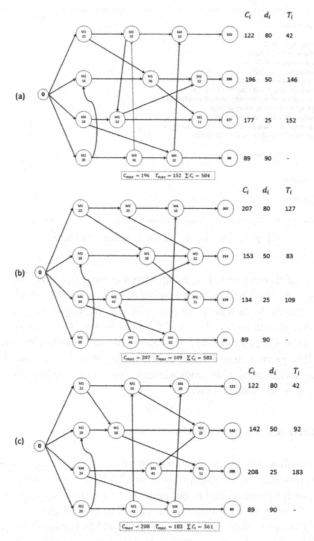

Fig. 5. Three non-dominated solutions at minimizing simultaneously $C_{max} T_{max}$ and $\sum C_i$

to increasing order to their due-date. Then, for the sequence of operations on machines is solved at considering the operation in route of the order jobs. It means that, if there exist an ordering of jobs, the sequence decisions solve the first operation of all them, then, the second and so on. In the improvement phase, initially, a random criterion is selected to create improving moves iteratively. When it is not possible to create a move using the selected criterion, it is penalized and a new criterion is selected. As soon as an improving move is generated for a penalized criterion, it could be considered to be selected. When all criteria are penalized, it implies that an improvement move cannot be created and the diversification phase is executed considering the last penalized criterion. Figure 6 describes the pseudo code of the improvement phase.

```
Input initial Solution
Current Solution ← initial Solution
CRT =∅
While (This running the algorithm) Do
    Fill the CRT vector with the k criteria
    While(There is a k criterion in CRT) Do
        Csel ← Random (Crt_i ∈ CRT)
        Determine the neighbors of the current solution that optimize Csel
        While (There is a neighbor that optimizes Csel) Do
            Select a neighbor of the current solution that optimizes Csel
            If (The neighbor is non-dominated) Then
                Update the set non-dominated solution
                Update de local and global optimal for the k criteria
                Current solution to the selected neighbor
            Else
                Remove the selected neighbor
            End If
        End While
        Remove Csel of CRT
    End While
    Go To the diversification phase
End While
```

Fig. 6. Pseudo code of the improvement phase

Several strategies were tested to escape from a local optimal solution. The best strategy consists on selecting a random number $\propto$ ($5 \leq \propto \leq 10$), which represents the number of generations. In each generation, a random critical operation x is chosen. After that, all f feasible insertions for $x(j - x - k)$ applying the HT conditions proposed by [20] are determined. Considering the f feasible insertions, a random number r ($1 \leq r \leq f$) is selected. The graph is transformed at performing the rth insertion. If the criterion is improved, the search goes to the improvement phase removing the penalization of all criteria. Else, a new generation is created.

7   Computational Experiments

To validate and evaluate the efficiency of our approach for the four criteria, the instances studied for the Job-shop scheduling problem in [22] have been considered and transformed to the conditions described in our approach using a parameter $f = 1.6$ to determine due date of jobs. Our algorithm was developed in Java language. The experiments were conducted on a PC with 3.40 GHz and 8 GB RAM during 300 s and ten times per instance. The Fig. 7 shows the results at performing our approach at minimizing makespan, maximum tardiness and total flow time (TFT) for the instance described Fig. 2. The Fig. 7(a) represents a txt file with the results. For example, the algorithm gets eight non-dominated solutions. Each solution shows the value of the criteria. Additionally, the metrics are separated by diversity and convergence. In 7(b), the eight non-dominated solutions are plotted on a three dimensional plane.

Determining parameters with considerations of maintenance activities and Set-up times was developed only one time. Then, they were saved in the original txt file. The process is as follows. For each instance, the number of maintenance activities per machine was determined randomly at selecting a number between 2 and 3. MA_m was determined at dividing the sum of its processing time per operation and the number of maintenance activities. Logically, it was ensured that this value would be greater or equal than the highest processing time. PM_m was fixed as a random number that belongs to the interval

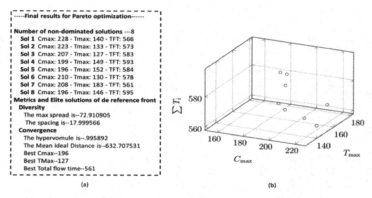

Fig. 7. Results for the instance at minimizing C_{max}, T_{max} and $\sum C_i$

from 12 to 15. The other times, random numbers from 1 to 9 were considered. The results are presented for combinations of regular criteria (see Table 1) in three different sets of criteria (Set_1, Set_2 and Set_3) see column S 1, 2 and 3 respectively. In Set_1, makespan (C_{max}) and maximum tardiness (T_{max}) are minimized. In Set_2 total flow time ($\sum C_i$) is added. Finally in Set_3 the total tardiness ($\sum T_i$) is introduced. The Table 1 illustrate the results for three instances (see column I) in the different sets, elite solutions are underlined and column N represents the number of non-dominated solutions.

Different analysis could be presented; they are illustrated in function of number of solutions (N), value of criteria and the metrics. Concerning to N, Set_3 generates more solutions than the others. It could be inferred that the addition of criteria leads to increase the solutions, which is evidenced that in the three instances Set_1 generates the fewest solutions. Logically to avoid the confusion for the decision maker a reduction procedure should be developed to ensure diversity and convergence. If the criteria are analyzed in the three sets, the performance of C_{max} and T_{max} is considered. Respect to C_{max} Set_1 gets the best makespan for one instance (see the instance abz6 underlined solution 1128 in Table 1) and in the other instances Set_3 performs better than the others. At analyzing T_{max} Set_3 arrives to better results. These analysis leads to affirm that adding criteria improves the quality of the front at minimizing the convergence. Besides, this conclusion could be extended by the case of $\sum C_i$ at analyzing Set_2 and Set_3 when adding $\sum T_i$ (see Table 1 at comparing $\sum C_i$ in both sets). The last facts confirm that Set_3 is the best combination of criteria analyzed to minimize, consequently, the quality metrics are illustrated with a representative number of solutions.

Our experiments reveal that optimizing in Pareto manner, different combinations of criteria could be executed to determine the best performance. In this case Set_3 is an excellent alternative for making decisions.

Table 1. Non-dominated solutions and quality metrics for the three sets

S	I	N	Solutions	MID	HV	D	S
1	abz6	6	[1236,184][1234,188][1295,179][1128,214][1215,191][1361,174]	1259,2	0,986	236,4	38,3
	la16	8	[1254,355][1217,360][1345,278][1176,402][1200,395][1218,359][1269,326][1272,318]	1292, 9	0,984	209,6	34,1
	orb5	2	[1199,349][1224,290]	1253,3	0,984	64,1	64,1
2	abz6	7	[1275,184,9580] [1273,182,9646] [1308,174,9760] [1224,183,9664] [1159,183,9686] [1158,183,9706] [1167,174,10098]	9812,8	0,98	539,4	127,0
	la16	14	[1359,270,10008] [1359,284,9965] [1359,287,9955] [1359,297,9951] [1296,443,9650] [1281,336,10205] [1334,308,9703][1264,417,9684] [1153,363,10053] [1218,360,10122] [1300,299,9765] [1331,299,9754] [1248,341,9697] [1358,394,9626]	9958,5	0,97	638,4	50,4
	orb5	8	[1294,360,8777] [1250,316,8974] [1252,318,8940] [1228,294,9164] [1187,330,8955] [1165,366,9151] [1164,365,9214] [1163,309,9621]	9186,3	0,98	857,1	137,2
3	abz6	12	[1167,151,9868,483] [1189,182,9884,470] [1202,181,9423,386] [1212,181,9361,388] [1204,181,9417,372] [1231,174,9448,359] [1250,159,9382,370] [1265,107,9371,350] [1258,146,9426,425] [1226,169,9627,404] [1270,112,9470,341] [1278,101,9505,340]	9603,7	0,976	559,3	53,0
	la16	36	[1141,366,9768,1539] [1231,273,9588,1206] [1267,268,9588,1306] [1257,299,9390,969] [1319,253,9401,980] [1257,299,9423,968] [1257,299,9334,1001] [1261,297,9010,823] [1263,299,8854,739] [1283,319,8868,663] [1199,378,9891,1362] [1208,346,9859,1370] [1222,410,9422,1240] [1212,337,9837,1380] [1221,330,9936,1461] [1145,330,10045,1572] [1147,329,10047,1566] [1152,329,9974,1493] [1152,329,9971,1501] [1212,350,9671,1191] [1301,244,9615,1369] [1216,330,9836,1586] [1169,346,9745,1386] [1169,348,9729,1370] [1192,334,9822,1443] [1302,232,9316,1071] [1244,232,9759,1309] [1235,348,9434,1053] [1318,215,9308,1005] [1308,205,9284,1040] [1326,223,9266,1037] [1278,202,9723,1254] [1277,202,9775,1267] [1312,204,9621,1224] [1288,212,9673,1204] [1214,344,9423,938]	9749,6	0,974	1533,8	71,9

(continued)

Table 1. (*continued*)

S	I	N	Solutions	MID	HV	D	S
orb5	34		[1239,330,8949,1406] [1255,321,8660,1203] [1175,386,8889,1296] [1181,362,8916,1244] [1173,385,8941,1281] [1242,308,8980,1196] [1180,361,8967,1427] [1158,370,8981,1441] [1244,310,8869,1150] [1162,365,9209,1476] [1162,365,9229,1462] [1168,311,9031,1183] [1160,373,9133,1347] [1160,373,9068,1385] [1166,373,9006,1394] [1182,363,8633,1155] [1184,365,8611,1165] [1177,320,8992,1311] [1177,320,9003,1290] [1180,323,8984,1323] [1181,324,8991,1313] [1213,356,8729,1200] [1213,356,8752,1199] [1161,362,9145,1534] [1161,362,9166,1523] [1233,376,8837,1002] [1215,358,8871,1036] [1261,327,8883,1048] [1234,300,8994,1161] [1189,332,8808,1272]	9119,1	0,975	828,9	43,9

8 Conclusion

This paper presented a local search algorithm to minimize regular criteria in the Job-shop Scheduling problem with maintenance activities, sequence dependent and set-up times using Pareto optimization. The best of our knowledge, the consideration of maintenance activity has not been studied for this kind of problem and it is scarce for other scheduling extensions. The algorithm is supported in the adaptation of estimation functions as extensions of the classic Job-shop scheduling problem and the proposition of the conjunctive graph. In its formulation, the properties of heads, tails and levels of operations have been considered. Computational results show the efficiency of our algorithm.

Finally, we are also extending our approach to the simultaneous optimization of multiple criteria and as perspectives the extension of our approach in other environments such as the flexible Job-shop Scheduling Problem. This research is supported by the project identified with the code 18-531-INT, which is financed by the Universidad de Ibagué (Colombia).

References

1. Zandieh, M., Khatami, A., Rahmati, S.: Flexible job shop scheduling under condition-based maintenance: improved version of imperialist competitive algorithm. Appl. Soft Comput. J. **58**, 449–464 (2017)
2. Rahmati, S., Ahmadi, A., Govindan, K.: A novel integrated condition-based maintenance and stochastic flexible job shop scheduling problem: simulation-based optimization approach. Ann. Oper. Res. **269**(1–2), 583–621 (2018)
3. Cassady, C., Kutanoglu, E.: Integrating preventive maintenance planning and production scheduling for a single machine. IEEE Trans. Reliab. **54**(2), 304–309 (2005)
4. Finke, G., Gara-Ali, A., Espinouse, M., Jost, V., Moncel, J.: Unified matrix approach to solve production-maintenance problems on a single machine. Omega (United Kingdom) **66**, 140–146 (2017)
5. Rebai, M., Kacem, I., Adjallah, K.: Earliness-tardiness minimization on a single machine to schedule preventive maintenance tasks: metaheuristic and exact methods. J. Intell. Manuf. **23**(4), 1207–1224 (2012)
6. Lei, D., Liu, M.: An artificial bee colony with division for distributed unrelated parallel machine scheduling with preventive maintenance. Comput. Ind. Eng. **141**, 106320 (2020)
7. Shen, J., Zhu, Y.: A parallel-machine scheduling problem with periodic maintenance under uncertainty. J. Ambient Intell. Humaniz. Comput. **10**(8), 3171–3179 (2018). https://doi.org/10.1007/s12652-018-1032-8
8. Pérez-González, P., Fernández-Viagas, V., Framinan, J.: Permutation flowshop scheduling with periodic maintenance and makespan objective. Comput. Ind. Eng. **143**, 106369 (2020)
9. Miyata, H., Nagano, M., Gupta, J.: Incorporating preventive maintenance into the m-machine no-wait flow-shop scheduling problem with total flow-time minimization: a computational study. Eng. Optim. **51**(4), 680–698 (2019)
10. Boufellouh, R., Belkaid, F.: Bi-objective optimization algorithms for joint production and maintenance scheduling under a global resource constraint: application to the permutation flow shop problem. Comput. Oper. Res. **122**, 104943 (2020)
11. Miyata, H., Nagano, M., Gupta, J.: Integrating preventive maintenance activities to the no-wait flow shop scheduling problem with dependent-sequence setup times and makespan minimization. Comput. Ind. Eng. **135**, 79–104 (2019)

12. Naderi, B., Zandieh, M., Fatemi Ghomi, S.: A study on integrating sequence dependent setup time flexible flow lines and preventive maintenance scheduling. J. Intell. Manuf. **20**(6), 683–694 (2009)
13. Khamseh, A., Jolai, F., Babaei, M.: Integrating sequence-dependent group scheduling problem and preventive maintenance in flexible flow shops. Int. J. Adv. Manuf. Technol. **77**(1–4), 173–185 (2014)
14. Ben Ali, M., Sassi, M., Gossa, M., Harrath, Y.: Simultaneous scheduling of production and maintenance tasks in the job shop. Int. J. Prod. Res. **49**(13), 3891–3918 (2011)
15. Naderi, B., Zandieh, M., Fatemi Ghomi, S.: Scheduling sequence-dependent setup time job shops with preventive maintenance. Int. J. Adv. Manuf. Technol. **43**(1–2), 170–181 (2009)
16. Rahmati, S., Ahmadi, A., Karimi, B.: Multi-objective evolutionary simulation based optimization mechanism for a novel stochastic reliability centered maintenance problem. Swarm Evol. Comput. **40**, 255–271 (2018)
17. Vela, C., Varela, R., González, M.: Local search and genetic algorithm for the job shop scheduling problem with sequence dependent setup times. J. Heuristics **16**(2), 139–165 (2010)
18. Bürgy, R.: A neighborhood for complex job shop scheduling problems with regular objectives. J. Sched. **20**(4), 391–422 (2017). https://doi.org/10.1007/s10951-017-0532-2
19. Mati, Y., Dauzère-Pérès, S., Lahlou, C.: A general approach for optimizing regular criteria in the job-shop scheduling problem. Eur. J. Oper. Res. **212**(1), 33–42 (2011)
20. García-León, A.A., Dauzère-Pérès, S., Mati, Y.: An efficient Pareto approach for solving the multi-objective flexible job-shop scheduling problem with regular criteria. Comput. Oper. Res. **108**, 187–200 (2019)
21. García-León, A.A., Torres Tapia, W.F.: A general local search pareto approach with regular criteria for solving the job-shop scheduling problem multi-resource resource flexibility with linear routes. In: Figueroa-García, J.C., Duarte-González, M., Jaramillo-Isaza, S., Orjuela-Cañon, A.D., Díaz-Gutierrez, Y. (eds.) WEA 2019. CCIS, vol. 1052, pp. 764–775. Springer, Cham (2019). https://doi.org/10.1007/978-3-030-31019-6_64
22. Singer, M., Pinedo, M.: A computational study of branch and bound techniques for minimizing the total weighted tardiness in job shops. IIE Trans. **30**(2), 109–118 (1998)

A Mathematical Model for the Optimization of the Non-metallic Mining Supply Chain in the Mining District of Calamarí-Sucre (Colombia)

Holman Ospina-Mateus[1]([✉]) [iD], Jairo Montero-Perez[1], Jaime Acevedo-Chedid[1] [iD], Katherinne Salas-Navarro[2] [iD], and Natalie Morales-Londoño[3] [iD]

[1] Department of Industrial Engineering, Universidad Tecnológica de Bolívar, Cartagena, Colombia
{hospina,jacevedo}@utb.edu.co, jairo.monteroperez@gmail.com
[2] Department of Productivity and Innovation, Universidad de la Costa, Barranquilla, Colombia
ksalas2@cuc.edu.co
[3] Department of Industrial Engineering, Fundacion Universitaria Tecnologico Comfenalco, Cartagena, Colombia
nmoralesl@tecnocomfenalco.edu.co

Abstract. This article presents a mathematical model of the Supply chain of non-metallic mining. The model considers uncertainty scenarios in materials, elements for capacity planning in a multilevel chain and with multiple products. The mathematical model is collaborative and maximizes the profits of the actors in the supply chain. The model is implemented in Calamarí-Sucre mining district (Colombia). The scenario is applied to the extraction, processing, storage, and distribution of limestone. To solve the model, the GAMS software was used through libraries of relaxed mixed nonlinear programming - RMINLP and the DICOPT solver. The results indicate that the greatest benefits occur in a scenario of the high provision of raw materials. The equity in the economic benefits show a dynamics of vertical integration in the sector. The model applied to non-metallic mining complexes helps determine optimal strategies and decisions in different echelons.

Keywords: Mining complex · Supply chain · Mineral · Non-metallic · Optimization · Mathematical model · Limestone

1 Introduction

The mining industry is a complex and dynamic system, immersed in an unstable market with little synergy [1]. [2, 3] Ensure that many companies need structural change for viability, through cost reduction, focus on productivity, value added, capital investment, and innovation. In this sense, the problems in the mining operations in their functional dimension, include the programming of the open pit and underground mine. The determining the optimal production schedule during the useful life of the deposit, the allocation and

J. C. Figueroa-García et al. (Eds.): WEA 2020, CCIS 1274, pp. 194–207, 2020.
https://doi.org/10.1007/978-3-030-61834-6_17

dispatch of the equipment of drag and load in the mine, the processing of the ore, and the transport. The complexity of the system effectively implies the routing and control of the movement of the material [4]. In Colombia, the productive chain of the non-metallic mining sector is oriented towards the exploration, exploitation, and commercialization of minerals such as sand, limestone, and clays [5].

In terms of the total value of world mineral production, for the year 2011, a 10% growth was evidenced in developed countries and 22% in developing countries [6, 7]. Worldwide, the reserve of non-metallic minerals has been increased [8, 9]. The countries that lead the world production, have achieved a solid development reaching significant levels of economic growth [5]. Latin America (Chile, Peru, Brazil, and Colombia) was one of the four regions of the world showed record growth in exports [10]. Mining is an economic activity of interest in Colombia, especially in the non-metallic sector [11]. The promotion of a set of strategic minerals such as Coal, gold, nickel, platinum, emeralds and construction materials, are considered critical for the productive and economic development of the country [12].

The main problems that affect mining performance are low levels of productivity, high production costs, and investment. For these problems, optimization models can be proposed that help the decision and the functional dimensions of the business. In decisions, capacity, efficient allocation of resources, constraints, and scheduling of operations can be considered. The use of mathematical models is a key tool for the design and implementation of supply chains [13]. [14] Define that stochastic programming methodology represents the best way to address problems and solutions within mineral supply chains. In the same way, [14] consider that the large mining operations are composed of several mines and processing plants, as well as storage sites, railways, ports and supply stations, each one with different capacities [14]. Pro-pose a stochastic model for strategic capacity planning in the global mining supply chain that includes operating zones, processing plants, multimodal transport, porting areas and final distribution [15]. Consider a method for modeling a complex supply chain using a combination of optimization techniques and simulation of discrete events [16]. Studied an unconventional approach to estimate mineral reserves throughout the chain, forecasting production and integrating stochastic simulation and optimization [17]. Developed an extension of the supply chain model of a mining complex with several mines, based on a multi-scenario method for mining production [18]. Designed a model for optimizing capacity planning considering future demand.

On the other hand, [19] developed in two scenarios the stochastic global model of optimization for the programming of the production of complexes of open-pit mining with uncertainty [20]. Developed a multi-objective optimization model for the selection of partners in mining companies [21]. Proposed a supply chain model for coal mine planning through linear programming for production programming [22]. Developed an extension of the supply chain model for a mining complex that contains several mines and operates simultaneously in operations with multiple rock types and processing flows [23]. Designed a model for the optimization of capacity planning in supply chains of minerals that tends to minimize the cost of infrastructure expansion [18]. Developed in two stages the global stochastic optimization model for programming the production of open pit mining complexes with uncertainty [24]. Developed a theoretical two-stage economic model to obtain the value of stored reserves for future processing minerals

This research offers a new mathematical model to optimize the activities of the mining chain that considers the method of extraction in quarries, reserves, processing, and distribution of non-metallic minerals, as well as the quality of the material extracted by the uncertainty of the deposit, analyzing the productive process, capacities and limited resources. In addition, provide a source of competitive advantage for planning and control of production under different scenarios. In This study, First, present the context of the problem (Sect. 1). Next, the elements of non-metallic mining are presented for the mathematical formulation (Sect. 2) and finally, the results (Sect. 3) and conclusions (Sect. 4) of the model and the application case.

2   Method

2.1   Overview

The object of study concentrates on the analysis of the non-metallic mining supply chain, which allows optimizing a mining complex. The model is structured in four levels that include *quarries* as suppliers, producers, and extracting associations of non-metallic minerals. In addition, there are *reserve zones* where different types of raw materials of non-metallic minerals are stored and mixed. *Processing plants* in which the production plants are located that transform the raw materials into finished products and *distributors* of finished products. Based on the reference models of [7] and [10] and the mining value chain in the technical architecture, Fig. 1 presents the conceptual model of the supply chain of non-metallic mining.

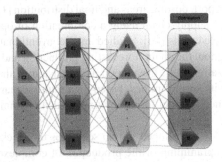

Fig. 1. Conceptual model of the supply chain of non-metallic mining.

In the following section the considerations and notation of the mathematical model are shown.

2.2   Fundamental Assumptions and Notation

The assumptions adopted for the development of the model were: i) There are multiple quarries, reserve areas, distributors and processing plants. The model has scenarios under uncertainty, according to the level of supply of raw materials: low, medium and high. ii) In the first level, non-metallic minerals are extracted as raw material, under different scenarios and precedence in mining terraces, in which there are decisions about the exploitation of these, including alternatives of transport from quarries to reserve zones and/or processing plants, attending to a maximum capacity level. There are amounts of shortages and surpluses. Likewise, exploitation, storage and transportation costs are related, penalties for shortages or surpluses, and, the inventory level at the end of each period. iii) In the second level, the storage of raw materials occurs, which includes the inventory level at the end of each period. Material handling costs are considered for the transfer of raw materials from the reserve areas to processing plants. iv) In the third level, decisions are made for the alternatives of operation in processing plants. The transformed products are transported to the final distributor according to the capacity levels. A quality factor is applied to the materials in process. Penalties for shortages or surpluses are also considered. v) The distributors relate the quantities of products to be sold (demand). The distributors select the transport system from the processing plants to the consumers.

2.3 Declaration of Indices

$e \in E$: Scenarios (1, 2, 3); $t, k \in T$: Periods of operational planning in the supply chain; $c \in C$: Quarries; $b, j \in B$: Extraction terraces in the quarries; $r \in R$: Reserve zones; $p \in P$: Processing plants; $a \in A$: Operation alternatives in the p processing plant; $n \in N$: Types of non-metallic minerals; $m \in M$: Final products of non-metallic minerals; $s \in S$: Transportation systems; $d \in D$: Distributors of non-metallic minerals.

2.4 Declaration of Variables

$M_{e,t}$ = Expected total benefits from the non-metallic mining supply chain in the scenarios s and the periods p (\$); $de_{e,t}$ = Discount benefit in the period t under the scenario e (\$); $dq_{e,t,c}$ = Discount at the quarry c in the period t under the scenario e (\$); $db_{e,t,d}$ = Discount profit on the distributors d in the period t under the scenario e (\$); $dp_{e,t,p}$ = Discount on the plants p in the period t and the scenario e (\$); $cop_{e,t,p,d,s}$ = Costs of transporting minerals from the processing plants p to the distributors d in the period t under the scenario e (\$); $cot_{e,t,c}$ = Costs of the exploitation in the quarry c in the period t under the scenario e (\$); $cop_{e,t,r,p}$ = Costs of handling minerals from the reserve zones r to plants p in the period t under scenario e (\$); $cos_{e,t,s}$ = Total transportation costs with the transport system s in the period t under the scenario e (\$); $coc_{e,t,p}$ = Costs of processing minerals in the processing plants p in the period t under the scenario e (\$); $com_{e,t,r}$ = Total cost of storage at the reserve zones r in the period t under the scenario e (\$); $comc_{e,t,c}$ = Total cost of storage at the quarry c in the period t under the scenario e (\$); $comp_{e,t,p}$ = Total cost of storage at the processing plants p in the period t under the scenario e (\$); $cocp_{e,t,c,p,s}$ = Costs of transport minerals in the system s from the quarry c to the processing plants p in the period t under the scenario e (\$); $cocr_{e,t,c,r,s}$ = Cost of transportation from the quarry c to the reserve zones r in the period t under the scenario e (\$); $incs_{e,t}$ = Total income per mineral sale in the period t and the scenario e (\$); $ingc_{e,t,c,n}$ = Income from sales of the n minerals in the quarries c in the period t under the scenario e (\$); $ingd_{e,t,d,m}$ = Income from the sale of minerals m in the distributor d in the period t under the scenario e (\$); $ingp_{e,t,p,m}$ = Mineral sales revenue m in the processing plants p in the period t under the scenario e (\$); $mpla_{e,t,r,p,n}$ = Mineral n sent the reserve zones r to plants p in the period t and the scenario e (Tons); $mtb_{e,t,d,m}$ = Tons of mineral m sold by the distributor d in the period t under the scenario e; $mct_{e,t,c,p,n}$ = Mineral n from the quarry c to plants p in the period t and the scenario e (Tons); $msr_{e,t,c,r,n}$ = Mineral n from the quarry c to reserve zones r in the period t and the scenario e. (Tons); $mxr_{e,t,n,r}$ = Minerals n stored in the reserve zones r in the period t under the scenario e (Tons); $matproce_{e,t,p,n}$ = Minerals n in the processing plants p in the period t and the scenario e (Tons); $penal_{e,t}$ = Penalty of the objective function in the period t and the scenario e (\$); $pct_{e,t,c}$ = Penalties for deviations from the production capacities of the quarries c in the period t under the scenario e (\$); $pce_{e,t,p}$ = Penalties for deviations from the capacities of the processing plants p in the period t under the scenario e (\$); $pecr_{e,t,s}$ = Penalties for deviations from the capacities in the transport system s in the period t and the scenario e (\$); $proct_{e,t,c}$ = Tons extracted in the quarries c in the period t and the scenario e; $propt_{e,t,p,a}$ = Tons outputs of the processing of the minerals of the processing plant p at the alternative of operation a in the period t under scenario e; $procp_{e,t,c,p,s}$ = Tons transported from the quarry c to plants p in the transport system s in the period t and the scenario e; $procr_{e,t,c,r,s}$ = Tons of products transported from the quarry c to reserve zones r in the transport system s in the period t and the scenario e; $propd_{e,t,p,d,s}$ = Tons transported from the processing plants p to the distributor d in the transport system s in the period t under the scenario e; $recmat_{e,t,p,m}$ = Tons of mineral product m recovered by different operating alternatives in the plants p in the period t under the scenario e; $tonvr_{e,t,c,r}$ = Tons sent from the quarry c to the reserve zones r in the period t and the scenario e; $tonvp_{e,t,c,p}$ = Tons sent from the quarry q to plants p in the period t and the scenario e; $tonst_{e,t,r}$ = Inventories in the reserve zones r in the period t under the scenario e (Tons); $tonps_{e,t,p}$ = Inventories in the processing plants p in the period t under the scenario e (Tons); $tonca_{e,t,c}$ = Level of inventories in the quarry c in the period t and the scenario e. (Tons); $toncs_{e,t,p}$ = Minerals processed in the processing plants p in the period t and the scenario e (Tons); $tonpla_{e,t,r,p}$ = Tons Sent from the reserve zones r to plants p in the period t and the scenario e (Tons); $VLA_{(e,t,p,a)_L}$ = Tons missing for the processing plant p in the period t under the scenario e and the alternative of operation a; $VL_{(e,t,c)_L}$ = Tons missing from the quarry c during the period t under the scenario e; $VU_{(e,t,c)_U}$ = Tons of surplus in the quarry c in the period t under the scenario e; $VUA_{(e,t,p,a)_U}$ = Tons exceeding the capacity associated with the operation alternative a at the processing plants p in the period t and the scenario e; $VUS_{(e,t,s)_U}$ = Tons exceeding the capacity in the transport system s in the period t and the scenario e; $VLS_{(e,t,s)_L}$ = Quantity of missing tons with respect to the capacity in the transport system s in the period t and the scenario e. (Ton); W = Total benefits in the non-metallic mining supply chain (\$); $X_{b,t,c,p,e}$ = Binary Variable that indicates if a terrace b is mined in the period t and sent to the plant p under the scenario e; $Xr_{b,t,c,r,e}$ = Binary Variable indicating if a terrace b is mined in the period t and sent to the Reserve Zone r under the scenario e; $Y_{t,p,a,e}$ = Binary Variable that indicates if a processing alternative a is implemented in the plant p in the period t under the scenario e; $Z_{t,p,d,s,e}$ = Proportion of the output tonnage of plant p transported to the distributor

d in the transport system s in the period t under the scenario e; $Zcp_{t,c,p,s,e}$ = Proportion of tons transported from quarries e to plants p in the period t in the transport system s under the scenario e; $Zcr_{t,c,r,s,e}$ = Proportion of tons transported from quarries c to reserve zones r in the transport system s in the period t under the scenario e.

2.5 Declaration of Parameters

$cp_{p,a}$ = Unit costs of processing in plant p with operation a ($/Ton); $CAPM_c$ = Production capacities in the quarry c (Tons); $CAPP_{p,a}$ = Processing capacity in the processing plant p using alternative a (Ton); $CAPS_s$ = Total capacity of the transport system s (Tons); $Capdis_d$ = Maximum capacity of the distributors d (Ton); cc_c = Unit costs of exploitation of the quarry c ($/Ton); $cm_{c,p}$ = Unit costs of transport of materials from the quarry c to the processing plants p ($/Ton); cs_r = Unit costs of storage of materials in the reserve zones r ($/Ton); $capres_r$ = Maximum capacity in the reserve zones r (Ton); $cmc_{c,r}$ = Unit costs of handling in the quarries c to reserve zones r ($/Ton); $cmr_{r,p}$ = Unit costs of material handling from the reserve zones r ($/Ton); csc_c = Unit costs of storage in the quarries c ($/Ton); csp_p = Unit costs of storage of minerals in the processing plants p. ($/Ton); $ctp_{p,d,s}$ = Unit costs of transport from the processing plants p to the distributors d using the transport system s ($/Ton); $Demdistrib_{e,t,d,m}$ = Demand m of the distributors d in the period t and the scenario e (Tons); $FFinos_{t,b}$ = Percentage factor of fines in the terraces b and the period t; $g_{b,e,n}$ = Percentage of minerals n in the mined terrace b and the scenario e; $ma_{b,e,t}$ = Mass of the extraction terrace b in the period t in the scenario e (Tons); $PELP_{(t,p,a)_L}$ = Unit cost of penalty associated with sub-deviation of production in operation a of the processing plant p in the period t ($/Ton); $PEU_{(t,c)_U}$ = Unit cost of penalty for excess of the production in the quarry c in the period t ($/Ton); $PEUP_{(t,p,a)_U}$ = Penalty cost associated with excess processing in operation a of the processing plant p in the period t ($/Ton); $prec_{c,n}$ = Unit sales price of mineral n in the quarry c ($/Ton); $PEL_{(t,c)_L}$ = Unit cost of penalty associated with sub-diversion of the quarry production c during the period t ($/Ton); $PELS_{(t,s)_L}$ = Penalty cost associated with non-compliance with the capacity of the transport system s in the period t($/Ton); $PEUS_{(t,s)_U}$ = Penalty cost associated with exceeding the capacity of the transport system s used in the period t ($/Ton); $Prob_e$ = Probability associated with each of the scenarios; $precd_{d,m}$ = Unit sales price of the product m in the distributors d ($/Ton); $precp_{p,m}$ = Sale price per unit of mineral product m of the processing plants p ($); $prot_{p,a,m}$ = Product proportion m recovered in the processing plants p with operation a; $Qual$ = Scale of maximum percentage of products with impurities in the processing plants; $Re_{p,a}$ = proportion input/output in the alternative of operation a of the processing plant p (Ton); $Tr_{p,d,s}$ = Binary parameter, if the output material of the processing plants p to the distributor using the transport system s [0-1]; $Trc_{c,p,s}$ = Binary parameter, if the output material in the quarries c be transported to plants p in transport system s [0-1]; $Trr_{c,r,s}$ = Binary parameter indicating if the output material in the quarries c be transport to the reserve zones r in the transport system s [0-1]; $tasd_e$ = Percentage discount rates per scenario.

2.6 Optimization Model

Once the variables have been defined, the formulation is as follows:

$$FObj \sim W = \sum_{t=1}^{T} \sum_{e=1}^{E} Prob(e) \cdot M_{e,t}, \text{ where } M_{e,t} = \frac{de_{e,t}}{(1 + tasd_e)^T} - penal_{e,t} \ \forall(e,t) \tag{1}$$

subject to :

$$de_{e,t} = \sum_{c=1}^{C} (dq_{e,t,c}) + \sum_{p=1}^{P} (db_{e,t,p}) + \sum_{d=1}^{D} (db_{e,t,d}) \forall(e,t) \tag{2}$$

$$dq_{e,t,c} = \sum_{n=1}^{N} (ingc_{e,t,c,n}) - ct_{e,t,c} - cc_{e,t,p} - \sum_{r=1}^{R} \sum_{s=1}^{S} (cr_{e,t,c,r,s}) \forall(e,t,c) \tag{3}$$

$$db_{e,t,p} = \sum_{m=1}^{M} (ingp_{e,t,p,m}) - cc_{e,t,p} - \sum_{r=1}^{R} cm_{e,t,r} - cp_{e,t,p}$$
$$- \sum_{c=1}^{C} \sum_{s=1}^{S} ctcp_{e,t,c,p,s} - \sum_{r=1}^{R} ctrp_{e,t,r,p} \ \forall(e,t,p) \tag{4}$$

$$bd_{e,t,d} = \sum_{m=1}^{M} ingd_{e,t,d,m} - \sum_{p=1}^{P} \sum_{s=1}^{S} ctpd_{e,t,p,d,s} \forall(e,t,d) \tag{5}$$

$$penal_{e,t} = \sum_{c=1}^{C} pct_{e,t,c} + \sum_{s=1}^{S} pts_{e,t,s} + \sum_{s=1}^{S} pcp_{e,t,s} + \sum_{s=1}^{S} pecr_{e,t,s} + \sum_{p=1}^{P} pcee_{e,t,p} \forall(e,t) \tag{6}$$

$$proct_{e,t,c} = \sum_{p=1}^{P} tonvp_{e,t,c,p} + \sum_{p=1}^{P} tonvr_{e,t,c,r} \forall(e,t,c) \tag{7}$$

$$tonvp_{e,t,c,p} = \sum_{b=1}^{B} (X_{b,t,c,p,e} * ma_{b,e,t}) \forall(e,t,c,p) \tag{8}$$

$$tonvr_{e,t,c,r} = \sum_{b=1}^{B} (Xr_{b,t,c,r,e} * ma_{b,e,t}) \forall(e,t,c,r) \tag{9}$$

$$tonca_{e,t,c} = tonca_{e,t-1,c} + proct_{e,t,c} - \left(\sum_{r=1}^{R} \sum_{p=1}^{P} \sum_{s=1}^{S} (procr_{e,t,c,r,s} + procp_{e,t,c,p,s}) \right) \forall(e,t,c) \tag{10}$$

$$tonca_{e,t,c} \le CAPM_c \forall(e,t,c) \tag{11}$$

$$procr_{e,t,c,r,s} = tonvr_{e,t,c,r} \times Zcr_{t,c,r,s,e} \forall(e,t,c,r,s) \tag{12}$$

$$procp_{e,t,c,p,s} = tonvp_{e,t,c,p} \times Zcp_{t,c,p,s,e} \forall(e,t,c,p,s) \tag{13}$$

$$tonst_{e,t,r} = tonst_{e,t-1,r} - \sum_{p=1}^{P} (tonpla_{e,t,r,p}) + \sum_{c=1}^{C} (tonvr_{e,t,c,r}) \forall(e,t,r) \tag{14}$$

$$tonst_{e,t,r} \le capres_r \forall(e,t,r) \tag{15}$$

$$tonps_{e,t,p} = \sum_{c=1}^{C} (tonvp_{e,t,c,p}) + \sum_{r=1}^{R} (tonpla_{e,t,r,p}) \forall(e,t,p) \tag{16}$$

$$tontp_{e,t,p} = tontp_{e,t-1,p} + \sum_{a=1}^{A} \left(prost_{e,t,p,a}\right) - \sum_{d=1}^{D} \sum_{s=1}^{S} propd_{e,t,p,d,s} \forall (e,t,p) \tag{17}$$

$$ttp_{e,t,p} \leq \sum_{a=1}^{A} CAPP_{p,a} \forall (e,t,p) \tag{18}$$

$$\sum_{p=1}^{P} tonpla_{e,t,r,p} \leq tonst_{e,t-1,r} \forall (e,t,r) \tag{19}$$

$$mct_{e,t,c,p,n} = \sum_{b=1}^{B} tonvp_{e,t,c,p} \times g_{b,e,n} \forall (e,t,c,p,n) \tag{20}$$

$$msr_{e,t,c,r,n} = \sum_{b=1}^{B} \left(tonvr_{e,t,c,r} \times g_{b,e,n}\right) \forall (e,t,c,r,n) \tag{21}$$

$$mxr_{e,t,n,r} = mxr_{e,t-1,n,r} - \sum_{p=1}^{P} \left(mpla_{e,t,r,p,n}\right) + \sum_{c=1}^{C} \left(msr_{e,t,c,r,n}\right) \forall (e,t,n,r) \tag{22}$$

$$\sum_{n=1}^{N} \left(mst_{e,t,n,r}\right) \leq capres_r \forall (e,t,r) \tag{23}$$

$$matproce_{e,t,p,n} = \sum_{c=1}^{C} \left(mct_{e,t,c,p,n}\right) + \sum_{r=1}^{R} \left(mpla_{e,t,r,p,n}\right) \forall (e,t,p,n) \tag{24}$$

$$\sum_{p=1}^{P} \left(mpla_{e,t,r,p,n}\right) \leq mxr_{e,t-1,n,r} \forall (e,t,r,n) \tag{25}$$

$$prost_{e,t,p,a} = tonps_{e,t,p} \times Y_{t,p,a,e} \times Re_{p,a} \forall (e,t,p,a) \tag{26}$$

$$propd_{e,t,p,d,s} = \sum_{a=1}^{A} \left(prost_{e,t,p,a} \times Z_{t,p,d,s,e}\right) \forall (e,t,p,d,s) \tag{27}$$

$$recmat_{e,t,p,m} = \sum_{a=1}^{A} \left(prost_{e,t,p,a} \times prot_{p,a,m}\right) \forall (e,t,m,p) \tag{28}$$

$$mst_{e,t,n,r} \times tonpla_{e,t,r,p} = mpla_{e,t,r,p,n} \times tonst_{e,t,r} \forall (e,t,p,n,r) \tag{29}$$

$$\sum_{p=1}^{P} \sum_{s=1}^{S} \left(propd_{e,t,p,d,s}\right) = \sum_{m=1}^{M} \left(Marb_{e,t,d,m}\right) \forall (e,t,d) \tag{30}$$

$$mtb_{e,t,d,m} \leq Demdistrib_{d,m} \forall (d,m,e,t) \tag{31}$$

$$Matdistrib_{e,t,d,m} \leq CAPDIS_d \forall (d,m,e,t) \tag{32}$$

$$Incs_{e,t} = \sum_{c=1}^{C} \sum_{n=1}^{N} \left(Ingc_{e,t,c,n}\right) + \sum_{p=1}^{P} \sum_{m=1}^{M} \left(Ingp_{e,t,p,m}\right) + \sum_{d=1}^{D} \sum_{m=1}^{M} \left(Ingd_{e,t,d,m}\right) \forall (e,t) \tag{33}$$

$$ingsc_{e,t,c,n} = \left(\sum_{p=1}^{P} \left(matecant_{e,t,c,p,n}\right) + \sum_{r=1}^{R} \left(matereser_{e,t,c,r,n}\right)\right) \times precioc_{c,n} \forall (e,t,c,n) \tag{34}$$

$$ingp_{e,t,p,m} = recmat_{e,t,p,m} \times preciop_{p,m} \forall (e,t,p,m) \tag{35}$$

$$ingd_{e,t,d,m} = Matdistrb_{e,t,d,m} \times preciod_{d,m} \forall (e, t, p, d, m) \tag{36}$$

$$cons_{e,t,s} = \sum_{c=1}^{C} \sum_{p=1}^{P} \left(cocp_{e,t,c,p,s} \right) + \sum_{c=1}^{C} \sum_{r=1}^{R} \left(cocr_{e,t,c,r,s} \right) + \sum_{p=1}^{P} \sum_{d=1}^{D} \left(copd_{e,t,p,d,s} \right) \forall (e, t, s) \tag{37}$$

$$comc_{e,t,c} = proct_{e,t,c} \times cc_c \forall (e, t, c) \tag{38}$$

$$coc_{e,t,p} = \sum_{a=1}^{A} \left(toncs_{e,t,p} \times cp_{p,a} \times Y_{t,p,a,e} \right) \forall (e, t, p) \tag{39}$$

$$com_{e,t,r} = tonst_{e,t,r} \times cs_r \forall (e, t, r) \tag{40}$$

$$comc_{e,t,c} = tonca_{e,t,c} \times csc_c \forall (e, t, c) \tag{41}$$

$$comp_{e,t,p} = tontp_{e,t,p} \times csp_p \forall (e, t, p) \tag{42}$$

$$corp_{e,t,r,p} = tonpla_{e,t,r,p} \times cmr_{r,p} \forall (e, t, r, p) \tag{43}$$

$$cocp_{e,t,c,p,s} = procp_{e,t,c,p,s} \times cm_{c,p} \forall (e, t, c, p, s) \tag{44}$$

$$cocr_{e,t,c,r,s} = procr_{e,t,c,r,s} \times cmc_{c,r} \forall (e, t, r, c, s) \tag{45}$$

$$cod_{e,t,p,d,s} = propd_{e,t,p,d,s} \times ctp_{p,d,s} \forall (e, t, p, d, s) \tag{46}$$

$$proct_{e,t,c} + VU_{e,t,c} - VL_{e,t,c} = \sum_{b=1}^{B} \sum_{p=1}^{P} \sum_{r=1}^{R} \left(CAPM_c \times X_{b,t,c,p,e} + CAPM_c \times Xr_{b,t,c,r,e} \right) \forall (c, t, e) \tag{47}$$

$$proct_{e,t,c} \leq CAPM_c \forall (c, t, e) \tag{48}$$

$$\sum_{p=1}^{P} \sum_{r=1}^{R} \sum_{n=1}^{N} \left(matcat_{e,t,c,p,n} + matersr_{e,t,c,r,n} \right) \leq CAPM_c \forall (c, t, e) \tag{49}$$

$$\sum_{p=1}^{P} \sum_{d=1}^{D} \left(propd_{e,t,p,d,s} \right) + VUS_{e,t,s} - VLS_{e,t,s} = \sum_{p=1}^{P} \sum_{d=1}^{D} \left(CAPS_s \times Z_{t,p,d,s,e} \right) \forall (s, t, e) \tag{50}$$

$$\sum_{p=1}^{P} \sum_{d=1}^{D} \left(propd_{e,t,p,d,s} \right) \leq CAPS_s \forall (s, t, e) \tag{51}$$

$$\sum_{c=1}^{C} \sum_{r=1}^{R} \left(procr_{e,t,c,r,s} \right) + VUSCR_{e,t,s} - VLSCR_{e,t,s} = \sum_{c=1}^{C} \sum_{r=1}^{R} \left(CAPS_s \times Zcr_{t,c,r,s,e} \right) \forall (s, t, e) \tag{52}$$

$$\sum_{c=1}^{C} \sum_{r=1}^{R} \left(procr_{e,t,c,r,s} \right) \leq CAPS_s \forall (s, t, e) \tag{53}$$

$$\sum_{c=1}^{C} \sum_{p=1}^{P} \left(procp_{e,t,c,p,s} \right) + VUSCP_{e,t,s} - VLSCP_{e,t,s} = \sum_{c=1}^{C} \sum_{p=1}^{P} \left(CAPS_s \times Zcp_{t,c,p,s,e} \right) \forall (s, t, e) \tag{54}$$

$$\sum_{c=1}^{C} \sum_{p=1}^{P} \left(procp_{e,t,c,p,s} \right) \leq CAPS_s \forall (s, t, e) \tag{55}$$

$$toncs_{e,t,p} + \sum_{a=1}^{A} \left(VUA_{e,t,p,a} \right) - \sum_{a=1}^{A} \left(VLA_{e,t,p,a} \right) = \sum_{a=1}^{A} \left(CAPP_{p,a} * Y_{t,p,a,e} \right) \forall (p, t, e) \tag{56}$$

$$toncs_{e,t,p} \le \sum_{a=1}^{A} CAPP_{p,a} \, \forall \, (p, t, e) \tag{57}$$

$$pct_{e,t,c} = PEU_{t,c} \times VU_{e,t,c} + PEL_{t,c} \times VL_{e,t,c} \forall (e, t, c) \tag{58}$$

$$pns_{(e,t,s)} = PEUS_{t,s} \times VUS_{e,t,s} + PELS_{t,s} \times VLS_{e,t,s} \forall (e, t, s) \tag{59}$$

$$pcp_{e,t,s} = PEUS_{t,s} \times VUScp_{e,t,s} + PELS_{t,s} \times VLScp_{e,t,s} \forall (e, t, s) \tag{60}$$

$$pcr_{e,t,s} = PEUS_{t,s} \times VUScr_{e,t,s} + PELS_{t,s} \times VLScr_{e,t,s} \forall (e, t, s) \tag{61}$$

$$pce_{e,t,p} = \sum_{a=1}^{A} \left(PEUP_{t,p,a} \times VUA_{e,t,p,a} + PELP_{t,p,a} \times VLA_{e,t,p,a} \right) \forall (e, t, p) \tag{62}$$

$$\sum_{c=1}^{C} \sum_{p=1}^{P} X_{b,t,c,p,e} - \sum_{k=1}^{K} \sum_{c=1}^{C} \sum_{p=1}^{P} X_{j,k,c,p,e} \le 0 \forall (b, t, j, e) \tag{63}$$

$$\sum_{c=1}^{C} \sum_{r=1}^{R} Xr_{b,t,c,r,e} - \sum_{k=1}^{K} \sum_{c=1}^{C} \sum_{r=1}^{R} Xr_{j,k,c,r,e} \le 0 \forall (b, t, j, e) \tag{64}$$

$$\sum_{t=1}^{T} \sum_{c=1}^{C} \sum_{p=1}^{P} X_{b,t,c,p,e} = 1 \forall (b, e) \tag{65}$$

$$\sum_{t=1}^{T} \sum_{c=1}^{C} \sum_{r=1}^{R} Xr_{b,t,c,r,e} \le 1 \forall (b, e) \tag{66}$$

$$\sum_{a=1}^{A} Y_{t,p,a,e} \le 1 \forall (t, p, e) \tag{67}$$

$$Z_{t,p,d,s,e} \le Tr_{p,d,s} \forall (t, p, d, s, e) \tag{68}$$

$$Zcp_{t,c,p,s,e} \le Trc_{c,p,s} \forall (t, c, p, s, e) \tag{69}$$

$$Zcr_{t,c,r,s,e} \le Trr_{c,r,s} \forall (t, c, r, s, e) \tag{70}$$

$$\sum_{s=1}^{S} \sum_{e=1}^{E} Z_{t,p,d,s,e} = 1 \forall (t, p, d) \tag{71}$$

$$\sum_{s=1}^{S} \sum_{e=1}^{E} Zcp_{t,c,p,s,e} = 1 \forall (t, c, p) \tag{72}$$

$$\sum_{s=1}^{S} \sum_{e=1}^{E} Zcr_{t,c,r,s,e} = 1 \forall (t, c, r) \tag{73}$$

$$\sum_{t=1}^{T} recmat_{e,t,p,m} \times FFinos_{t,b} \times X_{b,t,c,p,e} \le calidad * \sum_{t=1}^{T} recmat_{e,t,p,m} \forall (e, b, m, p, c) \tag{74}$$

$$Non - negativity \ condition \ for \ all \ variables \tag{75}$$

Equation (1) optimize profit (maximize discounted benefits) Eqs. (2) to (5) Calculate the total discounted benefit and each link. In the quarries, Eqs. (6) to (11) define the penalties associated with deviations, tons of raw materials, quantities to be sent from quarries to reserves or plants, tons in stocks and storage limitations, respectively. Equations (12) and (13) Calculate the tons transported from quarries to reserves or to processing plants. Equations (14) and (15) define the existing tons in reserves and storage limitations relative to the capacity level. Equations (16) to (18) determine the tons of minerals in process, quantities in stocks and storage limitations, respectively. The Eq. (19) Defines the mineral constraints sent from reserves. In Eqs. (20) and (21) The quantities are shown by type of mineral sent from quarries to plants or reserves. Equations (22) and (23) show amounts of materials per type in reserves and limiting capacities, respectively. Equations (24) to (30) Show restrictions on processing plants. Equations (31) and (32) define limiting agents in the distributors. Total revenues are shown from Eqs. (33) to (36). Equations (37) A (46) represent costs of transport, exploitation, processing and handling of materials. Equations (47) to (57) show deviations associated with the capacities in all the links. Equations (58) to (62) calculate the penalties associated with deviations. Equations (63) to (73) Restrict decision variables, with respect to block precedence, operation alternatives and transport systems. Finally, the restriction (74) is a quality condition.

3   Results

The model is implemented in the Calamarí-Sucre mining district (Colombia). The scenario is applied to the extraction, processing, storage, and distribution of limestone. To solve the model, the GAMS software was used through libraries of relaxed mixed nonlinear programming (RMINLP) and the DICOPT solver. 16 GB RAM Computer was used, with 1 TB HDD and 2.5 GHz Core i7 processor. The model has scenarios under uncertainty, according to the level of supply of raw materials: low (E1), medium (2) and high(3). In Fig. 2, the expected benefits are shown by scenario. The results show that in a high uncertainty scenario, the second period (second month) marks the planning of the echelons. From this period the provision of materials for the entire supply chain is guaranteed. In the results, the benefits cover the chain collaboratively. On the other hand, in a medium (E2) or low (E1) material supply scenario, the results are lower, especially in the third month, which means that in the cash flow the fines and costs are more limited income.

The equity in the economic benefits show a dynamics of vertical integration in the sector. It can be said that, in C7 the greatest benefits discounted are produced in a constant way and in C9 the worst yields are obtained. In the 5th month, under Scenario 1, it is only profitable to produce in the quarries C2 and C7. This is basically due to a higher production capacity, lower operating costs and the highest selling prices of raw materials. In P4, the highest discounted profits are produced and in P8, they are low. In Scenario 3, it is profitable to produce in P1, P2, P4, P5, P7, P8 and P10. For the distribution echelon, it is also profitable to sell under scenario 3, in which D4 generates the best discounted benefits and on D5 the worst yields are obtained. For its part, the penalties in the 2nd month are higher in a scenario of high provisioning (E3), in the 6th, in E2 and in the 5th, in E1, because it is the integration processes between various actors who participate in

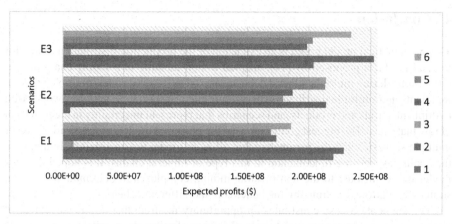

Fig. 2. Expected profits from supply chain scenarios ($)

the supply chain, the deviations of operational objectives are more difficult to manage, given the fluctuations in the different processes.

The revenues received in the supply chain are higher when there is a high level of provision (E3). Figure 3 shows the sales revenue of non-metallic minerals by periods and scenarios. The worst results are quantified on a stage with little projection quarries (E1). In quarries, in C7 and C2 the highest income is generated. In the processing plants under E3 and E1 the highest profitability in the sale of products is given in P4. However, the decisions based on the frequency of the sales can be focused on the analysis of P7. In Scenario 2, the behavior is better in P1 and P10. In all cases, sales have a better yield with the product gravel (M2), followed by the crushed 1 (M1), a situation that contrasts with the sales of Dust (M3). In Scenario 1 and 2, D3 has the highest income, by the high sales of granite (M4). On the other hand, under Scenario 3, the best results are generated in the whole echelon of distributors.

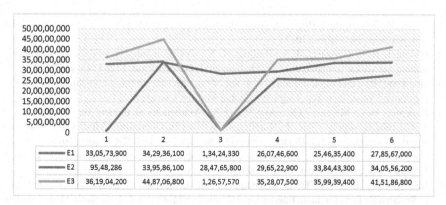

Fig. 3. Sales income of non-metallic mineral in the period t under the scenario e ($ COP)

4 Conclusion

The mathematical model posed is an extension of the production-distribution model for mineral products proposed by [14], adapted to non-metallic in a supply chain of four levels, considering multiple mineral deposits, mixed in Reserve zones, multiple processing plants and multiple distributors, using multiple transportation systems, works with multiple materials and products, and scenarios that represent uncertainty in the provision of raw materials. The biggest contribution of the proposed model is the consideration of multiple scenarios and the parameters that allow to model the uncertainty. In addition, the quality aspects are fundamental in this type of mineral chains. It is hoped that this model will contribute to the non-metallic mining complexes to determine an optimal strategy that allows maximizing the benefits in the different echelons.

The application case constitutes an opportunity to strengthen the management of operations in the programming of the exploitation of mineral deposits, processing and distribution in complexes or mining districts. For future work, it is necessary to include an additional echelon to analyses the behavior of the markets and the clients more deeply. Similarly, there can be more restrictions on capacity, quality, costs associated with this new echelon and probability distributions to model uncertainty, taking as a basis different policies of collaboration and integration in the chain. It may be interesting to consider the uncertainty of the demand of the retailer; multiple points of sales and the end uses of products of the chain. Considering that collaborative approaches can be presented among the agents, it is possible to take place in three ways, such as collaboration between non-metallic mineral deposits, collaboration between processing plants and collaboration between the Quarries and manufacturers. By increasing the complexity of the model, in the useful life of the deposits, it is possible to develop metaheuristics that allow to find an optimal solution, given the case as the floating cone algorithm and Lerchs-Grossmann using Gemcom Surpac and UPL.

References

1. Carter, B.: Boom, Bust, Boom: A Story About Copper, The Metal Rhat Runs the World, 1st edn. Scribner, New York (2012)
2. Pimentel, B.S., Gonzalez, E.S., Barbosa, G.N.: Decision-support models for sustainable mining networks: fundamentals and challenges. J. Cleaner Prod. 112, 2145–2157 (2016)
3. Hopwood, P.: Tracking the trends 2014: ten of the top issues mining companies will face in the coming year. Tech. rep. Deloitte e Global Mining, Canada (2014)
4. Pimentel, B.S., Mateus, G.R., Almeida, F.A.: Mathematical models for optimizing the global mining supply chain. In: Intelligent Systems in Operations: Models, Methods and Applications, B. Nag, Ed. Hershey, Pennsylvania, pp. 133–163. IGI Global (2010)
5. Cárdenas, M, Reina, M.: La minería en Colombia: Impacto Socioeconómico y fiscal. Fedesarrollo, Colombia, pp. 10–15 (2008)
6. Ericsson, M., Hodge, A.: Trends in the mining and metals industry. In: Mining's Contribution to Sustainable Development. International Council on Mining and Minerals (ICMM), London, UK, p. 16 (2012)
7. Measham, T.G., Haslam Mckenzie, F., Moffat, K., Franks, D.M.: An expanded role for the mining sector in Australian society? Rural Soc. 22(2), 184–194 (2013)

8. Xifengru, Houxilin, Chenerdong, Wangweiwei: Discussion in the mining industry of ecology and sustainable development. In: BMEI 2011 - Proceedings 2011 International Conference on Business Management and Electronic Information, vol. 1, pp. 81–83 (2011). http://doi.org/10.1109/ICBMEI.2011.5916879
9. March Consulting Associates Inc.: How To Successfully Access the Mining Supply Chain (2012)
10. Gómez, R., Correa, A.: Análisis del transporte y distribución de materiales de Construcción utilizando simulación discreta en 3D. Boletín de ciencias de la tierra - Número 30, Medellín, ISSN 0120 - 3630. pp 39-52 (2011)
11. Ministerio de Minas: Anuario estadístico minero 2007–2012 (2014). www.minminas.gov.co
12. UPME: El plan nacional para desarrollo minero visión 2019 (2006). www.upme.gov.co/Docs/PNDM_2019_Final.pdf
13. Salas Navarro, K., Chedid, J.A., Caruso, N.M., Sana, S.S.: An inventory model of three-layer supply chain of wood and furniture industry in the Caribbean region of Colombia. Int. J. Syst. Sci. Oper. Logistics 5(1), 69–86 (2018). https://www.tandfonline.com/doi/abs/10.1080/23302674.2016.1212428
14. Pimentel, B.S., Mateus, G.R., Almeida, F.A.: Stochastic capacity planning in a global mining supply chain. In: 2011 IEEE Workshop On Computational Intelligence in Production and Logistics Systems (CIPLS), pp. 1–8. IEEE (2011)
15. Bodon, P., Fricke, C., Sandeman, T., Stanford, C.: Modeling the mining supply chain from mine to port: a combined optimization and simulation approach. J. Min. Sci. 47(2), 202–211 (2011). https://doi.org/10.1017/CBO9781107415324.004
16. Dimitrakopoulos, R.: Strategic mine planning under uncertainty. J. Min. Sci. 47(2), 138–150 (2011)
17. Montiel, L., Dimitrakopoulos, R.: Stochastic mine production scheduling with multiple processes: Application at Escondida Norte, Chile. J. Min. Sci. 49(4), 583–597 (2013). https://doi.org/10.1134/S1062739149040096
18. Fung, J., Singh, G., Zinder, Y.: Capacity planning in supply chains of mineral resources. Inf. Sci. 316, 397–418 (2015). https://doi.org/10.1016/j.ins.2014.11.015
19. Goodfellow, R.C., Dimitrakopoulos, R.: Global optimization of open pit mining complexes with uncertainty. Appl. Soft Comput. 40, 292–304 (2016). https://doi.org/10.1016/j.asoc.2015.11.038
20. Ospina-Mateus, H., Acevedo-Chedid, J., Salas-Navarro, K., Morales-Londoño, N., Montero-Perez, J.: Model of optimization of mining complex for the planning of flow of quarry production of limestone in multiple products and with elements for the analysis of the capacity. In: Workshop on Engineering Applications, pp. 544–555. Springer, Cham, September 2017. https://link.springer.com/chapter/10.1007/978-3-319-66963-2_48
21. Montiel, L., Dimitrakopoulos, R.: Optimizing mining complexes with multiple processing and transportation alternatives: an uncertainty-based approach. Eur. J. Oper. Res. 247(1), 166–178 (2015)
22. Hennet, J.C., Arda, Y.: Supply chain coordination: a game-theory approach. Eng. Appl. Artif. Intell. 21(3), 399–405 (2008). https://doi.org/10.1016/j.engappai.2007.10.003
23. Zhao, Y., Wang, S., Cheng, T.C.E., Yang, X., Huang, Z.: Coordination of supply chains by option contracts: a cooperative game theory approach. Eur. J. Oper. Res. 207(2), 668–675 (2010). https://doi.org/10.1016/j.ejor.2010.05.017
24. Zhang, K., Kleit, A.N.: Mining rate optimization considering the stockpiling: a theoretical economics and real option model. Resour. Policy 47, 87–94 (2016). https://doi.org/10.1016/j.resourpol.2016.01.005

A Hybrid Algorithm to Minimize Regular Criteria in the Job-shop Scheduling Problem with Maintenance Activities, Sequence Dependent and Set-up Times

Andrés A. García-León$^{(\boxtimes)}$ ⓘ and William F. Torres Tapia ⓘ

Facultad de Ingeniería, Programa de Ingeniería Industrial,
Universidad de Ibagué, Ibagué, Colombia
{andres.garcia,william.torres}@unibague.edu.co

Abstract. The scheduling problems have been analyzed considering that the processing time of operations is known and normally without maintenance activities and set up times between jobs. Minimizing makespan is the most studied criterion, which does not consider important aspects for measuring the customer service like the due date and the importance between customers. Besides, the few level of publications based on regular criteria have not considered the maintenance activities and sequence dependent set-up times, which affects the finalization of jobs. In this paper, we propose a hybrid approach for minimizing regular criteria in the Job-shop Scheduling problem with maintenance activities and sequence dependent set-up times. It is an ant colony Min-Max system, which is improved with a local search algorithm at increasing the neighborhood. Our approach makes use of the disjunctive graph model to represent schedules and support the search for an optimal at reversing a critical arc that affects the criterion during the improvement phase and pheromone is supplied to the arcs that solve the problem if the global optimal is gotten. In the diversification phase, a parallel search of k ants is executed considering the pheromone on the arcs to escape of a local optimal and the best ant returns to improvement step. The quality of our approach is illustrated on known instances at adding information. The superiority respect to local search process and a classic ACO is evaluated. Finally, a reference of results is proposed for various regular criteria.

Keywords: Scheduling theory · Regular criteria · Maintenance activity ·
Sequence dependent · Set-up times · Local search · Ant colony optimization and
hybrid approach

1 Introduction

In modern industrial environments, the decisions of scheduling must lead to improve the productivity and the competitiveness simultaneously. Minimizing regular criteria at analyzing due date of jobs leads to optimize customer service. In scheduling theory, the Job-shop Scheduling Problem (JSP) and its extensions have attracted the interest to solve

© Springer Nature Switzerland AG 2020
J. C. Figueroa-García et al. (Eds.): WEA 2020, CCIS 1274, pp. 208–221, 2020.
https://doi.org/10.1007/978-3-030-61834-6_18

problems modeled in real configurations. This paper considers the JSP with maintenance activities, sequence dependent set-up times. This situation is typical of manufacturing activities, since, to maintain an efficient performance of machines needs periodically maintenance activities and normally the set-up times are affected by the complexity of the tasks between jobs (sequence dependent).

This paper addresses the minimization of regular criteria by a fast local search algorithm which uses the feasibility of transformations on a conjunctive graph at reversing a critical arc that belongs to the jobs which affect the criterion iteratively during the improvement process. In the diversification, a strategy based on Ant Colony Min-Max system avoids to escape of a local optimal. To validate the quality of the results, we have calculated various regular criteria to create a benchmark of results for future research. The paper is explained as follows. Section 2 presents a literature review, Sect. 3 describes and models the problem and an example is referenced to illustrate an optimal solution. Finally, Sect. 4 shows some computational experiments to illustrate the efficiency of our approach

2 Literature Review

The objective of the Job-shop Scheduling Problem is to determine a sequence of operations to be performed on machines to optimize an objective function. It assumes that an operation has to be processed exclusively on a unique machine, preempting operations is not allowed. It means that an operation cannot be interrupted once started and the machines are always available (see [1]). This last assumption is not possible to validate in many real industrial environments [2], for example maintenance activities (corrective and preventive), accidental failures, tool changes, availability of workers, availability of resources used by machines. The above reasons lead to the imposition of availability restrictions when planning production [3].

In recent years, the restriction of maintenance activities has been added to the scheduling problems. For example: Makespan in the Job-shop [4, 5] and in the flexible Job-shop in [6–8], machine downtime [9], multi objective optimization considering makespan and the total cost of maintenance [4], system reliability [10] and flexible maintenance [11]. Machine set-up times between jobs have been studied to solve industrial problems related to lithography, textile, container manufacturing and others [12]. In the formulation only few works aim to optimize regular criteria. For example, makespan in [13–15], maximum lateness, average tardiness, tardy jobs and total flow time in [16].

The best of our knowledge, there are no publications based on maintenance activities and, sequence dependent and set-up times simultaneously at minimizing regular criteria in the Job-shop Scheduling Problem. The main contribution of our paper is to develop a making decision tool at programing production to satisfy the customer service at minimizing regular criteria considering the completion time and the due date of jobs. The conception of our Hybrid solution approach is based on the estimation functions for the local search process described in [17] adapted to the conditions of the approach and a strategy inspired in Ant Colony Optimization principles for the diversification process, which allows escaping of a local optimum solution.

3 Problem Description and Modeling

The Job-shop scheduling problem "JSP" is modeled as follows. A set of n jobs $J = \{J_1, \ldots J_n\}$ are processed on a set $M = \{M_1, \ldots M_m\}$ of m machines that are available. Each machine can only process one job at a time. A job J_i is obtained at performing sequentially n_i operations in a fix route. Preempting operations is not allowed. It means that an operation cannot be interrupted once started. Each job J_i has a due-date d_i. The disjunctive graph proposed in [17] is used to represent the problem, which the n nodes ϕ_i represent the completion time of J_i and node 0 represent the start of the jobs and machines. When a solution is obtained at solving the disjunctive graph, it means at solving the sequence of operations to be processed on each machine some properties are possible. For example, for operation x, the processing time is p_x. The starting time of x is h_x ($h_x = L(0, x)$), that corresponds to the length of the longest path from 0 to x. The tail from a node x to the dummy node $\phi_i(q_x^i)$ is equal to $[L(x, \phi_i) - p_x]$ if a path exists from x to ϕ_i and $-\infty$ otherwise. A path from 0 to ϕ_i is called critical if its length is equal to C_i, and every node x belonging to this critical path is critical according to J_i. A critical node x for job J_i satisfies $h_x + p_x + q_x^i = C_i$. An arc belonging to the critical path of J_i is called critical if it connects two operations x and y assigned to the same machine and belong to different job. After obtaining the heads of the nodes of the graph, the criterion of a feasible schedule represented by the selection can be determined in $O(n)$ from the starting times of the dummy nodes. For instance, the makespan is obtained using the formula $C_{max} = \max C_i$. Additionally the tardiness (T_i), $T_i = \max(0, C_i - d_i)$. Then the maximum tardiness is $T_{max} = \max T_i$ and total tardiness (T) is the sum of the tardiness of jobs.

Concerning to the maintenance activities for machines, MA_m is the maximum frequency of maintenance operation on machine m, $A_{(x)}$ is the current frequency of maintenance operation on machine where x is performed $(MA_m \geq A_x)$. PM_m is the duration of the maintenance operation on m, S_{lkm} is the set-up time for preparing the machine m at changing from job l to job k, let ST_{lm} be the preparing time for the machine m for the job l, if l is the first assigned job to m or, if l is the assigned job after a maintenance operation on m. Finally, let TM_{lm} be the time for preparing the machine m for the maintenance operation as soon as m has finished an operation that belongs to job l.

The Fig. 1 and Fig. 2 illustrate an instance for a problem with four machines (M1, M2, M3 and M4) and four jobs (J1, J2, J3 and J4). Figure 1 illustrates a set of tables which information represents the times of maintenance activities. For example, considering the machine M1, the maximum frequency of maintenance operation is $MA_1 = 40$ (see frequency) and its duration $PM_1 = 6$ (see Maintenance time), the preparing times ST_{l1} where $l = 1$, 2 and 3 are respectively 5, 1 and 3 (see start). Besides the TM_{l1} are 3, 2 and 1 (see column Maint). The other values on the same table are the set up times, for example the set time for changing the machine from J1 to J2 is 3 (see the cell with the underlined 3).

Figure 2 shows a conjunctive graph that represents a solution for the proposed instance and it is explained by an example as follows. The first job has three operations (O11, O12 and O13). The processing time for O11 is 25 and it is performed on machine M3. The sequence of operations on M1 is O21, O12 and O33. For explaining the structure of times, the operation O21 is analyzed and the information is located in

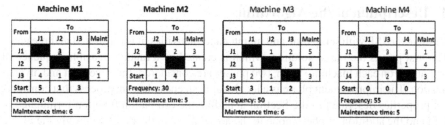

Fig. 1. Information of machines for the proposed instance (Color figure online)

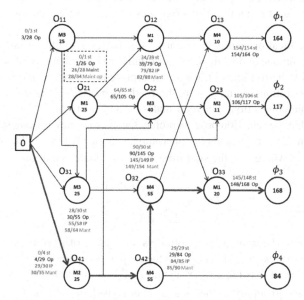

Fig. 2. Graph of the solution for the proposed instance

the dashed rectangle. O21 is the first operation in the sequence of M1, the $ST_{21} = 1$ (see start row in the table for machine M2 on Fig. 1). Therefore, if M1 starts at time 0, it finishes its preparing at time 1 (see letters in red color). After that, the O_{21} is processed between the time 1 and 26 since the processing time is 25 (see letters in black color). The operation is finished and the machine goes to a maintenance operation, since $MA_1 = 40$ and the processing time for O_{12} is 40, it implies that the sum of their processing time (25 + 40 = 65) must be lower than 40. M1 is prepared for a maintenance operation between the times 26 and 28 (see blue letters) and finally from 28 to 34 on M1 the maintenance operation is performed. At solving the graph, the completion time of jobs are $C_1 = 164$, $C_2 = 117$, $C_3 = 168$ and $C_4 = 84$. In this instance the makespan is 168, and the critical path that affects the criterion is highlighted in green color.

4 Description of the Algorithm

To solve the JSP with setup time and maintenance activities, it is illustrated in three parts. The first part is the initial solution, which is created by a random feasible sequence of operations on each machine. Then, two phases are considered: Improvement and diversification. The improvement phase is a local search steepest descent process that considers the properties described in the Section at adding the estimation function formulated in [17] and the addition of pheromone to the arcs that solve the problem if only the global optimal is improved. When it is not possible to create an improving move the diversification phase consists on a parallel search considering a number of ants that belong to a set K acording to the amount of pheromones of the feasible arcs and an evaporation process.

In the diversification phase, each ant $k \in K$ builds a solution following the track of artificial pheromone and analysis of information. The probability of selecting an arc is determined by the formula (1), where τ_{xy} represents the pheromones of the arc that connects the operations x and y, v is the road visibility, i is the index of the set of possible feasible connections between nodes. α and β are preference coefficients, if $\alpha > \beta$ means that the selection process prefers the pheromones, otherwise the start time of the operation y, τ_{xy} represents the pheromones in the arcs (x, y). The road visibility v is defined as $\frac{1}{w}$, where w is the start time of the candidate operation y.

$$P_{xy_i}^k = \frac{\left(\tau_{xy_i}^\alpha\right)\left(v_{xy_i}^\beta\right)}{\sum_{i=0}^{n}\left(\tau_{xyi}^\alpha\right)\left(v_{xyi}^\beta\right)} \tag{1}$$

After ants have been built their solutions, an update of pheromones is performed considering the expression (2), where ρ is the evaporation percentage, τ_{xy} is the amount of pheromones of all feasible arcs (x, y) and $\Delta\tau_{xy}^{Best}$ is defined in (3), which is defined as the pheromone to supply in the arcs (x, y) at considering the best ant (k^{Best}) and it is calculated by the inverse relation $\frac{1}{l_{best}}$, where l_{best} is the regular criterion obtained by k^{Best}.

$$\tau_{xy} = (1 - \rho)\tau_{xy} + \Delta\tau_{xy}^{Best} \tag{2}$$

$$\Delta\tau_{xy}^{Best} = \begin{cases} \frac{1}{l_{best}} \text{if the arc (x,y)} \in Best\ Ant \\ 0 \end{cases} \tag{3}$$

To avoid the permanence of the search in a local optimum, which is evidenced in an arc the track of pheromones is the most significant of all feasible arcs, We adopted the strategy inspired in [18] called NMAS. It controls the pheromones of all feasible arcs in the interval $[\tau_{min}, \tau_{max}]$. It is performed at the beginning at adding τ_{max} pheromones on all feasible arcs. When the level of pheromones is less than τ_{min}, this level is updated to τ_{max} which leads to explore underused arcs.

If the instance illustrated in Fig. 2 is considered to determine the optimal value for the makespan at performing the algorithm, the result is 162 (see Fig. 3). The Fig. 3 illustrates the graph and the printing of a txt file with the sequence of operations and their times.

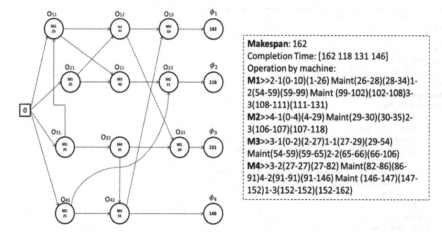

Makespan: 162
Completion Time: [162 118 131 146]
Operation by machine:
M1>>2-1(0-10)(1-26) Maint(26-28)(28-34)1-
2(54-59)(59-99) Maint (99-102)(102-108)3-
3(108-111)(111-131)
M2>>4-1(0-4)(4-29) Maint(29-30)(30-35)2-
3(106-107)(107-118)
M3>>3-1(0-2)(2-27)1-1(27-29)(29-54)
Maint(54-59)(59-65)2-2(65-66)(66-106)
M4>>3-2(27-27)(27-82) Maint(82-86)(86-
91)4-2(91-91)(91-146) Maint (146-147)(147-
152)1-3(152-152)(152-162)

Fig. 3. Representation of the best known solution for the proposed instance

5 Computational Experiments

To validate and evaluate the efficiency of our approach for the three criteria, the instances studied for the Job-shop scheduling problem in [19] have been considered and transformed to the conditions described in our approach. Our algorithm was developed in Java language and the experiments were conducted on a PC with 3.40 GHz and 8 GB RAM during 300 s per criterion and ten times per instance. The parameters related to ACO are three ants in the parallel search, $\rho = 6\%$, $\tau_{min} = 5 \times 10^{-4}$ and $\tau_{max} = 0.7$. In the Fig. 4 the pseudo code of the algorithm is described.

Determining parameters with considerations of maintenance activities and Set-up times was developed only one time. Then, they were saved in the original txt file. The process is as follows. For each instance, the number of maintenance activities per machine was determined randomly in the interval [2, 3]. MA_m was determined at dividing the sum of its processing time per operation and the number of maintenance activities. Logically, it was ensured that this value would be greater or equal than the highest processing time. PM_m was fixed as a random number that belongs to the interval [11, 14]. For the other times, random numbers from 1 to 9 were considered.

To illustrate the superiority of our hybrid approach, the makespan is calculated at executing separately the local search "LS" described in [17], the classic Ant Colony Algorithm "ACO" and the Hybrid Algorithm "HA" that is proposed in this paper. Additionally an ANOVA analysis is tested considering the three algorithms with the Relative Percentage Deviation "RPD", which is calculated by the expression $100(Av - BS)/BS$, where Av is the average of the solutions gotten by each algorithm, and BS is the best found solution considering the three algorithms together. The RPD is illustrated in Table 1, the ANOVA test with a confidence interval of 95% in Fig. 5 and the graph of means and intervals for each algorithm in Fig. 6 considering RPD.

```
Tc= 300 seconds //Running time
 Ta= 0 //Current time
 ρ = 0.07 //Evaporation factor
 F = Feasible arcs
 τ_xy_min = 5x10⁻⁴ //Minimum of pheromones
 τ_xy_max = 0.7 //Maximum of pheromones
 K = 3 //Number of ants
BestSolution= Null //Best global solution
While (Ta<Tc) Do
    BestAnt=Null //Best ant of the colony
    For each k ∈ K Do
        k.buildSolution //The ant builds the solution
        If((BestAnt=null) or (k.getCriterion < BestAnt.getCriterion))Then //Criterion comparison
            BestAnt= k //The best ant is updated
            If(k.getCriterion < BestSolution.getCriterion )Then
                BestSolution= k //Update best solution
            End if
        End If
    End For
    solution= BestAnt
    BestNeighbor=null // //Best neighbor
    call UpdatePheromone (solution, ρ, F , τ_xy_min, τ_xy_max) //Evaporating and adding pheromones
    solution.studyNeighborhood // The best neighbors are determined
    While(solution.getNeighborhood <> null) Do
        solution.transformGraph //The graph is transformed
        If(solution.getNeighborhood.getFirst.getCriterion < solution.getCriterion)
            solution= solution.getNeighborhood.getFirst// Update the solution
            BestNeighbor =solution // Update the best neighbor
            solution.studyNeighborhood
        Else
            solution.removeFirst
        End if
    End While
    If((BestNeighbor<>null) and (BestNeighbor.getCriterion < BestSolution.getCriterion)) Then
        BestSolution= BestNeighbor// Update the best solution
        call AddFeromona(BestNeighbor, τ_xy_max, F)// Adding pheromones
    End If
    Update Ta // Update the current time
End While
```

Fig. 4. Pseudo code for the hybrid algorithm

At analyzing Fig. 5 and Fig. 6, the results indicate that the means have statistically significant differences between the algorithms with a P value closeness to zero. It can conclude that the proposed algorithm is significantly better than LS and ACO. Considering only HA, it is executed for various regular criteria (see Tables 2, 3, 4 and 5) in three parts. First, in Table 2, makespan (C_{max}), the total flow time ($\sum C_i$) and the weighted completion time ($\sum w_i C_i$), where w_i is recorded in each instance file. In the second part, the criteria derived from the tardiness of jobs at considering the variations for d_i ($f = 1$, 3; 1, 5 and 1, 6) are calculated. The maximum tardiness (T_{max}) is illustrated in Table 3, Total tardiness in Table 4 and finally the weighted total tardiness ($\sum w_i T_i$) in Table 5. For each Table, column *Best* is the best solution, *Av* the average of the criterion and σ the standard deviation at executing ten running each criterion

Table 1. RPD at comparing the three algorithms

Instance	BS	LS		ACO		HA	
		Av	RPD	Av	RPD	Av	RPD
abz6	1086	1167,3	7,5	1142,8	5,2	1107,0	1,9
la16	1113	1203,3	8,1	1201,4	7,9	1151,4	3,5
la17	948	986,3	4,0	1009,8	6,5	968,6	2,2
la18	1001	1063,0	6,2	1075,6	7,5	1023,2	2,2
la19	1025	1141,3	11,4	1118,8	9,2	1053,2	2,8
la20	1065	1157,7	8,7	1178,0	10,6	1129,4	6,0
la21	990	1058,0	6,9	1078,4	8,9	1019,6	3,0
la22	943	1035,3	9,8	1004,6	6,5	956,4	1,4
la23	995	1066,0	7,1	1093,4	9,9	1013,2	1,8
la24	959	1017,0	6,0	1015,6	5,9	976,6	1,8
mt10	1192	1278,0	7,2	1287,4	8,0	1234,0	3,5
orb1	1327	1459,3	10,0	1427,6	7,6	1342,8	1,2
orb10	1250	1317,7	5,4	1373,8	9,9	1267,2	1,4
orb2	1097	1146,0	4,5	1175,0	7,1	1115,4	1,7
orb3	1282	1411,0	10,1	1353,2	5,6	1308,6	2,1
orb4	1246	1334,0	7,1	1398,2	12,2	1300,6	4,4
orb5	1126	1199,7	6,5	1189,2	5,6	1136,8	1,0
orb6	1273	1379,0	8,3	1383,4	8,7	1321,4	3,8
orb7	569	582,7	2,4	619,6	8,9	586,2	3,0
orb8	1203	1295,7	7,7	1266,8	5,3	1213,2	0,8
orb9	1185	1211,0	2,2	1326,2	11,9	1227,2	3,6

	Df	Sum Sq	Mean Sq	F value	P-Value
Algorithm	2	361.0	180.49	46	7.7e-13
Residuals	60	235.4	3.92		
Total	62	596.4			

Fig. 5. ANOVA test results

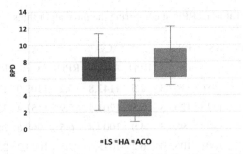

Fig. 6. Graph of means and intervals for the algorithms

Table 2. Results for the criteria C_{max} $\sum C_i$ and $\sum w_i C_i$

Instance	C_{max}			$\sum C_i$			$\sum w_i C_i$		
	Best	Av	σ	Best	Av	σ	Best	Av	σ
abz6	1086	1107	14,4	8975	9141,2	146,1	19148	19411,4	185,3
la16	1113	1151,4	25,1	8501	8716,9	112,5	17816	18272,8	317,0
la17	948	968,6	16,3	7690	7884,6	98,0	16649	16818,8	143,3
la18	1001	1023,2	15,4	8122	8293,7	81,4	17083	17217,0	116,8
la19	1025	1053,2	24,3	8626	8725,4	64,3	18820	18938,0	119,1
la20	1065	1129,4	38,2	8721	8864,3	90,7	17965	18315,2	212,6
la21	990	1019,6	25,2	8067	8182,2	66,9	16867	17027,6	101,1
la22	943	956,4	9,0	7997	8102,9	61,5	16934	16974,0	30,4
la23	995	1013,2	15,8	8379	8474,9	51,9	18011	18383,8	267,2
la24	959	976,6	11,1	8385	8496,6	84,0	17673	17743,4	72,7
mt10	1192	1234	25,3	9298	9406,2	119,5	18788	19225,4	285,0
orb1	1327	1342,8	11,2	9925	10114,8	154,6	21232	21648,8	318,6
orb2	1097	1115,4	18,4	8691	8784,2	54,2	19348	19587,0	152,1
orb3	1282	1308,6	19,4	9841	10012,8	103,4	20258	20593,8	285,2
orb4	1246	1300,6	39,9	10023	10152,3	111,9	20081	20860,0	199,1
orb5	1126	1136,8	7,8	8468	8506,9	44,4	18109	18552,6	251,8
orb6	1273	1321,4	33,0	9957	10104,0	88,8	20922	21080,0	165,9
orb7	569	586,2	13,2	4593	4651,0	55,9	9993	10096,0	77,8
orb8	1203	1213,2	8,8	8923	9061,4	127,5	18625	18798,6	148,6
orb9	1185	1227,2	25,7	9229	9294,6	56,4	19153	19408,2	149,3
orb10	1250	1267,2	16,9	9536	9834,1	145,2	20218	21058,0	260,0

Table 3. Results for the criterion T_{max}

Instance	f = 1, 3			f = 1, 5			f = 1, 6		
	Best	Av	σ	Best	Av	σ	Best	Av	σ
abz6	276	287,4	8,0	159	163,8	5,8	60	81,2	15,8
la16	340	352,2	8,2	208	232,0	22,3	165	186,6	17,8
la17	342	356,6	12,8	221	236,2	16,4	175	205,6	18,6
la18	310	334,4	16,4	191	217,6	17,3	152	170,2	15,5
la19	328	345,6	19,5	221	233,6	11,6	158	184,2	18,4
la20	348	358,6	12,7	216	238,6	15,9	149	176,8	21,3
la21	245	261,6	18,5	166	176,2	10,2	89	111,4	19,9
la22	298	311,4	11,4	212	226,6	11,2	158	167,4	8,4
la23	261	286,8	18,6	164	179,8	10,7	108	122,4	12,0
la24	315	328,6	9,2	199	217,8	13,1	156	168,8	10,8
mt10	508	534,6	16,1	391	420,6	17,2	362	369,2	4,4
orb1	559	579,8	14,8	444	448,6	4,1	356	410,0	31,1
orb2	354	392,8	29,9	239	274,4	22,8	221	232,4	21,1
orb3	538	570,0	18,6	427	454,4	20,5	396	408,6	14,3
orb4	535	557,2	17,2	355	438,0	23,3	321	393,6	13,4
orb5	472	483,0	8,2	319	352,8	36,0	279	309,6	19,4
orb6	503	542,4	25,6	400	413,6	11,6	332	349,6	15,7
orb7	245	255,2	8,6	176	209,6	20,1	179	188,8	9,3
orb8	532	584,4	44,9	480	496,6	10,5	410	438,6	16,4
orb9	451	502,2	30,5	341	415,6	26,5	292	349,6	32,2
orb10	481	523,0	24,9	394	415,2	19,1	338	356,0	18,8

Table 4. Results for the criterion $\sum T_i$

Instance	f=1,3			f=1,5			f=1,6		
	Best	Av	σ	Best	Av	σ	Best	Av	σ
abz6	1244	1395,0	98,5	382	518,8	97,0	147	222,6	61,0
la16	1710	1774,0	67,8	882	932,2	29,7	551	616,8	42,0
la17	1875	1927,4	38,5	975	1161,8	112,6	861	884,8	28,6
la18	1419	1583,2	95,1	661	747,6	57,5	390	459,2	45,0
la19	1687	1884,6	115,7	846	930,2	54,1	563	629,0	60,4
la20	1763	1854,0	92,3	969	1017,8	61,6	576	656,0	56,2
la21	1253	1303,8	39,9	464	534,8	55,8	178	235,6	45,2
la22	1552	1659,2	65,7	861	915,6	38,7	517	595,2	54,3
la23	1470	1560,8	61,1	544	673,4	77,2	179	295,8	72,8
la24	1711	1793,0	59,0	948	972,8	26,6	582	654,2	54,8
mt10	2616	2735,0	149,2	1634	1830,8	125,7	1316	1406,6	95,3
orb1	2995	3153,4	90,6	2232	2303,0	70,8	1764	1842,8	59,7
orb2	1946	2075,2	77,2	1101	1210,8	82,4	756	843,4	83,7
orb3	3165	3238,0	71,3	1995	2254,6	155,3	1805	1867,4	39,2
orb4	2691	2852,4	143,9	1467	1732,0	184,0	1455	1613,6	95,4
orb5	2149	2317,8	102,6	1407	1570,4	96,6	1107	1247,4	107,1
orb6	2651	2868,0	136,0	1723	1960,6	180,3	1446	1508,6	74,6
orb7	1416	1510,8	55,9	1097	1136,2	30,3	884	923,8	30,2
orb8	3117	3222,6	111,2	2280	2402,6	105,5	1939	2057,0	120,7
orb9	2580	2738,0	132,3	1624	1831,2	135,6	1145	1421,2	186,0
orb10	2448	2685,2	147,7	1781	1890,4	80,3	1417	1525,0	67,4

Table 5. Results for the criterion $\sum w_i T_i$

Instance	f = 1, 3			f = 1, 5			f = 1, 6		
	Best	Av	σ	Best	Av	σ	Best	Av	σ
abz6	2411	2576,0	156,8	741	899,4	125,8	218	373,0	117,7
la16	3359	3424,2	82,4	1596	1727,0	102,3	1009	1143,2	84,6
la17	3441	3607,8	174,6	1813	2002,4	118,2	1370	1480,4	96,7
la18	2833	2995,6	128,5	1376	1415,0	37,1	822	866,6	37,8
la19	3600	3627,0	31,5	1853	1931,0	67,9	1064	1229,6	106,7
la20	3196	3377,4	172,3	1469	1562,6	95,4	854	1018,2	117,1
la21	2073	2215,0	101,0	682	724,6	33,6	348	389,0	37,9
la22	2768	2902,4	84,0	1448	1578,2	101,2	916	979,4	43,0
la23	3019	3107,0	84,1	984	1214,0	159,2	443	635,4	120,5
la24	3280	3397,0	67,0	1561	1748,4	134,5	892	993,6	99,9
mt10	4797	5195,0	275,8	2752	3231,8	418,8	2020	2553,4	377,5
orb1	5595	6186,6	356,0	4191	4465,8	218,4	3281	3571,4	258,0
orb2	4489	4575,0	83,5	2529	2653,8	121,2	1690	1775,2	77,8
orb3	5442	5841,2	272,4	3101	3951,0	505,4	2825	3379,4	321,2
orb4	5189	5315,6	124,7	3335	3588,0	182,4	2448	2784,6	264,2
orb5	4380	4877,8	312,0	2972	3167,6	131,5	2187	2350,8	186,2
orb6	5624	5799,0	191,2	3249	3669,4	380,5	2469	2910,0	264,1
orb7	3100	3241,2	140,7	2103	2285,0	125,8	1754	1861,8	83,3
orb8	5902	6117,8	129,5	4079	4336,0	188,1	3716	3882,2	154,5
orb9	4074	4752,2	541,7	3182	3414,4	316,7	2178	2423,6	154,1
orb10	4855	5322,4	288,0	3462	3666,2	208,1	2659	2910,2	230,5

6   Conclusion

This paper presented a hybrid approach, which consist of a local search algorithm in the improving phase and Ant Colony Min-Max strategy in the diversification phase. To minimize regular criteria in the Job-shop Scheduling problem with maintenance activities, sequence dependent and set-up times. The best of our knowledge, these considerations have not been studied for this kind of problem and it is scarce for other scheduling extensions. The algorithm is supported in the adaptation of estimation functions as extensions of the classic Job-shop scheduling problem and the proposition of the conjunctive graph. In its formulation, the properties of heads, tails and levels of operations have been considered. Computational results show the efficiency of our Hybrid algorithm compared exclusively to the local search and Ant Colony algorithm.

Finally, we are also extending our approach to the simultaneous optimization of multiple criteria and as perspectives in other environments such as the flexible Job-shop Scheduling Problem.

This research is supported by the project identified with the code 18-531-INT, which is financed by the Universidad de Ibagué (Colombia).

References

1. Khoukhi, F., Boukachour, J., Alaoui, A.: The 'Dual-Ants Colony: a novel hybrid approach for the flexible job shop scheduling problem with preventive maintenance. Comput. Ind. Eng. 106, 236–255 (2017)
2. Avalos-Rosales, O., Ángel-Bello, F., Álvarez, A., Cardona-Valdés, Y.: Including preventive maintenance activities in an unrelated parallel machine environment with dependent setup times. Comput. Ind. Eng. 123, 364–377 (2018)
3. Lu, B., Zhou, X., Li, Y.: Joint modeling of preventive maintenance and quality improvement for deteriorating single-machine manufacturing systems. Comput. Ind. Eng. 91, 188–196 (2016)
4. Ben Ali, M., Sassi, M., Gossa, M., Harrath, Y.: Simultaneous scheduling of production and maintenance tasks in the job shop. Int. J. Prod. Res. 49(13), 3891–3918 (2011)
5. Naderi, B., Zandieh, M., Fatemi Ghomi, S.M.T.: Scheduling sequence-dependent setup time job shops with preventive maintenance. Int. J. Adv. Manuf. Technol. 43(1–2), 170–181 (2009)
6. Zandieh, M., Khatami, A.R., Rahmati, S.H.A.: Flexible job shop scheduling under condition-based maintenance: improved version of imperialist competitive algorithm. Appl. Soft Comput. J. 58, 449–464 (2017)
7. Jing, Z., Hua, J., Yi, Z.: Multi-objective integrated optimization problem of preventive maintenance planning and flexible job-shop scheduling. In: Proceedings of the 23rd International Conference on Industrial Engineering and Engineering Management. Atlantis Press, pp. 137–141 (2017)
8. Moradi, E., Fatemi Ghomi, S.M.T., Zandieh, M.: Bi-objective optimization research on integrated fixed time interval preventive maintenance and production for scheduling flexible job-shop problem. Expert Syst. Appl. 38(6), 7169–7178 (2011)
9. Naderi, B., Zandieh, M., Fatemi Ghomi, S.M.T.: A study on integrating sequence dependent setup time flexible flow lines and preventive maintenance scheduling. J. Intell. Manuf. 20(6), 683–694 (2009)
10. Rahmati, S.H.A., Ahmadi, A., Karimi, B.: Multi-objective evolutionary simulation based optimization mechanism for a novel stochastic reliability centered maintenance problem. Swarm Evol. Comput. 40, 255–271 (2018)
11. Lei, D.: Multi-objective artificial bee colony for interval job shop scheduling with flexible maintenance. Int. J. Adv. Manuf. Technol. 66(9–12), 1835–1843 (2013)
12. Shen, L.: A tabu search algorithm for the job shop problem with sequence dependent setup times. Comput. Ind. Eng. 78, 95–106 (2014)
13. Zhou, Y., Li, B., Yang, J.: Study on job shop scheduling with sequence-dependent setup times using biological immune algorithm. Int. J. Adv. Manuf. Technol. 30(1–2), 105–111 (2006)
14. Vinod, V., Sridharan, R.: Dynamic job-shop scheduling with sequence-dependent setup times: simulation modeling and analysis. Int. J. Adv. Manuf. Technol. 36(3–4), 355–372 (2008)
15. Naderi, B., Ghomi, S.M.T.F., Aminnayeri, M.: A high performing metaheuristic for job shop scheduling with sequence-dependent setup times. Appl. Soft Comput. J. 10(3), 703–710 (2010)

16. Chihaoui, F.B., Dridi, N., Hadj-Alouane, A.B.: Minimizing Lmax and Cmax in a job shop problem with sequence-dependent setup times. IFAC Proc. Vol. **39**(3), 75–80 (2006)
17. Mati, Y., Dauzère-Pérès, S., Lahlou, C.: A general approach for optimizing regular criteria in the job-shop scheduling problem. Eur. J. Oper. Res. **212**(1), 33–42 (2011)
18. Stützle, T., Hoos, H.: Improvements on the ant-system: Introducing the *MAX-MIN* ant system. In: Artificial Neural Nets and Genetic Algorithms, pp. 245–249. Springer, Vienna (1998). https://doi.org/10.1007/978-3-7091-6492-1_54
19. Singer, M., Pinedo, M.: A computational study of branch and bound techniques for minimizing the total weighted tardiness in job shops. IIE Trans. **30**(2), 109–118 (1998)

A Simple Yet Effective Algorithm to Compute Incremental All-Pairs Shortest Distances

Arturo Verbel[1], Nestor Rodriguez[2], and Sergio Rojas–Galeano[1(✉)]

[1] Universidad Distrital Francisco José de Caldas, Bogotá, Colombia
averbel@correo.udistrital.edu.co, srojas@udistrital.edu.co
[2] Formerly at Universidad Distrital Francisco José de Caldas, Bogotá, Colombia
nesterran@gmail.com

Abstract. Many activities of modern day living operate on the basis of graph structures that change over time (e.g. social networks, city traffic navigation, disease transmission paths). Hence, the problem of dynamically maintaining properties of such structures after modifying one of its edges (or links), specially for large-scale graphs, has received a great amount of attention in recent years. We address the particular case of updating all-pairs shortest distances upon *incremental* changes, i.e. recomputing shortest distances among all the nodes of a graph when a new or smaller shortcut between two nodes arises. We build upon the naive algorithm that visits all pairs of nodes comparing if the new shortcut shortens the distances, and propose a simple variation that instead chooses pairs of source and target nodes, only from the *affected* shortest paths. The new algorithm works with an optimal data structure, constant query time and worst-case $O(n^2)$ update cost, although our results on synthetic datasets hints at its practicality when compared with state-of-the-art approaches.

Keywords: All-pairs shortest distances · Dynamic incremental graphs

1 Introduction

Finding paths with shortest distances is a foundational problem in the analysis of graphs and has been extensively studied since the beginnings of computer science. In the case of graphs with static structure (i.e. fixed sets of nodes and edges) established algorithms such as Dijkstra's [8] and Floyd-Warshall's [11] are able to find effectively single–source and all–pairs shortest paths (known as SSSP and APSP respectively). Such algorithms are at the core of route planning technologies amply used in communication [17] and transportation networks [6, 9]. The growing size of these networks in recent years has motivated the proposal of more efficient strategies intended to cope with time limitations associated with such volumes, in particular, solving point-to-point shortest paths [5,12,15]. Usually in those scenarios the network structure is known and fixed, hence the

© Springer Nature Switzerland AG 2020
J. C. Figueroa-García et al. (Eds.): WEA 2020, CCIS 1274, pp. 222–229, 2020.
https://doi.org/10.1007/978-3-030-61834-6_19

aforementioned algorithms can be used to compute efficiently the distances from scratch, with a cost $O(n(m + n \log n))$, where n is the number of nodes and m is the number of edges in the graph (or $O(nm)$ in unweighted graphs).

A different problem where the graph structure changes dynamically over time, either by adding, removing or updating edges or nodes, has brought in new attention from researchers. Many activities of modern day living can be casted within such setting. Take for example wireless ad–hoc data networks, where routing paths are continuously changing depending on the availability of connected nodes (users or vehicles) [16]. Likewise, graphs of interactions happening in digital social networks [14] and mobile telephone calls [19] rapidly change their structure and therefore shortest paths or other interesting graph properties such as reachability, centrality or diameters, need to be maintained dynamically [4]. Navigation systems must deal with real-time traffic conditions so as to provide shortest routes recommendations [2]. The current COVID-19 pandemic is providing evidence that tracing contact transmission networks to estimate the expose to the virus as a function of distance to confirmed cases, is one of the more effective public health policies to contain the disease spread [13].

In this paper we focus on shortest–path distances over all–pairs of nodes of a directed graph upon *incremental* changes, i.e. on re-computing shortest distances among all the nodes of a graph when a new or a smaller shortcut between two nodes is inserted. We revisit the naive approach that examines all pairs of nodes to verify if the new shortcut shortens the distances [10], a strategy that takes $\Theta(n^2)$ time. We propose a simple variation that instead of traversing all combinations of target/source pairs, firstly filters only those nodes involved in the shortest paths that resulted *affected* with the new insertion. Although the worst-case update cost remains as $O(n^2)$, empirical evidence hints at a better average performance compared to the naive version and also comparable to recently proposed algorithms that likewise use the idea of restricting updates to the *affected* paths [20].

Notation. Let $G = (V, E, \omega)$ be a graph consisting of a set V of vertices or nodes, a set E of connecting edges, and a function $\omega : E \to \mathbb{R}^+$ assigning costs to each edge; $|V| = n$ and $|E| = m$. Let $D \in \mathbb{R}^{n \times n}$ be the all-pairs shortest distances matrix, with entries $d(s, t) < \infty$ being the distance of the shortest path connecting source node $s \in V$ to target node $t \in V$; if such a path does not exist then $d(s, t) = \infty$. We consider only updates consisting of insertions of a new or a smaller edge in terms of ω, that is, $\omega'(u, v) < \omega(u, v)$ for any $u, v \in V$. When this happens we denote by $\mathcal{A}_S$ the set of source nodes from the affected shortest paths whose target node is v; likewise we denote by $\mathcal{A}_T$ the set of target nodes from the affected shortest paths whose source node is u.

Problem Statement. Given $G = (V, E, \omega)$, $D = \{d(i, j)\}_{i,j=1}^n$ and $\omega'(u, v)$, find the resulting all–pairs shortest distances matrix $D' = \{d'(i, j)\}_{i,j=1}^n$ corresponding to $G' = (V, E', \omega')$.

2 Previous Work

The naive procedure comparing distances pairwise among all nodes of the graph is an algorithm that runs in $\Theta(n^2)$, originally proposed by Even and Gazit in 1985 [10]. The problem has attracted much attention since then. An algorithm that constraints the function ω to a an integer positive domain bounded by a constant C was proposed by Ausiello et al. [3]; its amortised running time is $O(n \log n)$. Afterwards, Ramalingam and Reps [18] proposed algorithms for incremental SSSP and APSP based on the idea of maintaining only the shortest paths *affected* by the edge update; basically they use a truncated version of Dijkstra's algorithm that traverses only the affected nodes, which in the worst-case is as costly as computing distances from scratch. Nonetheless, empirical studies have shown that their algorithms are well–performing in practice for real–life graphs [7].

More recently Slobbe, Bergamini and Meyerhenke [20] proposed novel SSSP and APSP algorithms for incremental edge also node insertions, both running in $O(n^2)$ worst–case time; their edge–update algorithms are improvements to Ramalingam and Reps algorithms, by simultaneously updating the distances from the affected source nodes, therefore avoiding repeating unnecessary truncated Dijkstra's executions. Despite their worst–case complexity, the authors show than empirically their algorithms achieve better performance than the baseline existing methods. Our study resembles this same approach, in that we also constraint the updating condition to the sets of affected sources and targets, although we focus on computing distances (not paths) and we use simpler algorithms and basic data structures. Our worst–case and empirical performance are nonetheless comparable with theirs. Lastly, a recent work reported by Alshammari et al. [1] also considers fully dynamic algorithms; their incremental algorithm maintains a forest of shortest path trees rooted in every node of the graph, that upon edge insertion updates distances in every tree using an adaptation of Dijkstra's algorithm; in the empirical study we conducted, our proposed algorithm also performs better in artificially generated graphs.

3 An Incremental APSD Algorithm

Broadly speaking, when a new edge with cost (length) $\omega'(u, v)$ is inserted (or replaced with a smaller length, if already exists), the algorithm checks if it is shorter than the current distance estimate $d(u, v)$ between these two nodes. If so, it updates this new distance for the edge $\overline{uv}$ and then checks which sub-paths are affected, from those starting in any other source node and ending at v, and from those starting at u and ending at any other target node in the graph. This is done with a linear-time loop that traverses every graph node k, recording those complying with the relaxing condition $(d(k, u) + \omega'(u, v)) < d(k, v)$ in a list of affected sources $\mathcal{A}_S$, and those complying with the relaxing condition $(\omega'(u, v) + d(v, k)) < d(u, k)$ in a list of affected targets $\mathcal{A}_T$.

The described step can be regarded as a filter that determines the actual affected pairs of distances that need to be updated. Since we keep distances in

---

Algorithm 1: abm $(D, \omega'(u, v))$

Input: All–pairs distance matrix $D = \{d(i,j)\}_{i,j=1}^{n}$, new decreased edge $\omega'(u, v)$
Output: Updated matrix D
if $\omega'(u, v) < d(u, v)$ then
  $\quad \mathcal{A}_S = \mathcal{A}_T = \emptyset$ // Lists of affected sources and targets
  $\quad$ for $k = 1 \ldots n$ do
  $\qquad$ if $(d(k, u) + \omega'(u, v)) < d(k, v)$ then $\mathcal{A}_S = \mathcal{A}_S \cup k$
  $\qquad$ if $(\omega'(u, v) + d(v, k)) < d(u, k)$ then $\mathcal{A}_T = \mathcal{A}_T \cup k$
  $\quad$ foreach $s \in \mathcal{A}_S$ do
  $\qquad$ foreach $t \in \mathcal{A}_T$ do
  $\qquad\quad d(s, t) = \min(d(s, t), d(s, u) + \omega'(u, v) + d(v, t))$

---

a square matrix D, indexed by the nodes of the graph in no particular order, the lists $\mathcal{A}_S$, $\mathcal{A}_T$ define in fact a subset of index nodes corresponding to a *block* of the matrix, namely the block of entries of *affected* distances. Thus, we call this algorithm the affected block matrix update (abm). The algorithm finishes traversing all-pairs in the block, updating only entries with shorter distances.

The time complexity of the algorithm is dominated by the double nested loop that traverses the lists of affected sources and targets. The size of these lists depend on how many elements are inserted during execution of the preceding loop, which in turn traverses all n nodes, that is, $|\mathcal{A}_S| \leq n$ and $|\mathcal{A}_T| \leq n$; since the actual sizes resulting because of an arbitrary decrease update are not known in advanced, hence we estimate a worst-case scenario for time complexity of $O(n^2)$. In practice, however, this cost may be usually smaller, as our empirical experiments suggest (see next section). This is because the size of the resulting block that needs to be updated is commonly much smaller than n^2. Besides, since the only data structure the algorithm uses to operate is the all-pairs distance matrix, its space complexity is also $O(n^2)$ with an optimal $O(1)$ query time.

4 Empirical Study

4.1 Synthetic Graphs

We created synthetic random graphs $G(n, p)$, consisting of n nodes and edges added at random between all possible $n \times n$ pairs with probability $0 < p < 1$. The weight of the edges is also randomly selected between $2 \leq \omega(u, v) \leq 10$. We tried $n \in \{100, 1000\}$ so as to account for small- and medium-size graphs, with densities $p \in \{0.01, \ldots 0.05, 0.1, \ldots 0.5\}$; edges are directed and no self-connections were allowed. For each combination (n, p), 30 different random graphs were generated; the algorithms were tested and results averaged over these instances in order to avoid biases arising in a single random graph.

In summary, 600 graphs were used in the empirical experiments. This collection of graph datasets is available at https://github.com/apspgraphincremental/graph-generated.

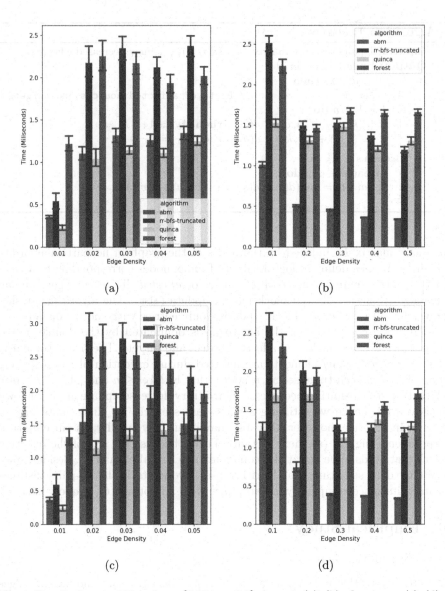

Fig. 1. Results for $n = 100$ and $p \in \{0.01, \ldots, 0.5\}$. **insert:** (a)–(b), **decrease:** (c)–(d).

4.2   Experiment Design

We performed experiments focusing on running times of a single edge update on the collection of the generated synthetic graphs. We compared the `abm` algorithm described above with the following algorithms: `even-gazit` [10], `quinca` [20], `rr-bfs-truncated` [20], and `forest` [1], which were chosen according to our literature review of Sect. 2, as the most relevant for the dynamic incremental All-pairs

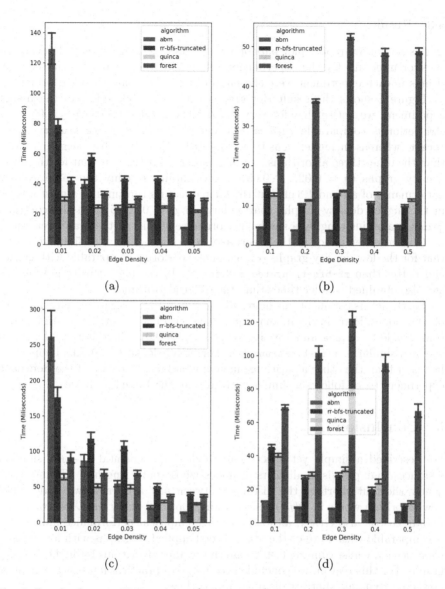

Fig. 2. Results for $n = 1000$ and $p \in \{0.01, \ldots, 0.5\}$. **insert:** (a)–(b), **decrease:** (c)–(d).

Shortest Distances problem. We defined two sets of experiments: **insert**, where a new edge is inserted between two randomly chosen (unconnected) nodes, and **decrease**, where the weight of a randomly chosen (existing) edge is decreased to $\omega'(u, v) = 1$.

The experiments were run on a Intel Core i5-8250U CPU, 1.60 GHz using 1 core and 16 GB of RAM, on an Ubuntu 20.04 LTS 64bit Server.

4.3 Results

In this section we report plot bars of average runtimes with standard deviations as error intervals, for the experiments described earlier. The three faster algorithms in each experiment were chosen in order to compare their performance.

Figure 1 shows the results for graphs with $n = 100$ nodes. In the **insert** experiment, we notice that for very low density graphs ($0.01 < p \leq 0.05$, (a)), `abm` performs comparable with `quinca` and better than `rr-bfs-truncated` and `forest`, whereas in higher density graphs ($0.1 < p \leq 0.5$, (b)), `abm` runs faster than the other three algorithms. An interesting observation is that for the lower density graphs ($p = 0.02, \ldots, 0.05$), `abm` maintains roughly the same average performance of around 1.3 ms but then it reduces its runtimes to almost a third in the higher density graphs (particularly in $p = 0.4, 0.5$). On the contrary, `quinca` maintains roughly a similar performance within all the graph densities.

On the other hand, in the **decrease** experiment with $n = 100$, we notice that for the low density graphs (c), again `abm` performs comparable with `quinca` and better than `rr-bfs-truncated` and `forest`. In the high density graphs (d), `abm` also obtained smaller times than the other algorithms.

Lastly, let us comment on the results shown in Fig. 2 regarding larger graphs of 1000 nodes. Here, in the **insert** experiment with low densities (a), `abm` behaves comparable to `quinca` and `forest` except on $p = 0.01$ where it takes longer in average, similarly to `rr-bfs-truncated`. For larger densities (b), `abm` happens to be faster than the other algorithms, including `quinca`. The case of the **decrease** experiment (c–d) follows a similar pattern than the **insert** scenario.

5 Conclusion

We described a simple yet effective method for incremental all-pairs shortest distances that pre-visits all pairs of nodes whose path length is affected when a new shortcut shortens the distance between any arbitrary two nodes. The new algorithm works in $O(n^2)$ space yielding optimal query time. Its worst-case update cost is also $O(n^2)$, although average empirical performance indicates it is comparable with state-of-the-art methods applied to graphs with low-density connectivity, whilst running faster than those other algorithms for higher-density graphs. For this reason, we conclude it could be of practical interest for many of nowadays dynamic shortest distance applications.

Regarding ideas for future work, we plan to extend our study to large-size graphs (10,000 or more nodes), including real-world data sets and to address the problem of updating the actual shortest paths, as well as other related dynamic operations, such as removing edges and adding or removing nodes.

References

1. Alshammari, M., Rezgui, A.: An all pairs shortest path algorithm for dynamic graphs. Comput. Sci. **15**(1), 347–365 (2020)

2. Ardakani, M.K., Tavana, M.: A decremental approach with the A* algorithm for speeding-up the optimization process in dynamic shortest path problems. Measurement **60**, 299–307 (2015)

3. Ausiello, G., Italiano, G.F., Spaccamela, A.M., Nanni, U.: Incremental algorithms for minimal length paths. J. Algorithms **12**(4), 615–638 (1991)

4. Bergamini, E., Meyerhenke, H., Staudt, C.: Approximating betweenness centrality in large evolving networks. In: ALENEX, pp. 133–146. SIAM (2015)

5. Delling, D., Goldberg, A.V., Pajor, T., Werneck, R.F.: Customizable route planning in road networks. Transp. Sci. **51**(2), 566–591 (2017)

6. Delling, D., Sanders, P., Schultes, D., Wagner, D.: Engineering route planning algorithms. In: Lerner, J., Wagner, D., Zweig, K.A. (eds.) Algorithmics of Large and Complex Networks. LNCS, vol. 5515, pp. 117–139. Springer, Heidelberg (2009). https://doi.org/10.1007/978-3-642-02094-0_7

7. Demetrescu, C., Italiano, G.F.: Experimental analysis of dynamic all pairs shortest path algorithms. ACM Trans. Algorithms (TALG) **2**(4), 578–601 (2006)

8. Dijkstra, E.W.: A note on two problems in connection with graphs. Numer. Math. **1**, 269–271 (1959)

9. Dunn, C.E., Newton, D.: Optimal routes in GIS and emergency planning applications. Area **24**(3), 259–267 (1992)

10. Even, S., Gazit, H.: Updating distances in dynamic graphs. Methods Oper. Res. **49**, 371–387 (1985)

11. Floyd, R.W.: Algorithm 97: shortest path. Commun. ACM **5**(6), 345+ (1962)

12. Henzinger, M., Krinninger, S., Nanongkai, D.: Decremental single-source shortest paths on undirected graphs in near-linear total update time. In: 2014 IEEE 55th Annual Symposium on Foundations of Computer Science (FOCS), pp. 146–155. IEEE (2014)

13. Keeling, M.J., Deirdre Hollingsworth, T., Read, J.M.: The efficacy of contact tracing for the containment of the 2019 novel coronavirus (COVID-19). medRxiv (2020)

14. Khopkar, S.S., Nagi, R., Nikolaev, A.G., Bhembre, V.: Efficient algorithms for incremental all pairs shortest paths, closeness and betweenness in social network analysis. Soc. Netw. Anal. Min. **4**(1), 1–20 (2014). https://doi.org/10.1007/s13278-014-0220-6

15. Lissovoi, A., Witt, C.: Runtime analysis of ant colony optimization on dynamic shortest path problems. Theoret. Comput. Sci. **561**, 73–85 (2015)

16. Liu, J., Wan, J., Wang, Q., Deng, P., Zhou, K., Qiao, Y.: A survey on position-based routing for vehicular ad hoc networks. Telecommun. Syst. **62**(1), 15–30 (2015). https://doi.org/10.1007/s11235-015-9979-7

17. Moy, J.T.: OSPF: Anatomy of an Internet Routing Protocol. Addison-Wesley Longman Publishing Co., Inc., Boston (1998)

18. Ramalingam, G., Reps, T.: An incremental algorithm for a generalization of the shortest-path problem. J. Algorithms **21**(2), 267–305 (1996)

19. Sarmento, R., Oliveira, M., Cordeiro, M., Tabassum, S., Gama, J.: Social network analysis in streaming call graphs. In: Japkowicz, N., Stefanowski, J. (eds.) Big Data Analysis: New Algorithms for a New Society. SBD, vol. 16, pp. 239–261. Springer, Cham (2016). https://doi.org/10.1007/978-3-319-26989-4_10

20. Slobbe, A., Bergamini, E., Meyerhenke, H.: Faster incremental all-pairs shortest paths. Technical report, Karlsruhe Institute of Technology, Faculty of Informatics (2016)

Bioengineering

Integration of Machine Learning Models in PACS Systems to Support Diagnostic in Radiology Services

Kevin Osorno-Castillo[2], Rubén D. Fonnegra[1,2]([✉]), and Gloria M. Díaz[2]

[1] Institución Universitaria Pascual Bravo, Medellín, Colombia
ruben.fonnegra@pascualbravo.edu.co
[2] Instituto Tecnológico Metropolitano, Medellín, Colombia
gloriadiaz@itm.edu.co, kevinosorno220486@correo.itm.edu.co,
http://www.pascualbravo.edu.co, http://www.itm.edu.co

Abstract. In recent years, machine learning models have been introduced to solve many problems in medical imaging, such as segmentation, classification, and disease prediction. Unfortunately, most of them are useless for the physician due that they are not available tools that are part of their workflow. At present, Picture Archiving and Communication Systems (PACS) are the standard platforms used in clinical environments to store and transmit electronic images and the reading reports. Therefore, the integration of the automatic analysis tools with these systems is required to allow validation by physicians and the use in clinical and medical research. This paper presents a simple way of adding the use of machine learning models for the automatic analysis of medical images in the radiological workflow using DICOM services provided by open source tools. An implementation case study is also presented, in which a deep learning architecture was trained for classifying chest X-ray images as normal, bacterial pneumonia or viral pneumonia, including in the last case images of COVID-19 patients.

Keywords: Medical imaging · Deep learning models · PACS integration · DICOM

1 Introduction

Conventionally, Clinical Decision Support Systems (CDSS) are information systems for supporting medical decisions at different levels in the clinical practice. They are mainly designed to help decision making based on the available data from patients, including clinical and imaging. Advances in computer science during the last 30 years have made possible the enhancements of CDSS, in a way that automated algorithms are used to attend, advise, diagnose, and follow up patients [1]. Moreover, the advances in artificial intelligence and machine learning algorithms had to lead the inclusion of models to efficiently estimate survival rate, diagnose different pathologies, determine relevant clinical findings, predict

© Springer Nature Switzerland AG 2020
J. C. Figueroa-García et al. (Eds.): WEA 2020, CCIS 1274, pp. 233–244, 2020.
https://doi.org/10.1007/978-3-030-61834-6_20

treatment procedures, among others. In the case of radiology systems, screenings, and other clinical data from patients is usually taken to estimate specific patterns to denote the existence of abnormalities according to the diagnosis protocol. However, the validation and use of these tools are frequently limited to experimental setups, due to the difficulty of integrating them into the applications used by the radiologists in clinical practices. A clear example of the lack of this integration was observed in the recent health emergency caused by the COVID-19 pandemic, which promoted the rapid development of machine learning-based solutions for supporting the detection and prognosis of the disease progression from chest imaging. However, the inclusion of such solutions in clinical environments seems not to be available in the same way [2].

Consequently, to bridge the gap between basic imaging scientists and physicians in both the clinical practice and the research settings, the implementation of strategies to run machine learning pipelines into the radiological workflow is required. To address this issue, several alternatives have been proposed. The first one, is the development of software packages or systems dedicated to solving specific problems related to image analysis of certain organs or diseases; some commercial examples are CADstream (Merge Healthcare Inc., Chicago, IL) or DynaCAD (Invivo, Gainesville, FL) for Breast MRI Analysis, and Syngo CXR CAD (Siemens HealthCare, Malvern, PA) for the chest image analysis [3]. In those cases, the extension for solving other medical imaging tasks is complicated since the algorithms that compose those tools are based on the specific requirements, and most of them are proprietary solutions. In other cases, researchers and commercial companies have proposed the use of web based solutions [4], which require radiologists or PACS operators upload the images to the Web application and to store the response as part of the radiological report. This is not only inefficient, but can also lead to human errors. Some researchers have proposed extensible software packages and frameworks that allow developers to create functional extensions under a platform, which handles the basic communication and visualization functions in medical imaging software. Some of them, such as MITK [5], Slicer 3D [6], and CAIPI [7], have gained a lot of recognition in the scientific community; however, as they are not really integrated into the workflow of the radiologist, its use is also limited. Additionally, developers require to learn specific programming tools for extending it. Finally, some authors have taken advantage of the acceptance of visualization software, such as Osirix (Pixmeo SARL, Geneva, Switzerland), to develop and distribute plugins that solving from general to specific problems, it is the case of Ribli et al. [8], who developed a plugin for the classification of lesions in mammography images.

In this work, a general framework to integrate radiology systems and machine learning models is described. In this case, a deep learning model is created in a widely use framework for this purpose (Tensorflow) to process a widely use medical imaging protocol (DICOM). After training, the model communicates with a radiology server to process medical imaging files and add the results as metadata to the original file, which is transmitted back. As a case of implementation for this approach, we use a deep learning architecture to detect normal, bacterial and viral pneumonia from patients with COVID-19. The architecture is based in ChexNet [9] after a lung segmentation, and it is able to classify among these categories, and create a synthetic risk heatmap as an embedded layer in the DICOM file. All this process is natively conducted using DICOM communication protocol. Besides, the machine learning model and the framework interface are developed independently using native Python. For this reason, the framework can be extensible and easy to implement with other trained machine learning models or algorithms.

2   Picture Archiving and Communication Systems

Picture Achieving and Communication Systems (PACS) have been developed with the aim of storing medical screenings and easing the communications among different devices and healthcare providers [10]. PACS are usually provided with CDSS for specific imaging tasks, as additional features developed by the system suppliers. Basically, a PACS is composed by three major groups of components: image acquisition devices (e.g.., computed radiography and magnetic resonance imaging scanners), storage and databases repositories (e.g., RAIDs, optical disks, etc.), and display and processing workstations. These components are integrated by a communications network and a database management system [11]. Their implementation offers benefits and direct impact in economical and security aspects, as they attend a workflow from the image acquisition to the final diagnosis or follow up. For instance, the information system is able to store the data maintaining high resolution, ease the accessibility, realize data analysis, create automatic or periodic reports, automatically anonymize, among others.

The DICOM Standard. The Digital Imaging and Communication in Medicine (DICOM) is the standard format for handling screenings in medical applications [12]. Besides, it also allows the storage of historical useful data such waveforms, reports and IDs to integrate different communication systems, including PACS. DICOM was first appear in 1993 and developed by the American College of Radiology (ACR) with the National Electrical Manufacturers Association (NEMA). It is based on layers, containing and upper layer protocol (ULP) implemented over TCP/IP that allows communication of messages, services, or information objects, which are stored in an information model based on tags, which maps a real-world medical examination into four levels named patient, study, series and image. Thus, a patient has one or more studies, each of them composed by one or more series, which in turn, may contain one or more images. Nowadays, the DICOM information model supports multiple data structures for different imaging modalities (such as Magnetic Resonance Imaging, Computer Tomography, Computer Radiography, Ultrasound, structured reporting, among others). For this reason, DICOM has become more popular in the imaging industry. In Mildenberger et al. [13], readers can to consult a complete historical review under DICOM format imaging and handling.

3   Proposed Framework

Figure 1 illustrates the general framework proposed in this paper, which adds a new component to the conventional radiological workflow based on PACS technologies. This component, named Machine Learning-boosted server consists of the trained machine learning models and other software components that make possible the integration with the PACS repositories and viewers of the radiological service. As it is illustrated, communication with the PACS Server and the DICOM viewers is enable by DICOM query and retrieve messages. Thus, this solution is supplier or DICOM viewer independent.

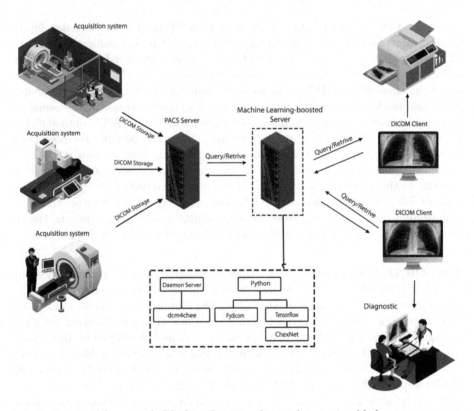

Fig. 1. Proposed framework. Machine Learning-boosted server is added as a component of the radiological framework by using simple query/retrieve DICOM messages

3.1   PACS Based Radiological Workflow

In Fig. 1 are showed the main components of a PACS based radiological workflow since medical images are captured by the acquisition systems. In general, this process is performed by a technician trained to handle the acquisition protocol according to examination requirements. Once an image (or sequence of images) is acquired, it is stored using the DICOM protocol into a local storage; then, these images are sent to the institutional PACS server in order to make them available for the radiological reading process as well as for long-term storage. In this step, technician can to generate post-processing images or other data useful to the diagnosis. From the DICOM viewers, physicians retrieve the studies to perform the image interpretation and to generate the diagnostic report, which is also stored in the PACS server. In the reading process, physicians can to use computer aiding diagnosis tools.

3.2 Machine Learning-Boosted Server

DICOM Server. The proposed framework consist in a DICOM server integrated to a conventional radiology workflow. The server is in charge of storing and launching machine learning models for the screenings and series processing when they are received. Furthermore, the server is the main link among the PACS and the DICOM client, using DICOM network protocols. For this, a DICOM listener is required to catch and store the files in real time through an specific port of the server. This service is constantly running in background, which means that it does not requires high computational capabilities.

Machine Learning Server. In case of the machine learning models, they do not need a special implementation to join the framework. Models can be implemented as they are usually are designed, trained, loaded and validated. For implementation purposes, a deep learning architecture is employed using widely accepted languages and frameworks for artificial intelligence. In our case, python 3.7 is used as programming language, CUDA 10.1 and cuDNN v7.6.4 are used for GPU accelerating computing, numpy, scipy, pillow, matplotlib, scikit-learn, scikit-image and pandas are used as complementary tools, tensorflow 2.0 is used for creating the neural network, pydicom is used for processing DICOM files. However, the framework is not limited and is completely extensible to custom setup by including other required libraries compatible with python 3.7 and tensorflow 2.0. The parameters and learning task for the deep learning model is described in the next section.

The DICOM Network Receiver. The DICOM listener stores received images in an assigned directory into the server. The Daemon process executes a bash script containing terminal commands to launch python each time an image is input. Once in python prompt, machine learning models read DICOM files to extract metadata, including patient information and screenings. Thereupon, images are converted in appropriate formats to be processed by machine learning algorithms to get an expected response. Finally, The final resulting image is added to the original DICOM file by appending a new "series description" and "series number". Thereupon, "pixel data" from the resulting image is appended for radiologist do not confuse it with the original image. Finally, as a preventive option; the original DICOM file and the DICOM with the results are responded to the client (PACS).

The use of this process ease different PACS task. Among them, the sequences reception, the process automation and the inclusion of machine learning or other statistics models. Besides, other open source modules and tools for massive data processing and analysis could also be natively included in the workflow.

4   Implementation Case Study

To evaluate the proposed framework, an implementation case study is presented evaluating a deep learning architecture to detect complications from COVID-19 patients. Severe acute respiratory syndrome coronavirus 2 (SARS CoV-2), also known as COVID-19 or HCoV-19 is a novel human coronavirus first appeared in late 2019 and emerged in Wuhan, province of Hubei, China. The disease has become pandemic and declared global emergency since February 2020 by World Health Organization (WHO) [14,15]. Infections with COVID-19 are spread all over the planet reporting at least than 8'860.331 confirmed cases and 465.740 deaths, by 22 June 2020 [16].

Reported symptoms for the disease are high temperature and a new, continuous cough. Other reported self-symptoms with strong correlation with COVID-19 are loss of smell and taste [15]. Nevertheless, the main reported complication related with COVID-19 patients is severe pneumonia, and it have caused the largest amount of deaths. For this reason, the proposed model is oriented to the detection of pneumonia from chest x-ray images as a tool to improve the diagnosis process. Despite the ideal task to perform is the prediction of COVID-19, this is not conducted in our work because of the lack of available data to train models. Moreover, the data used in to evaluate them was obtained as a collection of confirmed images of patients with pneumonia found in other finished works. To see further details, please reefer to Subsect. 4.2.

The tool is linked to our framework and fully evaluated in a real radiology environment.

4.1   Machine Learning Server Features

The DICOM server implemented in this work is DCM4CHEE based[1]. The package is linked to multiple useful open source modules and apps to develop medical pipelines. This tool is used to introduce a server for running machine learning in a conventional radiology workflow. DCM4CHEE is then used to create the listener, consisting in a service class provider (SCP) store. The listener receives DCM files in real time to be sent via DICOM network protocols. Files are then stored in a DICOM client; in this case, an Horos project client (Free DICOM

---

[1] Full details and documentation on DCM4CHEE can be found in https://www.dcm4che.org/.

Medical Image Viewer[2]). However, it is important to remark that the framework is not limited to this configuration (chosen for our case of implementation). It can also be extended to the use of other viewers that admit DICOM network communication protocols (Osirix, 3D Slicer, PostDICOM, among others). Moreover, since the server is capable of running python commands, a wide range of open source packages to read and process DICOM files would be available to use.

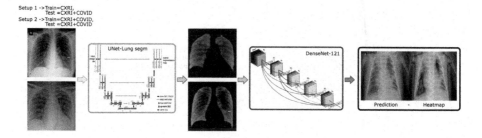

Fig. 2. Proposed deep learning-based framework.

4.2 Deep Learning Architecture

The proposed architecture is based in ChexNet [9]. Chexnet is a 121-layer architecture (originally based in DenseNet-121 [17]) trained on the ChestX-ray 14 dataset. The network inputs a x-ray imaging screening front-view lungs to detect 14 different pathologies (Atelectasis, Cardiomegaly, Consolidation, Edema, Effusion, Emphysema, Fibrosis, Hernia, Infiltration, Mass, Nodule, Pleural Thickening, Pneumonia, and Pneumothorax). In our case, a lung segmentation is applied to extract the appropriated region of interest from each image using a unet-based model previously trained[3]. The segmentation network has been trained using Montgomery County [18] and JSRT datasets [19]. The resulting pulmonary region is then passed to the DenseNet, where the last layer of the network is removed, and convolutional layers are taken as feature extractors. Therefore, two fully connected layers are added and retrained to recognize among 3 different classes (normal, bacterial pneumonia and viral pneumonia) using the Chest X-ray images database (CXRI) [20]. The database is generally split in train, test and validation sets. Besides, several images are included from patients diagnosed with pneumonia caused by COVID-19. These images were not taken from a database, but were found in published works in the state of the art reporting advances in COVID-19. A total of 382 images were collected reporting different types of coronavirus (SARS-CoV2, MERS-SARS). COVID-19 pneumonia

---

[2] Full details and documentation on Horos project can be found in https://horosproject.org/.

[3] Full details and results on the segmentation network can be found in https://github.com/imlab-uiip/lung-segmentation-2d.

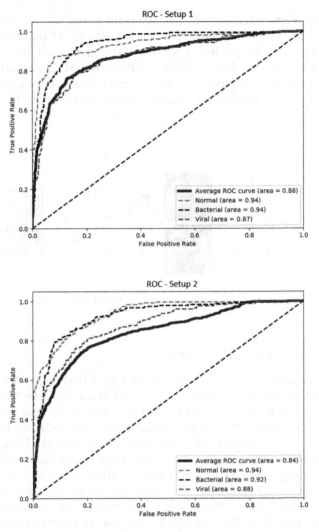

Fig. 3. Performance results in the classification of normal, viral pneumonia and bacterial pneumonia of computed chest radiographies for the experimental setup 1 (top), and 2 (bottom).

images were split in train and test set, and joined with their respective groups from the database. An evaluation on the test set using only CXRI database and CXRI + COVID pneumonia images is reported. A representation of the complete architecture can be found in Fig. 2. For training, adam optimizer is used with $\alpha = 0.001$ and default author proposed parameters $\beta_1 = 0.9$ and $\beta_2 = 0.999$ [21]. Finally, a minibatch of 10 is set.

5 Results

5.1 Distinguishing Viral from Bacterial Pneumonia Detection Using Deep Learning Models

The model was evaluated using two approaches. In the first (setup 1), train set only contains data from the CXRI database, and test set contained images from CXRI + COVID pneumonia images. In the second (setup 2), train and test sets contained CXRI + COVID pneumonia images in same proportions. During training, the loss is monitored to determine the best parameter combination for a correct classification. Therefore, only the model weights obtaining the lowest loss is selected as the best. Then, performance on the test set is obtained, extracting the area under the receiving operative curve (AUC) per class and average, sensitivity (SENS) and specificity (ESP). Besides, the receiving operative curve (ROC) is plotted. Figures 3 (top) and 3 (bottom) depict the results for both experiments and Fig. 4 shows the SENS and ESP scores for both setups. In both setups, similar SENS and ESP is achieved. However, a sightly higher viral AUC is obtained for setup 2, suggesting an existing differentiation among samples when including training data from pneumonia COVID. Despite, the model still does not obtain a significant improvement concerning viral patients. We believe this limitation is noticed due to the lack of available data for this kind of patients, since there is still no open access for imaging data to detect COVID. Therefore, the use of larger COVID data might increase performance of current models. Further research concerning this issues must be performed.

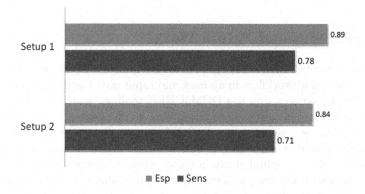

Fig. 4. Sensitivity (SENS) and specificity (ESP) scores for setup 1 and 2.

5.2 Machine Learning Boosted Server in Medical Workflow

After distinguishing among different types of pneumonia, the integration of this model in a real radiological workflow is performed. In this case, the DICOM listener receives multiple files and response back the original file with an additional layer containing the probability heatmap of damaged lung tissue. This layer is labeled as "colormap" in the response file. The file can then be visualized by the DICOM client using Horos. In Fig. 5, an example of a generated "colormap" layer using the deep learning model is displayed. Besides, the predicted label for the actual patient and the assigned probability to it is also written in red font in the top left of the image.

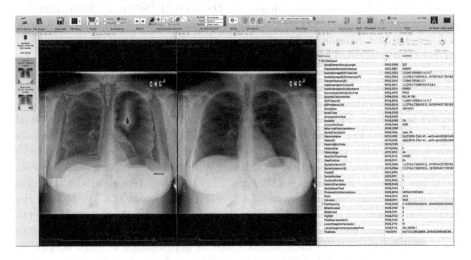

Fig. 5. The result of the implementation of the Machine Learning-boosted Server, here you can see the original and processed series with the prediction tag.

6   Conclusions and Future Work

This paper presents a framework that allows integrating machine learning models into the radiological workflow in an easy and rapid way. For doing so, a DICOM server is implemented using the DCM4CHEE toolbox, which provides retrieve and query services that are used to allows that results generated by the machine learning models be converted into DICOM images, reports or overlays, as part of an patient study or sequence. In this way, the PACS server will deploy this result as part of the original study in the diagnostic interpretation process.

The proposed framework was evaluated for developing and deploying a deep learning model trained to distinguish between normal, viral pneumonia and bacterial pneumonia in a computed chest radiography. The deep learning model was off-line trained and deployed in an IMac all-in-one with the macOS Catalina V. 10.15.4, in which a DICOM server was implemented using the DCM4CHEE toolbox. Additionally, The Horos software was used as PACS viewer, due it is one of the mos accepted open-source DICOM viewer in clinical environments. Results showed that the proposed framework allowed an easy and rapid integration of functional machine learning models, in a visual environment used by radiologist in their clinical practice.

As future work, we plan to evaluate the proposed framework with several perspectives. First, the use of different or multiple PACS clients as mentioned previously (Osirix, 3D Slicer, PostDICOM, among others). Second, the extensibility of the framework in terms of python open source modules and packages, beyond used in this work (Tensorflow, scikit-learn, etc.). Third, the evaluation of other image analysis tasks such as organ segmentation and region of interest classification in different imaging modalities (CT, MRI, etc.). Finally, the impact of using this strategies in the validation of machine learning models by radiologist or medical staff must be also evaluated.

References

1. Shortliffe, E.H., Sepúlveda, M.J.: Clinical decision support in the era of artificial intelligence. Jama **320**(21), 2199–2200 (2018)
2. Shi, F., et al.: Review of artificial intelligence techniques in imaging data acquisition, segmentation and diagnosis for COVID-19. IEEE Rev. Biomed. Eng. (2020)
3. Lin, T.W., Huang, P.Y., Cheng, C.W.C.: Computer-aided diagnosis in medical imaging: review of legal barriers to entry for the commercial systems. In: 2016 IEEE 18th International Conference on e-Health Networking, Applications and Services (Healthcom), pp. 1–5. IEEE (2016)
4. Mattonen, S.A., Gude, D., Echegaray, S., Bakr, S., Rubin, D.L., Napel, S.: Quantitative imaging feature pipeline: a web-based tool for utilizing, sharing, and building image-processing pipelines. J. Med. Imaging **7**(4), 042803 (2020)
5. Nolden, M., et al.: The medical imaging interaction toolkit: challenges and advances. Int. J. Comput. Assisted Radiol. Surgery **8**(4), 607–620 (2013)
6. Fedorov, A., et al.: 3d slicer as an image computing platform for the quantitative imaging network. Magn. Reson. Imaging **30**(9), 1323–1341 (2012)
7. Huellebrand, M., Messroghli, D., Tautz, L., Kuehne, T., Hennemuth, A.: An extensible software platform for interdisciplinary cardiovascular imaging research. Comput. Meth. Prog. Bio. **184**, 105277 (2020)
8. Ribli, D., Horváth, A., Unger, Z., Pollner, P., Csabai, I.: Detecting and classifying lesions in mammograms with deep learning. Sci. Rep. **8**(1), 1–7 (2018)
9. Rajpurkar, P., et al.: CheXNet: Radiologist-level pneumonia detection on chest x-rays with deep learning. arXiv preprint arXiv:1711.05225 (2017)
10. Liu, B.J., Huang, H.: Picture archiving and communication systems and electronic medical records for the healthcare enterprise. In: Biomedical Information Technology, pp. 105–164. Elsevier (2020)
11. Huang, H.K.: PACS and Imaging Informatics: Basic Principles and Applications. Wiley, Hoboken (2011)
12. Clunie, D.A.: DICOM Structured Reporting. PixelMed Publishing, Bangor (2000)
13. Mildenberger, P., Eichelberg, M., Martin, E.: Introduction to the DICOM standard. Eur. Radiol. **12**(4), 920–927 (2002)
14. Wu, F., et al.: A new coronavirus associated with human respiratory disease in China. Nature **579**(7798), 265–269 (2020)
15. Zhou, P., et al.: A pneumonia outbreak associated with a new coronavirus of probable bat origin. Nature **579**(7798), 270–273 (2020)
16. World Health Organization (WHO): Coronavirus disease (COVID-19) situation report-154. Data as received by who from national authorities by 10:00 CEST, 22 June 2020

17. Huang, G., Liu, Z., Van Der Maaten, L., Weinberger, K.Q.: Densely connected convolutional networks. In: Proceedings of the IEEE Conference on Computer Vision and Pattern Recognition, pp. 4700–4708 (2017)
18. Jaeger, S., Candemir, S., Antani, S., Wáng, Y.X.J., Lu, P.X., Thoma, G.: Two public chest X-ray datasets for computer-aided screening of pulmonary diseases. Quant. Imaging Med. Surg. 4(6), 475 (2014)
19. Shiraishi, J., et al.: Development of a digital image database for chest radiographs with and without a lung nodule: receiver operating characteristic analysis of radiologists' detection of pulmonary nodules. Am. J. Roentgenol. 174(1), 71–74 (2000)
20. Kermany, D.S., et al.: Identifying medical diagnoses and treatable diseases by image-based deep learning. Cell 172(5), 1122–1131 (2018)
21. Kingma, D.P., Ba, J.: Adam: A method for stochastic optimization. arXiv preprint arXiv:1412.6980 (2014)

Quantifying Irregular Morphology Electrograms in Atrial Fibrillation Using Fractional Fourier Domains

Alejandro Gómez-Echavarría[1], Juan P. Ugarte[2]([✉]) [iD], and Catalina Tobón[1] [iD]

[1] MATBIOM, Universidad de Medellín, Medellín, Colombia
[2] GIMSC, Universidad de San Buenaventura, Medellín, Colombia
juan.ugarte@usbmed.edu.co

Abstract. A fractional Fourier transform-based strategy is proposed for the analysis of morphological irregularities of 933 simulated electrograms recorded from a 3D simulated human atria under atrial fibrillation. Optimum fractional domains are considered to quantify the non-stationary features in the signals after preprocessing and segmentation. Optimum order maps obtained with the proposed strategy are compared with approximate entropy maps generated in previous studies. The results indicate that distinct types of electrical activity can be associated with different fractional domains and that the FrFT can be sensitive to different underlying propagation patterns where the approximate entropy exhibits uniform behavior.

Keywords: Atrial Fibrillation · Atrial electrograms · Fractional Fourier Transform · Irregular morphology signal

1 Introduction

Atrial fibrillation (AF) is a common arrhythmia that affects more than 33 million individuals globally with an increasing trend [4]. The AF is associated with morbidity and mortality, representing an important burden to the public health [13]. This pathology is characterized by a chaotic electrical activity over the atria that leads to abnormal increment of heart rate, reducing the ability of atrial contraction [4]. The study of the electrical activity during AF is commonly based on the analysis of intracardiac electrograms (EGM). Catheter ablation is a therapeutic technique used to electrically inactivate regions of the myocardium identified as arrhythmogenic by locally applying energy [21]. This approach relies on the analysis of EGM information related with underlying fibrillatory mechanisms. Therefore, a proper characterization of the AF mechanisms has important implications in the development of therapeutic strategies.

The AF mechanisms as rotors and multiple reentrant waves are related with areas of complex fractionated atrial electrograms and high dominant frequency (DF) [12,20]. Thus, the identification of atrial areas with these features may

J. C. Figueroa-García et al. (Eds.): WEA 2020, CCIS 1274, pp. 245–256, 2020.
https://doi.org/10.1007/978-3-030-61834-6_21

improve the ablation procedures success rates [22]. Considering the chaotic and non-stationary characteristic of the AF dynamics, applying robust EGM analysis techniques is important to extract the relevant information from the irregular electrical activity. Signal processing techniques have been proposed to localize and characterize the arrhythmogenic substrates such as EGM morphology analysis, [9,28], DF analysis [11,19] and organization measures [6,7,23]. Although these studies have contributed to the AF characterization, the non-stationary characteristics typical of the fribrillatory mechanisms requires new mathematical frameworks in order to improve the AF understanding.

In this work, a fractional Fourier transform (FrFT) based strategy is proposed to characterize EGM morphological irregularities using AF computational simulations. The FrFT is a time-frequency technique that extends the traditional Fourier transform (FT) to the entire time-frequency domain by using fractional powers of the FT operator $\mathcal{F}$. The temporal signal is decomposed using a linear frequency modulated function basis also known as *chirps* [2]. Therefore, this work presents a new time-frequency EGM analysis framework that uses the FrFT to measure the non-stationary characteristics embedded in the signal components associated with the irregular morphology.

2   Materials and Methods

2.1   Computer Modeling of Atrial Fibrillation

A realistic 3D model of human atria developed in a previous work [22] is used (Fig. 1(a)). The model includes fiber orientation, electrophysiological heterogeneity and anisotropy. The atrial surface is discretized into a hexahedral mesh with 52906 elements. To reproduce the electrical remodeling generated by AF, the maximum conductances of I_t, I_{K1}, I_{CaL} and I_{Na} ionic currents are modified in the cellular model developed by Nygren et al. [15]. Action potential propagation is modeled using the monodomain equation given by the following expression:

$$\nabla \cdot (D\nabla V_m) = S_m \left(C_m \frac{\partial V_m}{\partial t} + I_{ion} \right),\tag{1}$$

where V_m is the transmembrane potential, C_m is the membrane capacitance, S_v is the surface-to-volume ratio, D is the conductivity tensor, and I_{ion} is the total transmembrane ionic current. An AF episode of 10 s is generated by $S1$-$S2$ protocol. A train of stimuli is applied at the sinoatrial node area to simulate sinus rhythm ($S1$), at a basic cycle length of 1000 ms. After $S1$, a burst of six ectopic beats ($S2$) are applied near the right pulmonary veins at a cycle length of 130 ms. Through this protocol reentrant activity is generated, leading to fibrillatory conduction. During the simulated AF, plane waves, migratory rotors (Fig. 1(b)) of short duration (1 to 3 turns) and wave collisions (Fig. 1(c)) are observed.

A circular area of the posterior wall of the left atrium near to left pulmonary veins is selected (gray area in Fig. 1(a)), where different fibrillatory patterns

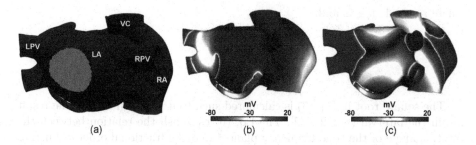

Fig. 1. AF simulated in a 3D model of human atria. (a) Circular gray area in the posterior wall of the left atrium (LA) where EGM are calculated. (b) Migratory rotor, and (c) wave collision in posterior wall of LA. RA: right atrium; VC: vena cava; LPV and RPV: left and right pulmonary veins.

can be observed. This region includes 933 elements. Pseudo-unipolar EGM at 0.2 mm from the atrial surface were recorded in this area each millisecond during the last 8 s of simulated AF. The extracellular potential (Φ_e), that corresponds to the input EGM for the analysis, is given by the following equation:

$$\Phi_e(\boldsymbol{r}) = -\frac{1}{4\pi}\frac{\sigma_i}{\sigma_e}\iiint \boldsymbol{\nabla}'V_m(\boldsymbol{r}')\cdot\boldsymbol{\nabla}'\left[\frac{1}{|\boldsymbol{r}'-\boldsymbol{r}|}\right]\mathrm{d}v, \qquad (2)$$

where $\boldsymbol{\nabla}'V_m$ is the spatial gradient of transmembrane potential V_m, σ_i is the intracellular conductivity, σ_e is the extracellular conductivity, $|\boldsymbol{r}'-\boldsymbol{r}|$ is the distance from the source point (x,y,z) to the measuring point (x',y',z') and $\mathrm{d}v$ is the differential volume.

2.2 Fractional Fourier Transform

In time-frequency analysis, a signal is represented in a plane where the time and frequency domains are orthogonal axes as depicted in Fig. 2(a). For a signal $x(t)$ along the time axis, its traditional FT $X(\omega)$ corresponds to the frequency axis, meaning a 90° rotation in the time-frequency plane. The FrFT of real order a, designated by the $\mathcal{F}^a$ operator, enables intermediate representations between time and frequency domains. The axis u is rotated within the time-frequency plane by an angle ϕ as illustrated in Fig. 2(b). Formally, the ath-order FrFT of a signal $x(t)$, is defined as follows [17]:

$$\mathcal{F}^a\{x(t)\} = x_a(u) = \int_{-\infty}^{\infty} K_a(t,u)x(t)\mathrm{d}t. \qquad (3)$$

The kernel $K_a(t,u)$ is given by the following expression:

$$K_a(t,u) = \begin{cases} A_\phi \exp\left[i\pi(u^2\cot\phi - 2ut\csc\phi + t^2\cot\phi)\right], \\ \delta(u-t) \quad \text{if } a \to 4n, \\ \delta(u+t) \quad \text{if } a \to 4n \pm 2, \end{cases} \qquad (4)$$

where $i^2 = -1$, $n \in \mathbb{Z}$ and:

$$A_\phi = \sqrt{1 - i \cot \phi},$$ (5)

$$\phi = \frac{a\pi}{2}.$$ (6)

The square root in Eq. (5) is calculated such that the argument of the result lies in the interval $(-\pi/2, \pi/2]$. The Eq. (6) establish the relation between the rotation angle of the time-frequency plane ϕ and the fractional order a. Further details about the FrFT can be found in [8, 26].

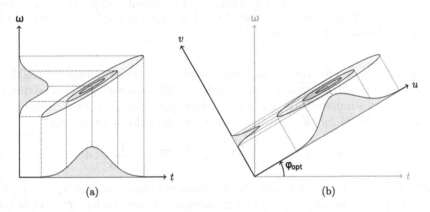

Fig. 2. Signal energy distributions: (a) time, frequency and time-frequency and (b) fractional domains. The ϕ_{opt} angle indicates the time-frequency plane rotation yielded by the FrFT that gives optimal alignment in the u domain and maximum compactness in the v domain.

The sampling-type DFrFT proposed by Ozaktas et al. [16] is used in this work for the analysis of the EGM signals. Under this scheme, the $x_a(u)$ samples are obtained from the $x(t)$ samples in a process whose computational complexity is $\mathcal{O}(N \log(N))$. This approach provides a better approximation to the continuous FrFT among the available formulations by generating a low deviation error. Since, it does not preserve the order additivity property, the inverse operation cannot be performed. Despite of this, the fast computation characteristic of this scheme is an attractive property for applications in which the inversion operation is not required.

2.3   Optimal FrFT Order Estimation

The irregular morphology of an EGM yields rapid changes in the signal. Such changes can be related with increasing or decreasing frequency variations as times evolves. Thus, the FrFT is used to detect non-stationarities within the signal. Figure 3 shows a diagram resuming the proposed EGM processing methodology based on the FrFT. Three main stages are established for studying the non-stationary behavior of fibrillatory EGM: preprocessing, moving windowing and FrFT optimal order search.

In order to extract the coarser time-varying waveform and enhance the activations characteristics of the EGM, the following preprocessing performed: Bandpass filtering at 40–250 Hz, rectification and Lowpass filtering 20 Hz [3]. This process extracts the relevant components of the local activations, producing a simplified waveform that describes the activations occurrence. When the absolute value is applied, the negative deflections of the EGM waveform become positive, generating high-frequency components in the signal that are smoothed with the low-pass filter. This type of pre-processing is commonly applied in electrophysiological procedures for DF analysis. After these steps, the signals are detrended and the Hilbert transform is obtained to generate a complex analytic signal. The Hilbert transform allows the computation of the single sided band fractional spectrum given by the FrFT.

The order of the FrFT is related to the linear frequency change of a signal. Given the chaotic characteristics of the electrical propagation during AF, the EGM have non-linear frequency modulated components. To effectively characterize the frequency modulations, a moving windowing strategy is proposed to obtain 16 signal intervals (segments) of 500 samples length (500 ms) where the frequency modulations of the EGM activations are assumed to be quasi-linear or less complex. The 500 ms segment is established as an analysis window since for smaller segments it is not possible to contain sufficient information on the periodicity of the signal, while for longer segments, the stationary components take on a greater representation.

The order of the FrFT, as an additional degree of freedom, provides flexibility for addressing the analysis of frequency-varying signals. Thus, proper order estimation is essential to accurately characterize the non-stationary EGM components that exhibit high energy concentration in optimal fractional domains [25]. The proposed method considers optimal fractional domains where high compactness of the signal energy is achieved, i.e. most of the spectrum energy concentrates in few coefficients. To illustrate this idea, Fig. 2(b) depicts the energy distribution of a linear frequency modulated signal in two fractional domains depicted by the u and v axes. The signal energy is represented in compact form over the v domain, requiring fewer coefficients than the other domains (t, ω and u) to represent the signal energy spread.

Providing the relation established in Eq. (6), the optimal order a_{opt} that corresponds to the maximum compactness for a linear frequency modulated signal is given by the following equation:

$$a_{opt} = 1 + \frac{2}{\pi}\phi_{opt}. \tag{7}$$

A criterion for measuring the compactness and a searching strategy are required. For this purpose, the maximum amplitude spectrum criterion and a coarse-to-fine searching algorithm are used as proposed in [27]. The energy spectrum is maximal when the signal is compactly represented in a fractional domain. Therefore, the amplitude spectrum $|x_a(k)|$ is also maximum. The cost function is defined by the following expression:

$$J(a) = \max\{|x_a(u)|\}, \tag{8}$$

where the estimation of the optimal transform order is given by $\hat{a}_{opt} = \underset{a}{\operatorname{argmax}}\{J(a)\}$.

The estimation of $J(a)$ requires the computation of the DFrFT for every order a. This could be computationally expensive for a large number of discrete values within the interval $[0,2)$. To reduce the number of DFrFT calculations the coarse-to-fine algorithm is applied. This algorithm computes an initial grid for $J(a)$ at values of a sparsely distributed to end with a finer grid around a_{opt} according to a desired accuracy [27]. The total number of required DFrFTs computations can be estimated using the following equation:

$$N_{FrFT} = \left(\frac{a_1 - a_0}{\Delta a_0} + 1\right) + \left(\frac{1}{\lambda} + 1\right)\left\lceil\frac{\log(\Delta a_0/\epsilon)}{\log(1/\lambda)}\right\rceil, \tag{9}$$

where a_0 and a_1 are the lower and upper bounds of the initial searching interval respectively, Δa_0 is the resolution of the initial grid, λ is a refinement factor, ϵ the desired accuracy and $\lceil\cdot\rceil$ is the ceiling function. The coarse-to-fine algorithm was configured with $a_0 = 0.5$, $a_1 = 1.5$, $\Delta a_0 = 0.01$ $\lambda = 0.1$ and $\epsilon = 0.001$ for this study.

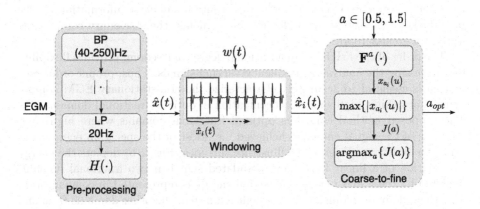

Fig. 3. Block diagram of the proposed EGM analysis method based on the FrFT.

2.4 Electrograms Irregularities Assessment and Electroanatomical Maps

The FrFT based processing procedure is applied to the set of 933 EGM obtained from the AF simulation. As the proposed method considers signals of 500 ms, the 8-s EGM are segmented in 16 intervals. Thus, for each EGM signal, 16 values of the FrFT order a_{opt} are obtained. In this manner, a dynamic assessment of the EGM morphology is achieved. Additionally, electroanatomical maps are built using the spatial information of the EGM recording sites within the selected atrial region. The a_{opt} values obtained for a given 500 ms interval are mapped to a false color scale. Accordingly, an FrFT electroanatomic map is obtained. In order to assess the obtained results, the approximate entropy (ApEn) is also calculated for each EGM and the corresponding maps are generated. The ApEn quantifies the degree of irregularity of a signal [18] and it has been reported to be useful in analyzing EGM irregularities during AF [23,24]. The ApEn is implemented following the configuration of a previous work [23].

3   Results

Figure 4 presents 12 EGM segments at different time intervals with their associated optimum order obtained from the proposed methodology. The Fig. 4(a) shows a segment with $\hat{a}_{opt} = 1$. The associated order indicates a quasi-periodic behavior with regular activations. The Fig. 4(b) depicts an interval where the activations maintain a regular morphology. However, the separations between successive activations decreases as time evolves. This behavior is interpreted as an increment in the frequency corresponding to a non-stationary behavior similar to the illustration in Fig. 2(b). This interval has a frequency varying feature that is characterized by the associated order of $\hat{a}_{opt} = 1.011$. The Fig. 4(c) shows a segment where the period between successive activations increase with the time. The electrical activity in this segment is characterized by $\hat{a}_{opt} = 0.990$, which indicates a decreasing trend in the activations frequency. The Figs. 4(d)–(f) show EGM segments with irregular morphology associated to $\hat{a}_{opt}$ values above 1. These intervals exhibit low amplitude activations, fragmentation of EGM, double activations and modulated frequency. The Figs. 4(g)–(i) show segments with a smaller degree of irregular morphology in comparison with the EGM segments presented in Figs. 4(d)–(f).

The distribution plot in Fig. 5 summarizes the results obtained by the proposed strategy. This visualization represents an estimation the density distribution of the obtained optimum order for each of the 16 time intervals over the 933 EGM [10]. For the intervals 5 and 9, the order of all the 933 EGM concentrates at $\hat{a}_{opt} = 1$, indicating regular activations. This suggests that the propagation wave in the registered area behaves uniformly between 2 to 2.5 s and 4 to 4.5 s. In the intervals 4 and 10 the orders are distributed normally within a small range around $\hat{a}_{opt} = 1$. This indicates the predominance of regular activations with few segments with irregular behavior. The segments of the interval 13 present a distribution concentrated at $\hat{a}_{opt} = 1$ and a heavy tail towars $\hat{a}_{opt} > 1$, which suggests few components with irregular behavior. A more complex behavior is evidenced in the intervals 3 and 11, in which $\hat{a}_{opt}$ value are mainly distributed above 1, indicating the presence of irregular EGM components. Intervals 2, 7, 8 and 15 show orders distributed normally within a wide range. This indicates irregular activations in the EGM and highlight the predominance of non-stationary signal components. Intervals 1, 6, 12, 14 and 16 show distributions with isolated lobes interpreted as areas with a non-uniform propagation.

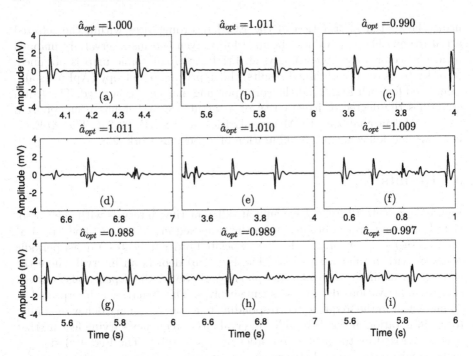

Fig. 4. Representative EGM segments with distinct morphological characteristics from the AF simulated episode. The corresponding FrFT optimal order is shown.

Representative electroanatomical maps are shown in Figs. 6. The maps correspond to consecutive 500 ms intervals. From left to right, the first two maps show two consecutive frames of the simulated electrical propagation within the specified interval The third and fourth maps correspond to the FrFT order and ApEn maps, respectively. A planar wave propagation is depicted in Fig. 6(c) corresponding to the interval 9. The optimum order map concentrates at $\hat{a}_{opt} = 1$ indicating regular activation (green color). Similarly, the ApEn map demonstrates low and uniform values. The Figs. 6(a), (b) and (d) describe non-uniform propagation patterns where the wave front bends, change the direction or collides within the interval. In these cases, the ApEn maps show low values, giving few information about the behavior of the propagation. However, the $\hat{a}_{opt}$ maps indicates non-stationary activity associated with the irregular morphology in the EGM, produced by the non-uniform propagation. Figure 6(e) describes a rotor whose tip travel over the registered area. In this case the $\hat{a}_{opt}$ and ApEn maps present values associated with the non-uniform propagation.

4   Discussion

This study proposes a new time-frequency EGM analysis that exploits the capabilities of the FrFT as indicator of morphological irregularities in the signals

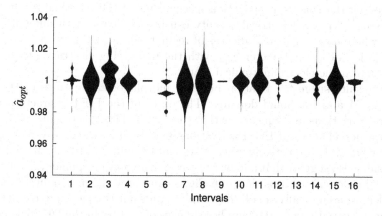

Fig. 5. Distribution plot of $\hat{a}_{opt}$ for each the calculated 500 ms interval of the 933 EGM

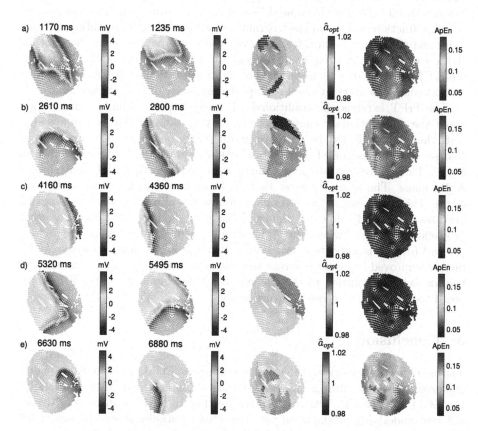

Fig. 6. Representative electroanatomical maps (columns 1 and 2) with their respective $\hat{a}_{opt}$ and ApEn maps. (Color figure online)

produced by the chaotic propagation mechanisms of the AF. The results show that distinct types of electrical activity can be associated with different FrFT orders, where $\hat{a}_{opt} = 1$ is an indicator of regular activation. There is also a possible relation of the parameter $\hat{a}_{opt}$ with the underlying electrical propagation as depicted in the electroanatomical maps.

The results suggest a relation between morphological features of the simulated EGM and fractional domains. The order of the FrFT characterizes the temporal variations of frequency within the signal. Thus, increasing or decreasing frequency changes of EGM activations may be associated to values of $\hat{a}_{opt}$ above or below 1, respectively. Such cases can be evinced in Figs. 4(b) and (c). The results also suggest that a higher degree of irregular morphology is related to fractional orders above 1 as shown in Fig. 5. Although the maximum changes in the order are numerically small, they imply significant changes in frequency variation, e.g. a variation of ±0.02 implies changes of $\pm31\,\mathrm{Hz}$ in the DF. This behavior can be associated to the rapid changes of the EGM signal. Other techniques that relies on the DF analysis, entropy measures and recurrence quantification analysis [1,5,14,23] have been used to address arrhythmogenic features such as complex fractionated atrial electrograms, single and double potentials, irregularity and atrial activation rates. However, these approaches do not account for of the frequency variations resulted from the fibrillatory episodes. Given that the FrFT can provide a quantification of such non-stationary behavior, it can be used as complementary analysis to improve the study of the AF mechanics.

The FrFT extends the traditional DF analysis [14], including information about the non-stationary components underlying the AF. The $\hat{a}_{opt}$ maps suggests that the FrFT may be sensitive to different propagation patterns, such as changes in the direction of propagation, colliding waves and rotors as shown in Fig. 6. This study also provides a comparison between the FrFT analysis and ApEn maps. The results suggest that both methods can highlight areas with rotors. The ApEn evinces a better characterization of rotors, which agrees with previous reports [24]. However, the FrFT-based methodology can highlight other propagation patterns where the ApEn exhibits a uniform behavior (Figs. 6(a), (b) and (d)). It is important to mention that the FrFT-based strategy can be further improved by using different window sizes with overlapping segments to provide better resolution to the analysis. Such developments in the FrFT proposed tool must be assessed in future studies.

5   Conclusion

The use of FrFT strategies for the analysis of cardiac EGM signals remains poorly explored, this work findings suggests that the FrFT can be used to characterize the EGM morphology. The results indicate that the FrFT can be sensitive to different underlying propagation patterns. Further studies should be conducted to assess the potential relation of the FrFT order and fibrillatory mechanisms.

References

1. Acharya, U.R., et al.: Application of nonlinear methods to discriminate fractionated electrograms in paroxysmal versus persistent atrial fibrillation. Comput. Meth. Prog. Bio. **175**, 163–178 (2019)
2. Almeida, L.B.: The fractional Fourier transform and time-frequency representations. IEEE Trans. Signal Process. **42**(11), 3084–3091 (1994)
3. Botteron, G., Smith, J.: A technique for measurement of the extent of spatial organization of atrial activation during atrial fibrillation in the intact human heart. IEEE Trans. Biomed. Eng. **42**(6), 579–586 (1995)
4. Chen, L.Y., Benditt, D.G., Alonso, A.: Atrial fibrillation and its association with sudden cardiac death. Circ. J. Official J. Japanese Circ. Soc. **78**(11), 2588–2593 (2014)
5. Cirugeda-Roldán, E.M., Molina Picó, A., Novák, D., Cuesta-Frau, D., Kremen, V.: Sample entropy analysis of noisy atrial electrograms during atrial fibrillation. Comput. Math. Methods Med. **2018** (2018)
6. Clayton, R.H., Nash, M.P.: Analysis of cardiac fibrillation using phase mapping. Card. Electrophysiol. Clin. **7**(1), 49–58 (2015)
7. Everett IV, T.H., Wilson, E.E., Verheule, S., Guerra, J.M., Foreman, S., Olgin, J.E.: Structural atrial remodeling alters the substrate and spatiotemporal organization of atrial fibrillation: a comparison in canine models of structural and electrical atrial remodeling. Am. J. Physiol. Heart Circ. Physiol. **291**(6) (2006)
8. Gomez, A., Ugarte, J.P., Tobón, C.: The fractional Fourier transform as a biomedical signal and image processing tool: a review. Biocybern. Biomed. Eng. (2020)
9. Jacquemet, V., et al.: Study of unipolar electrogram morphology in a computer model of atrial fibrillation. J. Cardiovasc. Electrophysiol. **14**(10 suppl.), 172–179 (2003)
10. Kampstra, P.: Beanplot: a boxplot alternative for visual comparison of distributions. J. Stat. Softw. Code Snippets **28**(1), 1–9 (2008)
11. Lin, Y.J., Tai, C.T., Chen, S.A.: Can mapping and ablation of atrial fibrillation be guided by frequency analysis of fibrillatory waves? J. Cardiovasc. Electrophysiol. **17**(SUPPL. 3), 44–49 (2006)
12. Mansour, M., Mandapati, R., Berenfeld, O., Chen, J., Samie, F.H., Jalife, J.: Left-to-right gradient of atrial frequencies during acute atrial fibrillation in the isolated sheep heart. Circulation **103**(21), 2631–2636 (2001)
13. Miyasaka, Y., et al.: Mortality trends in patients diagnosed with first atrial fibrillation. A 21-year community-based study. J. Am. College Cardiol. **49**(9), 986–992 (2007)
14. Ng, J., Kadish, A.H., Goldberger, J.J.: Effect of electrogram characteristics on the relationship of dominant frequency to atrial activation rate in atrial fibrillation. Heart Rhythm **3**(11), 1295–1305 (2006)
15. Nygren, A., et al.: Mathematical model of an adult human atrial cell: the role of K+ currents in repolarization. Circ. Res. **82**(1), 63–81 (1998)
16. Ozaktas, H.M., Ankan, O., Kutay, M.A., Bozdagt, G.: Digital computation of the fractional Fourier transform. IEEE Trans. Signal Process. **44**(9), 2141–2150 (1996)
17. Ozaktas, H.M., Kutay, M.A., Mendlovic, D.: Introduction to the fractional Fourier transform and its applications. Adv. Imag. Electron Phys. **106**, 239–291 (1999)
18. Pincus, S.M.: Approximate entropy (ApEn) as a regularity measure. In: Applications of Nonlinear Dynamics to Developmental Process Modeling, pp. 243–268 (1998)

19. Sanders, P., et al.: Frequency mapping of the pulmonary veins in paroxysmal versus permanent atrial fibrillation. J. Cardiovasc. Electrophysiol. **17**(9), 965–972 (2006)

20. Skanes, A.C., Mandapati, R., Berenfeld, O., Davidenko, J.M., Jalife, J.: Spatiotemporal periodicity during atrial fibrillation in the isolated sheep heart. Circulation **98**(12), 1236–1248 (1998)

21. Tan, A.Y., Li, H., Wachsmann-Hogiu, S., Chen, L.S., Chen, P.S., Fishbein, M.C.: Autonomic innervation and segmental muscular disconnections at the human pulmonary vein-atrial junction. Implications for catheter ablation of atrial-pulmonary vein junction. J. Am. College Cardiol. **48**(1), 132–143 (2006)

22. Tobón, C., Ruiz-Villa, C.A., Heidenreich, E., Romero, L., Hornero, F., Saiz, J.: A three-dimensional human atrial model with fiber orientation. Electrograms and arrhythmic activation patterns relationship. PLoS ONE **8**(2) (2013)

23. Ugarte, J.P., et al.: Dynamic approximate entropy electroanatomic maps detect rotors in a simulated atrial fibrillation model. PLoS ONE **9**(12), 1–19 (2014)

24. Ugarte, J.P., Tobón, C., Orozco-Duque, A.: Entropy mapping approach for functional reentry detection in atrial fibrillation: an in-silico study Juan. Entropy **21**(2), 1–17 (2019). https://doi.org/10.3390/e21020194

25. Zhang, Y., Zhang, Q., Wu, S.: Biomedical signal detection based on fractional fourier transform. In: 5th International Conference on Information Technology and Applications in Biomedicine, ITAB 2008 in conjunction with 2nd International Symposium and Summer School on Biomedical and Health Engineering, IS3BHE 2008, Shenzhen, China, pp. 349–352 (2008)

26. Zhang, Y.D., et al.: A comprehensive survey on fractional Fourier transform. Fundamenta Informaticae **151**(1–4), 1–48 (2017)

27. Zheng, L., Shi, D.: Maximum amplitude method for estimating compact fractional Fourier domain. IEEE Signal Process. Lett. **17**(3), 293–296 (2010)

28. Zlochiver, S., Yamazaki, M., Kalifa, J., Berenfeld, O.: Rotor meandering contributes to irregularity in electrograms during atrial fibrillation. Heart Rhythm **5**(6), 846–854 (2008)

Towards a Conceptual Framework for the Development of Artificial Muscles Using SMA

Paola Andrea Castiblanco(✉) ⓘ, Delio Alexander Balcázar-Camachoⓘ, José Luis Ramirezⓘ, and Astrid Rubianoⓘ

Universidad Militar Nueva Granada, Km 2 vía Cajica-Zipaquira, Bogotá, Colombia
u3900255@unimilitar.edu.co

Abstract. This work presents a conceptual framework for the design, development, and construction of artificial muscles as an actuator mechanism in bio-inspired systems. This framework is supported by current theories of soft robotics and the analysis of smart materials performance. Specifically, shape memory alloy materials (SMA) mathematical behavior is reviewed. Current Literature about these topics points to the experimentation as the main source for collecting the data and information of materials, that is required for the design of artificial muscles. The behavior of the materials can vary drastically when modifying simple variables in the workspace and the way of varying levels of temperature also influences its handling.

Keywords: Shape memory alloy materials · Biomechanics · Artificial muscle · Constitutive model

1 Introduction

The use of smart materials in the development of new devices applied to soft robotics has become the best option when looking for devices to build that have specific and bio-inspired skills [1]. This is because the field of soft robotics seeks the application of flexible and intelligent actuator systems, which adapt to new forms of manipulation, taking inspiration from living organisms [2]. In this case, there is the purpose of emulating the natural behavior of a muscle.

The importance of the research on artificial muscles is linked to new technologies in the health sector that seek to improve the quality of life of people who have suffered an event that makes them consider the use of a prosthesis that supplements the functions of a lost member of their body. The implementation of an artificial muscle could allow patients to a greater range of functions than those obtained from a common prosthesis after an amputation, to achieve the best possible operability concerning the lost limb.

To achieve that a device can naturally replace human muscles with an artificial mechanism, it can not only be applied in an actuator system of a possible upper or lower limb prosthesis. This requires complete analysis and study of human anatomy, in order to understand its operation and possible applications.

J. C. Figueroa-García et al. (Eds.): WEA 2020, CCIS 1274, pp. 257–267, 2020.
https://doi.org/10.1007/978-3-030-61834-6_22

This document compiles and analyzes various sources of information necessary to structure the frame of reference that is required for the development of artificial muscles using SMA. The study is divided into a review of the literature or state of the art, a conceptual framework to expose necessary concepts and the analysis of relevant factors for the construction and the operation of an artificial muscle. Finally, a discussion related to the information collected is presented.

2 Literature Review

Searching for information about SMA with the different types of scientific documents found (articles, theses, proceedings, books, among others), it is possible to identify some topics presented in Fig. 1. In this graph, it seems that the main pillars of the research are smart materials and SMA, and from these two keywords are derived for our research, such as a constitutive model, soft robotics, biomechanics, control, and muscle.

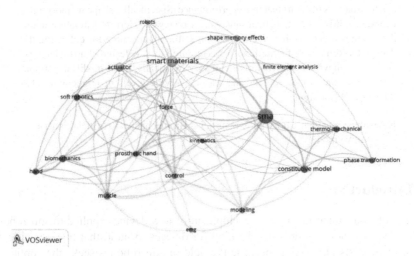

Fig. 1. Network analysis of state of art main topics

The information search method starts with identifying the thematic area of smart materials, then searching the specialized magazines for keywords in the area, such as "Smart Materials" and "Shape Memory Alloy", among others. A first filter was made of those documents that contain these keywords, after reading and analysis of their relevance the network map seen in Fig. 1 was built. 135 documents were considered to address topics related to smart materials, artificial muscles, and some of their implementations.

The documents were found in the most popular science databases such as ScienceDirect, Springer, and IEEE, among others. These main topics of the conducted review are developed in the next sections of this chapter.

2.1 Soft Robotics

Recent studies deal with changing the materials with which robots are made to achieve characteristics that are not possible with the use of rigid materials and that perform more specific tasks achieving a higher level of interaction with the environment [1]. Soft robots use different mechanisms with more skill than conventional robots [2]; as can be seen in Fig. 2, to explain their behavior, we must focus on several physical phenomena at the same time. Furthermore, these devices are based on structures found in nature, muscle models of different mammals, fish, plants, among others. So to carry out the application of a soft robotics system, we must understand the morphology and functionality of the different systems in nature.

In Nurzaman et al. [3] it is presented a summary of the fields of action in which soft robotics works: "scientific problems related to soft bodies, soft materials for robots, soft sensors and actuators, modeling and simulation of soft body techniques, manufacturing, and soft body control, interdisciplinary interaction between biology, medicine, materials, chemistry, and other disciplines, and soft robotics applications."

2.2 Smart Materials

"A smart material is a man-made engineering system that mimics nature's ability to react to external stimuli" [4]. These materials are classified as polymers or alloys.

Electroactive Polymers

EAP (Electroactive polymers), a type of polymer that reacts mechanically to electrical stimulation, among its main applications is its use as sensors and actuators, in addition to being the basis of some models of artificial muscles [5]. These can withstand great deformation when subjected to enormous forces, high resistance to fracture, and dampen vibrations. They divide into two groups: Electric and Ionic [6].

Electric Electroactive Polymers These are materials in which the action is caused by electrostatic forces between two electrodes that act on the polymer, resist high voltages, and function as a capacitor that causes the polymer to compress in thickness and expand in the area [6, 7].

Ionic These materials work due to the action caused by the displacement of ions within the polymer, low voltage values are needed for their operation, but they require more electrical power to be actuated and energy to keep the actuator in position. For example, of this type of polymers, we have IPMC. This material consists of a membrane of ionic polymer structured between two metal electrodes on each face; these are capable of translating the effort into electrical energy and vice versa, showing a low impedance. They work through electrostatic attraction, can be a useful application in the biological field, since collagen fibers are composed of ionic polymers with a neutral charge and can be adapted [8].

Shape Memory Alloy SMA

SMA are an alloy between metals that represents a special class of materials with very particular characteristics, among which is the effect of remembering or having "memory" of their shape, in addition to their Super-elasticity properties associated with their ability cushioning and outstanding fatigue resistance [9].

2.3 SMA Behavior and Modeling

SMA is formed by alloying various metals, and they can memorize or retain certain previously acquired information when it is under specific thermomechanical or magnetic conditions [10].

The shape memory effect is due to the transformation of one crystalline structure into another (austenite and martensite) the reorientation of these. When the material is heated, generally using an electric current in the wire, the martensite is transformed into austenite and the fiber contracts.

Subsequent cooling converts austenite back to martensite, and internal stresses return the material to the original shape. There are five significant phenomena in which the behavior of the SMA is explained [11], which evidence in with the stress-strain graphs of each effect: Super elasticity by transformation, Reorientation superelasticity, Shape memory effect by transformation, Shape memory effect by reorientation, and Bidirectional memory effect.

Some authors have focused on achieving a better understanding of why this material acts in this way, performing micro and macroscopic studies of the material, through the formulation of mathematical models using the creation of constitutive models, where the different observed phenomena of the material use to generate a response to its behavior.

The most complete study compiling the first developed mathematical models is shown in [12], where a database provides to make a first approximation to the SMA mathematical model.

At the microscopic level, the material volume fractions (austenite and martensite) are not considered in this formulation, and they are classified better for significant development than for quantitative description, making their experimental validation a complicated process to perform. One example of model is the proposed by Müller et al. [13].

The authors took advantage of some properties studied at the micro-level in combination with material characteristics that observe with the naked eye. These models implement laws of thermodynamics to describe transformation between phases. At the micro-level, they observe the response of the material in the behavior of subunits in the transformation, how the transformation from single crystal to polycrystalline is carried out. One example of model is the proposed by Müller et al. [14].

To carry out the construction of a mathematical model, it is necessary to take into account specific parameters so that a correct solution is reached, among which is, the values that are dependent on initial conditions with tension and temperature, the modification of the variables under initial conditions in each transformation to observe the hysteresis variation and the possibility of reversible transformation effects [12]. Some models were left out of the previous table and are shown in the following table because they were the most widely accepted models in the scientific community. These are one-dimensional, each obtained from different parameters, they do not depend on speed the deformation is evident, it works on a small scale, at each instant the thermodynamic state characterized by a set of internal and external variables, they only depend on the stress or deformation and its temporal change e.g.. Martensite transformation by stress, set of state variables, energy conservation, and Clausius-Duhem inequality proposed by Tanaka [15]. Based on some of the models previously proposed, some authors have focused on showing the experimental performance of the material and corroborating that the models are consistent [16, 17], where the objective of most is to formulate the stress-strain curves. Because the material varies over time, to develop each application, it is necessary to define an experimental protocol starting with the characterization of the material.

In Vantadori et al. [18], fatigue analysis of a special NiTi alloy is shown, where, using geometry analysis with a microscopic electron scanner, it shows the chemical composition. With an X-ray diffraction test, deformation data take during a certain number of times or cycles.

2.4 Human Muscle and Equivalent Models

In the human being, the muscle is a contractile organ that determines the shape and contour of the body, constitutes 40% of the body weight, and whose primary function is to be responsible for the movement of the body. Muscle has high blood and nerve irrigation that allows it to carry out the contraction process [19]. Each muscle makes up a large number of fibers that are located in an aligned manner, as shown in Fig. 5, where it is observed that the element. The most basic that makes it up is the sarcomere, up to the complete structure of the muscle.

There are three types of muscles (skeletal, smooth, and cardiac), and to establish the biomechanical requirements, the focus will be on the skeletal muscles, which are those that perform the movement using the bone system as support.

Two methods are discussed to develop a mathematical model that emulates the human muscle, the Hill equivalent model, and the finite element analysis. The latter model shows to be an excellent tool for measuring the behavior of muscles in action; however, the Hill model is more suitable for quantifying muscle behavior by making a comparison with mechanical elements [20].

Hill's model consists of an arrangement of elements that use descriptions of the elastic behavior of the muscle. It is composed of the representation of muscles in series with the tendon; the muscle is represented as a contractile element in parallel with the elastic element. The tendon is considered as the viscoelastic element; as a result, the tendon is modeled as a shock absorber in parallel with a spring [21].

The model chosen in [20] is the one proposed by Zajac [22], who considers that the angle generated in the model influences the kinematics of the mechanism and the force during movement. However, instead of using an elastic element to describe to the tendon, a shock absorber is used in parallel, in Fig. 2, the representation is shown, where: $CE =$ Contractile element, $Kpee =$ Parallel elastic element of the muscle, $Ksee =$ Elastic element in muscle series, $Ktee =$ Elastic Tendon Element, $b_{Tde} =$ Tendon damping element, and $\alpha_m =$ Penation angle.

3 Guidelines for the Development of Artificial Muscles Using SMA

Among the intelligent materials, the most commonly used in the biomechanical field are IPMC (Ionic Polymer.Metal Composite) and SMA (Shape Memory Alloy), this due to their mechanical properties, specifically in the stress levels and maximum force that

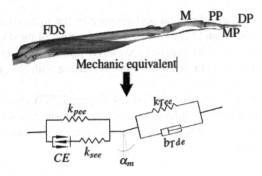

Fig. 2. Hill model to work [20]

these materials can be exposed to [10], since these are the only materials that reach the required force levels (up to 32N), compared to a bio-inspired system [20].

In the SMA literature, it is evident that most of the publications carried out seek to formulate or adapt different mathematical models from other authors that manage to explain the behavior of these materials, which presents dynamic, non-linear behavior which also varies depending on temperature levels. Other important studies are those where the material is formulated as an actuator system and more specifically its use in medical or biomechanical applications.

The first studies of this type of materials dating back to the '90 s where materials were analyzed and an attempt were made to determine a mathematical behavior, through the generation of constitutive models, which seek to group different physical phenomena in a single demonstration (Electrical, thermal, mechanical, etc.). These studies assume that the material to be modeled comes in a filament presentation, so its behavior can be observed in a single dimension, in order to simplify its analysis [23–25].

The works that relate the actuator systems mostly show that material characterization processes are carried out first and then design [26], also that each related document shows the development of a specific application [27–29].

Regarding control systems, they are made based on actuator systems, implementing different control techniques [28, 30], sometimes combinations of two or more techniques are presented, to overcome the particular difficulty of controlling this material [31]. Particularly when studying the system as an artificial muscle, topics related to the aforementioned are found, adding control methods based on biomechanical muscle models [16, 32, 33].

Below are some applications found in the literature concerning the SMA as an actuator system [10], which is easily integrated into any type of application and can replace conventional actuators if they know how to take advantage of its mechanical properties.

Li and Tian [34] shows the inverse model of an SMA actuator and its position control system with compensation the radial base function (RBF) that is used in nonlinear control models, seeking to verify the effectiveness of the control of the SMA with the RBF system through an experimental process, and its results are compared with a classic PID control.

3.1 SMA Control Methods

Doroudchi and Zakerzadeh [28] perform the rapid response control of a rotary actuator made with SMA, seeking to control the speed of the actuator, when current is applied to the material's wires, it undergoes a variation in its temperature which makes the pulley rotate, thanks Because in its configuration there are two cables when one cable is activated the other remains at rest and vice versa, which makes the actuator move in both directions.

Another case where control strategies for SMA-based actuator systems are addressed is shown in Khodayari et al. [31], where the control system of an SMA actuator for a gripper is performed, by using fuzzy logic and the implementation of a PID controller. Fuzzy logic is used to aid in material offset tasks to be sent to the controller. For the fuzzy controller, the gripper location values were entered and the necessary constants for the control were obtained as output. Using this combination to perform the control, it was observed that it has a very good performance, reducing the maximum over the peak and the stabilization time in the input signal of the actuator with SMA, besides, relatively smaller errors occur than those obtained with other different control.

3.2 SMA Applications in Biomechanics and Medicine

In the field of bioengineering, there are so many applications that a subdivision of the fields of action can be carried out, having, among the most important ones, support in prosthesis and orthosis systems, the elaboration of implements that help in medical emergencies, the elaboration of new tissues or parts that can be replaced in the human body, creation of tools for physical rehabilitation, dental, ocular or vascular supports, among many other options, all thanks to the biocompatibility properties of the human body that these intelligent materials have. [35–38].

When an intelligent material is implemented to a device that helps to supply motor functions of the human body, it is sought that the material works as an actuator and manages to make the operation of the device natural, thanks to its mechanical properties, analogously to the human body, this it behaves like the muscle, which is the one that gives support and that thanks to its contractions and retractions generate movement. This is why research is being done to try to emulate it and are called artificial muscles.

Peng et al. [39] work on the design methodology of a sensor-actuator structure implemented in artificial muscles with SMA, which seeks the reproduction and adoption of the operating mechanism of the musculoskeletal system.

Table 1 shows the comparison of mechanical properties of some candidate materials and the original human muscle, showing that the use of SMA provides quite profitable characteristics and design of a muscle fiber emulating the real one is carried out, verifying their behavior in working ranges.

Due to the mathematical complexity of the different existing models of intelligent muscles based on SMA, these systems comply with a non-linear behavior that poses a challenge when proposing to control any of its variables. So some authors have decided to combine or integrate different types of controllers for dynamic systems that suffer variations over time, as is the case of Zhang, Yin, and Zhu, [40] who propose a high-speed monitoring control for muscles made using SMA using the model of hysteresis of matter

Table 1. Comparison of the most used material mechanical properties [39]

Actuator type	Deformation (%)	Stress (MPa)	Energy density (KJ-m3)	Power density (W/Kg)	Reaction speed
Muscle	20(40)2	0.1(0.35)	8(40)	40(80)	Medium
EAP*	0.5(3.3)	3(15)	(5.5)	(2.56)	Medium
Engine	50	0.1	25	3	Fast
PZT*	(0.2)	(110)	(100)	(13)	Fast
SMA	5(10)	190(600)	10^3(10^4)	10^3(10^5)	Slow
SMA-AM	(20)	(12)	(1656)	(518)	Medium

*Electroactive Polymers (EAP), Piezoelectric Ceramic (PZT)

based on the sigmoid function.. This model performs self-measurement and operates silently, with potential for orthotic work especially on the ankle and foot in processes For physical rehabilitation, the model is limited by the slow response speed of the material, so a control strategy that helps should be sought. A forced cooling system is implemented to help accelerate speed without compromising its effectiveness and through experimental validation, an inverse model is obtained that indicates a mathematical model with which the control can be implemented.

The experimental results have shown that the responses of the artificial muscle in speed and accuracy improve with frequency tracking increased from 0.8 to 1 Hz, additionally, the tracking error was reduced by 82% when the initial angle of the ankle-foot configuration is satisfied.

4   Discussion

This work has reviewed different applications and models that allow the use of SMA in the elaboration of artificial muscles, by identifying the contributions of key authors of the topics involved in this process.

According to the research carried out, when working with SMA it is essential that an experimental characterization process to be carried out, and that the validity of these data must be confirmed by applying a constitutive model, this may be based on previous modeling studies It is also important to clarify that whenever performance tests are carried out, it would be pertinent to keep the test spaces fixed; changing them could generate changes in the environmental conditions that modify the experimental data collected.

In the process of designing an artificial muscle, much of the success of the process is the creation of a mechanism that manages to carry out the phase changes in a controlled manner and preferably in a short space of time, besides, a correct geometric arrangement of the filament will lead to optimizations in the travel capacity that the actuator can achieve.

Considering that the material can exceed temperatures of 90 °C, the selection of the material or mechanism that will support and grip the filament must withstand high temperatures, which represents a challenge in its manufacture.

Following the muscle model proposed by Hill [21], it is necessary to provide the mechanism with the elastic element such as the SMA filaments and additionally a contractile element that can be provided by a spring or an analogous mechanism that fulfills the function of helping the muscle to return to an original form.

The potential benefits of using the SMA in a specific application as an artificial muscle is evident in the values of force and effort that can be obtained in its transformation process, at this point the challenge is presented when achieving changes in the phase of the material because a special assembly is required to effectively regulate the temperature of the filament.

Further studies are required to verify the effects of different alloys in different modeling systems, considering various operating conditions that emulate the characteristics of biological systems. In this way, it will be possible to obtain approximations to the mathematical representations of these elements to be considered in bioinspired systems.

Regarding the possible implementation of SMA for the construction of artificial muscles, it is necessary to carry out a whole design and construction process under preset parameters that allow elaborating the muscle according to the expectations of operation that are presented in real life. Therefore it is necessary to start the process with the characterization of the material and the muscle that is required to build, in addition to performing the adaptation of the components of the whole prosthesis so that a synergy between all parties is achieved.

References

1. Laschi, C., Cianchetti, M.: Soft robotics: new perspectives for robot bodyware and control. Front. Bioeng. Biotechnol. (2014). 10.3389/fbioe.2014.00003
2. Trivedi, D., Rahn, C., Kier, W., Walker, I.: Soft robotics: biological inspiration, state of the art, and future research. Appl. Bionics Biomech. 5, 99–117 (2008). https://doi.org/10.1080/11762320802557865
3. Nurzaman, S., Iida, F., Laschi, C., Ishiguro, A., Wood, R.: Soft Robotics [TC Spotlight], vol. 20 (2013)
4. Lopez-Garcia, O., Carnicero, A., Ruiz Pablos, R.: Materiales inteligentes I/II: introducción a los materiales del siglo XXI, vol. 80 (2003)
5. Diab, M.O., et al.: Electromechanical model of IPMC artificial muscle. In: 2014 World Symposium on Computer Applications & Research (WSCAR), pp. 1–5 (2014). https://doi.org/10.1109/WSCAR.2014.6916820
6. Bar Cohen, Y.: Electroactive Polymer (EAP) Actuators as Artificial Muscles, 2°. The International Society for Optical Engineering, Bellingham (2004)
7. Polímeros Electroactivos (2018). https://www.hisour.com/es/electroactive-polymers-42852/
8. Akhtar, S.N., Cherusseri, J., Ramkumar, J., Kar, K.K.: Ionic polymer metal composites. In: Kar, K.K. (ed.) Composite Materials, pp. 223–249. Springer, Heidelberg (2017). https://doi.org/10.1007/978-3-662-49514-8_7
9. Cismasiu, C.: Shape Memory Alloys (2010)
10. Mohd Jani, J., Leary, M., Subic, A., Gibson, M.: A review of shape memory alloy research, applications and opportunities, vol. 56 (2014)

11. Moreno, L., Muñoz, M., Garrido, S., Blanco, D.: Materiales inteligentes: aleaciones con memoria de forma (SMA) (2009)
12. de la Flor López, S.: Simulación numérica y correlación experimental de las propiedades mecánicas en las aleaciones con memoria de forma. TDX (Tesis Dr. en Xarxa), June 2005
13. Müller, I., Xu, H.: On the pseudo-elastic hysteresis. Acta Metall. Mater. **39**(3), 263–271 (1991). https://doi.org/10.1016/0956-7151(91)90305-K
14. Patoor, E., Berveiller, M.: Micromechanical modelling of the thermomechanical behavior of shape memory alloys. In: Berveiller, M., Fischer, F.D. (eds.) Mechanics of Solids with Phase Changes. ICMS, vol. 368, pp. 121–188. Springer, Vienna (1997). https://doi.org/10.1007/978-3-7091-2660-8_5
15. Tanaka, K., Nishimura, F., Hayashi, T., Tobushi, H., Lexcellent, C.: Phenomenological analysis on subloops and cyclic behavior in shape memory alloys under mechanical and/or thermal loads. Mech. Mater. **19**(4), 281–292 (1995). https://doi.org/10.1016/0167-6636(94)00038-I
16. Ramirez, J., Rubiano, A., Castiblanco, P.: Soft driving epicyclical mechanism for robotic finger. Actuators **8**(3) (2019). https://doi.org/10.3390/act8030058
17. Zhu, P., et al.: Characterization and modeling of three-dimensional self-healing shape memory alloy-reinforced metal-matrix composites. Mech. Mater. **103**, 1–10 (2016). https://doi.org/10.1016/j.mechmat.2016.09.005
18. Vantadori, S., Carpinteri, A., Di Cocco, V., Iacoviello, F., Natali, S.: Fatigue analysis of a near-equiatomic pseudo-elastic NiTi SMA. Theoret. Appl. Fract. Mech. **94**, 110–119 (2018). https://doi.org/10.1016/j.tafmec.2018.01.012
19. Staugaard Jones, J.A.: Anatomía del ejercicio y el movimiento. Editorial Paidotribo (2014)
20. Ramirez, J.L.: Development of an artificial muscle for a soft robotic hand prosthesis, universite Paris Ouest (2016)
21. Hill, A.V.: The series elastic component of muscle. Proc. R. Soc. Lond. B Biol. Sci. **137**(887), 273–280 (1950). https://doi.org/10.1098/rspb.1950.0035
22. Zajac, F.E.: Muscle and tendon: properties, models, scaling, and application to biomechanics and motor control. Crit. Rev. Biomed. Eng. **17**(4), 359–411 (1989)
23. Abeyaratne, R., Sang-Joo, K., Knowles, J.K.: A one-dimensional continuum model for shape-memory alloys. Int. J. Solids Struct. **31**(16), 2229–2249 (1994). https://doi.org/10.1016/0020-7683(94)90208-9
24. Vivet, A., Lexcellent, C.: Micromechanical modelling for tension–compression pseudoelastic behavior of AuCd single crystals. Eur. Phys. J. - Appl. Phys. **4**(2), 125–132 (1998). https://doi.org/10.1051/epjap:1998251
25. Brinston, C.: One dimensional constitutive behavior of shape memory alloys: thermomechanical derivation with non-constant material function and redefined martensite internal variable. J. Intell. Mater. Syst. Struct. **4**, 229–242 (1993). https://doi.org/10.1177/1045389X9300400213
26. Bassil, M., Davenas, J., EL Tahchi, M.: Electrochemical properties and actuation mechanisms of polyacrylamide hydrogel for artificial muscle application. Sens. Actuators B Chem. **134**(2), 496–501 (2008). https://doi.org/10.1016/j.snb.2008.05.025
27. Wheeler, R.W., et al.: Engineering design tools for shape memory alloy actuators : CASMART collaborative best practices and case studies. In: SMASIS2016-9183, pp. 1–21 (2016)
28. Doroudchi, A., Zakerzadeh, M.R.: An experimental study on controlling a fast response SMA-actuated rotary actuator. In: 2017 5th RSI International Conference on Robotics and Mechatronics (ICRoM), pp. 144–149 (2017). https://doi.org/10.1109/icrom.2017.8466198
29. Drahoš, P., Kutiš, V.: Modelling and simulation of thermal field of SMA actuator. In: Proceedings of the 13th International Carpathian Control Conference (ICCC), pp. 131–136 (2012). https://doi.org/10.1109/carpathiancc.2012.6228629

30. Elahinia, M.H., Ashrafiuon, H., Ahmadian, M., Tan, H.: A temperature-based controller for a shape memory alloy actuator. J. Vib. Acoust. Trans. ASME **127**(3), 285–291 (2005). https://doi.org/10.1115/1.1898335

31. Khodayari, A., Zarefar, B., Kheirikhah, M.M., Mirsadeghi, E.: Force control of a SMA actuated gripper by using self tuning fuzzy PID controller. In: 2011 IEEE International Conference on Control System, Computing and Engineering, pp. 312–316 (2011). https://doi.org/10.1109/iccsce.2011.6190543

32. Jung, S., Bae, J., Moon, I.: Lightweight prosthetic hand with five fingers using SMA actuator. In: 2011 11th International Conference on Control, Automation and Systems, pp. 1797–1800 (2011)

33. Colorado, J., Barrientos, A., Rossi, C.: Músculos Inteligentes en Robots Biológicamente Inspirados: Modelado, Control y Actuación. Rev. Iberoam. Automática e Informática Ind. RIAI **8**(4), 385–396 (2011). https://doi.org/10.1016/j.riai.2011.09.005

34. Li, J., Tian, H.: Position control of SMA actuator based on inverse empirical model and SMC-RBF compensation. Mech. Syst. Signal Process. **108**, 203–215 (2018). https://doi.org/10.1016/j.ymssp.2018.02.004

35. Moura, T.D.O., Tsukamoto, T., de Lima Monteiro, D.W., Tanaka, S.: Hybrid MEMS-SMA structure for intraocular lenses. Sens. Actuators A Phys. **243**, 15–24 (2016). https://doi.org/10.1016/j.sna.2016.03.005

36. Teramoro Ohara, A.: Importancia clinica del punto austenitico final en la seleccion de las aleaciones de niquel-titanio para su aplicacion en arcos utilizados en ortodoncia. Rev. Odontol. Mex. **20**, 166–173 (2016)

37. Hoh, D.J., Hoh, B.L., Amar, A.P., Wang, M.Y.: Shape memory alloys: metallurgy, biocompatibility, and biomechanics for neurosurgical applications. Oper. Neurosurg. **64**(suppl_5), ons199–ons214 (2009). https://doi.org/10.1227/01.neu.0000330392.09889.99

38. Guo, S., Sun, X., Ishii, K., Guo, J.: SMA Actuator-based novel type of peristatic micropump. In: 2008 International Conference on Information and Automation, pp. 1620–1625 (2008). https://doi.org/10.1109/ICINFA.2008.4608263

39. Peng, C., Yin, Y.H., Hong, H.B., Zhang, J.J., Chen, X.: Bio-inspired design methodology of sensor-actuator-structure integrated system for artificial muscle using SMA. Procedia CIRP **65**, 299–303 (2017). https://doi.org/10.1016/j.procir.2017.04.016

40. Zhang, J., Yin, Y., Zhu, J.: Sigmoid-based hysteresis modeling and high-speed tracking control of SMA-artificial muscle. Sens. Actuators A Phys. **201**, 264–273 (2013). https://doi.org/10.1016/j.sna.2013.07.036

Exploring the Facial and Neurological Activation Due to Predetermined Visual Stimulus Using Kinect and Emotiv Sensors

Andrea Catalina Plazas-Molano, Mario Enrique Duarte-González,
Cristian Felipe Blanco-Díaz, and Sebastián Jaramillo-Isaza(✉)

Antonio Nariño University, Bogotá, Colombia
sebastian.jaramillo@uan.edu.co

Abstract. In recent years, technologies such as Kinect and Emotiv, combined with predetermined stimuli, have been widely used to perform studies in different fields such as neuromarketing, rehabilitation, medicine, among others. However, how facial and neurological activation parameters can be related has been little explored. This research aims to develop a way to synchronize data acquisition on both devices and find possible relationships between the data produced by facial tracking using the Kinect and the encephalographic signals obtained from the Emotiv. For this, an experimental design has been built with a population of 15 test subjects including both genders, who were exposed to a predetermined routine of images, which have been demonstrated and used by different neuroscience research centers since they can induce in humans emotions such as happiness, sadness, disgust or fear. Measurements were carried out in a controlled space, in total calm, away from any noise or interference that may affect data collection. Within the obtained results, it was identified some possible relationships between facial and encephalographic signals, as well as a dependent activation of the brain's areas with the stimuli presented, in both the time and frequency domain.

Keywords: Kinect · Emotiv · Neurostimulus · Neuroengineering · Facial tracking · EEG

1 Introduction

The human body is made up of innumerable receptors that allow it to generate responses to different stimuli [1–4]. Therefore, when these receptors are specifically stimulated, predetermined responses can be achieved in humans, including inducing feelings or emotions [5]. Over time, neurobiology has been looking for a universal definition of emotion, allowing the recognition of stimuli that provoke activation in the locomotor, facial, vocal, autonomous, and hormonal systems [6].

The search for ways to quantify and qualify the responses of human beings to stimuli that induce emotions has led to the development of tools for the acquisition of kinematic information which allows the recognition of facial configurations, however, the use of these tools to obtain Results have been negative for the research processes, since the

© Springer Nature Switzerland AG 2020
J. C. Figueroa-García et al. (Eds.): WEA 2020, CCIS 1274, pp. 268–280, 2020.
https://doi.org/10.1007/978-3-030-61834-6_23

use of this unique technique does not allow universal actions to be generalized within people in all situations [7], therefore, only facial configurations have been established for basic emotions: Happiness, Sadness, Fear, Disgust, Anger, and Surprise postulated by Paul Ekman [8], ruling out among them surprise and anger [9, 10]. A survey reveals that 80% of 149 scientists, who have published studies on this topic, points out that the emotions, mentioned above, are expressed in universal facial configurations [9].

On the other hand, this research seeks to quantify and qualify the kinematic and neurological information by combining these two techniques to obtain more forceful results in the induction of emotions at the facial and brain level.

The quantity available and the use of these tools that facilitate the study of emotional activations manifested in the different systems of the human body, have increased considerably in recent years thanks to their mass and relatively low cost. Within this group of tools, Kinect has been a revolutionary device in the human-machine relationship [11], making it increasingly friendly, easy and fast, and allowing it to be implemented in several applications [12]. Brain-Computer Interface (BCI) systems, more sophisticated tools, allow to quantify this type of interaction neurologically, and Emotiv is one of those tools. BCI systems extract the electroencephalography signals emitted by the brain [13].

The research was developed using functional codes that let the data acquisition process to be carried out for each of the tools: Kinect and Emotiv. These tools were manually and strategically synchronized to obtain homogeneous signals regarding the amount of data. A selected study group (ten men and five women) was tested under elaborate imaging routines based on the IAPS stimulus bank.

The signals, corresponding to the different Emotiv's channels and each Animation Unit of the Kinect tool, were obtained. These signals were compared, obtaining relationships between them regarding their activation. Besides, a density spectral analysis was performed for the encephalographic signals, getting concordant information in both the time and the frequency domain.

2   Materials and Methods

2.1   Subjects

This procedure was carried out with 15 volunteers (ten male and five female) with an average age $21,6 \pm 1,7$ years for men and $21,4 \pm 0,8$ for women.

2.2   Inclusion Criteria

All the volunteers are right-handed, without any considerable visual, neurological, cognitive, facial or other condition that could bias the obtained results. In agreement with the Declaration of Helsinki [14] and the Colombian resolution 8430 of 1993 [15] for experimental research in health topics, each of the subjects was requested to provide a signed informed consent expressing their voluntary participation in the present study and confirming to have understood the entire procedure, as well as the treating and use of the resulting data.

2.3 Visual Stimulus

A visual stimulus is an image or color that, when observed, produces a response due to the activation of the brain areas. This process is directly related to the representation of images in the retina and the encoding of information emitted to the nervous system, allowing the specific activation of brain areas and the emission of a characteristic response [16]. For this reason, a bank of predetermined images was used as stimuli for inducing induce one of the four basic emotions.

The International Affective Imaging System (IAPS) is a stimulus bank developed by the NIMH Center for Emotion and Attention (CSEA) at the University of Florida. This bank of stimuli is made up of various standardized images that comply with the characteristic of inducing emotions in people, in order to be used in different studies as well as providing parameters that an image must meet to be an inducer of each specific emotion allowing the creation of own image banks to carry out the studies.

In this project, three different models of visual routines were created with different images for each emotion. Each one made up of sequences of images characteristic of each emotion, each lasting 6 s when one minute of each emotion was completed. A black image, with a duration of 10 s, was presented for neutralizing.

2.4 Equipment and Software

Two information acquisition tools were used:

– *Emotiv Epoc+*

The EMOTIV EPOC+ is a portable, high resolution, 14-channel, low-cost EEG system. It was designed to take measurements in practical research applications and a bandwidth of 0.2–45 Hz, digital notch filters at 50 Hz and 60 Hz. It is compatible with all EMO-TIV software products. in charge of gathering encephalographic information, using free development codes in the Python environment (see Fig. 1), allowing the management and analysis of data through files in Excel format (.csv).

– *Microsoft Kinect V2*

The Kinect is a low-cost motion-sensing input device developed by Microsoft for home entertainment. The technology achieves this through the use of RGB cameras (color and monochrome), and an infrared (IR) projector and detectors [17]. This device has two versions Kinect v1 and Kinect v2, both of them with different features. It captures separate color and depth data at 30 Hz, but Kinect v2 does this task at a resolution of 1920 × 1080 for the color camera and 512 × 424 for the depth camera. Grace to its simplicity and its capability to perform real-time gesture recognition, speech recognition, and skeletal body detection, among others; this device has gained huge notoriety in the fields of biomechanics, robotics, and computer science [18]. Kinect V2 was the tool responsible for collecting facial information; it is working with a developer SDK to anchor it to Windows. This kit has different acquisition modes in various applications, such as basic audio, body, color, controls, coordinate mapping, depth, discrete gestures,

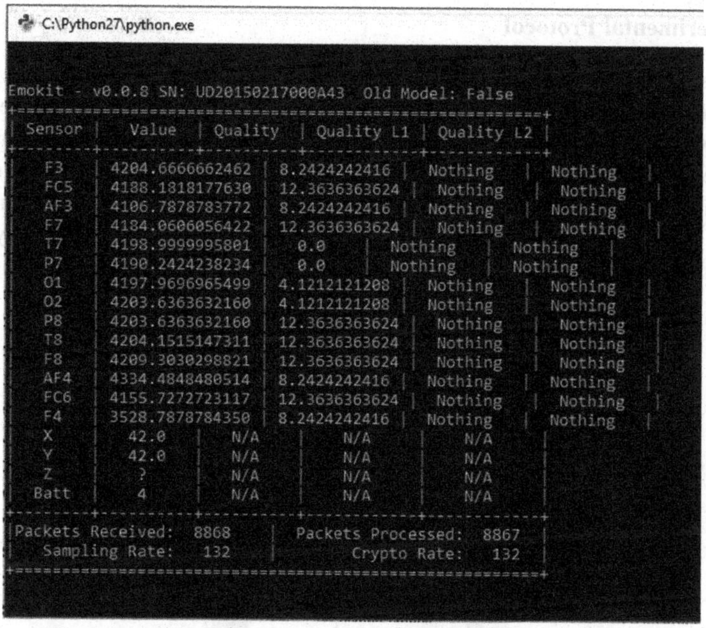

Fig. 1. Emotiv tool for data acquisition through the Python environment.

HD face, infrared, speech, and Kinect Fusion. Juan R. Terven developed the connection of the SDK kit with the Matlab environment [19], allowing the use of the FaceDemoHd program. Through this executable, it was possible to obtain a facial mapping p, as well as Animation Units directly related to the Action Units [20] established by the facial action coding system (FACS) [21] (Fig. 2).

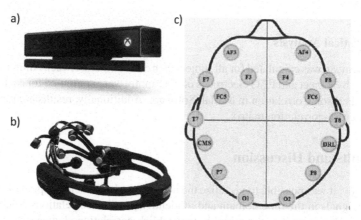

Fig. 2. Images representing a) Kinect sensor, b) Emotiv Epoc+ and c) Channel locations for the Emotiv system

2.5 Experimental Protocol

Both tools were synchronized to start data registering by using Matlab software. Both devices began recording, and visual stimulation was started by pressing the letter R on the keyboard. The different acquisition tools were located on the test subject. The procedure to be followed was explained, i.e., how the different stimuli were to be presented, and the concentration they should have for collecting the data. The stimuli were presented in a calm environment and isolated from external visual and auditory stimuli. The experimental setup using in this investigation is represented in Fig. 3.

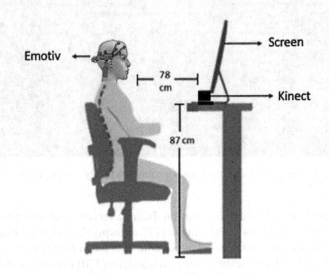

Fig. 3. Experimental setup for data acquisition.

2.6 Statistical Analysis

The grand mean was calculated for all subject then correlations between Animation Units measuring by Kinect and EEG electrodes of the Emotiv were computed for each emotion using the Pearson Correlation in Matlab Software. Additionally, results are represented using the cross-correlation matrix.

3 Results and Discussion

In this study, it was possible to visualize the neurological and facial responses of a study group as signals in the time domain and to identify possible correlations by comparing those data. However, it is not possible to establish correlations between test subjects regarding neurological or facial activation, since each individual has their own activation of perception of visual stimuli, that is, the emotional sense reflected in the obtained signals from both tools does not meet any behavioral characteristics among test subjects.

3.1 Comparative Analysis Between Emotiv Signals and Animation Units

Despite any code or software performed the synchronization of the Kinect and Emotiv acquisition tools, it was fully functional, allowing the obtain of homogeneous signals referring to the number of data of each signal among the different test subjects. Figure 4 represents the data 1347 points, as well as 17 Animation Units directly obtained from a male volunteer.

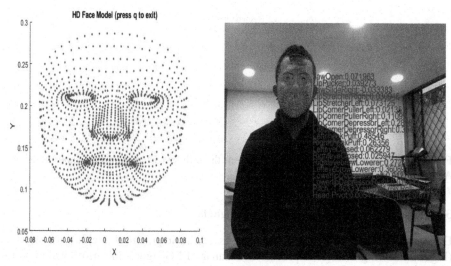

Fig. 4. Left image is a mapping of the 1347 points captured by the Kinect camera. Right image is an the 17 Animation Units that are linked to the FACS.

A graphic comparison was made of each channel of the Emotiv tool with the 17 Animation Units of the Kinect tool in the time domain, specifying each of the emotions evaluated, see Fig. 5.

The obtained results in the comparison analysis are drawn in Table 1. There are direct relationships between facial movements and EEG signals; however, in the population study, there were no identical facial movements or same neurological activity, even though the same visual stimulation routines had been presented.

When comparing the EEG signals with each of the Animation Units, it was observed that there are peaks in those signals that do not have any type of relationship with the facial response, that is, it was only possible to evaluate the response of the test subject to the stimulus by EEG signals, however, also found cases in which it was not possible to evaluate the test subject using these signals since no significant variations were found.

Perception of emotion in the brain is carried out in the limbic system in structures such as the amygdala, the ventral striatum and the hypothalamus [22]. These structures of the limbic system buried deep within the brain; this is why the activation of these structures cannot be registered using conventional EEG recorders like the BCI Emotiv system.

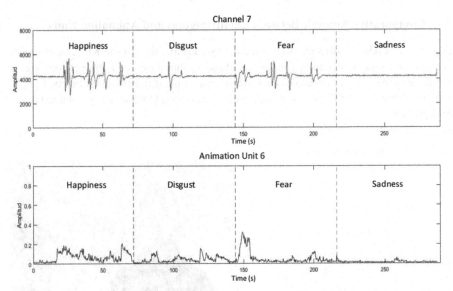

Fig. 5. Graph to make the comparison between the different Emotiv channels and the Kinect Animation Units.

3.2 Spectral Density Analysis of EEG Signals

EEGLAB Matlab environment tool generates a didactic graphical interface for the user (Fig. 5), allowing the user to process and manage EEG signals in various ways and to visualize graphs and models for interpreting the brain activity and its spectral density.

The obtained results in the frequency domain, through the power spectral density, are shown in Figs. 6 and 7. The correspondent spectral power value is assigned to each frequency range, and according to its magnitude, a color scale is defined. Those attributes allow obtaining the different activation diagrams by color range; it is observed that the study group's activation zones are generally in agreement with the different activation peaks in the time domain.

By means of the spectral density graphs it is possible to evaluate the concentration of this variable referring to each of the frequency bands. This density is mostly concentrated before 30 Hz, thus referring to the Delta, Theta, Alpha and Beta bands, the concentration in the Gamma band, that is, frequencies greater than 30 Hz, does not contain great activation with respect to the aforementioned. Taking into account that the concentration is in the values below 30 Hz, it is important to mention that its highest concentration is located generally within the totality of test subjects is the Delta and Theta band, that is, the study group have a characteristic spectral density in a range of low frequencies (Delta and Theta) related to visual stimuli emotion inducers.

Table 1. Results of the comparison of each channel of the Emotiv with each Animation Unit for each test subject.

	Emotiv Channels											
Kinect/Emotiv	AF3	AF4	F3	F4	F7	F8	FC5	FC6	O1	O2	P7	P8
AU1					MH5 MS5 MD7 FD3	MH10 FD3					MD4	
AU2	FS2					FD2						
AU3	MH9 FS2	MS7				MD7 MS7		MD7 MS7				
AU4	MH9 FS2											
AU5					MH1 MH5 FF2	MH1 MD3 FD2						
AU6	MF1 MH9 FS2	MF1 MS7 MD10	MF1	MF1	MF1 MH5 MH6 MD6 FD3	MF1 MH3 MD7 MH7 MH10 MD10 MF10 FD3	MD1 MF1	MS7				
AU7	MF1 MH9 MD10	MF1 MD10	MF1	MF1	MH1 MF1 MH5 MS5 FD3	MH1 MF1 MS3 FD3	MD10 MF1				MD4	
AU8	MH9				MH2 MH6 FF2						MD4	
AU9					MH1 MF1 MH6 MD6 MF6 FF2	MH1 MD3 MS3	MD1					
AU10	FS2											
AU11	MH9				MH2	MH3					MD4	
AU12	MH9 FF1 FS1	FD10			MH1 MH5 MS5 FS3 SF3		MD1					
AU13	MH9 MD10	MD10			MH1 MH5 MS5 FS3 FF3 FH3		MD1					
AU14	MD10										MD4	
AU15	MD10	MD10										
AU16	MF1	MF1 MF7 MS7 MD10	MF1	MF1	MH1 MF1 MH5 MF7 FF2 FS2	MH1 MF1 MD7 MF7		MD7 MF7			MD4	
AU17	MF1	MF1 MF7 MD10	MF1	MF1	MH1 MF1 MH5 MF7 FF2 FS2 FD2	MH1 MF1 MF7 FD2 FD3 FS3		MD7			MD4	

Animation Unit

MH = Male Happiness, MS = Male Sadness, MD = Male Disgust, MF = Male Fear
FH = Female Happiness, MS = Female Sadness, MD = Female Disgust, MF = Female Fear
# = Subject Number

3.3 Statistical Analysis

Pearson correlation coefficient show that each emotion has different response in both facial expression and EEG activation. Results are represented in Fig. 8. However, EEG correlations suggest that predetermined stimulus could induce different brain activation in the subjects. This fact insinuate that each emotion could be induced in the viewer by this method.

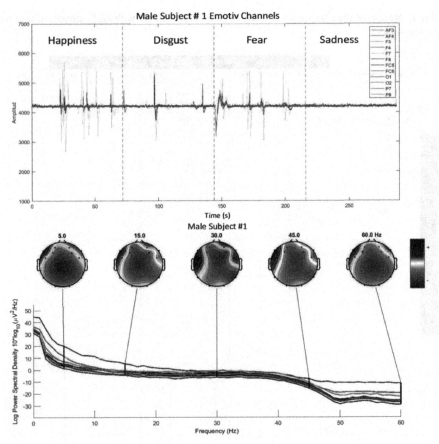

Fig. 6. Superior image represents the EEG signals captured by the 12 electrodes to be analyzed from Male Test Subject # 1 in the time domain, the dotted vertical lines indicate the beginning and end of each emotion stated at the top of it. Meanwhile the inferior image represents the spectral density of the 12 electrodes to be analyzed from Male Test Subject # 1, the upper diagrams refer to brain activation in the different areas. The black dots that appear on these are the electrode locations according to the Emotiv device.

In summary, according to our results, it is not yet possible to clearly distinguish emotions individually. However, it can be affirmed that the combined use of new specialized technologies in facial recognition and in the quantification of neuronal activation, can offer new approaches that help better to understand the responses of humans to predetermined stimuli.

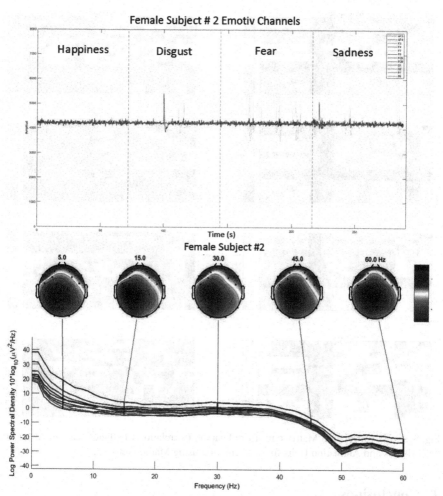

Fig. 7. Superior image represents the EEG signals captured by the 12 electrodes to be analyzed from Female Test Subject # 2 in the time domain, the dotted vertical lines indicate the beginning and end of each emotion stated at the top of it. Meanwhile the inferior image represents the spectral density of the 12 electrodes to be analyzed from Female Test Subject # 2, the upper diagrams refer to brain activation in the different areas. The black dots that appear on these are the electrode locations according to the Emotiv device.

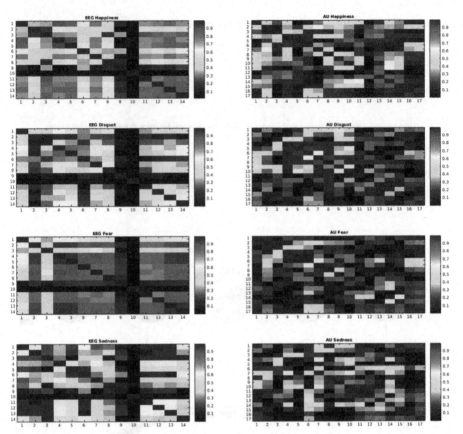

Fig. 8. Cross Correlation Matrix built from Pearson Correlation Coefficient computed for both EEG signals and Animation Units for each emotion using Matlab Software.

4   Conclusions

The found results with conventional analysis tools do not show a possible relationship between facial and neurological activation between subjects of the same gender, demonstrating that it is not a classification factor for the obtained results. The test subjects provide unique and unrepeatable signals between them. However, correlations coefficients suggest that each emotion could be induced using predetermined stimulus.

Increasing the number of subjects and using analysis methods such as computational intelligence and advanced statistics could help to establish more precise correlations between facial and neurological activation.

Future research in this field may include using more powerful equipment for recording EEG signals, such as BCI-type devices or advanced imaging techniques such as nuclear magnetic resonance (NMR). These new tools could increase the depth of the registry and provide relevant data on deep brain activity, which could be correlated with facial activation.

Acknowledgments. Authors want to thank to the Universidad Antonio Nariño for all the financial support to this work under the project number 2018218.

References

1. Lele, P.P., Sinclair, D.C., Weddell, G.: The reaction time to touch. J. Physiol. **123**, 187–203 (1954). https://doi.org/10.1113/jphysiol.1954.sp005042
2. Puntkattalee, M.J., Whitmire, C.J., Macklin, A.S., Stanley, G.B., Ting, L.H.: Directional acuity of whole-body perturbations during standing balance. Gait Posture **48**, 77–82 (2016). https://doi.org/10.1016/j.gaitpost.2016.04.008
3. González San José, M.L.: Metodología del análisis sensorial. In: Curso de Verano Viticultura y Enología en la D.O., pp. 85–96 (2008)
4. Llinás, R.R.: El cerebro y el mito del yo: El papel de las neuronas en el pensamiento y el comportamientos humanos (2003)
5. Palmero, F., Guerrero, C., Gómez, C., Carpi, A.: Certezas y controversias en el estudio de la emoción. REME **9**, 1–25 (2006)
6. Solís, F.O., Dichy, R.C., Parra, G.C., García, A.E.V., García, N.A.: Valencia, activación, dominancia y contenido moral, ante est{\'\i}mulos visuales con contenido emocional y moral: un estudio en población mexicana. Rev. española Neuropsicol. **5**, 213–225 (2003)
7. Chen, A.: Razones para prohibir el reconocimiento de emociones cuanto antes (2020)
8. Ekman, P.: Basic emotions. In: Handbook of Cognition and Emotion, no. 98, p. 16 (1999)
9. Barrett, L.F., Adolphs, R., Marsella, S., Martinez, A.M., Pollak, S.D.: Emotional expressions reconsidered: challenges to inferring emotion from human facial movements. Psychol. Sci. Public Interest **20**, 1–68 (2019). https://doi.org/10.1177/1529100619832930
10. Regader, B.: Estudio demuestra que las emociones básicas son cuatro, y no seis como se creía (2018)
11. Zhang, Z.: Microsoft kinect sensor and its effect. IEEE Multimedia **19**, 4–10 (2012). https://doi.org/10.1109/MMUL.2012.24
12. Wu, H.-H., Bainbridge-Smith, A.: Advantages of using a Kinect Camera in various applications. University of Canterbury (2011)
13. Cloyd, T.D., Pitt, J.C., Fuhrman, E.R., Laberge, A.F., Cloyd, T.D.: (r) Evolution in Brain - Computer Interface Technologies for Play: (non) Users in Mind (r) Evolution in Brain - Computer Interface Technologies for Play: (non) Users in Mind (2013)
14. Asociación Médica Mundial: Declaración de Helsinki: Principios éticos para las investigaciones médicas en seres humanos (1964)
15. Minsalud, R.N.: 8430 DE 1993. Por la cual se Establ. las normas científicas, técnicas y Adm. para la Investig. en salud. Minist. Salud Colomb., pp. 1–19 (1993)
16. Brenner, E., Smeets, J.B.J.: Chapter 4 - Accumulating visual information for action. In: Howard, C.J. (ed.) Temporal Sampling and Representation Updating, pp. 75–95. Elsevier (2017). https://doi.org/10.1016/bs.pbr.2017.07.007
17. Microsoft: Microsoft Kinect V2
18. Bauer, S., Wasza, J., Haase, S., Marosi, N., Hornegger, J.: Multi-modal surface registration for markerless initial patient setup in radiation therapy using microsoft's Kinect sensor. In: 2011 IEEE International Conference on Computer Vision Workshops (ICCV Workshops), pp. 1175–1181 (2011). https://doi.org/10.1109/ICCVW.2011.6130383
19. Terven, J.R.: Kinect 2 interface for Matlab (2017)
20. Regidor Serrano, M.: Reconocimiento de expresiones con Kinect (2015)

21. Hamm, J., Kohler, C.G., Gur, R.C., Verma, R.: Automated facial action coding system for dynamic analysis of facial expressions in neuropsychiatric disorders. J. Neurosci. Methods **200**, 237–256 (2011)

22. Pessoa, L.: On the relationship between emotion and cognition. Nat. Rev. Neurosci. **9**, 148–158 (2008)

Electrophysiological and Mechanical Approaches to the Swallowing Analysis

Juan Pablo Restrepo-Uribe[1], Sebastian Roldan-Vasco[1,2]([⊠]),
Estefania Perez-Giraldo[3], Juan Rafael Orozco-Arroyave[2,4],
and Andres Orozco-Duque[3]([⊠])

[1] Grupo de Investigación en Materiales Avanzados y Energía, Facultad de Ingenierías, Instituto Tecnológico Metropolitano, Medellín, Colombia
sebastianroldan@itm.edu.co
[2] Faculty of Engineering, Universidad de Antioquia, Medellín, Colombia
[3] Grupo de Investigación e Innovación Biomédica, Facultad de Ciencias Exactas y Aplicadas, Instituto Tecnológico Metropolitano, Medellín, Colombia
andresorozco@itm.edu.co
[4] Pattern Recognition Lab, Friedrich-Alexander-Universität, Erlangen-Nürnberg, Germany

Abstract. Alterations of the swallowing process at neurological and muscular levels can cause dysphagia. Its instrumental diagnosis is carried out by videofluoroscopy, which is invasive, expensive, and sometimes unavailable. Inexpensive and non-invasive alternatives have been proposed in several studies considering different biosignals including surface electromyography and accelerometry. Automatic approaches have been focused on unimodal analysis, disregarding the high complexity of the process. In this way, we performed a multimodal analysis of the swallowing process in 30 healthy individuals and 30 dysphagic patients, using surface electromyography and accelerometry-based cervical auscultation. Features in time, frequency, and time-frequency domains were extracted and selected for classification purposes. A support vector machine was used as a classifier, and hyperparameters were optimized by a grid search. The proposed scheme achieved an accuracy of 0.92 ± 0.07 in the best case. The performed method achieved promising results in terms of classification of dysphagic and healthy individuals, which could contribute to the development of non-invasive techniques of dysphagia screening.

Keywords: Dysphagia · Swallowing · Accelerometry · Surface electromyography · Classification · Feature selection

1 Introduction

The swallowing process involves well-coordinated neuromuscular activations to protect the airway while food is passing through the pharynx [1]. The swallowing is described as a sequential process with three phases: oral, pharyngeal, and esophageal [2]. Neuromuscular or neurogenic diseases often cause alterations

J. C. Figueroa-García et al. (Eds.): WEA 2020, CCIS 1274, pp. 281–290, 2020.
https://doi.org/10.1007/978-3-030-61834-6_24

in swallowing. Such alterations are known as dysphagia, which is a symptom of different conditions [3,4], including Alzheimer's disease, Parkinson's disease, myasthenia gravis, multiple sclerosis, amyotrophic lateral sclerosis, stroke, and others. Abnormal patterns in the oral and pharyngeal phases of swallowing originate oropharyngeal dysphagia. Epidemiological studies estimate that around 16–20% of the worldwide population suffers from dysphagia [5,6]. The dysphagia also produces malnutrition, dehydration, and laryngeal aspiration which can lead to pneumonia with subsequent death [7]. Furthermore, the oropharyngeal dysphagia has burdens at psychological and social levels, due to partial or total loss of autonomy as well as self-esteem [3,6].

The gold standard method to diagnose dysphagia is the Video-Fluoroscopic Swallowing Study (VFSS) which exposes the patients to X-rays [8]. This technique has limitations regard to ionizing radiation and costs, which limit its use in longitudinal studies when monitoring of the disease progression is required [9]. Other methods such as the clinical bedside swallowing evaluation depend on the examiner's experience [10,11]. These limitations motivate to explore new techniques for diagnosis and follow-up of dysphagia. Biosignals-based approaches have been studied for swallowing evaluation, since they have low cost, and they are non-invasive, are not time-consuming, and could be suitable to automated screenings. In this way, two types of biosignals were explored in this paper: surface electromyography (sEMG) and accelerometry-based cervical auscultation (ACC).

The automatic analysis of the ACC in swallowing has been widely addressed. Different features in time, frequency, and time-frequency domains, have been used for classification, segmentation, and identification of swallowing and non-swallowing related activities. A recent paper published a method to differentiate between swallowing and natural or false cough, through the application of support vector machines (SVM) and artificial neural networks. A classification performance of 90.3% was reported [12]. Other research used an artificial neuronal network to describe the hyoid bone movement with an accelerometer the signal was compared with videofluoroscopy, and the results showed that the use of non-invasive sensors offers an alternative for monitoring the hyoid bone during swallowing [13]. Otherwise, researches in the field of sEMG applied to dysphagia have been mainly focused on descriptive and statistical analyses of piecemeal deglutition and duration of swallowing [14,15]. Few works have addressed automatic analysis of sEMG signals in swallowing. In [16] the authors compared an artificial neural network with a SVM to identify the characteristics that best describe the swallowing process and detect the phases of swallowing. The results indicated that the time domain features are the most suitable to represent the swallowing process. The automatic segmentation of sEMG signals has been also explored. Recently, a scalogram based segmentation method in the time-frequency domain was developed and optimized for swallowing related muscles [17].

The signal segmentation is an important step prior to feature extraction and classification. Some researchers evaluated the signal segmentation with the use of artificial neural networks with information provided by a multi-sensor approach

(ACC, and nasal airflow), aiming to evaluate the segmentation performance, and to figure out which sensor combination is the most suitable for segmentation. This research found that the use of multi-sensor fusion is a promissory tool that should be more widely explored [18]. Other researchers evaluated the multi-sensor fusion with ACC, sEMG, and a microphone during swallowing. The system proved to be useful for detecting spontaneous swallowing, as well as to determine the frequency of swallowing and the mean time of spontaneous and voluntary swallowing. However, this work did not apply characterization and classification techniques [19]. In the same way, other researchers used and compared the multi-sensor fusion of sEMG, and cervical auscultation for detection of the frequency of spontaneous swallowing. The method determined that the acoustic sensor retrieved the highest performance [20].

In this way, we proposed a scheme to evaluate simultaneously sEMG and ACC during swallowing tasks, in order to compare the discrimination capability of such signals for dysphagia detection.

2 Materials and Methods

2.1 Subjects

The database was divided into two groups, one with 30 healthy subjects, (14 female and 16 male) with an average age of 29.46 ± 10.60 years old. The other group was formed with 30 patients with dysphagia, (11 female and 19 male) with an average age of 45.86 ± 15.00 years old. The volunteers were asked to sign an informed consent approved by the Ethics Committee of the Universidad Pontificia Bolivariana (Medellín, Colombia).

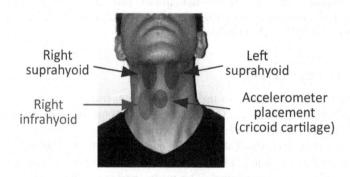

Fig. 1. Position of the accelerometer and sEMG electrodes

2.2 Data Acquisition and Signal Processing

The ACC signal was recorded with a DAQ 6215 (National Instruments) and a triaxial accelerometer sensor MMA7361 (NXP) located in the hyoid bone, with a sampling rate of 10 kHz, according to [21]. The sEMG signal was recorded with the Noraxon Ultium® EMG (Noraxon, USA) and the myoMUSCLE™ Software Module, with a sampling rate of 2 kHz. Three pairs of Ag/AgCl electrodes were located in the right and left suprahyoid muscles and right infrahyoid muscle, leaving the right infrahyoid muscle free to perform cervical auscultation and due to space limitations. The Fig. 1 shows the placement of the sensors. Subjects were asked to intake 10 mL of yogurt in one single drink.

Both kinds of signals were bandpass filtered with a Butterworth topology. The bandwidth of the sEMG was 10–500 Hz, while the bandwidth of the ACC was 0.1–3000 Hz [12,17]. The Fig. 2 shows an example of the analyzed signals.

In figure you can see the 6 signals acquired through ACC and sEMG.

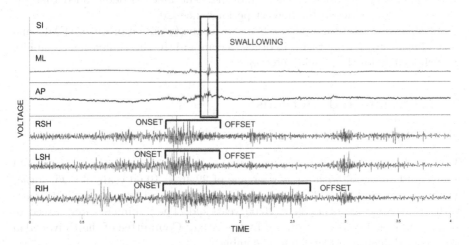

Fig. 2. ACC and sEMG signals during a swallowing task. Three axes of ACC are shown: SI (superior-inferior), ML (medial-lateral), and AP (antero-posterior). Three channels of sEMG are also shown: RSH (right suprahyoid muscles), LSH (left suprahyoid muscles), and RIH (right infrahyoid muscles)

2.3   Feature Extraction

The sliding window method was used for feature extraction, with frames of 200 ms and 25% overlapping for ACC, and frames of 250 ms and 40% overlapping for sEMG [22,23]. A set of 18 features was extracted in time, frequency, and time-frequency domains (see the Table 1). For each channel and feature, the sliding window method was applied. Thus, a feature related vector with length equal to the number of frames is retrieved. The mean, variance, skewness, and kurtosis were computed from such vector. In this way, the dimensions of the feature space are 6 channels × 18 features × 4 statistical moments.

2.4   Feature Selection and Classification

A grid search was used for the selection of the kernel, hyper-parameters tuning, and the feature selection with different methods. A SVM was used as a

Table 1. Extracted features

Domain	Features
Time	Variance (VAR)
	Root Mean Square (RMS)
	Integral (IEMG)
	Mean Absolute Value (MAV)
	Log detector (LOG)
	Wavelength (WL)
	Average Amplitude Change (ACC)
	Difference Absolute Standard
	Deviation Value (DASDV)
	Zero-Crossing (ZC)
	Willison Amplitude (WAMP)
	Myopulse Percentage Rate (MYOP)
Frequency	Frequency Ratio (FR)
	Mean Power (MNP)
	Total Power (TP)
	Mean Frequency (MNF)
	Median Frequency (MDF)
	Peak Frequency (PKF)
Time-Frequency	Wavelet Entropy (WENT)

classification model. Different kernels were assessed: linear, radial basis function (RBF), and sigmoid. Also, the hyperparameters C (penalty) and γ (kernel width) were optimized in the range 0.001–1000 with steps of one decade. For feature selection, three methods were assessed: univariate feature selection, recursive feature elimination, and sequential feature selection. The following parameters were changed in the grid search scheme: the feature selection mode, the parameter of the corresponding mode, the score function, the minimum number of features to select, and the number of features to select (groups of 54, 108, 162, 216, 270, 324 and 378 features). This process is illustrated in Fig. 3.

The database was divided into two sets, one for training (80%) and another for the test (20%). The training set was used for hyperparameters tuning of SVM and the feature selector methods. The grid search was carried out with the accuracy as optimization criterion. Also, the F_1 and the area under the ROC (AUC) were computed for each model. The test set was used for model validation using a cross-validation scheme.

3   Results and Discussion

Table 2 shows the optimal parameters of the evaluated models. Feature selection methods removed a different number of features, but to a greater extent

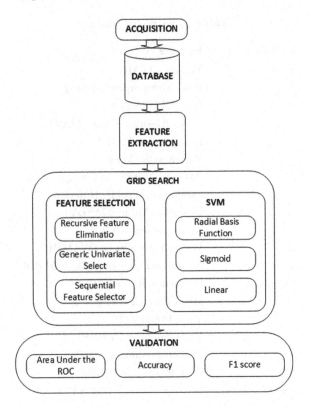

Fig. 3. Proposed methodology

sEMG related features. In the case of the generic univariate selection method, a set of 270 features was removed. Of these, 91 features correspond to the ACC signals and 179 of sEMG signals. Similarly, the recursive feature elimination removed 159 features, where 59 are from ACC, and 100 of sEMG. Finally, the sequential feature selection removed 162 features, 44 of ACC, and 118 of sEMG. The removed features correspond to all statistical moments in all channels. It suggests that none channel should be excluded without losing generalization. Our findings suggest that the use of features in different domains contribute to characterize the swallowing process.

The best parameters and hyperparameters that were evaluated in the test set achieved an accuracy of 0.83 and a F_1 score of 0.87. This result may be due to the reduced size to the database, or the number of subjects per class. The Table 3 summarizes the metrics obtained with the cross-validation scheme using the best parameters, where it is possible to see that the generic univariate selector overcomes the other techniques. Figure 4 presents the ROC curve of the generic univariate selection since this model showed to have the highest capability to find true positives compared with other models, that is, it has the best performance in terms of sensitivity.

Table 2. Optimal parameters obtained with for each feature selection method

Selection method	Parameter	Best parameter
Generic univariate selection	Kernel	rbf
	C	10
	γ	0.1
	Feature selection mode	χ^2
	Parameter of the corresponding mode	162
	Score function	k_best
Recursive feature elimination	Kernel	Linear
	C	1
	Minimum number of features to select	108
Sequential feature selector	Kernel	Linear
	C	0.01
	Number of features to select	270

Table 3. Performance measures evaluated in the cross-validation, for each model obtained with different feature selection methods.

Feature selection	Accuracy	f1 score
Generic univariate selector	**0.92 ± 0.07**	**0.91 ± 0.79**
Recursive feature elimination	0.85 ± 0.08	0.86 ± 0.97
Sequential feature selector	0.83 ± 0.1	0.84 ± 0.09

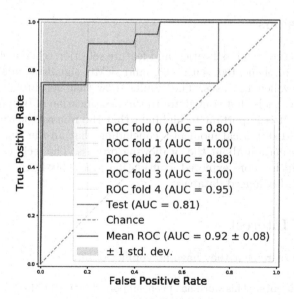

Fig. 4. ROC curve for the SVM classifier using the subset of features selected by the generic univariate method.

The main contribution of this paper is the use of a combination of features of sEMG and ACC in the classification of dysphagic patients. The sEMG and ACC signals provide features that describe the muscular activation and the movement of the hyoid bone, respectively. This work obtained results comparable to previous reports. For instance other researchers also evaluated patients with dysphagia by wavelet decomposition, linear discriminant analysis, and Bayesian classifier, applied on ACC signals. They achieved an accuracy of 90% in the detection of healthy and aspirated swallows [24]. Also, other work evaluated the classification of healthy and dysphagic subjects through the discriminant analysis, from ACC signals, using different consistencies of liquids. The accuracy was calculated for each consistency, and the highest accuracy (95.1%) was obtained with thick liquids [25]. The use of multi-sensor fusion contributes in some cases to reduce uncertainty and noise-related error, which it's would show that the complete elimination of the information collected by any of the sensors is not possible [26, 27]. The results of the multi-sensor fusion were comparable, however, it should be taken into consideration that this study analyzed two different dimensions of the swallowing process.

Future work will be focused on increasing the database to have balanced conditions for age and sex in the two groups, as well as to include different consistencies of the for swallowing assessment. Different features must be explored to identify swallowing phases and to evaluate the segment associated with swallowing in the multi-sensor fusion of ACC and sEMG. Furthermore, other classification models must be assessed to improve the detection of healthy and non-healthy swallows for dysphagia screening purposes.

4   Conclusions

In the present study, a classification and feature selection scheme of non-invasive biosignals was implemented, with ACC and sEMG signals acquired simultaneously during swallowing tasks. The results show that synchronous sEMG and ACC signals are tools that contribute to the identification of dysphagic subjects non-invasively. It is important to highlight that the removed features belong to all channels and statistical moments, concluding that all the channels contain, important information about the swallowing process. The techniques of feature selection should be more explored, considering more classifiers, features, and a more robust and balanced database.

Conflict of Interest

The authors declare that they have no conflict of interest.

Acknowledgements. This work has been supported by COLCIENCIAS - República de Colombia, research project No. 121077758144.

References

1. Clavé, P., Shaker, R.: Dysphagia: current reality and scope of the problem. Nat. Rev. Gastroenterol. Hepatol. **12**, 259 (2015)
2. Streppel, M., Veder, L.L., Pullens, B., Joosten, K.F.: Swallowing problems in children with a tracheostomy tube. Int. J. Pediatr. Otorhinolaryngol. **124**, 30–33 (2019)
3. Chen, D.F.: Dysphagia in the hospitalized patient. Hosp. Med. Clin. **6**, 38–52 (2017)
4. Suárez Escudero, J.C., Rueda Vallejo, Z.V., Orozco, A.F.: Disfagia y neurología: una unión indefectible? Acta Neurol. Colomb. **34**, 92–100 (2018)
5. Cichero, J.A.Y., Altman, K.W.: Definition, prevalence and burden of oropharyngeal dysphagia: a serious problem among older adults worldwide and the impact on prognosis and hospital resources. Nestle Nutr. Inst. Workshop Ser. **72**, 1–11 (2012)
6. Shapira-Galitz, Y., Drendel, M., Yousovich-Ulriech, R., Shtreiffler-Moskovich, L., Wolf, M., Lahav, Y.: Translation and validation of the dysphagia handicap index in Hebrew-speaking patients. Dysphagia **34**(1), 63–72 (2018). https://doi.org/10.1007/s00455-018-9914-7
7. Hsu, C.C., Chen, W.H., Chiu, H.C.: Using swallow sound and surface electromyography to determine the severity of dysphagia in patients with myasthenia gravis. Biomed. Signal Process. Control **8**, 237–243 (2013)
8. Miller, C.K., Maybee, J., Prager, J., Pentiuk, S.: Feeding and swallowing disorders. In: Kendig's Disorders of the Respiratory Tract in Children, 9th edn., pp. 1106–1113.e1. Elsevier Inc. (2018)
9. Armán, J.A., Lorente-Ramos, R.M., García, P.G., Lorduy, T.C.: Videofluoroscopic evaluation of normal and impaired oropharyngeal swallowing. Radiographics **39**, 78–79 (2019)
10. Wilson, R.D., Howe, E.C.: A of cost-effectiveness analysis screening methods for dysphagia after stroke. PM and R **4**, 273–282 (2012)
11. Cámpora, H., Falduti, A.: Evaluación y tratamiento de las alteraciones de la deglución. Rev. Am. Med. Respiratoria, 98–107 (2012)
12. Mohammadi, H., Samadani, A.A., Steele, C., Chau, T.: Automatic discrimination between cough and non-cough accelerometry signal artefacts. Biomed. Signal Process. Control **52**, 394–402 (2019)
13. Mao, S., Zhang, Z., Khalifa, Y., Donohue, C., Coyle, J.L., Sejdic, E.: Neck sensor-supported hyoid bone movement tracking during swallowing. Roy Soc. Open Sci. **6** (2019)
14. Vaiman, M.: Standardization of surface electromyography utilized to evaluate patients with dysphagia. Head Face Med. **3**, 1–7 (2007)
15. Ertekin, C., Aydogdu, I.: Neurophysiology of swallowing. Clin. Neurophysiol. **114**, 2226–2244 (2003)
16. Roldan-Vasco, S., Restrepo-Agudelo, S., Valencia-Martinez, Y., Orozco-Duque, A.: Automatic detection of oral and pharyngeal phases in swallowing using classification algorithms and multichannel EMG. J. Electromyogr. Kinesiol. **43**, 193–200 (2018)
17. Sebastian, R.V., Estefania, P.G., Andres, O.D.: Scalogram-energy based segmentation of surface electromyography signals from swallowing related muscles (2020)
18. Lee, J., Steele, C.M., Chau, T.: Swallow segmentation with artificial neural networks and multi-sensor fusion. Med. Eng. Phys. **31**, 1049–1055 (2009)

19. Afkari, S., et al.: Measuring frequency of spontaneous swallowing. Australas. Phys. Eng. Sci. Med. **30**, 313–317 (2007)
20. Crary, M.A., Sura, L., Carnaby, G.: Validation and demonstration of an isolated acoustic recording technique to estimate spontaneous swallow frequency. Dysphagia **28**, 86–94 (2013)
21. Sejdić, E., Steele, C.M., Chau, T.: A method for removal of low frequency components associated with head movements from dual-axis swallowing accelerometry signals. PLoS ONE **7**, 1–8 (2012)
22. Dudik, J.M., Kurosu, A., Coyle, J.L., Sejdić, E.: A comparative analysis of DBSCAN, K-means, and quadratic variation algorithms for automatic identification of swallows from swallowing accelerometry signals. Comput. Biol. Med. **59**, 10–18 (2015)
23. Roldan-Vasco, S., Perez-Giraldo, E., Orozco-Duque, A.: Continuous wavelet transform for muscle activity detection in surface EMG signals during swallowing. In: Figueroa-García, J.C., Villegas, J.G., Orozco-Arroyave, J.R., Maya Duque, P.A. (eds.) WEA 2018. CCIS, vol. 916, pp. 245–255. Springer, Cham (2018). https:// doi.org/10.1007/978-3-030-00353-1_22
24. Sejdic, E., Steele, C.M., Chau, T.: Classification of penetration-aspiration versus healthy swallows using dual-axis swallowing accelerometry signals in dysphagic subjects. IEEE Trans. Biomed. Eng. **60**, 1859–1866 (2013)
25. Lazareck, L.J., Moussavi, Z.M.: Classification of normal and dysphagic swallows by acoustical means. IEEE Trans. Biomed. Eng. **51**, 2103–2112 (2004)
26. Hackett, J.K., Shah, M.: Multi-sensor fusion: a perspective, pp. 1324–1330 (1990)
27. Lee, J., Steele, C.M., Chau, T.: Classification of healthy and abnormal swallows based on accelerometry and nasal airflow signals. Artif. Intell. Med. **52**, 17–25 (2011)

Genesis of Atrial Fibrillation Under Different Diffuse Fibrosis Density Related with Atmospheric Pollution. In-Silico Study

Laura C. Palacio[1] (iD), Juan P. Ugarte[2] (iD), Javier Saiz[3] (iD), and Catalina Tobón[1($\boxtimes$)] (iD)

[1] MATBIOM, Universidad de Medellín, Medellín, Colombia
ctobon@udem.edu.co
[2] GIMSC, Universidad de San Buenaventura, Medellín, Colombia
[3] CI2B, Universitat Politècnica de València, Valencia, Spain

Abstract. Atrial remodeling is a widely acknowledged process that accelerates the susceptibility to and progression of atrial fibrillation. An increasingly recognized structural component is atrial fibrosis. Recent studies have shown that air pollution increases the risk of heart arrhythmias, where the exposure to particulate matter (PM) contributes to the generation of myocardial fibrosis, increasing the cardiovascular risk. The density and patterns of fibrosis (interstitial, compact and diffuse) are relevant in abnormal conduction and vulnerability to cardiac arrhythmias. Taking into account that fibrosis has been widely reported as one of the consequences of PM exposure, in this work, we evaluated the effects of low and high diffuse fibrosis density on conduction velocity and arrhythmic propagation patterns. For this purpose, cellular models of atrial myocyte and fibroblast were implemented in a 3D model of the human atria. Low (6.25%) and high (25%) fibrosis densities were simulated in the left atrium and its effect on conduction velocity and fibrillatory dynamics was evaluated. Results showed a conduction velocity reduction of 71% associated with a high fibrosis density. At low fibrosis density, few reentries were observed. On the other hand, at high fibrosis density, irregular propagation patterns, characterized by multiple wavelets and rotors, were observed. Our results suggest that high diffuse fibrosis density is associated with a significant conduction velocity reduction and with chaotic propagation patterns during atrial fibrillation.

Keywords: Fibrosis · Air pollution · Atrial fibrillation · 3D models

1 Introduction

Atrial fibrillation (AF) is the most common sustained clinical arrhythmia [1]. The mechanisms of initiation and maintenance of AF include ectopic foci, multiple reentrant waves [2], and rotors [3]. The AF is characterized by a process of atrial remodeling, that includes electrical and structural alterations contributing to the formation of arrhythmogenic substrates [4, 5]. Recent studies have shown that external factors such as air pollution increases the risk of heart arrhythmias, where the exposure to particulate matter (PM) contributes to adverse remodeling and a worsening of myocardial fibrosis

© Springer Nature Switzerland AG 2020
J. C. Figueroa-García et al. (Eds.): WEA 2020, CCIS 1274, pp. 291–301, 2020.
https://doi.org/10.1007/978-3-030-61834-6_25

[6, 7], increasing the cardiovascular risk [8, 9]. Fibrosis represents excessive deposition of extracellular matrix proteins synthesized by fibroblast [10]. The density and patterns of fibrosis (interstitial, compact and diffuse) are relevant in abnormal conduction and vulnerability to cardiac arrhythmias [11], where the fibrosis extent is a hallmark of arrhythmogenic structural remodeling [5] and the progression of AF [12]. However, the mechanisms by which the type and density of fibrosis affects the conduction and electrical propagation patterns remains unclear.

The importance of the interaction between cardiomyocytes and fibroblasts in atria has been suggested recently. Observations on cultured atrial myocytes from AF patients, suggest that fibroblast proliferation might be an important factor in the worsening and irreversibility of cellular remodeling [13]. Additionally, the differentiation of fibrotic cells at the cellular level [14] and excess deposition of collagen at the tissue level [15], lead to complex interactions in cardiac tissue, setting the stage for AF initiation and maintenance in the fibrotic atria.

Experimentation and clinical studies of the effect of fibroblasts and its distribution on AF dynamics present ethical, complexity, and economic challenges. For this reason, computational modeling supplies a useful tool for integrating multiscale atrial data [16] and exploring the mechanisms underlying AF. In this sense, taking into account that fibrosis has been widely reported in the literature as one of the consequences of exposure to air pollution, we evaluate the effects of low and high fibrosis density on conduction velocity and fibrillatory dynamics. For this purpose, cellular models of atrial myocyte and fibroblast were coupled and implemented in a 3D model of human atria.

2   Methods

2.1   Mathematical Cell Models

The Courtemanche–Ramirez–Nattel [17] mathematical model was used for simulating the electrical behavior of human atrial cardiomyocyte. Cholinergic activity was included in the model by implementing the acetylcholine-dependent current equation developed by Kneller et al. [18]. The resting membrane potential is set to -81.2 mV. To reproduce the electrical remodeling generated by persistent AF, the maximum conductance of several ionic channels was modified differently in the right atrium than in the left atrium, as in a previous work [19] and according to experimental studies [20, 21]: the conductance of the transient outward potassium channel (I_{to}) is reduced by 45% and 75%, and ultrarapid outward channel (I_{Kur}) by 60% and a 45%, in the right and left atrium, respectively. The conductance of the delayed rectifier potassium channel (I_{Ks}) is increased by 150% in the right atrium and by 100% in the left atrium. In both atria, conductance of the inwardly rectifying potassium channel (I_{K1}) is increased by 100% and conductance of the current through the L-type calcium channel (I_{CaL}) is reduced by 65%.

The mathematical model of adult fibroblast proposed by MacCannell et al. [22] was implemented. The resting membrane for this model is -49.6 mV.

2.2   3D Model of Human Atria with Diffuse Fibrosis

A 3D model of human atria developed and validated in previous works was used [19, 23–25]. The model includes the main anatomical structures: left and right atria, pectinate muscles, crista terminalis, left and right atrial appendages, left and right pulmonary veins, superior and inferior caval veins, coronary sinus, Bachmann's bundle, fossa ovalis, tricuspid and mitral valve rings, and isthmus. It also includes realistic fiber orientation, electrophysiological heterogeneity and anisotropy in different regions (see Fig. 1A). The mesh is composed by 515010 hexahedral elements with uniform spatial resolution of 300 μm.

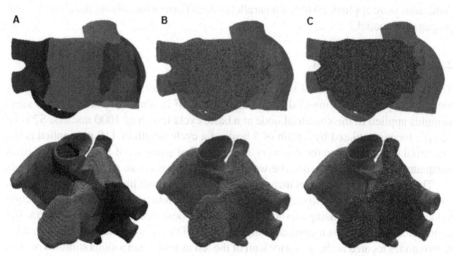

Fig. 1. 3D model of human atria, dorsal view (top) and frontal view (bottom). A) heterogeneous zones are shown with distinct colors. B) fibrosis density of 6.25%. C) fibrosis density of 25% density.

Low and high densities of diffuse fibrosis were incorporated into the 3D model by assigning the fibroblast model instead of the cardiomyocyte model to elements nodes in the left atrium. Based on previous work [26], the conductivity of fibroblasts was assigned to elements containing the fibroblast cell model in at least one of their nodes. The fibrosis densities were defined according to a clinical study [27]. Low fibrosis density (Fig. 1B) and high fibrosis density (Fig. 1C), were simulated assigning the fibroblast model to the 6.25% and 25% of the nodes in the left atrium, respectively. Such configurations correspond to the Utah stage 1 ($\leq$8.5% fibrosis) and Utah stage 4 (>21% fibrosis), respectively [27].

2.3   Model of Electrical Propagation

The electrical propagation in cardiac tissue is described by the monodomain equation as follows:

$$\frac{1}{S_v} \nabla \cdot (D \nabla V_m) = C_m \frac{\partial V_m}{\partial t} + I_{ion} + I_{st} \tag{1}$$

where, V_m is the transmembrane potential for both, cardiomyocytes and fibroblasts; C_m is the membrane capacitance, with values of 100 pF and 6.3 pF for cardiomyocytes and fibroblasts, respectively; I_{ion} is the sum of transmembrane ionic currents, which includes fifteen ionic currents for cardiomyocytes and four currents for fibroblasts; and I_{st} is the external stimulation current and it is only applied in the cardiomyocyte model; S_v is the surface-to-volume ratio and D is the conductivity tensor. The conductivity of fibroblasts was set to 0.078 mS/cm, corresponding to 30% of the cardiomyocytes conductivity, as suggested by [16].

The Eq. (1) was numerically solved using the finite element method implemented in the EMOS software [28], with a constant time step of 0.01 ms. Neumann boundary conditions were applied. EMOS is a parallel code in Fortran for solving the monodomain propagation model.

2.4 Stimulation Protocol

The S1–S2 standard protocol was applied to the 3D model. Each stimulus consists of rectangular pulses of 2 ms in duration and 28 pA/pF in amplitude. The S1 is a sinus stimulus applied to the sinoatrial node at a basic cycle length of 1000 ms. The S2 is an ectopic focus simulated by a train of 5 beats at a cycle length of 110 ms applied at the interatrial septum near to the coronary sinus. The first stimulus of S2 was applied to an adequate coupling interval (time between S1 and S2) to generate a unidirectional block.

The performed simulations include an AF episode without fibrosis, AF episodes with low and high fibrosis density. All simulations were conducted for 5 s. The conduction velocity was measured using two nodes located at the posterior wall of the left atrium. The conduction velocity was measured using the times of the action potential depolarization in two nodes located at the posterior wall of the left atrium when a sinus stimulus occurs.

3 Results

3.1 Effect of Fibrosis on Conduction Velocity

In the episode of simulated AF without fibrosis, the estimated conduction velocity in the posterior wall of left atrium was 62 cm/s. The conduction velocity for low and high fibrosis densities were 33 cm/s and 18 cm/s, respectively. These values correspond to reductions of 47% and 71%, respectively, with respect to AF without fibrosis. Therefore, a conduction velocity reduction of 45.5% is observed as the fibrosis density increases from 6.25% to 25%. The Table 1 summarizes the conduction velocity results.

3.2 Effect of Fibrosis Densities on Fibrillatory Dynamics

In the simulated AF episode without fibrosis, the S1–S2 protocol triggered the generation of two quasi-stable rotors (at ≈600 ms), one at the junction between the superior vena cava and the Bachmann bundle, and other between the superior vena cava and the posterior wall of the right atrium (Fig. 2A). Wavefront collisions were observed in the posterior wall of both atria. At ≈3500 ms, collisions were also observed in the superior wall of the left atrium, and a reentry was generated in the left appendage.

Table 1. Effect of fibrosis density on conduction velocity (CV).

Fibrosis density (%)	CV (cm/s)	CV reduction (%)
0%	62	–
6.25%	33	47%
25%	18	71%

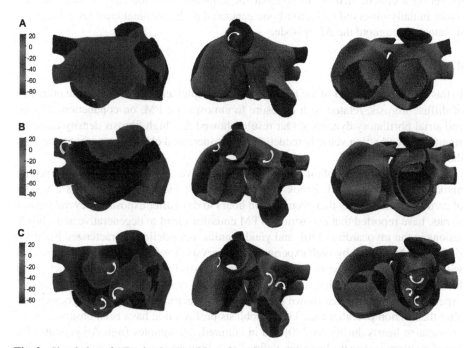

Fig. 2. Simulation of AF episodes A) without fibrosis and with B) low (6.25%) and C) high (25%) fibrosis density. The white arrows indicate reentry rotation direction.

In the simulated AF episode with low fibrosis density (6.25%), the quasi-stable rotors were observed at the junction between the superior vena cava and the Bachmann bundle, and between the superior vena cava and the posterior wall of the right atrium. Wavefront collisions also were observed in the posterior wall off both atria. However, additional reentrant activity was observed from the third second (Fig. 2B). At ≈3400 ms a rotor was generated in the superior wall of the left atrium, anchoring at the base of the left pulmonary vein. At the end of the simulation (at ≈4000 ms), a figure-of-eight reentry was observed in the base of the left pulmonary veins, colliding with a rotor generated in the base of the left appendage. At the end of the simulation (at ≈4000 ms), the two initially observed rotors remained at the right atrium, however, the rotor located at the junction between the superior vena cava and the Bachmann bundle migrated towards the terminal crest.

In the simulated AF episode with high fibrosis density (25%), a increased irregularity in the propagation patterns were observed. Initially, the same quasi-stable rotors were observed at the junction between the superior vena cava and the Bachmann bundle, and between the superior vena cava and the posterior wall of the right atrium. Wavefront collisions also were observed in the posterior wall off both atria. However, increased reentrant activity was observed from the third second. Wave fragmentations, collisions, rotors and figure-of-eight reentries were observed in the posterior and superior walls of the left atrium (Fig. 2C). The multiple reentrant waves collided with each other, triggering a chaotic activity throughout the simulation. In the right atrium, the two rotors initially observed and a third one generated at the terminal crest (at ≈3500 ms) remained throughout the AF episode.

4 Discussion

In this study, a 3D model of the human atria was implemented to evaluate the influence of diffuse fibrosis, related with exposure to atmospheric PM, on conduction velocity and atrial fibrillatory dynamics. Our results showed that high fibrosis density caused a significant conduction velocity reduction and an increased chaotic propagation patterns during AF.

Exposure to air pollution can contribute to adverse remodeling and worsening myocardial fibrosis [6, 7]. Brook et al. [29] suggest that PM inhalation is a trigger of cardiovascular events that occur within hours to days after exposure. Several studies in rats, have reported that exposition to PM emissions lead to degenerative and fibrotic lesions in the myocardium [30], and yields cardiac remodeling characterized by fibrosis [9, 31]. Motivated by such experimental observations of a cardiac condition related with air pollutants, this work simulates cardiac fibrosis by coupling cardiomyocyte and fibroblast models in the left atrium under a diffuse type distribution. Several animal experimental models have shown that fibroblasts electrically couple to myocytes and alter their action potential [32, 33]. Fibroblasts proliferation have been observed in in-vivo canine hearts during AF [10] and in cultured cell samples from AF patients [13, 34]. The fibrosis density has been defined as a biomarker to assess patients with AF [27]. Patients are staged in four categories according to the percentage of fibrosis quantified with magnetic resonance, relative to the left atrium volume, as follows: minimal or Utah stage I (<8.5%), mild or Utah stage II (8.6%–16%), moderate or Utah stage III (16.1%–21%), and extensive or Utah stage IV (>21.1%). In our work, the simulated low (6.25%) and high (25%) fibrosis density percentages correspond to values within the Utah stage I and IV, respectively. Therefore, the implemented model of fibrosis accounts for experimentally and clinically observed features during the AF remodeling process.

Structural remodeling of the atrial tissue contributes to the reduction of the conduction velocity, which is an important factor for establishing reentrant activity or conduction block [35]. Our results show that, as fibrosis density increase, the conduction velocity decrease. Zhan et al. [36] reported that fibroblasts can alter the conduction velocity with fibrosis densities of 40 and 45%, while our simulations showed that a density of 25% lead to a 71% conduction velocity reduction. These outcomes are in agreement with several experimental and simulation studies that found that fibroblasts can establish an electric coupling with myocytes leading to reduced conduction velocity [37–39].

Our simulated AF episodes suggests a close relationship between the reduced conduction, caused by a fibrosis density increase, with the augmented re-entrant and chaotic propagation. This behavior agrees with experimental and in silico studies, where decreased conduction velocity is associated with an increased risk of reentrant activity, leading to the establishment of AF [39, 40]. Fibroblast proliferation has also been observed in human atria in regions with altered conduction velocity [41], which can trigger AF by generating re-entrant activity [42]. Furthermore, our results indicate few reentries at low fibrosis density, while multiple reentrant waves at high fibrosis density. Such results are in agreement with reports of diffuse fibrosis leading to short-duration rotors at low fibrosis levels and multiple long-term reentrant waves at high fibrosis levels [39]. Additionally, our results evinced more irregular and chaotic fibrillatory dynamic in left atrium than right atrium, where quasi-stable rotors in right atrium were observed in all simulated AF episodes, and few reentries in left atrium at low fibrosis density. However, multiple waves reentries leading a chaotic AF dynamic were observed in left atrium at high fibrosis density. This is consistent with studies that have demonstrated the role of left atrial fibrosis in the genesis of AF [43, 44].

Computational simulations have become a powerful tool for studying the role that fibroblasts play in the AF [45, 46], and offer the possibility of studying how fibroblasts can change arrhythmia dynamics by reducing conduction velocity and introducing heterogeneities in the atrial substrate. Our findings, could serve as a scientific reference for the management of public policies aimed at mitigating the impacts of air pollution and, on the other hand, they could contribute to a better understanding of the role that diffuse fibrosis play at different densities in the fibrillatory dynamics, which could have implications in the development of atrial-selective therapeutic approaches. By means of simulation it is possible to suggest areas that can be ablated, in order to prevent the reentrant circuits that cause the arrhythmia.

4.1 Limitations

Variability between patients is a common clinical problem when diagnosing atrial arrhythmias, however, due to the high complexity that this entails, the simulated fibrosis distributions do not correspond to a reconstruction from patient-specific images. Our simulation results were obtained using a specific virtual atria model, albeit it includes a great number of anatomical and morphological details such as electrophysiology, anatomy, fiber direction, anisotropy and heterogeneity.

5 Conclusions

The results of our simulation study show that diffuse fibrosis, as an abnormal event related with exposure to atmospheric PM, reduces the conduction velocity and increase the re-entrant fibrillatory dynamics as fibrosis density increase.

Atrial myocyte and fibroblast coupling in a 3D model of the human atria, creates a substrate in which the dynamics of AF changes with the fibrosis density. By increasing the density of fibroblasts from low (6.25%) to high (25%), a significant conduction velocity reduction and multiple waves reentries leading a chaotic AF dynamic were observed in left atrium. These results and further in-silico studies can help to elucidate the mechanisms underlying fibrosis are required to develop therapies successful that ultimately translate to positive clinical outcomes for patients.

Acknowledges. This work was supported by Ministerio de Ciencia Tecnología e Innovación (Minciencias) from Colombia through grant No. 120677757994, and by the Dirección General de Política Científica de la Generalitat Valenciana PROMETEO/2020/043.

References

1. Nattel, S., Harada, M.: Atrial remodeling and atrial fibrillation: Recent advances and translational perspectives. J. Am. Coll. Cardiol. **63**, 2335–2345 (2014)
2. Kottkamp, H.: Human atrial fibrillation substrate: towards a specific fibrotic atrial cardiomyopathy. Eur. Heart J. **34**, 2731–2738 (2013)
3. Jalife, J.: Mother rotors and fibrillatory conduction: a mechanism of atrial fibrillation. Cardiovasc. Res. **54**, 204–216 (2002). https://doi.org/10.1016/S0008-6363(02)00223-7
4. Wijffels, M.C., Kirchhof, C.J., Dorland, R., Allessie, M.A.: Atrial fibrillation begets atrial fibrillation. A study in awake chronically instrumented goats. Circulation **92**, 1954–1968 (1995)
5. Allessie, M., Ausma, J., Schotten, U.: Electrical, contractile and structural remodeling during atrial fibrillation. Cardiovasc. Res. **54**, 230–246 (2002)
6. Newby, D.E., Mannucci, P.M., Tell, G.S., Baccarelli, A.A., Brook, R.D., Donaldson, K., Forastiere, F., Franchini, M., Franco, O.H., Graham, I., Hoek, G., Hoffmann, B., Hoylaerts, M.F., Künzli, N., Mills, N., Pekkanen, J., Peters, A., Piepoli, M.F., Rajagopalan, S., Storey, R.F.: ESC working group on thrombosis, european association for cardiovascular prevention and rehabilitation, ESC heart failure association: expert position paper on air pollution and cardiovascular disease. Eur. Heart J. **36**, 83–93b (2015)
7. Liu, Y., Goodson, J.M., Zhang, B., Chin, M.T.: Air pollution and adverse cardiac remodeling: clinical effects and basic mechanisms. Front. Physiol. **6**, 162 (2015)
8. Brook, R.D., Rajagopalan, S., Pope, C.A., Brook, J.R., Bhatnagar, A., Diez-Roux, A.V., Holguin, F., Hong, Y., Luepker, R.V., Mittleman, M.A., Peters, A., Siscovick, D., Smith, S.C., Whitsel, L., Kaufman, J.D.: Particulate matter air pollution and cardiovascular disease. Circulation **121**, 2331–2378 (2010)
9. de Oliveira-Fonoff, A.M., Mady, C., Pessoa, F.G., Fonseca, K.C.B., Salemi, V.M.C., Fernandes, F., Saldiva, P.H.N., Ramires, F.J.A.: The role of air pollution in myocardial remodeling. PLoS ONE **12**, e0176084 (2017)
10. Burstein, B., Qi, X.Y., Yeh, Y.H., Calderone, A., Nattel, S.: Atrial cardiomyocyte tachycardia alters cardiac fibroblast function: A novel consideration in atrial remodeling. Cardiovasc. Res. **76**, 442–452 (2007)
11. De Jong, S., Van Veen, T.A.B., Van Rijen, H.V.M., De Bakker, J.M.T.: Fibrosis and Cardiac Arrhythmias. J. Cardiovasc. Pharmacol. **57**, 630–638 (2011)
12. Akoum, N., Daccarett, M., McGann, C., Segerson, N., Vergara, G., Kuppahally, S., Badger, T., Burgon, N., Haslam, T., Kholmovski, E., Macleod, R., Marrouche, N.: Atrial fibrosis helps select the appropriate patient and strategy in catheter ablation of atrial fibrillation: a DE-MRI guided approach. J. Cardiovasc. Electrophysiol. **22**, 16–22 (2011)
13. Rücker-Martin, C., Pecker, F., Godreau, D., Hatem, S.N.: Dedifferentiation of atrial myocytes during atrial fibrillation: role of fibroblast proliferation in vitro. Cardiovasc. Res. **55**, 38–52 (2002)

14. Rohr, S.: Myofibroblasts in diseased hearts: New players in cardiac arrhythmias? Hear. Rhythm. **6**, 848–856 (2009)
15. Xu, J., Cui, G., Esmailian, F., Plunkett, M., Marelli, D., Ardehali, A., Odim, J., Laks, H., Sen, L.: Atrial extracellular matrix remodeling and the maintenance of atrial fibrillation. Circulation **109**, 363–368 (2004)
16. Zahid, S., Cochet, H., Boyle, P.M., Schwarz, E.L., Whyte, K.N., Vigmond, E.J., Jaı, P., Trayanova, N.A., Haı, M.: Patient-derived models link re-entrant driver localization in atrial fibrillation to fibrosis spatial pattern. Cardiovasc. Res. **110**(3), 443–454 (2016)
17. Courtemanche, M., Ramirez, R.J., Nattel, S.: Ionic mechanisms underlying human atrial action potential properties: insights from a mathematical model Ionic mechanisms underlying human atrial action potential properties: insights from a mathematical model. Am. J. Physiol. -heart Circ. Physiol. **275**, H301–H321 (1998)
18. Kneller, J., Zou, R., Vigmond, E.J., Wang, Z., Leon, L.J., Nattel, S.: Cholinergic atrial fibrillation in a computer model of a two-dimensional sheet of canine atrial cells with realistic ionic properties. Circ. Res. **90**, E73–E87 (2002)
19. Ferrer, A., Sebastián, R., Sánchez-quintana, D., Rodríguez, J.F.: Detailed anatomical and electrophysiological models of human atria and torso for the simulation of atrial activation. PloS One **10**(11), 1–29 (2015)
20. Van Wagoner, D.R., Pond, A.L., Lamorgese, M., Rossie, S.S., McCarthy, P.M., Nerbonne, J.M.: Atrial L-type Ca2+currents and human atrial fibrillation. Circ. Res. **85**, 428–436 (1999)
21. Caballero, R., de la Fuente, M.G., Gómez, R., Barana, A., Amorós, I., Dolz-Gaitón, P., Osuna, L., Almendral, J., Atienza, F., Fernández-Avilés, F., Pita, A., Rodríguez-Roda, J., Pinto, Á., Tamargo, J., Delpón, E.: In humans, chronic atrial fibrillation decreases the transient outward current and ultrarapid component of the delayed rectifier current differentially on each atria and increases the slow component of the delayed rectifier current in both. J. Am. Coll. Cardiol. **55**, 2346–2354 (2010)
22. Maccannell, K.A., Bazzazi, H., Chilton, L., Shibukawa, Y., Clark, R.B., Giles, W.R.: A mathematical model of electrotonic interactions between ventricular myocytes and fibroblasts. Biophys. J. **92**(11), 4121–4132 (2007)
23. Tobón, C., Ruiz-Villa, C., Heidenreich, E., Romero, L., Hornero, F., Saiz, J.: A three-dimensional human atrial model with fiber orientation electrograms and arrhythmic activation patterns relationship. PLoS One **8**, e50883 (2013)
24. Godoy, E.J., Lozano, M., García-Fernández, I., Ferrer-Albero, A., MacLeod, R., Saiz, J., Sebastian, R.: Atrial fibrosis hampers non-invasive localization of atrial ectopic foci from multi-electrode signals: a 3D simulation study. Front. Physiol. **9**, 404 (2018)
25. Martinez-Mateu, L., Romero, L., Ferrer-Albero, A., Sebastian, R., Rodríguez Matas, J.F., Jalife, J., Berenfeld, O., Saiz, J.: Factors affecting basket catheter detection of real and phantom rotors in the atria: a computational study. PLoS Comput. Biol. **14**, e1006017 (2018)
26. Gomez, J.F., Cardona, K., Martinez, L., Saiz, J., Trenor, B.: Electrophysiological and structural remodeling in heart failure modulate arrhythmogenesis. 2D simulation study. PLOS ONE. **9**, 1–12 (2014)
27. Daccarett, M., Badger, T.J., Akoum, N., Burgon, N.S., Mahnkopf, C., Vergara, G., Kholmovski, E., McGann, C.J., Parker, D., Brachmann, J., Macleod, R.S., Marrouche, N.F.: Association of left atrial fibrosis detected by delayed-enhancement magnetic resonance imaging and the risk of stroke in patients with atrial fibrillation. J. Am. Coll. Cardiol. **57**, 831–838 (2011)
28. Heidenreich, E.A., Ferrero, J.M., Doblaré, M., Rodríguez, J.F.: Adaptive macro finite elements for the numerical solution of monodomain equations in cardiac electrophysiology. Ann. Biomed. Eng. **38**, 2331–2345 (2010)

29. Brook, R.D., Rajagopalan, S., Pope, C.A., Brook, J.R., Bhatnagar, A., Diez-Roux, A.V., Holguin, F., Hong, Y., Luepker, R.V., Mittleman, M.A., Peters, A., Siscovick, D., Smith, S.C., Whitsel, L., Kaufman, J.D.: Particulate matter air pollution and cardiovascular disease. Circulation 121, 2331–2378 (2010)

30. Wold, L.E., Ying, Z., Hutchinson, K.R., Velten, M., Gorr, M.W., Velten, C., Youtz, D.J., Wang, A., Lucchesi, P.A., Sun, Q., Rajagopalan, S.: Cardiovascular remodeling in response to long-term exposure to fine particulate matter air pollution. Circ. Heart Fail. 5, 452–461 (2012)

31. Chen, T.-L., Liao, J.-W., Chan, W.-H., Hsu, C.-Y., Yang, J.-D., Ueng, T.-H.: Induction of cardiac fibrosis and transforming growth factor-β1 by motorcycle exhaust in rats. Inhal. Toxicol. 25, 525–535 (2013)

32. Gaudesius, G., Miragoli, M., Thomas, S.P., Rohr, S.: Coupling of cardiac electrical activity over extended distances by fibroblasts of cardiac origin. Circ. Res. 93, 421–428 (2003)

33. Burstein, B., Nattel, S.: Atrial fibrosis: mechanisms and clinical relevance in atrial fibrillation. J. Am. Coll. Cardiol. 51, 802–809 (2008)

34. Poulet, C., Künzel, S., Büttner, E., Lindner, D., Westermann, D., Ravens, U.: Altered physiological functions and ion currents in atrial fibroblasts from patients with chronic atrial fibrillation. Physiol. Rep. 4, e12681 (2016)

35. Camelliti, P., Borg, T.K., Kohl, P.: Structural and functional characterisation of cardiac fibroblasts (2005). https://pubmed.ncbi.nlm.nih.gov/15621032/

36. Zhan, H.Q., Xia, L., Shou, G.F., Zang, Y.L., Liu, F., Crozier, S.: Fibroblast proliferation alters cardiac excitation conduction and contraction: a computational study. J. Zhejiang Univ. Sci. B. 15, 225–242 (2014)

37. Maleckar, M.M., Greenstein, J.L., Giles, W.R., Trayanova, N.A.: Electrotonic coupling between human atrial myocytes and fibroblasts alters myocyte excitability and repolarization. Biophys. J. 97, 2179–2190 (2009)

38. Xie, Y., Garfinkel, A., Camelliti, P., Kohl, P., Weiss, J.N., Qu, Z.: Effects of fibroblast-myocyte coupling on cardiac conduction and vulnerability to reentry: a computational study. Hear. Rhythm. 6, 1641–1649 (2009)

39. Morgan, R., Colman, M.A., Chubb, H., Seemann, G., Aslanidi, O.V.: Slow conduction in the border zones of patchy fibrosis stabilizes the drivers for atrial fibrillation: insights from multi-scale human atrial modeling. Front. Physiol. 7, 1–15 (2016)

40. King, J.H., Huang, C.L.-H., Fraser, J.A.: Determinants of myocardial conduction velocity: implications for arrhythmogenesis. Front. Physiol. 4, 154 (2013)

41. Krul, S.P.J., Berger, W.R., Smit, N.W., Van Amersfoorth, S.C.M., Driessen, A.H.G., Van Boven, W.J., Fiolet, J.W.T., Van Ginneken, A.C.G., Van Der Wal, A.C., De Bakker, J.M.T., Coronel, R., De Groot, J.R.: Atrial fibrosis and conduction slowing in the left atrial appendage of patients undergoing thoracoscopic surgical pulmonary vein isolation for atrial fibrillation. Circ. Arrhythmia Electrophysiol. 8, 288–295 (2015)

42. Haissaguerre, M., Shah, A.J., Cochet, H., Hocini, M., Dubois, R., Efimov, I., Vigmond, E., Bernus, O., Trayanova, N.: Intermittent drivers anchoring to structural heterogeneities as a major pathophysiological mechanism of human persistent atrial fibrillation. J. Physiol. 594, 2387–2398 (2016)

43. Xiao, H.D., Fuchs, S., Campbell, D.J., Lewis, W., Dudley, S.C., Kasi, V.S., Hoit, B.D., Keshelava, G., Zhao, H., Capecchi, M.R., Bernstein, K.E., Bernstein, K.E.: Mice with cardiac-restricted angiotensin-converting enzyme (ACE) have atrial enlargement, cardiac arrhythmia, and sudden death. Am. J. Pathol. 165, 1019–1032 (2004)

44. Anyukhovsky, E., Sosunov, E.A., Plotnikov, A., Gainullin, R.Z., Jhang, J.S., Marboe, C.C., Rosen, M.R.: Cellular electrophysiologic properties of old canine atria provide a substrate for arrhythmogenesis. Cardiovasc. Res. 54, 462–469 (2002)

45. Tanaka, K., Zlochiver, S., Vikstrom, K.L., Yamazaki, M., Moreno, J., Klos, M., Zaitsev, A.V., Vaidyanathan, R., Auerbach, D.S., Landas, S., Guiraudon, G., Jalife, J., Berenfeld, O., Kalifa, J.: Spatial distribution of fibrosis governs fibrillation wave dynamics in the posterior left atrium during heart failure. Circ. Res. **101**, 839–847 (2007)

46. Saha, M., Roney, C.H., Bayer, J.D., Meo, M., Cochet, H., Dubois, R., Vigmond, E.J.: Wavelength and fibrosis affect phase singularity locations during atrial fibrillation. Front, Physiol (2018)

Characterizing ResNet Filters to Identify Positive and Negative Findings in Breast MRI Sequences

Diana M. Marín-Castrillón[1], Kevin Osorno-Castillo[1], Liliana M. Hernández[2],
Andrés E. Castro-Ospina[1], and Gloria M. Díaz[1(✉)]

[1] Instituto Tecnológico Metropolitano, Medellín, Colombia
{dianamarin121064,kevinosorno220486}@correo.itm.edu.co,
{andrescastro,gloriadiaz}@itm.edu.co
[2] Grupo de Investigación del Instituto de Alta Tecnología Médica (IATM),
Ayudas Diagnósticas Sura, Medellín, Colombia
mlhernandezp@sura.com.co

Abstract. Training of deep learning models requires large and properly labeled datasets, which make unfeasible using it for developing computer-aided diagnosis systems in medical imaging. As an alternative, transfer learning has shown to be useful to extract deep features using architectures previously trained. In this paper, a new method for classification of breast lesions in magnetic resonance imaging is proposed, which uses the pre-trained ResNet-50 architecture for extracting a set of image features that are then used by an SVM model for differentiating between positive and negative findings. We take advantage of the ResNet-50 architecture for introducing volumetric lesion information by including three consecutive slices per lesion. Filters used as feature descriptors were selected using a multiple kernel learning method, which allows identifying those filters that provide the most relevant information for the classification task. Additionally, instead of using raw filters as features, we propose to characterize it using statistical moments, which improves the classification performance. The evaluation was conducted using a set of 146 ROIs extracted from three sequences proposed for designing abbreviated breast MRI protocols (DCE, ADC, and T2-Vista). Positive findings were identified with an AUC of 82.4 using a DCE image, and 81.08 fusing features from the three sequences.

Keywords: Breast cancer · Transfer learning · Deep feature selection · Multiple kernel learning · ResNet

1 Introduction

Breast cancer is the leading cause of death from cancer among women around the world. In 2018, the World Health Organization (WHO) reported more than

This work was supported by MINCIENCIAS, Instituto Tecnológico Metropolitano and Ayudas Diagnósticas Sura (RC740-2017 Project).

2 million of new cases and 626,679 deaths from this disease [12]. The best strategy to improve the prognosis of this disease is the early detection, by which mammography screening is highly implemented in most countries [11]. However, mammography can fail in the detection of breast cancer in specific cases such as dense breasts and young women, reason for which the use of another image modalities has been suggested. From them, Magnetic Resonance Imaging (MRI) is one of the most sensitivity methods but its high-cost avoids its implementation as a screening method even in the moderate-risk population. High costs are associated to the acquisition and interpretation of a large set of image sequences, i.e., a full breast MRI protocol is composed at least of an Axial T1, an Axial T2, a STIR image, a DWI (Diffusion Weighted Image), six Dynamic Contrast Enhanced (DCE) images, and some post-processed generated sequences: ADC (Apparent diffusion coefficient) and six substracted images. Thus, the use of abbreviated MRI protocols, using only a few of them, has been evaluated as an reliable alternative [8].

Reducing diagnostic information could increase the uncertainty in the radiologist's interpretation, so computational methods that support the diagnosis decision have been developed for improving the sensitivity and reproducibility of this type of studies. Feature estimation, selection or extraction is the most challenging task for developing those systems, since there are lots of image descriptors and algorithms to perform these process according to the prior knowledge of the specific problem. Recently, deep Convolutional Neural Networks (CNN) have dealt with this issue thanks to their end-to-end workflow, which allows getting features automatically from the input data through multiple filters used in the convolutional layers. These features are used later in the classification process realized in the last CNN layers. By exploiting the ability of CNNs to estimate features automatically from 2D and 3D images, some works have been focused on using deep features in computer assisted diagnostic systems aiming to avoid hand-crafted feature engineering [10]. However, because deep learning methods require a lot of labeled data for training models, transfer learning has emerged as an alternative strategy, in which a pre-trained network can be used for extracting feature vectors that are then used for training conventional learning models such as Support Vector Machines (SVM), among others.

Antropova et al. [1] used 4096 features extracted by a pre-trained convNet network to train an SVM, which must distinguish between benign and malignant breast lesions from Regions Of Interest (ROI) at the second post-contrast of a DCE-MRI slice. Marrone et al. [9] investigated the fine-tuning of a pre-trained AlexNet and the complete training from scratch of the same ConvNet. In this case, all slices containing the lesion were independently classified, and final lesion class was decided by a voting strategy. In a similar way, features extracted from a pre-trained VGGNet were used for training SVMs to classify lesions as malignant or benign using maximum intensity projection images, an image resulting from post-processing the DCE images [2]. Other image modalities have been less used for this purpose, even when they are used by the specialist interpretation process. In [7], a pre-trained VGG19 network was used for characterizing and classifying breast lesions from diffusion-weighted images (DWI).

In this work, we propose a deep learning based strategy for aiding radiologists to differentiate between positive and negative findings in three selected MRI sequences, i.e., Axial T2, Second substracted post-contrast image, and the ADC map, which has been proposed as relevant to designing abbreviated protocols [8]. Thus, we aim to evaluate how a transfer learning based CAD system can support the detection of positive breast cancer-related lesions, using a single image sequence and a fusion of them.

2   Materials and Methods

Figure 1 illustrates the general components of the proposed approach. A pretrained ResNet50 network was used for generating a feature vector describing each region to be classified as was proposed in [6], that is to say, breast MRI Volumes of Interest (VOIs) were passed through this architecture with pre-trained weights in ImageNet. Since ResNet expected input is a 3-channel image, we input images corresponding to three contiguous slices that contain a VOI selected by the radiologist, which allows to taking advantage of volumetric information of MRI. Outputs from the convolutional layer were herein used; however, instead of to vectorize the 2D filters, we characterize it using the five statistic moments to reduce the dimension of the feature vector. Additionally, because a challenge in the use of pre-trained deep networks is the selection of the convolutional filters that will be used for characterizing the input image data, we use the multiple kernel method, as proposed in [3,4]. This method allows founding the most relevant information sources in a binary classification problem when it is solved using a set of kernel methods, in this case, the most relevant filters. Once filters are selected and feature vectors are generated, the last ones are used for training a classification model that discriminate between positive and negative lesions. We investigated the classification performance of two learning models, a classical SVM using a radial base function as kernel, and a Multiple Kernel Learning model.

2.1   Deep Feature Extraction

In the field of computer vision, many deep CNN architectures have been well trained for classifying a large number of objects. This models are publicly available and can be used as pre-trained models in other classification tasks, such as medical applications [13]. Therefore, aiming to get deep features from findings in breast MRI, we did transfer learning using a widely known CNN architecture to classify objects in RGB images, named ResNet-50 [6]. This architecture reported a very good performance in the original classification task but additionally requires a small number of operations in the forward process, in comparison with other CNN models trained to perform the same classification task [5].

Taking into account that ResNet was designed to receive as inputs 224×224 pixel RGB images and that MRI sequences are really image volumes, the ROI marked by radiologists were resized and used as a central slice from which were

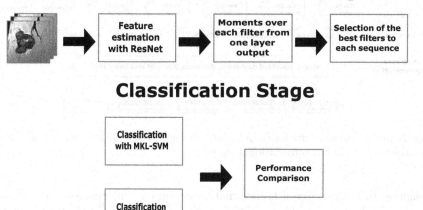

Fig. 1. Workflow of the proposed method to classify malign and benign findings in breast MRI

extracted regions in the same location but one slice after and one slice before. Thus, image volumes of size $224 \times 224 \times 3$ were input to the network. To get deep features from ResNet, all the findings in each sequence were passed through the network and features from five different blocks were taken. Figure 2 shows the architecture of the model and the size of each output considered for the analysis, which is determined by the number of filters. Specifically, we took features coming from convolutional layers through ResNet50 with 64, 256, 512, 1024 or 2048 filters, aiming to consider multiples representations levels. Therefore, ROIs can be initially represented by feature vectors resulting by vectorizing each group filter response, i.e., $56 \times 56 \times 64 = 200704$ which falls in a "curse of dimensionality" problem. Even more, the use of only one of those filters generates a vector with 3136 features, which is also large for the amount of training data. Thus, the feature vector dimension was reduced by the computation of five statistical moments (mean, standard deviation, variance, kurtosis, and skewness) over features coming from the filters of each block, obtaining a more compact representation as it is depicted in the Fig. 2.

2.2 Filter Selection

Once feature vectors were computed, filters that gives the best representation of findings were selected using an algorithm proposed as a feature group selector in [4], which uses Multiple Kernel Learning (MKL) for computing the relevance of each group of features for the classification task. In this algorithm, MKL allows to integrate information from multiples sources by a kernel-based similarity measure made between all data for each source independently, which implies

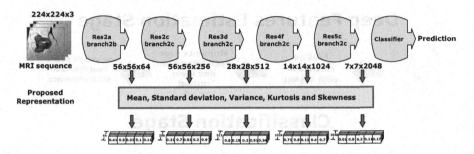

Fig. 2. ResNet architecture for deep feature estimation using first-order moments computation from filters at convolutional layers

assigning to each source a kernel that represents its information. In our case, we treat each feature group coming from every filter in the convolutional layers as a source during filters selection and Gaussian kernels were used to represent information from them, Eq. (1).

$$K(x_i, x_j) = \exp\left(\frac{-\|x_i - x_j\|_2^2}{\sigma^2}\right), \quad \sigma > 0 \tag{1}$$

where x_i and x_j are samples (ROI in the database) for $i, j \in 1, \ldots, N$ and σ is the kernel bandwidth.

The capacity of this method to represent information from multiples sources can be exploited by kernel-based classification algorithms as the Support Vector Machines (SVM) since the kernel function is fundamental to its performance and it can be implemented as a linear or no linear combination of multiple kernels as is shown in the Eq. (2).

$$K_\eta(x_i, x_j) = \sum_{m=1}^{P} \eta_m K_m(x_i^m, x_j^m) \tag{2}$$

where P is the number of information sources, features from each filter in a convolutional layer for our case.

As can be seen in Eq. (2), a weight η is related to each kernel, therefore it is also directly related to each filter or source. These weights are in the Δ domain shown in Eq. (3), and they are penalized in training taking values equal or near to zero when the filter relevance is low [14].

$$\Delta = \left\{ \eta \in \mathbb{R}_+^P : \sum_{j=1}^{P} \eta_j = 1, \ \eta_j \geq 0 \right\} \tag{3}$$

2.3 ROIs Classification

Feature vectors with the statistical moments from every selected filter were used to train learning models for classifying ROIs as positive or negative findings.

Two learning models that integrate information from the different filters were investigated in this work. The first classification approach was carried out using MKL as a classifier, aiming to represent information from all relevant filters for each sequence and integrate these sequences assigning a kernel to each one during the classification task. In the second model, a conventional SVM was used to classify positive and negative findings, concatenating features coming from all the relevant filters. The σ values assigned to each kernel and the C parameter of the SVMs were optimized using PSO, which is a metaheuristic algorithm that uses cooperative and stochastic methods to find the optimum working point of the function to be optimized, in this case, the performance measure of the SVM given by the geometric mean.

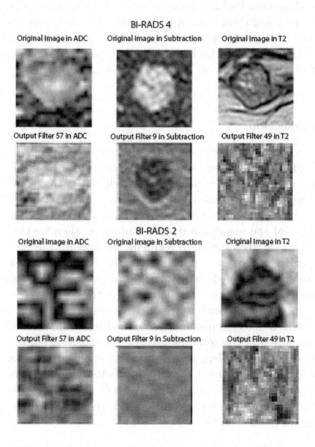

Fig. 3. Sample BI-RADS 4. Top row: Original Images in the three sequences. Bottom row: Output features from filter selected as the most relevant for each sequence.

3 Experimental Results

3.1 Database

A dataset with 146 VOIs was built during the diagnosis process carried out in 88 retrospective breast MRI studies by two experienced radiologists from Instituto de Alta Tecnología Médica de Medellín. Findings were marked by specialists with a box enclosing the mass on the center slice of the sequence in which each finding looks better, used sequences included ADC, T2-Vista, and Subtraction of T1 pre-contrast with T1 post-contrast after 2 min. Furthermore, to get each finding in every sequence, the bounding box containing the original marked ROI was projected to the other sequences using Horos software (https://horosproject. org/). During diagnosis, findings were categorized taking into account the Breast Imaging Reporting and Data System (BI-RADS). For this application, BI-RADS categorizations were grouped into two classes, where a class named negative findings has 61 ROIs categorized as BI-RADS one or two, and the other one, named positive findings, has 85 ROIS categorized as BI-RADS three, four or five.

3.2 Filter Selection

Filter selection was carried out on both filter representations, i.e., vectorized full filter and statistical moments based representations. Figure 4 shows performances given by the selection process. On the left side of the figure, which shows results from the statistical moments representation, it can be noted that if we add more than a certain amount of filters sorted from highest to lowest by relevance, the performance of the algorithm does not improve, then we can take just the first four, five and sixteen filters to estimate features on the ADC subtraction and T2, respectively. However, results from the full vectorized representation (right side) was not stable, whereby we could not set a specific number of filters as relevant for the classification task. Observing these results, we can say that information representation with statistical moments from each output's layer allows us to make a better representation of features from each filter, reducing, in turn, the number of deep features used in the classification stage and avoiding the dimensionality problem given by the relationship between the number of samples and features. Table 1 shows filters selected as relevant to represent positive an negative findings in each MRI sequence using the statistical moments representation and Fig. 3 shows outputs from kernels selected as most relevant for each sequence in one sample.

3.3 ROIs Classification

Selected filters, represented by the computed statistical moments, were used as inputs for training and evaluating the classification models. Two classification models were trained for each image sequence, i.e., an SVM and an MKL-SVM models. Additionally, in order to evaluate the effect of combining all image

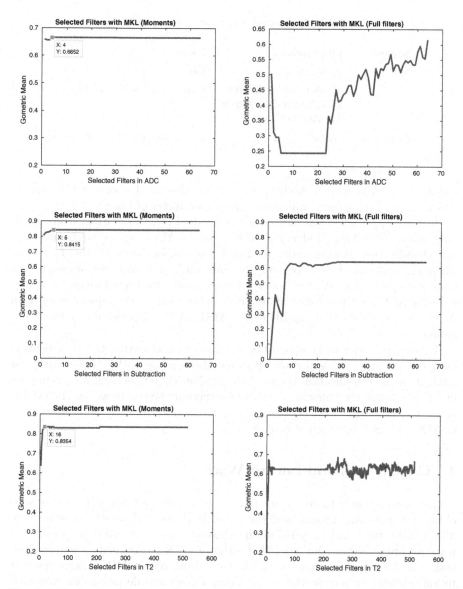

Fig. 4. Filters selection for each sequence using first-order moments and full data representations

sequences, two other algorithms were trained. In the first one, the features coming from the selected filters to each sequence were concatenated independently, considering each resultant array as an information source for the MKL-SVM model. In the second one, all features coming from all the relevant filters in all sequences were concatenated in an unique feature vector, which was used for

Table 1. Selected filters for each sequence

Sequence	Filter indices	Layer
ADC	22-30-44-57	Conv. Layer with 64 filters
T2	49-66-146-148-150-160 185-189-216-222-240-287 314-331-383-426	Conv. Layer with 512 filters
Subtraction	9-24-37-39-41	Conv. Layer with 64 filters

training the SVM model. Additionally as was described above, a PSO model was used for setting the σ values and the C parameter of the SVMs.

In both approaches was carried out a five-fold cross-validation, using stratified folds. The Area Under the ROC Curve (AUC) was used to measure the classification performance. In Fig. 5 the performance of the two classification approaches is reported. To this end, the best performance was obtained using MKL-SVM classifier for the second substracted image sequence, with an $AUC = 82.4\%$, followed by the combination of all sequences with an $AUC = 81.1\%$. Note that, in all cases, MKL-SVM outperforms to the SVM model.

Finally, In order to compare the results obtained during the classification applying the proposed approach with an end-to-end algorithm, fine-tuning was applied on the classification layers of the ResNet50 architecture, preserving the initial weights in the convolutional and maxpooling layers. However, the performances in validation were poor, obtaining an accuracy of 60%, 50%, and 66.7% in ADC, T2 and Subtraction respectively.

4   Conclusions and Future Work

In this paper, we investigate the use of transfer learning for characterizing regions of interest from MRI images, and the use of MKL for both to select the relevant filters to be used and to perform the classification of the ROI as positive or negative breast lesion. Our work shows that a CNN pre-trained on non-medical tasks can be used to extract image features from breast MRI images relevant to the radiologist interpretation, and overcoming the deep learning methods requirement of large labeled datasets, which are not readily available for breast MRI studies.

As previous works, we use transfer learning for generating feature vectors that then are used as inputs for training classical machine learning models. A challenging task in this strategy is to deal with the "curse of dimensionality" caused by the size of the filters. In this work, we proposed to characterize convolutional filter outputs using the statistic moments. Results showed that this strategy improves the classification performance but also allows to identify the most relevant features for the classification task.

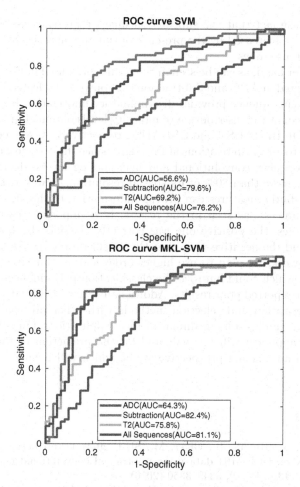

Fig. 5. Classification performance. Top: ROC curve and AUC for features from relevant filters using SVM. Bottom: ROC curve and AUC for features from relevant filters using MKL

We compared the classification performance using a classical SVM learning model vs a multiple kernel strategy that optimally combines several sources, each one related with a weighted kernel during classification task. Results showed that the use of MKL-SVM achieves the best performance in all cases, evidencing that it takes major advantage of the information provided by each one of the selected filters.

From the medical application point of view, results shown that the use of the Subtraction image outperforms the use of Axial T2 or ADC maps; even more, the use of this sequence alone shown a better classification than using them all together, which could be useful in the definition of abbreviated breast MRI protocols for reducing acquisition and interpretation costs. These results may be related to the fact that the subtraction image represents tissues' metabolic activity, which is increased by the presence of tumours and is represented in the image with intense tones.

On the other hand, as can be seen in the results presented in Fig. 3, visually, it can be interpreted in ADC and Subtraction that output of selected filters as most relevant for each sequence provides discriminatory information between classes, taking into account the distribution of intensity levels obtained in the malignant and benign ROI, BI-RADS 4 and BI-RADS 2 respectively. As for sequence T2, it is not possible to establish relations at first sight, since these are features obtained in several subsequent convolutional and max-pooling layers, during which the image has lost more than 80% of its spatial resolution. However, the gray level intensity distribution features can provide information to the algorithms in the classification process, as seen in the results. It is important to mention that for these samples, the positive one was correctly classified by both SVM and MKL-SVM, and the negative was correctly classified only by the latter.

As future work, we plan to use higher order features for characterizing the filter outputs, which could improve the classification performances of the image sequences that reported poor results. Additionally, we will evaluate the proposed filter characterization and selection methods with other pre-trained networks that had shown good results in similar medical applications. On the other hand, the proposed approach will be evaluated for the prediction of the final lesion malignancy in an ongoing prospective study, which will include biopsy-proven lesions.

References

1. Antropova, N., Huynh, B., Giger, M.: SU-D-207B-06: predicting breast cancer malignancy on DCE-MRI data using pre-trained convolutional neural networks. Med. Phys. **43**(6, Pt. 4), 3349–3350 (2016)
2. Antropova, N., Abe, H., Giger, M.L.: Use of clinical MRI maximum intensity projections for improved breast lesion classification with deep convolutional neural networks. J. Med. Imaging **5**(1), 014503 (2018)
3. Areiza-Laverde, H.J., Castro-Ospina, A.E., Hernández, M.L., Díaz, G.M.: A novel method for objective selection of information sources using multi-kernel SVM and local scaling. Sensors **20**(14), 3919 (2020)
4. Areiza-Laverde, H.J., Díaz, G.M., Castro-Ospina, A.E.: Feature group selection using MKL penalized with ℓ_1-norm and SVM as base learner. In: Figueroa-García, J.C., López-Santana, E.R., Rodriguez-Molano, J.I. (eds.) WEA 2018. CCIS, vol. 915, pp. 136–147. Springer, Cham (2018). https://doi.org/10.1007/978-3-030-00350-0_12
5. Canziani, A., Paszke, A., Culurciello, E.: An analysis of deep neural network models for practical applications. arXiv preprint arXiv:1605.07678 (2016)
6. He, K., Zhang, X., Ren, S., Sun, J.: Deep residual learning for image recognition. In: Proceedings of the IEEE Conference on Computer Vision and Pattern Recognition, pp. 770–778 (2016)

7. Hu, Q., Whitney, H.M., Edwards, A., Papaioannou, J., Giger, M.L.: Radiomics and deep learning of diffusion-weighted MRI in the diagnosis of breast cancer. In: Medical Imaging 2019: Computer-Aided Diagnosis, vol. 10950, p. 109504A. International Society for Optics and Photonics (2019)
8. Leithner, D., Moy, L., Morris, E.A., Marino, M.A., Helbich, T.H., Pinker, K.: Abbreviated MRI of the breast: does it provide value? J. Magn. Reson. Imaging (2018)
9. Marrone, S., Piantadosi, G., Fusco, R., Petrillo, A., Sansone, M., Sansone, C.: An investigation of deep learning for lesions malignancy classification in breast DCE-MRI. In: Battiato, S., Gallo, G., Schettini, R., Stanco, F. (eds.) ICIAP 2017. LNCS, vol. 10485, pp. 479–489. Springer, Cham (2017). https://doi.org/10.1007/978-3-319-68548-9_44
10. Murtaza, G., et al.: Deep learning-based breast cancer classification through medical imaging modalities: state of the art and research challenges. Artif. Intell. Rev. **53**(3), 1655–1720 (2019). https://doi.org/10.1007/s10462-019-09716-5
11. Narváez, F., Díaz, G., Poveda, C., Romero, E.: An automatic BI-RADS description of mammographic masses by fusing multiresolution features. Expert Syst. Appl. **74**, 82–95 (2017)
12. World Health Organization: Breast fact sheet. Technical report, International Agency for Research on Cancer (2018). http://gco.iarc.fr/today/data/factsheets/cancers/20-Breast-fact-sheet.pdf
13. Shin, H.C., et al.: Deep convolutional neural networks for computer-aided detection: CNN architectures, dataset characteristics and transfer learning. IEEE Trans. Med. Imaging **35**(5), 1285–1298 (2016)
14. Xu, Z., Jin, R., Yang, H., King, I., Lyu, M.R.: Simple and efficient multiple kernel learning by group lasso. In: Proceedings of the 27th International Conference on Machine Learning (ICML 2010), pp. 1175–1182. Citeseer (2010)

Sensor Network for Bipolar sEMG Detection and Angular Measurement for the Characterization of Foot Drop Pathology

Cecilia Murrugarra[1]([✉])[iD] and Santiago Noriega-Alvarez[1,2][iD]

[1] Electronics Engineering Program, Faculty of Engineering, Universidad El Bosque,
Bogota DC 110111, Colombia
cmurrugarra@unbosque.edu.co, santiago.noriega-alvarez@uni-ulm.de
[2] ULM University, Ulm, Germany

Abstract. The aim of this research work was to develop an embedded electronic sensing system, portable, wireless and wearable prototype that allowed to perform bipolar surface electromyography (sEMG) detection for the Tibialis Anterior (TA) and Peroneus Longus (PL) muscles and measure the angular displacement of the ankle-foot joint for the characterization of Foot Drop (FD) pathology through the establishment of a sensor network. Two Sensor Units were developed around a CPU responsible for receiving the sensors measurements in order to assemble data packets for transmission. The bipolar sEMG detection is carried out through an analogous conditioning module. The sEMG architecture allows to obtain the raw, rectified, and the envelope of the muscular signals. The angular displacement measurement consists in an inertial measurement system. A statistical analysis to validate the precision of the measurements regard to commercial instruments, showing a MSE of $5,27\%$ for the sEMG and a mean error $\leq \pm 1.5°$ for angular displacement measurements. Likewise, an analysis was implemented both in the time and frequency domain for bipolar sEMG detection, to assess the energetic distribution of the TA and PL muscle contractions, showing that the spectral information in the $10\text{--}300\,\mathrm{Hz}$ range and PSD oscillates in the $0\text{-}7\mathrm{e}\text{-}3\,\mathrm{dB/Hz}$ for a subject without FD pathology. The sensor network was implemented on the TA and PL in order to compare the transmitted and received information. The data collected and the experimental platform show the potential of the electronic prototype to measure physiological variables in real-time.

Keywords: Wearable sensors · Wireless transmission · sEMG · Foot drop · Sensing system

---

This work has been fund by Electronics Engineering Program and Faculty of Engineering of Universidad El Bosque with the research project PFI2020ES004.

J. C. Figueroa-García et al. (Eds.): WEA 2020, CCIS 1274, pp. 314–326, 2020.
https://doi.org/10.1007/978-3-030-61834-6_27

1   Introduction

Generally, the physio-pathological condition of Foot Drop (FD) is caused by circumstances that harm the muscles innervated by the deep peroneal nerve, for example, the Tibialis Anterior (TA) muscle [1]. The consequences of FD pathology commonly converge towards a remarkable movement restriction of the affected limb, making the foot tend to tilt downwards in a plantar flexion position. In the long term, this phenomenon causes the muscles associated with the movements of the joint complex of the ankle to degenerate; the most affected are usually the TA and Peroneus Longus (PL) muscles [2].

This fact awake a natural interest in measuring the muscular activity in the affected muscles. Bipolar surface electromyography (*bipolar sEMG*) is known as the procedure of recording the electrical activity of the muscles through two surface electrodes located over the skin on the surface of the muscle of interest [3]. Through bipolar sEMG it is possible to perform force studies and qualify muscle complexes, in routines or rehabilitation exercises where it is necessary to know the electrical behavior of the muscles, in the activation of prostheses by electromyographic signals. The success and efficiency of the bipolar sEMG are directly related to aspects of the muscle to be investigated, the quality of the supplies used, the electrode placement techniques, and the conditioning of the skin. Muscle attributes such as size, type, structure, and age have direct implications on the performance of bipolar sEMG [4]. Similarly, the quality and the type of electrodes used during the bipolar sEMG have essential connotations for the quality of the signals captured; for example, the use of gel for the improvement of electric transmission has been shown to generate good results in the signal acquisition and attenuation of the motion artifact noise [5]. This type of considerations earns relevance when bipolar sEMG is applied during dynamic muscle activation since the muscles tend to modify their length, reduce the force performed, and the electrodes move continuously from position [6].

As for the angular displacement measurement, there are three currently commonly used approximations: systems that incorporate encoders, flexible sensors, and inertial measurement unit systems. The system based on encoders is usually used to calculate variables such as displacement, velocity, or acceleration. This type of technology operates by counting the number of times an infrared beam is interrupted; in this way it is possible to count the steps, thus estimating angular rotation [7]. The encoders present an average error of $3.25°$ [8]. The flexible sensors act as variable resistors that change their resistive value depending on the degree of flexion of their surface [9]. Typically, this type of sensors requires an analog or digital conditioning stage to obtain the angular displacement made [10]. However, flex sensors tend to suffer mechanical wear and, due to their high average error (around $6.92°$), are not usually used in applications that require great precision [8]. Based on the current state-of-art angular sensing, the Inertial Measurement Unit (IMU) systems are projected as the most used alternative today for the measurement of angular displacement. The efficiency of the IMU sensors mainly due to the integration of accelerometers, gyroscopes, and magnetometers; by using the estimations of the embedded sensors, it is possible to reduce the error in the measurements [11] considerably. Additionally, one of the central advantages of IMU sensors is the fact that they can be installed anywhere in the body that manifests the angular rotation, which is why they are widely used in virtual immersion systems and as wearable sensors [12], and average error of 0.08° [8]. This research work was conceived to conceptualize, design, and develop an embedded electronic sensing system that would allow data to be transmitted wirelessly to a real-time visualization interface for the characterization of FD pathology.

2   Preliminary Considerations

At the time of designing the equipment, the following guidelines or attributes considered essential for the assessment of FD were established. (1) *Portability*: Considering that the operator will use the device for both static and dynamic exercises, the system should be portable and comfortable, which can be achieved through a modular architecture. (2) *Wireless transmission*: Should be critical since this contributes to the comfort of both the patient and the specialist, in addition to improving the usability of the system. and (3) *Signal processing interface*: Using a Unified Signal Processing Interface (USPI) as a real-time visualization tool that allows the use of the system in practically any scenario and customization of the rehabilitation routines based on the obtained records/registers, focusing the tool towards telemedicine field.

3   Sensor Unit

The hardware of the device consists of 5 modules integrated among them through a modular architecture. The bipolar sEMG detection (sEMG SU) for the TA and PL muscles is achieved through a conditioning circuit where the signal is filtered, rectified and integrated by the two sEMG channels while the angular displacement of sagittal and frontal planes (IMU SU) of the ankle-foot joint complex is measured with an IMU sensor at a sample rate of 1ksps and a resolution of 16 bits. The data records from bipolar sEMG and IMU sensor are processed by the Central Processing Unit (CPU). The bipolar sEMG detection is treated at a frequency of 1ksps and a resolution of 10 bits; the integration of the IMU sensor and the CPU requires an I^2C communication protocol in order for the micro-controller (μC) to search the IMU registers. The μC is in charge of assembling data packets which are stored in columns and then transmitted wirelessly through the RF transmission protocol to an USPI which is used, with a PC, as a real-time visualization platform. Figure 1 shows the general architecture of the SU as well as the experimental platform when using the device. Figure 1a shows the installation and arrangement of the SU in the user's body; the surface electrodes on the TA and PL muscles and the IMU sensor on the side of the instep. Figure 1b shows the integration of the modules within the system. The central core of the equipment is the CPU that allows to process and transmit the data registers. Table 1 presents the general technical characteristics of the SU, both for sEMG and IMU; from attributes of the Sensing Modules to mechanical aspects of the enclosure. Its possible to establish a sensor network constituted by three transmitters (TA, PL and IMU transmitters) and one universal receptor. A tree topology was designed to establish the communication chain between all the transceivers which is deeply describe in section *Transceiver Network.*

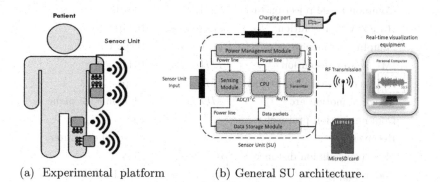

(a) Experimental platform   (b) General SU architecture.

Fig. 1. Block diagram and experimental platform of the system

3.1   Bipolar sEMG Module

The treatment of muscle signals is achieved through an analogous conditioning circuit implementing stages of instrumentation, filtering, rectification, smoothing and amplification. The instrumentation or differential stage is responsible for capturing the difference in amplitude of the contractions respect to a reference electrode, and amplifying it with a low level of signal-to-noise ratio; this stage has variable gain. Regarding the filtering architecture of the module, a high pass filter was used in cascade with a low pass filter to obtain the desired frequency spectrum. As the main features, they are active, second-order and Chebyshev topology filters with a cutoff frequency of 10 and 450 Hz respectively. Due to the frequency distribution of the TA and PL muscle information, a Notch filter 60 Hz was not used. The rectification and smoothing stages allows to obtain the rectified and smooth sEMG signals. This module has amplification stages distributed at the input and output of the circuit, the gain is adjustable through trimmers. Likewise, the circuit has a DC level shifter with the purpose of capturing the raw sEMG signal for the time and frequency domain study.

3.2   IMU Module

The prime core of this module is an *MPU6050* IMU sensor which incorporates a precision gyroscope and a tri-axial accelerometer. The estimation of the angular displacement is achieved through the measurement of partial angular rotations

Table 1. Electronic system technical specifications

Concept	Abbreviation	Value
sEMG channels	$sEMG_{ch}$	Up to 8
sEMG bandwidth	$sEMG_{bw}$	10 Hz–450 Hz
Max. gain	G	10000 V/V
Common mode rejection ratio	CMRR	130 dB
sEMG ADC resolution	$sEMG_{ADC}$	10 bits
Sampling frequency	$sEMG_{fs}$	1ksps/ch
IMU sensor resolution	IMU_{res}	16 bits
IMU sensor sampling frequency	IMU_{fs}	1ksps
Range of motion arc	MOV_{ARC}	±90° in each plane
Communication protocol	—	RF
Receiver	—	Personal computer
Max. transmission distance	d_{TX}	25 m
Power supply	V_S	3 Ah 1-cell Lithium
Autonomy of the system	—	16 h
Dimensions	—	5.2 × 3 × 3.6 (cm)
Weight	—	100 g

by the embedded IMU sensors; then the CPU applies a meticulous algorithm to find the angulation made with a low measurement error (this is generally known as indirect measurement); the mathematical algorithm is shown in *Central Processing Unit* section. This module needs to establish an I^2C communication protocol with the CPU in order to perform the data transfer; the protocol was configured at a speed of 400kbps (fast mode), synchronously and in a serial configuration to achieve a stable performance without loss of information. The IMU sensor is installed on the side of the instep of the user, fixed to a 3D printed piece and held by a velcro system; this allows to avoid incorrect positioning of the sensor.

3.3 Central Processing Unit (CPU)

CPU is designed around the *ATmega328P* microcontroller (μC). This system module processes the sEMG raw signal at a sampling frequency of 1ksps and a resolution of 10 bits (ADC). Some considerations must be taken into account when choosing the sampling frequency; due to the filtering frequency spectrum (10 to 450 Hz) we chose a sampling rate of 1ksps [13].

Regarding to the measurement of angular displacement, it is necessary to use the values of acceleration (accelerometer) and rotation (gyroscope) as complementary information to find a widely accurate value of the angular rotation. Using the expressions Eq. 1 and Eq. 2 is possible to determine the angular displacement from the acceleration values, where acc_x and acc_y denote the main axis of rotation; this method to calculate the angle is based on the fact that depending on the position of the IMU, the gravitational acceleration would be sensed over the respective axis.

$$\theta_x = tan^{-1} \frac{acc_x}{\sqrt{acc_y^2 + acc_z^2}} \tag{1}$$

$$\theta_y = tan^{-1} \frac{acc_y}{\sqrt{acc_x^2 + acc_z^2}} \tag{2}$$

$$\theta_x = \theta_{xo} + \omega_x \triangle t \tag{3}$$

$$\theta_y = \theta_{yo} + \omega_y \triangle t \tag{4}$$

$$Angle[0] = X(Angle[0] + Gyro_{angx}dt) + Y(Acc_{angx}) \tag{5}$$

$$Angle[1] = X(Angle[1] + Gyro_{angy}dt) + Y(Acc_{angy}) \tag{6}$$

Similarly, it is possible to use the values of rotation determined by the gyroscope, in order to estimate the angular displacement sensed by this transducer. Equation 3 and Eq. 4 work under the principle of measuring the actual and the future angle each fixed time step. Is possible to know how is the angular difference between two samples, i.e. the angular velocity. The integration of the expressions Eq. 1–Eq. 4 is achieved by modeling the gyroscope as a high pass filter and the accelerometer as a low pass filter. As can be seen in the expressions Eq. 5 and Eq. 6, the values of angular displacement are calculated as a vector, where the first element ($Angle[0]$) corresponds to the rotation made on the x axis and the second element ($Angle[1]$) concerns the rotation of the y axis. These expressions resemble the pitch and roll movements presented in drones or aircraft. One of the main advantages of implementing a model like the one presented above is that it avoids inaccuracies when abrupt measurements occur, either by a speed change in a short period of time or by sudden rotations.

Once the information from both physiological variables has been processed, the CPU assembles data packets for storage and transmission. An important characteristic is that the CPU requires that both variables have been measured and processed; otherwise, it discards the previous packet and performs the process again. This ensures data synchronization in both transmission and storage, thus avoiding loss of information.

3.4 Sensor Network

The sensor network consists of 4 transceivers, three of them operating as transmitters and a single receiver. The hardware used for the sensor network is the *NRF24L01* module. This hardware allows to establish up to 125 RF channels working independently; despite this, each single RF channel can have a total of 3125 modules communicating to each other within a extremely large node network. The *NRF24L01* module can handle three different data rates, 250*kbps*, 1 and 2*Mbps*. However, it has been used the maximum data rate in order to ensure the real-time visualization goal. Figure 2a shows the tree topology used in this project. *Node01*, *Node02* and *Node03* are the RF transmitters of the sensor network; taking into account that the sensor network is conceived as a passive tool, it has been decided that these elements only work in a single direction, which means that they only write the information sensed by the Sensing Module of each SU. By the other hand, the *Base00* is the global receiver of the network; this node receive the information related to the sEMG and the angular displacement and then processes this data for the USPI in order tho achieved the real-time visualization feature.

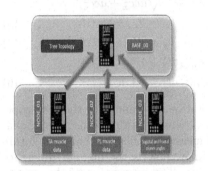 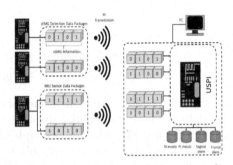

(a) Tree topology of the sensor network.

(b) Data transmission and reception diagram

Fig. 2. Topology of the sensor network and communications system diagram

3.5   Power Management Module

A Battery Management System (BMS) was implemented to protect the short circuit, overload, and over-discharge to the system boards. A Lithium-Ion (Li-Ion) battery is used to power all the modules of the system. The conditioning module designed in the bipolar sEMG requires negative supply, for which a single-to-dual-rail circuit was used. This circuit supplies symmetrical dual voltage with a current of 500 mA per rail. The digital level voltages of 5 V and 3.3 V were achieved through a *LM2596-ADJ* step-down (buck) DC-DC converter with an efficiency of 73% (typically).

3.6   Unified Signal Processing Interface (USPI)

USPI is the software designed to receive the data packets with the information of the TA and PL muscles and the angular displacement of the ankle-foot joint complex in the sagittal and frontal planes. The application was developed in Matlab in order to deploy a robust signal analysis. Among its most notable attributes, the application allows real-time visualization and grants to storage all the registered data. Figure 2b shows the data transmission and reception diagram; the USPI hear the transmitters at specific times, avoiding avalanche of data and optimizing the reading of each physiological variable.

4   Experimental Platform

The SU related to sEMG is attached directly to the muscle through the surface electrodes; this is possible since the PCB has incorporated the metal snap pieces of the electrode. This architecture allows adjust the ideal inter-distance between electrodes. Despite this, the motion noise is also considerably reduced. The SU related to the IMU sensor is installed on the user's instep, allowing measure the entire arc of movement of the subject; to achieve this, we used an ankle brace to generate a surface to attach the SU.

The Fig. 3 shows experimental platforms for both sEMG and angular displacement measurements. The Fig. 3a corresponds to the sEMG data verification in the Physiology Laboratory-Universidad El Bosque. Additionally, the SENIAM guidelines [14] were followed when placing the superficial electrodes over the muscles; recommendations related to electric transmission gel were also applied. Figure 3c illustrates the experimental configuration for the angular displacement data verification against a commercial mechanical goniometer.

(a) sEMG detection experimental platform   (b) Prototype installation on bicep muscle.   (c) Angular displacement

Fig. 3. Experimental platforms for sEMG and angular displacement measurements.

5   Results

5.1   IMU Sensor and Bipolar sEMG Data Verification

Data verification is that process to determine how accurate and stable our prototype's measurements are compared to a commercial instrument. Regarding the angular rotation measurement, a mechanical goniometer (Ez Read Jamar Goniometer-Manual medical goniometer) was used to perform the data verification. The procedure was based on comparing 5 sample measurements in each plane with both the goniometer and the IMU sensor, on determining the average error. For the verification of the bipolar sEMG data, a professional electromyograph (ADInstruments Powerlab recording unit, Teaching Series-26T) available in the physiology university laboratories was used. The envelope signal of the TA muscle was recorded both by the prototype and the professional instrument, to perform a robust statistical analysis and, among other things, finding the mean squared error (MSE) of the signals. The patient was asked to perform three contractions while sitting and lifting the instep of the ankle as steep as possible. As can be seen in Table 2, the average error, both in the sagittal and frontal planes, did not exceed 1.5°. This error behavior reflects a great sensor installation and calibration. About the bipolar sEMG, a linear interpolation was made due to the sampling frequency difference between instruments (1ksps for the prototype and 1.5ksps for the professional electromyograph). The MSE was also estimated between the signals. The data verification related to bipolar sEMG showed in Table 2 indicates that the first two contractions are considerably similar (1.02% and 7.71% respectively). However, the third contraction presents an MSE of 16.40%, being an appreciable difference. This behavior can be attributed to the divergence in the conditioning of the signal between both instruments. Figure 4 shows the graphs and charts obtained from the data verification process, both for bipolar sEMG as well as angular rotation. In Fig. 4a, the angular rotation registered by both instruments in both planes, continuously and simultaneously, is observed. Figure 4b and Fig. 4c show the two envelope signal registers from the TA muscle.

Table 2. Statistical analysis IMU sensor and bipolar sEMG. Nomenclature: G for goniometer, s for sagittal plane and f for frontal plane

Angular displacement data				
Plane	Test	G(s,f)	IMU(s,f)	Error(s,f)
	1	27.0°,14.0°	29.2°,14.3°	-2.2°, -0.3°
	2	17.5°,25.0°	17.3°,26.3°	0.2°, -1.3°
s,f	3	36.0°, 82.0°	37.9°,80.4°	-1.9°, 1.6°
	4	90.0°, 70.0°	87.5°,72.5°	2.5°, -2.5°
	5	0.0°, 43.0°	0.7°,41.8°	-0.7°, 1.2°
Avg error	-		-	**1.5°, 1.4°**

Bipolar sEMG data		
Measurement	Professional EMG	EMG module
Contraction #1 max amplitude	0.8867 mV	0.9007 mV
Contraction #2 max amplitude	1.0050 mV	0.9007 mV
Contraction #3 max amplitude	0.9703 mV	1.0050 mV
MSE Contraction #1	1.02%	
MSE Contraction #2	7.71%	
MSE Contraction #3	16.40%	

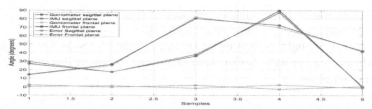

(a) Measurements between the mechanical goniometer, and the IMU sensor

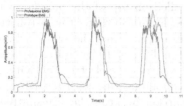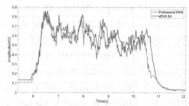

(b) Envelope signal of the bipolar sEMG of the TA muscleRegister 1   (c) Envelope signal of the bipolar sEMG of the TA muscleRegister 2

Fig. 4. Data verification results of the bipolar sEMG and the angular rotation in relation to a mechanical goniometer and a commercial electromyograph.

5.2 Frequency Study of the Bipolar sEMG

The prototype recorded the bipolar sEMG raw signal of the TA and PL muscles; the time and amplitudes values of the isometric contractions of each muscle were stored in the microSD card. *Matlab* software was used to perform all signal processing. First, the Eq. 7 of the Discrete Fourier Transform (DFT) was applied to obtain the representation of the function in the frequency domain. To estimate the Power Spectral Density (PSD) using the Eq. 8, where $X(f)$ represents the Fourier transform of $x(t)$. The total energy distribution as a function of the frequency decomposition of the $x(t)$ signal, and can be presented in Eq. 9.

$$X_k = \sum_{n=0}^{N-1} x_n e^{-i2\pi kn/N} \tag{7}$$

$$S_{xx}(f) = |X(f)|^2 \tag{8}$$

$$E = \int_{-\infty}^{\infty} S_{xx}(f) df \tag{9}$$

From the obtained results, Fig. 5 is elaborated, in which the energetic distribution of power during the muscle contractions can be observed. The region where the greatest power is manifested is in the range of 60 to 150 Hz; although this is a normal behavior, this region of frequency may change according to the muscle [15]. Figure 5a and Fig. 5b show the PSD of these muscle complexes. Is possible to observe that most of the spectral information is gathered around 10 to 350 Hz with a power per frequency unit in the 0-7e-3 dB/Hz for a healthy subject.

One of the most interesting behaviours of the TA and PL contractions are the co-antagonistic activations; this means that, when the TA muscle is activated, there is a slight activation of the antagonistic muscle (the PL muscle). This indicator can provide information about body's energy distribution against particular activities.

5.3   Sensor Network

The prototype design allows it to be installed on top of the muscle on interest in order to reduce motion noise sources. Figure 3b shows the installation of the prototype on the bicep muscle as an example. Using the same installation principle, two modules were equipped on the TA and PL muscles respectively; the purpose of this setup was to sense and transmit the electrical activity of the muscles using two independent RF units communicating with the RF receiver unit. Figure 6 shows a direct visual comparison between the transmitted and received signal for the TA muscle (raw and envelope of the signal). Despite there is no statistical or numerical connection between the respective transmitted and received signal, is possible to establish a direct similarity and affinity.

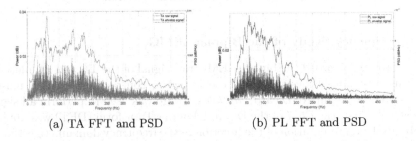

(a) TA FFT and PSD   (b) PL FFT and PSD

Fig. 5. Frequency domain study of the TA and PL muscle contractions

6   Discussion and Conclusions

The results presented both in the verification stage and in the frequency study of muscular contractions expose the potential of the system for the acquisition and treatment of physiological signals. Regarding data verification, the average error in the angular rotation ($\leq \pm 2°$) and the MSE in the bipolar sEMG (1.02%, 7.71%, and 16.4% respectively) reflect the accuracy of the system about much more expensive commercial instruments. Additionally, it is possible to conduct studies both in the time and frequency domain to find patterns and information that help to assess and rehabilitating FD pathology; moreover, this feature is enhanced taking into account that the size and modularity of the wearable system allow to establish a sensor network direct on top of the muscles of interest. This research work is presented as a new tool for the rehabilitation specialist. We

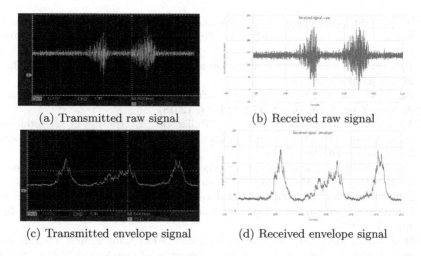

(a) Transmitted raw signal   (b) Received raw signal

(c) Transmitted envelope signal   (d) Received envelope signal

Fig. 6. Comparison regarding the transmitted and received raw and envelope signals

sought at all times to enhance its characteristic of being a passive, non-invasive and low-cost instrument that could be naturally integrated with the clinical specialist and help determine less obvious information to optimize the recovery time and rehabilitation routine adjustments. The design and development of this type of electronic system have the potential to open new scenarios in the characterization and assessment of pathological conditions; also, with its high capacity of data transmission and storage would allow the establishment of extensive and reliable databases of physiological variables for future studies and research.

References

1. Cengiz, A., Duygun, F.: New and unusual causes of foot drop. Med. Sci. Int. Med. J. **11**, 1 (2017)
2. Westhout, F., Pare, L., Linskey, M.: Central causes of foot drop: rare and underappreciated differential diagnoses. J. Spinal Cord Med. **30**(1), 62–66 (2007)
3. Merlo, A.: Technical aspects of surface electromyography for clinicians. Open Rehabil. J. **3**, 98–109 (2010)
4. Kupa, E., Roy, S., Kandarian, S., De Luca, C.: Effects of muscle fiber type and size on EMG median frequency and conduction velocity. J. Appl. Physiol. **79**(1), 23–32 (2017)
5. Arul, H.: A review on noises in EMG signal and its removal. Int. J. Sci. Res. Publ. **7**(5), 23 (2017)
6. Kazumi, M., Masuda, T., Sadoyama, T., Inaki, M., Katsuta, S.: Changes in surface EMG parameters during static and dynamic fatiguing contractions. J. Electromyogr. Kinesiol. **9**(1), 39–46 (1999)
7. Incze, I.I., Negrea, A., Imecs, M., Szabó, C.: Incremental encoder based position and speed identification: modeling and simulation. Acta Universitatis Sapientiae Electr. Mech. Eng. **2**, 27–39 (2010)

8. Khayani, S: Development of wearable sensors for body joint angle measurement. Master's thesis, University of Denver, 2199 S University Blvd, Denver, CO 80208, United States, 6 (2011)
9. Ting, S., et al.: An overview of the development of flexible sensors. Adv. Mater. **29**(33), 1700375 (2017)
10. Saggio, G., Orengo, G.: Flex sensor characterization against shape and curvature changes. Sens. Actuators, A **273**, 221–231 (2018)
11. Alonge, F., Cucco, E., D'Ippolito, F., Pulizzotto, A.: The use of accelerometers and gyroscopes to estimate hip and knee angles on gait analysis. Sensors (Switz.) **14**(5), 8430–8446 (2014)
12. Hol, J., Schon, T., Gustafsson, F., Slycke, P.: Sensor fusion for augmented reality. In: 2006 9th International Conference on Information Fusion, pp. 1–6 (2006)
13. Kilby, J., Prasad, K.: Analysis of surface electromyography signals using discrete Fourier transform sliding window technique. Int. J. Comput. Theory Eng. **5**(2), 321–325 (2013)
14. Stegeman, D., Hermens, H.: Standards for surface electromyography: the European project surface EMG for non-invasive assessment of muscles (SENIAM). Surface electromyography application areas and parameters. In: Proceedings of the Third General SENIAM Workshop on Surface Electromyography, Aachen, Germany, 11 Jan, pp. 108–112 (1998)
15. Strazza, A. et al.: Time-frequency analysis of surface EMG signals for maximum energy localization during walking. In: EMBEC NBC 2017, pp. 494–497. Springer, Singapore (2018)

Military Applications

Infrastructure Estimation for a Freight/Personal Transport Operation with an Electric Boat on the Magdalena River

Camilo Vélez[✉], Daniel Villa, and Alejandro Montoya

Departamento de Ingeniería de Producción, Universidad EAFIT,
Carrera 49 No 7 Sur–50, Medellín, Colombia
{cvelezg10,dvillab,jmonto36}@eafit.edu.co

Abstract. Nowadays, electric mobility is an attractive alternative to the traditional internal combustion mobility. Electric mobility presents benefits in the reduction of greenhouse gas emissions and noise pollution. This mobility has been studied in the context of urban areas as they usually have better connections to the power grid; however, it is necessary to study the implementation of electric mobility in the context of rural areas as well. In this way, we introduce a study performed on a river route in a region of Colombia. This route consists of a round trip between Magangué and Pinillos, two municipalities on the banks of the Magdalena river. The study aims to determine the necessary infrastructure to perform the operation with an electric boat (EB). This infrastructure is defined as the location and sizing of Photovoltaic-assisted Charging Stations (PVCSs) and the EB battery capacity. For finding the infrastructure, we propose a constructive heuristic. After running this heuristic, we found a feasible solution. In this solution, one PVCS is installed with an energy storage system of 46 kWh and an area of 29 m^2 of photovoltaic modules. The battery capacity for the EB was 207 kWh.

Keywords: Electric boat · Infrastructure sizing ·
Photovoltaic-assisted Charging Station · River transport operation

1 Introduction

The transport sector significantly contributes to the CO_2 emissions. For instance, in Latin America, in 2005, this sector accounted for 34.1% of the total CO_2 emissions [16]. For this reason, Electric Vehicles (EVs) are gaining importance in the last years. These vehicles present the advantage that they are free of polluting gas emissions. Nowadays, electric mobility solutions have been thought mainly for urban areas due to their driving range, the availability of the electric infrastructure to install charging stations (CSs), and the high concentration of polluting gases in those areas. Nevertheless, the use of electric mobility, in rural

© Springer Nature Switzerland AG 2020
J. C. Figueroa-García et al. (Eds.): WEA 2020, CCIS 1274, pp. 329–337, 2020.
https://doi.org/10.1007/978-3-030-61834-6_28

areas, could be interesting considering that CO_2 is a global problem. More-over, using internal combustion vehicles pollutes natural resources, and usually the fuel is more expensive in those areas because of high logistic costs. Recent developments on battery technologies and Photovoltaic-assisted Charging Stations (PVCSs) make feasible the implementation of the electric mobility in rural areas. Developments on battery technology impact the driving range limitations making it possible to perform longer routes, and developments on PVCSs allow accessing zones where there is no connection to the grid.

The river transport operation is one of the possibilities for implementing the electric mobility in rural areas considering its relevance in regions such as Latin America. For example, in the Amazonas region, around 90% of the transportation is made by river means due to the lack of access for ground vehicles [6,11]. Additionally, in countries like Brazil, river transport operations transport 6% of the total freight flow. In Colombia, more than 3.4 million tons of freight and more than 3.7 million passengers are moved by river means [3]. The river transport operations with Electric Boats (EBs) have different benefits such as the reduction of CO_2 emissions and pollution in water sources. Some initiatives for implementing EBs in the latin american context have been made. Such is the case of [11] who successfully tested some EBs for passenger transportation in communities across the Putumayo river, following routes of up to 60 km. [2] assessed the feasibility of performing some fluvial operations with EBs with self photovoltaic generation in the Napo river, deeming most of them as feasible, while indicating that some cargo operation could require external charging operations during their routes.

With these considerations, in the frame of the "Energética 2030" project [9], there is a plan to implement a river transport operation with EBs on Magdalena River, in Colombia. This operation consists in a round trip starting at the municipality of Magangué and returning from the municipality of Pinillos moving freight and passengers. Given that in some settlements of the Magdalena River there is no connection to the grid, this problem will consider the use of PVCSs.

For implementing this operation with EBs, we must first estimate the required infrastructure. This estimation consists in deciding the location and sizing of the PVCSs and determining the EB battery capacity aiming to minimize the total investment cost. To solve this optimization problem, we initially propose a constructive heuristic. With this heuristic, it is feasible to solve the problem considering the features of this particular river transport operation and the complexities of the electric mobility such as nonlinear charging functions, photovoltaic (PV) generation curves, among others. In this paper, we present the solution of this problem for the case of the round trip Magangué - Pinillos, on the Magdalena River, Colombia.

2   Literature Review

When an electric mobility transport operation is being designed, one of the focuses is to determine the optimal locations and sizing of CSs. In the literature, most of the studies focus on the location and size of conventional CSs for the urban context such as the studies presented in [15,20,22]. Nonetheless, recent studies have been oriented to location and sizing of CSs including the use of Renewable Energy Sources (RESs) such as photovoltaic generation and wind power. [14] presented a model for determining CS location and sizing including operative features, such as RESs and vehicle-to-grid. They use a mathematical formulation as well as a heuristic approach due to the NP-hard nature of the problem. Meanwhile, [21] developed a multi-objective model considering location and sizing of CSs, and they also included RESs and Energy Storage Systems (ESSs) in the decision-making. [1] introduced a location problem of CSs for reducing energy losses considering PV uncertainty and stochastic behaviour of the EVs. [17] used a search algorithm to minimize the investment costs in photovoltaic modules and ESSs for a set of off grid PVCSs required to supply another stochastic energy demand from EVs.

From the perspective of transport operation planning with EBs (or electric ships), to the best of our knowledge, there are only two related works. In terms of strategic planning, [23] presented a Mixed-Integer Linear Programming (MILP) formulation for electric ship CS locations. They estimated the CS locations, to then determine their capacities. In terms of operative planning with EBs, [19] presented a MILP formulation for an EB in a river transport operation. They considered charging decisions accounting for nonlinear charging functions and battery degradation costs. However, as far as we know, there is no literature that simultaneously considers PVCS locations and sizing as well as EB battery capacity determination.

3 Problem Description

The Magdalena River is one of the main rivers in Colombia. One important port on this river is located in the municipality of Magangué. This municipality is the origin and the destination of different routes that travel from and towards different settlements (henceforth nodes) influenced by the river. Nowadays, there is one important route on the Magdalena River that is currently being performed using an Internal Combustion Boat (ICB) and that could be performed with an EB. Currently in this route, an ICB goes from Magangué to the municipality of Pinillos and returns. To perform this route with an EB, it is required to estimate the location and size of the PVCSs as well as the EB battery size aiming to minimize the total investment cost. This cost is defined as the sum of the PVCSs and EB battery costs. A feasible solution of this problem should ensure the autonomy of the EB, and that the total time of the route is less than a time limit T_{max}. We assume that the EB travels at a constant speed, and therefore the travel time is constant. However, the total charging time depends on the EB battery size and the size of the PVCSs. The latter is because the charging time at any PVCS depends on the charging power supplied by the PVCS, which is related with the PVCS size. This means that some infrastructure configuration (i.e., EB battery size and, the location and size of the PVCSs) might not meet the time limit constraint. Besides, we assume that the EB departs with its battery fully charged from Magangué. Considering that Magangué is connected to the national grid the EB can charge during the night at the origin using a domestic charging station.

In this problem, the set B represents the battery capacities that can be installed in the EB. The parameter c is the unitary cost of the EB battery. For the location of the PVCSs, there is a set N of candidate nodes between Magangué and Pinillos. In this problem, we consider PVCSs with an ESS, which is a battery that stores the energy generated by the solar panels. The set P represents the area of solar panels that can be installed in each PVCSs. There is a proportional relationship between the solar panel area and the capacity of the ESS. The parameter f indicates the capacity of the ESS (in kWh) for one square meter of solar panel. The main costs of the PVCSs are the solar panels and the ESSs.

In this problem, we only consider such costs for the PVCSs. The parameters g and h represent the unitary cost of solar panels and the unitary cost of the ESS. Considering that we use PVCSs in this problem, we included a parameter that models the solar radiation behavior. To model this behavior, we use a set E of solar irradiance values during the day (measured in W/m^2 and including the efficiency of the panel). For estimating the charging time of the EB at the PVCS, we consider the energy generated by the PVCS and the nonlinear behavior of the charging process. For modeling the nonlinear behavior, we use a piecewise linear approximation as in [13], and the data of the breakpoints is taken from [18]. In this problem, it is important to consider that the size of the EB battery affects the energy consumption of the EB due to the weight of the battery. The function $\phi(\cdot)$ estimates the energy consumption between each pair of nodes depending on the EB's weight.

The goal of this research is to smartly determine the battery size for an EB as well as the location and sizing of PVCSs to be installed for a the fluvial transport operation. The objective function for this problem is then to minimize the total investment costs on the components. As previously mentioned, a feasible solution to the problem must allow a route to be finished within the time limit T_{max} while meeting the EB's energy autonomy.

4 Solution Approach

As stated in [17], due to the nature of the problem, it is reasonable to use heuristic solution methods for transportation problems with EVs and off grid PVCSs. For that reason, we propose a constructive heuristic as our solution approach. It is worth pointing out that the global minimum can't be guaranteed with this heuristic, it simply is a first approach to solve the problem.

Algorithm 1 describes the general structure of the constructive heuristic. The heuristic starts by iterating through the set B of EB battery size (line 3). At each iteration i, another iterative process is performed through the set P of solar panel areas (line 4). Using the solar panel area P_j and the parameter f, we estimate the capacity of ESSs (line 5). Then, the heuristic uses a procedure called EvaluateFeasibility (line 6). This procedure evaluates the feasibility of the route considering the EB battery size (B_i), solar panel area of the PVCSs (P_j), ESS capacity (q), the irradiance data (E), the time limit (T_{max}), and the function for estimating the energy consumption ($\phi(\cdot)$). To estimate the charging decision (where and how much to charge), EvaluateFeasibility uses a simple rule where the EB charges at the last node in which its energy level is still positive. The charging process finishes when the EB battery reaches a level that is either enough for completing the route or its maximum capacity is reached. This procedure returns a boolean value indicating the feasibility of the evaluated solution, and the set $U \subseteq N$ that represents the PVCSs where the EB charged following the aforementioned simple rule. In other words, the set U represents the selected nodes for installing PVCSs. If the solution is feasible (line 7), the total cost of the solution is estimated (line 8). After that, if the cost of the current solution is lower than that of the best-found solution (line 9), the latter is updated (lines 10 to 13). The algorithm then continues with the next inner-loops iteration. After completing the outerloop we retrieve the best solution (line 20) in terms of the EB battery size (b), the area of the solar panels for the PVCSs (p), the nodes selected for installing PVCSs (U'), and the investment cost (Best).

Algorithm 1. Constructive heuristic general structure

1: **function** HEURISTIC(N, B, P, E, f, c, g, h, T_{max}, $\phi(\cdot)$)
2:     $Best \leftarrow \infty$
3:     **for** $i \leftarrow 1$ to $|B|$ **do**
4:         **for** $j \leftarrow 1$ to $|P|$ **do**
5:             $q \leftarrow f \times P_j$
6:             $< U, o > \leftarrow EvaluateFeasibility(B_i, P_j, q, E, T_{max}, \phi(\cdot))$
7:             **if** $o = true$ **then**
8:                 $ec \leftarrow c \times B_i + |U| \times (g \times P_j + h \times q)$
9:                 **if** $ec < Best$ **then**
10:                     $Best \leftarrow ec$
11:                     $b \leftarrow B_i$
12:                     $p \leftarrow P_j$
13:                     $U' \leftarrow U$
14:                 **end if**
15:             **end if**
16:         **end for**
17:     **end for**
18: **end function**
19:
20: **return** $b, p, U', Best$

---

5   Computational Experiment

In this section we present the results obtained after applying our approach to solve the Magdalena River transport operation case, for the route Mangangué

- Pinillos - Magangué. The heuristic was implemented on Java (jdk-1.8.0_211). The computational experiment was run on a computer with an AMD Ryzen 5 2500U processor (with 8 cores at 2.0 GHz) and 8 GB of RAM running Windows 10 x64. For the case study we used the next general parameters:

- $N = \{1, ..., 6\}$ denotes the set of candidate nodes between Magangué and Pinillos.
- $T\{\}$ denotes the set of moments of the day, where each value equals to the equivalent minutes of the day.
- The value of the radiation e_t at the moment $t \in T$ is an average value, which is obtained using the data of the studied region reported in [10].
- $B = \{27, 28, ..., 280, 281\}$ denotes the set of the EB battery capacities (in kWh). In this case $B_{i+1} - B_i = 1 \forall i \in \{1, ..., |B|\}$, where $|B| = 155$. The minimum value of set $B(B_1)$ is the value such that the EB may travel between each pair of nodes. The maximum value of set $B(B_{155})$ is the value such that the EB is able of performing the entire route Magangué - Pinillos - Magangué without requiring to charge energy in an intermediate PVCS.
- $P = \{5, 6, ..., 79, 80\}$ denotes the set of PV array sizes, where each value is measured in m^2. In this case $P_{i+1} - P_i = 1m^2 \forall i \in \{1, ..., |P|\}$, where $|P| = 76$. The minimum value of set $P(P_1)$ is the minimum required area for a PV array for a CS of this type. The maximum value of set $P(P_{76})$ is the maximum area for a PV array that is feasible to install at the candidate nodes for installing a PVCS.
- The parameter that relates the ESS capacity with the area of the PV array of the PVCS is f = 0.77 kWh/m^2 [4].
- The unitary cost of the EB battery is c = 300 USD/kWh [7,8].
- The unitary cost of solar panels is g = 90 USD/m^2 [5].
- The unitary cost of the ESS is h = 150 USD/kWh [4].
- The function $\phi(\cdot)$ for estimating the energy consumption is the Yokoyama's function presented in [12].

After running the algorithm with the aforementioned parameters, only one PVCS was installed on the route with 29 m^2 of PV modules and 46 kWh of ESS. The selected EB battery capacity was 207 kWh. With these characteristics, the EB departs from Magangué fully charged and arrives at Pinillos with an energy level of 113.16 kWh without charging at the PVCS. During the return trip the EB stops at Panceguita (node names are listed in Fig. 1) with an energy level of 21.74 kWh. At this node, the EB charges 33.17 kWh, which takes 2.47 h using a charging power of 22 kW during the first segment of the charging function. Finally, the EB arrives at Magangué with an empty battery after 4.99 h (4 h and 59.4 min), complying with both the autonomy and time constraints. The results are shown in Fig. 1. The investment costs are indicated in Fig. 2.

The objective function (total cost) was 74.910 USD. The EB battery cost accounted for 82.9% of such cost. The remaining 17.1%, which represents the cost of the PVCS and its components, dedicated 9.21% to the ESS. This indicates that 92.11% of the total investment cost is directed to energy storage. As previously

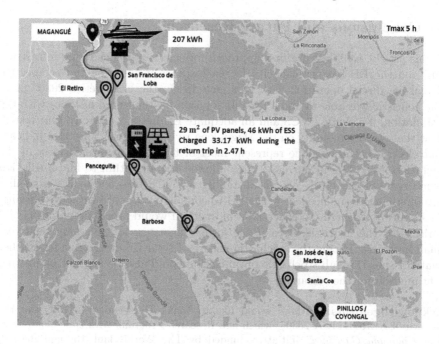

Fig. 1. Test instance depiction, route, nodes, and PVCS characteristics.

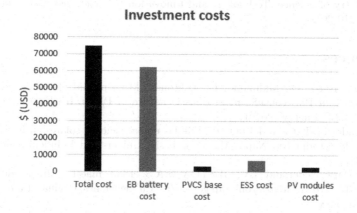

Fig. 2. Investment costs.

stated, the maximum battery capacity for the EB would have allowed it to perform the whole round trip without needing to charge. It can therefore be seen that reducing such battery capacity via installing PVCSs for one in-route charging operation decreased the overall installation costs, as doing so was not required to complete the route.

6 Conclusions and Future Research

In this article, we studied a first approach for selecting the charging infrastructure and the EB battery capacity for an instance inspired on the perspective of real life fluvial operation with EBs included in the "Energética 2030" plan. The heuristic was able to find a feasible solution for the tested instance with the installation of a single PVCS and an adequate EB battery capacity. Our results show that electric mobility on the Magdalena river is feasible. They also indicate that electric batteries alone represent most of the total investment cost of the operation, over 92% in our case. This allowed the algorithm to find a solution which reduces the total cost via installing a PVCS in order to use a smaller battery that the one needed by the EB to complete the route without charging.

As future research, an exact solution method would provide a point of comparison for the heuristic, even if the former manages to solve only relatively small instances. Facing the stochastic nature of solar irradiance due to weather related issues through stochastic optimization could also be another interesting continuation for the research.

Acknowledgements. Authors would like to thank Universidad EAFIT and the alliance "ENERGETICA 2030", which is a Research Program, with code 58667 from the "*Colombia Científica*" initiative, funded by The World Bank through the call "778-2017 Scientific Ecosystems". The research program is managed by the Colombian Ministry of Science, Technology and Innovation (Minciencias) with contract No. FP44842-210-2018.

References

1. Ali, A., Raisz, D., Mahmoud, K., Lehtonen, M.: Optimal placement and sizing of uncertain PVs considering stochastic nature of PEVs. IEEE Transactions on Sustainable Energy (2019)
2. Alvarado, L.: Estudio del potencial de las embarcaciones solares en la Amazonía: Caso de estudio Río Napo. Master's thesis, Universidad Politécnica de Madrid (2017)
3. ARCADIS Nederland BV, JESYCA S.A.S: Plan maestro fluvial de Colombia 2015 (2015). https://onl.dnp.gov.co/es/Publicaciones/Paginas/Plan-Maestro-Fluvial.aspx
4. Autosolar: Batería Estacionaria 600Ah 6V Ultracell UZS600-6 (2020). https://autosolar.es/baterias-estacionarias/bateria-estacionaria-600ah-6v-ultracell-uzs600-6
5. Autosolar: Panel Solar 335W 24V Policristalino ERA (2020). https://autosolar.es/panel-solar-24-voltios/panel-solar-335w-24v-policristalino-era
6. Bara Neto, P., Sánchez, R., Wilmsmeier, G.: Amazonía: hacia un desarrollo sustentable e integrado (2007)
7. Battery University: Cost of mobile and renewable power (2017). https://batteryuniversity.com/learn/article/bu_1006_cost_of_mobile_power
8. Bloomberg New Energy Finance: Electric Cars to Reach Price Parity by 2025 (2017). https://about.bnef.com/blog/electric-cars-reach-price-parity-2025/
9. Icetex: Colombia Científica (2017). http://colombiacientifica.gov.co/colombia/

10. IDEAM: Promedio horario de la radiación (Wh/m^2) (Sincelejo) (2020). http://atlas.ideam.gov.co/basefiles/RadiacionPDF/Sincelejo.pdf
11. Jaimurzina, A., Wilmsmeier, G., Montiel, D.: Eficiencia energética y movilidad eléctrica fluvial: soluciones sostenibles para la Amazonía. In: CEPAL (2017)
12. Minami, S., Yamachika, N.: A practical theory of the performance of low velocity boat. J. Asian Electr. Veh. **2**(1), 535–539 (2004)
13. Montoya, A., Guéret, C., Mendoza, J.E., Villegas, J.G.: The electric vehicle routing problem with nonlinear charging function. Transp. Res. Part B: Methodol. **103**, 87–110 (2017)
14. Quddus, M.A., Kabli, M., Marufuzzaman, M.: Modeling electric vehicle charging station expansion with an integration of renewable energy and vehicle-to-grid sources. Transp. Res. Part E: Logist. Transp. Rev. **128**, 251–279 (2019)
15. Sadeghi-Barzani, P., Rajabi-Ghahnavieh, A., Kazemi-Karegar, H.: Optimal fast charging station placing and sizing. Appl. Energy **125**, 289–299 (2014)
16. Timilsina, G.R., Shrestha, A.: Factors affecting transport sector CO2 emissions growth in Latin American and Caribbean countries: an LMDI decomposition analysis. Int. J. Energy Res. **33**(4), 396–414 (2009)
17. Ugirumurera, J., Haas, Z.J.: Optimal capacity sizing for completely green charging systems for electric vehicles. IEEE Trans. Transp. Electrif. **3**(3), 565–577 (2017)
18. Uhrig, M., Weiß, L., Suriyah, M., Leibfried, T.: E-mobility in car parks-guidelines for charging infrastructure expansion planning and operation based on stochastic simulations. In: EVS28 (2015)
19. Villa, D., Montoya, A., Ciro, J.M.: The electric boat charging problem. Production **29**, e20190067 (2019)
20. Wang, G., Xu, Z., Wen, F., Wong, K.P.: Traffic-constrained multiobjective planning of electric-vehicle charging stations. IEEE Trans. Power Delivery **28**(4), 2363–2372 (2013)
21. Wang, S., Luo, F., Dong, Z.Y., Ranzi, G.: Joint planning of active distribution networks considering renewable power uncertainty. Int. J. Electr. Power Energy Syst. **110**, 696–704 (2019)
22. Zhang, H., Moura, S.J., Hu, Z., Song, Y.: PEV fast-charging station siting and sizing on coupled transportation and power networks. IEEE Trans. Smart Grid **9**(4), 2595–2605 (2016)
23. Zhang, W., Yan, X., Zhang, D.: Charging station location optimization of electric ship based on backup coverage model. TransNav Int. J. Mar. Naviga. Saf. Sea Transp. **11**(2), 137–141 (2017)

Simulation of Single and Twin Impinging Jets in Cross-flow of VTOL Aircrafts (Review)

César A. Cárdenas R[1]($\boxtimes$), Carlos Andrés Collazos Morales[2],
Juan Carlos Amaya[3], Yaneth Patricia Caviativa Castro[1],
and Emiro De-la-Hoz-Franco[4]

[1] Universidad Manuela Beltrán, Vicerrectoría de Investigaciones,
Bogotá, Colombia
[2] Grupo de Ciencias Básicas y Laboratorios, Universidad Manuela Beltrán,
Bogotá, Colombia
[3] Universidad Manuela Beltrán, Departamento Ingeniería Electrónica,
Bogotá, Colombia
[4] Universidad de la Costa, Departamento de Ciencias de la Computación y
Electrónica, Barranquilla, Colombia
cesar.cardenas@docentes.umb.edu.co

Abstract. When operating near the ground beneath a Vertical/Short Take-Off and Landing (VSTOL) aircraft a complex turbulent 3D flow is generated. This flow field can be represented by the configuration of twin impinging jets in a cross-flow. Studying these jets is a significant parameter for the design of VTOL aircraft. This flowfield during very low speed or hover flight operations is very complex and time dependent. An important number of experimental researches and simulations have been carried out to be able to understand much better these flows related with powered lift vehicles. Computational Fluid Dynamics (CFD) approach will be used in this paper work for simulation purposes of a single and twin impinging jet through and without crossflow.

Keywords: VSTOL · Impingement jet · CFD · Crossflow

1 Nomenclature

- D: Diameter of the jet
- H: Height of the crossflow channel
- H/D: Blockage ratio
- k: Turbulence kinetic energy
- Re: Reynolds number
- S: Distance between the jet along transversal direction
- U: Horizontal Velocity
- V: Vertical Velocity
- V_j/U_o: Velocity ratio

© Springer Nature Switzerland AG 2020
J. C. Figueroa-García et al. (Eds.): WEA 2020, CCIS 1274, pp. 338–349, 2020.
https://doi.org/10.1007/978-3-030-61834-6_29

- X: Horizontal Coordinate
- Y: Vertical Coordinate
- Z: Transverse Coordinate
- W_c: Crossflow Velocity
- j: Jet exit Value
- 0: Crossflow Value

2 Introduction

A successful design of a VTOL aircraft will require an important mixture of propulsive lift system technology with some high speed aircraft characteristics. The VTOL aircraft configuration embraces several performance requirements as well as airframe configuration variables and lift system options. The major operational requirements of a VTOL aircraft which are responsible for the complex design are the vertical and transition flight conditions. These flight modes require a good understanding of the forces and moments to which the vehicle is subjected. These induced forces and moments as described in [11] which act in and out of ground effect, usually come up as a result of two well understood flow phenomena. These are jet entrainment and the formation of jet flow fountains. The jet entrainment effect occurs both in and out of regions influenced by the presence of the ground. It is regularly underlined as the distance between the nozzle exit and the ground. Fountains characteristics are influenced by the jet impingement points and angles. Due to the upward jet flow within the fountain, the performance of the propulsion system is reduced in consequence of exhaust gas ingestion. The turbulent flowfield strongly depends on the airframe and nozzle geometry along with the spacing of the aircraft structure to the ground plane. The flowfield configuration of a VTOL aircraft hovering in ground effect is shown in Fig. 1 [11]. There are different complexities related to the 3D flow generated underneath a VTOL aircraft. If the Harrier design configuration is considered, 1t will be important to provide some details about the jets coming out from the rear and front nozzles. Warm air from the fan is exhausted from the front nozzles as a hot/air fuel mixture from the engine is exhausted from the rear nozzles. The jets created impinge on the ground and move radially which form a ground jet flow. Headwind during hover opposes the jet flow. All this multiple jet interaction produces a flow separation and formation of an upwash fountain that strikes the underside of the fuselage. If the aircraft is sufficiently close to the ground the inlet can ingest ground debris and hot gases HGI from the fountain and ground vortex. This HGI can cause a sudden of thrust loss (lift). Additionally, the high speed jet flow along the ground can also entrain the ambient flow resulting in a low pressure region underneath the vehicle leading to what is known as "suckdown" effect which was mentioned earlier. Flowfields associated with geometrically simplified models such as single, double or multiple impinging jet with or without crossflow have been studied.

3   Research Approaches

The importance of being able to predict both the mean flow and unsteady features provides a relevant parameter for the design and development of future aircraft. In Fig. 1 the interaction phenomena of a VTOL aircraft in hover operation is shown. Other important features described in some jet impingement studies is firstly the fact that as flow moves away radially, a radial wall jet is formed. Wall jets are commonly accompanied by pressure loads which are high and unsteady. This can cause a significant ground erosion. Secondly, for beneficial purposes related to STOVL aircraft design, how the temperature of jet influences impingement jet characteristics needs still more research. Regarding the impinging jet structure it depends on the design Mach number, that is, nozzle geometry, nozzle pressure ratio, distance between nozzle exit and so on. Studies carried out by [2] late 1990 s described three different flow regimes as follows:

1. Primary flow region or jet free region.
2. Jet impingement zone.
3. Wall jet region.

The flow of single or multiple jet has had an important relevance in many engineering situations. Examples such as the discharge of exhaust gases from a chimney into a the atmosphere or liquids waste into water, film cooling of turbine blades, and so on. Additionally, if the cross flow is confined and the jet to crossflow is high, a complexity is introduced by jet impingement. The most practical relevant issue is the flow beneath a short takeoff/vertical landing (VSTOL) aircraft while operating close to the ground. In this condition the lift jets interact in such a strong way with the ground and crossflow forming a ground vortex that wraps around the impingement regions and an upwash fountain which results from the collision of wall jets. These phenomema can lead to engine thrust losses, reingestion of exhaust gases. Recently, several research papers have focused on the study of what is known as HGI (Hot Gas Ingestion). Later in this paper this topic the HG issue will be described a bit more in detail. Studying impingement jets in crossflow provides a basic understanding of the essential dynamics of these situations. The measurements were got in a water flow rig (water channel) under isothermal conditions. They do not represent the compressibility effects and coupling of the energy equation. However, they certainly allow the analysis of the turbulence structure and give a suitable test case to validate the physical modelling of the turbulent structure of VSTOL jets. Previous jet impingement studies were done just for single jets. These attempts showed that numerical schemes of high order and very fine meshes have got to be used to get accurate solutions. In one of the researches from [13,16] for the twin jet case the QUICK scheme was used to evaluate the convective terms and computational method performance. The water tunnel basic configuration was set up as also described in [13,16]. The Reynolds numbers and crossflow velocities of flow studies were given to allow VSTOL applications simulations. Single and twin jets were studied. This research has been the basis of many numerical studies from 90s onwards. The main reason why experimental studies have been carried out in a water tunnel is that some of the fluid mechanics issues of a VTOL flow are at enough low mach number what it makes the incompressible study justifiable. When considering computational studies of this kind, jet to crossflow velocity is a very important parameter since it controls the location of the ground vortex. More recent studies consider and includes other issues to get a much better understanding of these type of flows. Computational Fluid Dynamics (CFD) using the Reynolds Averaged Navier-Stokes (RANS) approach along with a Reynolds Stress Model (RSM) have been used to study these flows. Using a RSM model offers a relationship between the computational efficiency of a two equation turbulence model and accuracy closer to that of Large Eddy Simulation (LES). It will not be as accurate as LES, though. The mean velocity profiles are reasonably well predicted by both the standard $k - \epsilon$ model and the RSM with slightly better prediction by the RSM. However, Reynolds stress prediction by the RSM is poor which indicates that to capture the detailed unsteady flow features an LES would be required. There are different complexities with this flow created underneath the aircraft. The one considered as the main area of concern is the HGI issue. The ingestion possibility of hot gases back into the engine inlet. It can cause a dramatic loss of lift and a temperature increase. The HGI comes from the interaction of the impingement jet on the ground which is recirculated either in an upwash fountain or when there is a headwind. The upwards flow creates a vortex back to the inlets. It was found that the HGI into the inlets depend on the aircraft configuration and wind speed. These interaction effects have been considered as operational problems even an aerodynamics instability has been observed. Regarding HGI phenomenon it was also discovered that when hovering out of ground effect the jet streams that supports the aircraft induce suction pressures on the lower surfaces producing a down load. As it descends into ground effect, the jet streams impinge on the ground and form a radial wall jet flowing outward from the impingement points.

It was concluded that not only the upwash fountain but also ground vortex are involved in HGI. In [4, 12]. From the experimental study developed by [13, 16] different conclusions were drawn. The upwash fountain flow is created from collision of the jets with the ground plate; intense velocity fluctuations are observed in the shear layers surrounding the impingement regions from the jets and the upwash fountain. [3], worked with three different flow cases. One crossflow and equal jet velocities, another had no crossflow and unequal jet velocities, and the other had a crossflow and equal jet velocities. [3, 16] did two numerical studies using LES: twin impinging jets in a crossflow and twin impinging jets through a crossflow but including intake geometry. The LES results agree much better with the experimental data than the results obtained from the $k - \epsilon$ model. The second simulation was picked out to match the one carried out by [3], in their study about HGI. The conclusions were that the simulation unsteadiness was due to the flapping motion of the fountain, coupled with the impingement process. It was also observed that the results showed promise for LES value for application to multiple impinging jet cases when using real aircraft geometry.

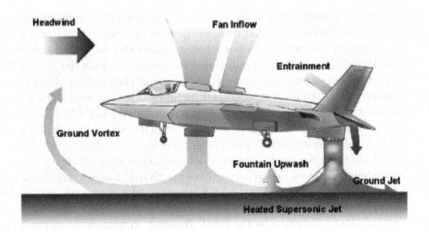

Fig. 1. Flowfield about a VTOL aircraft hovering in ground effect [11]

Likewise, a LES of a single impinging jet in cross-flow was done by [3,15,16]. It was compared to the LES results with a RANS-based $k - \epsilon$ model. It was demonstrated that the LES gave better results and its superiority of the LES approach over the RANS approach with a $k - \epsilon$ solution. Therefore, the above review shows that the results obtained from the $k - \epsilon$ model are not as accurate as LES but the computational cost of LES is still too high.In addition, It has been proved that the RSM model fails to predict the vortex attachment to the impingement jet. Although the current approach offers advantages over the $k - \epsilon$ model for gross flowfield approximations. Therefore as further investigation LES approach is recommended on issues such as the unsteady fountain, flow distortion and swirl in the intake. In addition, It has been proved that the RSM model fails to predict the vortex attachment to the impingement jet. This the reason why more research of this approach will be required to model these flow cases. In LES of a complete Harrier aircraft in ground effect by [15] and [16], a recent review done is quoted regarding jet induced effects for VSTOL. A summary of different attempts throughout several years to apply CFD tools in this type of application is mentioned. It seems that since the 1980s there has been some relevant CFD research into flows relevant to this aircraft. Not much work has been known for complete aircraft simulations, though. It looks like it has been due to the complexity of the HGI. Other studies such as the one performed by [18], present a fountain pattern layout as a result of the HGI effect. This is considered as the HGI governing mechanisms. Basically, it might be recognized that any mechanism may dominate depending on several factors such as onset flow direction, crossflow ratio (ratio of onset flow to jet speed), aircraft height, fuselage geometry, nozzle configuration. The fountain upward flows acting below the engine intake are assumed to be the responsible for the increase in engine intake temperatures [18].

It has also been concluded by other research papers that work related to the effect of the nozzle to plate spacing, jet angle and its influence on the pressure distribution, Reynolds number, nozzle to nozzle centerline spacing, velocity components, kinetic energy, for twin jet investigations has been really little [1]. Additionally, some other features have been studied such as stagnations points. In ground effect it is considered in other investigations that the behaviour prediction of the flow is given in a logical order from the aircraft lift jet exits to the free jets, jet impingement points, wall jets, fountain bases known as stagnation lines, and fountain upwash flow followed by impact on the aircraft structure undersurface. [11]. The suckdown flow has been also taken into consideration based upon the turbulent entrainment of both free jets and wall jets in ground effect and free jets out of the ground effect. [11]. It seems that parameters such as jet angle nozzle plate, nozzle to nozzle spacing have a significant influence on the sub atmospheric region. However, in this work it is considered that there have been certainly different works about twin jets lately. Furthermore, the focus of other researchers have been on heat transfer with compressible fluid characteristics and air as the working fluid for other industrial applications rather than particularly VTOL jets. It has been noticed that even the geometries models applied would not match with the ones used in studies done for instance by [15,20], in which besides some feed pipes, even an additional intake has been employed to deal with HGI. Indeed, jets in crossflow have been widely examined. Nonetheless, the main focus of investigations like the one described has been basically to study the presence of sub atmospheric region between two jets and the effect of nozzle/plate spacing features. [1], do not consider a water tunnel. The experimental device employed in this study is shown in Fig. 1. Moreover, the schematic for the twin jets is shown in Fig. 2. In an interesting investigation by [13], a computational approach is presented to study the behaviour of three twin-jet configurations handled by flow features which are based upon impingement jets on a flat plate and jet-jet interaction. These cases were taken as incompressible. One subjected to crossflow, another one is transonic. The important fact with his type of configurations is that all of them are closely related to VSTOL operation while operation close to the ground and at low speed. As it has been pointed out earlier in this work, single or twin/multiple impinging jets on a solid surface and subjected to crossflow have a very relevant importance for operational characteristics of VSTOL as operating in ground proximity. Once again in this research study, important consideration to fountain features is given. As wall jets collide as a result of impinging interaction, fountains come up showing that the turbulent structure have a strong influence on their behaviour. Besides, according to [13], any crossflow creates jet deflection and ground vortex on the impinging wall. In another research paper done by [8], the heat transfer coefficient has been considered for both impinging jets in cross flow and without cross flow and the way the jet to plate spacing influences on it. For instance some researches have found that when increasing cross flow, heat transfer performance decreases.

Besides, it was also found that the highest heat transfer coefficients are at jet-to-plate spacings between 5 and 6 jet diameters for high Reynolds numbers (higher than 70.000) and at a jet-to-plate spacing of 3D for low Reynolds numbers (aprox. 35. 000) with crossflow. The experimental equipment used by [8], is also a wind tunnel rectangular shaped with a 12 jet diameter. Another considerable variable studied has been the temperature effect in inclined jets in crossflow. It is a different approach since a fume is injected in the jets and the study objective is the interaction between them at certain jet angle, [17]. However, parameters as the ones taken in [1], were also examined (nozzle spacing). The most interesting issue of this research work in agreement with [17], is the possibility of having different arrangements for jet nozzles: tandem, side by side, staggered and opposed. It may be a bit controversial as [15,16,21], have also carried out investigations by employing similar layouts. VTOL fountain flow characteristics were also investigated by [20,20] by applying a LES approach. Once again, the flow is assumed as incompressible and governed by the Navier- Stokes equations. Some other variables such as excitation effect were taken into consideration. Its mainly focus is to find out about the interaction of the impinging jets and influence on the engine performance as studied by [17–20] employed a QUICK scheme to discretize the convective terms in the Navier-Stokes equations as the Adams-Bashforth scheme was used for the solution in time. Similarly, a finite difference scheme of second order was also used for space and time. It appears the mean jet exit is disturbed which can provide a possibility to capture data of the flow dynamics of large structures. Another similar research carried out by [20], but then main focus was on the excitation effects on the VTOL upward fountain. Again, the dominant equations employed are the Navier-Stokes equations taking an incompressible flow and a LES procedure. In this case the VTOL fountain created is disturbed at jet exits. The authors also focused on solving a three dimensional problem rather than a two dimensional one. The interaction description of how this fountain is originated is also discussed in the same way as in [15,18]. Furthermore, the differences between this fountain and free jets causes are also studied since they are considered as not well understood. The large scale structures are used to find out about how they interact closer to the fountain and when included into it. According to [19,20], there are different space and time disturbances in turbulent flows which are created due to the interaction of the fountain of the neighboring jets.

4   Numerical Procedures

The governing equations implemented in these studies are the ones derived from the fundamental physical principles such as conservation laws for mass, momentum and energy. Most of the studies carried out with these kind of jets match with the experiments done with water as the fluid material so the flow is incompressible. These governing equations are three dimensional and time dependent. They can be solved directly with mesh to capture every details of turbulent flow. This method is known as Direct Numerical Simulation (DNS) which is has a very high computationally demand and especially for high Reynolds number flow it is almost impossible to perform a DNS with the current computing power.

To simplify these calculations the RANS (Reynolds Average Navier-Stokes) approach has been taken. The governing equations are time-averaged so the results obtained are time-averaged quantities. RANS with a turbulence model can provide a reasonable prediction of the ground vortex and turbulent mean flow. However, it is not able to provide data on issues such as the unsteady fountain, flow distortion and swirl in the intake. In addition, It has been proved that the RSM model fails to predict the vortex attachment to the impingement jet. This the reason why more research of this approach will be required to model these flow cases. Another math approach that could be explore and proposed for further studies could be based in [5, 6, 9, 10].

4.1 RANS Equations

The governing equations taken are as follow:

Mass Conservation Equation

$$\frac{\partial U_i}{\partial x_i} = 0 \tag{1}$$

Momentum Equation

$$\frac{\partial U_i}{\partial x_i} + \frac{\partial (U_i U_j)}{\partial x_j} = -\frac{1}{\rho}\frac{\partial P}{\partial x_i} + \left[\nu \frac{\partial U_i}{\partial x_j}\right] - \frac{\partial (u_i u_j)}{\partial x_j} \tag{2}$$

Reynolds Stress Model RSM

$$\frac{\partial \overline{u_i u_j}}{\partial t} + \frac{\partial (\overline{U}_k \overline{u}_j u_j)}{\partial x_j} = -\overline{u_i u_k}\frac{\partial U_j}{\partial x_k} + \overline{u_i u_j}\frac{\partial \overline{U}_i}{\partial x_k}$$

$$+ \frac{\partial}{\partial x_k}\left[\nu\frac{\partial \overline{u_i u_j}}{\partial x_k} - \overline{u_i u_j u_k} - \frac{\overline{p}}{\rho}\overline{u_i \delta_{jk} + u_j \delta_{ik}}\right]$$

$$+ \left[\frac{p}{\rho}\frac{\partial u_i}{\partial x_j} + \frac{\partial u_j}{x_i}\right] - 2\nu\overline{\frac{\partial u_i}{\partial x_k}\frac{\partial u_j}{\partial u_k}} \tag{3}$$

Because of some numerical instabilities, the following simplified model has been considered:

$$\frac{DR_{ij}}{D_t} = \frac{\partial R_{ij}}{\partial t} + C_{ij} = P_{ij} + D_{ij} - \epsilon_{ij} + \Pi_{ij} + \Omega_{ij} \tag{4}$$

4.2 Pressure Strain Model

The following pressure - strain model was proposed by [7] where $C_1 = 1.8, C_2 = 0.60, C_1' = 0.5, C_2' = 0.3$

$$\varphi_{ij}1 = C_1\rho\frac{\epsilon}{k}\overline{(u_iu_j)} - \frac{2}{3}\delta_{ij}k \tag{5}$$

$$\varphi_{ij}1 = C_2\left[P_{ij} + C_{ij} - \frac{2}{3}\delta_{ij}(P - C)\right]$$

$$\varphi_{ijw} = -C_1\left[\overline{u_ku_m}n_kn_m\delta_{ij} - \frac{3}{2}\overline{u_ku_i}n_kn_j - \frac{3}{2}\overline{u_ku_j}n_kn_i\right]\frac{0.4k^{3/2}}{\epsilon d}$$

$$+C_2\left[\varphi_{km,2}\,n_kn_m\delta - ij - \frac{3}{2}\varphi_{ik,2}n_kn_j - \frac{3}{2}\varphi_{jk,2}n_kn_i\right]\frac{0.4k^{3/2}}{\epsilon d}$$

4.3   Dissipation Transport Equation Model

$$\frac{\partial(\rho\epsilon)}{\partial t} + \frac{\partial\rho\epsilon U_i}{\partial x_i} = \frac{\partial}{\partial x_i}\left[\left(\mu + \frac{\mu_t}{\sigma_\epsilon}\right)\frac{\partial\epsilon}{\partial x_i}\right] + \frac{1}{2}C_{1\epsilon}P_{ii} - \frac{\epsilon}{pk}C_{\epsilon 2}\frac{\epsilon^2}{k} \tag{6}$$

where $\sigma_\epsilon = 1.0$, $C_{1\epsilon} = 1.44$, $C_{2\epsilon} = 1.92$

The domain employed by [14,16,21] has been a 1.50.10.5 m domain. Both square and circular jet inlet geometry has been tested. An additional intake has been also included as shown in Fig. 7. The mesh with the intake case in shown in Fig. 8 as well. The average values taken for Reynolds have been from 60.000 to 105.000. Jet and crossflow velocities of about 3 and 0.1 m/s have been applied as inlets boundaries. Shear stresses have been taken as zero. Other boundaries details have been implemented based upon the research paper by [14,16]. As an outflow boundary, a zero gradient has been applied on the outlet face. Furthermore, simplified geometries have been taken to be able to make the flow problem fluid representative of the most important components of a VSTOL aircraft flowfield ground issues. In [1], the mathematical model involves similar mathematical models as in [14,16], conservation of mass, momentum turbulent kinetic energy and turbulent energy dissipation. Equations solved by using a volume difference method. The numerical solution is managed by SIMPLE method. The numerical method and geometries employed in [13] are based on the investigations developed by [14–16]. Particularly, a comparison among all these models is done. (Compressible - incompressible twin jet, incompressible twin jet in cross flow). In the research performed by [17], the flow was also assumed as turbulent, incompressible and three dimensional applying the Navier-Stokes equations to describe the conservation laws of momentum, mass and energy as in for instance [14,16] and so on. The geometry taken is even very close to the one outlined by [14,16,21] Fig. 4. The considerable difference is that it is a wind tunnel rather than a water one, though. It is show in Fig. 4. In [18], the meshing process was done based upon a previous CAD model which was then imported to the ICEMCEFD grid generator. It looks like a hexa mesh type is the best option because the cell faces are aligned with the direction of the flow. A tetra mesh was employed specifically for the less important regions and is not suitable for LES calculations because of the importance to avoid rapid changes in the mesh density. it was thought important to use hexa mesh to solve variables such as the ground vortex, the fountain upwash flows, and the flows along the underside of the aircraft. The solver used in this experimental work was the URANS (Unsteady Reynolds averaged Navier Stokes) and then the URANS Spalart-Allmaras (SA) turbulence model which shows how the HGI features affect the profiles of the engine intake temperatures. Later, in this same research work is pointed out a code description which involves a HYDRA code developed by Rolls-Royce and some partner universities. Its aim is to solve unstructured meshes with some specific data structure. In addtion, turbulence is modelled using either the Spalart-Allmaras or $k - \epsilon$ turbulence models, and that an additional Smagorinsky based LES is also available.

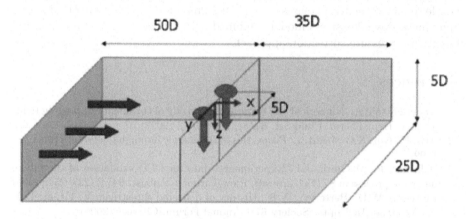

Fig. 2. Twin jet configuration, [14,16] for a LES study of twin jets in crossflow

5   Results and Conclusions

Many of the outcomes presented in these investigations have considered uniform inlet boundary conditions. Some results have shown that there have not been actually so far any improvements over the steady RANS, and particularly did not capture some important unsteady features due to turbulence. So, it is evident that some important turbulent unsteady features can only be captured by LES. However, the RSM models show some improvements over the k-e model. Also, significant improvements of RSM over eddy-viscosity have been noticed. For instance, in Large eddy simulation of twin impinging jet in crossflow by [14,16,21], a remarkable perspective shown states that RANS method could predict a large scale of unsteadiness issues in the ground vortex. Nonetheless, it will not improve the prediction of the near field. When LES is used, a Strouhal number of about 0.1 is taken. Other algorithms to study the behaviour of these flows have been applied. One of them is the Rolls Royce CFD code hydra, Fig. 15. It was implemented in LES crossflow simulation of twin impingements jets again by [14,16]. It includes a RANS unstructured and compressible solver. The computational domain used in LES have been the same water tunnel described in the research papers pointed in this work, Fig. 6. Additionally, in spite of the scarce information about the flow field experimental data for VTOL aircraft in ground effect, this research review attempts to compile the most remarkable features for twin impinging simulation. Very important conclusions could be drawn from [1]. A sub atmospheric region is created with jets of higher Reynolds number and at lower nozzle to plate spacing. Pressure grows when Reynolds number increases. Therefore, the sub atmospheric region becomes stronger. Pressure at primary and secondary stagnations points comes reduces as the nozzle to plate spacing increases as well as Reynolds number decreases. Likewise, turbulent kinetic energy increases in each vortex region. It decreases when the jet angle and/or the nozzle to plate spacing increases. The results presented by [13], were obtained by applying a Reynolds stress model combined with a higher-order approximation based on a pressure-correction approach.

References

1. Abdel-Fattah, A.: Numerical and experimental study of turbulent im- pinging twin-jet flow. Exp. Therm. Fluid Sci. **31**(8), 1061–1072 (2007)
2. Alvi, F., Iyer, K.G., Ladd, J.: Properties of supersonic impinging jets. In: November 1999
3. Behrouzi, P., McGuirk, J.J.: Experimental data for CFD validation of the intake ingestion process in STOVL aircraft. Flow Turbul. Combust. **64**(4), 233–251 (2000)
4. Bertelsen, W.D., Bertelsen, W.R.: History of deflected slip-stream VTOL aircraft. In: American Helicopter Society 61st Annual Forum. Citeseer (2005)
5. Collazos, C., et al.: State estimation of a dehydration process by interval analysis. In: Figueroa-García, J.C., López-Santana, E.R., Rodriguez-Molano, J.I. (eds.) WEA 2018. CCIS, vol. 915, pp. 66–77. Springer, Cham (2018). https://doi.org/10.1007/978-3-030-00350-0_6
6. Collazos, C.A., et al.: Detection of faults in an osmotic dehydration process through state estimation and interval analysis. In: Misra, S., et al. (eds.) ICCSA 2019. LNCS, vol. 11620, pp. 699–712. Springer, Cham (2019). https://doi.org/10.1007/978-3-030-24296-1_56
7. Gibson, M.M., Launder, B.E.: Ground effects on pressure fluctuations in the atmospheric boundary layer. J. Fluid Mech. **86**(3), 491–511 (1978)
8. Goldstein, R.J., Behbahani, A.I.: Impingement of a circular jet with and without cross flow. Int. J. Heat Mass Transf. **25**(9), 1377–1382 (1982)
9. Cárdenas R., C.A., et al.: Correction to: quadrotor modeling and a PID control approach. In: Tiwary, U.S., Chaudhury, S. (eds.) IHCI 2019. LNCS, vol. 11886, pp. C1–C1. Springer, Cham (2020). https://doi.org/10.1007/978-3-030-44689-5_26
10. Jiménez-Cabas, J., et al.: Robust control of an evaporator through algebraic riccati equations and DK iteration. In: Misra, S., et al. (eds.) ICCSA 2019. LNCS, vol. 11620, pp. 731–742. Springer, Cham (2019). https://doi.org/10.1007/978-3-030-24296-1_58

11. Patel, K., Shah, H., Dcosta, M., Shastri, D.: Evaluating neurosky's single-channel EEG sensor for drowsiness detection. In: Stephanidis, C. (ed.) HCI 2017. CCIS, vol. 713, pp. 243–250. Springer, Cham (2017). https://doi.org/10.1007/978-3-319-58750-9_35

12. Kuhn, R.E.: Review of Basic Principles of V/STOL Aerodynamics. National Aeronautics and Space Administration, Washington, D.C. (1960)

13. Leschziner, M.A., Ince, N.Z.: Computational modelling of three-dimensional impinging jets with and without cross-flow using second-moment closure. Comput. Fluids **24**(7), 811–832 (1995)

14. Li, Q., Page, G.J., McGuirk, J.J.: Large-eddy simulation of twin impinging jets in cross-flow. Aeronaut. J. **111**(1117), 195–206 (2007)

15. McGuirk, J., et al.: Simulation of an impinging jet in a cross flow using an LES method. In: 2002 Biennial International Powered Lift Conference and Exhibit, p. 5959

16. Page, G.J., McGuirk, J.J.: Large eddy simulation of a complete Harrier aircraft in ground effect. Aeronaut. J. **113**(1140), 99–106 (2009)

17. Radhouane, A., Mahjoub Saïd, N., Mhiri, H., Bournot, H., Le Palec, G.: Dynamics of the flowfield generated by the interaction of twin inclined jets of variable temperatures with an oncoming crossflow. Heat and Mass Transf. **50**(2), 253–274 (2013). https://doi.org/10.1007/s00231-013-1241-9

18. Richardson, G.A., Dawes, W.N., Savill, A.M.: An unsteady, moving mesh CFD simulation for Harrier hot-gas ingestion control analysis. Aeronaut. J. **111**(1117), 133–144 (2007)

19. Rizk, M.H., Menon, S.: Large-eddy simulations of axisymmetric excitation effects on a row of impinging jets. Phys. Fluids **31**(7), 1892–1903 (1988)

20. Rizk, M.H., Menon, S.: Large-eddy simulations of excitation effects on a VTOL upwash fountain. Phys. Fluids Fluid Dyn. **1**(4), 732–740 (1989)

21. Worth, N.A., Yang, Z.: Simulation of an impinging jet in a cross flow using a reynolds stress transport model. Int. J. Numer. Methods Fuids **52**(2), 199–211 (2006)

Computational Analysis of the IN718 Material Microstructure (Nickel-Based INCONEL Superalloy): Potential Applications in the Military Industry

Fabián Garay[1]([🖂]) [iD], Gustavo Suárez[2] [iD], Karina De la Hoz[2] [iD], Elvis Urraya[2] [iD],
Paula Loaiza[2] [iD], Luis Javier Cruz[2] [iD], Alejandro Ángel[2] [iD],
and Moisés David Ortells[1] [iD]

[1] Escuela de Infantería, Ejercito Nacional de Colombia, Bogotá, Colombia
fsgrairan@gmail.com, cienciatecnologia.esinf@cedoc.edu.co
[2] Grupo de Investigación Sobre Nuevos Materiales, Facultad de Ingeniería, Universidad
Pontificia Bolivariana, Medellín, Colombia
{gustavo.suarez,elvis.urraya,paula.loaiza,luis.cruz,
Alexandra.de,alejandro.angelc}@upb.edu.co

Abstract. The alloy IN718 (Ni-Fe superalloy) hardened by precipitation, possesses an extensive use for applications both in the aeronautical and military industry due to its good castability, weldability and corrosion resistance, and excellent mechanical properties. In this research, computational simulations were developed to analyze the behavior of an IN718 microstructure subjected to conditions of mechanical stress. An elastic-linear model was established and implemented on IN718 probes with different percentages of the incorporated elements. (Ni-Fe-Cr). Mechanical properties, Young modulus and Poisson ratios were determined for each component of the material. The constitutive equations were solved by the Finite Difference Method (F.D.M). The computational implementations for the two probes were made in Matlab. The results displayed an excellent mechanical contribution from each component of the alloy, increasing the mechanical properties of the alloy evidently. This research can ease the analysis of microstructured alloys with the implementation of computational techniques that facilitate the analysis of mechanical behavior, varying the percentages of each element of the alloy and confirm the various possibilities of applications in the military industry.

Keywords: Superalloys · High temperature alloys · IN718 nickel-based superalloy · Modeling and simulation · Finite differences (MDF) · Military industry

1 Introduction

Inconel 718 is an alloy that can be age hardened, it is comprised mainly by Nickel, Chromium and Iron, with fundamental properties, such as high tensile strength and creep, and it is designed with the intention of withstanding a wide range of high corrosive

© Springer Nature Switzerland AG 2020
J. C. Figueroa-García et al. (Eds.): WEA 2020, CCIS 1274, pp. 350–359, 2020.
https://doi.org/10.1007/978-3-030-61834-6_30

environments, pitting and stress corrosion. It is characterized by its ease of manufacture, excellent resistance to welding and fracture toughness after the latter. These types of materials require computational analyses that help evince and understand its mechanical performance.

1.1 Nickel-Based Superalloys (IN718)

Nickel-based superalloys can be found in the hotter parts of the metal, which is why its use is common in this area of metallurgy [3]. In the International Nickel Study Group (INSG) report from April of 2013, it is remarked that this superalloy corresponds to around 50% of the weight of modern aviation engines, this is mainly due to its high stability characteristics and the possibility of improving its strength and superficial stability with Chromium and Aluminum alloys [1]. The alloy between Ni-Fe gives as a result the superalloy IN718 that can be hardened by precipitation, within its properties the ones that stand out are castability, weldability and its potential mechanical properties and corrosion resistance, which is why it can be seen widely used in the aerospace industry [11]. Figure 1 shows the computational model of the Inconel 718 microstructure.

Fig. 1. Voxels model of the Inconel 718 microstructure [11].

1.2 Micromechanical Model of the Fatigue Behavior of a Nickel-Based Superalloy

In the research carried out by Segurado in 2016 a computational tool was developed to predict the fatigue life of the Inconel 718 superalloy based on cyclic behavior models of the superalloy through finite element simulations of representative volumes (RVEs) of the polycrystalline microstructure, with which Fatigue Indicating Parameters (FIPs) were obtained. The model consisted of a phenomenological relationship between the number of cycles to initiate fatigue, the FIP values, local plastic deformation and the formation of Persistent Slip Bands (PSB); as a result, the predictions of the model were accurate with respect to the potential model for high and medium applied deformation ranges, showing the ability of the tool to estimate the life of the material in these cases allowing to reduce the number of tests required [11].

1.3 Multiscale Modeling of the Mechanical Behavior of IN718 Superalloy Based on Micropillar Compression and Computational Homogenization

In this study, a multiscale model of the IN718 polycrystalline material is made with the purpose of determining its effective mechanical properties, for that it is made use of a computational homogenization of a representative volume element of the microstructure built from the grain size distribution, shape and orientation of the material; the simulation was made under a crystalline plasticity model, and was validated by a comparison with experimental tests made on the material. As a result of the comparative assessment, the model successfully predicted the compression of the wrought IN718 [5].

1.4 Slip System Characterization of Inconel 718 Using In-Situ Scanning Electron Microscopy

Within the different methods of characterization of the IN718 there is the In-Situ Scanning Electron Microscopy (SEM), in this study the slip system and tension identification of the superalloy to which the slip systems of the superalloy activated was characterized, as a result, there are between 60 to 90 s to obtain the images equivalent to a displacement rate of 0.004 mm/s and a deformation rate of 10–3/s. Between other aspects taken into account, there is the grain orientation of the surface to identify the orientations of the slip planes and the Schmid factor as an indicator of shear stress; as a result this factor is approximately zero which indicates an orientation that is hard to use for the activation of a particular slip system, there were also grain 17 slip bands that were found with a factor of Schimd of 0.46 (the highest) and two activated slip systems in grain 52 and in grain 64 [4].

1.5 Prediction of Mechanical Properties of Superplastic Inconel 718 Using Artificial Neural Networks

This work makes use of an artificial neural network (ANN) with a two-layer architecture on the materials science field for the estimation of the mechanical properties of the Inconel 718 superalloy and the prediction of said properties, the algorithm that was selected for the optimization process was backpropagation; the use of ANN showed as a result the correlation between various stress flow values obtained as a function of the speed and temperature of formation, localized plastic instability effects, computations of exponentials of hardening of work h and sensitivity to deformation [7].

1.6 IN718 in the Military Industry

The IN718 superalloy is not excluded of its potential in the military industry, within its most highlighted uses in this sector one can find, manufacturing of military aircraft gas turbines, submarines and military electric engines [10]. In the aerospace sector there have been studies carried out to evaluate the most adequate parameters of welding to be applied on IN718 for space applications, gas turbine manufacture and aviation engines which require a high strength and creep resistance, in Enrico Lertora's research from 2014, the main application focused in the manufacturing of components for helicopter engines [8].

Other researches have evaluated the effects of heat treatment in this superalloy to ballistic impact and fail mechanisms, for the said task it was made use of the evaluation of deformation rates and measurement of velocities required for penetration with Ti-6-4 projectiles of 12.5 mm of cylinder diameter and 25.4 mm of length that impact flat plates in the range of 150–300 m/s; as a result an annealed IN718 was able to absorb more than 25% of the energy in comparison to aged materials [9]. Some armory companies such as Altemp Alloys Inc develop alloy products of high performance and able to withstand high temperatures for reaction engines, structures, vehicles and vessels that protect the armed forces, highlighting its high resistance and durability, its corrosion resistance, creep, and high wear out levels [2]. Figure 2 shows a military platform whose caterpillar traction system has been manufactured with the superalloy IN718.

Fig. 2. Superalloy applied in a military vehicle with caterpillar traction [2].

2   Materials and Methods

The micromechanic behaviors can be developed through formulations [12]:

Models based on the mechanics of materials in which a tension field and uniform deformations in the constituents is assumed as a simplified hypothesis.

Models based on the classic elasticity theory that provide formulations of bounded problems. These require the use of numerical methods tools for the estimation of the tensions and deformations at a micromechanic level.

Empirical models based on curve fitting of data obtained experimentally.

In this research, elasticity models were implemented for each constituent material complementing the theory with a Voxels' design that considers the percentage of grains of each material in the probes. In this way the representation of the phenomenon is improved [11, 12].

For the development of this research the Matlab program was used in the process of simulation an microstructural analysis for 2 probes of the material, to accomplish this, a mathematical modeling was made where design and loads were considered, and finally, the computational considerations were taken into account. Next, the mentioned phases are detailed.

2.1 Mathematical Modeling

A constitutive model was worked out defined by Hooke's law applied in the analysis of isotropic elastic-linear materials [6].

The formulation of the constitutive law is defined as [6]:

$$\sigma_{ij} = C_{ij}\varepsilon_j \tag{1}$$

Hooke's law of elasticity, which is described as:

$$E_m A_t \left(\frac{\partial^2 u}{\partial x^2} + \frac{\partial^2 u}{\partial y^2} \right) = P \tag{2}$$

Where:

E_m modulus of elasticity of the material from the alloy, $m = 1, 2, 3 \ldots, 12$
A_t transverse area of the probes used for the mechanical tests.
P internal pressure product of the material's properties.
u displacements due to micro-strains of the material.
C material's constitutive properties matrix.
σ stress of the material.
ε strains of the material

Using numerical techniques to solve the partial differential equation, it can be shown that:

$$E_m A_t \left(\frac{A_{i,i+1}u_{i,i+1} - 2A_{i,i}u_{i,i} + A_{i,i-1}u_{i,i-1}}{hx^2} + \frac{A_{i,i+51}u_{i,i+51} - 2A_{i,i}u_{i,i} + A_{i,i-51}u_{i,i-51}}{hy^2} \right) = P \tag{3}$$

And by solving the system, the following equation is obtained:

$$\frac{u_{i,i+1}}{hx^2} - \frac{2u_{i,i}}{hx^2} + \frac{u_{i,i-1}}{hx^2} + \frac{u_{i,i+51}}{hy^2} - \frac{2u_{i,i}}{hy^2} + \frac{u_{i,i-51}}{hy^2} = \frac{P}{E_m A_t} \tag{4}$$

Where:

hx, hy: represent the numerical partitions of the F.D.M.

Being the latter, the equation implemented in the software Matlab to model the micrometric behavior considering the properties of each material from the alloy.

The behavior of the material subjected to plane tensile stress was analyzed. The properties of the incorporated materials were the following (Table 1).

Table 1. Properties of the implemented material.

N°	Material type	Young's modulus E_m [pa]	Poisson radio: ν [−]
1	NICKEL	$2 \times 10\char`\^11$	0,3
2	CHROME	$2,79 \times 10\char`\^11$	0,21
3	MOLYBDENUM	$3,29 \times 10\char`\^11$	0,293
5	NIOBIO	$1,05 \times 10\char`\^11$	0,35
6	COBALT	$2,09 \times 10\char`\^11$	0,32
7	ALUMINUM	$7 \times 10\char`\^10$	0,33
8	MANGANESE	$1,98 \times 10\char`\^11$	0,24
9	SILICON	$4,7 \times 10\char`\^10$	0,42
10	COPPER	$1,3 \times 10\char`\^11$	0,34

2.2 Design and Loads Considerations

A two flat sheet geometry was designed with dimensions 0.15 m × 0.048 m, 0.148 m × 0.046 m, respectively. The boundary conditions were established in terms of loads to assess the micromechanical behavior of the Inconel 718, the designs can be seen in Fig. 3.

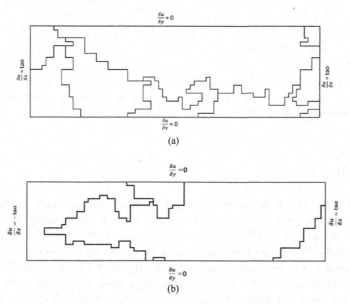

Fig. 3. Micro-mechanical structural model for the two plane layers (a) and (b).

2.3 Computational Considerations

Two uniform numerical reticles with rectangular elements were made with a total of 1800 and 1702 to represent the behavior of the problem in this nodal location. The reticle shapes were defined based on the adjustment of shapes of the geometry over the reticles.

Two algorithms were implemented in Matlab to solve the problem described by the physical laws of behavior of the phenomenon, using the Finite Different Method (FDM). In Fig. 4 it can be seen the result of the definition of the uniform reticles for each sheet. The Voxels model is built from the distinction of the different materials through the occupation of the micro grains within the structure. Each color characterizes the material that comprises the alloy. The number of grains in each component is identified through cells and at the same time described by the mechanical properties of each material, Fig. 4.

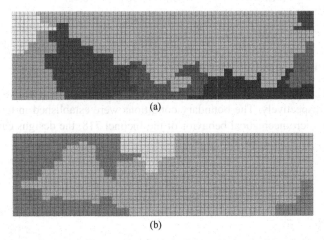

Fig. 4. Definition of the uniform numerical reticles (a) and (b), purple=molybdenum, blue=chromium, yellow=silicon, green=aluminum, pink=nickel, brown=copper, niobium=red, golden=magnesium, gold=cobalt.

3 Results

The simulations of the material behavior were obtained for two different configurations, the configuration of Fig. (4a), values of strain in terms of displacement were obtained within the range of [0.55, 0.95] mm, and for the model (4b) of [0.78, 0.92] mm. See Fig. (5a) and (5b). The polychromatic range describes the distribution of energy of deformation that achieves each component within the alloy. The greater the deformation in terms of displacements, the polychromatic range tends to a red spectrum of colors and the lower the deformation in terms of displacements, the polychromatic range tends to a blue spectrum of colors.

The maximum displacements of the material were localized in the nickel, silicon and chromium grains Fig. 6.

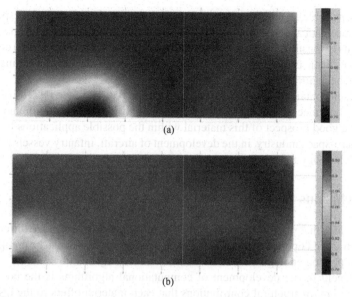

(a)

(b)

Fig. 5. Simulations of the material behavior with configurations: (a) and (b).

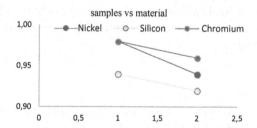

samples vs material

●—Nickel   ○ Silicon   ●— Chromium

Fig. 6. Numerical results of the maximum values of the materials in samples (a) and (b).

Aluminium coupled with copper and molybdenum grains was the combination that presented the best mechanical behavior in the tests (u =0.76). Following, the aluminium coupled with nickel grains presented a good mechanical behavior (u =0.85).

4 Analysis

The simulations showed a good behavior of the material Inconel 718 subjected to traction loads. Probe (a) indicated a better elastic behavior with an alloy comprised of a greater number of different material components, nevertheless plate (b) displayed a greater mechanical resistance.

From the results it can be seen that Nickel contributed with an elastic behavior, in the same way as Aluminium. Each contribution to the alloy from the metallic components of the plane plates can be seen in the simulations. For each probe different percentages were considered with the purpose of visualizing its contribution to the alloy.

It was possible to validate what was reported in the literature with respect to the excellent mechanical performance of the alloy, evident improvements due to each of the components of the alloy, in the same way the results indicate that Nickel (Ni) contributed with a more elastic behavior than the rest of the elements of the alloy providing a greater dissipative behavior of the deformation energy.

The results obtained from the microstructural simulations of the IN718-based superalloy, the good mechanical performance, machinability, tensile strength and low cost, confirm the good prospect of this material within the possible applications for the military and aero-space industry, in the development of aircraft, infantry vessels and general defense technology for the Colombian National Army.

5 Conclusions

The algorithms that were implemented provide the possibility to analyze different material properties and operating conditions. The mathematical model can be complemented with other phenomenological conditions in a versatile way.

The benefit of the development of computational algorithms is the possibility to analyze the micro-structural contributions that each material offers to the tested alloy. This research contributes with additional knowledge in the experimental processes that are being developed in alloys under a micro-structural scope.

The computational implementations ease different mechanical behavior analyses, varying the percentages of each element of the alloy, moreover experimental testing costs could be reduced.

References

1. Akca, E., Gursel, A.: A review on superalloys and IN718 nickel-based INCONEL superalloy. 3(1) (2015). https://doi.org/10.21533/pen.v3i1.43
2. Altemp Alloys INC.: Alloys for military and defense - nickel based alloys. https://www.altempalloys.com/defense.html. Accessed 18 June 2020
3. Betteridge, W., Heslop, J.: The Nimonic Alloys and other Nickel-Base High- Temperature Alloys. Edward Arnold, New York (1974)
4. Boehlert, C.J., et al.: Slip system characterization of Inconel 718 using in-situ scanning electron microscopy. Adv. Mater. Process. **168**, 41–45 (2010)
5. Cruzado, A., et al.: Multiscale modeling of the mechanical behavior of IN718 superalloy based on micropillar compression and computational homogenization. Acta Mater. **98**, 242–253 (2015). https://doi.org/10.1016/j.actamat.2015.07.006
6. Gere, J.M.: Timoshenko. Resistencia de materiales (2002)
7. Huang, Y., Blackwell, P.L.: Prediction of mechanical properties of superplastic Inconel 718 using artificial neural networks. Mater. Sci. Technol. **18**(10), 1104–1108 (2002). https://doi.org/10.1179/026708302225006016
8. Lertora, E., et al.: Mechanical behaviour of Inconel 718 thin-walled laser welded components for aircraft engines. Int. J. Aerosp. Eng. **2014**, 721680 (2014). https://doi.org/10.1155/2014/721680
9. Pereira, J.M., Lerch, B.A.: Effects of heat treatment on the ballistic impact properties of Inconel 718 for jet engine fan containment applications. Int. J. Impact Eng. **25**(8), 715–733 (2001). https://doi.org/10.1016/S0734-743X(01)00018-5

10. Pollock, T.M., Tin, S.: Nickel-based superalloys for advanced turbine engines: chemistry. Microstruct. Prop. J. Propuls. Power. **22**(2), 361–374 (2006). https://doi.org/10.2514/1.18239
11. Segurado, J., et al.: Un modelo micromecánico del comportamiento en fatiga de una superaliación de Base Niquel. In: ANales de Mecánica de la Fractura 33. pp. 1–7 (2016)
12. Hyer, M.W.: Stress Analysis of Fiber-reinforced Composite Materials. DEStech Publications Inc., Lancaster (2008)

Simulation, IoT and Networks

Development of an IoT Platform for Monitoring Electric Vehicle Behaviour

Santiago Echavarría[1]([✉]), Ricardo Mejía-Gutiérrez[1], and Alejandro Montoya[2]

[1] Design Engineering Research Group (GRID), Universidad EAFIT,
Carrera 49 No 7 Sur–50, Medellín, Colombia
{sechava4,rmejiag}@eafit.edu.co
[2] Departamento de Ingeniería de Producción, Universidad EAFIT,
Carrera 49 No 7 Sur–50, Medellín, Colombia
jmonto36@eafit.edu.co

Abstract. Batteries are the largest contributor to the high value of electric vehicles. The lack of knowledge about the effect of driving style, charging strategies, and routes taken on battery degradation rests on the lack of real operating data describing these factors. For this reason, the design of a monitoring system that collects such information is proposed. Initially, in a variable prioritization stage, a functional analysis identifies the system variables and potential information collection points. Additional vehicle sensor information is collected through an OBD-II (The OBD term, stands from the acronym of "On Board Diagnosis (OBD)") port data-logger. Subsequently, the function to data method prioritizes and reduces the set of variables for each operating state. Then, a finite state machine selects the set of monitoring variables accordingly. With this result, the instrumentation architecture of the vehicle is defined, as well as the development of a data-oriented web application, which allows visualizing, using different approaches, the variables previously defined.

Keywords: Electric vehicle · IoT · Variable selection · Monitoring · Instrumentation · Data visualization

1 Introduction

Electric Vehicles (EV) have become a popular transportation option due to their low operation costs, exemption from environmental containment, tax benefits, and the elimination of emissions. Such emissions are responsible for heart, lung, and cardiovascular diseases World Health Organization (WHO). However, such growth has led to many questions from potential buyers. Among them, two main reasons stand out, the high price and the battery degradation. Regarding the price, batteries are the biggest contributor to the acquisition and maintenance value of these vehicles. To compete in price with a combustion engine vehicle, electric vehicle batteries should go from $208 per kWh (NISSAN Leaf (NL)

© Springer Nature Switzerland AG 2020
J. C. Figueroa-García et al. (Eds.): WEA 2020, CCIS 1274, pp. 363–374, 2020.
https://doi.org/10.1007/978-3-030-61834-6_31

24 kWh reference, at the time of this writing) to below \$100 per kWh [1]. Moreover, this price must be associated with a lower manufacturing cost and a longer useful life.

In terms of battery degradation, According to Soon [2], the health status State of Health (SoH) of a battery can be defined as $SoH = C(dis, act)/C(dis, init)$. Where $C(dis, act)$ is the maximum amount of energy the battery can deliver in operation in a complete discharge at the current time, and $C(dis, init)$ is the factory rated capacity of the battery. The main causes are electrolyte decomposition, contact loss in the active material, and Corrosion on the current collector [3]. These causes are related to operation variables such as: charge and discharge currents [4], depth of discharge [5], temperatures [6], State of Charge (SoC), overloads, and over discharges [7].

Battery degradation cannot be measured with conventional sensors [7]. For this reason, various estimation methods have been developed based on battery terminals measurements, such as voltage, current, temperature, and operating times. To that aim, Murnane [8] stated that using the enhanced coulomb counting method along with the universal SOC algorithm, the estimation error in SoH does not exceed 2%.

Since SoH tells about the current state of the battery, Remaining Useful Life (RUL) models predict how many cycles it takes until a degradation limit is reached. These allow the characterization of battery usage and the generation of use strategies. To obtain accurate estimates, it is necessary to record the evolution of SoH over time.

Regarding the existing RUL estimation models for EV applications, Pelletier [7] presented battery degradation models. However, factors such as road, traffic, and environmental conditions, make them inaccurate for a real driving application due to variations in input parameters. To this aim, data driven models have been developed. However, most of them have been made in laboratory environments: Nuhic [9] developed discharge cycles in battery testers to simulate standard driving cycles. On the other hand, Barré [10] developed an estimation method based on real driving data, but ignored the effect of topographic conditions, charging profiles, and it is developed with only one vehicle and driving style which reduces its external applicability.

Besides, RUL estimation models made from driving cycles developed in Europe and Asia will likely fail to produce proper results in Latin America due to the differences in road infrastructure. To reference this issue, according to the World Economic Forum, Colombia ranks 120th out of 138 countries worldwide. In synthesis, evidence shows a lack of models for EV lithium-ion battery life estimation model that includes topographical road factors, charging, and driving behavior based on real operation data.

In synthesis, the existing battery RUL estimation models for EV generate uncertainty for real-world applications since they ignore key factors regarding diverse users and road conditions. Besides, it is not possible to determine the causes of degradation using such models. Therefore, this lack of information hinders taking corrective actions to preserve high-value components such as the battery.

This study aims to develop a monitoring and data collection system that captures the most significant information concerning the listed inputs, in order to create a baseline for the development of a battery RUL estimation model. Initially, in a variable prioritization phase, a functional analysis identifies the system variables and potential information collection points. Vehicle sensor information is collected through an OBD-II port data-logger. Subsequently, the function to data method prioritizes and reduces the set of variables for each operating state. Then, a finite state machine selects the set of monitoring variables accordingly. With this result, the instrumentation architecture of the vehicle is defined. Finally, the development of a data-oriented web application that allows visualizing, using different approaches, the resulting variables is presented.

2 State of the Art

For the aim of this paper, two categories of monitoring related topics were reviewed: driving behavior detection and instrumentation for battery health monitoring.

Regarding driver behavior recognition literature, different classifications can be found. For example, Smith [11] monitored 76 vehicles using a GPS reception data-logger, there, position, speed, and acceleration data were obtained. The study aimed to identify driving patterns in people of different gender, education, age, and profession. Among the results obtained, a classification of power consumption patterns into 8 groups is obtained, depending on the type of road. However, the use of a standalone GPS module ignores the effect of environmental conditions. Conditions such as rain and light, affect driving patterns, see [12,13]. Furthermore, Johnson [14] classified driving behavior into two main groups, aggressive and non-aggressive. To achieve this, they used the smartphone sensors to determine characteristics such as turns, aggressive acceleration, aggressive braking, lane changes, and excessive speed. These features were extracted using gyroscope and accelerometer data. However, the dependency of the driver's smartphone is not a suitable solution for a real-world application.

As for monitoring the health status of vehicles in operation, Myall's [15] research recorded the health status performance of 283 NL over 7 years, using a data-logger connected to the vehicle's CAN port. The results give a relationship between degradation and time of use. However, due to the lack of additional sensors, it is impossible to establish the causes of degradation. On the other hand, Eider [16] used a data-logger connected to the OBD-II port of the vehicle to extract CAN data of SoH, SoC, and ambient temperature. This paper aimed to relate the charge current and temperature to degradation but ignored the effect of the running state in the degradation. Similarly, Johnson and Trivedi [17] develop an in-vehicle application using an android tablet and a OBD-II decoder to interpret can frames regarding SoC and Current consumption. In contrast Sousa [18] developed a mobile application based on data obtained from Bluetooth sensor nodes. In this paper, the authors demonstrated that Bluetooth outperforms against other wireless communications protocols such as Zigbee and

RFID in EV applications. As for the purpose of the instrumentation, it aimed to extend battery life by sending notifications to the driver about overloads in charging and over-discharge in operation.

In conclusion, the main drawbacks of the reviewed work are as follows: They do not contemplate the effect of topological conditions [19] in battery behavior. Also, none of the methods take into account the environmental factors that affect driving behavior. Moreover, they do not contain a prioritization of measurable variables. Finally, they ignore the identification of operational states. This means that, for example, the system will monitor the same variables both in operation and in idle.

3   Instrumentation Infrastructure Design

This section consists of the development of the in-vehicle sensor network and data acquisition. The purpose of this design process consists of determining the variables to be monitored, in order to build an efficient sensor network that can collect the necessary information for facing the presented challenges in Sect. 1.

3.1   Analysis of Measurable Variables

The tool used for this analysis is called Function to Data Matrix (FDM) [20]. It aims to find the most relevant variables of a system according to its Functional Analysis (FA) and the main objective of the monitoring process. The first part consists of analyzing the main purpose of the instrumentation. For this case of study, the proposed system is a model 2019 NL and the goal is to correlate the battery degradation with charging behavior, driving behavior, and topological conditions as seen in Sect. 1.

Then, a Goal to Function Tree (GFT) defines the purpose of the instrumentation. Figure 1 represents the identified functions based on the NL technical information.

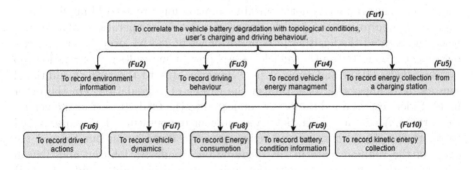

Fig. 1. Goal to function diagram

The arrange of basic functions from the tree in Fig. 1 is $F = (Fu2, Fu5, Fu6, Fu7, Fu8, Fu10)$. Then, according to the procedure in [20], the resulting weight vector for the basic functions is:

$$Wu = (0.25, 0.25, 0.125, 0.125, 0.083, 0.083, 0.083)$$

The following step consists in the development of the FA of the system, where inputs and outputs of energy, matter, and information, links to each other by terms of functions. The purpose is to find the variables present in the system assuming that each flow has an associated variable. A total number of 81 variables were identified in the FA of the system which is presented in Fig. 2.

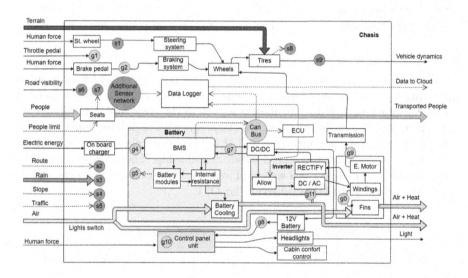

Fig. 2. Simplified FA

The grouping of information flows is done by identifying two main sensor networks. The first one consists of the vehicle's CAN bus, which gathers information about the sensor nodes (g_i) embedded in the vehicle (blue nodes in FA). Such sensors are distributed among the main systems such as the battery, engine, built-in charger, inverter, and cabin. Then, information is extracted by the Open Vehicle Monitor Open Vehicle Monitoring System (OVMS) programmable data logger, which can also send and receive information by HTTP protocol through the Global System for Mobile communication (GSM).

Since the sensors embedded within the original vehicle design aim to ensure its control and safe operation, the second sensor network is composed of auxiliary sensor nodes (s_i) (orange nodes in FA). They aim to gather information about factors affecting energy consumption and driving behavior as stated in Sect. 2.

To build the FDM, it is necessary to define the operating states in which the vehicle can be found depending on the functions it is performing. Each basic function from the GFT is evaluated in every Operative Stage (OS) to determine their correlation. Table 1 shows the proposed states and their relation to the basic functions.

Table 1. Operative states

Action	Operative state	$Fu1$	$Fu5$	$Fu6$	$Fu7$	$Fu8$	$Fu9$	$Fu10$
Run - Forward - No regenerate	OS1	1	0	1	1	1	1	0
Run - Backward - No regenerate	OS2	1	0	1	1	1	1	0
Run - Forward - Regenerate	OS3	1	0	1	1	0	1	1
Stop - On - Charge	OS4	1	1	0	0	0	1	0
Stop - On - No charge	OS5	1	0	0	0	0	1	0
Stop - Off - No charge	OS6	1	0	0	0	0	1	0

Once the operating states are defined, a FDM is constructed for each unique operating state in terms of basic functions (OS1, OS3, OS4, and OS6). Initially, all the variables are listed in the matrix as well as the basic function weights vector. Then, the relationship that each variable has with each basic function of the GFT is evaluated in the range $R = [0, 1, 2, 3]$ being 0 unrelated, 1 weak relationship, 2 medium relationship, and 3 strong relationship. Then, the importance of each variable is calculated as a weighted average of the evaluation scores. Table 2 shows the prioritized FDM evaluation for OS1.

Table 2. Example of sorted FDM: case of OS1

Node	Metric	Variable description	0.25	0.25	0.125	0.125	0.083	0.083	0.083	Score
s2	m	GPS altitude	3	0	2	2	2	0	0	1.42
g7	kW	Main battery momentary power	0	0	3	3	3	3	0	1.25
s2	km/h	GPS speed over ground	3	0	3	1	0	0	0	1.25
s2	°	GPS latitude	3	0	2	1	1	0	0	1.21
s2	°	GPS longitude	3	0	2	1	1	0	0	1.21
g7	Wh/km	Main battery momentary consumption	0	0	3	2	3	3	0	1.129
g9	km	Vehicle odometer	0	0	3	2	3	3	0	1.129
g5	V	Main battery momentary voltage	0	0	2	2	3	3	0	1.00
g5	A	Main battery momentary current	0	0	2	2	3	3	0	1.00
g5	km	Ideal range at 100% SOC & current conditions	1	0	2	0	3	3	0	1.00
g5	%	State of charge	0	1	2	0	3	3	0	1.00
g5	%	State of health	0	1	2	0	3	3	0	1.00
g10	String	Active drive profile code (vehicle specific)	0	0	3	3	3	0	0	1.00
g10	°C	Ambient temperature	3	0	0	0	0	3	0	1.00
g1	%	Drive pedal state [%]	0	0	3	3	3	0	0	1.00
g9	RPM	Motor speed	0	0	3	3	3	0	0	1.00
g9	m/s^2	Vehicle acceleration	0	0	3	3	3	0	0	1.00
g9	km/h	Vehicle speed	0	0	3	3	3	0	0	1.00
g7	Ah	Main battery coulomb used on trip	0	0	2	1	3	3	0	0.88
g7	kWh	Main battery energy used on trip	0	0	2	1	3	3	0	0.88
s8	psi	TPMS average pressure	1	0	0	3	3	0	0	0.88
s7	#	Occupants	0	0	2	3	3	0	0	0.88
s6	Lux	Road light	3	0	1	0	0	0	0	0.88
g5	°C	Main battery momentary temperature	1	0	1	1	1	3	0	0.83
g10	Bool	HVAC state	1	0	2	0	3	0	0	0.75

A threshold criteria of $Threshold = 0.6 * MAX(Score(OS_i))$ is defined for every FDM. Therefore, it should be noted that each operating state has both different variables and a number of variables since it depends on the maximum score. Given the above, Fig. 3 shows the implementation of Finite State Machine (FSM) in order to optimize the volume of the information sending. This implementation sends, based on the current OS, a different set of variables to be monitored in a different sending frequency.

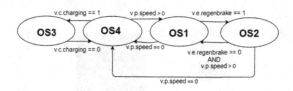

Fig. 3. EV monitoring FSM

3.2   Vehicle Instrumentation

Taking as a starting point the resulting variables within the established threshold, it is noted that from the complementary instrumentation proposed in the FA (Fig. 2), only the following sensors are needed in the vehicle (Table 3).

Table 3. Components selection

Node	Variable	Technical need	Value	Unit	Selection
s_2	Longitude	To measure topological information	0–360	°	GPS antenna
s_2	Latitude	To measure topological information	0–180	°	GPS antenna
s_2	Elevation	To measure topological information	0–3500	MAMSL	GPS antenna
s_6	Road illumination	To detect the effect of the Road illumination in driving behaviour	0–1000	lux	LDR sensor
s_7	Number of occupants	To find the impact of the people's weight on the energy consumption	0–1	Boolean	FSR seat occupancy sensor

Once the additional sensors are defined, it is necessary to develop an architecture that incorporates them into the vehicle. The choice for the auxiliary data-logger is the ESP32 due to its wide application range in IoT. The ESP32 communicates with the OVMS by the WIFI network provided by the OVMS. This network allows the ESP32 update via post requests, the information of additional sensors to the OVMS in JSON format.

For the user detection, the ESP32 generates a user login interface in the driver phone accessible by a QR in WIFI station mode. It also pulls the existing users list using GSM communication with the server.

Finally, the OVMS collects the information obtained from the vehicle via the OBD-II port, the information obtained from the additional sensors, and the topographic information from a GPS antenna connected to an additional port and makes a POST request to the server via HTTP using the GSM network. Figure 4 presents the vehicle network architecture.

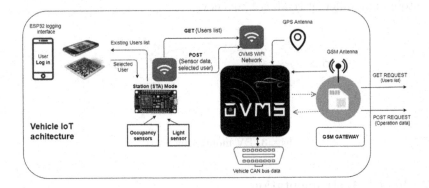

Fig. 4. Vehicle IoT architecture

4 Preliminary Approach for the Cloud Platform Implementation

4.1 Proposed Architecture

To store the operation data and have user interaction with it, is necessary to develop a database as well as a web application in a cloud server. For this aim, the Model-View-Controller (MVC) architecture [21] arises from the need to separate the user presentation from the program logic and data storage, in order to make data-based applications easier to scale. Figure 5 illustrates such architecture in the context of this case study.

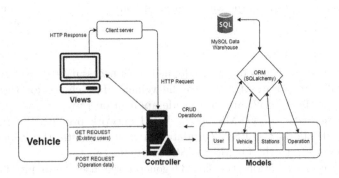

Fig. 5. Application architecture

Such architecture is implemented in a Linux server with python using the Flask framework for web development, The controller handles the incoming POST request from the vehicle and tells the Model to perform CRUD operations in the database. It also handles user requests from the web application and interacts with the view model to select and display the requested information. Section 4.2 presents the database architecture implemented in the server.

4.2   Database Architecture and Implementation

With the variables defined in all the OS in Sect. 3.1, the next step is to model this data in the database for its storing and manipulation. Relational Database Management System (RDMS) is used for this purpose. Figure 6 represents the data architecture implemented in order to fit the RDMS requirements. To query the operation data, the operation table has as columns the variables presented in Sect. 3.1, a unique ID, a timestamp, a user ID, a vehicle ID, a station ID if its charging, and an operational state. To query the data, it is possible to select a vehicle or a user, the time window to be analyzed, and the set of variables to be monitored. The engine of the database is developed in MySQL running in the main server. Concerning the proposed MVC architecture, The model consists of a set of defined classes that interacts with the MySQL tables structure using the SQLAlchemy object-relational mapping model to avoid using plain SQL statements.

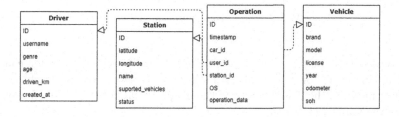

Fig. 6. Database architecture

4.3   FrontEnd Development and Preliminary Monitoring Results

When entering the application URL for the first time, the GUI[1] front-end is displayed. There, the user can interact with the data in two main sections. The first one is an interactive xy graph developed using (Plotly^{TM}) scientific library [22]. There, it is possible to visualize the behavior of any pair of variables of the proposed in Sect. 3.1 as well as the associated boxplot of the y axis variable. There, a time window must be defined for the data display. Finally, the next section consists of the geospatial representation of the data implemented through DECK.GL developed by UBER^{TM}. This section allows to graph in real-time, layers

---

[1] Graphical User Interface.

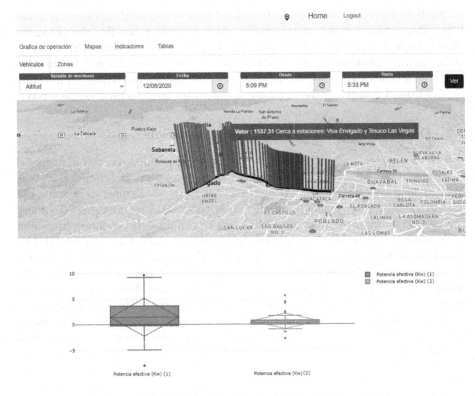

Fig. 7. Data visualization in the GUI

that represent data sets. The layers included are the circle layer for charging stations, line layer for routes, and column layer for the selected variable values. Figure 7 presents the visualization of the height variable for a route on a specific day in the maps section.

Finally, box-plots in the GUI presented in Fig. 7 represents measured effective power output for an aggressive and non aggressive driving profiles in route tests. Interquartile ranges for non aggressive driving style are typically 0.77 kW, and for aggressive style having a broader range of 3.88 kW. in terms of standard deviation, the values are typically 1.49 kW and 3.71 kW respectively. Maximum values of 5.62 kW and 9.62 kW respectively also allow to differentiate between driving profiles.

5   Conclusions and Future Work

Literature review shows that integral electric vehicle monitoring systems including actors such as people, vehicles, charging stations, routes, as well as environmental conditions, have not been implemented yet. Also, visualizing real-time variables in a 3D map, is not evident from the works analyzed in EV context.

This makes it difficult to understand and characterize the behavior of electric mobility in cities.

The implementation of FSM for identifying operating states in the design of the monitoring system, allows to disaggregate the operation information, making it easier to filtrate and classify for further analysis. A reduction in the number of variables of 69.1% 69.1 % 74.1% 86.4% is achieved for the operational states OS1 OS2 OS3 OS4 respectively, without missing valuable information.

Regarding the future work, it is first necessary to evaluate SoH estimation models to verify the values delivered by the vehicle Battery Management System (BMS). Then, a data processing stage follows, including data cleaning, clustering of user driving and charging behaviors, and routes identification. Then, the modeling of a degradation profile according to the resulting classifications and the experimental validation must be performed, to make recommendations that help increase battery life, and doing so, make Electric vehicle investments more attractive.

Acknowledgements. Authors would like to thank Universidad EAFIT to support this research through the Research Assistantship grant from project 952-000029. This research has been also developed in the framework of the "ENERGETICA 2030" Research Program, with code 58667 in the "Colombia Científica" initiative, funded by The World Bank through the call "778-2017 Scientific Ecosystems", managed by the Colombian Ministry of Science, Technology and Innovation (Minciencias), with contract No. FP44842-210-2018.

References

1. Delucchi, M.A., Lipman, T.E.: An analysis of the retail and lifecycle cost of battery-powered electric vehicles. Transp. Res. Part D Transp. Environ. **6**(6), 371–404 (2001)
2. Ng, K.S., Moo, C.-S., Chen, Y.-P., Hsieh, Y.-C.: Enhanced coulomb counting method for estimating state-of-charge and state-of-health of lithium-ion batteries. Appl. Energy **86**(9), 1506–1511 (2009)
3. Vetter, J., et al.: Ageing mechanisms in lithium-ion batteries. J. Power Sources **147**(1-2), 269–281 (2005)
4. Rodriguez, R.: A study on the impact of driver behavior on the energy consumption of electric vehicles in a virtual traffic environment. Ph.D. thesis, University of Michigan-Dearborn (2020)
5. Guena, T., Leblanc, P.: How depth of discharge affects the cycle life of lithium-metal-polymer batteries. In: Twenty-Eighth International Telecommunications Energy Conference, September 2006
6. Rezvanizaniani, S.M., Liu, Z., Chen, Y., Lee, J.: Review and recent advances in battery health monitoring and prognostics technologies for electric vehicle (EV) safety and mobility. J. Power Sources **256**, 110–124 (2014)
7. Pelletier, S., Jabali, O., Laporte, G., Veneroni, M.: Battery degradation and behaviour for electric vehicles: review and numerical analyses of several models. Transp. Res. Part B Methodol. **103**, 158–187 (2017)
8. Murnane, M., Ghazel, A.: A closer look at state of charge (SOC) and state of health (SOH) estimation techniques for batteries. Analog Dev. **2**, 426–436 (2017)

9. Nuhic, A., Terzimehic, T., Soczka-Guth, T., Buchholz, M., Dietmayer, K.: Health diagnosis and remaining useful life prognostics of lithium-ion batteries using data-driven methods. J. Power Sources **239**, 680–688 (2013)
10. Barré, A., Suard, F., Gérard, M., Riu, D.: A real-time data-driven method for battery health prognostics in electric vehicle use. In: Proceedings of the 2nd European Conference of the Prognostics and Health Management Society, pp. 1–8 (2014)
11. Smith, R., Shahidinejad, S., Blair, D., Bibeau, E.L.: Characterization of urban commuter driving profiles to optimize battery size in light-duty plug-in electric vehicles. Transp. Res. Part D Transp. Environ. **16**(3), 218–224 (2011)
12. Hogema, J.H.: Effects of rain on daily traffic volume and on driving behaviour. Technical report, Transportation Research Board (1996)
13. Konstantopoulos, P., Chapman, P., Crundall, D.: Driver's visual attention as a function of driving experience and visibility. Using a driving simulator to explore driver's eye movements in day, night and rain driving. Accid. Anal. Prev. **42**(3), 827–834 (2010)
14. Johnson, D.A., Trivedi, M.M.: Driving style recognition using a smartphone as a sensor platform. In: 2011 14th International IEEE Conference on Intelligent Transportation Systems (ITSC), pp. 1609–1615. IEEE (2011)
15. Myall, D., Ivanov, D., Larason, W., Nixon, M., Moller, H.: Accelerated reported battery capacity loss in 30 kWh variants of the Nissan leaf. Energy & Fuel Technology (2018)
16. Eider, M., Bodenschatz, N., Berl, A., Danner, P., de Meer, H.: A novel approach on battery health monitoring. In: Conference on Future Automotive Technology (2018)
17. Khorsravinia, K., Hassan, M.K., Rahman, R.Z.A., Al-Haddad, S.A.R.: Integrated OBD-II and mobile application for electric vehicle (EV) monitoring system. In: 2017 IEEE 2nd International Conference on Automatic Control and Intelligent Systems (I2CACIS), pp. 202–206. IEEE (2017)
18. Sousa, R.A., Monteiro, V., Ferreira, J.C., Nogueiras Melendez, A.A., Afonso, J.L., Afonso, J.A.: Development of an IoT system with smart charging current control for electric vehicles. In: IECON 2018–44th Annual Conference of the IEEE Industrial Electronics Society, pp. 4662–4667. IEEE (2018)
19. De Cauwer, C., Van Mierlo, J., Coosemans, T.: Energy consumption prediction for electric vehicles based on real-world data. Energies **8**(8), 8573–8593 (2015)
20. Fernandez-Montoya, M.: Information management method based on a knowledge management (km) approach for human supervisory control systems (2017)
21. Selfa, D.M., Carrillo, M., Del Rocio Boone, M.: A database and web application based on MVC architecture. In: 16th International Conference on Electronics, Communications and Computers (CONIELECOMP 2006), p. 48 (2006)
22. Plotly Technologies Inc.: Collaborative data science (2015)

Computational Simulation of Stress Distribution in a Magnesium Matrix Composite Reinforced with Carbon Nanotubes

Mateo Duarte[1], Miguel Alvarez[1], Andres López[1], Luis Portillo[1], Gustavo Suárez[1(✉)], and Juliana Niño[2]

[1] Grupo de Investigación sobre Nuevos Materiales, Universidad Pontificia Bolivariana, Cir.1 70-01, 050031 Medellín, Colombia
{mateo.duarte,miguel.alvarezm,andresd.lopez,luis.portillo,
gustavo.suarez}@upb.edu.co
[2] Grupo de Investigación en Ingeniería Aeroespacial, Universidad Pontificia Bolivariana, Cir.1 70-01, 050031 Medelín, Colombia
juliana.nino@upb.edu.co

Abstract. The development of composite materials has brought with it global questions about its behavior on materials science where the computational simulations have the methodology to increase the knowledge about them. To exemplify the usefulness of the computational methodologies in simulations of mechanical characterization, one of the newest composite materials is used in a tensile test, this material is a magnesium matrix composite reinforcement with carbon nanotubes (CNTs). Furthermore was implemented a constitutive model to a linear-elastic behavior with the inclusion of Elasticity Modulus and Poisson Ratio properties. The computational model has been developed in Matlab software and includes the design of five reticules with 2500 nodes and insertions of 0%, 1%, 4%, 8%, and 12% of carbon nanotubes. Additionally, the finite difference method (FDM) has been applied and showed that carbon nanotubes improve mechanical properties of monolithic magnesium alloys achieving an 80% decrease in the displacement of the composite, also ensure the pertinence of the computational simulations for the future of the materials science.

Keywords: Carbon nanotubes · Computational simulation · Metal matrix composite · Matlab · Magnesium

1 Introduction

The aerospace, aeronautical and automotive industries in the last years have been focused on the research of composite materials where the specific properties have gained popularity for application in wings, fuselages, boat construction, and racing car bodies [1]. The above is supported with history of the aeronautical

© Springer Nature Switzerland AG 2020
J. C. Figueroa-García et al. (Eds.): WEA 2020, CCIS 1274, pp. 375–386, 2020.
https://doi.org/10.1007/978-3-030-61834-6_32

applications where the main objectives are focused on the weight decrease and improved in mechanical properties, for example, the magnesium was widely used on aircraft parts between 1940's to 1980's as control surfaces, wheels, actuators, etc, also currently is used in some parts of helicopters as gearbox, but non like primary structure of aircrafts [2].

Furthermore, the automotive industry uses these materials to decrease specific fuel consumption and greenhouse emission as CO_2, in the same way, the reduction in weight improves on the necessary power to operate [3]. However, magnesium alloys have problems in its volatility, also in manufacture methods and price [4] but with the new era of composites and ideas focused in the development of materials that combined two or more materials for obtain the main properties of the constituents the magnesium can be a ideal material for new applications [5].

In general, the composite materials depend upon factors in matrix and reinforcement properties when particularly the selection of these components integrates symbiosis to improve performance and reliability [6]. Wherefore, the materials research has been focused on the evolution of physical and mechanical properties achieving through the adoption of metal matrix composites (MMCs) and the used in carbon nanotubes for reinforcement showing high specific strength and specific elastic modulus over their monolithic alloys (magnesium, aluminum, titanium, and others) [7].

The use of the term metal matrix composite caused the incorporation of the main metals alloys families that represent the highest properties on specific characteristics where the magnesium was an ideal candidate being one of the lightest structural engineering materials, more than materials such as steel and aluminum [10]. For these reasons, when it comes to engineered materials, magnesium is one of the most effective due to its good mechanical properties and low density [11].

The inclusion of magnesium on metal matrix composites (MMCs) has taken into account the application of ceramic reinforcement such as carbon nanotubes (CNTs) [12] or Silicon Carbide (SiC) particles [13]. Furthermore, the particular use of CNTs in metal matrix composites has been generated by the height properties in tensile strength, Young's modulus, and compressive strength in values of 300 GPa, 0.4–1.3 TPa, and 100 GPa respectively [14].

Accordingly, several authors have researched about the properties of magnesium matrix composites reinforced with carbon nanotubes and compare the values of metal and MMCs mechanical properties, for example, Zet et al. [15] increase the tensile strength in a 30,8% compared to that in the AZ31 Mg alloys, also, Izasa et al. [16] increase in elastic modulus in 90% for the composites reinforced with 1% of CNTs and Sie Ching Tjong includes an increase of 42% in yield stress of the AZ31B by adding 0.95 vol % MWNT [7].

Another material that uses CNTs as reinforcement is aluminum where the properties increase by 50% and 23% on tensile strength and stiffness respectively compared with monolithic aluminum alloys. A.M.K. Esawi say that 5% CNTs the highest mechanical properties are achieved, but the best relationship between percentage and increase in properties is found in 2% of CNTs [8]. On the other hand, A.M.K. Esawi in other research concluded that the mechanical properties not only depend on the introduction of CNTs but also length and diameter have a fundamental role [9].

However, the obtention of these properties turn around specific manufacturing processes with challenges that researchers confront in the generation of MMCs, for instance, stir casting manufacturing required control in temperature, time and speed stirring variables [17]. Hence, numerical simulations have been developed experimental procedures applicable in the research of failure in fiber reinforced composites [18], bending test in composites [19], and others.

Moreover, mathematical simulation has a good approximation in research focused on the prediction of elastic modulus in nanocomposites and reveals that the analytical models are capable of establishing real values of the mechanical properties in composites [20]. On the other hand, the simulation of tensile strength in hybrid materials represents approximations in maximum stress where the nonlinear models include reasonable prediction of the degradation in laminar composites. Another, significant factor is that graphics simulation generates a representation of the evolution in the material with the application of the tensile strength [21], being an aspect with the ability to amplify the value of computational simulations.

This paper presents a tensile strength computational simulation of a metal matrix composite made of AZ31 magnesium alloy matrix and carbon nanotube reinforcement where the percent of carbon nanotube changes in values of 0%, 1%, 4%, 8%, and 12%. Accordingly, strength mapping is performed by the applications of planar tensile strength methods and the influence of carbon nanotubes in MMCs in mechanical properties is determined.

2   Materials and Methods

2.1   Composite Requirements

The selection of MMCs materials is base on the aeronautical and aerospace necessities, where the materials development is focused on the light-weight materials with high specific properties (property/density) [22]. For this reason, magnesium attracted attention as a good matrix material for MMCs, similarly, the discovery of carbon nanotubes and its physical properties make the material an ideal reinforcement candidate [23]. Considering the foregoing, the main properties of these materials are shown in Table 1 and Fig. 1, represent a real illustration of magnesium and CNTs.

Table 1. Main properties of selected materials [24–26]

Material	Density (g/cm^3)	Young's Modulus (GPa)	Yield Strength (GPa)
AZ31B Mg Alloy	1.7	44.8	0.244
Carbon Nanotubes	1.8–2	1000	20–100

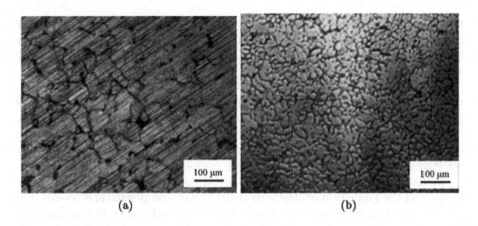

(a)   (b)

Fig. 1. a) AZ31 magnesium alloy b) AZ31 with 1 wt% MWCNT [15].

The regards taken account in algorithm are: i) all CNTs are dispersed homogeneous on magnesium matrix and ii) exist a coherent interface bonding between CNTs reinforcement and magnesium AZ31 matrix [27].

2.2 Constitutive Laws

The Hooke's law predicts the deformation that a material will undergo when subjected to a stress, this law only applies to materials that have elastic properties, among them are metals. The generalized Hooke's laws extend this concept to all axes of the cartesian plane as well as to the cross sections, in Eq. 1 [28] the mathematical expression for a flat plate is observed, assuming no deformation in the z axis.

$$\begin{Bmatrix} \sigma_x \\ \sigma_z \\ \tau_{x_z} \end{Bmatrix} = \begin{pmatrix} C_{1_1} & C_{1_2} & 0 \\ C_{1_2} & C_{2_2} & 0 \\ 0 & 0 & C_{6_6} \end{pmatrix} \begin{Bmatrix} \xi_x \\ \xi_z \\ \gamma_{x_z} \end{Bmatrix} \tag{1}$$

Where σ_x and σ_y are normal stress while τ_{x_z} is shear stress. ξ_x, ξ_y and γ_{x_z} are deformation in x, y and transverse, respectively. C_{1_1} and C_{1_2} are related with known constant, specifically Young's modulus(E) and Poisson ratio(v). Taking into account the above and a sum of force in x axis, where the equilibrium is applied can be obtained the Eqs. 2 and 3.

$$\sum F(x) = 0 \tag{2}$$

$$(N + dN) + b(x)dx - N = 0 \tag{3}$$

By simplifying and solving Eq. 3, Eq. 5 can be obtained, where N is the axial force and A in the area.

$$\frac{dN}{dx} + b(x) = 0 \tag{4}$$

$$N = \sigma A \tag{5}$$

Moreover, the definition of strain in materials science are in the Eq. 6.

$$\sigma = E\xi = E\frac{du}{dx} \tag{6}$$

On the other hand, using Eq. 6 into Eq. 4, Eq. 7 was obtained and with mathematical solution Eq. 8 was developed.

$$N = EA\frac{du}{dx} \tag{7}$$

$$\frac{d}{dx}\left(EA\frac{du}{dx}\right) + b = 0 \tag{8}$$

In the same way, the mathematical solution was applied to two dimensions model (x and y axis) obtained Eq. 9, this is Poisson equation, a differential equation that was mathematically solved, as show the Eq. 10.

$$\frac{\partial^2 u}{\partial x^2} + \frac{\partial^2 u}{\partial y^2} = \frac{\beta}{k} \tag{9}$$

$$\frac{1}{hx^2}U_{ii+1} - 2\frac{1}{hx^2}U_{ii} + \frac{1}{hx^2}U_{ii-1} + \frac{1}{hy^2}U_{ii+8} - 2\frac{1}{hy^2}U_{ii} + \frac{1}{hy^2}U_{ii-8} = \frac{\beta}{k} \tag{10}$$

$$r = \frac{1}{hx^2} \; ; \; s = \frac{1}{hy^2} \tag{11}$$

2.3 Computational Simulation

The mathematical model implementation was performed in Matlab software where, employing the definition of a 2500 nodes grid and the inclusion of magnesium AZ31B as a matrix with CNTs reinforcement in percentages of 0%, 1%, 4%, 8%, and 12% have executed a simulation taking into account the sequences shown in Fig. 2. This algorithm implementation includes sample and materials requirements, also generates the relation between constitutive equations and composites properties to obtain a real behavior of the sample displacement in a tensile test of 250 MPa.

Furthermore, the sample dimensions have been represent in a square with 0.1 m and the 2500 nodes were distributed in a 50 × 50 grid as shown in Fig. 3, where carbon nanotubes have been dispersed in homogeneous conditions on a magnesium matrix composite. Similarly, the gray color have been used in magnesium matrix and black color in carbon nanotubes, on the other hand, in the characteristics of the nodes includes the development of the Laplace equation mentioned in the Eq. 10.

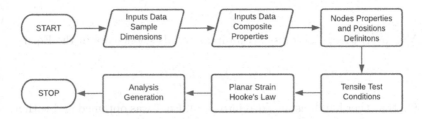

Fig. 2. Mathematical model flow chart.

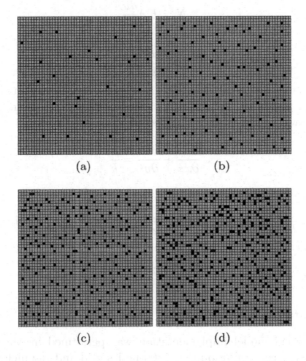

Fig. 3. Grid sample with (a) 1% CNTs and (b) 4% CNTs (c) 8% CNTs and (d) 12% CNTs.

3   Results and Discussion

For the displacement analysis, the methodology described above (Sect. 2.3) has used. Figure 4, shows the reference sample that was made in monolithic magnesium AZ31B alloy (0% of CNTs) where the maximum displacement value is 1 mm and has focused on the tensile stress sides (right and left). This value can be considered as the sample displacement for the magnesium stress limit and will be a reference for the inclusion of CNTs reinforcement.

The main changes in the original sample are the inclusion of 1%, and 4% of CNTs as shown in Fig. 5, where at first sight the CNTs generate a different displacement in the sample. Moreover, the maximum displacement value decrease

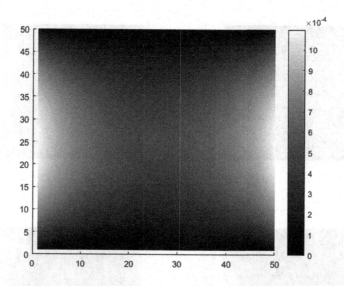

Fig. 4. Monolithic magnesium AZ31B alloy displacement in meters.

by 40%, and 65% for 1%, and 4% in CNTs reinforcement, respectively. Otherwise, the CNTs highlight in the composite for the low values in displacement and this is due to the high mechanical properties that the material has.

In Section 5a of Fig. 5, demonstrates that a low percentage of CNTs can decrease the near sections displacement in 50% regarding the central points in the Monolithic magnesium AZ31B alloy. Another important aspect is the effect of the CNTs distribution around the matrix, where on the case 5b of Fig. 5, a homogeneous reinforcement can achieve a reduction in the areas that are involved with the maximum displacement, this factor includes the requirements of a good dispersion of the reinforcement.

To determinate limits in volume reinforcement and comparate low and high values have been made two extra samples of 8% and 12% as shown in Fig. 5, cases 5c and 5d . The computational simulation demonstrates that the CNTs in these percentages can distribute the stress around 80% of sample area in low values where the displacement decrease by 75%, and 80% for 8%, and 12% of CNTs reinforcement, respectively. Also, the influence of the tensile test with 250 MPa does not affect the mechanical conditions of these samples and justify the use of CNTs in the main composite materials.

The results on different values of reinforcement demonstrate that the carbon nanotubes in low concentration can perform good improvements on monolithic materials and the values of 1% or 4% with a homogeneous dispersion are enough to the increase in an important mechanical strength.

Finally, in relation to the influence in the displacement sample with the percentage of CNTs, a graph has been made as shown in Fig. 6. This graph represents the increase in mechanical properties of the composite with the addition of more percentage of carbon nanotubes where the low volumetric percentage to

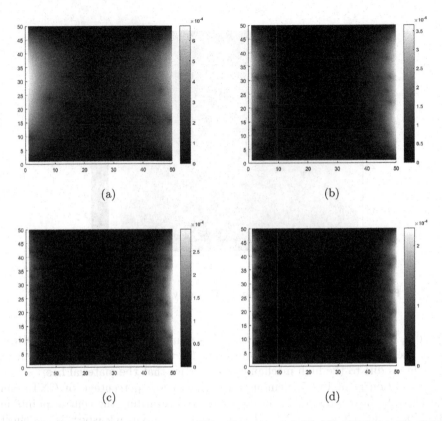

Fig. 5. Displacement simulation with (a) 1% CNTs and (b) 4% CNTs (c) 8% CNTs and (d) 12% CNTs in meters.

get better characteristics make the CNTs an ideal reinforcement for de MMCs. An inverse logarithmic curve is making as a result of addition CNTs, where the line decrease through left to right due to the addition of reinforcements, therefore the strain decrease too.

Take into account Fig. 6, a decrease in deformation is presented when the percentage of CNTs increases, this analysis proposes that in the relation stress-strain the last one reduces its value at the same stress parameter of 250 MPa and supports an increase in elasticity modulus. The above can be corroborated with other authors, for example, C. Isaza obtained an increase of 66%, 88%, and 90% of elasticity modulus for 0.25%, 0.5 and 1% of CNTs into MMC, respectively [16]. These increases in elasticity modulus allow in turn to obtain a value in the change of deformation when 250 MPa of stress is applied, resulting in that 41.3%, 46.8% and 46.8% are the percentages of strain reduction that have 0.25%, 0.5% and 1% of CNTs into the matrix compared with pure Mg. Also, the deformation values for 1% of CNTs have a discrepancy of 13.23% compared with C. Isaza research [16].

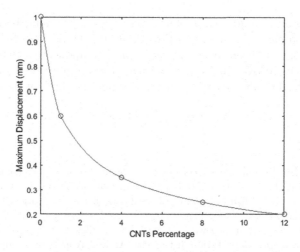

Fig. 6. Relation between reinforcement percentage and the maximum displacement in the sample.

On the other hand, the variation of the values between this research and other authors [29, 30] is determined by the stress transmission behavior, where an adequate alignment and dispersion of CNTs into magnesium matrix is necessary for great mechanical properties, also, another factor is the interface phase, where the materials should be coherent or semi-coherent. However, as mentioned in Sect. 2, the computational simulation establishes these components and can be determined as ideals.

4 Conclusions

Given the results, a clear trend can be observed that the CNTs generate a greater resistance on the magnesium alloy AZ31B, this resistance, in turn, is reflected with a less deformation in the figures built with the algorithm, therefore, a higher concentration of CNTs the material undergoes less deformation, where the reinforcement absorbing the energy due to its high mechanical performance. Moreover, the deformations obtained are found within the elastic region, Hooke's law being validated as a mathematical method to find the deformations in the nodes.

The mathematical simulation demonstrates that computational tools can implement algorithms to provide a first approach to the materials science knowledge. These implementations defined the importance of carbon nanotubes dispersion in an uniformly form on the matrix composite, which can be seen in Fig. 5a, 5b, 5c, and 5d, also in future research will be important to the inclusion of other limits in the interaction between CNTs and magnesium to obtain a model that is closer to reality. Certainly, some of the limitations are the interface behavior between matrix and reinforcement, also dispersion and alignment of CNTs that depends on the manufacturing process.

The future outlook for this material turns around manufacturing processes where a line production would allow the evolution of aeronautics and automotive industries for the application in main structural components as wings, fuselage, and others. Also, MMCs are new knowledge and computational simulation can be a fundamental tool for complementing the main research of these composites materials.

References

1. Soutis, C.: Introduction: engineering requirements for aerospace composite materials. In: Irving, P.E., Soutis, C. (eds.) Polymer Composites in the Aerospace Industry. Woodhead Publishing, Cambridge (2015). https://doi.org/10.1016/B978-0-85709-523-7.00001-3
2. Wardlow, G.D.: A changing world with different rules–new opportunities for magnesium alloys?. In: Presentation at the 64th Annual World Magnesium Conference, Vancouver, BC, Canada, 13th–15th May 2007 (2007)
3. Oak Ridge National Laboratory, Transportation Energy Data Book, 34th ed. Oak Ridge, TN, Oak Ridge National Laboratory (2015). http://cta.ornl.gov/data/chapter4.shtml
4. Joost, W.J., Krajewski, P.E.: Towards magnesium alloys for high-volume automotive applications. Scripta Mater. **128**, 107–112 (2017). https://doi.org/10.1016/j.scriptamat.2016.07.035. ISSN 1359-6462
5. Shetty, N., Shahabaz, S.M., Sharma, S.S., Divakara, S.: A review on finite element method for machining of composite materials. Compos. Struct. (2017). https://doi.org/10.1016/j.compstruct.2017.06.012
6. Shirvanimoghaddam, K., Hamim, S.U., Akbari, M.K., et al.: Carbon fiber reinforced metal matrix composites: fabrication processes and properties. Compos. A Appl. Sci. Manuf. **92**, 70–96 (2017). https://doi.org/10.1016/j.compositesa.2016.10.032. ISSN 1359-835X
7. Tjong, S.C.: Recent progress in the development and properties of novel metal matrix nanocomposites reinforced with carbon nanotubes and graphene nanosheets. Mater. Sci. Eng. R Rep. **74**(10), 281–350 (2013). https://doi.org/10.1016/j.mser.2013.08.001. ISSN 0927-796X
8. Esawi, A.M.K., Morsi, K., Sayed, A., Taher, M., Lanka, S.: Effect of carbon nanotube (CNT) content on the mechanical properties of CNT-reinforced aluminium composites. Compos. Sci. Technol. **70**(16), 2237–2241 (2010)
9. Esawi, A.M.K., Morsi, K., Sayed, A., Taher, M., Lanka, S.: The influence of carbon nanotube (CNT) morphology and diameter on the processing and properties of CNT-reinforced aluminium composites. Compos. A Appl. Sci. Manuf. **42**(3), 234–243 (2011). https://doi.org/10.1016/j.compositesa.2010.11.008. ISSN 1359-835X
10. Rashad, M., Pan, F., Zhang, J., Asif, M.: Use of high energy ball milling to study the role of graphene nanoplatelets and carbon nanotubes reinforced magnesium alloy. J. Alloy. Compd. (2015). https://doi.org/10.1016/j.jallcom.2015.06.051
11. Che, Q., Wang, K., Wang, W., et al.: Microstructure and mechanical properties of magnesium-lithium alloy prepared by friction stir processing. Rare Met. (2019). https://doi.org/10.1007/s12598-019-01217-2
12. Han, G., et al.: The influence of CNTs on the microstructure and ductility of CNT/Mg composites. Mater. Lett. (2016). https://doi.org/10.1016/j.matlet.2016.06.021

13. Wang, X.J., Hu, X.S., Wu, K., Wang, L.Y., Huang, Y.D.: Evolutions of microstructure and mechanical properties for SiCp/AZ91 composites with different particle contents during extrusion. Mater. Sci. Eng., A **636**, 138–147 (2015). https://doi.org/10.1016/j.msea.2015.03.058. ISSN 0921-5093
14. Behera, D.R., Das, S.R., Jha, R.: An Overview of the Properties and Biomedical Applications of Multi-Walled Carbon Nanotubes (2020). https://doi.org/10.2139/ssrn.3548429
15. Zeng, X., Zhou, G., Xu, Q., Xiong, Y., Luo, C., Wu, J.: A new technique for dispersion of carbon nanotube in a metal melt. Mater. Sci. Eng., A **527**(20), 5335–5340 (2010). https://doi.org/10.1016/j.msea.2010.05.005. ISSN 0921-5093
16. Merino, C.A.I., Sillas, J.E.L., Meza, J.M., Ramirez, J.M.H.: Metal matrix composites reinforced with carbon nanotubes by an alternative technique. J. Alloy. Compd. **707**, 257–263 (2017). https://doi.org/10.1016/j.jallcom.2016.11.348. ISSN 0925-8388
17. Kandpal, B.C., Kumar, J., Singh, H.: Manufacturing and technological challenges in stir casting of metal matrix composites-a Review. Mater. Today Proc. **5**(1), 5–10 (2018). https://doi.org/10.1016/j.matpr.2017.11.046. ISSN 2214-7853
18. Koyanagi, J., Sato, Y., Sasayama, T., Okabe, T., Yoneyama, S.: Numerical simulation of strain-rate dependent transition of transverse tensile failure mode in fiber-reinforced composites. Compos. A Appl. Sci. Manuf. **56**, 136–142 (2014). https://doi.org/10.1016/j.compositesa.2013.10.002. ISSN 1359-835X
19. Badriev, I.B., Makarov, M.V., Paimushin, V.N.: Mathematical simulation of nonlinear problem of three-point composite sample bending test. Procedia Eng. **150**, 1056–1062 (2016). https://doi.org/10.1016/j.proeng.2016.07.214. ISSN 1877-7058
20. Charitos, I., Drougkas, A., Kontou, E.: Prediction of the elastic modulus of LLDPE/CNT nanocomposites by analytical modeling and finite element analysis. Mater. Today Commun. **24**, 101070 (2020). https://doi.org/10.1016/j.mtcomm.2020.101070. ISSN 2352-4928
21. Kashfi, M., Majzoobi, G.H., Bonora, N., Iannitti, G., Ruggiero, A., Khademi, E.: A study on fiber metal laminates by using a new damage model for composite layer. Int. J. Mech. Sci. (2017). https://doi.org/10.1016/j.ijmecsci.2017.06.045
22. Zhang, X., Chen, Y., Hu, J.: Recent advances in the development of aerospace materials. Prog. Aerosp. Sci. **97**, 22–34 (2018). https://doi.org/10.1016/j.paerosci.2018.01.001. ISSN 0376-0421
23. Li, H., Dai, X., Zhao, L., et al.: Microstructure and properties of carbon nanotubes-reinforced magnesium matrix composites fabricated via novel in situ synthesis process. J. Alloy. Compd. **785**, 146–155 (2019). https://doi.org/10.1016/j.jallcom.2019.01.144. ISSN 0925-8388
24. Gzyl, M., Rosochowski, A., Boczkal, S., Olejnik, L.: The role of microstructure and texture in controlling mechanical properties of AZ31B magnesium alloy processed by I-ECAP. Mater. Sci. Eng., A **638**, 20–29 (2015). https://doi.org/10.1016/j.msea.2015.04.055. ISSN 0921-5093
25. Castro, F., Jiang, Y.: Fatigue life and early cracking predictions of extruded AZ31B magnesium alloy using critical plane approaches. Int. J. Fatigue **88**, 236–246 (2016). https://doi.org/10.1016/j.ijfatigue.2016.04.002. ISSN 0142-1123
26. Cha, J., Jin, S., Shim, J.H., Park, C.S., Ryu, H.J., Hong, S.H.: Functionalization of carbon nanotubes for fabrication of CNT/epoxy nanocomposites. Mater. Des. **95**, 1–8 (2016). https://doi.org/10.1016/j.matdes.2016.01.077. ISSN 0264-1275
27. Song, Y.S., Youn, J.R.: Modeling of effective elastic properties for polymer based carbon nanotube composites. Polymer **47**, 1741–1748 (2006). https://doi.org/10.1016/j.polymer.2006.01.013. ISSN 0032-3861

28. Kuo, S.-Y., Shiau, L.-C.: Buckling and vibration of composite laminated plates with variable fiber spacing. Compos. Struct. **90**, 196–200 (2009). https://doi.org/10.1016/j.compstruct.2009.02.013. ISSN 0263-8223
29. Han, G., Wang, Z., Liu, K., Li, S., Du, X., Du, W.: Synthesis of CNT-reinforced AZ31 magnesium alloy composites with uniformly distributed CNTs. Mater. Sci. Eng., A **628**, 350–357 (2015). https://doi.org/10.1016/j.msea.2015.01.039. ISSN 0921-5093
30. Goh, C.S., Wei, J., Lee, L.C., Gupta, M.: Simultaneous enhancement in strength and ductility by reinforcing magnesium with carbon nanotubes. Mater. Sci. Eng., A **423**(1–2), 153–156 (2006). https://doi.org/10.1016/j.msea.2005.10.071. ISSN 0921-5093

Computational Simulation of Franz Diffusion Cell Method for Bacterial Nanocellulose Wound Dressings

Shaydier Argel Pérez(ID), Daiver Estiven Jiménez Gutiérrez(ID),
Alexander León Ramírez(ID), Samuel Villa Alvarez(ID),
Marlon Andr´es Osorio Delgado(ID), Isabel Cristina Castro Herazo(ID),
and Gustavo Suárez Guerrero$^{(\boxtimes)}$ (ID)

Grupo de Investigación sobre Nuevos Materiales, Universidad Pontificia Bolivariana,
Cir.1 70-01, Medellín, Colombia
gustavo.suarez@upb.edu.co

Abstract. In this paper, computational simulations were used to analyze the thermo-electro-diffusive behavior of the povidone-iodine (PVI) and the acetylsalicylic acid (ASA) embed in a nanocellulose wound dressing. Mathematical models were determined with Fourier's law for the thermal model, Maxwell's equations for the electric phenomena and Fick's law to model the diffusive behavior to simulate the Franz cell (FC) method. Also, 6 computational models were built to determine effectivity of the FC method in the skin, considering flux conditions for the drug delivery, temperature, and electric conditions. For this models, numerical reticules were designed for the implementation of algorithms using MATLAB and the mathematical equations were solved using Finite Difference Method (FDM). The results showed an appropriate behavior of the diffusive process, were the diffusion of PVI and ASA through epidermis was observed, also in the electric simulation it was observed that the current travel only through the primary layers of the skin; moreover, after the simulation of two thermic processes: heating plate and water bath, the latter proved to be the method that could be more appropriate for applying heat in Franz cells. The results obtained in this paper can provide predictions that could guide future in vitro experimental tests in a more assertive way, also it will allow predicting the behavior of the release of drugs from wound dressings. Also, the algorithms used, and computational tests were a powerful tool that contributes to a more assertive experimental methodology.

Keywords: Franz diffusion cell · Wound dressings · Computational simulation · Matlab

1 Introduction

Nowadays is crucial to develop wound dressings that can maintain a moist wound environment and provide oxygenation, as well as generate biological signals that help the healing process. A promising material for the development of dressings is bacterial cellulose (BC), which is a biocompatible, natural and non-toxic hydrogel [1]. Nevertheless,

© Springer Nature Switzerland AG 2020
J. C. Figueroa-García et al. (Eds.): WEA 2020, CCIS 1274, pp. 387–397, 2020.
https://doi.org/10.1007/978-3-030-61834-6_33

BC in its natural state does not have biological signals such as anti-inflammatory, antimicrobial or analgesic compounds [2], therefore, it must be loaded with active ingredients or medicines that can help the treatment of wounds. Among the active compounds that have the potential to generate a bioactive dressing that interacts and benefits the wound surface promoting its healing are acetylsalicylic acid, for its anti-inflammatory and analgesic properties, and povidone-iodine for its antimicrobial capacity [3–6]. In the development of wound dressings, it is essential to understand the release mechanism of the active ingredients in environments simulating human skin and its physiological conditions. Accordingly, the Franz cell method is used [7, 8], where the desorption can be evaluated in aqueous media, in the presence or absence of skin samples, under conditions of body temperature [9, 10]. In this work, a computational simulation of the Franz cell method was performed, in a desorption study of povidone iodine and acetylsalicylic acid from bacterial cellulose wound dressings as well as, thermal diffusion on the cell [11] and electric distribution of charge through the skin [12]. A further mathematical approach for modelling is diffusion models which consist of partial differential equations describing drug delivery in space according to Fick's laws of diffusion [13]. Furthermore, the thermic and electric behavior was studied using Gauss's law for electric fields and the heat equation to improve the desorption process of povidone iodine and acetylsalicylic acid.

2   Description of the Model

2.1   Model Geometries

Two geometries were designed for the development of this work. The first one was a cellular material considered for drug and electrical diffusion simulation and the model used in this article was an extended skin model which is based on the two-dimensional *Brick-and-mortar model*, with a simplified representation of the five constitutional skin layers [14]. The resulting geometry of the skin model is showed in Fig. 1(a) were the change of the brick size along the height can be appreciated. The second one was a vertical Franz cell of form indicated in Fig. 1(b), only the bottom chamber was considered for drug and thermal diffusion simulation.

2.2   Model Equations

Thermal Diffusion Model. The behavior of the Franz cell subjected to heating in a water bath, and over a heating plate were analyzed, according to Fourier Law [15].

$$q = -k\nabla T \tag{1}$$

Where q is the heat flow, k the conduction coefficient and T the temperature. Assuming an isotropic medium, Fourier law leads to the heat equation which was used for the numerical simulation:

$$\frac{dT}{dt} = \alpha\nabla T \tag{2}$$

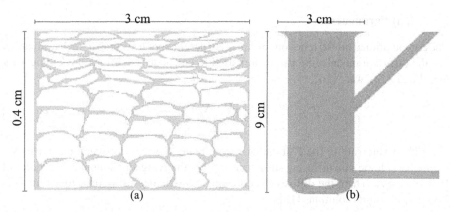

Fig. 1. (a) Geometry of skin. (b) Geometry of Franz cell.

Where T is the temperature in the skin and α is the thermal diffusivity.

Drug Diffusion Model. The behavior of the skin and Franz cell subjected to drug diffusion was analyzed. It was assumed that transport in each skin phase and in the Franz cell is due to Fick´s second law of diffusion [13].

The passive diffusion process of a chemical from a region of high concentration to low concentration in the skin is described by Fick's first Law of diffusion at steady state:

$$J = -D\frac{\Delta C}{x} \tag{3}$$

The steady state flux (Jss) through the skin can be described as

$$J_{ss} = -D\frac{AT\Delta C}{h} \tag{4}$$

Where Q is the amount of solute, D is the penetrant diffusivity in the membrane, A is the area of the membrane considered, T is time, ΔC is the penetrant concentration gradient across the membrane, and h is the membrane thickness (path length).

Electric Diffusion Model. The behavior of the skin when subjected to an electric current with a certain voltage was analyzed. Electric current flow is assumed to be defined by one of the Maxwell's equations (Gauss's law for electric fields).

Gauss's law in electromagnetism allows us to determine the electric flux, or electrostatic flux, this is a scalar quantity that expresses a measure of the electric field that crosses a certain surface. In this case we will work with its gradient to arrive at the space charge density.

$$\frac{\varepsilon_0}{E} = \rho, E = -\nabla V \tag{5}$$

Where ε_0 is the dielectric coefficient, V is the dielectric potential and ρ is the surface charge density.

2.3 Input Parameters

The computational model relies on several input parameters according to each evaluation. For the diffusive models, the parameters used to calculate the diffusion coefficient for the PI and ASA were [16]:

$$r_A = \frac{(V_m/N_A)^{\frac{1}{3}}}{2} \tag{6}$$

With A referring to the PVI and ASA, r_A being the radius of each molecule, V_m the molar volume of a diffusing substance and N_A the Avogadro's number for moles of PVI and ASA. Then, the diffusive coefficient was obtained using the Stokes-Einstein equation for dilute solutions [16]:

$$D = \frac{k * T}{b * \pi * r_A * n_B} \tag{7}$$

With D being the diffusive coefficient, k is the Boltzmann's constant, T is the temperature, b is a constant dependent on the size of diffusive molecules, and n_B is the dynamic viscosity of water.

For the heat model, the heat conduction of water at 20 °C found on the literature. Finally, for the electric model the skin was considered as a surface without space charge density and the skin's dielectric constant was also obtained from the literature. Finally, Table 1 summarizes coefficients found for the simulations.

Table 1. Coefficients used in simulations.

Coefficient	Value	Units
ASA Diffusion	5.489E-10	m^2/s
PI Diffusion	7.855E-10	m^2/s
Heat conduction of water at 20 °C	0.600	W/mk
Dielectric coefficient of skin	1.00	F/m

2.4 Numerical Technique and Computational Modeling

The MATLAB program was used to provide the solutions and run the simulation for the partial differential equations that describe the phenomena. Here, two geometries were designed according to 2.1. Later, in each one of the geometries, a numerical grid was created to represent the behavior of the problem. The lattice shape was defined based on the fit of the geometry shape. Boundary conditions were established in terms of flux [mol/s*m²], heat [W/mK], temperature [K] and voltage [V], to evaluate the behavior of Franz cell or skin.

For the simulation of the diffusive behavior in skin showed in Fig. 2(a), Neumann conditions were applied throughout the borders, a Dirichlet condition for the cell walls was used assuming no concentration on both lateral and inferior borders with no diffusive flux, and for the top border a flux of 2.57×10^{-6} mol/s*m^2 for the PVI diffusion and 2.85×10^{-6} mol/s*m^2 flux for the ASA diffusion were used.

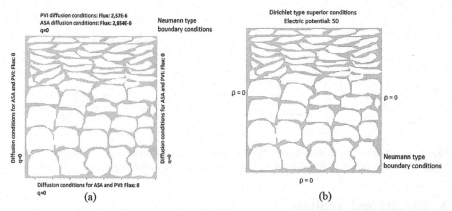

Fig. 2. (a) Distribution and values of frontier conditions of diffusive model on skin. (b) Distribution and values of frontier conditions of electrical model on skin.

For the electric behavior showed in Fig. 2(b), the boundary conditions for the cell walls is a Dirichlet condition with no electric potential, both lateral borders and the inferior border have a Neumann condition with no surface charge and the superior border has a Dirichlet condition with an electric potential of 50 V.

Furthermore, in the diffusive model of the Franz cell, Dirichlet conditions were applied throughout the borders, both lateral and inferior borders with no concentration, and for the top border a Neumann condition were used with fluxes of 2.57×10^{-6} mol/s*m^2 for the PVI diffusion and 2.85×10^{-6} mol/s*m^2 flux for the ASA diffusion, as showed in Fig. 3(a).

For the thermal behavior in Franz Cell a Neumann condition with no heat flux was used for the top and right borders. For the remaining borders, a Neumann condition with a heat flux of 15657.15 W/m^2 and a heat transfer coefficient of 50 W/m^{2}k was used when simulating the water bath. On other hand, in the heat plate model a Dirichlet condition for the same borders was used using a temperature of 313.15 K. This distribution is showed in Fig. 3(b).

Finally, an algorithm was implemented to solve the problem described by the laws of the physical behavior of the phenomenon using finite differences numerical method.

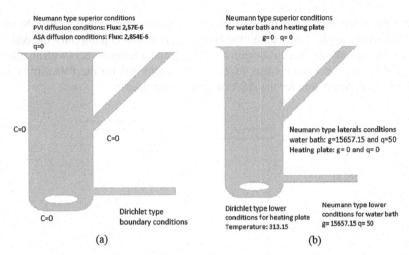

Fig. 3. (a) Distribution and values of frontier conditions of diffusive model on Franz cell. (b) Distribution and values of frontier conditions of thermal model on Franz cell.

3   Results and Analysis

3.1   Drug Diffusion Throughout the Skin

Information related to the simulation of the diffusion of two active compounds in skin through an intercellular route was obtained.

Povidone Iodine. Figure 4(a) shows the diffusion of the povidone-iodine through the skin. An accumulation of the drugs was observed on the surface of the skin, with minimal penetration. Additionally, povidone accumulates a lot in the interstices of the cell, this can be associated with the molecule being large, with a molecular weight of 364.95 g/mol, which would hinder its journey through the intermediate space [17]. Actually, this behaviour could be expected in experimental processes due to the presence of cholesterol, ceramides, and free fatty acids that are in the intermediate space that could hinder the passage of the large lipophobic molecules of povidone-iodine [4, 18].

Acetylsalicylic Acid. Figure 4(b) shows that similar to the behaviour of povidone-iodine, ASA accumulates on the skin's surface, however, greater penetration of the compound is noted compared to the penetration of povidone-iodine. Additionally, the accumulation in the interstices indicates that a more extensive diffusion will be given through the skin [19].

In this manner, in experimental processes the ASA is going to diffuse more through the skin, as much for its diffusion coefficient as for the behaviour evidenced in this simulation [20], and this is shown in Fig. 4, where the concentrations are higher in the ASA, with a maximum of 4000 while the PVI has lower values around 2500. Finally, the simulations show that the higher values of concentration at 30°C was obtained at 0.01 mm from the surface, as in both cases the diffusion did not go beyond the epidermis.

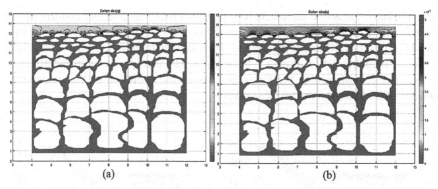

Fig. 4. (a) Behavior of PI concentration on skin model. (b) Behavior of ASA concentration on skin model.

3.2 Effect of an Electric Current in the Skin

Figure 5 shows how the electric current is conducted only through the outermost layers of the skin. By applying the voltage in the outer layers of the skin an electric field is generated in them, a better diffusion can be evidenced thanks to the electro-permeabilization, this increases the permeability of the cell membrane as a function based on electrical impulses. These impulses are distributed through the non-homogeneous structure of the skin, with the various layers creating a system like multiple resistors connected in series, giving rise to an electric field which increase electro-permeability [21].

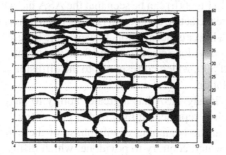

Fig. 5. Behavior of voltage on skin model.

3.3 Drug Diffusion Behavior on Franz Cell

Information related to the simulation of the diffusion of two active compounds in Franz cell was obtained.

Povidone Iodine. Figure 6(a) shows the simulation of the desorption of povidone-iodine from a BNC wound dressing placed in the upper part of a Franz cell. It shows that the concentration begins to unfold from the top of the cell to the inside of the cell, since it seeks a balance the active ingredient travels from a part with a higher concentration to one with a lower concentration. As was previously said, diffusion in the top of the Franz cell can be observed, where is possible to appreciate the transition from a concentration of 1800 to a concentration around 400, only in what corresponds to one centimeter of the Franz cell; furthermore, the figure also shows the evolution of the concentration behavior of PVI through the surface curves.

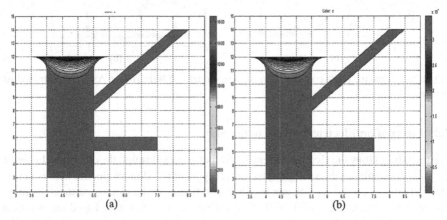

Fig. 6. (a) Behavior of PI concentration through Franz cell. (b) Behavior of ASA concentration through Franz cell.

Acetylsalicylic Acid. In Fig. 6(b) can be seen that the ASA has a behavior similar to that povidone-iodine, where the active compound is observed to travel towards the interior of the cell where there is a lower concentration, however, the difference is that the diffusion was lower compared to povidone since it started from a concentration of 20,000 to reach only a concentration of 500, which corresponds to the diffusion in one centimeter of the Franz cell in the simulation.

As mentioned previously, ASA has a greater ability to pass through the skin than povidone-iodine, which is represented by a higher concentration of ASA in the upper part of the Franz cell at the beginning of this phase of the experiment, however, this diffuses slowly in the water, contrary to povidone, which diffuses more quickly due to its solubility in water [3], while it can present a slower diffusion due to the presence of alcohol and glycerin in its formulation.

3.4 Thermal Behavior on Franz Cell

Thermal Diffusion. Behavior of the temperature into the Franz cells with thermal bath and heating plate methods was obtained in the computational simulation, and results are described below. The aim of this simulation was assessing which of the two ways is the most appropriate for the Franz cell method.

Heating Plate Method. Figure 7(a) shows the computational simulation behavior of the heating plate method in the Franz cells. Uniform heating is observed but only in the inferior part of the cell, where the plate is placed in the simulation and in experiments, represented in the distribution of the contour lines of temperature. The superior part of the cell shows no change in temperature. As the temperature is an indicator of molecular movement, an increase in this variable could improve the drug diffusion [22]. However, drug diffusion starts at the top of the Franz cell, so the effect of temperature in this heating method is not relevant at the start of the experiments. If heating starts before the experiment, ensuring a more homogeneous temperature in the cell, the effect may be relevant and observable. For this, a computational simulation using transient modeling equations could be worked.

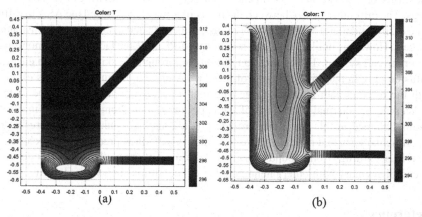

Fig. 7. (a) Behavior of temperature in Franz cell with heating plate method. (b) Behavior of temperature in Franz cell with thermal bath.

Thermal Bath Method. Computational simulation behavior of thermal bath method in Franz cells is shown in Fig. 7(b). It was observed that uniform heating begins in the cell walls, where the thermal bath has contact with the Franz system and was distributed inside the cell. Uniformity is represented with the distribution of contour lines, which are drawn homogeneously throughout the cell. This temperature behavior is an indicator that this variable will have an initial impact on drug diffusion, contrary to what was observed on the heating plate. In fact, a computational simulation of the problem observed with transient equations, which exemplify the natural evolution of the phenomenon, would indicate that the thermal bath would reach thermal equilibrium more quickly compared to the heating plate.

As mentioned on the heating plate, the molecular movement produced by the increase in temperature could improve the diffusion of the drug. The theory indicates that the increase in temperature in a medium increases the kinetic energy of the molecules, causing them to move faster and more frequently, which directly affects the speed of diffusion [22]. The more homogeneous the temperature in a medium, the more experimentally visible this effect will be. Therefore, according to the results obtained in the simulation, a higher diffusion speed is expected using a thermal bath, while a lower speed is expected with the heating plate, in this way a thermal bath is the more appropriative way of heat the Franz cell, which explains the reason why this method and the use of external jackets through which heated water flows are the most used when carrying out experimental tests [23].

4 Conclusions

In this paper, studies about thermal, electrical, and drug diffusive behavior for dermis and Franz cells were carried out using the development of mathematical models, as well as biophysical and structural conditions seeking a resemblance to real dermal models. The diffusive behavior in both skin and Franz cells showed similarities between the two drugs. The difference in size between the molecules may have caused the ASA to diffuse more easily, and therefore there is more through the skin and at the start of diffusion into the cell. However, unlike ASA, the solubility of PI in water facilitates its mobility in the Franz cell system. The application of voltage through the skin showed an electrical diffusion only in the primary layers of the skin. A more uniform heating was observed with the thermal bath method, suggesting that it is appropriate for this type of tests, by keeping the thermal conditions of the experiment more homogeneous. Finally, the results obtained in this paper can provide predictions that could guide future in vitro experimental tests in a more assertive way, also it will allow predicting the behavior of the release of drugs from wound dressings. Additionally, the mathematical model could be complementary with other phenomenological conditions in a versatile way.

References

1. Osorio, M., et al.: Novel surface modification of three-dimensional bacterial nanocellulose with cell-derived adhesion proteins for soft tissue engineering. Mater. Sci. Eng. C **100**, 697–705 (2019). https://doi.org/10.1016/j.msec.2019.03.045
2. Moritz, S., et al.: Active wound dressings based on bacterial nanocellulose as drug delivery system for octenidine. Int. J. Pharm. **471**(1–2), 45–55 (2014). https://doi.org/10.1016/j.ijpharm.2014.04.062
3. Wiegand, C., et al.: Antimicrobial functionalization of bacterial nanocellulose by loading with polihexanide and povidone-iodine. J. Mater. Sci. Mater. Med. **26**(10), 1–14 (2015). https://doi.org/10.1007/s10856-015-5571-7
4. Nesvadbova, M., Crosera, M., Maina, G., Filon, F.L.: Povidone iodine skin absorption: an ex-vivo study. Toxicol. Lett. **235**(3), 155–160 (2015). https://doi.org/10.1016/j.toxlet.2015.04.004
5. Preston, S.J., Arnold, M.H., Beller, E.M., Brooks, P.M., Buchanan, W.W.: Comparative analgesic and anti-inflammatory properties of sodium salicylate and acetylsalicylic acid (aspirin) in rheumatoid arthritis. Br. J. Clin. Pharmacol. **27**(5), 607–611 (1989)
6. Darby, I.A., Weller, C.D.: Aspirin treatment for chronic wounds: potential beneficial and inhibitory effects. Wound Repair Regen. **25**(1), 7–12 (2017). https://doi.org/10.1111/wrr.12502
7. Franz, T.J.: Percutaneous absorption. on the relevance of in vitro data. J. Invest. Dermatol. **64**(3), 190–195 (1975). https://doi.org/10.1111/1523-1747.ep12533356
8. Franz, T.J.: The finite dose technique as a valid in vitro model for the study of percutaneous absorption in man. Curr. Probl. Dermatol. **7**, 58–68 (1978). https://doi.org/10.1159/000401276

9. Lasso Reyes, J.C., Ruiz Durango, J.F.: Optimizacion metodologica para estudios de permeabilidad in vitro empleado los modelos de celda de franz horizontal y vertical. Universidad Icesi (2017)
10. Zsikó, S., Csányi, E., Kovács, A., Budai-Szűcs, M., Gácsi, A., Berkó, S.: Methods to evaluate skin penetration in vitro. Sci. Pharm. **87**(3), 19 (2019). https://doi.org/10.3390/scipharm8703 0019
11. Tateo, F., et al.: The in-vitro percutaneous migration of chemical elements from a thermal mud for healing use. Appl. Clay Sci. **44**(1–2), 83–94 (2009). https://doi.org/10.1016/j.clay. 2009.02.004
12. Gelker, M., Müller-Goymann, C.C., Viöl, W.: Permeabilization of human stratum corneum and full-thickness skin samples by a direct dielectric barrier discharge. Clin. Plasma Med. **9**, 34–40 (2018). https://doi.org/10.1016/j.cpme.2018.02.001
13. Paul, A., Laurila, T., Vuorinen, V., Divinski, S.V.: Thermodynamics, Diffusion and the Kirkendall Effect in Solids. Springer, Berlin (2014). https://doi.org/10.1007/978-3-319-074 61-0
14. Prausnitz, M.R., et al.: Skin barrier and transdermal drug delivery. Dermatology **3**, 2065–2073 (2012)
15. Liu, I.S.: On fourier's law of heat conduction. Contin. Mech. Thermodyn. **2**(4), 301–305 (1990). https://doi.org/10.1007/BF01129123
16. Reeks, M.W.: Stokes-einstein equation. In: A-to-Z Guide to Thermodynamics, Heat and Mass Transfer, and Fluids Engineering, Begellhouse (2011)
17. de Mattos, I.B., et al.: Delivery of antiseptic solutions by a bacterial cellulose wound dressing: uptake, release and antibacterial efficacy of octenidine and povidone-iodine. Burns **46**(4), 1–10 (2019)
18. Wickett, R.R., Visscher, M.O.: Structure and function of the epidermal barrier. Am. J. Infect. Control **34**(10), S98–S110 (2006)
19. Moser, K., Kriwet, K., Naik, A., Kalia, Y.N., Guy, R.H.: Passive skin penetration enhancement and its quantification in vitro. Eur. J. Pharm. Biopharm. **52**(2), 103–112 (2001). https://doi. org/10.1016/S0939-6411(01)00166-7
20. Pereira, G.R., et al.: Evaluation of skin absorption of drugs from topical and transdermal formulations. Artic. Braz. J. Pharm. Sci. **52**(3), 527–544 (2016). https://doi.org/10.1590/ s1984-82502016000300018
21. Pavšelj, N., Miklavčič, D.: Resistive heating and electropermeabilization of skin tissue during in vivo electroporation: a coupled nonlinear finite element model. Int. J. Heat Mass Transf. **54**(11–12), 2294–2302 (2011). https://doi.org/10.1016/j.ijheatmasstransfer.2011.02.035
22. Delpierre, G.R., Sewell, B.T.: Temperature and molecular motion (2002)
23. Estévez, T., Aguilera, A., Sáez, A., Hardy, E.: Diseño y validación de una celda de difusión para estudios de liberación in vitro de biomoléculas. Biotecnologia Aplicada **17**(3), 187–190 (2000)

Portable and Mobile System Connected to a Web Application for the Measurement of Air Quality in the City of Bogotá Associated with Particulate Matter and Meteorological Variables

Daniel Santiago Becerra Casas[1], Carlos Felipe Reyes Bello[1],
Juan Sebastian Rubiano Labrador[2(✉)], and Oscar Arnulfo Fajardo Montaña[3]

[1] Electronic Engineering Department Microelectronics Research Hotbed, Central University,
Bogota, Colombia
{dbecerrac1,creyesb}@ucentral.edu.co
[2] Electronic Engineering Microelectronics Research Hotbed, Central University,
Bogota, Colombia
jrubianol@ucentral.edu.co
[3] Environmental Engineering Department, Central University, Bogota, Colombia
ofajardom@ucentral.edu.co

Abstract. The advance of communication and sensor technologies has driven the development of surveillance systems that help to significantly improve the living conditions and health of living beings. The difficulty in accessing data, the high cost of conventional monitors and the low scalability of conventional air quality monitoring networks in Bogotá have motivated the development of air quality monitoring devices, communication and connectivity technologies supported by the Internet of Things (IoT) and the integration of a low cost wireless sensor network for easy access to the public. This document presents the development of a portable device for the monitoring of Bogotá's air quality index (IBOCA) associated with the ultrafine PM2.5 and PM10 materials, the measurement of meteorological variables (temperature, relative humidity and atmospheric pressure) and the acquisition of geolocation The air quality monitoring device (AirQDev) performs a triangulation of the user's geographic location by means of its geographic coordinates where he will have a personalized space within a web platform (UCAirQNet) to consult and download his measurements at any time, to follow up through the platform and a detailed search of how polluted the area where he performs his usual routes is. With this research, it was determined that the use of low-cost portable devices to monitor air quality has an important impact on citizen participation by providing real-time information about their environment, in addition to generating awareness in the community about the diagnosis of the most recurring contamination routes and the need to take citizen actions to mitigate this public health problem.

Keywords: Air monitoring · Fine particulate matter · IoT · PM10 · PM2.5 · IBOCA · Mobile monitoring · Mobile sensors network

© Springer Nature Switzerland AG 2020
J. C. Figueroa-García et al. (Eds.): WEA 2020, CCIS 1274, pp. 398–408, 2020.
https://doi.org/10.1007/978-3-030-61834-6_34

1   Introduction

Breathing good air is a fundamental right, a right that is violated every day, since 90% of humanity breathes polluted air, it is estimated that about seven million people die from air pollution, equivalent to 7.6% of deaths worldwide [1]. In national terms, the figures are not very encouraging since, according to the National Observatory of health (ONS; For its acronym in Spanish) of the National institute of health (INS; For its acronym in Spanish), the technical report "Environmental Disease Burden in Colombia" for 2019 indicates that 17,579 people die in the country as a result of exposure to air and water in poor conditions, which represents 8% of the total annual mortality in Colombia. The same report emphasizes a measure for solving the air quality problem, "increasing monitoring units for environmental risk factors" [2].

The use of monitoring networks for air pollution around the world has become more important in the last decade, particularly in Bogotá due to the continuous warnings from local government and environmental entities about poor air quality. During the period from the second half of 2019 to the first quarter of 2020, the city government issued a yellow alert and an orange alert, followed by drastic measures such as restricting vehicle mobility by license plate and regulating the operation of factories with high levels of fixed emissions, among others [3].

The pollutant that most affects air quality in urban areas is fine particulate matter (PM2.5), made up of particles 2.5 μm in size or less. Most vehicles, mainly those that use diesel fuel, are responsible for the emission of this pollutant. Because PM2.5 is so small and light it remains suspended in the air, making it more likely that humans will inhale it, causing respiratory diseases, cerebrovascular [4], and cardiac diseases, which can lead to heart attacks, lung diseases, aggravating asthma and bronchitis [5]. Student scientific initiatives in the implementation of monitoring campaigns offer a great potential for a wealth of information that is composed of a large amount of data. In this case, the Universidad Central Air Quality (UCAirQ) project focuses on the calculation of the Bogota Air Quality Index (IBOCA; For its acronym in Spanish, Indice Bogotano de Calidad del Aire), thanks to the measurement of particulate matter PM2.5, PM10 and the measurement of meteorological variables such as relative humidity, temperature and atmospheric pressure. These data are represented graphically in a web application, which allows monitoring through a general display panel by subnet, general by variable and specific by monitoring device developed and an interactive map updated thanks to the location of the device, tracing a route of pollution during the trips that are made during the measurement of the variables mentioned, in order to make studies on geographical behaviors corresponding to the Bogota Air Quality.

2   Materials and Methods

The monitoring device prototype (AirQDev) in its first version is designed to monitor particulate matter (PM1.0, PM2.5 and PM10), ambient temperature, relative humidity, atmospheric pressure, internal temperature and geographical position in order to calculate the Bogota Air Quality Index (IBOCA) for the ultra-fine material PM2.5 and to give a visualization of its state in a moment of time both in the device and in a web application, where you can make instantaneous consultations about the state of the air while you make your habitual routes, download the data to make later studies with them and consult the historical of measurements taken by the device.

2.1 Variables for Measuring the IBOCA

In order to calculate the IBOCA, certain data related to parameters that affect air quality are considered. The Bogotá Environmental Secretariat considers that it can be represented by specific concentrations of pollutants such as PM10 and PM2.5 particulate matter, carbon monoxide, ozone, sulfur oxide, and nitrogen dioxide [6].

The main air pollutant in Bogotá is the particulate matter emitted by each of the sources, whether mobile or fixed, corresponding to a conglomerate of solids and liquid waste floating in the air. The main way to study them is by their micrometric size (um), so they are divided into two groups:

– **Coarse Particles (PM10):** Formed by mechanical processes, civil works, pollen, mold, dust and wind currents produced by the passage of cars, its diameter is in the range of 2.6–10 (um/m^3).
– **Fine Particles (PM2.5):** They do not exceed 2.5 (um/m3) in concentration, they are produced mainly by any combustion phenomena, wood burning, power plants, forest fires, biomass burning and industrial processes.

Meteorological variables are very important to provide relevant information about specific air conditions, they turn out to be useful for the validation of simulation models of the atmospheric conditions in which pollutants can be concentrated or mobilized. Humidity in the air must be measured since it is to a great extent a fundamental factor in the transformation of the physical properties of air. Relative humidity is described as the fraction between the weight of water vapors in a volume of air and the weight of saturated vapor in the same volume. The temperature represents a scalar magnitude, measurable, directly related to the internal energy conditions of the system.

Finally, the measurement of atmospheric pressure is carried out since accompanied by meteorological data such as atmospheric temperature and relative humidity that is significant to be able to carry out an analysis in time, the meteorological conditions can be clearly determined and even forecasts can be made, therefore, the capacity to make good decisions to mitigate atmospheric pollution related to meteorological factors can be obtained.

2.2 Bogota Air Quality Index (IBOCA)

The Bogota air quality index is a dimensionless indicator, calculated from concentrations of air pollutants, it is homologous to the international air quality index ICA, with the difference that it is designed for the average concentrations of the city evaluating the pollutants on a scale of 1–100 while the ICA evaluates using a scale of 1–600 [6].

The IBOCA is designed with the objective of establishing an informative parameter so that the population has clarity on how healthy or unhealthy the city's air is, informing about alerts, air pollution emergencies, health effects on the population, and articulating joint actions between the city's health and environmental control entities [7, 8]. This parameter is established by the district secretary of environment and disseminated by the air quality monitoring network of Bogotá (RMCAB; For its acronym in Spanish, Red de Monitoreo de Calidad del Aire de Bogotá). Table 1 below shows the condensed information corresponding to particulate matter concentrations (PM10 and PM2.5) with units of ug/m3 related to an IBOCA dimensionless index, an associated air quality adjective and a prevention, warning or emergency response as appropriate.

Table 1. Bogotá air quality index IBOCA focused on particulate matter. (Source [7])

Attributes of IBOCA			Concentration Ranges of the Contaminant	
Numerical ranges - colors	Air quality status	Action and response status	PM 10 8 h (ug/m^3)	PM2.5 8 h (ug/m^3)
0–10	Favorable	Prevention	(0–54)	(0–12)
10,1–20	Moderate	Prevention	(55–154)	(12,1–35,4)
20,1–30	Regular	Yellow alert	(155–254)	(35,4–55,4)
30,1–40	*Bad*	Orange alert	(255–354)	(55,5–150,4)
40,1–60	*Very bad*	Red alert	(355–424)	(150,5–250,4)
60,1–100	*Dangerous*	Emergency	(425–604)	(250,5–500,4)

Based on Table 1, An algorithm is developed to associate the data measured by the particulate material sensor with a state of air quality, making use of the general equation to calculate the air quality index adjusting the values for Bogotá. [6]:

$$IBOCA = \frac{I_{Hi} - I_{Lo}}{BP_{Hi} - BP_{Lo}}(C - BP_{Lo}) + I_{Lo} \qquad (1)$$

The final value of the IBOCA is reported in the web application and displayed on the monitor of the device, storing it in the cloud along with the location by coordinates, date and time of measurement, this with the aim of determining points and road spaces in the city with higher rates of pollution.

3 AirQDev - Air Quality Monitoring Device

3.1 Design

The air quality monitoring device we call **AirQDev**, is built with a particulate material sensor which in turn incorporates a temperature sensor, relative humidity, an air pressure sensor and an internal temperature sensor. In the communication stage the AirQDev is supported by a 2G/3G connection to the GSM network through a SIMCard installed in the module SIM800V2 module, this module has a double functionality in the device, first, provides the geographic location of the user carrier. And second, it performs the communication with the web application we call **AirQNet** (Fig. 1).

Fig. 1. AirQDev device (Source: own elaboration).

The design of the structure of the AirQDev prototype was made thinking about a portable, resistant and easy to use device. To achieve this, the prototype was manufactured with 3D printing technology based on PLA polymer. This is a material that has properties of resistance to compression and traction, it is an insulating material, built with the minimum distance between layers (< 1 mm) avoiding the filtration of humidity and air currents inside it, also it is resistant to temperatures up to 55°C (with higher temperatures it starts to vitrify) and its composition is based on recyclable plastic.

Today, the latest technologies have contributed to implement many solutions for Air Quality monitoring that become more accurate, faster acquisition and display, smaller and much more accessible to people. The AirQDev monitor combined with the use of the web application has a cost that ranges from 150 USD to 200 USD which comparing with the high cost instrumentation in official monitoring stations offers a new opportunity for the communities to get involved in the air quality sampling.

3.2 Data Acquisition and Transmission

Data acquisition is performed synchronously every twenty-five (25) s, while data transmission and signal quality queries take an average time of five (5) s, thus having a sampling time of thirty (30) s. As the AirQDev prototype has the feature of being for portable use, it can be used in walking, cycling, in a private vehicle or public transport. Therefore, in consideration that on average a person walks at a speed of 2 m/s [9] and in Bogota if a vehicle drives at an average speed of 6.7 m/s, during peak hours [10].

During the journey that a citizen makes to get to her place of work or study, which on average can last up to 2 h and at the end of her day, the same time is assumed [11], there would be approximately 480 samples (points) with more than 4000 data per day, for each of the sensor nodes that will feed the network, and a route that will determine how polluted the air is that is breathed in her routine route, which will vary the distance between the sensor points depending on the speed at which one advances.

For the location, a query is made to the GPRS module by means of the AT command protocol, in order to know the geographical coordinates of latitude and longitude. The communication of the device with the web server of the AirQNet is made thanks to the implementation of a data buffer sent by the POST method, having as base the HTTP protocol, which with the help of the PHP programming language. This transfer protocol is the system by which requests for access to a page and the response with the content are sent.

The device performs a first filtration of the collected information, making sure that the data frame does not come empty or null, in order not to overload the database of truncated information. If the first filter gives a positive result, a TOKEN is received, which corresponds to a 16-byte variable that is used as an identity checker and is the main branch of the database hosting the registered data.

As soon as the database detects the arrival of the data, it is automatically read by the web server, which carries out a processing of the data to verify on the one hand that it is not empty data and does not affect the process. On the other hand, filter them depending on the needs of the user visiting the web application. This process is explained in Sect. 4.

Since data transmission and the location query have a high priority, a query of the signal quality value is performed, this task will be executed asynchronously to ensure that there is an optimal signal for the proper functioning of the device, being between optimal signals a range between 10–30, this value represents a magnitude called RSSI, given in dBm, which would be from −93 dBm to −53 dBm [12].

3.3 Energy and Battery Autonomy

The AirQDev device was designed to be a portable device, since inside it includes a package of three 3.6 V batteries, 2150 mAh, the system provides a total voltage of approximately 10.8 V, with a constant battery capacity of 2150 mAh. All stages of the prototype are adapted to work with low consumption elements, reaching a maximum consumption of 400 mA, according to the formula of battery life, this allows us to guarantee a constant functionality of 5.3 h, this result was estimated thanks to the equation [13].

$$Vb * lb = Wb \qquad 10.8\,V * 2.150\,A = 23.22\,W \tag{2}$$

$$Vb * lc = Wc \qquad 10.8\,V * 0.4\,A = 4.32 \tag{3}$$

$$H = \frac{Wb}{Wc} \qquad \frac{23.22\,W}{4.32\,W} = 5.375\,h \tag{4}$$

The result of the ratio of the battery power to the power consumed will result in the hours of battery life [13].

4 Data Processing and Visualization

The platform is also synchronized with a real time database in which the information of the measurements made by the users and the monitoring devices (AirQDev) is stored, so that at the sampling frequency the data sensed in the database will be reflected and processed both by the device, in an OLED screen (see Fig. 3), and by the web platform that will present the results to the user in the most dynamic way.

4.1 Display on the AirQDev

In order to show the measurements that are being sensed and the calculation of the IBOCA that is being processed, these data are presented in an OLED screen of 0. 96 inches (128 x 64 pixels), this display module will additionally include a graphical conversion of the remaining battery voltage in four lines, the 3G signal quality obtained at the time in a four vertical bar signal representation, the particulate matter in its three concentrations and weather variables, and the IBOCA air quality status (see Table 1), a processing that determines whether or not good air quality is currently available (Fig. 2).

Fig. 2. AirQDev display (Source: own elaboration).

The layout of the information is made based on the arrangement of pixels on the screen and is located according to a matrix. The data on the display is updated at intervals of 30 to 40 s and is specified after the sensed data has been sent to the platform. On the other hand, battery voltage and 3G signal power data are acquired asynchronously during 3-min and 10-s time intervals, respectively, so that, when a variation in one of the values acquired immediately before is detected, it will be updated on the screen and, if necessary, alerts will be issued regarding the device's charge and the low quality of the signal.

4.2 Web Application

The construction of the web application is based on JavaScript language as a website event controller, so the updating of data, graphics and display of them is done automatically in order to always have the information updated according to the measurements of the online devices. AirQnet is initially developed in Spanish as the initial language, but with the deployment process it is intended to implement an API for automatic translation in the different languages.

4.2.1 Data Base

The data is anchored to the cloud database offered by Google's FireBase, this database is used because it has the characteristic of being a real-time database, that is, every time it detects a change in the data, it will be reflected in the web application in milliseconds. In addition, the database continues to work even if for some reason the connection is lost, saving data in memory until the connection is re-established. It has the advantage of being scalable as needed, working multiplatform (a single database serves Android, iOS and web) and multilingual having the possibility of working in more than 5 programming languages [14].

The database of AirQNet has two main branches one will save the users information called AirQUsers and other will save the devices data called AirQData, and they are related when a user acquires or has an AirQDev, then the database structure would then share the devices identifiers to define that relationship.

4.2.1.1 Reading Captured Data

The data that is written to the database can be read in various ways, depending on the need, and worked with according to the type of traffic to be worked with. In the application, this reading is done in two important ways.

– First, the data are organized according to the date on which the data are collected. The date is in UTC (Universal Time Coordinated) format as complete as possible, that is, the date has day, month, year, hour, minute and second (YYYY-MM-DDThh:mm), this in order to be able to filter the data from the most current to the oldest.
– The second one is a general reading of the data, here the data does not go through any kind of filtering and it is done in order to have a complete visualization of all the data, and with them to be able to graph histograms, or that the user can filter all this information according to one or another range, to visualize two or more data at the same time, etc.

4.2.2 Data Processing

The way the data is read from the database allows to have in real time the amount of data that the devices write in it and also as from the AirQDev prototypes a processing of the data is done, a release to discard data that are out of range and, a calibration to match the data with the testing tests performed for Bogotá, the web platform reduces its processing to inspecting whether or not the data it is collecting from the database is empty and the rest of the data is collected as it is found in the database. The data, after being brought from the database, is stored in arrays or vectors to be used as appropriate and, with the assurance that these are constantly being updated.

4.2.3 Display of the Data

In the web application there are two graphs, one shows the real time value of each of the variables that are being sensed, that is, the last one registered in the database. The other graph is a histogram where the last 24 h of devices behavior are shown in a summarized way. There is also a section where users can interact with the data, so that they can filter and sort the data by time, variables or by network. In addition, there is a section for displaying each device registered in the database individually, where you can see all the sensing records individually, that is, a history of the data on particulate matter, meteorological variables and IBOCA calculation, in addition to its air quality route, an individual map with the georeference points taken.

5 System Integration and Results

The implementation and testing of the system is based on the deployment of two sensing devices in the city of Bogota in two phases, the first one carried out from two fixed points in order to have comparison of the collected data and performance tests in two different environments, the first AirQDev prototype located in the town of Suba and the second one in the town of Puente Aranda. This phase allowed the validation of the communication between the sensing device and the Web application. For the second phase, tests were conducted on the operation of the geolocation system, for which four short bike rides of about 4 km were made, thus proving the energy independence of the device and its connection quality for sending data and geolocation in motion.

Fig. 3. Diagram of the basic functioning of the system (Source: own elaboration).

The web application is ready to provide all the information collected by the devices and display it to the users. It's divided into 6 main sections:

- Network: Shows the main dashboard, with the data and summary graphs of the last 24 h, depending on the server time. Classified in a total or subnet summary.
- Live Map: Shows the data in a dynamic map, showing the last 8 h of each one of the Online devices.
- Statistics: It is a section that allows you to filter, organize and visualize the information according to user requirements.
- Docs: Shows information of the prototype's enclosure.
- Auth/Register: Section dedicated to control the start and registration of users.
- AirQDev - Details: Shows statistics and relevant information of each AirQDev.

The web application has been initially developed in Spanish but in the future, it is expected to be available in different languages.

The PMS5003 sensor, used to determine air pollution has a detection range of 0.3 to 10 ug/m^3 and a manufacturer's declared accuracy of ±10 ug/m^3. Sensors (PMS) show more variability at low concentrations of particulate matter and can be affected by meteorological conditions such as temperature and relative humidity, so it is recommended to have these conditions measured in order to determine their influence on final measurements.

5.1 Visualization of Information and Graphical Analysis of Data

In the developed application, data can be analyzed independently, knowing that there are three subnetworks (mobile, fixed bottom and fixed track), eight variables (IBOCA 10, IBOCA 2.5, PM 10, PM 2.5, PM 1.0, temperature, relative humidity, atmospheric pressure) and the geolocation of the prototype. Therefore, the user will have a great variety of graphic information, among the most relevant are those presented in the overview of the main dashboard, which has histograms of the behavior of the last 24 h of the entire network, as well as the immediately "new" data (the last to be added to the database) of the variables.

The graphs in this overview allow a quick look at the air quality, as well as the pollutants and environmental variables, in order to determine at what time of the day is when the highest concentration of pollutants in the air is present, regardless of the location, since the overview does not filter the data by subnetwork. The current value, because it is so changeable, can only be taken as a reference of operation and communication between the devices and the web server because, in such a case that you have a large number of devices per network, turned on and sensing at the same time, this "current" value would change every second (or less) with a new value found in the database (Fig. 4).

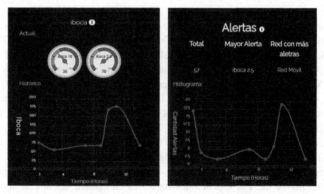

Fig. 4. Web application: current graphics and histogram for IBOCA 10 and IBOCA 2.5,: graph of total alerts (Source: own elaboration).

Knowing the limits of each of the variables, it is possible to know when the PM10 and PM2.5 are or are not on alert for overexposure, which results in IBOCA 10 and IBOCA 2.5 indexes being alerted. If a count is made of the number of times the data was alerted in an hour, then another histogram can be constructed that reports the total number of alerts received in the last 24 h, as well as which variable was most alerted and which network had more alerts. Thus, deducing which of the 3 networks is the most polluting and the reason for its high number of alerts.

6 Conclusions and Future Works

It is ratified that the prototype AirQDev developed can be the base for new studies about the quality of the air in the capital, in the same way, it is demonstrated that it can have the capacity and the necessary dynamism in the information to be able to communicate to the citizenship about the conditions of the air that they breathe, presenting the information in a scale regulated by the governmental entities of the city corresponding to the IBOCA associated to the particulate matter (PM).

This work exposes the viability of the use of low-cost sensorics for particulate matter in the implementation of community monitoring networks, in order to make possible the acquisition of data to inform the population, since these device monitors are the most cost-effective means to improve the low number of certified monitoring stations, their high monetary cost and their low scalability. During the implementation process it was determined that, thanks to the use of a portable monitoring device, it is possible to determine the routes or roads in the city that have more pollution, as well as to diagnose the time slots in which it is more unsafe to travel, in terms of air pollution.

For future research, it is necessary to carry out a calibration process of the devices. It is proposed to take a reference instrument, preferably the one used by the Bogotá Air Quality Monitoring Network, in order to obtain an optimal balance between the cost and precision variables of the measurement systems.

References

1. OMS. Nueve de cada diez personas de todo el mundo respiran aire contaminado. 4 (2018)
2. ONS. Carga de enfermedad ambiental en Colombia. Inf. Técnico Espec. 10 177 (2018)
3. Bogotá, S.: de ambiente de. Reporte de la calidad del aire en Bogotá: lunes 9 de marzo (2020)
4. Leiva, M.A., Santibañez, D.A., Ibarra, S., Matus, P., Seguel, R.: A five-year study of particulate matter (PM2.5) and cerebrovascular diseases. Environ. Pollut. **181**, 1–6 (2013)
5. Zhao, C., et al.: Respiratory exposure to PM2.5 soluble extract disrupts mucosal barrier function and promotes the development of experimental asthma. Sci. Total Environ. **730**, 139145 (2020)
6. Instituto de Hidrología, M. y E. A. Formato Común Hoja Metodológica Índice de calidad del aire (ICA) Formato Común Hoja Metodológica. Ideam, pp. 1–8 (2012)
7. SDA. Índice Bogotano de Calidad del Aire - IBOCA. Obs. Ambient. Bogotá, pp. 1–6 (2015)
8. Bogotá, A.: mayor de. Por condiciones regulares en calidad del aire se mantiene Alerta Amarilla en Bogotá (2020)
9. Order, Z.: Velocidad (m/ s), pp. 14–15 (2007)
10. Melgarejo, C.: Movilidad quiere que la velocidad máxima en Bogotá sea de 50 km/h. EL TIEMPO **1**, 4 (2018)
11. FM, L.: Cuánto tiempo gastan los bogotanos en llegar a sus trabajos y volver a casa La FM **1**, 3 (2018)
12. M2M support.net. AT commands. At+csq. Available at: https://m2msupport.net/m2msupport/atcsq-signal-quality/. Accessed 4 April 2020
13. Coelectrix. Calcular Autonomía de una Batería. 5 (2019). https://coelectrix.com/calcular-la-autonomia-de-una-bateria#:~:text=FórmulaparacalcularlaautonomíadeunaBatería,-Hayuna fórmula&text=(Vb)voltajedelabatería,deduracióndelabatería. Accessed 8 March 2020
14. Google. Data base Documentation. 2020. Available at: https://firebase.google.com/docs/?gclid=CjwKCAjwrcH3BRApEiwAxjdPTZacDmLoudigl1cNbKAWPB3YJgp1qmdkwF3s 9Q1Jx3RMokVmPycwCxoCkDEQAvD_BwE

Web Application for the Teaching of Anatomy and Physiology of the Respiratory System: Usability Measurement and Metrics

Luis Felipe Buitrago-Castro⊕, Maria Bernarda Salazar-Sánchez(✉)⊕, and Alher Mauricio Hernández-Valdivieso⊕

Bioinstrumentation and Clinical Engineering Research Group - GIBIC, Bioengineering Department, Engineering Faculty, Universidad de Antioquia UdeA, Calle 70 No. 52-21, A.A. 1226, Medellín, Colombia
{luis.buitragoc,bernarda.salazar,alher.hernandez}@udea.edu.co

Abstract. Usability testing is a measure of quality in the area of technology tool development, which allows evaluating the response that a potential user has when facing the tool for the first time. This paper aim is to assess the usability of a web application about Anatomy and Physiology of the Respiratory System developed for teaching-learning in programs offered in the area of Health Sciences by higher education institutions in Colombia. The usability test was conducted based on the MUSiC methodology, which evaluates the following attributes: effectiveness, efficiency, satisfaction, ease of use, memorability, and errors. The instrument developed consisted of 26 questions divided into two categories: solving tasks (4 items) and level of satisfaction (22 items). The trial involved 43 volunteers (38% women, 62% men), including undergraduate students and professionals. The effectiveness of the tool in the different contexts of use proposed exceeded 70%, which is an excellent result for the first potential end-users - software interaction test. However, the satisfaction of the users on solving tasks suggests we include guide boxes in specific modules for facilitating more the development of some tasks (e.g., simulation). In summary, the results obtained show the anatomy and physiology web application can be used intuitively and efficiently, by the academic community related to health sciences.

Keywords: Usability test · Health education · Software applications

1 Introduction

The educational process, as a phenomenon of interaction and exchange whose sole purpose is to generate strategies aimed at cause learning [1], that does not create faculties in the educated, but cooperates in their unfold and precision [2], has been evolving over the years. Thus, the idea of an education where those involved, teachers and students, are physically separated but connected by different means has taken strengthen just as new technologies have been developed [3]. According to the Mobile of Economy, currently, 49% of the world population is connected, estimating that the use of mobile devices

© Springer Nature Switzerland AG 2020
J. C. Figueroa-García et al. (Eds.): WEA 2020, CCIS 1274, pp. 409–419, 2020.
https://doi.org/10.1007/978-3-030-61834-6_35

will be 5.2 billion by 2019 [4]. This has led to a growing interest among educators in acquiring tools to facilitate the teaching-learning process [5], a trend that has boosted and encouraged the development of technological aids. That provides educational environments in which students can take advantage of their learning in a practical way based on experience [6]. A task that is highly complex due to the features that are expected from the tool, such as support database, comprehensive content, elements for interactive sessions, sending notifications, ease of login, and a friendly user interface [7].

In order to ensure that applications are user-friendly and easy to use for their target population, many developers conduct usability testing [8]. Whose basic principles according to the International Standard Organization (ISO) are to generate [9]: (1) ease of learning, understood as the comfort with which a user can interact effectively; (2) flexibility, referring to the range of possibilities with which information can be exchanged with the system; and (3) robustness, which implies the degree of support provided to the user to achieve its objectives. Given the relevance of these principles in the design of applications, multiple models have been proposed to evaluate the degree of usability as accurately as possible, clearly considering what should be measured and how it should be measured. Within these models can be found: (1) ISO 9241-11 [10], which measures the level at which objectives are achieved, the resources invested in accomplishing them, and the degree to which the user finds the use acceptable; (2) MUSiC (Metrics for Usability Standards in Computing) [11], where measures can be taken such as effectiveness in the suggested tasks, time efficiency, and proportion of the productive period; (3) QUIM (Quality in Use Integrated Measurement) [12], which is broken down into factors that it ranks, specifying criteria and metrics; and finally (4) SANe (The Skill Acquisition Network) [13], which assumes a user interaction model defining tasks, device dynamics and procedures for task execution; among others.

These methodologies are expected to show the degree of acceptance of the application before it is actively used by the target population. However, they are models that were developed in the context of desktop applications, whose characteristics may differ widely from those existing in web or mobile apps [14]. Therefore, one of the challenges is to adapt the models to the particular needs of the web environment and development, selecting the metrics that show the ease or difficulty that the user has when interacting with the web tool [15]. Because, unlike desktop or mobile applications, web applications can be accessed from any browser or device, over a local network or the Internet, they require no installation and can be in the cloud, not on the device accessing it [16].

Therefore, the main objective of this article is to advance in the usability testing of a technological tool designed and developed for teaching and learning of the respiratory system in higher education programs in Colombia. Tool composed of both theoretical and simulation elements, so it is of vital importance to know the effectiveness, efficiency, and user satisfaction to achieve a specific objective, ensuring the high quality of the tool. Taking into account the above and understanding the value of adapting the usability evaluation methodology to ensure the high quality of technological tools that involve teaching-learning processes, this paper also addresses the metrics used to evaluate and analyze such intuitiveness and ease of use.

2 Methods

2.1 Web Application

The application of Anatomy and Physiology of the Respiratory System (see Fig. 1) is a tool to support the teaching-learning process in programs with traditional methodology. Structured in a modular way, it focuses on conceptualizing the main structures and functions of the respiratory system, following a learning line that takes the student from the understanding of the clinical conditions of a healthy person to the identification of patterns associated with different pathologies. The web application has three main modules: (1) ventilation, which seeks to contextualize the student within the mechanical properties of the system; (2) breathing, which addresses the processes and concepts related to gas exchange; and (3) physiopathology, which conceptualizes and simulates the behavior of the respiratory system in high-impact diseases such as ASTHMA, Chronic Obstructive Pulmonary Disease (COPD) and Acute Respiratory Distress Syndrome (ARDS).

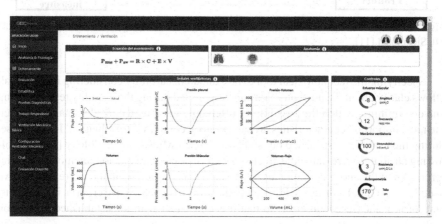

Fig. 1. Web application interface. The application allows the training and evaluation of the students, in addition to interaction with the teacher through a chat.

The web application uses different pedagogical strategies through which it provides content and clinical scenarios for the reinforcement of skills and knowledge, including within the functionalities simulation and variation of clinical parameters, as well as theoretical elements organized in diagrams, concept maps, and interactive illustrative images.

2.2 Usability Test

Considering the context of use and the objectives of the web application to be evaluated, the methodology of the MUSiC model was adapted [11], which considers the inclusion of specific tasks and time efficiency in the axis of the same. The methodological strategy used for the usability test is shown in the Fig. 2 and responds to the following three characteristics: (1) the product to be evaluated is the web application Anatomy and

Physiology of the Respiratory System; (2) the context of use will be the learning of an academic-clinical content and clinical simulation, and (3) the objectives will be to know the degree of understanding, use, and the difficulty presented by the user when interacting with the web application.

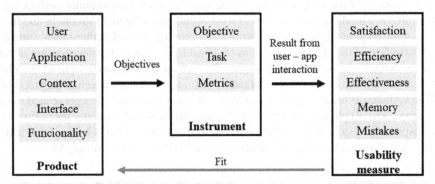

Fig. 2. The methodological framework of the usability test according to what is suggested in the MUSiC model [11].

Specifying the technological tool to be evaluated, carefully considering its potential, allows clarity about the attributes that can be assessed during the usability test. Selecting and determining, within the possibilities offered by the tool, a typical scenario in which the most important characteristics are taken into account in the evaluation. In this sense, during the usability test carried out and based on the MuSIC methodology [11], the following attributes were defined: Effectiveness, efficiency, satisfaction, memorability, and errors. All of the above in the context of the target population, so that it is a representative sample of potential end-users. For which, the tasks to develop have criteria, instructions, and form of measurement clear, so that it is consistent with the established evaluation metrics.

Thus, the instrument developed consisted of 26 questions divided into two categories: task execution (4 questions) and level of satisfaction (22 questions). The latter was subcategorized as follows: task execution, ease of use of the application, information provided, graphic interface, and functionality.

2.3 Usability Measurement and Metrics

The specific characteristics that the web application must meet in terms of usability were associated with the requirements necessary for the adequate provision of the services for which it was designed. The attributes defined as fundamental, their definition with an expected quality relation, and the metrics used in each attribute are shown in Table 1.

2.4 Experimental Design

For the selection of the study population, the following inclusion criteria were proposed: (1) Professional or professional training in the area of health sciences; (2) person with

Table 1. Definition of the usability measures used in the test within the context of the web application of Anatomy and Physiology of the Respiratory System

Attribute	Definition	Metric
Effectivity	The number of tasks carried out (Quantity) and quality with which they have been solved (Quality)	✓ Tasks carried out in the time allotted ✓ Percentage of completed tasks
Effectiveness	The amount of time a user is able to complete a task. It gives information about the intuitiveness of the tool	✓ Time spent completing the task ✓ Productive time
Satisfaction	Measure of tool acceptance, which varies on a scale from 0 to 100. It gives an account of the user's conformity with their experience	✓ Level of difficulty presented ✓ Preferences
Ease of use	Relationship between the user's sense of learning and the time it takes to complete a task	✓ Amount of training ✓ Learning curve
Memorability	The ease with which the user navigates through the tool	✓ The number of steps or clicks used to complete the task
Errors	The number of errors made during the test	✓ The number of mistakes made

advanced management of information and communication technologies, and (3) professional or professional training with previous knowledge in the subject matter covered by the web application.

Thus, 43 volunteers, including undergraduate students and professionals (teachers), aged between 19 and 35 years (38% women, 62% men) participated. All the volunteers read and signed the informed consent, according to the regulations by the Bioethics Committee Medical Research Institute, Faculty of Medicine, University of Antioquia, Medellín - Colombia (F-017-00, Act No. 011, May 2019). Before starting the test, the responsibilities of project researchers, data use, and data protection compliance of all the participants following Law 1581 of 2012 and Decree 1377 of 2013 were highlighted.

2.5 Statistical Analysis

The present study is of a descriptive type, whose variables of interest are quantitative (discrete) or qualitative (nominal measurement scale). Statistical measures such as mean (μ), standard deviation (σ), and coefficient of variation (CV) are applied to the data to analyze the user's response during their interaction with the different modules of the web application and their level of satisfaction using that application.

3   Results

In order to approach a usability measure, the designed test collected the data related to: (1) the completion or not of the tasks set out in the usage scenarios; (2) the time required by the participant to complete each task; (3) the number of errors made in performing the task; and (4) satisfaction with interacting with the application. The tasks defined taking into account the characteristics of the web application and the objectives of the usability test, are related in Table 2.

Table 2. Tasks set for the usability test of the web application of Anatomy and Physiology of the Respiratory System.

Task	Context of use	Protocol
1	Information search	1.1 Start the timer 1.2 Enter to the training section 1.3 Go to the topic of physiopathology 1.4 Open the ventilatory signals information 1.5 When you have completed the task, stop the timer, and write down the time spent
2	Identification of structures	2.1 Start the timer 2.2 Go to the topic of ventilation 2.3 Open the ventilating muscles illustration 2.4 Explore each muscle 2.5 When you have completed the task, stop the timer, and write down the time spent
3	Simulation	3.1 Start the timer 3.2 Go to the topic of breathing 3.3 Stand in the controls section and set an altitude of approximately 2500 msn and a breathing rate of 16 3.4 Go to the monitoring section and read the inspired oxygen pressure value 3.5 When you have completed the task, stop the timer, and write down the time spent
4	Functionality	4.1 Start the timer 4.2 Go to the topic of ventilation 4.3 Zoom in on the ventilatory signal corresponding to pleural pressure 4.4 Return the ventilating signal to the initial view 4.5 When you have completed the task, stop the timer, and write down the time spent

In Table 3 it is evident that at least 80% of users completed any of the four tasks posed in the usability test successfully. Task 2 was the least difficult task and was completed by all participants, while Task 3 was the most challenging and was not completed by eight users, i.e., 19% of the sample. This result is corroborated by the time used to execute the tasks, in which Task 3 took an average of 125 s, which represents the longest time for completion of the assigned activity, following the protocol described in Table 2. Unlike the shorter time spent on Task 1 and Task 2, where users spent on average less than 75 s.

Table 3. The number of users and time spent (maximum value, minimum, average, and deviation) in the realization of the tasks indicated in the usability test.

Task	Number of users		Time spent (s)	
	Completed tasks	Unfinished tasks	Min, Max	Mean $\pm\,\sigma^2$
1	42 (98%)	1 (2%)	40.00, 100.0	72.09 $\pm$ 39.64
2	43 (100%)	0 (0%)	40.00, 80.00	74.84 $\pm$ 32.06
3	35 (81%)	8 (19%)	80.00, 140.0	125.0 $\pm$ 47.20
4	37 (86%)	6 (14%)	50.00–80.00	85.98 $\pm$ 47.47

In terms of the distribution density of the number of errors made and the time spent by users (see Fig. 3), it was found that 70% made between 0 and 1 error, 77% between 0 and 1 error, 81% between 0 and 4 errors, 75% between 0 and 1 error for Task 1, Task 2, Task 3 and Task 4, respectively. These results corroborate that Task 3 presented the highest degree of difficulty; there are users who made more than five errors, which was the maximum value of mistakes for the other tasks. This may be because Task 3 required the simulation of a clinical scenario to report the final value of a clinical variable, which was affected if the user fully complied with the protocol indicated for that task in Table 2.

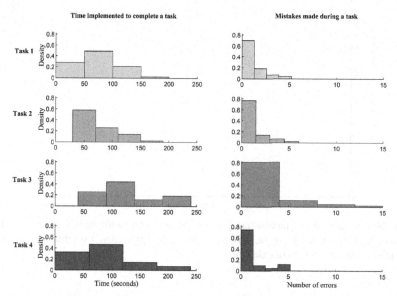

Fig. 3. Distribution of the population in terms of the time taken to complete a task (first column) and the number of errors made during a task (second column). The tasks are represented in the rows of the graph.

Concerning the time spent by the users, it was expected that the completion of the tasks would require less than 100 s, considering that none of the volunteers knew the learning tool previously. The results obtained can be seen in Fig. 3, where the density concentrated on the first two bars for Tasks 1, 2 and 4, indicates that at least 77% of the users took a maximum of 100 s to complete the assigned task. This does not occur in Task 3, where only 26% finished the task in less than 90 s.

Finally, users were consulted for their level of satisfaction (category) on a scale from 0 to 100%, and the results are shown in Fig. 4. The questions addressed the following subcategories: (1) task development, (2) ease of use of the application, (3) information provided, (4) graphical interface, and (5) functionality. The results highlights that most users present a medium to high satisfaction with their interaction with the evaluation tool in each subcategory. When calculating the average values, it was found that the lowest level of satisfaction is related to performance during the execution of the task (68.83%) and the highest level to the design of the graphic interface (86.94%). However, the satisfaction expressed with respect to the different functions available in the tool (80.23%), the ease of using the web application (75.08%), and the quality of the information provided in the different scenarios addressed in the test (74.57%) was also relevant.

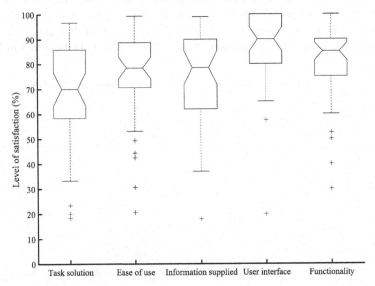

Fig. 4. Boxplot of user satisfaction (category) when interacting with the web application in five subcategories (1) task development, (2) ease of use of the application, (3) information provided, (4) graphic interface, and (5) functionality.

4 Discussion

Usability testing, as a measure of quality in software development, has been conducted by multiple authors in different areas of knowledge [17–21]. The final objective is to show the capacity of the tool to facilitate comfortable navigation for the user. Thus, according to the conceptualization of the ISO, this measure is divided into three basic principles that are: ease of learning, flexibility, and robustness [9]. Principles that were observed in this work through the attributes shown in Table 1, these were specified and configured according to the web application nature. In this sense, the results shown in Table 3 show an increase in the difficulty of solving Tasks 3 and 4, because these are tasks whose main objective is the simulation, and not the information search as Tasks 1 and 2, which provides valuable information for improving the controls and intuitiveness of technological assistance in evaluation. However, a study carried out by Jeff Sauro with 1200 users concludes that the average efficiency in carrying out a task is 78% [22] so that what is obtained in this study, both individually and globally, could be considered as very good. And as Wicaksono mentions [23], a "good" measure of effectivity depends on the intended context of use for the tool.

On the other hand, the lowest effectiveness was obtained for Task 3, with an average duration of 125 s, this suggests that developers should include more specific elements that facilitate the simulation for users in their first interaction, even more so when efficiency has been shown to be a susceptible measure since the failure of only a few users can cause this to decline significantly [23], as takes into account the performance of all participants during all tasks.

In line with the two previous measures, we analyzed the number of errors that the participants made when carrying out the different tasks, a measure that is important as it can affect the productivity of the users during the use of the application [24]. The results obtained (see Fig. 3) highlight that most participants made between 0 and 1 mistake, which is not a significant number of errors. As long as a large number of errors are made, it means that the user must spend time to find out how to correct them [25]. Given the low number of errors in 77% of users (<2), the high intuitiveness of the tool can be inferred, which has an impact on increasing the efficiency of user-application interaction.

Finally, concerning the degree of satisfaction shown by users (ver Fig. 4), which was low in terms of task performance (68.83%), it suggests the inclusion of more visible icons in the application environments that allow the simulation of clinical scenarios. Much more so when the web application nature is to teach professionals training on a specific topic.

5   Conclusions

The use of the proposed methodology allowed a usability analysis of the web application of Anatomy and Physiology of the Respiratory System developed by the GIBIC research group in terms of the attributes: effectiveness, efficiency, satisfaction, ease of use, and the number of errors. Where the definition of the context of use and survey in a representative population proved high users satisfaction ($>70\%$) with the different functions available in the tool, graphic interface, and the quality of the information provided in the clinical scenarios.

Acknowledgments. This work was partially supported by COLCIENCIAS under Grant "CT 450-2018 - Desarrollo de aplicaciones móviles para el aprendizaje del sistema respiratorio: Conceptos básicos, diagnóstico de enfermedades, terapia y rehabilitación - recursos provenientes del Sistema

General de Regalías fondos de CTeI de la Gobernación de Antioquia, administrados a través del patrimonio autónomo fondo nacional de financiamiento para la ciencia, la tecnología y la innovación Francisco José de Caldas" (Colombia); and by Universidad de Antioquia under Grant 2018-20133 (Medellín, Antioquia, Colombia).

Conflict of Interest. The author(s) declare(s) that there is no conflict of interest regarding the publication of this paper.

References

1. Contreras, J.: Enseñanza, currículum y profesorado introducción crítica a la didáctica, 2nd ed. Madrid (1994)
2. Ausubel, D.P., Novak, J.D., Hanesian, H.: Psicología educativa: Un punto de vista cognoscitivo, 2nd ed. México D.F (1990)
3. Kiryakova, G.: Review of distance education. Trakia J. Sci. **7**(3), 29–34 (2009)
4. GSMA Corporate: The mobile Economy (2020)
5. Hsu, Y., Ching, Y.: Mobile app design for teaching and learning: educators' experiences in an online graduate course. Int. Rev. Res. Open Distance Learn. **14**(4), 117–139 (2013)
6. Eady, M.J., Lockyer, L.: Tools for learning: technology and teaching strategies. In: Hudson, P. (ed.) Learning to Teach in the Primary School, p. 71. Queensland University of Technology, Australia (2013)
7. Rajput, M.: 10 Important Educational Mobile App Features That Boost The Learning Process - eLearning Industry, 08 July 2017. https://elearningindustry.com/10-educational-mobile-app-features-boost-learning-process. Accessed 05 May 2020
8. Kumar, B.A., Goundar, M.S., Chand, S.S.: Usability guideline for mobile learning applications: an update. Educ. Inf. Technol. **24**(6), 3537–3553 (2019). https://doi.org/10.1007/s10639-019-09937-9
9. Figuero, M.A.A.: Calidad en la Industria del Software. La Norma ISO-9126 (2012)
10. International Organization for Standard: Ergonomic requirements for office work with visual display terminals (VDTs.) - Part 11: Guidance on usability, vol. 1998 (1998)
11. Macleod, M., et al.: The MUSiC performance measurement method. Behav. Inf. Technol. **16**(4/5), 279–293 (1997)
12. Seffah, A., Kececi, N., Donyaee, M.: QUIM: a framework for quantifying usability metrics in software quality models. In: Proceedings - 2nd Asia-Pacific Conference on Quality Software, APAQS 2001, pp. 311–318 (2001)
13. Macleod, M.: Usability : practical methods for testing and improvement. In: Proceedings of the Norwegian Computer Society Software Conference, pp. 1–4 (1994)
14. Zhang, D., Adipat, B.: Challenges, methodologies, and issues in the usability testing of mobile applications. Int. J. Hum. Comput. Interact. **18**(3), 269–292 (2005)
15. Enriquez, J.G., Casas, S.I.: Usabilidad en aplicaciones móviles. Inf. Científicos Técnicos UNPA **5**(2), 25–47 (2014)
16. Bruno, V., Tam, A., Thom, J.: Characteristics of web applications that affect usability: a review. In: Proceedings of OZCHI 2005, vol. 122, pp. 1–4 (2005)
17. Swaid, S.I., Suid, T.Z.: Usability heuristics for M-commerce apps. In: Ahram, Tareq Z., Falcão, C. (eds.) AHFE 2018. AISC, vol. 794, pp. 79–88. Springer, Cham (2019). https://doi.org/10.1007/978-3-319-94947-5_8
18. Bandi, A., Heeler, P.: Usability testing: a software engineering perspective. In: 2013 International Conference on Human Computer Interaction, ICHCI 2013 (2013)

19. Abuhlfaia, K., De Quincey, E.: The usability of E-learning platforms in higher education: a systematic mapping study. In: Proc. 32nd International BCS Human Computer Interaction Conference, HCI 2018, July 2018

20. Zha, R.: Improving the usability of mobile application user review collection. Tampere University (2019)

21. Arain, A.A., Hussain, Z., Rizvi, Wajid H., Vighio, M.S.: Evaluating usability of M-learning application in the context of higher education institute. In: Zaphiris, P., Ioannou, A. (eds.) LCT 2016. LNCS, vol. 9753, pp. 259–268. Springer, Cham (2016). https://doi.org/10.1007/978-3-319-39483-1_24

22. Sauro, J.: MeasuringU: What Is A Good Task-Completion Rate? (2011). https://measuringu.com/task-completion/. Accessed 08 May 2020

23. Wicaksono, S.A., Firdausy, D.R., Saputra, M.C.: Usability testing on android application of infrastructure and facility reporting management information system. J. Inf. Technol. Comput. Sci. 3(2), 184 (2018)

24. Shneiderman, B.: Designing the User Interface: Strategies for Effective Human-Computer Interaction, 4th edn. Pearson, Boston (2004)

25. Tan, J.: FOUUX-a framework for usability & user experience. Blenkinge Institute of Technology (2009)

A Computational Prototype for Electromagnetic Field Pollution Maps in Colombia

Osberth De Castro[1]([📧]) [iD], Angela Becerra[2], Mauricio A. Polochè[3][iD], and Yamil Buenaño[2]

[1] Electronics Engineering, Universidad El Bosque, Bogotá, Colombia
occastro@unbosque.edu.co
[2] Systems Engineering, Universidad de San Buenaventura, Bogotá, Colombia
ybuenano@usbbog.edu.co
[3] Electronics Engineering, Universidad de San Buenaventura, Bogotá, Colombia
mpoloche@usbbog.edu.co

Abstract. This work presents a first computational prototype for Electromagnetic Field (EMF) pollution visualization, as a geographic map for human exposure estimation to potentially harmful levels of electromagnetic radiation. The map is a computational tool including a mobile application that uses a basic EMF mathematical model for estimating levels of exposure in two geographic dimensions based on a limited collection of antennas information from Bogotá City. Our application is intended to be an inexpensive first solution for EMF pollution analysis. This paper shows a first mobile prototype as a result, based on standard free tools, such as Google Maps API and its drawing tools and open access EMF emitters databases.

Keywords: Pollution · Data visualization · Electromagnetic field · Antennas · Mobile maps

1 Introduction

The study of health risks associated to excessive electromagnetic radiation exposure on humans is a topic of research interest in health and environment institutions around the world. More than 1500 studies on those risks have been published or are currently in progress, as [1] and [2], including considerations by the World Health Organization [3]. This field of research can be separated in two main categories: effects on human body of electromagnetic radiations, and environmental levels of exposure. The later comprises the analysis of levels and distribution of artificial electromagnetic radiation emissions in populated areas due high concentration of antennas for radio communications and broadcasting.

Supported by Grant PFI2020ESCV036 *Mapas de Exposición a la Radiación Electromagnética para Colombia Mediante Modelado Computacional*, Faculty of Engineering, Electronics Engineering Program, Universidad El Bosque, Bogotá, Colombia.

1.1   Pollution Maps

Pollution maps are very useful analysis tools for regulatory institutions and epidemiology research. We can find temperature, CO_2 emissions, air and water quality maps available worldwide. On the other hand, EMF exposure maps are not as easy to find. Powerful tools are available for Radio frequency propagation analysis, such as Radio Mobile and ICS Telecom [4], that offer coverage mapping, and many other features based on simulations, and can be used as input for exposure analysis. However, the specific effort for exposure risk analysis has become a matter of field measuring as the main tool for mapping, given the wide range of radio frequency sources and, some times, the lack of information about all the sources installed. After a representative set of measures have been made, gaps between measures are usually filled using statistical analysis, like interpolation and other techniques, as in [5], in Spain, [6] in Colombia and [7] in The Netherlands.

Regulatory Context. According to the World Health Organization, in [8], there is no data regarding regulations for electromagnetic radiation emissions in Colombia. Nevertheless, the Colombian Spectrum National Agency (ANE, for *Agencia Nacional del Espectro*), has made a couple of efforts in [9] and [10], to establish mechanisms for measuring electromagnetic propagation patterns and potential risks, in order to test whether Colombia complies with safety recommendations by IEEE in [11] and [12], and by the UIT in [13] and [14]. The construction of technological tools that help with the regulation effort is a very important research field in Colombia.

1.2   The Computational EMF Pollution Project

Measuring EMF pollution for map construction is a costly endeavor, due to the massive amount of points for a city such as Bogotá. Colombia is a country with an specific need for inexpensive but effective tools, so the aim of the this project as a whole is to create such inexpensive EMF exposure mapping tool, based on mathematical modeling, and not on bare measurements. The final tool consists of an application with mobile and desktop capacities that works with a dedicated server for a massive amount of mathematical calculations and available geo-localization and mapping on-line tools. It not only will show static, previously calculated results, but also will be interactive, so an authorized user can add a new radiation source and see the results promptly. The project is an independent multidisciplinary academic effort, but open to future collaboration with public or private organizations for which all the results and tools will be available. The first result shown in this paper is a prototype mapping front-end capable of computing local EMF maps using free available tools such as Google Maps API. The server side of the system and the information gathering for antenna databases are subject of ongoing and further work.

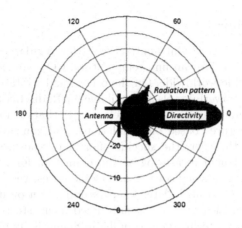

Fig. 1. Radiation pattern example.

2 Mathematical Model

The main sources of non-ionizing electromagnetic radiation in our urban environment are telecommunication and broadcasting antennas, so this work focuses on them. In a radiation system we have a sinusoidal voltage source connected to a conductor, whose energy produces a charge distribution of electric field and magnetic field. When these fields arrive by the conductor to the antenna, the radiation will occur and the electric field and the magnetic field propagate through the air. In this propagation, three relevant parameters can be found:

- Directivity
- Radiation Pattern
- Bandwidth

These parameter are the key to determine how much energy an antenna can irradiate and where in space that energy is sent to by a single antenna. Figure 1 is an example of radiation pattern, showing directivity and distribution of irradiated energy. From this parameters, the transferred energy per area unit can be computed, as power density or Poynting vector that is defined as Eq. 1.

$$P = E \times H = \frac{P_t}{4\pi d^2} \tag{1}$$

Where E is electric field intensity in V/m, and H is magnetic field intensity in A/m [15]. This power density can also be calculated for any point in space too, in terms of power and distance, where P_t is the antenna terminal power, d is the distance between the antenna and the desired point, and P is the power density expressed in W/m^2 [16].

In this work we deal with multiple antenna types, so analyzing a specific antenna in an area depends heavily on characterization of magnetic and electric field at place of observation, but also the multiple contributions of energy by the antennas in an urban area have to be taken into account.

Table 1. Electromagnetic spectrum areas

Region	Sub-region	Frequency	Wavelength
Radio	High frequency	3 MHz–30 MHz	>10 m
	Very high frequency	30 MHz–300 MHz	>1 m
Microwaves	Ultra high frequency	300 MHz–3 GHz	>0.1 m
	Super high frequency	3 GHz–30 GHz	>0.01 m
	Extra high frequency	30 GHz–300 GHz	>1 mm
Infrared		300 GHz–348 THz	>780 nm
Visible light		38 4THz–789 THz	>380 nm

Table 2. Cellular technology frequencies

System	Frequency
2G/GSM	900 MHz–1800 MHz
3G/WCDMA	900 MHz–2100 MHz
4G/LTE	800 MHz–2600 MHz

2.1 Propagation Model by Path Loss

When a signal propagates in space, an average level can be received and measured at a specific location. When different average signal levels are recorded, a model can be generate in terms of dB [17]. This model is called **Path Loss**, and describes the attenuation pattern in space. This model is given by Eq. 2, [18,19].

$$\overline{PL}[dB] = PL(d_0) + 10Blog_{10}\left(\frac{d}{d_0}\right) \qquad (2)$$

Where $\overline{PL}$ is the average path loss at the distance d from antenna to receiver in meters, $PL(d_0)$ is the path loss reference at distance d_0, and B is an coe that describes how average path loss increases with distance. Other path loss models with empirical adjustments have been developed given geometry and irregularity of geographical terrain or urban and rural areas, such as Longley-Rice's model [20] that calculates transmission loss relative to free space loss over irregular terrain, Edwards-durkin's model [21] that only predicts irregular terrain and losses caused by obstacles, Okumura's model [22] that predicts taking into station antenna heights, Hata's model [23] that is a graphical extension of loss data provided by Okumura's and Walfisch-Bertoni's model [24] that consider the impact of rooftops and building height. This work focused on Okomura's model because is largely used in our application context.

2.2 Algorithmic Approach

Using the previously explained model, knowing the amount of nearby antennas, and considering, at first, omni-directional arrays for each technology, gain and

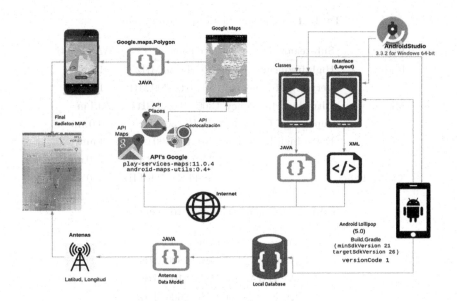

Fig. 2. Application software architecture.

path loss, the total amount of EMF radiation is the summatory of all contributions of each antenna in a specific point, computing the power density on it as in Eq. 3.

$$P_{total} = \sum_{n=1}^{p} P_n \qquad (3)$$

This sum has to be done for each *pixel* of the map, so the size of the sample and the resolution of the map has to be controlled for a local computing application. In the case of cities such as Bogotá, any given zone can contain tens of emitters. For our application, the resolution of the map has been established at 24×14, due to hardware limitations of local computing and API restrictions. On further developments, including a computing server side and a better mobile device, this resolution can grow. The results for each point is compared with standards and recommendations and colored accordingly.

3 Regulatory Component

This work is focused on cellular base stations, the most common radiation sources of electromagnetic waves in open space. In this case, IEEE C95.1-1991 (IEEE standard for safety levels with respect to human exposure to radio frequency electromagnetic fields, 3 kHz to 300 GHz) [12] and norms of the ICNIRP such as 1999/519/CE [25].

Table 1 shows the main areas of the electromagnetic spectrum. However, cellular base stations only cover the microwave range, as shown in Table 2. Any

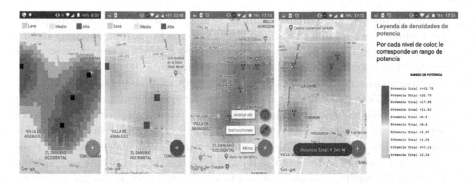

Fig. 3. Application screen, showing progressive versions, notification, dragging and a help screen. (Color figure online)

cellular base station comprises one or more antennas that concentrate their emissions to frontal-horizontal directions from its structure, and low emissions to all other directions, as in Fig. 1, constructing an array of electromagnetic sources.

4   Software Product Development

From the product development stand point, international software standards have been used, which are flexible and sustainable, as Scrum [26, 27] and [28]. Scrum allow us to work in cycles of iterative development. This first version has basic front-end working functionality and in every new iteration new ones shall be added. Nevertheless, fixed development stages as requirement analysis, product launch and others were fulfilled.

4.1   Incremental Development

A sequential testing protocol was established for decision making, including the following steps:

1. **API and tools testing and evaluation and selection.** Several tools were tested for development, and the specifically for mapping and drawing activities. For general development, the Android Operating System was used, Android Studio was selected as a main developing tool, and Google Maps API, including the Polygon API was selected as first drawing solution.
2. **Architecture and platform testing.** Figure 2 shows the software architecture for the App. The Architecture testing was made in order to adjust computation parameters and API capacity for our application. Some adjust were critical due to the amount of calculation done locally in this version, but it was confirmed that every tool complied to the app minimum requirements.
3. **Drawing Activity Testing.** Some testing and adjust was made for the drawing Activity in the app. For example, the Google Polygon tool is not

made for massive amount of small figures, so it impacted the smartphone performance in zooming in and out. It was decided to use no zooming in this first prototype. Every polygon would represent a *pixel* on the map, so a the application resolution was adjusted to this limitation.

4. **Computation Activity Testing.** In the best case scenario, The App calculates the Power Density for every visible pixel in the map, and display an associate color code in real time. However, every computation includes every aspect described on past sections, every contribution and every distance for every pixel to be painted. The amount of operations escalates fast with resolution and antenna sources in the database, and is limited by the smartphone processing capacity, so some features were adjusted in order to keep the user interface comfortable. For instance, it was decided that computation of the map only takes place by user click (touch) and not in every zoom or drag of the map. If the user only drags the map, the app won't calculate or show the color layer, until the user executes a click/touch in the center of the area he or she wants to analyze.

5. **Integration Testing.** Once all prototype features were adjusted and tested, an integration testing was made, in order to ensure the app has usability under the specified requirements.

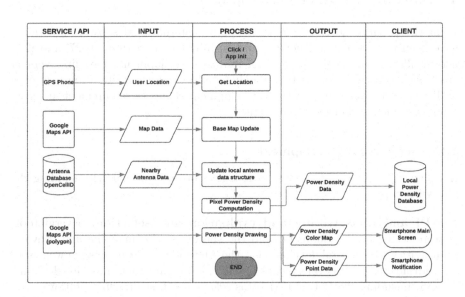

Fig. 4. Application main process flow.

5   Results

The main result of this work is a prototype for the EMF pollution App, as a first step to build a system for Radiation Exposure Maps in Colombia, with the following specifications:

5.1   Software Architecture

In Fig. 2 shows the software architecture for the Application, with the following components:

- Lollipop 5.0 Android Operating System
- Java Activities Programming for Power Density computing and drawing.
- Local Testing Database.
- Google Maps API and Services, including Polygon Tools for Drawing.

5.2   Process Flow

In Fig. 4, the process flow, inputs and outputs are shown. In this version, a very simple processing has been implemented, allowing future flexibility, due to the heavy computation involved. We can see that the computation for the map is made from a user click, and produces useful data and visualization.

5.3   User Interface

The user interface is simply enough, resembling any special map application, with a direct representation plus some button features. In Fig. 3 four version of app screens are shown. The final version is shown in the center. To the left first testing versions are shown, and to the right we can see two other views of the final User interface, including a first help screen and a result of dragging the map and obtain a particular lecture for the click point. The user interface also consist of:

- Splash screen
- Menu
- Help screen
- pdf manual download

5.4   Power Density Representation

In Fig. 3 the color code is shown. At the most left we can see solid colors from green to red used to represent Power Density values according with a scale shown at the most right, not showing the geographic google map behind. The same code was used in final versions but using transparency in order to allow a detailed localization map. The power density in this example ranges from 2.5 to 30 W/m^2. It's very important to clarify that in this prototype version, antenna data is not accurate.

5.5   Antenna Database

The first choice for testing of the app is the use of a local Antenna Database. Once everything is working correctly, a open cellular tower database was used, called OpenCellID[1]. This database is not necessarily accurate due to it's collaborative management, but it's a great tool for testing the access to millions of towers and adjust the computing sample size for the app. This Database allowed us to test the app on a variety of cities, showing consistency of behavior.

5.6   Computational Complexity

Usage Experiments with the tool has shown that the computational complexity has to be managed according to the resolution and zoom, given the calculations are local, and device dependent. A calculation server side solution is needed in order to make the app device independent.

6   Conclusion

In this work, a Radiation Map application was designed and constructing, as a first prototype for further development for radiation level easy visualization. Given relevant source data, such as antennas database and other emitters, it can display a color coded map for Power density levels in a flexible way, but with computing restrictions. The objective was achieved successfully, and will serve as a feedback tool for constructing specific databases for Colombian cities and study the impact of this emitters, in order to aid further regulation.

6.1   Further Work

Back-End. In order to make all the mathematical model computation possible, our app needs a large amount of data input regarding every relevant EMF source geolocation and characterization. This information can be obtained using public crowd sourced databases like OpenCellId [29], OpenSignal [30], RadioCells [31], CellMapper [32] and others. These provide free API access and services for developers. However, field work is also needed in order to achieve close to real accuracy. Colombian public institutions can provide regulatory information and enterprise antennas data, and more detailed antenna information will be obtained using on site visual inspection. The next step is to create and manage a more reliable specific data source, by constructing a custom Back-end. This back-end solution allows also the implementation of remote power density computation. A model were the phone doesn't have to calculate, but consume power density data from it's own server is better, adding the power of massive storage for power density data for analysis.

---

[1] https://opencellid.org.

Field Measurements. A special case for information gathering and validation are on site EMF measurement. On the information gathering stage, measurement allow us to characterize antenna parameters like directivity and Power density, when no official information is available. On validation stage, EMF exposure are made so we can validate the mathematical model, and also adjust its parameters. of measuring and easily updateable.

References

1. Röösli, M., Frei, P., Mohler, E., Hug, K.: Systematic review on the health effects of exposure to radiofrequency electromagnetic fields from mobile phone base stations. Bull. World Health Organ. **88**(12), 887–896 (2010)
2. Rodríguez-Martín, B., Bielsa-Fernández, P.: Asociación entre las radiaciones de teléfonos móviles y el riesgo tumoral en personas adultas. Gaceta Sanitaria (1426) (2017)
3. OMS. OMS—Campos electromagnéticos y salud pública: teléfonos móviles (2014)
4. Fratu, O., et al.: Comparative study of Radio Mobile and ICS Telecom propagation prediction models for DVB-T. In: IEEE International Symposium on Broadband Multimedia Systems and Broadcasting, BMSB, August 2015 (2015)
5. Gonzalez-Rubio, J., Najera, A., Arribas, E.: Comprehensive personal RF-EMF exposure map and its potential use in epidemiological studies. Environ. Res. **149**, 105–112 (2016)
6. Rodríguez, C., Forero, C., Boada, H.: Electromagnetic field measurement method to generate radiation map. In: Proceedings of the 2012 IEEE Colombian Communications Conference (COLCOM), Cali, Colombia. IEEE (2012)
7. Bolte, J.F.B., Eikelboom, T.: Personal radiofrequency electromagnetic field measurements in The Netherlands: exposure level and variability for everyday activities, times of day and types of area. Environ. Int. **48**, 133–142 (2012)
8. World Health Organization. Global health observatory data repository: existence of standards data by country (2014)
9. Agencia Nacional del Espectro. Sistema Nacional de Monitoreo de Campos Electromagnéticos (2013)
10. Agencia Nacional del Espectro - Grupo EMC-UN. Herramienta para la predicción y gestión del espectro radioeléctrico en entornos urbanos. Technical report. Asociación Nacional del Espectro, Bogotá (2016)
11. IEEE Standards Coordinating Committee 28. IEEE C95. 1–1992: IEEE standard for safety levels with respect to human exposure to radio frequency electromagnetic fields, 3 kHz to 300 GHz, vol. 2005. IET (2006)
12. IEEE C95.1-2005. IEEE standard for safety levels with respect to human exposure to radio frequency electromagnetic fields, 3 kHz to 300 GHz (2006)
13. Telecommunication standardization sector of ITU. K.52: Guidance on complying with limits for human exposure to electromagnetic fields. Series K: Protection Against Interference (2017)
14. Telecommunication Standardization Sector of ITU. K.83: Monitoring of electromagnetic field levels. Series K: Protection Against Interference (2011)
15. Balanis, C.A.: Antenna Theory: Analysis and Design, 3rd edn. Wiley, Hoboken (2005)
16. Yacoub, M.D.: Foundations of Mobile Radio Engineering. CRC Press, Boca Raton (1993)

17. Rappaport, T.S.: The wireless revolution. IEEE Commun. Mag. **29**, 52–71 (1991)
18. Rappaport, T.S., Sandhu, S.: Radio-wave propagation for emerging wireless personal-communication systems. IEEE Antennas Propag. Mag. **36**(5), 14–24 (1994)
19. Seidel, S.Y., Rappaport, T.S.: Site-specific propagation prediction for wireless in-building personal communication system design. IEEE Trans. Veh. Technol. **43**(4), 879–891 (1994)
20. Longley, A.G., Rice, P.L.: Prediction of tropospheric radio transmission loss over irregular terrain, a computer method. Technical report. Institute for Telecommunication Sciences, Boulder, Colorado (1968)
21. Durkin, J., Edwards, R.: Computer prediction of service areas for V.H.F. mobile radio networks. In: IEEE (ed.), Proceedings of the Institution of Electrical Engineers, pp. 1493–1500. IET (1969)
22. Okumura, Y., Ohmori, E., Kawano, T., Fukuda, K.: Field strength and its variability in VHF and UHF land-mobile radio service. Rev. Electr. Commun. Lab. **16**(9), 825–73 (1968)
23. Hata, M.: Empirical formula for propagation loss in land mobile radio services. IEEE Trans. Veh. Technol. VT **29**(3), 317–25 (1980)
24. Walfisch, J., Bertoni, H.L.: A theoretical model of UHF propagation in urban environments. IEEE Trans. Antennas Propag. **36**(12), 1788–1796 (1988)
25. Council Recommendation: Council Recommendation of 12 July 1999 on the limitation of exposure of the general public to electromagnetic fields (0 Hz to 300 GHz). Technical report. The Council of the European Union (1999)
26. Takeuchi, H., Nonaka, I.: The new new product development game. Harvard Bus. Rev. **64**(1), 137–146 (1986)
27. Poppendieck, M.: Principles of lean thinking. IT Manag. Sel. **18**, 1–7 (2011)
28. Poppendieck, M., Poppendieck, T.: Introduction to Lean software development: practical approaches for applying lean principles to software development. In: Extreme Programming and Agile Processes in Software Engineering, p. 280 (2005)
29. Unwired Labs: OpenCell Id, the world's largest open database of cell towers (2019). https://opencellid.org
30. OpenSignal Limited. OpenSignal analytics 2019. https://www.opensignal.com
31. OpenBMap. RadioCells, open-source community project for cell tower and Wifi locations 2019. https://radiocells.org
32. CellMapper. Cell mapper, cellular provider maps (2019). https://www.cellmapper.net

Object Extraction and Encoding for Video Monitoring Through Low-Bandwidth Networks

Franco Stramana[1,3], Juan Pablo D'amato[1,2(✉)], Leonardo Dominguez[1,2], Aldo Rubiales[1,3], and Alejandro Perez[1,3]

[1] PLADEMA, Universidad Nacional del Centro de la Provincia de Buenos Aires, Tandil, Argentina
juan.damato@gmail.com
[2] National Council Scientific Technical Research, CONICET, Buenos Aires, Argentina
[3] Comisión de Investigaciones Científicas, CICPBA, La Plata, Argentina

Abstract. Surveillance cameras in smart cities generate a dramatic amount of data each day, that must be transferred through communication channels. Most of this information is useless, just images of static scenarios that must be observed by thousands of monitor people. Even though there are plenty of algorithms that helps to automatically classify this information, the computational effort is still concentrated on transporting (coding/decoding) those images.

This work aims to present the first results of applying an efficient software analyzer and encoder for static cameras that struggles to reduce computational effort and data generation. For this purpose, a combination of background segmentation and classification algorithms are used, which separate the moving objects from background and tag them using convolutional neural networks. For storing, a hyper-image organization structure is proposed, used for describing such objects in a minimal way. To have efficient algorithms, GPUs and multi-core processors are used. Several tests were carried out, on long video sequences, showing the amount of bandwidth that is reduced compare to other traditional encoders.

Keywords: Video processing · GPGPU · Video encoders · Smart Cities

1 Introduction

Security is one of the major priorities of government policy. The fear and uncertainty that high levels of violence and crime induce in society are motivating the development of new technologies to aid citizen security. This situation worsens in large cities, where violent events are more frequent. Actually, there are known systems and methods that help to solve the problem. To face this problem, large

© Springer Nature Switzerland AG 2020
J. C. Figueroa-García et al. (Eds.): WEA 2020, CCIS 1274, pp. 431–441, 2020.
https://doi.org/10.1007/978-3-030-61834-6_37

monitoring centers are being built, based on CCTV technology. This technology involves the deploy of a network of video cameras distributed throughout the cities, with exclusive connectivity, management and video recording software. In the center, there are groups of people watching and reporting any event related to crime and accidents. In this context, automated video analysis systems helps to organize and detect events on video cameras, without the exclusive attention of people. These systems take encoded video images, like [1] apply certain analysis algorithms and generates tags indicating which class of object are present in the scene. This kind of analysis is extremely useful to reduce the stress and attention effects of people who are observing many hours videos each day.

On the other side, there still exists lot of computation issues to overcame, in order to have an efficient video system. The first one that is considered in this work is the amount of computational effort dedicated to encode/decode video, necessary to reduce image size. Very known formats encoders, like MP4 or the newer one MP5, reduces files size about 1 MB each 25 MB. Data is encoded on the camera, transmitted through a network and played on the monitor center. In general, many of these data is useless: the cameras are observing static scenes with no-activities. Some initial ideas propose to activate the recording once there is a movement, but as cameras are in general located outside, they're are affected by climate such as wind, rain or light, resulting in a constantly activation.

The main idea of this work is to use already installed surveillance cameras and add them computational capabilities in order to provide more informations. As a complex scene is observed, only moving objects should be evaluated. In that case, a pipeline running on parallel architectures such as GPUs is implemented, separating the background from the background and evaluating only tracked objects. Variations of the VIBE algorithms are used for the separation of the movement with respect to the background. In an initial stage, the algorithms that allow determining will be trained with a large number of video images, extracting lighting variation parameters according to the time range and also be able to characterize the movement by intensity. Only objects of interest are stored or transmitted to the monitor center. These detected object through different frames are encoded using a hyper-image structure, reducing considerably the amount of bandwidth required.

To compare the results, the size of the generated file and the efficiency of the processing will be taken into account and compared with other state-of-the-art algorithms, currently included in the videoLan distribution (VLC). Efficiency will also be compared with GPU encoding algorithms, measured in the number of frames per second. Various experiments were carried out to verify the usefulness of the algorithms, especially in the conservation of the shape of the objects compared with manual segmentation of free databases.

This paper is organized into five sections. Section 2 summarizes the state of the art and considers existing tools with similar purposes. Section 3 describes the developed architecture and encoding format. Section 4 shows preliminary results. Finally, Section 5 offer conclusions and future work.

2   State of the Art

As a result of enhanced computation power from current market processors, there are abounding video surveillance systems available and recent bibliography addressing real time people tracking, making it a deeply studied subject.

Considering integral existing solutions, [2] makes a review of 18 commercial surveillance systems, and a summary of the most used algorithms for object detection, tracking, classification, event detection and trajectory reconstruction. Regarding algorithms, works such as [3] describe some common methods for object detection and tracking. In [4], an interesting comparison between multiple detectors is made, where it is concluded that a combination of them can be useful to reduce the rate of false positives without compromising real-time analysis. More recently, in [5], general strategies for vehicles tracking and classification from video were reexamined. When the scenes are noisy, and with plenty of objects, new approaches are required.

2.1   Actual Encoders: Strength and Failures

The HVEC video codec applies the same idea of intra and interframe prediction (frames) used in all standards since H261. An algorithm to generate a video stream under this standard generally applies the following steps. First, each image of a video is separated into rectangular blocks. The first image of a sequence is encoded using an intra-frame prediction (analogous to JPEG) without dependencies on other images. Next, inter-frame prediction modes are applied for the following frames. The interframe predictive mode process consists of selecting motion data using displacement vectors to predict how each block has moved. The encoder and decoder generates an interframe prediction by applying a motion compensation, which is transmitted as part of the information. The remainder of the prediction, which is the difference between the original and the predicted one, is transformed using a spatial function, such as DCT or DST (discrete transform of Cosine and Sine respectively). The resulting coefficients are normalized, binarized, encoded by entropy (Huffman type compression) and transmitted along with the predicted information. An outline of how it works is the one presented below, described in [6].

Certainly, compression algorithms based on this specification can generate extremely compact files (a ratio of 1:50 or even greater) with respect to the original video. Most of the current security cameras, support some of these algorithms (x264 or x265) natively, in order to be able to transmit video in real time with low latency. Unfortunately, when you want to work with video analytic, algorithms often fail because of the amount of artifacts generated. Even as the predictions of intra and interframe residues differ considerably, the form of binarization changes, dragging errors of the type of "intermittent pixels", "fuzzy edges" and others in time. The result is a lower rate of positive detections and a large number of false positives.

The Challenges and Opportunities of Video-Surveillance. When you want to work with videos abroad, other difficulties associated with the complexity of the scenes are added, such as changes in global lighting in different climatic situations, movements in areas of low interest and large differences in contrast. There are some works that propose working with images in a uniform space [7], reducing the presence of shadows. This approach is interesting, especially when the same area is observed for a long time. Other repeated cases that generate false positives are when there are objects that move repetitively and should be omitted. For these cases, the extended VIBE [8] can be applied using a scheme of elimination of blinking.

The connectivity of the network through which the cameras must be accessed is often of low bandwidth, so in general it works with lower image quality, in order to maintain a higher viewing rate. The following Fig. 1 shows 2 cases of errors in two consecutive images. On the one hand (in the orange rectangle) the artifacts of block work are distinguished; in red an error of differences between pixels by binarization.

As presented in [1], the system includes cameras designed for this application, powerful software that provides consistent and reliable results and a computer (Digital Processing Unit) designed to handle the fast processing required.

Even though there are commercial solutions which solve a considerable amount of the issues involved, they are not always correctly adapted to legislation and country-specific interests. In addition to this, the "proprietary software" model they present works against the digital government model, which pretends to be open and transparent.

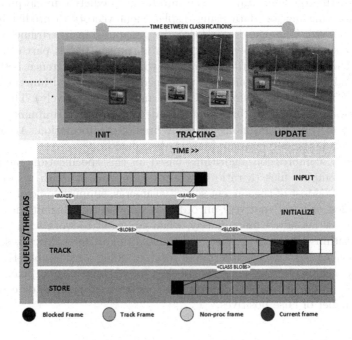

Fig. 1. Parallel tracking architecture (Color figure online)

Furthermore, these systems generally follow a centralized scheme, where all the analysis is performed in a monitoring center, requiring very specific equipment. Given that the cost of embedded processors has decreased considerably, it is natural to consider a distributed design for image processing in order to scale the system rapidly. Under this scheme, solutions must coexist with multiple connected devices which perform analysis on site, reporting only when an irregular situation is detected. In these cases, to achieve an architecture with the ability to adapt to multiple situations in a simple way, it is vital to count with an accessible, transparent and inter-connected platform.

3   Proposal

Our project emerges as an answer to social demands regarding security and in a close relationship with the continuous rise of camera installations in public spaces. This work proposes a distributed platform for managing and sharing IP cameras with embedded processing via different kinds of networks, taking advantage of a collaborative philosophy aimed to achieve a general goal: public safety. This platform, that was already presented in [9], is extended to support plate recognition.

The platform takes into consideration the automation and integration of tasks related to the detection and tracking of objects and individuals with multiple video cameras. The innovative design of the platform allows for the usage of various analysis techniques depending on the situation, which can even execute on different devices (servers, micro-PCs, embedded systems). That is why its architecture is open and distributed, making it able of processing "in situ" to enhance reactivity. Only relevant events are transmitted to a central server, improving scalability without de-creasing global performance.

Our proposal is an "object based compressor". Basically, different algorithms try to segment moving objects, generating two information layers, one for detected objects the other representing the background. This information can be compressed with different techniques based on the classic ones on blocks of images (such as x264) or others that preserve the shape of objects, even at different rates and compression qualities. When it is desired to store information while maintaining the shape of the objects, it is better to use a representation of the vector type, similar to that used for geometric objects.

The layered structure is expected to serve at the same time as a "tag", for other stages of video analysis. In addition to the dissemination of the results, it is intended that the algorithms developed can be used to improve compression and video transmission, especially in a monitoring platform that is being developed at this University.

To accomplish this task, we propose to analyze each new frame from a camera stream in multiple ways. First, a fast object detector is applied to the regions of interest, to discern moving parts of the image from the static scene. This constitutes the real-time pipeline, and gives as an output an enriched stream with metadata that can outline detected objects. After the detection of a potential object, more complex characteristics are detailed. This new analysis stage involves computationally expensive algorithms (for example, object recognition algorithms); for that reason, it is executed asynchronously. This constitutes the deferred pipeline. Finally, detected objects and associated analysis results are stored in a distributed database that can be accessed from any interested device in the network.

3.1 Pipeline

The first step in fast event detection is to localize motion in series of consecutive frames. This problem is well studied in the field of background subtraction algorithms. Many solutions can calculate image pixels' variation [10]. Methods vary in effectiveness and computational complexity. Currently, the platform makes use of a version of ViBe [11] to improve results. In order to reduce this complexity, a tracking based method was used. Only moving objects, that came close to the camera are evaluated. Other object properties, such as color, type or brand are of interest, so they whole object is analyzed.

When cameras are placed on outdoors, factors associated with variations of time of the day, cloud conditions and time of the year are exacerbated. To counteract these effects, motion windows are used as mentioned in [12]. Their goal is to apply a logical operation to process only movements detected inside the window dimensions and filter the ones outside.

Given the computational cost, a dedicated processor is required to execute this task. To improve global efficiency, processing was extracted to the video-camera location. Watertight cabinets were designed to that end, with the capacity to allocate a mini-PC connected directly with the camera. The PC performs the analysis of the objects and communicates the results to the central server, along with the video frame. The output of this step is a set of pixels (grouped or not) that have been classified as relevant to further describe objects in motion.

Object characteristics are then described using tracking techniques, such as its size, velocity direction, and last positions. If an object size is considerably small (too few pixels), it is not considered for further analysis. Otherwise, it is uniquely identified inside the network, registered in the system, and assigned for pending characterization. Object tracking is then based on motion detection events from the real-time pipe-line. After an object detection, a new message under the topic new object is created, which includes the object ID, a cropped portion of the image where the object was found and, if necessary, any information obtained as a result of the analysis (for example, direction and speed).

3.2 Hyperimage Generation

For storing the object during different consecutive frames in an optimal way, we detect the corresponding bounding box of each object on each frame and a organizing them in a global unique image using nesting algorithms. The method of solving the nesting problem is proposed from highly documented heuristics, such as Bottom-Left (BL) [13]. The BL heuristic successively places the rectangular pieces in the position of the deepest possible canvas and then moves

Algorithm 1. Encoding algorithm

1: **procedure** UPDATEOBJECTSTATE(*newObjects, histObjects*)
2:     new, keep = mergeTracked(newObjects, histObjects)
3:     **for** $d \in new$ **do**
4:         $Trackert = init(d.box)$
5:         $keep \leftarrow push(t)$
6:     **for** $d \in keep$ **do**
7:         **if** $d.life \leq 0$ **then**
8:             storeObject(d);
9:             $keep \leftarrow remove(d)$
10:    *return* keep
11:
12: **procedure** FRAMEEVALUATOR   ▷ Scheduler thread
13:    $History \leftarrow new()$
14:    **while** *true* **do**   ▷ this runs on a synchronized thread
15:        $Objects, frame \leftarrow dequeue(queueTrack)$
16:        $active \leftarrow updateObjectState(Objects, History)$
17:        **for** $o \in active$ **do**   ▷ Process next frames
18:            $couldUpdate \leftarrow o- > update(R, frame);$
19:            **if** $couldUpdate = True$ **then**
20:                $o.setNewPosition(o.objectRectangle)$
21:            **else**   ▷ Probably, the object has left the scene
22:                $d- > life- = 1$

---

them completely to the left. The Best-Fit (BF) heuristic [14] applies a dynamic arrangement of the pieces as opposed to the permutation of the elements proposed in the previous heuristics, using the area. The algorithm analyzes the set of available spaces and selects for each place the piece that best suits, if any. This allows the algorithm to make informed decisions about what the next element will be and where it should be assigned. A natural implementation of this strategy is executed in quadratic time as well.

In [13] is presented BLD which is an improved BL strategy, where objects are ordered according to some criteria (height, width, perimeter and area) and the algorithm selects the piece that obtains the best result. An improvement is the BLD * heuristic [15], where a list of objects is constructed according to certain criteria (height, width or other) in decreasing form. The BLD strategy repeats different locations with using previously contact locations. Its algorithm improves other heuristic and meta heuristic algorithms based on the BL strategy reported in the literature. In [16], we presented an improvement of pBLD, using parallel architectures, that is currently applied in this work.

In this work, we unify the way that the algorithms are invoked. The algorithm takes a list of bounding boxes (B) of a detected object through several frame and an initial canvas(C) is used to locate the images. Best locations are stored in a list S. For choosing the location of each bounding box, an algorithm A (that

Algorithm 2. Nesting algorithm

1: **procedure** NESTING(B, C, M, A)
2:    sort(B)
3:    **while** !empty(B) **do**
4:        $b \leftarrow choose(B)$
5:        $pos \leftarrow selectBestLocation(b, C, M, A)$
6:        $B \leftarrow P - b$
7:        $S \leftarrow S + b, pos, r$
8:        return S

---

could be BF, BLD, BL) generates the potential locations and the evaluation criteria, trying to fit in the best place.

Each strategy, gives different possible locations and different criteria to place the next piece. Depending on the strategy, the algorithm will find the best location for each cut on the canvas and try to locate it. To notice, the algorithm is simplified, also only test rotations in two cases: original or 90° left rotated.

Images are saved as JPEG and cuts locations are stored in a JSON format and published on the platform. For retrieving and visualizing such data, a decoder application is implemented with AngularJS, accessible from mobile devices and in low bandwidth conditions. The resulted images looks like Fig. 2.

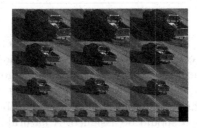

Fig. 2. Sample of a bunch of nested cuts for an object in different times

4 Encoding Performance Evaluation

The goal of a first series of test was to assess the impact of processing in real-time video images, trying to encode videos coming from cameras in different situations. The input video comes in 1920 × 1080 resolution, at about 30 frames-per-second (30fps). The algorithms run on an industrial PC, with an Intel i5 7500 processor, 8 GB of RAM and a Nvidia 1050gtx, using OpenCL for GPU programming.

The first series of test, compare the different methods to generate the hyperimage. Implementing the different strategies explained above. The main canvas for locating the images has a fixed size of 2600 × 2600 pixels. We compare the

METHOD	BOTTOM LEFT	BOUNDING BOX	RASTER BOUNDARY
OCCUPANCY	75%	26%	19%
SPEED	320MS	460MS	1017MS

Fig. 3. Comparison of different location methods

time for generating such image, and the occupancy ratio of locating each cut respect to the original canvas size. Some results are shown in Fig. 3.

In general, the "bottom left" strategy is faster, but tries to use the canvas vertically, which is not so practical for later storing. The "raster boundary" method is the optimal one, but spends too much time respect to the other. We found that the "bounding box" method is the best, even that gives some blank spaces.

A second series of tests were concerned with different camera locations, in order to evaluate performance. We used three camera locations, each one corresponding to a different points of view and time of the day. We evaluate about 45 min of Full HD video (1920 × 1080 pixels) at 30fps, encoded either on h264 and h265 and are compared to the real information extracted with our method for describing objects. To understand the scene, we propose a *complexity* criteria that describes it, that is the mean amount of moving objects per frame. The higher the amount of moving objects, the more the information the frame carries.

The experiments that were carried out are shown in Table 1.

Table 1. Encoding performance

	Complex	Original		h265 encoder		Our proposal	
		Size	FPS	Size	FPS	Size
Case 1 (Night)	0.1	502 MB	25.0	110 MB	42.0	18 MB
Case 2 (Route)	1.6	720 MB	15.0	605 MB	15.0	622 MB
Case 3 (Avenue)	2.8	1.8 GB	10.0	1.42 GB	7.0	1.2 GB

As expected, the results show that in case there are few objects in scene, the amount of valuable information is lower and the compression rate higher. In case the scene is crowded, as the avenue one, the compression rate is lower. Even though, our method stills compressed information about 50% higher than original h264 and 30% respect to h265.

5   Conclusions

In this work, a first approach of an object-based encoder for existent surveillance cameras is presented. Our open source platform is used for distributing image streams through 4G networks. The algorithm runs on parallel hardware that operate multiple cameras and sensors, to support comprehensive security management. The first results are reasonable in performance, reaching near a real-time encoded and classification detection, even for high resolution images. The compression rate is high, about 50% respect to actual video encoders such as h264 and h265, which leads to minimal connection requirements.

On the other side, there are several cases that should be included and considered. For instance, when objects are only visible for few frames or in case they are very small and detector omits them. Also, background encoded is not fully implemented. The next version of the encoder will include both features. Even more, the hyper-image could be compressed even more, using self-similitude removal which leads to a more optimal size reduction.

Acknowledgements. The current project has received grants from the National Scientific and Technical Research Council (CONICET), project PICT-2016-0236.

References

1. Dominguez, L., Perez, A., Rubiales, A., Damato, J., Barbuzza, R.: A GPU-accelerated LPR algorithm on broad vision survillance cameras. J. Inf. Syst. Eng. Manag. **3**(3), 1–7 (2018)
2. Smeulders, A.W., Chu, D.M., Cucchiara, R., Calderara, S., Dehghan, A., Shah, M.: Visual tracking: an experimental survey. IEEE TPAMI **36**(7), 1442–1468 (2014)
3. Fan, H., Ling, H.: Parallel tracking and verifying: a framework for real-time and high accuracy visual tracking. In: IEEE International Conference on Computer Vision, pp. 5486–5494 (2017)
4. Ojha, S., Sakhare, S.: Image processing techniques for object tracking in video surveillance-a survey. In: International Conference on Pervasive Computing, p. 1 (2015)
5. Sobral, A., Vacavant, A.: A comprehensive review of background subtraction algorithms evaluated with synthetic and real videos. Comput. Vis. Image Underst. **122**, 4–21 (2014)
6. Shaikh, S.H., Saeed, K., Chaki, N.: Moving object detection using background subtraction. In: Shaikh, S.H., Saeed, K., Chaki, N. (eds.) Moving Object Detection Using Background Subtraction. SCS, pp. 15–23. Springer, Cham (2014). https://doi.org/10.1007/978-3-319-07386-6_3

7. Hadi, R., Sulong, G., George, L.: Vehicle detection and tracking techniques: a concise review. Sig. Image Process. Inte. J. (SIPIJ) **5**(1), 1–12 (2014). https://doi. org/10.5121/sipij.2014.5101
8. Zivkovic, Z., van der Heijden, F.: Efficient adaptive density estimation per image pixel for the task of background subtraction. Pattern Recogn. Lett. **27**(7), 773–780 (2006)
9. Dominguez, L., Perez, A., Rubiales, A., Damato, J., Barbuzza, R.: Plataforma abierta de gestión de cámaras ip y aplicaciones móviles para la seguridad civil ciudadana. Revista lbérica de Sistemas y Tecnologías de Información (2016)
10. Schick, A., Bauml, M., Stiefelhagen, R.: Improving foreground segmentations with probabilistic superpixel Markov random fields. In: 2012 IEEE Computer Society Conference on Computer Vision and Pattern Recognition Workshops (CVPRW), pp. 27–31 (2012)
11. Piccardi, M.: Background subtraction techniques: a review. In: 2004 IEEE International Conference on Systems, Man and Cybernetics, vol. 4, pp. 3099–3104 (2004)
12. Bouwmans, T., Javed, S., Sultana, M., Jung, S.K.: Deep neural network concepts for background subtraction: a systematic review and comparative evaluation. Neural Netw. **117**, 8–66 (2018)
13. Hopper, E., Turton, B.: An empirical investigation of meta-heuristic and heuristic algorithms for a 2D packing problem. Eur. J. Oper. Res. **128**, 34–57 (2001)
14. Burke, E., Kendall, K., Whitwell, G.: A simulated annealing enhancement of the best-fit heuristic for the orthogonal stock-cutting problem. J. Comput. **21**, 505–516 (2009)
15. Lesh, N., Mitzenmacher, M.: Bubble search: a simple heuristic for improving priority-based greedy algorithms. Inf. Process. Lett. **97**, 161–169 (2006)
16. D'Amato, J., Mercado, M., Heiling, A., Cifuentes, V.: Un método de optimización proximal al problema de nesting de piezas irregulares utilizando arquitecturas en paralelo. Revista Iberoamericana de Automática e Informtíca industrial, pp. 1697–1712 (2013)

Partial Contraction Analysis for a DC Microgrid with Modular DC-DC Buck Power Converters

Christian Erazo Ordoñez[1]([✉])(iD), Daniel Muñoz Guzman[1](iD),
and Cristian Ocampo Blandon[2]

[1] Facultad de Ingeniería Mecánica, Electrónica y Biomédica,
Universidad Antonio Nariño, Bogota, Colombia
{christian.erazo,dmunoz166}@uan.edu.co
[2] R&D Department, Meero, Paris, France
cristian@meero.com

Abstract. DC microgrids have emerged as an appropriated solution to the world energy crisis by integrating renewable energy sources, storage devices and modern loads. One of the most critical issues of the DC microgrids is to remain stable after being subject to large disturbances such as changes in loads, switching operation modes and short circuit faults. In this paper we exploit contraction analysis of switching systems to guarantee proper performance and global stability of a DC microgrid integrated by a set of controlled DC-DC buck power converters. Analytical results of global stability for an all-to-all network of N DC-DC power converters in terms of the coupling strength are presented and validated numerically for a set of eight power converters.

Keywords: DC microgrids · Contraction tools · Global stability

1 Introduction

The coupling of non-conventional distributed generators (DGs) such as solar-photovoltaic panels, wind turbines, fuel cells along with energy storage systems (ESS) and loads is becoming a very popular efficient and flexible energy distribution system [9]. These microgrids are highly used in rural territories or places with difficult access where the usual power distribution network cannot reach or there is not enough generation due to the costs of connecting them to the main grid [12,15]. One of the most critical issues of the DC microgrids is to remain steady after subjecting a large disturbance such as change in loads, witching of operation mode and short circuit faults. So, for safe operation of MGs in all operating modes, dynamic behavior and transient stability of DCMG

This work was supported in part by University Antonio Nariño through the research project 2018216, and in part by the Council of the National research training (COLCIENCIAS) under the grant Call for PhD studies abroad Number 529.

© Springer Nature Switzerland AG 2020
J. C. Figueroa-García et al. (Eds.): WEA 2020, CCIS 1274, pp. 442–450, 2020.
https://doi.org/10.1007/978-3-030-61834-6_38

acquire relevant importance [14]. Power converters play an important role in operation of a DC microgrid. They not only insure proper local operation, but also enable interconnection between different units of a DCMG. It is well known that a power converter acting as a load adds nonlinear effects caused by constant power behaviors which could make the system unstable. So it should be considered in the control strategy.

The small gain theorem is the most common approach to study stability of DC microgrids [7]. The full system model is broken down into two subsystems, a load subsystem and a source subsystem then by studying the ratio impedance of both subsystems, stability conditions over the microgrid can be obtained [10]. Nevertheless, stability results rely on linearizations for modelling and analysis switching power converters in DC microgrids, therefore stability results are valid only around the operation point [4]. Recently in [1] was proposed a control synthesis for a DC-DC buck power converter based on contraction analysis [6]. The authors proposed a coordinate transformation to guarantee the switching vector fields are contracting which implies the controlled DC-DC power converter is globally stable. Following these ideas, we extend the contraction analysis to a network of N coupled DC-DC buck power converters in order to determine sufficient conditions over the coupling gain so that we can guarantee global stability for the whole network through partial contraction analysis. In particular, after offering a contextualization in Sect. 2, in Sect. 3 we prove global exponential stability of a network of N coupled buck converters. The effectiveness of the proposed methodology is validated through numerical simulations in Sect. 4.

2 Mathematical Preliminaries

In this section we present the network model that describes the interaction between each power converter. We assume that each converter exchanges information with all its neighbors, commonly known as consensus protocol. Tools for the stability analysis of switched systems are provided below.

2.1 Microgrid Structure

Let us consider a microgrid of N controlled buck power converters governed by

$$\begin{aligned} \dot{x}_i &= A_i x_i + B_i u_i - \sigma \sum_{j=1}^{N} (x_i - x_j) \\ y_i &= H_i x_i \end{aligned} \tag{1}$$

where $x_i = [x_{i1}\ x_{i2}]^T$ is the state vector with x_{i1}, x_{i2} denoting voltage across the i-th capacitor and the current flowing through the i-th inductor. The last term in the right hand Eq. (1) involve the network topology with a coupling strength denoted by σ. The control goal of each system is to regulate the output to a desired value via a switching control law $u_i = \frac{1}{2}(1 - \text{sgn}(H_i x_i))$. The constant matrices A_i, B_i and H_i are given by

$$A_i = \begin{bmatrix} -1/RC & -1/C \\ -1/L & 0 \end{bmatrix}, B_i = \begin{bmatrix} 0 \\ E/L \end{bmatrix},$$

$$H_i = \begin{bmatrix} h_1 & h_2 \end{bmatrix}$$

(2)

Parameters R, C and L stand for resistance, capacitance and inductance, respectively. E is the voltage provided by the power source. The scheme of a single controlled buck power converter is depicted in Fig. 1. The dynamics of a single controlled buck converter are shown in Fig. 2 for the set of parameters: $R = 20\,\Omega$, $L = 2\,\text{mH}$, $C = 40\,\text{mF}$, $E = 40$ and $v_{ref} = 8\,\text{V}$.

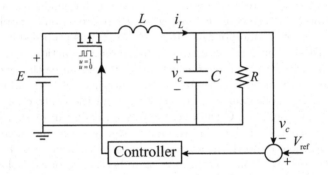

Fig. 1. Schematic diagram of a DC-DC buck power converter.

2.2   Contraction Analysis of Switched Systems

Switched (or bimodal) Filippov systems are dynamical systems $\dot{x} = f(x)$ where $f(x)$ is a piecewise continuous vector field having a codimension-one submanifold *switching manifold* $\Sigma := \{x \in \mathbb{R}^n : h(x) = 0\}$ as its discontinuity set [5,16]. Hence a bimodal Filippov system can be defined as

$$\dot{x} = f(x) = \begin{cases} f_1(x) & \text{for } x \in R_1, \\ f_2(x) & \text{for } x \in R_2, \end{cases}$$

(3)

where $f_1(x) : \mathbb{R}^n \mapsto \mathbb{R}^n$ and $f_2(x) : \mathbb{R}^n \mapsto \mathbb{R}^n$ are smooth vector fields and the two disjoint regions $\mathcal{S}_1 = \{x \in \mathbb{R}^n : h(x) > 0\}$ and $\mathcal{S}_2 = \{x \in \mathbb{R}^n : h(x) < 0\}$. We assume the solutions of system (3) are defined in the sense of Filippov, i.e. admitting sliding motions [5]. Recently in [6], the authors proposed sufficient conditions for convergence of any two trajectories of a switched system towards each other. The resulting sufficient conditions for a switched system, to be exponentially stable in a certain set, are stated in the following theorem, see [6] for a complete proof.

Theorem 1. *Let $\mathcal{C}$ be a forward invariant set. The piecewise bimodal system is incremental exponentially stable in $\mathcal{C}$, with convergence rate $\alpha := \min\{\alpha_1, \alpha_2\}$,*

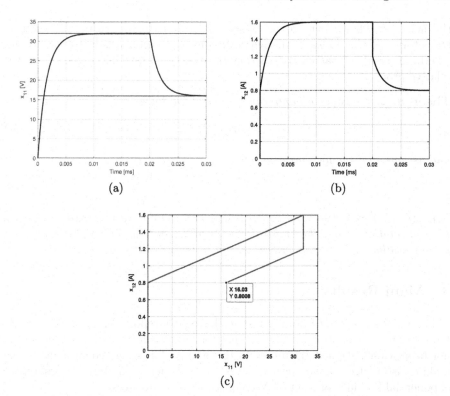

Fig. 2. Numerical simulations of a single system (1) with $i = 1$, $v_{ref} = 15$ during $t < 5\,\text{ms}$ and $v_{ref} = 8$ for a $t > 5\,\text{ms}$: (a) Voltage regulation and (b) Phase portrait. Initial conditions were set $(x_{11}, x_{12}) = (0, 0)$

if there exist some norm in $\mathcal{C}$ with associated matrix measure $\mu(\cdot)$, such that for some positive constants c_1 and c_2

$$\mu\left(\frac{\partial f_1}{\partial x}(x)\right) \leq -\alpha_1, \quad \forall x \in \bar{R}_1 \tag{4}$$

$$\mu\left(\frac{\partial f_2}{\partial x}(x)\right) \leq -\alpha_2, \quad \forall x \in \bar{R}_2 \tag{5}$$

$$\mu\left([f_1(x) - f_2(x)] \cdot \nabla h(x)\right) = 0, \quad \forall x \in \Sigma. \tag{6}$$

Hence, according to Theorem (1) a switched system (3) is exponentially stable if their vector fields $f_1(x)$ and $f_2(x)$ fulfill the conditions (4), (5) and (6).

A powerful extension of contraction theory to study convergence of a network of agents is the concept of *partial* contraction firstly introduced in [18], further references can be found [2,8]. This is based on the use of some auxiliary system or virtual system whose particular solutions are the solutions of each node in the network. Then if the virtual system is proved to be contracting then all trajectories of the nodes in the network converge exponentially to each other. The basic result of partial contraction can be stated as follows (see [8] for the relative proof).

Theorem 2. *Consider a nonlinear system of the form*

$$\dot{x} = f(x, x, t) \tag{7}$$

and assume that the auxiliary system

$$\dot{y} = f(y, x, t) \tag{8}$$

is contracting with respect to y. If a particular solution of the auxiliary system (8) is a solution of (7), then all trajectories of the system (7) verify this property exponentially. The original system is said to be partially contracting

3   Main Results

Exponential stability of Filippov systems have been reported in literature [3, 13], however the exponential stability studies for large scale switching systems have not been widely studied. Therefore in this section following the ideas of [1] and making use of the *virtual system* we derive sufficient conditions to guarantee exponential stability of a set of N coupled power converters.

Theorem 3. *Consider a set of N homogeneous buck power converters coupled by a diffusive protocol with coupling gain σ described in equation (1). Then, if the coupling gain is selected so that*

$$\sigma > \frac{\alpha}{N} - \frac{1}{2NR}\sqrt{\frac{L}{C}} \tag{9}$$

then, global stability is guaranteed for the network.

Proof. According to [1] after a normalization and a coordinate transformation process, the equations of the single buck power can be rewritten as

$$\begin{bmatrix} \dot{z_1} \\ \dot{z_2} \end{bmatrix} = \begin{bmatrix} -\gamma/2 & \rho \\ \rho & -\gamma/2 \end{bmatrix} \begin{bmatrix} z_1 \\ z_2 \end{bmatrix} + \begin{bmatrix} 1 \\ -\gamma/(2\rho) \end{bmatrix} u \tag{10}$$

where $\gamma \doteq \frac{1}{R}\sqrt{\frac{L}{C}}$ and $\rho \doteq \sqrt{4 - \gamma^2}/2$. An auxiliary system for the network model (1) can be chosen as

$$\dot{y} = \begin{bmatrix} -\frac{\gamma}{2} - \sigma N & -\rho \\ \rho & -\frac{\gamma}{2} - \sigma N \end{bmatrix} y + \begin{bmatrix} 1 \\ \frac{\gamma}{2\rho} \end{bmatrix} u + \sigma \sum_{j=1}^{N} x_j \tag{11}$$

Let us rewrite the auxiliary system into the piecewise form with the vector fields defined as

$$f_1(y) = \begin{bmatrix} -\frac{\gamma}{2}y_1 - \rho y_2 - \sigma N y_1 + \sigma \sum_{j=1}^{N} x_{j1} + 1 \\ \rho y_1 - \frac{\gamma}{2}y_2 - \sigma N y_2 + \sigma \sum_{j=1}^{N} x_{j2} - \frac{\gamma}{2\rho} \end{bmatrix} \qquad (12)$$

$$f_2(y) = \begin{bmatrix} -\frac{\gamma}{2}y_1 - \rho y_2 - \sigma N y_1 + \sigma \sum_{j=1}^{N} x_{j1} \\ \rho y_1 - \frac{\gamma}{2}y_2 - \sigma N y_2 + \sigma \sum_{j=1}^{N} x_{j2} \end{bmatrix}, \qquad (13)$$

and the switching surface is $\Sigma = \{x \in \mathbb{R}^2 : H(x) = 0\}$. Then, the Jacobian of the virtual is given by

$$J_1(y) = J_2(y) = \begin{bmatrix} -(\gamma/2 + \sigma N) & -\rho \\ \rho & -(\gamma/2 + \sigma N) \end{bmatrix}, \qquad (14)$$

Therefore, from the Theorem 1 it follows that the trajectories of the nodes in the network (1) exponentially converge towards each other if

$$\begin{aligned} \mu_2(J_1) &= \mu_2(J_2) \\ &= \left(\begin{bmatrix} -(\gamma/2 + \sigma N) & -\rho \\ \rho & -(\gamma/2 + \sigma N) \end{bmatrix} \right) \leq -\alpha, \ \alpha > 0, \\ &= \max \left\{ \sigma N + \frac{1}{2R}\sqrt{\frac{L}{C}}, \sigma N + \frac{1}{2R}\sqrt{\frac{L}{C}} \right\}. \end{aligned} \qquad (15)$$

the condition (6) reads

$$\begin{aligned} \mu_2 &([f_1 - f_2] \cdot \nabla h(x)) \\ &= \mu_2 \left(\begin{bmatrix} 1 \\ -\gamma/(2\rho) \end{bmatrix} \cdot \begin{bmatrix} h_1 & -h_1\gamma/(2\rho) \end{bmatrix} \right) \\ &= \min \left\{ 0, -h_1 \left(1 + \gamma^2/(2\rho) \right) \right\} \end{aligned} \qquad (16)$$

Since $\min \left\{ 0, -h_1 \left(1 + \gamma^2/(2\rho) \right) \right\} = 0$, we can conclude that if the coupling gain is chosen as $\sigma > \frac{\alpha}{N} - \frac{1}{2NR}\sqrt{\frac{L}{C}}$, the network of buck power converters (1) becomes exponentially stable with convergence rate given by α.

4   Numerical Validation

In order to validate the results of Theorem 3, we consider a network of $N = 8$ DC-DC power converters with the following set of parameters: $L = 2\,\text{mH}$, $C = 40\,\text{mF}$, $E = 40\,\text{V}$ and $v_{ref} = 8\,\text{V}$. For the computations we assume a resistance load of $R = 20\,\Omega$ and a reference current of $i_{ref} = v_{ref}/R = 1.6\,\text{A}$. With these parameters $\gamma = 0.35$ and $\rho = 0.98$, thus the switching surface is given by

$$H_i = (h_{i1}, h_{i2})x_i = \begin{pmatrix} -4.4 \times 10^{-3} & 1.74 \end{pmatrix} \cdot \begin{pmatrix} x_{i1} - v_{ref} & x_{i2} - i_{ref} \end{pmatrix}^T \qquad (17)$$

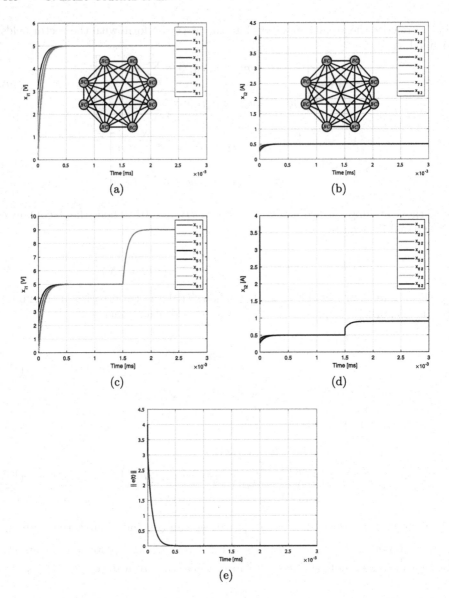

Fig. 3. Numerical simulation of a network of eight power converters for a coupling parameter $\sigma = 7$, with random initial conditions. Numerical simulations were carry out making use the numerical solver for Filippov systems presented in [11].

By using the measure μ_2 induced by the 2-norm (see Appendix A), global stability with convergence rate $\alpha = 4$, can be guaranteed if the coupling parameter is selected as $\sigma > 0.279$.

Figures 3 (a) and (b) show the numerical evolution of the voltage and current for each power converter. The output voltages and currents reach the steady state close to $0.5ms$ and $0.25ms$ with no overshoot, respectively. The time trace of the output voltage in response to a drastic change in the reference voltage v_{ref}, for each converter is depicted in Fig. 3 (c), indicating the network is able to remain stable for the new value of the reference output. In order to quantify the error between trajectories of all power converters $e(t) = [e_1(t)\,e_2(t), \ldots, e_N(t)]^T$, we compute

$$e_i(t) = x_i(t) - \frac{1}{N}\sum_{j=1}^{N} x_j(t). \tag{18}$$

Hence, we say that the network (1) is globally stable if

$$\lim_{t\to\infty} \|e(t)\|_2 = 0. \tag{19}$$

The norm of the error between trajectories displayed in Fig. 3 (d) goes to zero, confirming the analytical results.

5 Conclusions

We presented an approach based on contraction theory to determine globally stability of a DC microgrid integrated by a set of controlled DC-DC buck power converters. The methodology allows to determine sufficient conditions over the coupling parameter so that the network remains globally stable. The theoretical results were illustrated through a small network of DC DC power converters demonstrating the effectiveness of the proposed methodology, even under drastic changes in the reference signals. Future work will be aimed at extending the approach for different typologies of the network, considering different dynamics for each node in the network.

A   Matrix measures

The matrix measure (Vidyasagar 2002) [17] associated to a matrix A is listed in Table 1.

Table 1. Standard Matrix measures

Vector Norm, $\|\cdot\|$	Induce Matrix Norm $\|\cdot\|$	Matrix Measure $\mu(\,\cdot\,)$
$\|x\|_1 = \sum_{i=1}^n \|x_i\|$	$\|A\|_{i1} = \max_j \sum_{i=1}^n \|a_{ij}\|$	$\mu_1(A) = \max_j \left[a_{jj} + \sum_{i\neq j} \|a_{ij}\| \right]$
$\|x\|_2 = \left(\sum_{i=1}^n \|x_i\|^2\right)^{1/2}$	$\|A\|_{i2} = \left[\lambda_{\max}(A^T A)\right]^{1/2}$	$\mu_2(A) = \lambda_{\max}\frac{A^T+A}{2}$
$\|x\|_\infty = \max_{1<i<n} \|x_i\|$	$\|A\|_{i\infty} = \max_i \sum_{j=1}^n \|a_{ij}\|$	$\mu_\infty(A) = \max_i \left[a_{ii} + \sum_{j\neq i} \|a_{ij}\| \right]$

References

1. Angulo-Garcia, D., Angulo, F., Osorio, G., Olivar, G.: Control of a DC-DC buck-converter through contraction techniques. Energies **11**(11), 3086 (2018)
2. di Bernardo, M., Fiore, D., Russo, G., Scafuti, F.: Convergence, consensus and synchronization of complex networks via contraction theory. In: Lü, J., Yu, X., Chen, G., Yu, W. (eds.) Complex Systems and Networks. UCS, pp. 313–339. Springer, Heidelberg (2016). https://doi.org/10.1007/978-3-662-47824-0_12
3. Biemond, J.B., Postoyan, R., Heemels, W.M.H., van de Wouw, N.: Incremental-stability of hybrid dynamical systems. IEEE Trans. Autom. Control **63**(12), 4094–4109 (2018)
4. Erickson, R.W., Maksimović, D.: Fundamentals of Power Electronics. Springer, Boston, MA (2001). https://doi.org/10.1007/b100747
5. Filippov, A.F.: Differential Equations with Discontinuous Righthand Sides, vol. 18. Springer, Dordrecht (1988). https://doi.org/10.1007/978-94-015-7793-9
6. Fiore, D., Hogan, S.J., Di Bernardo, M.: Contraction analysis of switched systems via regularization. Automatica **73**, 279–288 (2016)
7. Gu, Y., Li, W., He, X.: Passivity-based control of DC microgrid for self-disciplined stabilization. IEEE Trans. Power Syst. **30**(5), 2623–2632 (2014)
8. Jouffroy, J., Slotine, J.J.: Methodological remarks on contraction theory. In: 43rd IEEE Conference on Decision and Control, CDC, vol. 3, pp. 2537–2543. IEEE (2004)
9. Kumar, J., Agarwal, A., Agarwal, V.: A review on overall control of DC microgrids. J. Energy Storage **21**, 113–138 (2019)
10. Middlebrook, R.D., Cuk, S.: A general unified approach to modelling switching-converter power stages. In: 1976 IEEE Power Electronics Specialists Conference, pp. 18–34. IEEE (1976)
11. Piiroinen, P.T., Kuznetsov, Y.A.: An event-driven method to simulate filippov systems with accurate computing of sliding motions. ACM Trans. Math. Softw. (TOMS) **34**(3), 13 (2008)
12. Prinsloo, G., Mammoli, A., Dobson, R.: Customer domain supply and load coordination: a case for smart villages and transactive control in rural off-grid microgrids. Energy **135**, 430–441 (2017)
13. Rejeb, J.B., Morărescu, I.C., Girard, A., Daafouz, J.: Stability analysis of a general class of singularly perturbed linear hybrid systems. Automatica **90**, 98–108 (2018)
14. Shuai, Z., et al.: Microgrid stability: classification and a review. Renew. Sustain. Energy Rev. **58**, 167–179 (2016)
15. Ubilla, K., et al.: Smart microgrids as a solution for rural electrification: ensuring long-term sustainability through cadastre and business models. IEEE Trans. Sustain. Energy **5**(4), 1310–1318 (2014)
16. Utkin, V., Guldner, J., Shi, J.: Sliding Mode Control in Electro-Mechanical Systems, vol. 34. CRC Press, Boca Raton (2009)
17. Vidyasagar, M.: Nonlinear systems analysis. SIAM (2002)
18. Wang, W., Slotine, J.J.E.: On partial contraction analysis for coupled nonlinear oscillators. Biolog. Cybern. **92**(1), 38–53 (2003)

Power Applications

Optimization of the Orientation of Vertical Surfaces Based on Geographic Parameters for Solar Energy Harvesting

Cristian C. Ospina-Metaute[2](✉), Esteban Betancur[1], Luis F. Medina-Garzón[2], José Ignacio Marulanda-Bernal[2], and Alejandro Velásquez-López[1]

[1] Design Engineering Research Group (GRID), Universidad EAFIT, Carrera 49 No 7 Sur–50, Medellín, Colombia
{ebetanc2,avelasq9}@eafit.edu.co
[2] Departamento de Ciencias Física, Universidad EAFIT, Carrera 49 No 7 Sur–50, Medellín, Colombia
{cospin26,lfmedinag,jmarulan}@eafit.edu.co

Abstract. The solar energy potential of vertical façades in Building Integrated Photovoltaics (BIPV) systems represents an alternative for a sustainable development that has been analyzed in different countries but not yet in Colombia. This study analyzes the energy potential of vertical surfaces for four cities in Colombia by optimizing the orientation of the vertical panels using a clear sky radiation model. The results highlight the need for positioning vertical surface designs given the variation of optimal azimuthal angles for each city during both morning and afternoon. In addition, the energy generation potential of vertical façades with respect to horizontal solar panels is analyzed considering the maximum energy received and its alignment with the energy demand curve. Angular deviation tolerances with respect to the optimum angle are also found showing Sincelejo City to be more sensitive to changes than Medellin, Rionegro and Bogota.

Keywords: BIPV · Optimization · Photovoltaic · Solar energy · Solar façade · Solar panel orientation

1 Introduction

The solar energy is the most abundant and renewable resource to supply the global energetic demand and allow a transition to non polluting technologies such as Photovoltaic (PV) systems. For future success of photovoltaics one of the key areas is the Building Integrated Photovoltaics (BIPV) technology [24]. BIPV are functional elements for building structures that replace conventional building materials with PVs (e.g. rooftops or façades), thus reducing material, installation costs, and reaching aesthetical, economical and technical solutions [20].

At present, façades applications represent 20% of BIPV market [21] with a growth trend due to the development of compact urban environments and

© Springer Nature Switzerland AG 2020
J. C. Figueroa-García et al. (Eds.): WEA 2020, CCIS 1274, pp. 453–464, 2020.
https://doi.org/10.1007/978-3-030-61834-6_39

higher buildings with reduced available areas for horizontal PV installations. Hence, PV vertical façades turn to be a feasible solution to meet the buildings' energy requirements as they consider more available area than the roofs for horizontal panels. For instance, Fig. 1 illustrates how the façade can easily surpass the rooftop area on average residential buildings. Other benefits of vertical panels may include maintenance cost reductions and a better distribution of energy along the day [14], considering that combined with horizontal photovoltaic systems or vertical bifacial panels the daily generation power curve may flatten. However, PV façade generation implies lower irradiation averages and its efficiency can be affected by the shading effect due to installation angles, surrounding obstacles or non-optimal orientations, which makes clever decisions during the design phase to be mandatory.

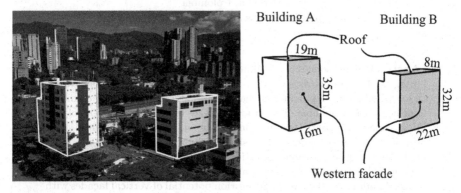

Fig. 1. Approximate dimensions of residential buildings in Medellin. The facades area is notably larger than the roof area. The Western-Façade/Roof area ratio is estimated around 1.8 and 4.0 for building A and B respectively.

Colombia has a significant photovoltaic potential due to its tropical location [10]. However, it has regional differences that affect the incidence of solar radiation, such as the landscape, altitude, average rainfall [23] and other climatic conditions mainly related to certain altitude levels, which are known as thermal floors. The majority of the population in Colombia resides in three main thermal floors characterized by its altitudes: hot (0–1000 Metres Above Mean Sea Level (MAMSL)) with 80% of the territory; tempered (1000–2000 MAMSL) with 10% of the territory and cold (2000–3000 MAMSL) with 7.9% of the territory. Also, the solar energy distribution varies greatly throughout the year, then, in order to harvest this energy, it is essential to understand its spatial and temporal distribution. With the growth of PV applications in Colombia, new regulations are being implemented [15, 19] in recent years. Horizontal PV arrays are predominating the market, and vertical PV installations are not explored yet. Therefore, the vertical generation harvesting in building façades, or vertical solar farms is studied.

The solar potential has been explored by optimizing the orientation of a PV panel based on economical and energy generation factors, such as the maximum electric energy production, maximum incident solar irradiance or maximum absorbed solar irradiance, module inclination and panel shading [1,8]. Other authors consider the minimimal variance of the power produced in a given time period and optimum times in order to adjust the tilt angle for specific locations instead of using sun-tracking systems which are complex and expensive [6]. The annual potential, economical issues, the impact of the urban context and shadowing effects on roof and façades are also included in these studies [3]. Statistical radiation models are also commonly used to find optimal orientations [22]. Also, available software is used to obtain the best radiation models in different geographical locations covering a wide range of latitudes such as Saudi Arabia, Korea, Morocco, among others as can be shown in the state-of-the-art by Ullah et al. [25].

Regarding the solar energy harvesting on vertical façades, other approaches and tools have been used to estimate the performance and factors that affect their generation in an urban scale as reported in [16]. Nowadays, the approaches to study the vertical solar potential consider the building's morphology and urban structure [12]. The state-of-the-art studies on this area include analytical and Geographical Information System (GIS) models combined with technologies to obtain detailed landscape information like Light Detection And Ranging (LiDAR) and Digital Surface Model (DSM) developing accurate strategies to calculate and visualize the roof and façade solar potential [4,7]. Other methods that include Airborne Laser Scanning (ALS), Mobile Laser Scanning (MLS), finite element method and ray-tracing algorithms [13] have been developed in order to make more accurate solar radiation analyses. The use of specialized software like EnergyPlus and Windperfect is also reported by [9].

The above-mentioned methods use the solar position formulae, radiation models and climatological data on tilted surfaces, considering the components of beam, diffuse, and reflected radiation, as well as geographic parameters, economical issues, orientation techniques and geometry analysis of buildings on fixed and tilted surfaces [17].

In contrast to the proposed approaches, there are neither similar studies for Colombia and its vertical façades energetic potential, nor the use of the optimization of orientation and their energy generation as a design factor. Hence, this paper evaluates the energetic potential of vertical surfaces in Colombia by means of optimizing the orientation of a vertical panel for different cities located on each of the main thermal floors. The main purpose is to identify the optimal azimuth angle for every location, and how the energy generation depends on geographical parameters assuming clear sky conditions. The optimal orientation of the vertical surface to obtain the greatest amount of energy throughout the year is calculated. This article describes in Sect. 2 the tools used to develop the algorithm and the corresponding mathematical model. In Sect. 3, the results obtained with the algorithm are shown. Finally, Sect. 4 presents the analysis of how this optimization can be useful to design a vertical façade or surface in different thermal floors.

2 Materials and Methods

To study the optimum orientation of vertical surfaces, an optimization code is developed using Python language and the PVLib package [2] to model PV systems. To assess the potential of vertical generating surfaces on the three main thermal floors, one location on each floor is considered: Medellin, Rionegro and Sincelejo; and a fourth city, Bogota, is included for comparative purposes. The assumed geographical locations are listed in Table 1.

Table 1. Geographical coordinates of every city considered in this study.

City	Latitude	Longitude	Altitude (MAMSL)
Sincelejo	9.31	−75.39	200
Rionegro	6.52	−75.59	2200
Medellin	6.25	−75.56	1495
Bogota	4.64	−74.24	2640

To determine the apparent solar position several parameters must be defined such as the angle of declination, δ; the angle of angular elevation, α, between the horizontal and the position of the sun defined as $\alpha = 90° - \phi - \delta$, where ϕ is the latitude; and the azimuthal angle Φ which is the position of the sun on the horizontal plane measured with respect to the North.

To find the optimal orientation for each location, the azimuth angle of a vertical façade is varied from 0° to 359° with 1° steps within a one-year range from January 1, 2019 until December 31, 2019. Then, the solar position is obtained based on the geographic parameters from 4:00 am until 9:00 pm (with 10min steps) using the PVLib method "solarposition.get_solarposition". The azimuth of the vertical surface is defined as the angle between the north cardinal point and the normal vector of the flat surface.

The direct intensity of incident light I_i on a module with a 90° vertical tilt and arbitrary orientation is calculated using Ineichen Clear Sky Radiation Model [11] with the PVLib function clearsky.ineichen(). This model is mainly defined by Eq. 1.

$$I_i = bI_0 e^{(-0.09AM(T_{LK}-1))} \tag{1}$$

where I_i is the direct incident beam radiation, b is a multiplicative coefficient $b = 0.664 + 0.163/f_{h1}$ and $f_{h1} = exp(-altitude/8000)$, I_0 the normal incidence extraterrestrial irradiance, AM the altitude corrected air mass and T_{LK} the Linke turbidity coefficient.

The surface incident energy is conditioned by its location, the climatic conditions of the site, the angle of incidence of the solar beam and the angle of inclination of the module (see Fig. 2). When the light beam is perpendicular to the panel, the power density is maximum, but the incident sunlight varies continuously with the solar beam angle. The incident perpendicular direct radiation component on an inclined surface I_{nm} with fixed azimuthal angle is found based on Fig. 2 as shown in the Eq. 2.

$$I_{nm} = \frac{I_h \sin (\alpha + \beta)}{\sin (\alpha)} \tag{2}$$

where α is the elevation angle of the sun, β is the angle of inclination of the solar module and I_h is the solar radiation measured on a horizontal surface, defined as the sine of the incident radiation, $I_h = I_i \sin(\alpha)$.

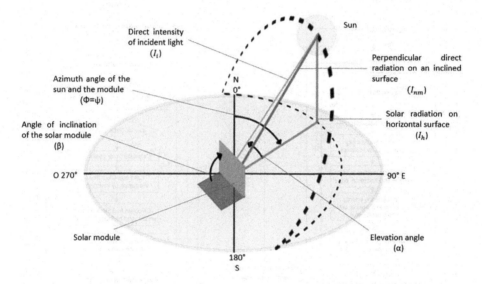

Fig. 2. Solar radiation on a tilted surface, adapted from [5].

In the situation of an arbitrarily tilted and oriented panel, the calculation of I_{nm} in the module becomes more complex as given by Eq. 3.

$$I_{nm} = I_i \left[\cos (\alpha) \sin (\beta) \cos (\psi - \varPhi) + \sin (\alpha) \cos (\beta) \right] \tag{3}$$

where α is the sun elevation angle, β is the module tilt angle, $\varPhi$ is the sun azimuth angle and ψ is the azimuthal angle that the module faces.

By implementing Eq. 3, the incident direct energy received by the vertical surface is obtained and the diffuse component calculated by Ineichen model is added. Finally, the energy is calculated for each azimuth angle using a trapezoidal integral of the irradiation. The yearly energy for each azimuth angle at each location, including the minimum and maximum values, is stored in a database. In Fig. 3, the flow diagram of the developed algorithm is depicted.

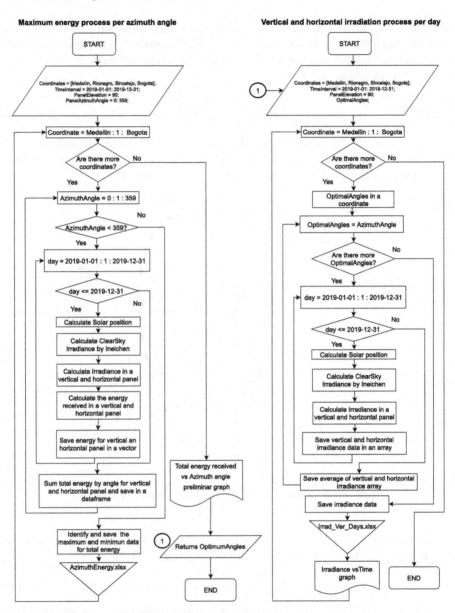

Fig. 3. Flowchart of the optimization code for the orientation of vertical surfaces.

3   Results

For each thermal floor, the algorithm is run for horizontal and vertical surfaces, varying the azimuth angle for the latter. The accumulated energy for each azimuth angle during every day of the year is used to determine a fixed optimum azimuth angle to orientate PV modules and, therefore, harvest more energy. The results are shown in Fig. 4.

A significant difference in the total accumulated incident energy between the cities located on each thermal floor is noticed. Sincelejo, located at a lower altitude (200 MAMSL), shows the lowest values of energy obtained both vertically and horizontally, while Bogota, located at a higher elevation (2,640 MAMSL), shows the highest total accumulated energy with respect to the other floors considered. The energy assessment considering the optimal orientations found for every location is reported in Table 2.

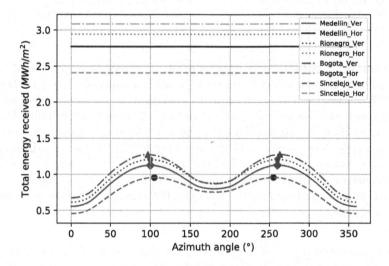

Fig. 4. Total energy obtained on each geographic location during one year according to the variation of the azimuth angle of the panel.

Furthermore, the optimal azimuth angles reported in Table 2 show the disparity of the angles between thermal floors, except for Medellin and Rionegro that present equal angles given their geographical proximity, their difference in altitude determines a higher accumulated energy for Rionegro. This reinforces the idea to locally optimize the orientation of BIPV applications with vertical façades for each region, instead of adopting the same orientation angle for all regions of Colombia. Also, Table 2 shows the ratio of energy received by a horizontal panel to a vertical panel, indicating that the generation for a vertical panel with both sides considered is 20%, 18%, 19% and 18% less than the horizontal one for Sincelejo, Rionegro, Medellin and Bogota, respectively.

In addition, to make better use of energy in façades it is necessary to take into account the angular tolerances with respect to the optimal azimuthal angle, since the angular mismatches in the analyzed geographies produce an energy loss with increasing parabolic behavior for each shifted angle in all places considered in this study. Therefore, by assuming a threshold of $1kWh/m^2$ of energy loss received

Table 2. Total energy obtained (during one year) with the panel optimal azimuth angle for every city considered.

City	Optimal Azimuth angles (°)		Total energy received (MWh/m²)		Vertical to horizontal ratio[b]
	Morning	Afternoon	Vertical[a]	Horizontal	
Sincelejo	105	255	0.96	2.41	0.80 : 1
Rionegro	100	260	1.21	2.94	0.82 : 1
Medellin	100	260	1.12	2.77	0.81 : 1
Bogota	97	263	1.27	3.09	0.82 : 1

[a] The total energy received by the vertical panel is reported for one side.
[b] The vertical position energy considers the sum of morning and afternoon, both are equivalent.

at the surface due to angular misalignment, it is recommended for Medellin, Rionegro and Bogota to not exceed $\pm 2°$, while for Sincelejo, $\pm 3°$, as shown in the Table 3. Also, as shown in Table 3, if a deviation of $\pm 10°$ is exceeded, received energy losses could be up to $\approx 8.96 kWh/m^2$, $\approx 11.47 kWh/m^2$, $\approx 11.82 kWh/m^2$ and $\approx 12.81 kWh/m^2$ for Sincelejo, Rionegro, Medellin and Bogota, respectively.

The hourly average irradiance for both vertically tilted and horizontal surfaces was obtained for each analyzed thermal floor as shown in Fig. 5; it is noted that the curves are consistent with the results of Fig. 4, in which Bogota is found to produce the highest energy, and Medellin, Rionegro and Sincelejo in respective decreasing order.

Table 3. Loss of energy in kWh/m^2 (during one year) per angle offset relative to the optimal value of the azimuth angle for each location.

City	$\pm 1°$	$\pm 2°$	$\pm 3°$	$\pm 10°$
Sincelejo	≈ 0.13	≈ 0.43	≈ 0.90	≈ 8.96
Rionegro	≈ 0.12	≈ 0.46	≈ 1.02	≈ 11.47
Medellin	≈ 0.19	≈ 0.60	≈ 1.23	≈ 11.82
Bogota	≈ 0.16	≈ 0.56	≈ 1.21	≈ 12.81

It is also observed from Table 4, that peaks are generated around 8:20am and 3:40pm, for both morning and afternoon, respectively. These maximum peaks coincide with high energy demand points in the typical Colombian energy demand curve during the morning and during the afternoon for all sectors. For a typical household energy demand curve the optimal azimuth angle for the morning matches with a maximum energy demand point, while in the afternoon the optimum angle it is not at the highest point but in a growing energy demand point [18]. Hence, the implementation of vertical power generation surfaces is beneficial to help supply the point of maximum demand and generate a better distribution in the power demand curve, mainly in the residential sector.

4   Discussion

The accumulated energy results using the clear sky model in the algorithm (Fig. 4) is consistent with respect to the simulated geographical characteritics of the thermal floors analyzed. It is coherent that the energy is greater at thermal floors further from the sea level, because the air mass that the radiation must overcome is less than when closer to the sea. This is due to the relationship between the air mass and the optimal path of a solar ray normal to the terrestrial surface (or zero zenith angle) and the altitude above sea level.

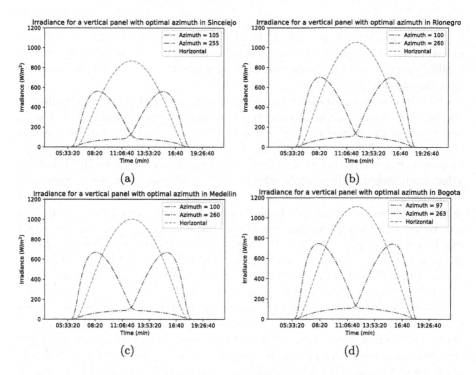

Fig. 5. Irradiance vs. time (a) Sincelejo. (b) Rionegro. (c) Medellin. (d) Bogota.

Additionally, comparing the accumulated energy between Sincelejo and Bogota from the clear sky algorithm and the Colombian atlas of solar, ultraviolet and ozone radiation provided by the Institute of Hydrology, Meteorology and Environmental Studies (IDEAM in spanish) [10], it is noticeable that there is an opposite behavior of available radiant energy in these cities. Since Sincelejo is in the Colombian Caribbean, a region characterized for its high solar radiation [23], it should have a value higher than Bogota. However, the lower values in Sincelejo are explained by the clear sky algorithm that does not consider the climatological factors such as the atmosphere composition.

Table 4. Average irradiance with optimum azimuth angle for every city considered.

City	Vertical average irradiance (W/m^2)						Horizontal average irradiance (W/m^2)	
	Morning			Afternoon				
Sincelejo	8:40 am	105°	563.27	3:20 pm	255°	559.51	12:00 pm	935.94
Rionegro	8:20 am	100°	702.41	3:40 pm	260°	699.32	12:00 pm	1118.24
Medellin	8:20 am	100°	669.62	3:40 pm	260°	668.52	12:00 pm	1060.32
Bogota	8:10 am	97°	746.37	3:40 pm	263°	742.98	12:00 pm	1165.31

Also, from Fig. 4, it is evident that for all the explored locations, the minimum values correspond to azimuth angles close to 0° and 180°, due to the smaller effective area for radiation capture when the sun moves from east to west throughout the day.

This approach of optimizing the azimuth angle of a vertical panel for different regions of Colombia allows to identify the optimal orientation required for a better use of the incident energy on a vertical surface, which can be a design criterion for performing energy façade installations in new or existing buildings. Moreover, it is a tool that contributes to strengthen and promote BIPV both in urban environments where vertical façades are an alternative of power generation given the limitation of horizontal space, as in places far from the national system or whose access to energy is complex like rural areas. A vertical system may receive less radiation than a horizontal one, but it can have a bigger area, which can be even doubled if both sides are used. Nevertheless, the implementation of vertical generation surfaces must be carefully analyzed for being sensitive to external factors such as shading effects from nearby obstacles or non-optimal orientations that can affect its generation efficiency.

Although this study is carried out assuming clear sky conditions, it gives clear lights towards promising results that can be used in the Colombian territory. However, it is necessary to integrate meteorological databases, electrical generation models using photovoltaic systems with real parameters, and economic models that show the feasibility of the optimization model. Thus, the optimization model could get more robust and versatile, in order to serve as an analysis and design tool for energy façades in Colombia or other countries.

5   Conclusions and Future Work

An algorithm for optimizing the orientation of a vertical PV surface was developed for applications as BIPV systems using a clear sky radiation model. Three places in Colombia were studied: Medellin, Rionegro and Sincelejo located at the three main thermal floors, and a fourth, Bogota for comparison reasons. Medellin an Rionegro's optimal azimuth angles for the morning and afternoon where found to be 100° and 260°; 97° and 263° for Bogota, and 105° and 255° for Sincelejo in relation to the energy accumulated along the year. Furthermore, along with these optimal angles is the irradiance curve for each location, showing two maximum peaks that are aligned with the hours of maximum energy demand of the demand curve for all sectors in Colombia and the typical residential energy demand curve. Moreover, Sincelejo has been found to be the least sensitive city for angle deviation from the optimal angle with values up to $\pm 3°$, while Medellin, Rionegro and Bogota are more sensitive, varying up to $\pm 2°$. In addition, for the analyzed cities it is found that, eventhough a vertical panel receives less energy than a horizontal one, vertical areas on buildings can be bigger than the roof's. This also shows viability for other generation options on vertical surfaces such as bifacial panels.

As future work, it will be incorporated the meteorological data from each place in the Colombian territory of interest, including analyses with real photovoltaic systems and the development of an analysis of energy potential based on economical data. Additionally, the relationship between thermal comfort and the orientation of a vertical surface for the regulation of the temperature inside the building. Finally, in the context of the project funding this research (refered to in the acknowledgements) two living-labs are going to be built in the cities of Medellin and Sincelejo, with some of its vertical façades adopting the suggested orientation angles, which are going to be used to validate this model.

Acknowledgements. Authors thank Universidad EAFIT and the alliance "ENERGETICA 2030", which is a Research Program coded 58667 from the "*Colombia Científica*" initiative, funded by The World Bank through the call "778-2017 Scientific Ecosystems". The research program is managed by the Colombian Ministry of Science, Technology and Innovation (Minciencias) with contract No. FP44842-210-2018.

References

1. Al Garni, H.Z., Awasthi, A., Wright, D.: Optimal orientation angles for maximizing energy yield for solar PV in Saudi Arabia. Renew. Energy **133**, 538–550 (2019)
2. Andrews, R.W., Stein, J.S., Hansen, C., Riley, D.: Introduction to the open source PV lib for python photovoltaic system modelling package. In: 2014 IEEE 40th Photovoltaic Specialist Conference (PVSC), pp. 0170–0174. IEEE (2014)
3. Brito, M., Freitas, S., Guimarães, S., Catita, C., Redweik, P.: The importance of facades for the solar PV potential of a Mediterranean city using LiDAR data. Renew. Energy **111**, 85–94 (2017)
4. Catita, C., Redweik, P., Pereira, J., Brito, M.C.: Extending solar potential analysis in buildings to vertical facades. Comput. Geosci. **66**, 1–12 (2014)
5. Honsberg, C.B.S.: Photovoltaics education (2019). www.pveducation.org
6. Despotovic, M., Nedic, V.: Comparison of optimum tilt angles of solar collectors determined at yearly, seasonal and monthly levels. Energy Conver. Manage. **97**, 121–131 (2015)
7. Desthieux, G., et al.: Solar energy potential assessment on rooftops and facades in large built environments based on Lidar data, image processing, and cloud computing. methodological background, application, and validation in Geneva (solar cadaster). Front. Built Environ. **4**, 14 (2018)

8. Díez-Mediavilla, M., Rodríguez-Amigo, M., Dieste-Velasco, M., García-Calderón, T., Alonso-Tristán, C.: The PV potential of vertical façades: a classic approach using experimental data from Burgos, Spain. Solar Energy **177**, 192–199 (2019)
9. Hsieh, C.M., Chen, Y.A., Tan, H., Lo, P.F.: Potential for installing photovoltaic systems on vertical and horizontal building surfaces in urban areas. Solar Energy **93**, 312–321 (2013)
10. Institute of Hydrology, M., (IDEAM), E.S.: Atlas of solar radiation, ultraviolet and ozone of Colombia (2020). http://atlas.ideam.gov.co/visorAtlasRadiacion.html
11. Ineichen, P., Perez, R.: A new airmass independent formulation for the linke turbidity coefficient. Solar Energy **73**(3), 151–157 (2002)
12. Jakubiec, J.A., Reinhart, C.F.: A method for predicting city-wide electricity gains from photovoltaic panels based on LiDAR and GIS data combined with hourly daysim simulations. Solar Energy **93**, 127–143 (2013)
13. Kaynak, S., Kaynak, B., Özmen, A.: A software tool development study for solar energy potential analysis. Energy Build. **162**, 134–143 (2018)
14. Khan, M.R., Hanna, A., Sun, X., Alam, M.A.: Vertical bifacial solar farms: physics, design, and global optimization. Appl. Energy **206**, 240–248 (2017)
15. López, A.R., et al.: Solar PV generation in Colombia-a qualitative and quantitative approach to analyze the potential of solar energy market. Renew. Energy **148**, 1266–1279 (2020)
16. Martín, A.M., Domínguez, J., Amador, J.: Applying LiDAR datasets and GIS based model to evaluate solar potential over roofs: a review. AIMS Energy **3**(3), 326–343 (2015)
17. Ouria, M.: Solar energy potential according to climatic and geometrical parameters of cities and buildings: a case-study from Tabriz city-iran. Urban Clim. **28**, 100469 (2019)
18. Pimm, A.J., Cockerill, T.T., Taylor, P.G.: The potential for peak shaving on low voltage distribution networks using electricity storage. J. Energy Storage **16**, 231–242 (2018)
19. Rodríguez-Urrego, D., Rodríguez-Urrego, L.: Photovoltaic energy in Colombia: current status, inventory, policies and future prospects. Renew. Sustain. Energy Rev. **92**, 160–170 (2018)
20. Shukla, A.K., Sudhakar, K., Baredar, P.: A comprehensive review on design of building integrated photovoltaic system. Energy Build. **128**, 99–110 (2016)
21. Shukla, A.K., Sudhakar, K., Baredar, P.: Recent advancement in BIPV product technologies: a review. Energy Build. **140**, 188–195 (2017)
22. Stanciu, C., Stanciu, D.: Optimum tilt angle for flat plate collectors all over the world-a declination dependence formula and comparisons of three solar radiation models. Energy Conver. Manage. **81**, 133–143 (2014)
23. Taba, M.F.A., Mwanza, M., Çetin, N.S., Ülgen, K.: Assessment of the energy generation potential of photovoltaic systems in Caribbean region of Colombia. Period. Eng. Nat. Sci. **5**(1) (2017)
24. Tripathy, M., Sadhu, P., Panda, S.: A critical review on building integrated photovoltaic products and their applications. Renew. Sustain. Energy Rev. **61**, 451–465 (2016)
25. Ullah, A., Imran, H., Maqsood, Z., Butt, N.Z.: Investigation of optimal tilt angles and effects of soiling on PV energy production in Pakistan. Renew. Energy **139**, 830–843 (2019)

Preliminary Sizing of a Propulsion Unit for an Electrically-Powered Vessel Using a Screw Propellers Performance Comparison Tool

Juan-David Mira[✉], Santiago Gómez-Oviedo, Esteban Betancur, and Ricardo Mejía-Gutiérrez

Design Engineering Research Group (GRID), Universidad EAFIT, Carrera 49 No 7 Sur–50, Medellín, Colombia
{jdmirap,esgomezo,ebetanc2,rmejiag}@eafit.edu.co

Abstract. The sizing of the power to be installed in a vessel depends on the desired Effective Power (P_E) and how efficient the energy conversion process is carried out in each of its components. Screw type are the most widely used propellers and their selection determines to a greater extent the overall efficiency of the unit. An interactive tool that accelerates the selection of the most efficient propeller for two different series, the Gawn and the B-Wageningen, is presented and is used for a design case of study where the required P_E of an electrically-powered vessel is known. The comparative analysis provided by the tool allowed to determine a difference in performance parameters of almost 10% between different propellers series, to estimate the installed power values, and to characterize the geometrical parameters for a commercial selection approach.

Keywords: Interactive selection tool · Electrically-powered vessel · Propeller performance · Propulsion design

1 Introduction

When designing a vessel, cruising speed and the demand for cargo and/or passenger transport capacity are taken as a starting point to dimension and define the shape of the hull, which must allow it to act safely and stably in the different static and dynamic situations. It must also exercise the least possible opposition to forward movement. Once the geometry of the boat is known, it is subjected to hydrodynamic studies to estimate the thrust necessary for its displacement. Thrust and velocity define the power that must be delivered to the vessel in order to meet its operating requirements. Most existing vessels make use of propulsion units incorporating internal combustion engines (ICE), using a fossil fuel energy source that presents 100 times more energy density (KWh/kg) than, for example, a battery that powers the propulsion unit of an electric boat. Therefore, energy efficiency becomes a mandatory and determining factor for the design

© Springer Nature Switzerland AG 2020
J. C. Figueroa-García et al. (Eds.): WEA 2020, CCIS 1274, pp. 465–476, 2020.
https://doi.org/10.1007/978-3-030-61834-6_40

of an electric boat [8]. The calculation of the power needed to drive an electric boat must consider the different components that make up the propulsion unit (Motor-Transmission-Propeller). Their losses translate into an increase in the installed power capacity. The Fig. 1 schematically illustrates the propulsion flow of energy and the main efficiencies and losses.

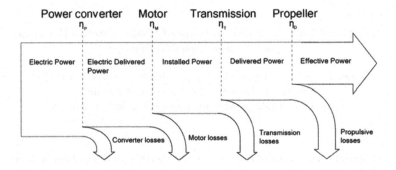

Fig. 1. Losses associated with an electric propulsion unit.

Screw propellers are the most commonly used propellants and their selection is one of the most important stages in the design process, since it determines to a greater extent the overall efficiency of the unit. For the propeller selection, the designer has a variety of options, and his goal is to find the most efficient one, which provides the required performance and minimizes energy losses.

2   Literature Review

2.1   State of the Art

Different computer tools have been developed to help finding the most suit-able propeller in terms of performance characteristics. These characteristics are expressed through propeller series diagrams or regression polynomials data that allow interpolation and optimization within traditional propeller geome-tries [4,9]. The collected information is the result of experimental tests in open water with different propeller models that vary geometrical parameters such as Pitch Ratio (P/D), Blade Number (Z), and Blade Area Ratio (A_E/A_O) that define the standard series. The data of standard series is used by the numerical analysis software as a benchmark [18]. Gaafari *et al.* in [7] developed a computer program for optimal design of the B-Series marine propeller considering cavita-tion, material strength and propeller thrust limitations. Tanaka and Yoshida in [19] developed a software that allows the generation of non-dimensional charts consisting of a base scale and a set of superimpositions for a series of propellers. For their part, Benini [2] proposed an optimization method that helps design-ers to determine the optimal configuration of a propeller by maximizing the efficiency of the propeller and the thrust coefficient through the use of evolutionary algorithms. On the other hand Matulja *et al.*[16] applied the advantages of Artificial Neural Networks(ANN) to the problem of optimal screw helix selection by using the B-Wageningen series polynomial expression data as a set of weight values to train an ANN that provides the selection of the screw helix with maximum efficiency. Gómez-Oviedo and Mejía-Guitérrez in [12] presented a methodology for the selection of the propeller according to the definition of an electric motor suitable for a given context. A computational tool is implemented as a support to determine the efficiency of a propeller. It is common to find in studies that seek the optimal propellant the use of the information available for the B-series since they are the most extensive and widely used series [4]. There are additional propeller series for which information is available such as the Gawn-series [18]. Including this other type of propeller series in the research allows for a more accurate selection, not only by evaluating series whose central application include most merchant ship types such as the B-Wageningen series but also by considering the Gawn-series propellers that are commonly applied to ferries, warships, small crafts and higher speed crafts [18].This study makes use of an interactive tool, developed by [12], that speeds up the selection of the most efficient propeller. Two different types of propeller families are considered, the Gawn-series and the B-Wageningen series, maximizing the efficiency values and allowing a comparative analysis of these two types of series. The previously optimized values are used for the preliminary design and the approximation to a commercial selection of the propulsion unit of an electric boat.

2.2   Theoretical Framework

When a propeller is located in the ship, the flow around the hull is modified at the location point. This causes an increase in the resistance experienced by the hull. It also modifies the wake initially generated by the bare hull and therefore the average water speed through the propeller which will not be the same as the boat speed. These two effects are taken together as an input to measure the hull efficiency. The other effect of combining the hull and the propulsion unit is that the flow through the propeller (or a variation thereof) is not uniform [10]. The above losses are quantified by the Quasi-propulsive coefficient (η_D) defined by the Eq. 1 [4,10,18].

$$\eta_D = \eta_O \times \eta_H \times \eta_R \tag{1}$$

Where η_O is the efficiency of the propeller in open water, η_H the efficiency of interaction with the hull and η_R the relative rotation efficiency. The efficiency of the hull is expressed by the Eq. 2 [3,10,18], where t and w are dimensionless coefficients known as the thrust deduction factor and the wake factor respectively.

$$\eta_H = \frac{1-t}{1-w} \tag{2}$$

The thrust deduction factor (t) accounts for the change in the resistance of the boat due to the presence of the propeller. The factor w or wake fraction accounts for how much the performance of the propeller is affected by the hull ahead of it, this modifies the speed of the fluid around it by creating a wake that disturbs the fluid ahead of the propeller. The factors t and w are defined as follows in Eq. 3 [3,10,18],

$$t = \frac{T - R_T}{T} \qquad\qquad w = \frac{V_S - V_a}{V_S} \qquad (3)$$

where, V_S is the speed of the ship, V_a is the average propeller forward speed, which differs from the ship's speed, V_S. This difference in speed is the result of the shearing of the fluid caused by the acceleration towards the stern or rear of the boat from the water mass in front of the propeller and is known as the "Slip-ratio". T is the thrust generated by the propeller and R_T is the total resistance (both expressed as units of force). In addition, "Slip-ratio" is given by the Eq. 4, where P is the pitch (fixed feed distance for each turn) and n is the angular speed of rotation of the propeller [10].

$$Slip\ Ratio = \frac{Pn - V_a}{Pn} \qquad (4)$$

There is a high degree of complexity in determining the deduction factors involved in calculating the Effective Power (P_E), many of these factors evade the possibility of accurate analyses and there is no completely satisfactory method of analysis for the quantitative measurement [10]. For the propeller analysis, experimental models have been developed, they consist of measuring the performance characteristics of the propellers in a tank by means of a towed mechanism, providing efficiency, thrust and torque curves. The principal aim in carrying out systematic propeller tests is to provide a data base to help the designer understand the factors which influence propeller performance [4]. The most commonly tested propellers are the B-Wageningen series and the Gawn-series [18]. The Wageningen B-Series is a general purpose and the most extensive propeller series. The series encompasses a total of 120 propellers with systematic variations of Z, A_E/A_O, and P/D, ogival sections are used from 60% of the radius to the blade tip [3,6]. The Gawn series is a set of 37 three-bladed propellers with P/D between 0.4 and 2.0 and expanded area ratios from 0.2 to 1.1. This series also covers a wide P/D range which makes it applicable to high-speed and naval vessels [4]. Parameters of the propeller like Z, Propeller Blade Area Ratio (A_E/A_O), Pitch Ratio (P/D) are varied systematically, into the Eqs. 5 and 6, in order to obtain the maximum efficiency for a given advance coefficient (J). The regression coefficients C^T, C^Q and the terms s, t, u and v are presented by [18] and will be used as a database for the comparative tool to be developed.

$$K_T = \sum_{s,t,u,v} C^T_{s,t,u,v} (J)^s (P/D)^t (A_E/A_O)^u (Z)^v = \frac{T}{\rho n^2 D^4} \qquad (5)$$

$$K_Q = \sum_{s,t,u,v} C^Q_{s,t,u,v} (J)^s (P/D)^t (A_E/A_O)^u (Z)^v = \frac{Q}{\rho n^2 D^5} \qquad (6)$$

$$J = \frac{V_a}{nD} \qquad\qquad \eta_O = \frac{TV_A}{2\pi nQ} = \frac{J}{2\pi} \frac{K_T}{K_Q} \qquad (7)$$

The dimensionless parameters Thrust Coefficient (K_T), Torque Coefficient (K_Q), Advance Coefficient (J) and Propeller Coefficient (η_O) are given by the Eqs. 5, 6, 7, respectively and define the performance of the propellers, are common to all designers and allow comparison of performance [18]. T is the thrust, ρ is the fluid density and D is the propeller diameter.

3   Methodology

In this study, an interactive tool that accelerates the selection of the most efficient propeller is implemented for two different series, the Gawn series and the B-Wageningen series, by reducing the time required to perform calculations, maximizing the efficiency values and allowing a comparative graphic analysis of these two types of series that provide guidelines for a correct selection.

It is based on the algorithm developed by Gómez-Oviedo and Mejía-Guitérrez in [12] that defines the sequence of instructions for the model to calculate the efficiency of a propeller operating in open water. Two essential calculation stages for the design are added at the beginning and end of the calculation model. The mentioned stages were included as subroutines, together with an environment for the calculation of variables and intermediate values needed for the calculation process. As a first step, the "Subroutine 1" computes the optimal diameter D for the P_E to be transmitted by the propeller, based on Crouch's Propeller Method in [9]. A Diameter-HP-RPM chart is generated by the tool making use of Eq. 8 for RPM ranges between 500 and 4500, propeller diameters between 6 and 60 inches [in], and powers between 10 and 3000 horsepower [HP]. This chart allows to define the operation point for the characteristics of the motor-transmission subset at the optimal RPM and provides the optimal diameter that the propeller should have for the defined conditions (see Fig. 4(a)).

$$D = \frac{632.7 \times HP^{0.2}}{RPM^{0.6}} \qquad (8)$$

As a next step, and taking as input the result of the "Subroutine 1", the tool allows the designer to continue interactively performing intermediate calculations of the "Slip-ratio" (Eq. 4), average propeller forward speed V_a, wake fraction (Eq. 3) and hull efficiency (Eq. 2) variables required to compute J and η_D. Here, the "Subroutine 2" optimization is executed taking J as an input parameter. The tool uses the iterable data set from the Gawn and B-Wageningen series for the calculation and executes the estimation of the K_T, K_Q and η_O coefficients of the propeller by iterating the different values of the polynomials presented in Eqs. 5 and 6 and maximizing the results. In this way, the optimal propeller for each of the series is determined and a graphic result of the dimensionless performance variables is generated in a single image map allowing the designer to identify the cut-off points for K_T and K_Q as well as the efficiency difference ($\Delta\eta$) values between the two series. The geometrical parameters P/D, A_E/A_O and Z associated with each of the optimal propellers found in each series are also computed and displayed at the top of the image map (see Fig. 5). Finally, knowing the optimal propeller, the designer can continue with the calculation of the η_D (Eq. 1) that allows the sizing of the propulsion unit. The Fig. 2 shows the detailed flow chart for the computation tool by grouping the stages in subroutines 1 and 2, intermediate calculations and final results.

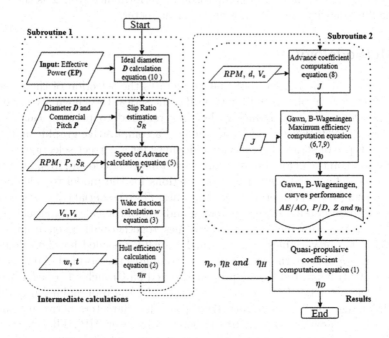

Fig. 2. Flow chart of interactive computation tool.

4   Case Study

The river transport options have taken great relevance throughout history, especially in Latin America and the Caribbean region, which have the highest density of navigable rivers in the world. Colombia, located in the north of South America, has a total of 24,725 km of waterways [1,13]. The Magdalena is the main river of Colombia and has a total of 125 municipalities around its banks, the municipality of Magangué is one of them. This municipality has a potential of 39,172 fluvial passengers per month. It is there where the case study boat operates. The case study context has particularities, mainly related to the need for low operating costs, high velocity and high energy consumption. These factors are analyzed by Mira *et al.* in [17] through the implementation of a Quality Function Deployment (QFD) tool.

4.1 Determination of the Installed Power

The definition of the power to be installed is expressed as a function of the efficiencies involved as shown in Eq. 9. The dimensioning problem is then translated into the calculation of P_E that will be an input for this case of study together with each of the coefficients of the chain of efficiencies. Typical values found in the literature allow for the estimation of the power converter, power transmission and main machinery efficiencies. The Table 1 summarizes the typical values reported, these will be used for the sizing of the unit. This study then concentrates on the calculation of the quasi-propulsive coefficient using the calculation tool developed.

$$Installed\ Power\ (PI) = \frac{Effective\ Power\ (PE)}{\eta_D} \times \frac{1}{\eta_M} \times \frac{1}{\eta_T} \times \frac{1}{\eta_P} \qquad (9)$$

Table 1. Typical efficiency ranges

Component		Efficiency [%]
Power converter η_P [14]		98%
Motor η_M [15]		95%
Transmissions	Gears η_T [3–5,18]	95%
	Shaft η_H [3,4,18]	98%

4:2 Input Data

As input for the sizing of the propulsion unit for the vessel, an estimate of the required power for monohull geometry (see Fig. 3(a)) of the glide currently operating in the project's interference zone (see Fig. 3(b)). The electrical power at a given speed, which for the case study has been defined as 55 km/h, is calculated for Giraldo *et al.* in [11]. As a result, the calculations estimate that **119 kW** of P_E is required [11]. This and other input data are summarized in the Table 2.

To determine the pitch (P) of the propeller and to approximate the results to a commercial selection, the supplier Yamaha is taken as a reference and its local commercial offer of propellers of the Yamaha XTO® is analyzed.

With the data provided by the local supplier Yamaha®, the estimation of the "Slip-ratio" is made, at the beginning of the intermediate calculation stage. Once the results have been obtained, it is verified that the selected P/D is adequate for the type of ship and the defined speed according to the Eqs. 10, 11 and 12 where Kts is the boat speed measured in knots. These formulas were derived by Geer in [9] and have been reported to work well with a wide variety of vessels.

$$Maximum\ Pitch\ Ratio = 0.52 \times (Kts^{0.28}) \qquad (10)$$

$$Minimum\ Pitch\ Ratio = 0.39 \times (Kts^{0.23}) \qquad (11)$$

$$Average\ Pitch\ Ratio = 0.46 \times (Kts^{0.26}) \qquad (12)$$

Table 2. Parameters for P_I estimation

Parameter	Value	Units
Boat length over all	7.91	m
Boat beam	2.2	m
Boat draft	0.54	m
Boat displacement	3.6	tons
Speed range	0–17	m/s
Cruise speed	15	m/s
Pitch Yamaha XTO® propellers	15–25	in
Effective power requirement	119	kW

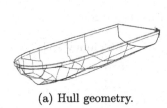

(a) Hull geometry.   (b) Typical Boat

Fig. 3. Study vessel.

5 Results

The comparison of performance characteristics between Gawn and B-Wageningen series is presented. The results of the operating point in terms of diameter D and RPM for the effective power to be delivered (119 kW $\cong$ 160 HP) are shown in Fig. 4. The rotation speed of **2500 RPM** and **16 inches** of propeller diameter are established by means of the program.

17 inches is taken as the value for the pitch P of the propeller, which offers the lowest slip ratio. This value $P/D = 1.06$ is within the interval limited by the minimum and maximum limits specific to the vessel $0.85 < P/D < 1.35$ and 0.05 units below the average value. The values for V_a, w, η_H and J are calculated by the tool and are summarized in the Table 4. For $J = 0.57375$ "Subroutine 2" starts, the tool evaluates the whole set of propellers existing for each one of the series by computing K_T and K_Q values for all the possible combinations and maximizing the results for η_O. The optimal result values are shown graphically in Fig. 5(a) for B-Wageningen series and Fig. 5(b) for Gawn series and summarized in Table 3.

The optimal B-Wageningen series has an efficiency of 75.5% while the Gawn one presents a value of 66.2%. There is a difference of 9.35% between the two values (see Fig. 6). An analysis of the other parameters shows that the propeller of the B-Wageningen series has a constructive result of $Z = 2$ when the optimiza-

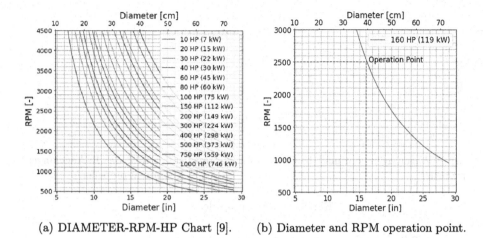

(a) DIAMETER-RPM-HP Chart [9].   (b) Diameter and RPM operation point.

Fig. 4. Computing propeller operation parameters

Table 3. Optimal Values

Item	B-Wageningen series propeller	Gawn series propeller
J	0.57375	0.57375
P/D	0.7	0.9
A_E/A_O	0.3	0.2
Z	2	3
η_O	75.56%	66.20%
Difference Δ_η	9.354 %	

tion is made on the whole set of possible propellers for this series, result which is not commonly found in the commercial offer of manufacturers for this range of diameters and power. On the other hand, the Gawn series propeller has a construction parameter of $Z = 3$ and a P/D value of 0.9, which is much closer to the estimated value of 1.06 than the B-Wageningen series, which is 0.7. The choice of number of blades is discussed by Molland *et al.* in [18], there is evidence that the number of blades is governed mainly by the effects of propeller-excited vibration and, particular, vibration frequencies and the effects on efficiency. Four blades are the most common, and changing to three blades would typically lead to an increase in efficiency of about 3% for optimum diameter (1% for non-optimum diameter), whilst changing to five blades would typically lead to a reduction in efficiency of about 1%. Gerr in [9] on his part refers that three-bladed propellers have proven to be the best compromise between balance, blade area and efficiency.

In order to extend the analysis further and to provide a greater number of elements for the correct selection, the tool is used again only including the

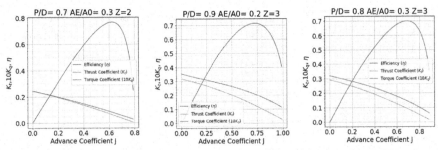

(a) B-Wageningen optimal (b) Gawn optimal propeller (c) 3-Blade B-Wageningen
propeller   optimal propeller

Fig. 5. Optimal propeller results.

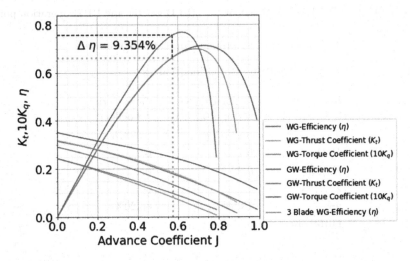

Fig. 6. Computation tool results: K_T, K_Q and efficiencies of resulting propellers

propellers with $Z = 3$ for the B-Wageningen series. The result is a propeller with
$P/D = 0.8$ and a value of 66.11% of efficiency for the case of study operation
point (see Fig. 5(c)), which equals the performance value of the optimal Gawn
series propeller. Based on the above, the Gawn series propeller is selected and
its efficiency and associated parameters are used by the tool to calculate η_D as
shown in Eq. 1. The value of $\eta_D = 0.668$ (see Table 4) together with the other
efficiency values (see Table 1) are used for the calculation of the Installed Power
resulting in 197.7 kW and a Electric Power sizing of 201.7 kW.

Table 4. Output computation values

Item	Result	Units
Slip Ratio	0.46	[-]
Forward Speed V_a	32.13	[ft/s]
Wake Fraction w	0.36	[-]
Hull Efficiency η_H	1.03	[-]
Advance coefficient J	0.57375	[-]
Quasi-propulsive coefficient η_D	0.668	[-]
Installed Power	**197.78**	[kW]

6   Conclusions and Future Work

The tool presented in this study allowed the authors to facilitate the process of sizing the power to be installed in an electric boat. The inclusion of the data from the two series of propellers in the calculation, allows the designer to find comparative differences in the performance parameters, on the case study was $\Delta\eta = 9.35\%$ for the optimum efficiency values. An approach to the characteristics under which propellers are manufactured and marketed locally allows to conclude that the propeller of the B-Wageningen series that has higher efficiency cannot always be applied, besides evaluating the constructive geometrical parameters for the same effects. A Gawn series propeller was selected and the efficiency value of $\eta_O = 66.20\%$ allows to estimate an installed power of 197 kW. The database for commercial propellers is being developed. In this case, a family of different options, that do not directly coincide with the Gawn or B-Wageningen series may arise, and the models should be modified to estimate operating efficiencies for these new options. The propeller manufacturers do not provide enough efficiency data for particular cases. Therefore, this tool will give better insights to the propeller selection and efficiency estimation on the design stages.

Acknowledgements. Authors would like to thank Universidad EAFIT and the alliance "ENERGETICA 2030", which is a Research Program, with code 58667 from the "*Colombia Científica*" initiative, funded by The World Bank through the call "778-2017 Scientific Ecosystems". The research program is managed by the Colombian Ministry of Science, Technology and Innovation (Minciencias) with contract No. FP44842-210-2018.

References

1. Arcadis Nederland, B.V., Jesyca S.A.S: Plan Maestro Fluvial de Colombia 2015. Technical report, Ministerio de Transporte (2015)
2. Benini, E.: Multiobjective design optimization of B-screw series propellers using evolutionary algorithms. Marine Technol. SNAME News **40**(4), 229–238 (2003)

3. Birk, L.: Fundamentals of Ship Hydrodynamics. Wiley, New Orleans (2019)
4. Carlton, J.S.: Marine Propellers and Propulsion, 2nd edn. Butterworth-Heinemann, Oxford (2007)
5. Ehsani, M., Gao, Y., Emadi, A.: Modern Electric, Hybrid Electric and Fuel Cell Vehicles, 2nd edn. CRS Press, Florida (2010)
6. Ekinci, S.: A practical approach for design of marine propellers with systematic propeller series. Brodogradnja **62**(2), 123–129 (2011)
7. Gaafary, M.M., El-Kilani, H.S., Moustafa, M.M.: Optimum design of B-seriesmarine propellers. Alexandria Eng. J. **50**(1), 13–18 (2011). https://doi.org/10.1016/j.aej.2011.01.001
8. Galindo, N.: Impacto de la incorporación del vehículo eléctrico en la integración de energías renovables en el sistema eléctrico. Ph.D. thesis, Universidad Carlos III de Madrid (2010)
9. Gerr, D.: Propeller Handbook. McGraw-Hill, International Marine, New York (1989)
10. Gillmer, T.C.: Introduction to Naval Architecture, 1st edn. E. & F. N. Spon Ltd., London (1982)
11. Giraldo Pérez, E., Gaviria, G., Betancur, E., Osorio Gomez, G., Mejía-Guitérrez, R.: Influence of energy consumption on battery sizing of electric fluvial vessels : a Colombian case study. In: Fifteenth International Conference on Ecological Vehicles and Renewable Energies (EVER) (2020)
12. Gomez, S., Mejía-Guitérrez, R.: An interactive tool for propeller selection according to electric motor exploration: an electric boat design case study. In: IEEE Transportation Electrification Conference and Expo (2020)
13. Jaimurzina, A., Wilmsmeier, G.: La movilidad fluvial en América del Sur. CEPAL–Serie Recursos Naturales e Infraestructura, p. 79 (2017)
14. Lee, E.C.: Review of Variable Speed drive technology, p. 13 (2001)
15. Lu, S.M.: A review of high-efficiency motors: specification, policy, and technology. Renew. Sustain. Energy Rev. **59**, 1–12 (2016). https://doi.org/10.1016/j.rser.2015.12.360
16. Matulja, D., Dejhalla, R., Bukovac, O.: Neural network selection of a maximum efficiency ship screw propeller. In: 13th Congress of International Maritime Association of Mediterranean, vol. 62, 12–15 October 2016 (2016)
17. Mira, J.D., et al.: Preliminary design tools applied to a solar powered vessel design : a South American river analysis. In: Fifteenth International Conference on Ecological Vehicles and Renewable Energies (EVER) (2020)
18. Molland, A.F., Turnock, S.R., Hudson, D.A.: Ship Resistance and Propulsion. Cambridge University Press, Cambridge (2011). https://doi.org/10.1017/cbo9780511974113. Butterworth-Heinemann
19. Tanaka, H., Yoshida, Y.: An approach to transformation of non-dimensional diagrams into nomograms and its application to new propeller design system. WIT Trans. Built Environ. **68**(1), 91–102 (2003)

Simplified Method to Compare the Performance of a Solar Cell Under Different Optical Conditions and Orientations

Juan Pablo Giraldo-Pérez[1]([✉]), Juan Sebastian Orrego-García[2],
Cristian C. Ospina-Metaute[2], and Alejandro Velásquez-López[1]

[1] Design Engineering Research Group (GRID), Universidad EAFIT,
Carrera 49 No 7 Sur–50, Medellín, Colombia
{jgiral95,avelasq9}@eafit.edu.co
[2] Physics Engineering Department, Universidad EAFIT,
Carrera 49 No 7 Sur–50, Medellín, Colombia
{jorreg13,cospin26}@eafit.edu.co

Abstract. The electrification of the modern world will increase the relevance of Renewable Energy Sources (RES). Specifically, Photovoltaic (PV) technologies are expected to be the fastest developing energy generation source. Given the efficiency challenges that these technologies come with, it is necessary to create techniques that allow improving and maximizing their power generation. This paper presents a simple approach to compare the performance of solar cells, using Short-Circuit Current (Isc), Open-Circuit Voltage (Voc) and taking advantage of Internet of Things (IoT) technologies to create a device capable of comparing the performance of multiple cells and plotting real-time results at the same time. Two experiments are carried out to compare different optical covers and different orientations, where according to the device's measurements, a flat cover performed 11.5% better than a triangular cover, and western oriented cells performed 18.7% better that eastern oriented ones. Thus, the device was capable of giving insights for design decisions.

Keywords: Solar cell · Comparison · Performance · I-V curve · Open-circuit voltage · Short-circuit current

1 Introduction

The global energy demand curve will change dramatically over the next decades as industries such as transport and heat production start switching from fossil fuels to electricity as their main power source. To meet this increase on the electrical demand, renewable energy sources, especially Photovoltaic (PV) and wind, will rapidly expand and are expected to fulfill as much as 80% of the demand by 2050 [7]. Although these technologies are an important step towards the world's decarbonization and have a wide range of advantages, they also

© Springer Nature Switzerland AG 2020
J. C. Figueroa-García et al. (Eds.): WEA 2020, CCIS 1274, pp. 477–488, 2020.
https://doi.org/10.1007/978-3-030-61834-6_41

present new challenges, specially in the field of energy efficiency. These electric generation sources depend on external variables such as the climate to determine the amount of energy that they are able to produce.

Specifically talking about PV technologies, the solar cell is the base of its power generation. Solar cells are photo-electronic devices capable of transforming solar radiation into electric energy, generating power without moving parts nor secondary polluting products, making it a clean energy source. There are remarkable developments on PV materials and manufacturing methods, each with specific mechanisms to improve light conversion into electrical energy. Nowadays, semiconductor materials in the form of a p-n junction such as silicon, dominate the market [20,24], reaching power conversion efficiencies up to 29.1% in research labs [13] and 24.4% in commercial modules [14]. The main downside of this renewable energy technology is that it can only produce energy during the daytime, and also that its power generation is not constant as it depends on variables such as irradiance and temperature [5].

In order to evaluate the performance of such technologies, it is necessary to measure their voltage and current variation. The result of plotting these measurements is called the I-V curve. Figure 1 shows an example of how an I-V curve looks and its main points. This curve can then be used to determine the main characteristics of a solar cell as follows:

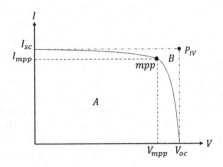

Fig. 1. IV curve of solar cell.

- Maximum Power Point (MPP): Point at which the cell achieves its maximum efficiency.
- Short-circuit current (I_{SC}): Current obtained when the voltage across the terminals is zero.
- Open-circuit voltage (V_{OC}): Voltage across the terminals when the net current in the device is zero.
- Fill factor (FF): Ratio between the maximum power from the solar cell and the product of V_{OC} and I_{SC}. Graphically, in Fig. 1, it is defined as the relation of the area of rectangle A and B.

– Efficiency: Ratio between the energy output from the solar cell and the input energy from the sun. It depends on the spectrum and intensity of the incident sunlight and the temperature of the solar cell.

Given the long process and effort of scientific research and engineering needed to make a significant progress in the field of solar cells efficiency, it becomes necessary to use the existing technologies in the most proper manner to maximize the power generation. Solar cells perform differently when exposed to different environmental conditions. As mentioned before, temperature [12] and irradiance [5] have a direct impact on their output energy, furthermore, various studies have found that variables such as dust accumulation [18], humidity[11], shading [2], optical mechanisms used for light trapping [23] and orientation [6] also directly affect the efficiency and energy production of solar cells.

Each solar cell technology performs differently under different scenarios, therefore, to enhance the power generation, it is essential to perform preliminary studies to identify the correct combination of variables that better suit each solar cell technology. Commercially, there are several devices designed to characterize the solar cells behavior. However, these instruments are expensive and acquire data for only one cell. Table 1 presents examples of different models, prices and technical details for some commercial I-V curve tracers.

Table 1. I-V curve tracers [1, 4, 9, 19, 21].

PV analyzer model	Price (US$)	Specifications				Company	Sweep time (s)
		PV voltage range (V)	Voltage resolution (mV)	Current resolution (mA)	I-V trace points		
SOLAR-600	3,000	0–60	10	10	-	Amprobe	3
PVA-1500V2	9,895	0–1500	25	2	100–500	Solmetric	0.05–2
PV210	2,595	0–1000	100	10	-	Seaward	-
I-V500W	4,495	0–1500	100	10	-	HT-Instruments	5
FTV200	4,129	0–1000	100	10	500	Chauvin-Arnoux	-

In research, authors have described and used different simplified I-V curve tracers [10, 16]. The main methods used are: variable load, capacitive load, electronic load, four-quadrant supply, DC-DC converter and bipolar power amplifier [8, 25]. The difference between these methods are accuracy, sweep speed, maximum rating and resolution.

However, the downside of these devices and methods include complexity, price and the fact that they are designed to evaluate one cell or module at a time. When multiple cells need to be assessed simultaneously, for instance to compare their performance with different optical arrangements or orientations, it is necessary to have as many measuring instruments as cells being compared, which is not cost-effective. In addition, these measurement instruments are not stand-alone, meaning that they require the presence and manipulation of the user to start, operate, retrieve and save data.

In this paper we present an alternative to these devices. In contrast with the approaches found in the State of Art (SoA), we propose a method based on an instrument capable of performing comparisons by only measuring Open-Circuit Voltage (Voc) and Short-Circuit Current (Isc). These two points of the I-V curve are easily measured without the need of specialized equipment. Furthermore, the proposed device has the capability of connecting to the internet to send real time measurements to an Internet of Things (IoT) platform, enabling new test opportunities.

2   Materials and Methods

Two SunPower C60 5" ×5" mono-crystalline silicon cells connected in series are used, each with a maximum voltage of 0.58V, an output power of 3.42W and an efficiency of 23%. These cells are embedded in the cover of a solar brick, a power generating device for vertical facades developed at Universidad EAFIT [3,22]. The necessities of comparing the performance of different types of solar brick covers, each with a different optical profile, and finding the best orientation for the generation of solar energy with vertical modules has encouraged the development of the previously mentioned device.

As seen in Eq. 1, the maximum power generated by a solar cell can be defined as a function of its Voc, Isc and Fill Factor (FF).

$$P_{MaxOut} = V_{OC} * I_{SC} * FF \tag{1}$$

The proposed methodology is based on the fact that the solar cells being compared are the same reference, hence, when under the same climatic conditions, they share the same FF given that it mainly depends on temperature [15], irradiance [5] and the manufacturing techniques and materials used to make the cells [17]. As shown in Eq. 2, considering a constant and same FF for both cells (for comparison reasons), measuring Voc and Isc would be sufficient to find which one generates more energy. In this case, E_{ratio} represents the relation between the energy generated by both cells.

$$E_{ratio} = \frac{\int_{t_i}^{t_f} P_{C1}dt}{\int_{t_i}^{t_f} P_{C2}dt} = \frac{\int_{t_i}^{t_f} FF_1 * V_{OC1} * I_{SC1}dt}{\int_{t_i}^{t_f} FF_2 * V_{OC2} * I_{SC2}dt} = \frac{\int_{t_i}^{t_f} V_{OC1} * I_{SC1}dt}{\int_{t_i}^{t_f} V_{OC2} * I_{SC2}dt} \tag{2}$$

It is important to clarify that the "Energy" being calculated with Eq. 2 does not correspond to the MPP nor any point of the IV curve but to the point P_{IV} from image Fig. 1, which is strictly being used for comparison purposes.

The designed device has as its goal to measure Voc and Isc and consists of three subsystems (i) control, (ii) measurement and (iii) communication, which are explained as follows.

2.1   Control

This subsystem is in charge of controlling the measurement equipment, acquiring and saving the data. An Arduino^{TM} Uno is used for this task, due to its availability, versatility and low price. It also incorporates all the necessary hardware such as analog inputs, digital inputs/outputs and compatibility with a bast list of sensors.

As mentioned before, the goal of the device is to compare the performance of various units of the same solar cell with different covers and orientations, which is the main reason to include a multiplexed system. In order to assess multiple cells at the same time they are connected to a series of MOSFETs that are switched on and off by the Arduino^{TM}, this way it is able to control which cell is being evaluated at a certain instant of time. Since only Voc and Isc are being measured, each cell can be evaluated in less than a second. After evaluating one cell, the algorithm switches the MOSFET that corresponds to the next one; thus the cycle continues until the last cell is evaluated.

2.2   Measurement

Open-Circuit Voltage. To measure Voc, one of the analog input pins of the Arduino^{TM} is used. In order to utilize the entire range of sensitivity of this pin (Max. 5 V with a 4.9 mV resolution) and to ensure that the signal is more reliable, an operational amplifier is used. A Non-inverting configuration is set on the amplifier to generate a gain of the voltage generated by the cell.

Short-Circuit Current. The current sensor ACS714, made by Pololu, is used to measure Isc. This sensor has a working current range between -5A and 5A, is electrically centered at 2.5 V when no current is passed through it and has a gain of 185 mV/A. As a complement to this sensor, one voltage divider and two operational amplifiers are used. The first amplifier is configured as a subtractor (differential amplifier), and is connected to the sensor and to the voltage divider, thus re-centering the signal at 0 V. The second operational amplifier is configured as Non-inverting and set to a gain that allows to connect it to an analog input of the Arduino^{TM} microprocessor where the measurements are saved.

2.3   Communication

This subsystem is responsible for sending the acquired data to an IoT platform. In this case, a SIM900 GSM module is used, and is capable of connecting into a mobile network and establishing communication to an online server. It connects to the Arduino^{TM} UNO through Serial communication, allowing it to send data to the GSM module every time that a new measurement is taken. After reading the data, the SIM900 sends a HTTP request to the IoT server, where the data can be seen in real time, plotted and analyzed. The platform also allows downloading the acquired data as a CSV file for further processing and analysis.

This subsystem allows the device to be placed and used anywhere as long as there is a mobile network connection. Furthermore, if several devices are used simultaneously and located on different places, it allows the data to be centralized in a single database without the need of a physical connection between the devices.

Figure 2 shows a flowchart diagram of the information throughout the process, Fig. 3 represents the electronic schematic of the assembled prototype.

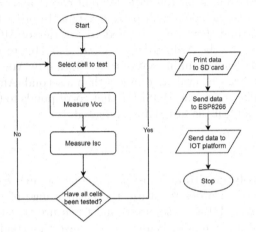

Fig. 2. Algorithm's flow diagram.

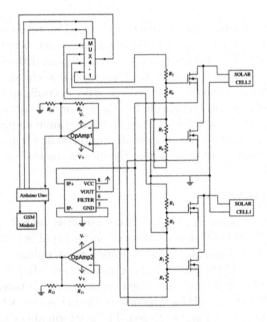

Fig. 3. Final prototype schematic.

2.4 Validation

In order to validate the instrument, a SOLAR-600 IV curve tracer is used. Both devices are connected to the same solar cell and programmed to take measurements every minute. Finally, 129 points were acquired, and its data processed in order to check its matching. Figures 4a and 4b show the scatter graphs that are obtained after plotting the instrument's and Solar-600's results.

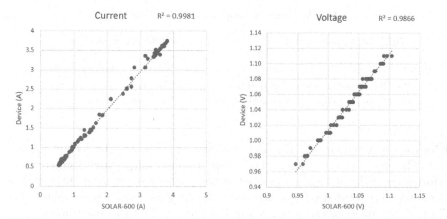

(a) Scatter plot of Isc taken with SOLAR 600 (X axis) and the device (Y axis).

(b) Scatter plot of Voc taken with SOLAR 600 (X axis) and the device (Y axis).

Fig. 4. Voltage and current measurement validations.

The validation experiment shows that the coefficient of determination (R^2) is 0.9981 and 0.9866 for Isc and Voc respectively, meaning that the relation between the device's and SOLAR-600's Voc and Isc measurements is strong.

2.5 Experiment Design

Two experiments were set up at Universidad EAFIT (Medellin, Colombia) in order to compare the performance of solar cells with different optical and orientation conditions. For both experiments the time interval between measurements is set to one minute and the operating time is three days, for a total of six days.

Optical Variation. Four modules with Mono-Crystalline C60 solar cells (used on the previously mentioned solar brick) are used (Fig. 5). Each module has two solar Cells connected in series, a transparent front cover and a white foam backsheet. Two modules have a flat front cover, while the other two have a triangular profiled front cover.

The modules are placed beside each other, in vertical position with an azimuth angle of 286° so that they receive direct sunlight during the afternoon (Fig. 6a). These conditions are synthesized in Table 2.

Fig. 5. Modules used in the experiment.

Table 2. Experiment 1 setup, comparison of different front covers.

Module	Solar cell	Cover	Back-sheet	Position	Azimuth
A & B	Mono-Crystalline x2	Flat-Transparent	White Foam	Vertical	286°
C & D	Mono-Crystalline x2	Triangular-Transparent	White Foam	Vertical	286°

Orientation Variation. The same modules are used for the second experiment. The objective is to change their orientation to evaluate and compare their performance with the results obtained in the previous experiment. In this case the modules are rotated 180° so that the cells get direct radiation in the morning (Fig. 6b). Table 3 synthesizes the conditions presented for this experiment.

Table 3. Experiment 2 setup, comparison of different orientations.

Module	Solar cell	Cover	Back-sheet	Position	Azimuth
A & B	2 X Mono-Crystalline	Flat-Transparent	White Foam	Vertical	106°
C & D	2 X Mono-Crystalline	Triangular-Transparent	White Foam	Vertical	106°

3   Results and Discussion

A total of 8606 points where retrieved from the IoT platform, each containing the measurements of Voc and Isc for each module. Table 4 synthesizes the results for both experiments after integrating their product (Voc.Isc) along time. The results are divided into two categories, one comparing the performance of the cells with different optical profiles and one comparing the performance under different orientations.

Figure 7 shows an example of how the voltage and current graph looks for each module on each experiment. As expected, Voc remains constant throughout the experiments while Isc changes as a function of irradiance. On experiment 1 (modules with an azimuth of 286°) the Isc stays bellow 1A during the morning, and after 12:00 pm, when the sun's irradiance directly reaches the cells, the Isc increases up to 4.8A. Experiment 2 shows an opposite behaviour, since the Isc peak occurs in the morning, and after 12:00pm it remains below 1A.

(a) Experiment 1, 286° orientation.

(b) Experiment 2, 106° orientation.

Fig. 6. Implemented experiments.

Table 4. Results of experiments 1 & 2.

Module	Energy (Wh)		Total energy (Wh)	Relationship between Experiment 1 and Experiment 2
	Experiment 1	Experiment 2		
A	49.02	42.19	91.21	1.16
B	46.68	39.07	85.75	1.19
C	42.32	35.06	77.38	1.20
D	44.17	37.18	81.35	1.18

3.1   Influence of the Optical Profile

The measurements obtained by the device give evidence of the differences of the overall energy generated by the two types of optical profiles under study.

The overall differences in power generation indicate that the flat optical profile (Modules A & B) is 11.5% more efficient than the triangular profile (Modules C & D) for both experiments, as shown in the Table 4. That is, the sum of the energy for the same profiles' typologies in the tests shows that the flat modules generated a total energy of $176.96\,Wh$ while the triangular generated $158.73\,Wh$.

3.2   Influence of Orientation

To identify the influence of orientation Eq. 2 is used. In this case, as the optical covers will not be taken into account, results of all modules for each experiment are added and then compared. Experiment 1 generated a total of $182.19\,Wh$ and experiment 2 $153.5\,Wh$.

$$E_{ratio} = \frac{\int_{t_i}^{t_f} P_{exp1}dt}{\int_{t_i}^{t_f} P_{exp2}dt} = \frac{182.19\,Wh}{153.5\,Wh} = 1.187 \tag{3}$$

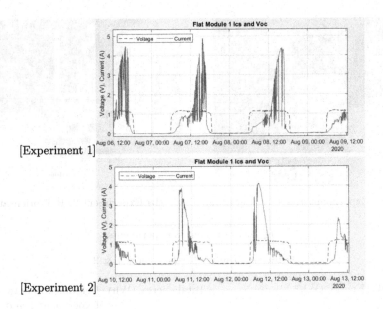

[Experiment 1]

[Experiment 2]

Fig. 7. Isc.Voc vs time curves - module A.

The ratio result indicates that experiment 1 was 18.7% more efficient, meaning that for this case the azimuth angle of 286° is better for vertical solar energy harvesting compared to the 106° angle.

4 Conclusions and Future Work

This paper proposed a new method to compare the performance of solar cells by only measuring Isc and Voc, and enabling the use of IoT technology. Two experiments were designed and implemented to show the use of the methodology. The objective of both experiments was to compare cells under different optic conditions (flat vs triangular profile) and different orientations (286° vs 106° azimuth angles).

According to the results, despite the fact that the triangular cover was expected to improve the performance of the solar cells, they actually performed 11.5% better when they had the flat covers on. This could be caused by the larger thickness of the triangular profile. Further research needs to be done in order to fully understand the causes of this result. Nevertheless, the device and methodology reached the goal of giving insights about such covers performance.

As for the orientation, results show that for the specific period of time in which the experiments were carried out, the conditions for the azimuth angle of 286° were better. Both experiments show how the methodology of using Voc and Isc to compare the performance of solar cells can be used and give relevant information about how it changes when cells are subjected to different conditions.

The implementation of the IoT platform was successful. Field tests on different locations can now be performed for extended periods of time given that the device is stand-alone and capable of sending data over a mobile network, reaching the objective of comparing solar cells exposed to different conditions.

The fully operative device had a total cost of approximately 70USD, which is much affordable than the solar cells curve tracers. This makes the proposed circuit an attractive and cost-effective option for solar cells comparison.

Although the validation experiment indicates that the coefficient of determination (R^2) is 0.9981 and 0.986 for current and voltage respectively, giving validity to the measurements and guaranteeing its reliability on the fields tests carried out, it is necessary to design and perform more experiments to confirm the validity of the proposed methodology.

Acknowledgements. Authors would like to thank Universidad EAFIT and the alliance "ENERGETICA 2030", which is a Research Program, with code 58667 from the "*Colombia Científica*" initiative, funded by The World Bank through the call "778-2017 Scientific Ecosystems". The research program is managed by the Colombian Ministry of Science, Technology and Innovation (Minciencias) with contract No. FP44842-210-2018.

References

1. Amprobe: SOLAR 600 Solar Analyzer (2010), rev. D
2. Bayrak, F., Ertürk, G., Oztop, H.F.: Effects of partial shading on energy and exergy efficiencies for photovoltaic panels. J. Clean. Prod. **164**, 58–69 (2017)
3. Betancur, M., Camargo, V., Betancur, J., Velasquez-Lopez, A., Marulanda, J., Toro, V.: Recubrimiento con elementos optoelectrónicos, 11 March 2016. https://sipi.sic.gov.co/, colombia Patent, ref. 16064118
4. Chauvin Arnoux: FTV200SOLAR PANEL TESTERSI-V Tracer (2012), rev. D
5. Cuce, E., Cuce, P.M., Bali, T.: An experimental analysis of illumination intensity and temperature dependency of photovoltaic cell parameters. Appl. Energy **11**, 374–382 (2013)
6. Despotovic, M., Nedic, V.: Comparison of optimum tilt angles of solar collectors determined at yearly, seasonal and monthly levels. Energy Conv. Manage. **97**, 121–131 (2015)
7. DNV G: Maritime forecast to 2050: Energy transition outlook 2017. DNV GL, Høvik, Norway (2017)
8. Duran, E., Piliougine, M., Sidrach-de Cardona, M., Galan, J., Andujar, J.: Different methods to obtain the I–V curve of PV modules: a review. In: 2008 33rd IEEE Photovoltaic Specialists Conference, pp. 1–6. IEEE (2008)
9. HT Instruments: I-V500wRel. 1.01–06/03/19I-V curve tracer and IVCK tester up to 15A or 1500VDC (2019), rev. D
10. Luna, J.G.P., Coria, L.A.M., Iniesta, S.A., Xochimitl, S.J., González, A.E.J.: Modulo trazador de curvas para caracterizar elementos o dispositivos en la gama de nanoamperes. SOMI Congreso de Instrumentación (2014)
11. Mekhilef, S., Saidur, R., Kamalisarvestani, M.: Effect of dust, humidity and air velocity on efficiency of photovoltaic cells. Renew. Sustain. Energy Rev. **16**(5), 2920–2925 (2012)

12. Moharram, K.A., Abd-Elhady, M.S., Kandil, H.A., El-Sherif, H.: Enhancing the performance of photovoltaic panels by water cooling. Ain Shams Eng. J. **4**(4), 869–877 (2013)
13. (NREL) N.R.E.L.: Best research-cell efficiency chart (2019)
14. (NREL) N.R.E.L.: Champion photovoltaic module efficiency chart (2019)
15. Qu, H., Li, X.: Temperature dependency of the fill factor in PV modules between 6 and 40 °C. J. Mech. Sci. Technol. **33**(4), 1981–1986 (2019). https://doi.org/10.1007/s12206-019-0348-4
16. Ramaprabha, R., Jubair, S., Suhas, K., Lokesh, A.: Design and implementation of efficient curve tracer for photovoltaic system under partial shaded conditions. Int. J. Electr. Eng. Inf. **7**(1), 140 (2015)
17. Reusch, M., Bivour, M., Hermle, M., Glunz, S.W.: Fill factor limitation of silicon heterojunction solar cells by junction recombination. Energy Procedia **38**, 297–304 (2013)
18. Saidan, M., Albaali, A.G., Alasis, E., Kaldellis, J.K.: Experimental study on the effect of dust deposition on solar photovoltaic panels in desert environment. Renew. Energy **92**, 499–505 (2016)
19. Seaward Electronic: PV210 Solar PV tester and I-V curve tracer (2018), rev. D
20. Singh, R.: Why silicon is and will remain the dominant photovoltaic material. J. Nanophotonics **3**(1), 032503 (2009)
21. Solmetric Corporation: Solmetric PVA-1500 Brochure (2018), rev. D
22. Velasquez-Lopez, A., et al.: Elemento estructural tipo ladrillo que permite la fijación de elementos eléctricos, ópticos, electrónicos y electromecánicos, 10 November 2014. https://sipi.sic.gov.co/, Colombia Patent, ref. 14248214
23. Wang, D., Cui, H., Su, G.: A modeling method to enhance the conversion efficiency by optimizing light trapping structure in thin-film solar cells. Solar Energy **120**, 505–513 (2015)
24. Zhang, Y., Stokes, N., Jia, B., Fan, S., Gu, M.: Towards ultra-thin plasmonic silicon wafer solar cells with minimized efficiency loss. Sci. Rep. **4**, 4939 (2014)
25. Zhu, Y., Xiao, W.: A comprehensive review of topologies for photovoltaic I–V curve tracer. Solar Energy **196**, 346–357 (2020)

Speed Estimator Design of an Induction Motor Using an Adaptive Neuro-Fuzzy Inference System (ANFIS)

Jesus Enrique Salamanca Jaimes, Jorge Luis Diaz Rodríguez[✉],
and Jaime Antonio Gonzalez Castellanos

Universidad de Pamplona, Pamplona, Colombia
jexuz27@gmail.com, jdiazcu@gmail.com, gcjaime@gmail.com

Abstract. This paper deals with the speed estimation of an induction motor (IM) based on an Adaptive Neuro-Fuzzy Inference System (ANFIS) for the speed control of the induction machine using the sensorless control technique. The estimation technique ANFIS was reviewed, as well as its implementation detailed. Firstly, the induction motor was simulated with the transformations that allow obtaining the components of the voltages and currents in the direct and quadrature axes. Then the sensorless control method was simulated. Finally, to verify the experimental results, the speed at the output of the ANFIS estimator and the induction motor were compared.

Keywords: Induction motor · Speed estimation · Sensorless control · ANFIS

1 Introduction

The induction machines are used mostly in all types of industrial applications due to the availability of the AC electric power supply as a primary energy source. Thus, the induction motor plays the principal role in modern technological and industrial development. Initially, the DC motors massively used in applications where simple control of motor speed was required, despite the brushes and all de drawbacks associated with its presence. With the advent and develop of power electronics, the number of applications in which the induction motor expanded widely.

Some speed control methods for the induction motors use different control strategies as neural networks [1], sliding mode control [2] and so on. Also different motor control methods such as scalar control [3] or the vector control [4].

The vector control method aims to emulate the behavior of the DC machine since the motor's three-phase coordinate system decoupled into a two-phase rotary coordinate system (as a DC motor) by using the Clarke and Park transformations [5]. This control method allows optimal and effective motor speed control under different loading conditions.

For speed control of an induction motor requires to get measure of the rotor shaft speed. For this reason, commonly use optical encoders or sinusoidal resolvers.

J. C. Figueroa-García et al. (Eds.): WEA 2020, CCIS 1274, pp. 489–500, 2020.
https://doi.org/10.1007/978-3-030-61834-6_42

The resolvers encode the shaft position information by providing a pair of sine and cosine waves signals. Thus, to determine the position information, appropriate phase demodulation algorithms must be applied to sinewave signals [6].

The use of additional external electronic devices such as photosensors and tacho-generator reduces the robustness and reliability of the system and increases its cost. Therefore, it has been an increasingly motivation toward the use of sensorless techniques (without encoder or resolver). By the developing of digital algorithms, known as observers, to estimate the speed of the rotor through the measure of the electrical variables in the motor stator as voltages and currents, even the magnetic flux.

Some methods of rotor speed estimation of the induction motor have been developed, such as the use of Extended Kalman Filter (EKF) [7], Neural Networks (ANN) [8], Adaptive Referential Model Systems [9], Fuzzy Logic [10], and so on. Therefore, we proposed to apply an adaptive neuro-fuzzy inference system to estimate the rotor speed of the induction motor, evaluating its reliability and performance.

2 Induction Motor Modeling

Induction motors are AC electrical machines that can essentially be of two types according to the type of rotor: squirrel cage or wound rotor. In the wound rotor induction motor can access the rotor currents by means of the stator brushes and in this way the torque characteristic of the motor could be modified with some ease, in consideration this type of rotor is larger than the cage rotor of squirrel and require more maintenance due to wear associated with brushes and slip rings.

Therefore, it is not common to use this type of rotor in induction motors, in this way the term induction motor is generalized to the alternating current machine that uses a squirrel cage rotor [11]. So it is of great importance to obtain a mathematical model for the induction motor (Fig. 1), which allows us to implement in a simulation environment and thus useful to study the behavior of the induction machine when used together with devices. electronic switching, speed controls, among other transient processes.

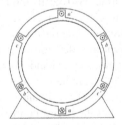

Fig. 1. Schematic representation of a three-phase induction motor.

To simplify the model, considering:

1) Uniform air gap.
2) Linear magnetic circuit.
3) Identical stator windings, spatially distributed to produce a spatial sine m.m.f.

4) Rotor coils or bars arranged so that, the rotor m.m.f. waveform can be considered as a spatial sine waveform that possess the equal number of poles as the m.m.f waveform of the stator voltages [12].

To develop the model, it is necessary to use Clarke transforms in to the induction motor power supply to obtain two 90° phase-shifted voltages ($\alpha\beta 0$ components) from the three-phase voltages (*abc* components), which are 120° phase-shifted. Subsequently, the Park transformation is performed to obtain the *dq* axes (direct and quadrature) voltages. Therefore, taking into account that the motor parameters are measured with respect to the stator windings, the equations for the voltages of a three-phase machines are [14]:

$$v_{qs} = p\lambda_{qs} + \lambda_{ds}\omega + r_s i_{qs} \tag{1}$$

$$v_{ds} = p\lambda_{ds} - \lambda_{qs}\omega + r_s i_{ds} \tag{2}$$

$$v'_{qr} = p\lambda'_{qr} + \lambda'_{dr}(\omega - \omega_r) + r'_r i'_{qr} \tag{3}$$

$$v'_{dr} = p\lambda'_{dr} - \lambda'_{qr}(\omega - \omega_r) + r'_r i'_{dr} \tag{4}$$

Where λ are the flux linkages. The v_{qs}, v_{ds} are the stator quadrature and direct axis voltages. The v'_{qr}, v'_{dr} are the voltages in the rotor, which will be assumed zero considering that the rotor is short-circuited in the squirrel cage. Also, ω is the angular speed in the arbitrary reference system and ω_r is the angular rotor speed rotor [12].

$$i_{qs} = \frac{1}{X_{ls}}\left(\Psi_{qs} - \Psi_{mq}\right) \tag{5}$$

$$i_{ds} = \frac{1}{X_{ls}}(\Psi_{ds} - \Psi_{md}) \tag{6}$$

$$i'_{qr} = \frac{1}{X'_{lr}}\left(\Psi'_{qr} - \Psi_{mq}\right) \tag{7}$$

$$i'_{dr} = \frac{1}{X'_{lr}}\left(\Psi'_{dr} - \Psi_{md}\right) \tag{8}$$

Where i_{qs}, i_{ds} are the stator currents on quadrature and direct frames, i'_{qr}, i'_{dr} are the rotor currents referred to the stator. Since $\Psi_{qs} = \omega_e \lambda_{qs}$, then ω_e being the electrical angular speed at rated frequency and Ψ_{qs}, Ψ_{ds}, Ψ'_{qr}, Ψ'_{dr} are de magnetic flux [12].

$$\Psi_{mq} = X_m\left(i_{qs} + i'_{qr}\right) \tag{9}$$

$$\Psi_{md} = X_m\left(i_{ds} + i'_{dr}\right) \tag{10}$$

By replacing Eqs. 1–4 in 5–8 and solving, obtaining [12]:

$$\Psi_{qs} = \frac{\omega_e}{p}\left[v_{qs} - \frac{\omega}{\omega_e}\Psi_{ds} + \frac{r_s}{X_{ls}}\left(\Psi_{mq} - \Psi_{qs}\right)\right] \tag{11}$$

$$\Psi_{ds} = \frac{\omega_e}{p}\left[v_{ds} + \frac{\omega}{\omega_e}\Psi_{qs} + \frac{r_s}{X_{ls}}(\Psi_{md} - \Psi_{ds})\right] \tag{12}$$

$$\Psi'_{qr} = \frac{\omega_e}{p}\left[v'_{qr} - \left(\frac{\omega - \omega_r}{\omega_e}\right)\Psi'_{dr} + \frac{r'_r}{X'_{lr}}\left(\Psi'_{mq} - \Psi'_{qr}\right)\right] \tag{13}$$

$$\Psi'_{dr} = \frac{\omega_e}{p}\left[v'_{dr} + \left(\frac{\omega - \omega_r}{\omega_e}\right)\Psi'_{qr} + \frac{r'_r}{X'_{lr}}\left(\Psi_{mq} - \Psi'_{dr}\right)\right] \tag{14}$$

$$Te = \frac{nP}{4\omega_e}\left[\Psi'_{qr}i'_{dr} - \Psi'_{dr}i'_{qr}\right] \tag{15}$$

$$\omega_r = \frac{P(T_e - T_l)}{2pJ\omega_e} \tag{16}$$

$$\theta_r = \frac{\omega_r}{p} \tag{17}$$

2.1 Simulation of the Induction Motor Model

The simulation of the induction motor model as well as the speed estimator were developed in Simulink from the Matlab© environment. For the application of the equations that build the induction motor model, it is necessary to obtain the supply voltages on the corresponding dq frames. The Clarke and Park transformations were performed using the blocks available in the Simulink libraries. The subsystem of Fig. 2 requires the three-phase voltages that supply the motor stator, as well as the speed, to obtain the voltages v_{ds} and v_{qs}.

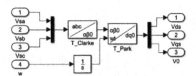

Fig. 2. Clarke and Park transformations.

Figure 3 shows the block diagram of the simulated motor model. It has as input parameters: the three-phase supply voltages, the demanded load torque on the rotor shaft and the reference frame.

The reference frame could be selected:

- Synchronous reference frame, where $w = w_e$.
- Rotor reference frame, where $w = w_r$.
- Stator reference frame, where $w = 0$.

Figure 4 shows the stator and rotor currents on the direct and quadrature axes, the electromagnetic torque and the rotor speed for no-load operation, using the rotor speed as reference frame ($w = w_r$).

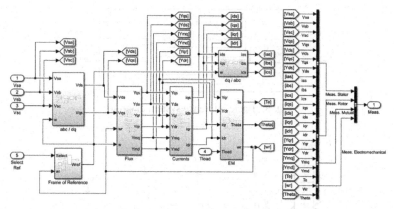

Fig. 3. Induction motor model in *Simulink/Matlab*®.

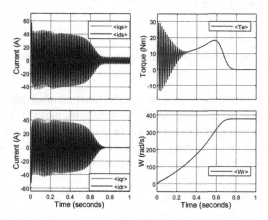

Fig. 4. a) *dq* stator currents. b) electromagnetic torque. c) *dq* rotor current d) rotor speed.

3 Adaptive Neuro-Fuzzy Inference System (ANFIS)

Using a hybrid learning procedure, the proposed ANFIS can construct human-knowledge based input-output mapping (in the form of fuzzy if-then rules) and stipulated input-output data pairs [13].

Primarily setting parameters of activation functions are used in a similar way to the weights of artificial neural networks, this allows self-tuning of rules and membership functions. Figure 5 basically represents a fuzzy inference system [14].

Fuzzy mapping can be represented through a fuzzy association matrix and then moved to activation regions. It can be represented by ANFIS-like networks that can be used correctly for decision mapping in a properly trained fuzzy inference system [14].

Figure 6 shows the ANFIS topology as an adjustable network, in this type of networks fixed nodes appear as circles and adaptable nodes as tables, adjusting in the training process. Also shows a segmentation of a fuzzy system emulated through an adaptive neural network.

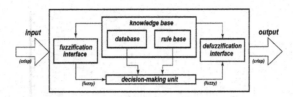

Fig. 5. Basic inference system diagram.

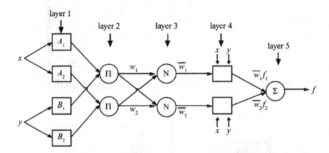

Fig. 6. ANFIS network for the emulation of the inference system.

Layer 1 is for adjusting the parameters of the input membership function. Layers 2 and 3 of the network is for carrying out fuzzy operations, meanwhile layers 4 and 5 are those that carry out a weighting to obtain the output of f system [14].

Assuming that the given training data set has P inputs, we can define the measure error (or energy function) as the sum of the squared errors [13]:

$$E_p = \sum_{m=1}^{L} \left(T_{m,p} - O_{m,p}^L\right)^2 \tag{18}$$

Where T is the desired output vector, L the number of layers and O is the output current vector, therefore the measure of error is [13]:

$$E = \sum_{p=1}^{P} E_p \tag{19}$$

The error rate for the output node in can be calculated from the equation above using the descending gradient method, as:

$$\frac{\partial E_p}{\partial O_{i,p}^L} = -2\left(T_{i,p} - O_{i,p}^L\right) \tag{20}$$

For internal nodes k the error rate can be derived by the chain rule [13]:

$$\frac{\partial E_p}{\partial O_{i,p}^k} = \sum_{m=1}^{k+1} \frac{\partial E_p}{\partial O_{m,p}^{k+1}} \frac{\partial O_{m,p}^{k+1}}{\partial O_{i,p}^k} \tag{21}$$

In this case the error rate of an internal node can be expressed as a linear combination of the error rates of the nodes in the next layer. Using alpha as the network adjustment parameter, we obtain [13]:

$$\frac{\partial E_p}{\partial \alpha} = \sum_{O* \in S} \frac{\partial E_p}{\partial O^*} \frac{\partial O^*}{\partial \alpha} \tag{22}$$

Where S is the set of nodes whose outputs depend on *alpha*. The derivative of the global error measure E with respect to *alpha* is [13]:

$$\frac{\partial E}{\partial \alpha} = \sum_{p=1}^{P} E_p \frac{\partial E_p}{\partial \alpha} \tag{23}$$

The expression for the *alpha* parameter is:

$$\Delta \alpha = -\eta \frac{\partial E}{\partial \alpha} \tag{24}$$

Where η is the learning rate that can be expressed as [13]:

$$\eta = \frac{q}{\sqrt{\sum \alpha \left(\frac{\partial E}{\partial \alpha}\right)^2}} \tag{25}$$

Where q is the step size or length of each gradient transition in the parameter space. This parameter can be varied to change the rate of convergence [13].

4   ANFIS Based Speed Estimator

Several investigations have been conducted with Adaptive Neuro-Fuzzy Inference Systems applied to rotating electrical machines, such as Bonde and Dhok [15], who propose a speed control scheme for the induction motor based on ANFIS. Tripura and Srinivasa [16], propose an intelligent control for a DC motor using ANFIS, Osorio, Molina, Ponce, and Romero [17], propose a model of the induction motor with ANFIS. Nevertheless, this research is focused on developing an ANFIS system that allows estimating the induction motor speed without the need to attach a physical speed sensor to the motor shaft. For this reason, the speed was obtained with the motor voltage and current measurements, that aim to improve the reliability and to reduce maintenance costs using sensorless control.

To develop the estimator, a scalar control was implemented to vary the speed of the induction motor. This control method generates the three-phase voltages that feed the stator of the induction motor. Figure 7 shows the proposed block diagram. In the motor model, the currents in the stator of the induction machine are taken, which will be the estimator inputs together with the three-phase supply voltages. In the estimator, the estimated speed is obtained, which is compared with the speed of the motor model w_r.

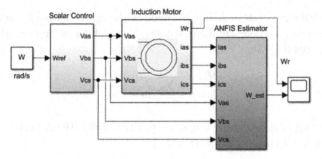

Fig. 7. IM Scalar Control with rotor speed estimator.

The ANFIS speed estimator was developed using *Matlab's ANFIS* tool, as shown in Fig. 8. The trend of the data corresponding to the desired output speed can be observed. Stator voltages (*Vas, Vbs* and *Vcs*) and stator currents (*Ias, Ibs* and *Ics*) are used as inputs. After training the Adaptive Inference System, an estimated output is obtained with a 40.4% error with respect to the desired output.

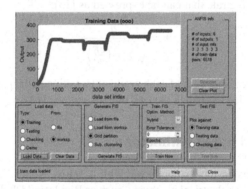

Fig. 8. Matlab ANFIS tool

Figure 9a shows the set-point of the rotor speed. Figure 9b shows the actual rotor speed (*black-colored*) and the estimated rotor speed (*red-colored*). The last was pre-filtered using a Butterworth low-pass filter at 100 rad/s cut-off frequency. Although the rotor speed was estimated and followed the rotor reference speed, its level of accuracy is low. The root means square error (RMSE) is a quantitative performance index commonly used to evaluate the estimation methods. Besides, such a method amplifies and penalizes strongly enough those errors of greater magnitude [18], the expression used to quantify the RMSE is shown in Eq. 26. The RMSE value of the estimator response is 22.6 rad/s concerning the desired output W_r. The average relative error in the steady-state is 2.5%, rising to 35% for speed transitions.

$$RMSE = \sqrt{\frac{1}{n} \sum_{i=1}^{n} (W_{est} - W_r)^2} \qquad (26)$$

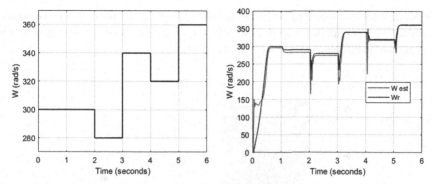

Fig. 9. a) Speed set-point of the control loop. b) Speed estimation using three-phase input data. (Color figure online)

Due to the aforementioned drawbacks, it is chosen to implement the rotor speed estimator using the stator voltages and currents in the direct and quadrature axes, reducing the number of inputs from six (V_{as}, V_{bs}, V_{cs}, I_{as}, I_{bs}, I_{cs}) up to four inputs (V_{ds}, V_{qs}, I_{ds}, I_{qs}). Simplifying the architecture of the adaptive inference system and would decrease the data to be processed, achieving less error in the output of the ANFIS estimator.

The ANFIS tool allows assigning different types of membership functions for the fuzzy inference system, such as: triangular, trapezoidal, Gaussian, Sigmoidal, among others. The estimator error was evaluated according to the membership functions available using the input data on the *dq* reference frames. Table 1 shows the respective errors for each membership function using only three epochs in training. According to this the type of membership function to be used in the estimator is the *gaussmf* with an error in the estimation of only 5.68%. A Butterworth low-pass filter is then applied to the output to reduce noise and smooth the response, reducing the error shown in Table 1.

Table 1. Rule-base.

Membership functions	Error (%)
Trimf	8.67
Trapmf	27.2
Gbellmf	6.44
Gaussmf	5.68
Gauss2mf	10.39
Pimf	30.95
Dsigmf	9.21
Psigmf	9.21

Additionally, it is chosen to increase the number of training periods to decrease the error percentage respecting the desired output. It is evident that increasing training periods produces a minimum decrease in the error percentage, in the order of thousandths of a percentage per applied period, as well as a significant increase in training time. The topology of the inference system shown in Fig. 10.

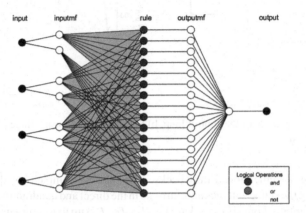

Fig. 10. ANFIS estimator topology.

The number of rules is determined by the expression a^n, where a is the number of membership functions and n is the number of entries in the system, obtaining 16 rules. Figure 11 shows the rule base of the adaptive inference system with Gaussian membership functions.

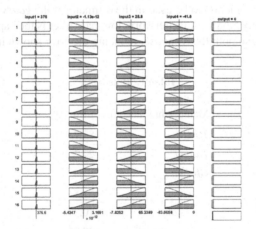

Fig. 11. ANFIS rule base.

Figure 12a shows the estimator output for the first 2 s and Fig. 12b for the remaining 4 s to better visualize the response, W_{est} (red-colored) and the desired output, W_r (black-colored). Using the data at the input on the dq reference axes. It is observed that the estimated speed tends to be very close to the speed of the induction motor. This obviously improves its accuracy, it can be verified by comparing it with the estimated speed, with the data in the three-phase input shown in Fig. 9b.

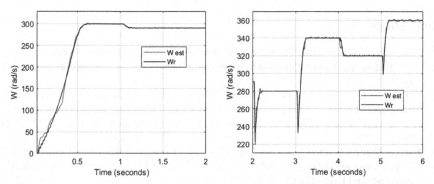

Fig. 12. a) Speed estimation 0-2 s *dq* input data. b) Speed estimation 2-6 s *dq* input data. (Color figure online)

Figure 12a shows the output of the rotor speed estimator with a load of 10 Nm, applied one second after the motor startup. There is a slight decrease in output response, typical of the scalar control method used, even under load conditions the estimator closely follows the desired output. According to Eq. 26, the RMSE value is 3.9 rad/s, much lower than the 22.6 rad/s of the previous case study. At motor starting a higher error was observed in the estimator response. At speed transitions, the relative error does not exceed 5%, a much lower percentage than the error observed in Fig. 9a which was sometimes up to 35%. A considerable reduction can also be observed in the steady-state relative error, which is 0.26% on average, compared to the estimator using three-phase data where the average error was 2.5%. From the above, a major improvement is evidenced by using as input data the magnitudes in the *dq* reference frame (V_{ds}, V_{qs}, I_{ds}, and I_{qs}) instead of the three-phase magnitudes (V_{as}, V_{bs}, V_{cs}, I_{as}, I_{bs}, and I_{cs}).

5 Conclusions

It was observed that the estimated output follows with a high degree of precision and accuracy at the speed of the induction motor with minimal steady-state errors, adaptive systems based on fuzzy logic can be a useful alternative to sensorless control systems, replacing physical measurement on the motor shaft. This reduces additional acquisition and installation costs, as well as the number of maintenance man-hours.

It is important the use of Clarke and Park transformations to simplify the speed estimator. This allows to reduce the Adaptive Fuzzy Inference System inputs from 6 to 4. Achieving a less complex network architecture and also fewer computation operations, rules and membership functions, which in fact reduce considerably the output error.

It was found that with increasing training periods, the output error of the adaptive inference system does not decrease significantly, which must be evaluated for each particular case.

Thus, filtering the output response of the speed estimator is essential, as it allows a major noise reduction and steady-state oscillation as well, which could be significant depending on the control strategy applied.

References

1. Martínez Quintero, C., Díaz Rodríguez, J.L., Pardo García, A.: Application of neural networks to AC motors speed control. Revista Colombiana de Tecnologías de Avanzada 2(20), 113–118 (2012)
2. Bermeo, W.L., De Sousa, A.B., Fernandez, T.R., Honório, D.A., Nogueira, L.L., Barreto, L.: Sliding model control applied in current loop for a DSP- based position control applied to squirrel-cage induction motor. Revista Colombiana de Tecnologías de Avanzada 1(27), 26–32 (2016)
3. Jinl, S., Wang, Z., Zhul, L., Zong, M., Zhang, F.: Constant V/Hz control based on DSP for open winding doubly-fed wind power generator. In: IEEE Transportation Electrification Conference and Expo (ITEC), pp 822–827 (2016)
4. Alzate Gómez, A., Escobar Mejía, A., Torres, C.: Control vectorial de la máquina de inducción. Scientia et Technica 3(43), 55–60 (2009)
5. Li, W., Xu, Z., Zhang, Y.: Induction motor control system based on FOC algorithm. In: IEEE 8th Joint International Information Technology and Artificial Intelligence Conference, pp 1544–1548 (2019)
6. Ye, G., Zhao, G., Liu, H., Lu, B.: Precise phase demodulation algorithm for sinusoidal encoders and resolvers. IEEE Trans. Industr. Electron. 67(10), 8778–8787 (2019)
7. González, J., Silveira, M., Pacheco, J.: Comparación de la red neuronal y el filtro de Kalman en la estimación de velocidad del motor de inducción. I Congreso Iberoamericano de Estudiantes de Ingeniería Eléctrica (2004)
8. Gallo, M., Gonzalez, J.A., Diaz, J.L., Velazco, J.A.: Estimation of the induction engine speed using neural networks. Revista Colombiana de Tecnologías de Avanzada 1(29), 111–117 (2017)
9. Kumar, B., Chauhan, Y.K., Singh, S.P.: MRAS based speed estimation strategies for induction motor drives: a review. In: 7th India International Conference on Power Electronics, Patiala, pp 1–4 (2016)
10. Divandari, M., Rezaei, B., Amiri, E.: Indirect speed estimation of high speed brushless DC motor drive using fuzzy logic current compensator. In: 2017 IEEE International Electric Machines and Drives Conference, Miami, pp 1–6 (2017)
11. Chapman, S.J.: Máquinas eléctricas, 5th edn. McGraw-Hill, México (2012)
12. Orille, A.L., Sowilam, G.M.A., Valencia, J.A.: A new simulation of symmetrical three phase induction motor under transformations of park. Comput. Ind. Eng. 37, 359–362 (1999)
13. Jang, J.S.R.: ANFIS: adaptive-network-based fuzzy inference system. IEEE Trans. Syst. Man Cybern. 23(3), 665–685 (1993)
14. Ponce Cruz, P.: Inteligencia artificial con aplicaciones a la ingenieria, 1st edn. Alfaomega, México (2010)
15. Bonde, S., Dhok, G.: ANFIS control scheme for the speed control of the induction motor. Int. J. Eng. Res. Appl. 4(3), 35–39 (2014)
16. Tripura, P., Srinivasa, Y.: Intelligent speed control of DC motor using ANFIS. J. Intell. Fuzzy Syst. 26(1), 223–227 (2014)
17. Osorio, J., Molina, A., Ponce, P., Romero, D.: Induction motor model with ANFIS. In: Electronics, Robotics and Automotive Mechanics Conference (2011)
18. Masoud, I., Sahiner, A., Ozturk, M.: Temperature and pressure based estimation of daily global solar radiation over turkey using fuzzy logic modeling. Int. J. Recent Sci. Res. 10(01), 30559–30565 (2019)

Photovoltaic Array Fault Detection Algorithm Based on Least Significant Difference Test

Luis Diego Murillo-Soto[✉][iD] and Carlos Meza[iD]

Costa Rica Institute of Technology, Cartago 30101, Costa Rica
{lmurillo,cmeza}@tec.ac.cr
http://www.tec.ac.cr

Abstract. One major concern in solar systems is the health of the solar installation, specifically related to the undetected faults in the photovoltaic array. Any fault in the array could provoke power losses in the system and may generate security risks for the operative and technical personnel.

The present paper proposes a novel fault detection and location algorithm in PV arrays. The algorithm is validated using numerical simulations of a PV array with the following faults: diode short circuit, open circuit, degradation of the parasitic serial resistance, and partial shadows.

The proposed fault detection algorithm is based on the idea that a set of quasi-identical PV modules produces statistical equivalent results when faced with the same stimulus such as irradiance and temperature. All the modules should be connected at the same maximum power point tracker (MPPT). If there is one element affected by one fault its measurements will be different from the unaffected modules. The authors present a pseudo-code for this idea and tested in Simulink®. The obtained results show the proposed algorithm can detect and locate faults occurring in the solar array with a delay of 3 samples.

Keywords: Fault location in solar array · Least significant difference test · Real time algorithm

1 Introduction

The production engineers in photo-voltaic (PV) plants are always interested in the yield because this is part of the return on investment, a key economic indicator. To calculate it accurately, the monitoring systems is nowadays an obligation, an extended review is shown in [14]. On the other hand, undetected faults could down the power production [24] and the efficiencies [20].

This work was supported by scholarship program of the Costa Rica Institute of Technology and the VIE project 5402-1341-1701.

© Springer Nature Switzerland AG 2020
J. C. Figueroa-García et al. (Eds.): WEA 2020, CCIS 1274, pp. 501–515, 2020.
https://doi.org/10.1007/978-3-030-61834-6_43

The fault detection techniques applied to solar systems are a growing field with many proposals such as the ones mentioned in [15,23]. These techniques according to [16] can be classified as (1) image analysis and (2) electrical characterization. Imaging methods are currently expensive and time-consuming, whereas electrical characterization is cheaper and more flexible [3], however, the selection of the technique depends on the type of failure mode, for instance, the delamination of Ethylene Vinyl Acetate (EVA) could be more evident with imaging analysis than electric analysis. The electrical characterization can be further divided into the following techniques:

- signal processing and statistical methods (e.g.., [10,26])
- $i - v$ curve characteristics analysis (e.g.., [2,5,18])
- power losses analysis (e.g.., [6,11])
- current and/or voltage measurements (e.g.., [7,19,21]).
- artificial intelligent methods (e.g.., [4,12])

There are many types of faults that can be studied at the PV module level ([13]) or at the PV system level ([1,15]). Generally speaking, these faults can be classified according to their event duration as temporal or permanent. Faults occur in different parts of the PV system, e.g.., at the DC side or at the AC side of the solar system. The faults at the DC side can be further classified as inverter failures or solar array failures. The faults in the solar array also can be clustered in the following groups: short circuits, open circuits, mismatches, short circuit to ground, bypass diode failure, electric arcs, bridging, asymmetrical short circuits. The detailed explanation of these failure modes can be found in [15].

This study focuses on the detection of five common faults in solar arrays, i.e., internal degradation, internal open circuit, module's short circuit, string open circuit and shadows.

This paper is particularly interested in the statistical methods because they don't depend on the identification of the model-base of the solar module. This means that it is not necessary to know the model's parameters, instead, the statistical methods work only with the behavior of the signals. In this work, these signals are PV string currents and the differential voltage of the modules.

This work is divided into six sections as following: the photovoltaic model used to generate the synthetic data is presented in Sect. 2. The proposed algorithm based on the least significant difference test is presented in Sect. 3, the simulated experiment, the results obtained and the analysis are presented in Sects. 4, 5 and 6 respectively.

2   System Modeling

2.1   PV Module Model

The electrical behavior of a PV module is modeled using the five-parameter model described in [22,25] which comprises of Eqs. (1), (3) and (4). The description of the parameters used in the aforementioned expressions is shown in Table 1 and their implementation in Simulink® is illustrated in Fig. 1 (Table 2).

$$I = I_{ph} - I_s \left(e^{\left(\dfrac{V + IR_s}{aV_t} \right)} - 1 \right) - \dfrac{(V + IR_s)}{R_p} \tag{1}$$

$$V_t = \dfrac{N_s kT}{q} \tag{2}$$

$$I_{ph} = (I_{ph,n} + K_I \cdot \Delta_T) \cdot \dfrac{G}{G_n}, \ \Delta_T = T - T_n, \tag{3}$$

$$I_s = \dfrac{I_{ph,n} + K_I \cdot \Delta_T}{e^{\left(\dfrac{V_{oc,n} + K_V \cdot \Delta_T}{aV_t} \right)} - 1}, \tag{4}$$

Table 1. Parameters for the PV model used. (Standard Test Conditions (STC): Irradiance of 1000 W/m², a temperature 298.15 K and an air mass of 1.5.)

Parameter	Description
I	Current generated by the PV module
V	Voltage drop across the PV module
a	Ideality factor
R_s	Serial resistance, considered constant
R_p	Parallel resistance, considered constant
N_s	Number of cells in series in the PV module
V_t	Thermal voltage defined according to (2)
I_{ph}	Photocurrent defined according to (3)
I_s	Diode saturation current defined according(4)
k	Boltzmann constant (1.38×10^{-23} J/K)
q	Charge of the electron (1.6×10^{-19} C)
T	Temperature of the p-n junction
T_n	Temperature at Standard Test Conditions (STC) ($T_n = 298.15$ K)
$I_{ph,n}$	Photocurrent measured at STC
K_I	Short circuit current thermal coefficient
G	Perpendicular irradiance to the module
G_n	Irradiance at STC ($G_n = 1000$ W/m²)
K_V	Thermal coefficient for the open circuit voltage
$V_{oc,n}$	Open circuit voltage measured at STC

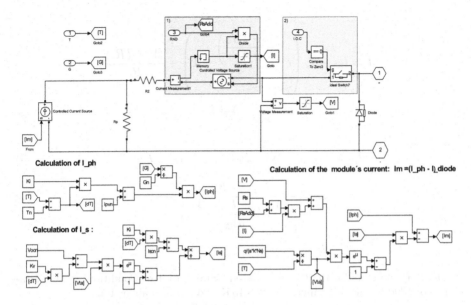

Fig. 1. Solar module implemented in Simulink® according to [25]

2.2 Fault Modeling

The proposed fault detection algorithm has been constructed to be effective with faults related with internal degradation, internal open circuit, module's short circuit, string open circuit and partial shadowing. Such sub-optimal conditions have been simulated as described below:

- Internal degradation: According to [2] the PV module degradation causes an increase in the internal series resistance. This effect is modeled using a controlled voltage source in series with the PV module internal resistance as shown in the light orange box of Fig. 1. The value of the additional resistance can be modified during the simulation (Using port 3 called RND shown in Fig. 1).
- Internal open circuit: This fault is simulated with controllable normally-close (NC) single-pole-single-throw (SPST) switch in series with R_s resistance as shown in Fig. 1 (light green box). Port 4 (IOC signal) shown in Fig. 1 allows to activate this switch during the simulation time.
- Module's short circuit: This condition is emulated similarly than the open-circuit failure. A controllable normally-open (NO) SPST switch is included at the output of a PV module in parallel with the bypass diode, as shown with the green blocks Fig. 2.
- String open circuit: A controllable NC SPST switch is included between modules in a string to emulate the string open circuit faults. The aforementioned switches are colored blue in Fig. 2.
- Partial shadowing: This suboptimal condition is simulated modifying the irradiance magnitude in each PV module, labeled G in Fig. 1 and 2.

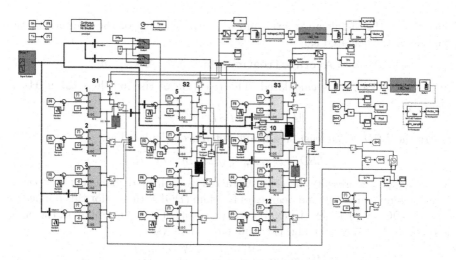

Fig. 2. Simulated test bench for the faults in the solar array

3   Proposed Algorithm

The proposed algorithm is based on the Least Significant Difference (LSD) test explained in [17] used to determine if the difference between two averages is statistically significant. This technique applies to a set of quasi-identical elements, such that, given a set of n elements generates $n(n-1)/2$ comparisons to determine which of them is different.

To apply the LSD technique to the PV array detection algorithm we construct a matrix A, (5), consisting of m rows of n columns,i.e.,

$$\mathbf{A}\,[k,i] = \begin{pmatrix} a_{1,1} & a_{1,2} & \cdots & a_{1,n} \\ a_{2,1} & a_{k,i} & \cdots & a_{2,n} \\ \vdots & \vdots & \ddots & \vdots \\ a_{m,1} & a_{m,2} & \cdots & a_{m,n} \end{pmatrix} \qquad (5)$$

Each row represents an electrical measurement (e.g.. voltage, current or power) perform on each of the n possible PV modules that are part of the analyzed array. Thus, each column represents measurement data from the same PV module (called treatments) taken at different instants. The number of samples m recorded in the treatment is fixed, and this is the size of the moving window. According to the aforementioned definition, the LSD is formulated as (6).

$$\begin{aligned} \mathbf{H_0} &: \bar{a}_i = \bar{a}_j \\ \mathbf{H_1} &: \bar{a}_i \neq \bar{a}_j \\ \alpha &= 0.05 \\ \forall i, j &\in \{n\}, |i \neq j \end{aligned} \qquad (6)$$

where α is the significance level and $\bar{a}_i$ is the average of the samples in the treatment i, calculated as:

$$\bar{a}_i = \mathbf{AverageTreatment}[i] = \Sigma_{k=1}^m \mathbf{A}[k,i]/m, \tag{7}$$

in the same way, $\bar{a}_j$ is calculated. The rejection of the null hypothesis $\mathbf{H_0}$ is given by:

$$\|\bar{a}_i - \bar{a}_j\| > LSD \quad | \, i \neq j, \tag{8}$$

where the LSD is the least significant difference calculated as,

$$LSD = t_{\alpha/2, mn-n} \sqrt{2\, MSerror/m}. \tag{9}$$

The $t_{\alpha/2, mn-n}$ represents the value extracted from the T-distribution for specific level of significance $\alpha/2$ and degrees of freedom (DOF). Hence, for this particular case the DOF is given by the expression $(mn - n)$. The mean square of the error is presented as $MSerror$ and is calculated as follows,

$$MSerror = \frac{SSTotal - SSTreatment}{mn - n}, \tag{10}$$

where $SSTotal$ is the total sum of squares, i.e.,

$$SSTotal = \Sigma_{i=1}^n \Sigma_{k=1}^m (\mathbf{A}[k,i])^2 - \frac{TotalSum^2}{mn}, \tag{11}$$

and the $SSTreatment$ is calculated as,

$$SSTreatment = \frac{\Sigma_{i=1}^n \left(\Sigma_{k=1}^m \mathbf{A}[k,i]\right)^2}{m} - \frac{TotalSum^2}{mn}, \tag{12}$$

finally, the $TotalSum$ is obtained as,

$$TotalSum = \Sigma_{i=1}^n \Sigma_{k=1}^m \mathbf{A}[k,i]. \tag{13}$$

For all the $n(n-1)/2$ LSD tests, a square matrix of size n, called $\mathbf{Alarm}[\cdot]$, is needed to record the binary results. One alarm activates when the following condition holds

$$\mathbf{Alarm}[i,j] = \begin{cases} True & \text{if } \|\bar{a}_i - \bar{a}_j\| > LSD \\ False & \text{if } \|\bar{a}_i - \bar{a}_j\| \leq LSD \end{cases}, \quad \forall i,j \in \{n\}, |i \neq j. \tag{14}$$

Finally, the detection of the fault event in the element i occurs when that element generates $(n-1)$ true alarms. This can be formulated as follows,

$$\mathbf{Fault}[i] = \wedge_{j=1}^{n-1} \mathbf{Alarm}[i,j], \quad \forall i,j \in \{n\}, |i \neq j, \tag{15}$$

this last equation allow us to locate that the i-element has statistically abnormal behavior with respect to the rest of elements analyzed. Notice that the $\mathbf{Fault}[\cdot]$ vector has size of $(1 \times n)$.

The foregoing expressions are integrated into an algorithm for the detection of faulty PV modules in an array. The pseudo-code of this algorithm is presented in (1), where lines 6–15 show how $MSerror$ is calculated. The LSD is obtained in line 15 where the T-value selected automatically for an α equal to 0.05 and $(nm-n)$ degrees of freedom. Lines 17 to 20 represent the alarm detection segment and the fault location defined in (15) is implemented from line 21 to 29.

Algorithm 1: Fault location algorithm base on LSD Test

---

1 *Input data:* **A** of size $m \times n$
2 *Output data:* **Fault** of size $1 \times n$
3 *InternalVariables:* **AverageTreatment, SumVector, Alarm,** *TotalSum*
   SumSamplesSquared, SumVectorSquared, SSTotal, SSTreatment, MSerror row,
   col
   /* For all the internal variables put to zero   */
4 ∀ *InternalVariables* ← **0**
   /* This line define the size ot input matrix   */
5 $[row, col] \leftarrow SIZE(\mathbf{A})$
   /* This block calculates the Mean Square Error (MSerror)   */
6 **for** *i=1:col* **do**
7   **for** *k=1:row* **do**
8   **SumVector**[i]← **A**[k,i] +**SumVector**[i]
9   *SumSamplesSquared*←(**A**[k,i])^2+*SumSamplesSquared*
10   **AverageTreatment**[i]← **SumVector**[i]/*row*
11   *SumVectorSquared* ← (**SumVector**[i])^2+*SumSamplesSquared*
12   *TotalSum*← **SumVector**[i]+*TotalSum*
13 $SSTotal \leftarrow SumSamplesSquared - TotalSum^2/(row\ col)$
14 $SSTreatment \leftarrow SumVectorSquared/row - TotalSum^2/(row\ col)$
15 $MSeror \leftarrow (SSTotal - SSTreatment)/(row\ col - col)$
   /* This line calculates the Least Significant Difference   */
16 $LSD = t_{(0.025, row\ col-col)}\sqrt{2MSerror/row}$
   /* This calculates if the pairwise differences are significant   */
17 **for** *i=1:col* **do**
18   **for** *j=i+1:col* **do**
19   **if** *ABS(AverageTreatment[i]-AverageTreatment[j])>LSD* **then**
20   **Alarm**[i,j]←1

   /* This finds the element that is different among the pairwise   */
21 **for** *i=1:col* **do**
22   **for** *j=i+1:col* **do**
23   **Fault**[i]←**Fault**[i] + **Alarm**[i,j]
24   **for** *k=1:i* **do**
25   **Fault**[i]←**Fault**[i] + **Alarm**[k,i]
26   **if** *Fault[i]/(col-1)=1* **then**
27   **Fault**[i]← 1
28   **else**
29   **Fault**[i]← 0

---

4   Case Simulated

The simulated test bench to prove the LSD algorithm consists of three strings with four solar modules each one, such as it is shown in Fig. 2. The three strings are tagged as S1, S2, S3 and the modules position are tagged sequentially, these tags are calculated with the position (i, j) in the array as $((j - 1) \cdot 3 + i)$, where j is the column and i is the row.

The parameters used for the simulated PV modules correspond to data of the KC200GT PV module according to Villalva [25] and summarized in Table 2. It is important to mention, that the panels in the simulated model should not consider equals, in practice, solar panels from the same production batch don't generate the same output power because there are mismatches provoked by defective materials or small changes in the manufacturing lines. This electric mismatch is evident in the measurement of the output power, normally the power losses are proportional to the variance of the maximum power point current, this is $Losses(\%) \propto \sigma^2_{Imp}$, and typically this power loss is around 0.5% in [9], for this study to simulate this condition the parameter R_s change according to the normal distribution using a standard deviation of 0.5% or $R_s/200$.

Table 2. Value of the parameters the PV module

Parameter	Value
$I_{ph,n}$	8.215 A
I_s	9.825e-08 A
R_s	$\mathcal{N}(0.221, 1.1\text{E-}3)$ Ω
R_p	415.405 Ω
$V_{oc,n}$	32.9 V
a	1.3
N_s	54
K_V	$-1.230\text{e-}1$ V/K
K_I	3.180e-3 A/K

The stimulus signals of the simulated plant are divided into two groups, the ambient, and the fault variables. The standard test condition was chosen to simulate the operation point, this irradiance value is $1000 \, \text{W/m}^2$ and cell temperature of 298.15 K. It is evident that the solar irradiance change during the day, but in tropical countries, with clear skies, from 9:00 am to 3:00 pm, the irradiance change to little in periods less than 36 s, hence the irradiance model could be considered in average constant for a few seconds as in this experiment (21 s). For instance, the irradiance in Cartago, Costa Rica, on March 15, at 9 am could be $930.01 \, \text{W/m}^2$ after 36 s the irradiance has increased only 0.0181%, thereafter at midday, this percentage decrease to only 0.000021%. On the other hand, the irradiance over the solar array has small deviations provoked by dust, dew, or variations in the atmosphere. To capture these effects, the irradiance is modeled as a normal distribution with a standard deviation of 2.5, $\mathcal{N}(1000,2.5)$ for every solar panel. The generation of these random numbers was implemented by the Matlab software using a 32-bit multiplicative congruential generator as described in [8].

During the simulation time, the solar array is affected by the different faults twice in several locations. Each fault has a duration of one second and always start in odd seconds. The fault location and the order is set randomly. Table 3 shows the order of the faults applied, the starting and the ending time, the string location, the module position (i, j) in the array, and its tag number. With these information the signals vector is built, inside Fig. 2, the gray box called *Signal Builder1* generates the faults commands.

Table 3. Programmed faults applied to the PV plant.

	Fault type	Interval (Sec)	String	Module position	Tag
F1	Short-circuit	1–2	1	(1,1)	1
F2	Internal O.C	3–4	3	(1,3)	9
F3	Shadow (100 W/m^2)	5–6	1	(4,1)	4
F4	Degradation ($\uparrow 2R_s$)	7–8	2	(2,2)	6
F5	String O.C	9–10	2	(3,2)	7
F6	Internal O.C	11–12	1	(3,1)	3
F7	Degradation ($\uparrow 2R_s$)	13–14	3	(4,3)	12
F8	String O.C	15–16	3	(2,3)	10
F9	Shadow (100 W/m^2)	17–18	2	(1,2)	5
F10	Short-circuit	19–20	3	(3,3)	11

In order to detect/locate the faults, all the modules have a voltage sensor connected in parallel to their output terminals, also, each string has a current sensor. With these voltage and current signals two LSD test algorithms can be applied to detect and locate the faults in simulation time, i.e, real time, the orange boxes in the Fig. 2 haves the implementations. If the current signals are used the LSD algorithm indicates the string where the fault occurs, for this case the matrix **A** has size of(4×3) samples.

On the other hand, if voltage signals are used then the LSD algorithm locates the fault inside the solar array, i.e., it indicates which PV module is faulty, the matrix **A** built has a size of (4×12) samples, notice that in both cases, the window size or the number of samples in the treatment is four samples. These two cases demonstrate that this algorithm can be applied to different types of measurements, the orange boxes in Fig. 2. The current and voltage signals are sampled by the zero order hold every 0.1 s and after applying the LSD algorithm a moving average filter is applied in order to prevent false positives, i.e,

$$Result_i = \lfloor (sample_i + sample_{i-1})/2 \rfloor \quad . \tag{16}$$

5   Results

Every fault listed in Table 3 affects the output power of the solar array, their voltages and currents. Normally, the severity in terms of output power is related with the fault type, for instance, degradation failures {F4,F7} affect less the outcome power than open-circuit faults {F5,F8}, this can appreciated in the Fig. 3. The solar array was operated in a suboptimal and fixed point, the idea was to observe clearly the changes in the electrical variables measured with the certainty that no other variable is affecting the circuit. For example, the increase and reduction of the power was caused by the fault itself and not by the maximum power point tracker algorithm. Another reason is that in the maximum power point for this array configuration (4 × 3) panles, the short circuit faults {F1, F10} causes that the blocking diode opens and the string currents decreases to zero. Such situation was avoided for the sake of the clarity of the analysis.

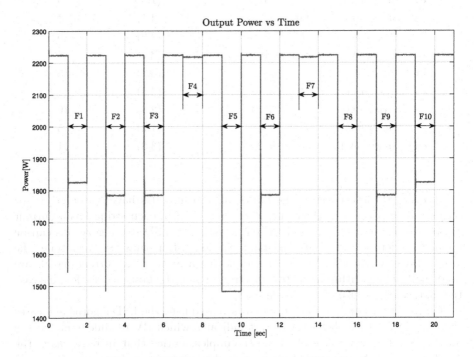

Fig. 3. Behavior of the output power of the array

Figure 4 shows the results of the LSD algorithm for the string currents. It can be observed that the sequence of the fault location was correct. The faults occurred in the following string order $\{1, 3, 1, 2, 2, 1, 3, 3, 2, 3\}$, the same shown in the chart of Fig. 4. It is also interesting to see that the results have a sample delay of 3 samples and this depends directly of the data processing related with the size of the window chosen in the algorithm (number m).

In the same way, when the LSD algorithm was applied to the voltage signals, it locates correctly the faulty module. The faults were applied to specific modules in the following order: $\{1, 9, 4, 6, 7, 3, 12, 10, 5, 11\}$. As can be seen in Fig. 5 the sequence of the faults was correctly decoded by the algorithm.

A very important aspect of the LSD algorithm is the detection of the un-fault situations, this means the capability of the algorithm to detect that there aren't faults affecting the solar array. In Fig. 4 and 5 this ability of the algorithm can be observed. Another positive characteristic of this algorithm is capable to detect five different faults no matter the fault type was. This doesn't mean the algorithm is infallible, special care has to be taken when simultaneous faults of the same type occur because this situation can hide the faults. The aforementioned can be explained as follows, two or more faulty elements could be producing statically equivalent signals between them hence the algorithm can not distinguish the faulty modules because any of them could fulfill the Eq. (15). This disadvantage is being solved in the next version of the algorithm.

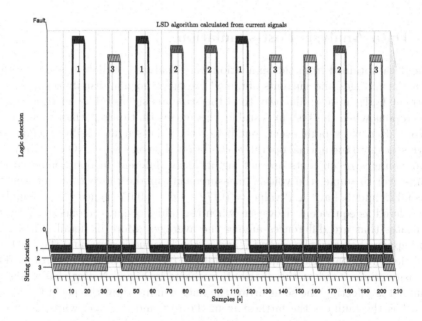

Fig. 4. Results of the LSD algorithm with current signals

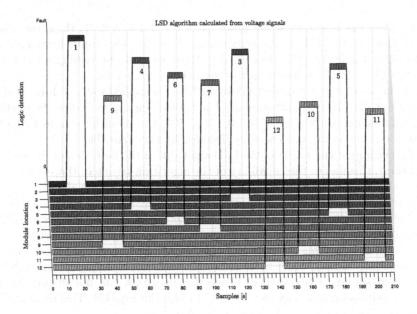

Fig. 5. Results of the LSD algorithm with voltage signals

6 Data Analysis Post-simulation

The data obtained from the simulation were analyzed off-line, it is easy to find that the voltages and currents obtained present a normal distribution with and without faults in a similar way than the stimulus signals. The analysis is done by sections when the system is stable, this means that data gathered can not be mixed after every fault event, but before the events it is possible because this corresponds to the normal operative condition. The one-way ANOVA determines that voltages or currents are not significantly different in operations without faults. For example, the voltage measurements in the range time between the second 2 and 3 have a P-value $= 0.172 > \alpha = 0.05$, hence they should be considered as equivalent. However, when the faults occur, the one-way ANOVA indicates that are differences among the averages. More in detail, when fault F4 happens between the second 7 and 8, the P-value is zero, and the LSD test and the Tukey pairwise compassions indicate the presence of three groups. This is easily appreciated in the distribution charts in Fig. 6. Notice that when the fault F4 is affecting the solar array, the data coming from the panel 6 (the one who has the fault) is the farthest from the rest and is alone, while the others measurements are grouped in two clusters, the group of the normal panels, and the groups of the affected panels.

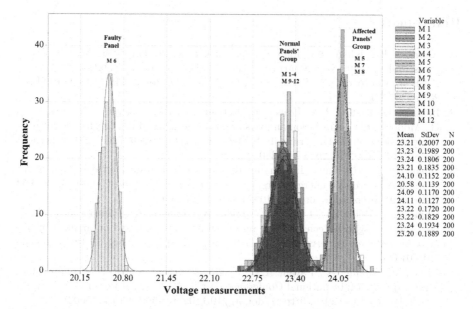

Fig. 6. Distribution of the voltage measurements when the fault F4 is stable.

7 Conclusion

The intention of the presented algorithm is processing in real-time current or voltage measurements to distinguish one offset from the averages. The algorithm is based on the least significant difference test to detect faulty modules on the PV array. This is capable to detect and locate different fault types, also it detects when the fault has been solved and it does not produce false detection. The algorithm has a delay due to the data processing that is limited to 4 measurement samples and does not affect the interpretation.

The algorithm has been tested with five different failures distributed randomly in the array. The results are satisfactory but special care must be taken because only one failure can occur at a time, this is explained because the criteria to accept or reject faults is too severe and the simultaneous faults don't pass it. However, we are working on the next version to correct this by changing the Eq. (15).

This novel lightweight algorithm can be used in embedded systems or microcontrollers because it requires low data processing power and is completely independent of any physical model of a solar module that may be difficult to solve in real-time.

References

1. Alam, M.K., Khan, F., Johnson, J., Flicker, J.: A comprehensive review of catastrophic faults in PV arrays: types, detection, and mitigation techniques. IEEE J. Photovolt. **5**(3), 982–997 (2015). https://doi.org/10.1109/JPHOTOV. 2015.2397599
2. Bastidas-Rodriguez, J.D., Franco, E., Petrone, G., Ramos-Paja, C.A., Spagnuolo, G.: Model-based degradation analysis of photovoltaic modules through series resistance estimation. IEEE Trans. Ind. Electron. **62**(11), 7256–7265 (2015). https://doi.org/10.1109/TIE.2015.2459380
3. Chen, H., Yi, H., Jiang, B., Zhang, K., Chen, Z.: Data-driven detection of hot spots in photovoltaic energy systems. IEEE Trans. Syst. Man Cybern. Syst. **PP**, 1–8 (2019). https://doi.org/10.1109/TSMC.2019.2896922
4. Chine, W., Mellit, A., Lughi, V., Malek, A., Sulligoi, G., Massi Pavan, A.: A novel fault diagnosis technique for photovoltaic systems based on artificial neural networks. Renew. Energy **90**, 501–512 (2016). https://doi.org/10.1016/j.renene. 2016.01.036
5. Chine, W., Mellit, A., Pavan, A.M., Lughi, V.: Fault diagnosis in photovoltaic arrays. In: 2015 International Conference on Clean Electrical Power (ICCEP), pp. 67–72. IEEE, June 2015. https://doi.org/10.1109/ICCEP.2015.7177602
6. Chouder, A., Silvestre, S.: Automatic supervision and fault detection of PV systems based on power losses analysis. Energy Convers. Manage. **51**(10), 1929–1937 (2010). https://doi.org/10.1016/j.enconman.2010.02.025
7. Davarifar, M., Rabhi, A., El Hajjaji, A.: Comprehensive modulation and classification of faults and analysis their effect in DC side of photovoltaic system. Energy Power Eng. **5**(04), 230 (2013)
8. Devroye, L.: Sample-based non-uniform random variate generation. In: Proceedings of the 18th Conference on Winter Simulation, pp. 260–265 (1986)
9. Evans, R., Boreland, M., Green, M.A.: A holistic review of mismatch loss: from manufacturing decision making to losses in fielded arrays. Solar Energy Mater. Solar Cells **174**, 214–224 (2018). https://doi.org/10.1016/j.solmat.2017.08.041
10. Garoudja, E., Harrou, F., Sun, Y., Kara, K., Chouder, A., Silvestre, S.: Statistical fault detection in photovoltaic systems. Solar Energy **150**, 485–499 (2017). https://doi.org/10.1016/j.solener.2017.04.043
11. Huang, C., Wang, L.: Simulation study on the degradation process of photovoltaic modules. Energy Convers. Manage. **165**(March), 236–243 (2018). https://doi.org/ 10.1016/j.enconman.2018.03.056
12. Huang, Y., Lu, J., Liu, C., Xu, X., Wang, W., Zhou, X.: Comparative study of power forecasting methods for PV stations. In: 2010 International Conference on Power System Technology, pp. 1–6. IEEE, October 2010. https://doi.org/10.1109/ POWERCON.2010.5666688
13. Kontges, M., et al.: Review of failures of photovoltaic modules. Technical report (2014). ISBN 978-3-906042-16-9
14. Madeti, S.R., Singh, S.N.: Monitoring system for photovoltaic plants: a review. Renew. Sustain. Energy Rev. **67**, 1180–1207 (2017). https://doi.org/10.1016/j.rser. 2016.09.088
15. Madeti, S.R., Singh, S.: A comprehensive study on different types of faults and detection techniques for solar photovoltaic system. Solar Energy **158**(August), 161–185 (2017). https://doi.org/10.1016/j.solener.2017.08.069

16. Mellit, A., Tina, G., Kalogirou, S.: Fault detection and diagnosis methods for photovoltaic systems: a review. Renew. Sustain. Energy Rev. **91**, 1–17 (2018). https://doi.org/10.1016/j.rser.2018.03.062
17. Montgomery, D.C.: Design and Analysis of Experiments, 5th edn. Wiley, New York (2001)
18. Murillo-Soto, L.D., Figueroa-Mata, G., Meza, C.: Identification of the internal resistance in solar modules under dark conditions using differential evolution algorithm. In: 2018 IEEE International Work Conference on Bioinspired Intelligence (IWOBI), pp. 1–9. IEEE (2018). https://doi.org/10.1109/IWOBI.2018.8464197
19. Murillo-Soto, L.D., Meza, C.: Diagnose algorithm and fault characterization for photovoltaic arrays: a simulation study. In: Zamboni, W., Petrone, G. (eds.) ELECTRIMACS 2019. LNEE, vol. 615, pp. 567–582. Springer, Cham (2020). https://doi.org/10.1007/978-3-030-37161-6_43
20. Murillo-Soto, L.D., Meza, C.: Fault detection in solar arrays based on an efficiency threshold. In: 2020 IEEE 11th Latin American Symposium on Circuits & Systems (LASCAS), pp. 1–4. IEEE (2020)
21. Pei, T., Hao, X.: A fault detection method for photovoltaic systems based on voltage and current observation and evaluation. Energies **12**(9), 1712 (2019). https://doi.org/10.3390/en12091712
22. Petrone, G., Ramos-Paja, C.A., Spagnuolo, G., Xiao, W.: Photovoltaic Sources Modeling. Wiley Online Library, New York (2017)
23. Triki-Lahiani, A., Bennani-Ben Abdelghani, A., Slama-Belkhodja, I.: Fault detection and monitoring systems for photovoltaic installations: a review. Renew. Sustain. Energy Rev. **82**, 2680–2692 (2018). https://doi.org/10.1016/j.rser.2017.09.101
24. Vergura, S., Acciani, G., Amoruso, V., Patrono, G., Bari, P.: Inferential statistics for monitoring and fault forecasting of PV plants, pp. 2414–2419 (2008)
25. Villalva, M.G., Gazoli, J.R., Ruppert, E.F.: Modeling and circuit-based simulation of photovoltaic arrays, vol. 14, p. 1 (2009)
26. Zhao, Y., Lehman, B., Ball, R., Mosesian, J., de Palma, J.F.: Outlier detection rules for fault detection in solar photovoltaic arrays. In: 2013 Twenty-Eighth Annual IEEE Applied Power Electronics Conference and Exposition (APEC), pp. 2913–2920 (2013). https://doi.org/10.1109/APEC.2013.6520712

Experimental Modelling of DC Motor for Position Control Systems Involving Nonlinear Phenomena

David González-Morales[1(✉)], Olimpo García-Beltrán[2],
Yeison Alejandro Aldana-Rodríguez[1], and Oswaldo López-Santos[1]

[1] Facultad de Ingeniería, Universidad de Ibagué, Carrera 22 Calle 67, Ibagué 730002, Colombia
david.gonzalez@unibague.edu.co

[2] Facultad de Ciencias Naturales y Matemáticas, Universidad de Ibagué, Carrera 22 Calle 67, Ibagué 730002, Colombia

Abstract. Nonlinear phenomena in the dynamic behavior of DC motors are commonly disregarded in speed regulation systems because it has a constant operation point or a reduced range of variation. Therefore, in the majority of applications, a second order linear model is enough to design the required controllers. However, in angle positioning systems involving DC-motor based actuators, deviation of linear models becomes unacceptable because the impact of non-linearities accentuates. This paper presents a method for experimental modelling of DC motor bidirectional dynamic following three main steps: i) obtaining input-output measurements from multiple experiments using chirp signals as input stimulus; ii) to produce a family of Hammerstein-Wiener type models using software tools for parametric system identification, and iii) to synthesize a unique model from superposition analysis of both the nonlinear gains and the root loci of the linear part. Validity of the obtained model is demonstrated using simulation results showing its potential application in engineering practice.

Keywords: Position control systems · DC motor · Experimental modeling · Hammerstein-Wiener model · Nonlinear modeling · Dead-zone nonlinearity

1 Introduction

Angular positioning systems can be implemented by employing pneumatic, hydraulic and electromechanical actuators depending not only on the required torque, speed and precision but also on the available energy source. Autonomous and portable applications are limited to the use of electrical energy provided by batteries then focusing actuator alternatives to DC motors [1]. The selection of the adequate motor technology depends not only on physical limitations such as size and weight but also on precision, cost and maintenance requirement. Among the well-known DC motor types, stepper motors offers high precision and easy use as main advantages but requires the use of specialized drives and filters to smooth the negative effect of its pulsating current in the lifetime of the batteries. This last aspect has in turn a negative effect in the size, weight and cost of the

© Springer Nature Switzerland AG 2020
J. C. Figueroa-García et al. (Eds.): WEA 2020, CCIS 1274, pp. 516–528, 2020.
https://doi.org/10.1007/978-3-030-61834-6_44

entire device [2]. Then, permanent magnet DC motors represent the lower cost solution for many applications because of its high availability in the market in several models and the high level of standardization of the needed accessories [3, 4]. The dynamics of DC motors are commonly modelled by means of a second-order linear transfer function involving mechanical and electrical time constants representing the motor dynamics and gains representing the drive and sensor behavior. However, this model is highly dependent on the operation point and then models involving nonlinear phenomena can be more suitable [5].

The friction is one of the parameters considerably affecting linearity of motor dynamics. It shows a slight increment proportional to the velocity and exhibits a starting value different to zero (Coulomb friction) which also depends on the motion direction. Also, an asymmetric discontinuity is present in motor dynamics because the input voltage required to start its movement is higher than the one required to sustain it. However, a complete modelling of these phenomena is practically impossible because manufacturers do not provide enough information about these highly uncertain parameters. This difficulties push for development of nonlinear models [6].

Model identification methods seems to be a key alternative to work with an improved accuracy when designing controllers for DC-motor based positioning systems. These methods are based on either on-line or off-line analysis of data obtained from measurements of the input and output signals. The on-line methods operates simultaneously with the control system involving algorithms such as the Extended Kalman Filter (EKF), the Improved Least Square Method (LS) and Artificial Neural Networks (ANN) allow a higher precision at expenses of a higher complexity and computational cost [7–10]. Although, there exists a great difference between on-line and off-line methods, these works are used as a part of the reference frame of this paper because the use of nonlinear models. The off-line methods generally try to establish an input-output relationship to define the parameters through subsequent measurements or tests developed in different conditions. For these methods, the key aspect is the selection of adequate input signal, the implementation of adequate instrumentation and the use of specialized and robust computational tools. Some of the documented applications of the off-line methods used to identify nonlinear models of DC motors are presented chronologically below.

Cong et al. conducted tests by exciting the input of a DC motor and analyzing the data from it and its corresponding output, and making use of the genetic algorithms (GA) with global optimization character and the simplex method [11]. Wu presented an open circuit method, performing measurements of the speed and position of a DC motor, from a stepped voltage input, estimating mechanical and electrical time constants as well as friction. In this work, the speed response was expressed as a power series expansion with coefficients related to the motor parameters to be estimated [12]. Robet et al. proposed a method for dynamic direct and inverse identification models (DIDIM). This method is a closed loop output error approach mixed with the reverse dynamic identification model. Each step of the iterative Gauss-Newton regression procedure (EO method) is simplified to a linear regression that is solved with the Inverse Dynamic Identification Model (IDIM) technique [13]. Buechner et al. proposed an automated identification of the parameters of the permanent magnet DC motor separating two different experiments obtaining results with errors lower than 10% comparing with the real behavior of the system [14]. Differences between methods are the setup required to perform experiments including sensors and instruments, the signals used as stimulus, the methods used to compute the models and assess their accuracy and their computational cost. Although, several approaches have been conducted from research, simplify obtaining nonlinear models is still a challenge.

The contribution of this paper can be framed into the off-line identification methods differing from previous works on the specificity of the following steps:

1. To perform experiments using **chirp signals** as input stimulus with a constant amplitude for each experiment;
2. To produce a family of **Hammerstein-Wiener type models** using software tools for parametric system identification, and
3. To synthesize a **unique model from superposition analysis** of both the nonlinear gains and the root loci of the linear part.

The rest of the paper is organized documenting the step-by-step procedure of the proposed method using a DC motor integrated into a spectrophotometer as case study [15]. Firstly, Sect. 2 describes the experimental setup and methodology used to obtain black-box input-output measurements. After that, in Sect. 3, the obtained data is processed to generate a family of nonlinear models using identification tools. Section 4 is devoted to obtain a unified model. Then, simulated results validate the proposal in Sect. 4 and the conclusions of the work are developed in Sect. 5.

2 Experiment Setup and Proposed Methodology

To apply the proposed method, the elements shown in Fig. 1 were used. A simple LabVIEW application is used to create the stimulus signals on a computer and transfer them to an Arduino UNO microcontroller through serial communication. The PWM signal to be applied to the H-bridge. Two output channels are used, one indicating the direction and the other generating the PWM signal at 2.5 kHz. The H-bridge generates the voltage levels corresponding to each pulse width and applies them to the DC motor. A NI DAQ-USB 6002 data acquisition card is used to acquire the system output signals. Two analog input channels were used, one for PWM signal, which is obtained through a low-pass filter that allows to know its main component value, and a second analog channel to capture the output signal of frequency-to-voltage converter. Two signal sweeps are performed for each experiment. The acquisition is made using a sampling time of 1 ms. In terms of control, the plant is composed by four elements (highlighted using blue contours): a motor drive using a full-bridge converter using Pulse Width Modulation (PWM), a DC motor, an encoder as speed sensor and a frequency-to-voltage transducer which allows to produce a continuous signal as an instantaneous speed reading.

The off-line system identification experiments require input signals with varying features such as amplitude, frequency and off-set, among others. Then, depending on the studied system, selected signal must stimulate different working ranges to produce an output signal rich in information about the behavior of the system for further processing. The use of swept-sine signals in nonlinear systems identification was introduced by

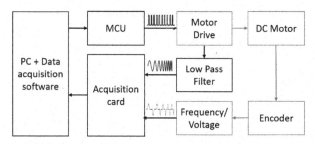

Fig. 1. Block diagram of the identification experiment.

Novak et al. in 2009 [16]. Considering the bandwidth of the motor and the existence of a nonlinear gain behavior, we have considered the chirp signal shown in Fig. 2 extending experiments for multiple amplitudes (a constant amplitude by experiment). Eight experiments were performed with amplitudes (V_m) ranging from around 65% to 90% of the nominal motor voltage (3 V) into a frequency range ($f_{min} - f_{max}$) between 0.5 and 10 Hz, which are swept upwards in about 10 s.

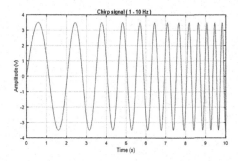

Fig. 2. Chirp signal with constant amplitude (100%) and frequency ranging from 1 to 10 Hz.

Figure 3 shows the measurements obtained from input-output signals. As it can be noted in the output signal, the system has an evident non-linear behavior for input values around zero. In this case, the system has a nonlinear dead zone, which means that no movement is produced until a certain value is exceeded at the input side. This gives an idea of the structure that the nonlinear system model can have.

3 Obtaining Nonlinear Models from Identification Tools

3.1 Model Hypothesis (Hammerstein-Wiener)

The MATLAB System Identification Toolbox is chosen to perform the tasks of estimating the system models from the previously obtained experimental input and output data. The tool allows obtaining models that represent nonlinear systems with coefficients that are calculated using relationships between input and output measured data. Considering the nature of the system and the observed behavior of the output signal, it is deduced that a

520   D. González-Morales et al.

Input and output signals

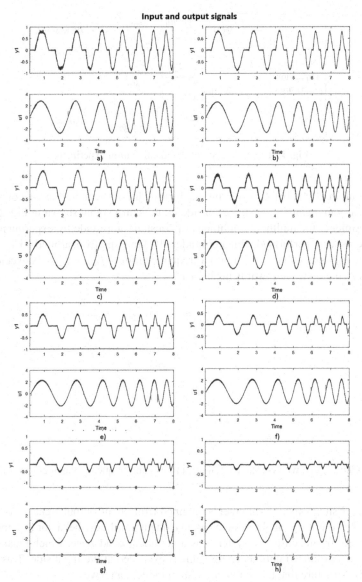

Fig. 3. Detail of the applied and obtained signals for each identification experiment.

practical solution is to use a model representation that differentiates between linear and non-linear parts, which can be achieved by means of a Hammerstein-Wiener model. This last is a type of non-linear model composed by one input nonlinearity, one linear part and one output non-linearity. This model is suitable for modelling electromechanical systems, radiofrequency components, audio processing systems and chemical processes [17]. The first performed experiment aims to determine the nonlinearities that better fit the model (see Table 1).

Table 1. Fit (%) of the model using different input nonlinearities.

Nonlinear function (input side)	Fit (%)
Piecewise linear	80.20
Saturation	76.65
Dead zone	84.38
Wavelet network	79.50
1-D polynomial	81.54

A system estimation check is made using the non-linearity options available in the tool. The highest fit (%) corresponds to the dead zone nonlinearity with 84.38%, which suggests that the form presented in Fig. 4 is the appropriate configuration.

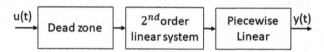

Fig. 4. Proposed Hammerstein-Wiener nonlinear model.

About the linear component, it corresponds to a discrete-time second-order linear system with two poles, one zero and a constant gain which are defined using the structure (1) and taking parameters listed in Table 3 for different models.

$$H(z) = \frac{a(z+b)}{z^2 + cz + d} \tag{1}$$

Figure 5 depicts a graphical comparison between the experimental output data and the model output data when identical stimulus is applied. For the selected case, a chirp signal with an amplitude of 2.125 V (H7) was used, the obtained fit is 84.18%. The similarities and differences between the signals can be appreciated, allowing us to assess successfulness of the procedure.

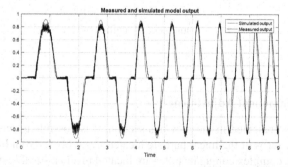

Fig. 5. Measured output compared with the output of the identified system.

Table 2 shows the results of the performed experiments, relating the value of the input amplitude to the linear part parameters and the fit (%) obtained for each one of the produced models.

Table 2. Measured output compared with the output of the identified system.

Experiment	a	b	c	d	V_m (V)	Fit (%)
H1	0.013611	1.0930	−1.667	0.7163	2.875	87.60
H2	0.027755	1.0180	−1.497	0.5779	2.750	90.96
H3	0.037354	0.9769	−1.409	0.5108	2.625	88.74
H4	0.026935	1.0390	−1.542	0.6149	2.500	88.24
H5	0.042097	0.9672	−1.386	0.4959	2.375	91.40
H6	0.043164	0.9692	−1.387	0.4992	2.250	89.60
H7	0.049421	0.9469	−1.342	−1.3420	2.125	84.18
H8	0.047066	0.9663	−1.387	0.4943	2.000	79.70

4 Obtaining a Unified Nonlinear Model of the Motor

Table 2 shows slight differences in the model dynamic behavior of the system for different experiments, then for different amplitudes of the stimulus signal. To complete the identification process, the analytical fit procedure defined by steps in Table 3 is performed to synthesize a unified model.

Table 3. Steps required to obtain a unified model.

Ref.	Step
1	Linear component adjustment
2	Input nonlinearity adjustment
3	Output nonlinearity adjustment
4	Synthesis of the unified model

4.1 Linear Component Adjustment

From the results presented in the previous section, it is possible to model the regions where poles and zeros of the linear part are located. As it observed in Fig. 6, for all the experiments, the complex conjugate poles are located inside a small region of the plane (highlighted in yellow) far to the unitary circle boundary, while the zeros are located into a region of minor influence. Taking into account the four extreme points delimiting the region where the roots are located, only four "limit" models are maintained as it is also shown in Fig. 8 (LS8, LS7, LS4 and LS1).

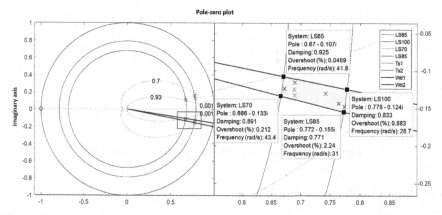

Fig. 6. Detail of the location of the roots in the new four linear systems. (Color figure online)

4.2 Input Nonlinearity Adjustment

The second step consist on analyze the input non-linearity so that a unified function can be obtained as well. The input nonlinearity has been identified as a dead zone. Table 4 shows the upper and lower starting values for the dead zone of each obtained model highlighting the limits used to obtain the unified model. A graphic representation of the limit dead zones obtained from single experiment identification besides the unified version are shown in Fig. 7.

Table 4. Values of the dead zone nonlinearities identified in the systems.

System convention	Lower DZ	Upper DZ
NLHW1	−1.5286	1.6634
NLHW2	−1.5015	1.6463
NLHW3	−1.4894	1.6306
NLHW4	−1.4615	1.6047
NLHW5	−1.4507	1.6191
NLHW6	−1.3847	1.5391
NLHW7	−1.3168	1.4578
NLHW8	−1.1880	1.3392

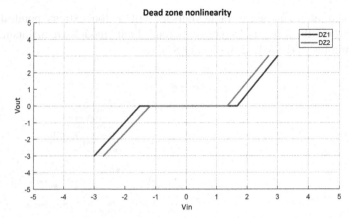

Fig. 7. Representation of DZ1 and DZ2 and the unified DZ.

4.3 Output Nonlinearity Adjustment

The behavior of the systems is then analyzed to define the gain function that will be included in the piecewise linear type output nonlinearity. Using the MATLAB ident tool, individual gain values are determined which make the output amplitude of each experiment similar to the amplitude of the simulated output. Since the analysis of the linear part of the system model has been performed considering normalized transfer functions, the dependency of the gain of the operating points has been transferred to the non-linearity of the output. Consequently, it is possible to define a piecewise linear gain function for each model as shown in Table 5. The resulting two extreme piecewise linear functions producing a region for memoryless nonlinear gain is depicted in Fig. 8.

Table 5. Gains of each identified system for DZ1 and DZ2.

Identified system	Input amplitude	DZ1 Gain	DZ2 Gain
NLHW100	2.90	0.90	0.80
NLHW95	2.75	0.93	0.82
NLHW90	2.62	0.95	0.84
NLHW85	2.52	0.95	0.82
NLHW80	2.38	0.96	0.81
NLHW75	2.26	0.97	0.81
NLHW70	2.14	0.98	0.80
NLHW65	1.99	0.98	0.81

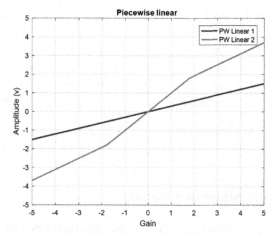

Fig. 8. Piecewise linear for the case with DZ1.

4.4 Unified Model Synthesis

After having four linear systems, two dead-zone values and two piecewise linear gain functions, the new non-linear Hammerstein-Wiener models are tested. This procedure results in eight new non-linear models named: NLS65DZ1, NLS65DZ2, NLS70DZ1, NLS70DZ2, NLS85DZ1, NLS85DZ2, NLS100DZ1 and NLS100DZ2. The models are tested with each input voltage signal from the original experiments and the fit percentage is evaluated as it is suggested by Fig. 9.

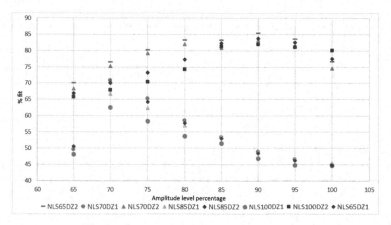

Fig. 9. Fit percentage for each input amplitude.

It can be concluded that the system that has performed best in the tests is the NLS65DZ2 which parameters are listed in Table 6.

Table 6. Obtained unified nonlinear Hammerstein-Wiener model.

Model stage	Type	Parameters
Input nonlinearity	Dead zone	Upper limit: 1.3392 Lower limit: −1.1880
Linear system	2nd order	$H(z) = \dfrac{0.013611(z+1.093)}{z^2 - 1.667z + 0.7163}$
Output nonlinearity	Piecewise linear	Points in x = −5, 1.8, 1.8, 5 Points in y = −3.7, −1.8, 1.8, 3.7

5 Validation and Simulated Results

By applying the same stimulus input signals as the ones used in the first step of identification to compare the Unified Model (UM) versus H2, H3, H5 and H7 identified systems, the results depicted in Fig. 10 were obtained. As it can be observed, the simulated waveforms have a good quality and are closer to the measured ones. The fit percentages are satisfactory, having for the case of H2 model 90.55% vs 85.29 in the UM%, in H3 model 89.8% vs 86.89% for the UM, in H5 model 89.94% vs 88.75% for the UM and, in H7 model 81.02% vs 81.24% for the UM.

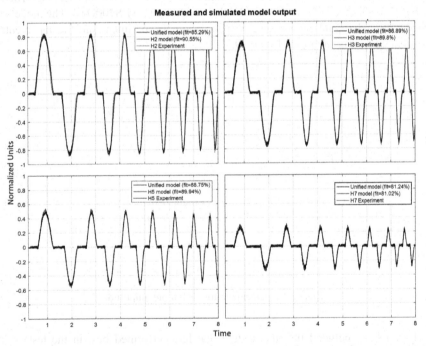

Fig. 10. Results comparing the obtained model with experiments and H2, H3, H5, H7 models.

6 Conclusions

A method improving experimental modeling of DC-motors from for a wide set of operation conditions was developed. The experimental modeling allows to integrate the nonlinearities of the system into two memoryless nonlinear functions using the Hammerstein-Wiener form. The presented results confirm that by combining computational analysis and rule-based heuristic analysis, the contained result can be improved arriving to a simplified model able to be used in control design. Multiple experiments were performed using a chirp signal with different amplitudes but maintaining the same frequency range and the sweep time.

The fit percentage obtained in the unified model are higher than 80% which is a very important results considering that models derived from individual experiments show fit percentages between 79% and 91%.

Acknowledgments. This research was funded by the *Ministerio de Ciencia, Tecnología e Innovación de Colombia (MinCIENCIAS)* under grant number 130774559056".

Conflicts of Interest. The authors declare no conflict of interest.

References

1. Wach, P.: Brushless DC motor drives (BLDC). In: Dynamics and Control of Electrical Drives, pp. 281–380. Springer, Heidelberg (2011). https://doi.org/10.1007/978-3-642-20222-3_4
2. Jones, D.W.: Stepping Motors Fundamentals. http://ww1.microchip.com/downloads/en/App notes/00907a.pdf
3. Metal Gearmotor. https://www.tme.eu/Document/9f1749ca4c948cf20b4136b6210055fb/POLOLU-1447.pdf
4. Tipsuwanporn, V., Piyarat, W., Tarasantisuk, C.: Identification and control of brushless DC motors using on-line trained artificial neural networks. In: Proceedings of the Power Conversion Conference-Osaka 2002 (Cat. No.02TH8579), vol. 3, pp. 1290–1294 (2002). https://doi.org/10.1109/PCC.2002.998159
5. Robet, P.Ph., Gautier, M., Jubien, A., Janot, A.: Global identification of mechanical and electrical parameters of DC motor driven joint with a fast CLOE method. In: 2013 IEEE/ASME International Conference on Advanced Intelligent Mechatronics, pp. 1205–1210 (2013). https://doi.org/10.1109/AIM.2013.6584258
6. Lu, S., Jingzhuo, S.: Nonlinear Hammerstein model of ultrasonic motor for position control using differential evolution algorithm. Ultrasonics **94**, 20–27 (2019). https://doi.org/10.1016/j.ultras.2018.12.012
7. Kara, T., Eker, İ.: Nonlinear modeling and identification of a DC motor for bidirectional operation with real time experiments. Energy Convers. Manag. **45**, 1087–1106 (2004). https://doi.org/10.1016/j.enconman.2003.08.005
8. Rahim, N.A., Taib, M.N., Yusof, M.I.: Nonlinear system identification for a Dc motor using NARMAX approach. In: Asian Conference on Sensors, 2003, AsiaSense 2003, pp. 305–311 (2003). https://doi.org/10.1109/ASENSE.2003.1225038
9. Bature, A.A., Muhammad, M.G., Abdullahi, A.M.: Identification and real time control of a DC motor (2013). https://doi.org/10.9790/1676-0745458

10. Liceaga-Castro, J.U., Siller-Alcalá, I.I., Jaimes-Ponce, J., Alcántara-Ramírez, R.A., Arévalo Zamudio, E.: Identification and real time speed control of a series DC motor. Math. Probl. Eng. **2017**, 7348263 (2017). https://doi.org/10.1155/2017/7348263

11. Cong, S., Guodong, L., Feng, X.: Parameters identification of nonlinear DC motor model using compound evolution algorithms. Lecture Notes in Engineering and Computer Science, vol. 1 (2010)

12. Wu, W.: DC motor parameter identification using speed step responses. Model. Simul. Eng. **2012**, 189757 (2012). https://doi.org/10.1155/2012/189757

13. Robet, P.-P., Gautier, M., Jubien, A., Janot, A.: A New Output Error Method for a Decoupled Identification of Electrical and Mechanical Dynamic Parameters of DC Motor-Driven Robots (2012)

14. Buechner, S., Schreiber, V., Amthor, A., Ament, C., Eichhorn, M.: Nonlinear modeling and identification of a dc-motor with friction and cogging. In: IECON 2013 - 39th Annual Conference of the IEEE Industrial Electronics Society, pp. 3621–3627 (2013). https://doi.org/10.1109/IECON.2013.6699711

15. González-Morales, D., Valencia, A., Díaz-Nuñez, A., Fuentes-Estrada, M., López-Santos, O., García-Beltrán, O.: Development of a low-cost UV-Vis spectrophotometer and its application for the detection of mercuric ions assisted by chemosensors. Sensors **20**, 906 (2020). https://doi.org/10.3390/s20030906

16. Novák, A., Simon, L., Kadlec, F., Lotton, P.: Nonlinear system identification using exponential swept-sine signal. IEEE Trans. Instrum. Meas. **59**, 2220–2229 (2010). https://doi.org/10.1109/TIM.2009.2031836

17. Wills, A., Schön, T.B., Ljung, L., Ninness, B.: Identification of Hammerstein-Wiener models. Automatica **49**, 70–81 (2013). https://doi.org/10.1016/j.automatica.2012.09.018

Author Index

Printed in the United States
By Bookmasters